READINGS
in MEDICAL
SOCIOLOGY

READINGS
in MEDICAL
SOCIOLOGY

EDITED BY
David Mechanic

 THE FREE PRESS
A Division of Macmillan Publishing Co., Inc.
NEW YORK

THE FREE PRESS
A Division of Macmillan Publishing Co., Inc.
866 Third Avenue, New York, N.Y.   10022

Library of Congress Catalog Card Number: 79-7578

Printed in the United States of America

printing number

1   2   3   4   5   6   7   8   9   10

Library of Congress Cataloging in Publication Data

Main entry under title:

Readings in medical sociology.

Includes bibliographical references and index.
1. Social medicine—Addresses, essays, lectures.
I. Mechanic, David   date
RA418.R374   1979   362.1'08   79-7578
ISBN 0-02-920700-2

Contents

Preface

Because medical sociology is a growing field, there has been an outpouring of collections of articles and essays for the general reader as well as the student. Most such collections, however, offer no coherence of perspective, no sense of how the field is expanding, or even a feeling of excitement as the field narrows its focus on certain issues and begins to achieve mastery over them. I trust that the present volume is of another genre.

This collection of twenty-nine readings has been assembled to achieve a variety of goals. No twenty-nine selections by themselves can cover the scope or varied concerns of the increasing numbers of scientists working in medical sociology, health-services research, behavioral medicine, and public health. Thus, as a first goal, this book has been put together to be fully compatible with David Mechanic, *Medical Sociology*, 2d ed. (New York: Free Press, 1978). Indeed, it includes many of the selections I ask my own students to read, and it can easily be used with my text in a course on medical sociology. The listing of Suggested Parallel Reading shows the way I assign these readings relative to the various chapters in *Medical Sociology*.

This collection has also been designed to stand by itself in introducing students to important research questions, policy issues, and methodological approaches. I have given high priority to pieces that convey the excitement of the field but also the uncertainty of our knowledge and the needs for further exploration. That this is not a parochial collection is suggested by the fact that the twenty-nine readings come from twenty-four different sources. Only two highly esteemed journals—*Science* and the *New England Journal of Medicine*—provide more than one. Moreover, the work represented here comes in about equal parts from sociologists, psychiatrists and other physicians, and other behavioral and biological scientists.

Because of the variety of sources and the diversity of authors, the pieces collected here show, naturally, variety and diversity of writing and editorial styles. Beyond basic typographics, no attempt has been made to impose an artificial consistency of style on this collection. For the readers' convenience, all notes and references have been gathered at the end of each piece, where authors' acknowledgments also appear. Abstracts, lists of index terms, and authors' professional affiliations at the time of original publication have been omitted. Unless otherwise noted, methods of documentation, numbering systems, and other such matters of style are here reproduced as in original sources.

Many of the selections presented here raise important controversies that are central to the field and that are conducive to promoting constructive and interesting class discussion. Thus, I purposely include examples of theoretical strategies and political positions with which I personally disagree. My criteria for selection were the quality and interest of the piece, not the author's alignment with any particular theoretical approach, political position, or methodological standpoint. Indeed, I have tried to convey the diversity of the field by choosing authors who bitterly disagree with each other on central issues.

In opting for the airing of differences, I do not endorse the position that all work is equal. For example, in the methodological area I include an overrepresentation of studies that involve field experiments and that use "hard" dependent measures, as compared with people's responses to one or another set of items on a questionnaire. I have done so because I believe that the field of medical sociology will advance more readily if such work is emulated than if we continue to depend so heavily on questionnaire-type investigations. I hope to impress the student with the fact that many alternatives are possible and that there is no single way to improved knowledge and understanding.

Finally, I should draw attention to the fact that the articles selected span a period of twenty-five years, although most are fairly recent. There is a dangerous belief that all of the best work and the best thought is whatever is most contemporary. In areas of policy and present-day description, the work must be recent, but in terms of analytic and theoretical thinking or in innovative methodology, many of the older works are far superior to those that are most current. We do ourselves and the field a disservice when we ignore some of the very fine work done years ago but still unsurpassed.

Suggested Parallel Reading

The following scheme, a fourteen-week program, shows topical parallels between the pages of David Mechanic, *Medical Sociology*, 2d ed. (New York: Free Press, 1978), and the readings collected here.

Week 1 General Perspectives on
Man Health, and the Environment

      Medical Sociology, pp. 1–92

      Readings 1 and 2

Week 2 Concepts of Health and Disease

      Medical Sociology, pp. 95–117

      Readings 7, 8, and 9

Week 3 Methods of Sociomedical Research:
Study of Mortality

      Medical Sociology, pp. 118–80

      Reading 6

Weeks 4 & 5 Morbidity and Epidemiology

      Medical Sociology, pp. 181–221

      Readings 3, 4, 15, and 16

READINGS
in MEDICAL
SOCIOLOGY

Introduction

In the past two decades the field of medical sociology has grown enormously both in volume of research and writing and in breadth of reach. Although most medical sociologists in the 1950s worked on social aspects of mental disorders and their consequences, they are now concerned with almost every aspect of health and medical care. In the 1960s and 1970s the federal government became more involved in the financing and regulation of medical care, and funding and opportunities became available for behavioral scientists to study such matters as the determinants of health and illness, reaction to disorder, and the functioning of health-care institutions. With increasing sophistication of medical science and technology and growing complexity of medical-care organization, the need for better understanding of social and behavioral issues became more apparent. Medical sociologists thus examined such areas as social factors in the causation of disease, illness behavior and help seeking, access to medical care and the delivery of services, patterns of disease and mortality, and ethical, political, and organizational matters.

Sociologists who became involved in medicine approached the area from two points of view.[1] Some saw medicine as one more social institution in which to study and test hypotheses of sociological import, but not necessarily with practical relevance. Others were interested in medical sociology primarily as an applied endeavor, hoping to make some contribution to social betterment and the reduction of suffering. Both groups have contributed, and the field of medical sociology is an amalgam of their efforts.

Medical sociology by its very character depends on the efforts of many disciplines, because its concerns are broad and largely problem oriented. Work in many of these related disciplines overlaps medical sociology,

1

and it is important to be aware of related fields and the extent to which similar types of study are carried out under different rubrics. The areas most closely overlapping medical sociology are the fields of social epidemiology, health-services research, behavioral medicine, medical anthropology, and social psychiatry. Social epidemiology is basically a perspective and methodology used by workers from a variety of medical and behavioral fields. When the emphasis of such study is on social factors in disease, it is of interest to the medical sociologist regardless of the disciplinary affiliation of the investigator. In contrast, health-services research is a substantive field of interest. It overlaps medical sociology to the extent that the problem area deals with social aspects of the organization, provision, and outcomes of health services.

Behavioral medicine is a relatively new field involving behavioral factors in disease and treatment. The field provides a focus for nonclinical psychologists and social psychologists interested in the role of emotions, personality, and living styles in health and disease. Many investigators who identify with the field of behavioral medicine are especially interested in such matters as stress and disease, type A personality and coronary heart disease, biofeedback, and the use of behavior-change strategies in treatment and rehabilitation.

Social psychiatry deals primarily with the study of social factors related to the causes or progression of mental disorders, processes of psychiatric help seeking, and social variables affecting the organization of psychiatric services, treatment, and rehabilitation. Medical anthropologists, in contrast, share many concerns with their counterparts in sociology, but their focus is more on folk health practices, cultural factors in definitions of and responses to health and disease, and minority cultural groups. A variety of other subfields give special attention to the relevance of their disciplines for health: medical economics, medical geography, medical ecology, and medical ethics. In short, there is a wide range of relevant literatures that may inform issues studied by medical sociologists.

Medical sociologists bring a wide variety of perspectives, theories, typologies, and methods to the various problems they study. Mechanic's *Medical Sociology*, 2d ed. (New York: Free Press, 1978) reviews these in detail. There are, however, a limited number of basic ideas that run through many problem areas and types of analysis in medical sociology, and understanding some of these will provide the student with an effective way of thinking about and integrating the selections in this volume.

Social Epidemiology as a Perspective

A fruitful way of examining disease patterns is to study populations, identifying those who are ill and ascertaining what differentiates them from those who remain well. The study of health, disease, disability, and impairment in populations is called epidemiology, and this approach can be used not only to describe disease patterns but also to test varying hypotheses as to the ways in which factors such as social stress, family instability, social deprivation, unemployment, and behavior patterns affect the occurrence and persistence of disease. Epidemiology provides excellent clues as to possible influences on patterns of morbidity. When such clues are identified they direct more focused study not only in populations, but in the clinic and experimental laboratory as well.

The epidemiologist attempts to define and measure as effectively as possible some health or disease indicator. Case finding may be pursued through interviews, health examinations, or diagnostic tests. After identifying those affected, the epidemiologist then tries to find influences that predict the existing pattern. A classic historical example is the work of John Snow, who, by studying the pattern of occurrence of cholera in several areas of London, was able to trace the outbreak of an epidemic to a contaminated water source. In this case, epidemiological study resulted in the control of the spread of disease well before the bacteria causing it were discovered. More current examples of epidemiology include the study of health habits and behavior in the occurrence of coronary heart disease, the role of smoking in the occurrence of lung cancer and a variety of other health problems including heart disease, the influence of environmental pollution on the occurrence of cancer, and the impact of working with asbestos, vinyl chlorides, and other industrial substances on rates of disease and death.

Social Selection in the Processes of Seeking Help

Social selection is a ubiquitous process. People are continually making selections as to where to live, what kinds of work to do, whom to marry, and what types of group to join. People are also socially selective in the ways they define illness, cope, and use a great variety of available formal and informal sources of help, including doctors, hospitals, and medical facilities.

Processes of selection into medical care are usually studied under the rubric of illness behavior, which is influenced by such factors as sociocultural learning experiences, life problems and social stress, and the availability of varying kinds of medical and other helping facility.

Only a fraction of persons with symptoms or illness in any given month actually seek medical care, and for every person who does there are usually others with comparable symptoms who do not. Moreover, the symptoms most frequently seen by physicians are relatively simple and common ones, not very different from the illnesses of many people who do not seek medical assistance. The study of illness behavior deals with two very practical concerns. (1) Why do people with serious illness who need care delay or fail to seek it? (2) Why do people with relatively simple, common, and mild symptoms come to the physician, when experience should have taught them that they are likely to get well with simple self-care and without the physician's intervention? Reading 5 in this volume, on the ecology of medical care, describes the pathways into care, while reading 12, on the presentation of bodily complaints, provides some conceptions of help-seeking behavior.

Just as patients select themselves into care, so do physicians select what patients will be hospitalized, when referrals to other physicians will take place, and when such procedures as surgery will be necessary. Although we like to think that such decisions reflect simply the severity of the patient's illness and the need for more complex types of care, studies indicate that there is great variability in decision making and that the use of such resources as hospitals, surgeons, and other types of facility reflects their availability in any area, financial incentives and pressures, the attitudes and values of the decision maker, and situational factors affecting medical practice. Understanding these decisions from a sociological perspective is as important as understanding differences among patients in definitions of and responses to illness. Different aspects of this area are discussed in readings 17 through 20, which consider the macro system of health care.

Causes of Illness, Course of Illness, and Processes of Seeking Help

In both the medical and sociological literature there is frequent confusion among the factors that cause an illness or problem, the factors that affect what happens to that illness or problem over time, and the factors that affect whether or not the person seeks help and the types of assistance that are sought. Although the same factor can affect all three (cause, course, and help seeking), often very different influences account for each of these outcomes. In thinking about problems, it is extremely important to be as clear as possible about the causes of a condition, its course over time, and the patterns of help seeking that take place.

Consider some examples. In the case of schizophrenia, causes are unknown, although there is a reasonable body of evidence that indicates that there is an important genetic component.[2] Such evidence shows a greater concordance in schizophrenia among identical as compared with fraternal twins, and indicates that infants of schizophrenic mothers placed in foster situations following birth are more likely to develop a schizophrenic syndrome than foster children similarly placed who were the offspring of nonschizophrenic mothers. Because the concordance rate for schizophrenia in identical twins is considerably less than 100 percent (which would be expected if schizophrenia were simply a genetically transmitted disease), current views support the notion that the syndrome we call schizophrenia is a product of an inherited vulnerability interacting with other social and psychological factors. There is much disagreement about the other factors that are important, but such influences as social stress, distorted family interaction and communication, and rigidity of value structures that inhibit adaptation have all been posited as possible contributors.

Although our understanding of the causes of schizophrenia is limited, in recent years we have learned a great deal about factors affecting its course. It has been well documented, for example, that custodial care of the schizophrenic patient in large mental hospitals in which they engaged in little activity and responsibility resulted in an elaboration of their problem and an erosion of their capacities to resume community living.[3] These secondary disabilities associated with the manner in which the schizophrenic is handled have been called institutionalism. Existing studies suggest that schizophrenic patients can do reasonably well in the community if they are kept involved and active, if they receive social support, if they are insulated from extreme stress or high emotional involvement, and if they are properly treated with psychoactive drugs. Such factors may make the difference between becoming a totally disabled person unable to assume any community or self responsibility and becoming a person capable of living a reasonable life in the community. The extent to which community adjustment is possible depends on the network of services available to the patient and may have little to do with the factors that cause schizophrenia in the first place.

Whether schizophrenic patients seek care, when they seek care, and the types of care they receive are related to different factors depending on the manner in which the condition manifests itself, the attitudes, knowledge, and tolerance of the patient or significant others, and the organization of services in the area. Patients of lower socioeconomic status are more likely than those more affluent to become involved in public situations involving the intervention of social agencies and police. Affluent patients are more likely to come into contact with and be processed by private physicians. While poor people more generally receive care at mental-health centers, mental hospitals, and public clinics, those with higher incomes or with good insurance coverage are more likely to be cared for by private psychiatrists and through community general hospitals. Because the pathways into care may differ from one social group to another, studies of schizophrenic patients as well as other ill persons must sample patients from a variety of institutions providing care.

The epidemiological distinction between incidence and prevalence has an important relationship to the distinction between *causes* and *course*. Incidence refers to new cases during a specified time interval, while prevalence includes all known cases at any point in time. The prevalence rate thus includes both incidence (new cases) and continuing cases. It should follow from this discussion that an investigator who wishes to study *causes* of a condition must study new cases, because examination of the total cases (prevalence) tends to confuse those factors contributing to new cases with those other factors that affect the persistence of the condition. In the example of schizophrenia, the incidence rate is relatively low.

Because there is no cure for schizophrenia, however, the prevalence rate is many times the incidence rate, since it includes significant numbers of patients who developed the condition in the past and who continue to have it. In reality, defining a new case is often a difficult methodological problem.

Social Selection versus Social Causation

Our old friend, social selection, reappears and, as will soon be evident, is relevant to many central problems in understanding the occurrence of disease and mortality and in evaluating treatment and therapeutic environments. Consider the finding that persons who are single, divorced, or widowed have higher mortality from a variety of diseases than persons who are married. One possibility is that the dissolution of marriage is extremely disruptive to health, increasing the probability of illness and death. An alternative hypothesis is that persons who remain single or those whose marriages dissolve are on the average quite different types of people. Perhaps they were sick in the first place, making it more difficult for them to marry or limiting their choice of suitable mates. Or perhaps those who get divorced are the types willing to take risks in health situations and marriage. While the relationship between marital status and mortality tends generally to be less impressive for the widowed, even here alternative selection hypotheses are plausible. Perhaps persons who are less healthy marry others who are also unhealthy, accounting for widowhood on the one hand and poor health on the other. This is not the place to review the abundant research on marital status and illness. Suffice it to say that in all likelihood the findings in the literature represent the effects of both social causation and social selection processes.

There is an almost endless variety of problems in medical sociology in which it becomes necessary to weigh the effects of social selection against social causation. Are the higher death rates in Nevada as compared with Utah[4] a reflection of the fact that the Mormon population of Utah (with prohibitions on smoking and drinking and encouragement of moderation in living) encourages a style of life conducive to health and longevity; or are these differences better explained by a large migration of persons to Nevada who have unhealthy life styles and who are prone to risk taking and violence? Is the relationship between poverty and chronic illness a result of the causal influence of poverty on health or a result of the fact that people who are chronically ill face work and income difficulties because of their health status? Is the link between low socioeconomic status and schizophrenia a result of adverse circumstances contributing to the occurrence of the disorder, or is the explanation that schizophrenics fail to be upwardly mobile or are downwardly mobile because of the debilitating effects of the condition? Is the finding in some studies that patients do better in health-maintenance organizations than in more conventional medical settings a result of the quality of care provided by such organizations, or of the fact that such organizations attract patients who are healthy, more health conscious, and more concerned about taking care of their health?

Indeed, social selection is such a ubiquitous process that some scientists argue that only through experimentation and the randomization of patients can firm knowledge be acquired.[5] This is a very limited and restrictive view, however, and much understanding can be acquired through nonexperimental studies, but this view does emphasize that social selection is an important determinant of social outcomes and must be taken into careful consideration. Charles Darwin changed the face of the world with his theory of social selection in explaining the origin of the species, and it is not too farfetched to suggest that selection is as important in social processes as it is in the biological realm.

Behavior of Patients and Health Personnel as Adaptive Responses

Many factors affect the way people behave. These include their social and cultural upbringing, their capacities, knowledge, and understanding, social expectations, and the pressures of the moment that affect their responses. While the literature in medical sociology is extensive in discussing social and cultural determinants of behavior, it is less complete in examining the way situational pressures and incentives affect behavior and decision making, and the way these are structured by different types of social organization. In examining behavior in medical contexts it is important not only to look at the definition of social roles, values, and attitudes, but also to examine the way the pressures of the situation push decision making in one direction or another. It is this focus on the adaptiveness of behavior that constitutes an important viewpoint in medical sociology.

For example, Mark Field has described the situation of the physician in the Soviet Union in the period following World War II.[6] The Soviets suffered many losses during the war, and the postwar period was a time of reconstruction requiring all available manpower. The work demands subjected many people to considerable social stress from which they sought relief. One legitimate way of obtaining relief from work obligations was to receive medical certification of illness, and many patients came to physicians seeking such sickness clearances. The doctors, acting as sympathetic agents, provided patients with medical excuses that allowed them to miss work. Such sickness certification was sufficiently widespread that the Soviets rationed the number of sickness clearances a physician could issue, thus controlling the release of necessary industrial manpower. In this context, both patients and the state were attempting to manipulate the sick role in their own interests. Patients under stress used a variety of means to try to get doctors to serve as their agents in gaining release from activities, while the state was attempting to manipulate sickness definitions to insure industrial needs being met. Both patients and government officials were attempting to adapt to their problems by manipulating the institution of medicine.

Consider another example. Studies of physicians working on a fixed stipend, such as salary or capitation, show that they deal with their medical responsibilities in different ways than fee-for-service physicians.[7] The structure of payment affects the doctor's response in that it provides incentives to work longer or shorter hours, to deal with patients more quickly or at a more leisurely rate, or to opt for doing more or less during periods of uncertainty. Physicians paid the same amount regardless of the number of patients they see are likely to try to see all their patients within a limited span of time, while those who have a financial incentive for every additional patient consultation are more likely to expand the amount of time they spend seeing patients. Just as a fixed stipend creates incentives for doing as little as necessary, a fee-for-service system induces a tendency to be more active in situations of uncertainty. Doctors with comparable training, values, and experience will behave differently depending on the financial and social structure within which they work.

Similar types of adaptive response are common among medical students and house officers, as they are among students in general. Studies of students indicate that they often face expectations that are impossible to meet.[8,9] Professors have idealistic notions about what they expect the student to learn and the amount of work they would like the student to do in their courses. They hope that the students will seek learning and understanding in a broad sense and will not gear their study responses merely to passing exams or getting through the course. Students, however, who often face the anxieties of "making it" and who do not have enough time to meet all demands made on them, will try to develop strategies of "getting through." They come to concentrate on materials they believe are more likely to be on their tests, to give greater emphasis to courses in which they know the professor is tough, or to build their course schedule so that there are trade-offs between difficult and easier courses. They might purposely select an easy course, not because they think they will learn the most in it, but to raise their grade-point average or increase the chances of getting into graduate school. The point is that all of us respond to the pressures of the environments we live in, our notions of our capacities and weaknesses, and our sense of threat and reward. These responses and the way they form constitute the study of adaptive behavior, and such study is essential in understanding people's responses to health and illness and their behavior in medical settings.

The Ideal and the Real

All organizations tend to have a formal set of goals, responsibilities, and ideologies about the way they do their work and serve their clients and the public, and about the value of their product. Although such formal definitions and ideologies may convey some sense of the organization and the way it functions, there often is a large discrepancy between the way an organization purports to function and the way it really does. Have mental hospitals existed in the past to serve psychiatric patients or to protect the community from disturbing and disruptive persons? Are the vigorous efforts of the American Medical Association against chiropractic mainly attempts to eliminate quacks, or do they result from a desire to avoid competing practitioners? Is the expansion of many new medical technologies mainly an effort to improve the quality of patient care, or primarily intended to increase the profits of medical industries and doctors? Is the emphasis on the deinstitutionalization of mental-patient care primarily motivated to give mental patients more humane and effective treatment environments or to limit the necessary institutional expenditures on such patients? Is the rapid development of coronary bypass surgery an example of the wonders of medical technology in extending life and promoting greater comfort, or is it being promoted in part to allow highly trained surgeons to keep busy with remunerative types of practice? None of these questions has a simple or clear-cut answer. In each case there are discrepancies between the ideologies promoted by interested groups and the realities. Only through careful study of medical developments and medical situations does it become possible to assess accurately the impact of medical organization. Understanding discrepancies between formal definitions of organizational programs and what actually takes place depends on more than identifying self-serving rhetoric. In many situations the formal goals are widely shared by organizational personnel, who have a sincere desire to achieve the stated objectives. A variety of factors, however, may lead to modifications of behavior, including the existing reward structure and the way it affects them, problems associated with work performance, the need to reduce uncertainty that is stressful, and the difficulties of achieving necessary cooperation. Most health personnel want to provide good care, to treat patients in a humane way, and to be responsive, but often the impediments of organizational requirements, workload, limited resources, disagreeable patients and colleagues, and fears and insecurities make it difficult to translate desires into reality. Understanding the world as patients and health personnel see it increases our ability to design organizations and programs that are effective.

References

1. Robert Straus. "The Nature and Status of Medical Sociology." *American Sociological Review* 22 (April 1957): 200–204.
2. David Rosenthal. *Genetic Theory and Abnormal Behavior*. New York: McGraw-Hill, 1970.
3. J. K. Wing. *Reasoning about Madness*. Oxford: Oxford University Press, 1978.
4. Victor R. Fuchs. *Who Shall Live? Health, Economics, and Social Choice*. New York: Basic Books, 1974.

5. A. L. Cochrane. *Effectiveness and Efficiency: Random Reflections on Health Services.* London: Nuffield Provincial Hospitals Trust, 1972.

6. Mark G. Field. *Doctor and Patient in Soviet Russia.* Cambridge, Mass.: Harvard University Press, 1957.

7. David Mechanic. *The Growth of Bureaucratic Medicine: An Inquiry into the Dynamics of Patient Behavior and the Organization of Medical Care.* New York: Wiley-Interscience, 1976.

8. Howard S. Becker, Blanche Geer, Everett C. Hughes, and Anselm L. Strauss. *Boys in White: Student Culture in Medical School.* Chicago: University of Chicago Press, 1961.

9. David Mechanic. *Students under Stress: A Study in the Social Psychology of Adaptation.* New York: Free Press, 1962.

I

Man, Health, and the Environment

The first four readings sketch the broad relationships between health and society and illustrate that the ways in which man lives and adapts have impact on disease and death.

Reading 1 comes from a book by René Dubos, an eminent microbiologist and for many years a professor at Rockefeller University in New York City. Dubos, an erudite and well-informed scientist, points to the fact that health and happiness are elusive goals because they depend on values, understandings, and people's aspirations that are always changing. It is these aspirations and goals, and the social environment that is developed in pursuing them, that constitute the major causative factors in disease. Dubos illustrates with considerable clarity that the major breakthroughs in the control of disease resulted more from social reform than from any specific medical knowledge. As a medical scientist, Dubos appreciates both the great advantages that flow from science and its limitations, and it is this appreciation that provides a profound introduction to the relationships between environment and disease. The entire book from which this selection has been made is highly recommended, as are some other books by Dubos: *Man Adapting* (New Haven: Yale University Press, 1965) and *The White Plague: Tuberculosis, Man and Society*, written jointly with Jean Dubos (Boston: Little, Brown, 1952).

Although it is essential to take a broad perspective, broadness itself entails risk because it requires mastery over many types of subject matter. Dubos's work illustrates this. While it is enriching and erudite, he sometimes lapses into overstatement of his argument. For example, in the excerpt selected, Dubos tells us that one of every four citizens will have to spend at least some months or years in a mental asylum, but careful review of existing data on mental hospitalization in the United States or elsewhere would not substantiate this claim. Serious students must learn that even the best scholars occasionally make errors, and being a good student requires an ability to read and think critically, to check one set of discussions and arguments against another, and to retain a certain skepticism. The student must also learn that a factual error does not necessarily invalidate a larger argument. Whatever errors of detail Dubos might make, he offers us a powerful perspective that is extremely valuable in understanding issues of health and disease.

John Powles, in his discussion of the limitations of modern medicine, reading 2, follows up on issues that Dubos raises, but evaluates in more detail and in a more empirical way the advantages to health that have resulted from the rise of modern medicine, and discusses its likely future limitations in promoting health and longevity. He raises important questions about whether curative medicine as we know it can be expected to have major future impact.

Joseph Eyer, who represents one of the new breed in the field, embraces a radical perspective of health and health care, but unlike many young radicals who specialize in political rhetoric and sloppy scholarship, he brings to his studies both methodological sophistication and a careful digestion of the evidence. In reading 3 Eyer considers one of the major plagues of modern life—elevated blood pressure—which, if not adequately treated, results in more serious disease and an early death. Hypertension constitutes one of the most prevalent serious illnesses in modern nations, and Eyer argues quite persuasively that its prevalence reflects the nature of our civilization. Eyer goes well beyond his data in presenting a radical viewpoint, but nevertheless it is a perspective of some importance, and worth understanding. We still know far too little about hypertension; the evidence is not all in. Various investigators are examining hypotheses concerning genetic influences, diet, stress, and many other factors. Eyer points out the importance of taking a broad view of hypertension as well as a more focused one.

The final reading in this section, by Lester Breslow, addresses the issue of how we can prevent illness and enhance health. Breslow illustrates that although we do not yet know the causes of many major diseases, we have identified important risk factors that are highly correlated with them. By developing programs to reduce risk factors such as smoking, poor diet, lack of exercise, and excessive drinking, we increase the probability of keeping people healthy. The position that Breslow presents in reading 4 is one dear to the hearts of social epidemiologists. Recall the discussion in the introduction of the studies of cholera in London by John Snow. Although Snow could not identify the actual organism that caused cholera, his knowledge of the pattern of disease allowed effective intervention by closing down the water pump on Broad Street, which was the source of contaminated water. By identifying risk factors, modern epidemiologists similarly can contribute to the prevention of disease despite our incomplete knowledge of causation. In some areas like smoking, for example, we have made some progress in controlling an important risk factor related to lung cancer, heart disease, and many other health problems. The risk factor approach is not certain, given the incompleteness of our knowledge, but it is prudent.

The Mirage of Health

René Dubos

The nineteenth-century reformers naïvely but firmly believed that, since disease always accompanied the want, dirt, pollution, and ugliness so common in the industrial world, health could be restored simply by bringing back to the multitudes pure air, pure water, pure food, and pleasant surroundings—the qualities of life in direct contact with nature. There is no doubt that this philosophy, unsophisticated in terms of modern science, was nevertheless immensely effective in overcoming many of the disease problems brought into being by the Industrial Revolution. All contemporary observers expressed the view that the general conditions of health in Western Europe and in North America were much better during the second half of the nineteenth century than they had been before the social reformers began clearing up the mess caused by the sudden growth of industrial cities. And the improvement clearly began long before the modern era in medicine was ushered in by the germ theory of disease.

Although the laboratory scientist was only the laborer of the eleventh hour in the campaign against disease that began a century and a half ago, he occupies now the center of the stage everywhere, and practically all recent progress has been the result of his work. The nineteenth-century reformers had immense practical achievements to their credit, but the science of which they boasted was usually made up of catchwords. By preaching the virtues of pure air, pure water, and pure food they had gone far toward eliminating infection and improving nutrition, but their success had been due more to zeal in the correction of social evils than to understanding of medical problems. The original contribution of the laboratory scientist was to reformulate the problems of disease in more precise terms and to uncover by

SOURCE: René Dubos, *Mirage of Health: Utopias, Progress, and Biological Change* (New York: Harper & Row, 1959), pp. 17–23. Volume 22 of World Perspectives Series, planned and edited by Ruth Nanda Anshen. Copyright © 1959 by René Dubos. Reprinted by permission of Harper & Row, Publishers, Inc.

analysis the properties that lay hidden behind the word "pure"—so alluring yet so vague. And what the scientist uncovered was far more complex than the most subtle imaginings of all philosophers, humanitarians, and social reformers. He found among other things that poisons and germs of disease could lurk unseen in fragrant air and in limpid water and that the most tasty food, even though natural and pure, might be deficient in essential growth factors or be so unbalanced as to cause metabolic misery.

As the result of the scientist's labors, it became clear that the instincts of health postulated by Virey involved in final analysis all the complex and interrelated controls of physiological function. This new understanding, even though still so incomplete today, has yielded new and more convenient techniques for the control of some of man's ancient plagues. The time has passed when explorers on land or at sea have to depend on heavy loads of lemons and animal food in order to protect themselves against scurvy and other deficiency diseases. A few small packages of snythetic vitamins can now make an adequate diet out of proteins, carbohydrates, fats, and water. A dash of chlorine and an effective filtration bed will make any water supply more typhoidproof than the most sparkling streams brought from high mountains. There is no longer any reason to fear that bad air will kill men with yellow fever in the Brazilian jungle or with Carrion's disease in the Peruvian Andes. The knowledge that these diseases are caused by parasites transmitted through mosquitoes has led to protective measures far more effective than the traditional practices of natives in those regions.

But while modern science can boast of so many startling achievements in the health fields, its role has not been so unique and its effectiveness not so complete as is commonly claimed. In reality, as already stated, the monstrous specter of infection had become but an enfeebled shadow of its former self by the time serums, vaccines, and drugs became available to combat microbes. Indeed, many of the most terrifying microbial diseases—leprosy, plague, typhus, and the sweating sickness, for example—had all but disappeared from Europe long before the advent of the germ theory. Similarly, the general state of nutrition began to improve and the size of children in the labor classes to increase even before 1900 in most of Europe and North America. The change became noticeable long before calories, balanced diets, and vitamins had become the pride of nutrition experts, the obsession of mothers, and a source of large revenues to the manufacturers of colored packages for advertised food products.

Clearly, modern medical science has helped to clean up the mess created by urban and industrial civilization. However, by the time laboratory medicine came effectively into the picture the job had been carried far toward completion by the humanitarians and social reformers of the nineteenth century. Their romantic doctrine that nature is holy and healthful was scientifically naïve but proved highly effective in dealing with the most important health problems of their age. When the tide is receding from the beach it is easy to have the illusion that one can empty the ocean by removing water with a pail. The tide of infectious and nutritional diseases was rapidly receding when the laboratory scientist moved into action at the end of the past century.

The great increase in over-all expectancy of life during the past hundred years in the Western world is properly quoted as objective evidence of improvement in the general health condition. It is often overlooked, however, that this increase has been due not so much to better health in the adult years of life as to the spectacular decrease in infant mortality. The control of childhood diseases, in turn, resulted more from better nutrition and sanitary practices than from the introduction of new drugs. It is remarkable, in contrast, that little practical progress has been made toward controlling the diseases that were not dealt with by the nineteenth-century reformers. Whereas the Sanitary Revolution did much to eliminate the most common microbial diseases, it has had no counterpart in dealing with the ailments of the adult years of life and of old age.

The nineteenth-century sanitarians believed that health and happiness could be found only through a return to the ways of nature. Modern man, probably no wiser but certainly more conceited, now claims that the royal avenue to the control of disease is through scientific knowledge and medical technology. "Health is purchasable," proclaimed one of the leaders of American medicine. Yet, while the modern American boasts of the scientific management of his body and soul, his expectancy of life past the age of 45 is hardly greater today than it was several decades ago and is shorter than that of many European people of the present generation. He claims the highest standard of living in the world, but 10 per cent of his income must go for medical care and he cannot build hospitals fast enough to accommodate the sick. He is encouraged to believe that money can create drugs for the cure of heart disease, cancer, and mental disease, but he makes no worth-while effort to recognize, let alone correct, the mismanagements of his everyday life that contribute to the high incidence of these conditions. He laughs louder than any other people, and the ubiquitous national smile is advertised ad nauseam by every poster or magazine, artist or politician. But one out of every four citizens will have to spend at least some months or years in a mental asylum. One may wonder indeed whether the pretense of superior health is not itself rapidly becoming a mental aberration. Is it not a delusion to proclaim the present state of health as the best in the history of the world, at a time when increasing numbers of persons in our society depend on drugs and on doctors for meeting the ordinary problems of everyday life?

Should Virey come back to this world he probably would experience mixed reactions concerning the success of science in substituting precise knowledge for the lost instincts of health. He would marvel, of course, at the inexhaustible spring of new facts uncovered by the scientific method and at man's skill in converting knowledge into power. He probably would ask himself, on the other hand, whether he and the Encyclopedists had not taken too much for granted in assuming that knowledge could be equated with vision and wisdom. He would see evidence that scientific civilization threatens to ruin or even to destroy life and creates much unhappiness whenever it ignores or fails to respect the ethical and emotional values that men prize above life itself. He would find thoughtful men—untutored persons as well as sophisticated scholars—fearing that a day may come after all when "he that increaseth knowledge increaseth sorrow," because it is easier for the scientific mind to unleash natural forces than for the human soul to exercise wisdom and generosity in the use of power. Even among the most optimistic he would perceive a disturbing awareness that the solution of the problems of health and happiness— indeed, their very formulation—will prove far more complex than had been antici- pated by scientists a few generations ago.

There is no reason to doubt, of course, the ability of the scientific method to solve each of the specific problems of disease by discovering causes and remedial proce- dures. Whether concerned with particular dangers to be overcome or with specific requirements to be satisfied, all the separate problems of human health can and will eventually find their solution. But solving problems of disease is not the same thing as creating health and happiness. This task demands a kind of wisdom and vision which transcends specialized knowledge of remedies and treatments and which apprehends in all their complexities and subtleties the relation between living things and their total environment. Health and happiness are the expression of the manner in which the individual responds and adapts to the challenges that he meets in everyday life. And these challenges are not only those arising from the external world, physical and social, since the most compelling factors of the environment, those most commonly involved in the causation of disease, are the goals that the individual sets for himself, often without regard to biological necessity. Nor can the problem be usefully stated by advocating a return to nature.

It is possible that the haunting memory of the golden age is more than a fond illusion. As suggested by Lewis Mumford, the interglacial periods may have pro- vided a relatively idyllic environment of ease and abundance, breathing spells in the midst of tropical luxuriance that contrasted with the recurrent hardships of the glacial periods contemporary with man's early development. Furthermore, it is also probable that a few people now and then in limited periods of history have enjoyed relative peace in a fairly constant physical and social environment. These periods of relative static equilibrium probably correspond to the era of tranquility of which the Yellow Emperor spoke, which primitive people often evoke in their legends, and which the philosophers of the Enlightenment had in mind when they pleaded for harmony with the ways of nature. But the state of equilibrium never lasts long and its characteristics are at best elusive, because the word "nature" does not desig- nate a definable and constant entity. With reference to life there is not one *nature*; there are only associations of states and circumstances, varying from place to place and from time to time.

Living things can survive and function effectively only if they adapt themselves to the peculiarities of each individual situation. For some sulphur bacteria nature is a Mexican spring with extremely acid water at very high temperature; for the reindeer moss, it is a rock surface in the frozen atmosphere of the arctic. Nature for fishes is ocean, lake, or stream, and for the desert rat it is a place where never a drop of water is available. The word "nature" also means very different things to different men.

2

On the Limitations
of Modern Medicine

John Powles

One of the more striking paradoxes within modern medical culture lies in the contrast between the enthusiasm associated with current developments and the reality of the decreasing returns to health for rapidly increasing efforts. As this paradox involves both the technical and nontechnical aspects of medicine, any attempt to unravel it must involve an exploration of both. It must also investigate the whole medical culture, encompassing as it does a complex web of explanations and activities accepted by both doctors and their patients.

In this chapter we shall attempt to explore the origins and dynamics of this paradox. In demonstrating that the paradox is real, the argument will move to an assessment of the current status of modern man's efforts to gain technical mastery of disease. It will then go on to explore the complex interaction of the technical and nontechnical aspects of modern medicine.

Diminishing Returns

It seems unnecessary to demonstrate the optimism that underlies contemporary confrontation with disease. News stories of fresh battles won are frequently relayed through the mass media to a public that has grown to expect such victories. More frequent still are stories of new and more powerful weapons that will ensure future conquests. While most are aware that cancer and heart disease remain to be subdued, few doubt the ultimate outcome.

Nor is it necessary to document in detail the rapid pace of medical inflation—especially in the last two decades. In England and Wales the number of hospital

SOURCE: Robert L. Kane, ed., *The Challenges of Community Medicine* (New York: Springer, 1974), pp. 89–122. Copyright © 1974 by Springer Publishing Company, Inc., New York. Used by permission.

FIGURE 1. Mortality Trends over the Last Century, England and Wales (with Recent Expenditure Trends)

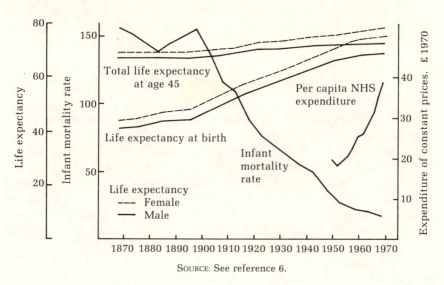

SOURCE: See reference 6.

workers increased by 70 percent over the two decades up to 1969 (1). By comparison, the increase in total workforce was only 10 percent (2). In the Soviet Union in the period 1940 to 1968, the number of physicians in relation to population increased more than threefold and the number of days spent in hospital in relation to population increased more than two and a half times (3). In the United States, per capita health expenditures rose from $79 to $324 in the two decades up to 1969/70 (4). This was an increase of 310 percent over a period in which the consumer price index rose only by around 60 percent (5).

What has been the result of these redoubled efforts? Do they provide grounds for optimism to a purely rational man? Figure 1 shows the trends in the major mortality indices in England and Wales for the 100 years up to 1970. Note that it is precisely during the last two decades—when scientific medicine is alleged to have blossomed and when the quantity of resources allocated to medical care has been rapidly increased—that the decline in mortality associated with industrialisation has tapered off to a virtual zero.

Whilst it is true that female life expectancy is continuing to increase marginally, the picture for men is very sobering. Although more are surviving the infectious diseases of childhood in England and Wales than was the case three decades ago, their prospects once they have reached adulthood are hardly better. The gap between male and female life expectancies has widened with marked social consequences. This can be shown by trends in a national "mean period of widowhood" (figures for England and Wales) (7,8). Thus the slight gains in female life expectancy are serving to increase the number of lonely old women. Such gains are a mixed blessing.

	1930–1932	1948–1950	1966–1968
Mean difference in age at marriage	2.58	3.39	2.63
+	+	+	+
Mean difference in life expectancy *at age of marriage (say 25)*	3.01	4.10	5.62
	=	=	=
"Mean period of widowhood"	5.59 years	7.49 years	8.25 years

The major technical failure of modern medicine has been its inability to reduce premature death in men. In several countries, male death rates in middle age have actually been rising; in others, they are failing to decline (9,10). In England and Wales it is the poor who seem to have gained least. The age-specific death rates for unskilled workers over the age of 50 were probably higher in 1959–63 than they had been in the depression years 1930–32 (11). Nearly twice as many men as women currently die in middle age in England and Wales, and 90 percent of this excess mortality in men can be attributed to heart disease, lung cancer, and bronchitis (12).

Some will object that there is more to life than the avoidance of death and that trends for lethal conditions may not be reflected in trends for nonlethal illness. Death statistics are, however, the most reliable figures that are comparable over time. In England and Wales the best information on trends in illness are returns for the employed male population on sick-leave from work. Morris has reviewed these from the 1920s to the early 1960s and concluded that "sick absence rates in men show no improvement" (13). He made a more detailed examination of trends in the 1950s which showed "an appreciable rise of chronic sickness among men in their late fifties, and a very substantial one, amounting to 30 percent in men in their early sixties" (14). More recent figures for the period 1962/3 to 1968/9 show an overall increase of 20 percent in days lost, with the most marked increases in absence attributed to cardiovascular disease, respiratory diseases (other than bronchitis and tuberculosis), diseases of the musculoskeletal system, and accidents, poisoning, and violence (15). Whilst these figures may be reflecting an increasing tendency not to work when feeling unwell, trends by disease category are broadly parallel to known mortality trends. At the very least, these data fail to support an optimistic interpretation of the recent health experience of middle-aged men.

Two final qualifications to this critical review of the recent gains from medical technology need to be made. First, technology exists not only to prevent and cure illness but also to help sick people cope with their illness. There have been many gains in symptom relief—the anti-allergy, asthma-relieving, and pain-killing drugs are obvious examples. Second, given the close relationship in the long term between the regulation of population and health, oral contraceptives, intrauterine devices, and improved abortion techniques are significant gains.

However, the overall outcome of the recent contest with disease is hardly the success story it is so widely believed to be. It is now necessary to enquire why this has been so.

The Human Experience of Disease

What is the nature of the contemporary disease burden? What has been the relative impact on it of changes in life style and medical activities? Is the current medical strategy appropriate to the task it faces? For at least 99 percent of the duration the genus *Homo* has inhabited the earth, he has lived by hunting and gathering. This way of life was presumably also shared by the preceding prehominids. Of the 50,000-odd generations in the last million years of human history, only about 400 have lived since agriculture was first adopted. With agriculture came dramatic changes in diet, population density, and patterns of daily life. These exposed the human organism to stresses that were, in evolutionary terms, novel. It is unlikely that there has been any major biological change in man since the Neolithic revolution (16). Such genetic change is even more highly improbable with respect to the more recent adoption of urban and advanced industrial patterns of life. The selection pressures associated with hunting and gathering were predominant in determining man's genetic constitution. It is therefore reasonable to take the functioning of the human organism under such circumstances as the baseline in discussing the impact of civilisation and medical technology on the health of man. While it may be argued that behavioural flexibility provides the very basis of man's success as a species, it is man's biological adaptability that is being questioned here. It must be recognised, however, that the two interact.

Infection

At first glance, it is the infectious and parasitic diseases whose decline has been so evident in recent times. Together they constitute a group of diseases where modern man seems clearly to have "improved on nature." What, however, was the baseline situation? Can we know anything with confidence about the impact of infection on hunter-gatherer man?

There are several reasons for believing that the burden of infection was considerably lighter on hunter-gatherer man than in advanced agricultural civilisations such as preindustrial Europe. First, birth spacing seems to be wider (three to four years as compared to two to three) and completed family size smaller (three to five compared to four to six) (17). Smaller family size means a smaller proportion of infants and children dying before reproductive age. The second consideration is that population sizes and densities would usually not have been sufficient to sustain those infections specific to man that conferred lasting immunity. This assumption, based on theoretical epidemiological considerations, is confirmed by the frequently reported vulnerability of contemporary hunter-gatherer populations to introduced infections of this kind. Fenner has suggested that cholera, measles, smallpox, poliomyelitis, and many viruses invading the upper respiratory tract are post-Neolithic developments (18). Low population densities and shifting camps would also have reduced the contagiousness of bowel infections such as those caused by the salmonellae. A third factor pointing to a lesser burden of infection is the higher host resistance likely to have been conferred by the generally better nutritional status of hunter-gatherers when compared to advanced agricultural populations. The good nutritional status generally enjoyed by hunter-gatherers has frequently been noted (19,20). Whilst population numbers are likely to have been ultimately regulated by food supplies, there generally appears to have been a good measure of "reserve capacity." Under hunting and gathering conditions. a diverse and usually well-balanced diet results. Brothwell has noted that a single pair of tibiae are alone suspicious of deficiency disease in the very large number of prehistoric skeletons that have been examined. By contrast, 7 percent of the 233 skeletons in the St. Brides Church series (London c. 1750 to 1850) show some degree of rickets (21).

In summary, the transition from hunting and gathering to agriculture almost certainly led to a significant increase in the burden of infectious disease. With industrialisation this burden has largely been abolished. Virtually all of the decline in the death rate in England and Wales in the second half of the last century was in deaths registered as being due to infection—half of them to tuberculosis (22). Thus it is to the changes that led to a decline in infections that we largely owe our current standard of health. McKeown has endeavoured to assess the probable causes of this decline since it first began in the second half of the eighteenth century (22). Medical treatments available then were unlikely to have altered for the better the course of many illnesses. Two other major factors would appear to have been general environmental conditions and nutrition. While the sanitary reforms of the mid-nineteenth century led to a decline in bowel infections, it is difficult to see how other environmental changes could have worked to reduce infection. The concentration in the new industrial cities would appear to have favoured the transmission of tuberculosis. McKeown therefore settles for improved nutrition as the factor most likely to have been operating to reduce deaths in the period since that reduction first began in the second half of the eighteenth century. This is consistent with known increases in agricultural productivity at that time. Perhaps the starchy cereals on which the population had long been dependent were now supplemented by more vegetables and meat. The dietary balance that had been forfeited with the Neolithic revolution was restored. However, improvement in living standards could only have been sustained by birth control:

> If the birth rate in England and Wales had remained at the level of 1870, the population today would be 140 million instead of 46 million, with effects on the standard of living and health that can be imagined. . . . Although the improvement in health was initiated by increased food supplies, without limitation of numbers the advance would soon have been eliminated. Viewed historically, the balance between food and population size on which health depends owes less to increase of food than to control of numbers (23).

It is ironical that the single measure that was to prove most critical for the sustained improvement of the health of the British people—birth control—was not merely overlooked by the medical profession, but was vigorously opposed by them (24).

The contribution of medical intervention in individuals—both preventive and curative—is much more difficult to assess. Razzell has argued for the importance of vaccination against smallpox (25) but the proportion of the total decline in mortality that could be attributed to this one disease is unlikely to be great. In McKeown's assessment, the contribution of clinical medicine was not significant until the second quarter of this century (23). By this time the larger proportion of the total decline in mortality had already been achieved.

It is widely believed that the introduction of antibiotics and effective immunisation campaigns marked a dramatic breakthrough in the fight against infectious diseases. Whilst this may have been true in particular cases—for example, immunisation against diphtheria—their contribution to the total decline in mortality over the last two centuries has been a minor one. Most of the reduction had already occurred before they were introduced and there was only a slight downward inflection in an otherwise declining curve following their introduction. (See Figure 2.)

This account of the changing impact of infectious disease throughout the three main phases of human history—hunting and gathering, agricultural, and industrial—has demonstrated the major importance for health of man's interactions with his environment. The provision of food, sanitary control, and the regulation of births have been the three central factors.

This is not to underrate the recently acquired capacity to intervene in individuals by means of immunisation and antibiotics. But it does put that capacity into perspective.

The Diseases of Civilisation

In industrialised countries cardiovascular diseases and neoplasms account for two-thirds of total mortality in both sexes, and in Japan for 50 percent (10).

Those diseases which appear to have increased relative to the posited natural state of man will now be considered. A central issue is whether this increase is a real one or simply the result of people living long enough to succumb to degenerative processes. In other words, are they the universal consequences of the aging of the

FIGURE 2. Deaths of Children under 15 Years Attributed to Scarlet Fever, Diphtheria, Whooping Cough, Measles (England and Wales)

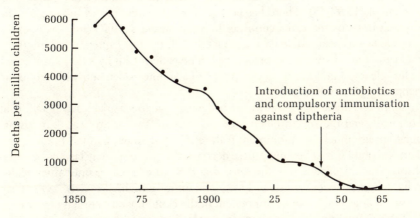

Source: Porter, R. R. The contribution of the biological and medical sciences to human welfare. *Presidential Addresses of the British Association for the Advancement of Science,* Swansea Meeting, 1971. Published by the British Association, 1972, p. 95.

human organism or are they, in large measure, the consequences of changes in behaviour associated with economic development? There is also the related issue of whether the way of life affects the overall rate of aging as distinct from the development of particular diseases. However, the evidence on this latter issue would be very difficult to obtain, so this analysis will be concerned with particular categories of disease.

Cardiovascular disease of a degenerative kind is manifested by two principal changes that progress with age—degeneration of the arterial walls and rising blood pressure. These two changes tend to occur together but need not do so. The underlying causal mechanisms may well be different in each case and so may the final lethal event. Kuller and Reisler have attempted to explain these interactions (26). High levels of arteriosclerosis combined with hypertension tend to produce a high incidence of both heart attacks and strokes (as in U.S. Negroes). Arteriosclerosis without high blood pressure tends to be associated with a high incidence of heart attacks and an intermediate level of strokes (as in U.S. whites). Hypertension unaccompanied by high levels of coronary arteriosclerosis tends to be associated with a high incidence in strokes but not heart attacks (as in Japan).

Reliable information on the prevalence of arteriosclerosis is only available by direct examination of the arteries at autopsy, but indirect evidence is provided by the level of serum cholesterol. Information on blood pressure is more readily available. Some of these data for contemporary hunter-gatherers is listed in Table 1 (27–40). Evidence for former hunting and gathering groups who have changed their way of life is not included. While it would be unwarranted to conclude from this evidence that hunter-gatherers are free from degenerative cardiovascular disease, the evidence certainly points towards its incidence being low. It is also interesting to note that in most of these groups blood pressure and serum cholesterol do not tend to increase with age.

There is now a very large body of data on the epidemiology of ischaemic heart disease which shows a general tendency for it to increase with increasing economic development (41,42,43). There has been a very substantial rise in the age-specific death rates in many industrial countries in recent decades (10). While many of the way-of-life factors responsible have been identified, the full sequence and interrelation of causal events remain to be clarified. The pattern with hypertension seems a little less clear-cut and there are exceptions to a simple association with economic development (44,45,46,47).

In summary, there are grounds for believing that the marked degeneration of arterial walls and the rise in blood pressure with age that are typical of industrial populations are much less prominent features of aging under natural (hunting and gathering) conditions. Therefore, these degenerative processes may be characterised as diseases of maladaptation in the sense that they arise "because our earlier evolution has left us genetically unsuited for life in an industrialised society" (42). They constitute a large and growing component of the contemporary burden of disease.

In Table 2 an attempt has been made to identify the relative impact of the major categories of disease in contemporary Britain, as indicated by different measures (48–52). The relative impact of the killing disorders may be assessed by calculating the years of a national "total life" (say to age 85) that are lost from each cause. In

TABLE 1. Some Data on Signs of Degenerative Cardiovascular Disease in Hunter-Gatherers

Groups	Authors	Systolic Blood Pressure		Serum Cholesterol		Comments
		Level at age 40	Increase with age?	Level	Increase with age?	
Australian aborigines	Casley-Smith (27) (review) Abbie & Schroder (28) Schwartz & Casley-Smith (29) Sewartz & others (30)	<120	slight	low to moderate	no	Exception is high blood pressure recordings from groups on Gulf of Carpentaria by Croll (27)
Malayan aborigines	Polunin (31)	(low)	no	—	—	
Bushmen (Kalahari)	Kaminer & Lutz (32) Bronte-Stewart & others (33) Truswell & Hansen (34) Tobias (35)	c.115	no	low	no	Circumstantial evidence of arteriosclerosis and sudden death with chest pain in (33). See text.
Hadzas (Tanzania)	Barnicot & others (36)	c.120	slight	low	no	Most had adopted a settled way of life within the previous 3 years
Pygmies (Congo)	Mann & others (37)	c.130	slight	low	no	Contact with agricultural Bantus. Plantain, sweet potato and rice prominent in diet.
Amerindians of the Brazilian Mato Grosso	Neel & others (38) Hugh-Jones & others (39) Lowenstein (40)	<115	no	low	slight	

TABLE 2. Major Components of the Contemporary Disease Burden in Britain

	K=Killing D=Disabling	Years of "Total Life" Lost (i.e., to Age 85) (E&W, 1968)		Years of "Working Life" Lost (i.e., Ages 15–64) (E&W, 1968)		Days Certified Sickness Absence (GB, 1969)		N.H.S. Expenditure (E&W, 1961/2)	General Practitioner Consultations (from Fry, 1966)	Hospital Bed Use (E&W, 1968)	
		M	F	M	F	M	F	M&F	M&F	M	F
		%	%	%	%	%	%	%	%	%	%
1. Cardiovascular (including cerebrovascular)	K&D	35	33	21	16	14	9	10	10	10	12
2. Respiratory (including TB)	K&D	15	12	13	13	28	19	10	33	8	5
3. Neoplastic	K	20	23	16	23	1	1	4	—	5	5
4. Congenital and perinatal (including mental handicap)	K&D	10	11	20	23	—	—	5	—	22	14
5. Accidents and violence	K&D	7	4	13	7	7	4	4	—	5	4

Condition	D	(a)	(b)	(c)	(d)	(e)	(f)	(g)	(h)	(i)	(j)
6. Mental and nervous	D	—	—	—	—	13	18	15	12	34	35
7. Musculoskeletal	D	—	—	1	1	12	11	4	8	3	4
8. Digestive	D	—	1	1	1	7	5	6	10	5	3
9. Symptoms and ill-defined conditions	D	—	—	—	—	9	12	4	—	3	3
10. Others		12	16	16	17	9	21	38 (including: dental—9 maternity—7)	27 (including: skin—10 preventive—10)	5	15 (including: maternity—9)
Total Rates (100%)		223	141	66	34	16,659	17,586	£665.4m	4–6	6.97	8.46
		per 1,000 population per year				per 1,000 at risk per year		attributed to specific diseases out of a total of £900m	per person per year	per 1,000 population	
					(48)		(49)	(50)	(51)		(52)

E&W = England and Wales, GB = Great Britain
Sources: Given under References. Numbers indicated at base of each column.

27

England and Wales in 1968 more than 20 percent of such "total loss" was due to cancer. In males, 40 percent of this loss was in turn due to one cancer—cancer of the lung (48). This is almost entirely caused by tobacco smoking (53). Cancer of the colon and rectum is the second commonest cancer in men and a major one in women in many industrialised countries (54). Burkitt has noted that its incidence appears to increase with economic development (55). The incidence in U.S. Negroes is comparable to that for U.S. whites and is around 10 times greater than that estimated for rural Africans. The removal of dietary fibre and a high intake of refined carbohydrates that is typical of diets in industrialised countries is associated with a much slower transit of food through the gut. Burkitt argues that this may be significant not only in the aetiology of large bowel cancer but also for other large bowel diseases associated with economic development—for example, appendicitis and diverticulitis (56,57). If this were so they would all fit neatly into the category of diseases of maladaptation.

For many cancers, however, the picture is less clear-cut. Cancer of the cervix and stomach have both been declining in many industrialised countries. Doll has reviewed the geographical distribution of cancer (54) and has recently commented:

> The marked differences in cancer incidence in different countries and the changes that have been noted in the experience of migrant groups when they move from one country to another are among the many pieces of evidence suggesting that most cancers are due to environmental factors. It follows that most cancers are, in principle, preventable (58).

Higginson of the International Agency for Cancer Research has estimated that 80 percent of all cancer has its aetiology in man's relation to his environment (59). There is little information on cancer incidence in hunter-gatherers.

So far an attempt has been made to show that diseases of maladaptation are probably responsible for a major proportion of premature deaths in industrial populations. Disease of this kind may also be responsible for a good deal of morbidity and discomfort. Upper respiratory infections spread much more easily where large numbers are gathered together (18). Smoking and air pollution are responsible for much chronic bronchitis (53,60). The chemicalisation of the human environment may well be leading to further untoward effects which are not yet apparent (61). Diabetes (62) and dental caries (21) both appear to be associated with a diet rich in refined carbohydrates. Even varicose veins appear to be associated with industrialisation (63). It will be seen from Table 2 that mental and nervous disorders are major causes of general practitioner and hospital utilisation, health service expenditure, and absence from work. Much inappropriate and distressing anxiety and depression result from the stresses of modern life (64). Recent research has also linked greater experience of significant life events (e.g., promotion, marriage, divorce, change of residence and occupation) with greater vulnerability to illnesses, such as ischaemic heart disease (65,66). Although cancer is not usually thought of as a stress disease, the incidence of breast cancer has recently been associated with personality type and past experience of stressful events (67). Findings such as these suggest that a biological and not just emotional price is being paid for the individual mobility which is often regarded as one of the greatest benefits of industrialisation.

Other Diseases

The category of disease in which way-of-life factors do not seem to have major significance is, by definition, a residual one. Its size will depend on the proportion of disease that is deemed neither to be caused by those infections that have decreased nor by those diseases which have increased since Paleolithic times. It is likely to include a significant minority of all cancer, many metabolic disorders, a certain proportion of infection—especially that caused by microbes such as streptococci, staphylococci, and coliforms, which are ubiquitous in the human environment—and most congenital disorders. If organic causes are demonstrated to be predominant in schizophrenia, it also may fit within this category. The question of trauma is a little different. The damage that industrial populations are sustaining from the mechanical violence they have unleashed upon themselves—especially in the forms of the motor car, industry, and mechanised warfare—may lead one to think of this as a disease of civilisation. On the other hand, hunting and other injuries are likely to have been frequent causes of death in Paleolithic times.

To summarise: Industrial populations owe their current health standards to a pattern of ecological relationships which serves to reduce their vulnerability to death from infection and to a lesser extent to the capabilities of clinical medicine. Unfortunately, this new way of life, because it is so far removed from that to which man is adapted by evolution, has produced its own disease burden. These diseases of maladaptation are, in many cases, increasing.

We may now move forward to the following two questions: What has been the strategy for tackling these new diseases? Why has it not been more successful?

The Current Medical Effort

Ischaemic heart disease is the paradigmatic disease of maladaptation; the response to it typifies wider trends within medicine. The major thrust of the medical response to this problem has been towards the hospital treatment of heart attack. This has been elaborated in complex and expensive intensive cardiac care units. For the U.S.A. it has been estimated that 3,000 such units were established by the end of 1971 and that they were using 10 percent of all trained nurses (68). And yet this major effort has been mounted in the absence of convincing evidence of benefit. The only randomised controlled trial which has compared treatment at home with hospital treatment, with which this author is familiar, failed to show any benefit from hospital treatment (69).

A consideration of the natural history both of the acute episode and of the underlying process points to the implausibility of significant gain from the hospital treatment of heart attack. Results from Belfast and Edinburgh indicated that because of the suddenness of death "about 50 percent of fatal heart attacks are outside the possible reach of medical treatment. In such cases hope must lie with prevention" (42). Moreover, the individual who has survived one acute episode is still a coronary-prone individual much more likely than average to succumb to another.

Why then this apparent technological overreach in the response to heart disease? Was it just a simple mistake encouraged by genuine gains in other fields? Or has the perception of the problem been seriously hampered by the character of contemporary medical thinking? If so, in what way is this thinking limited?

Thomas McKeown has noted the extent to which the contemporary medical effort is based on an engineering approach to the improvement of health:

> The approach to biology and medicine established during the seventeenth century was an engineering one based on a physical model. Nature was conceived in mechanistic terms, which led in biology to the idea that a living organism could be regarded as a machine which might be taken apart and reassembled if its structure and function were fully understood. In medicine, the same concept led further to the belief that an understanding of disease processes and of the body's response to them would make it possible to intervene therapeutically, mainly by physical (surgical) chemical, or electrical methods (23).

In view of the limited effectiveness of this approach, it is worth examining its origins. At least four things have been important. They are: 1) the nature of the doctor-patient relationship, 2) the limitation of medical theory to the "biology of the individual," 3) the germ theory of disease, and 4) institutional and political factors.

Given the traditional form of doctor-patient interaction, it was inevitable that doctors would strive to get better and better at intervening in their patients' illnesses. This is the historical foundation of the engineering approach. When doctors drew from the emerging biological science of the nineteenth century, they chose that strand which had the most obvious relevance to their ability to treat their patients: They chose what Crombie refers to as the "science of the organised individual" and were singularly uninfluenced by the other strand—"the science of populations." This theoretical bias is the second important factor (70). In medicine this theoretical foundation lent support to the view that it was the doctor's role to intervene chemically (by drugs) or physically (by surgery) in order to restore the patient's disordered system or systems to normal.

The extent to which human population biology—for example, evolutionary theory, historical demography, and medical ecology—has failed to influence medical theory is quite remarkable. The resulting inability to deal theoretically (as distinct from statistically) with biological phenomena at levels of organisation above a single organism has left medical theory seriously deficient. Medicine has deprived itself of the only possible theoretical basis on which criteria for man's biological normality could rest. It hesitates to call progressive health-compromising processes—such as arterial degeneration, rising blood pressure, and the tendency towards diabetes—"diseases," because they are associated with a way of life it feels bound to accept as normal. The limits of normality in blood pressure are endlessly debated. The serious issue of whether a bodily change that is induced by our way of life and predisposes to overt disease should be regarded as pathological has been reduced to the trivial one of whether the distribution of blood pressures in the population is unimodal or bimodal. It hardly needs to be added that the debate gains its significance not from a felt need to prevent the development of the abnormal but from the assumed imperative to knock it into line with drugs.

With little understanding of the way of life to which man is biologically adapted, modern medicine is unable to predict the possible harmful consequences of departures from it. It was surprised to find that the repeated inhalation of tobacco smoke actually harmed the lungs and caused cancer. Until quite recently it was not widely suspected that large bowel cancer, a major cause of cancer death, might be associated with dietary habits that have diverged a long way from those of our forbears. The fourteenth edition of Bailey and Love's famous *A Short Practice of Surgery*, published in 1968, contains 15 pages of discussion on cancers of the colon and rectum (71). Much of it is naturally concerned with operative techniques for the removal of the tumours. In the case of rectal cancer it includes a paragraph and a diagram on the complete removal of all pelvic organs (under the appropriate heading "More Extensive Operations"). In contrast to this readiness to consider drastic attempts at cure there is no discussion of aetiology and there is no acknowledgment of the possibility that these cancers might be caused by our way of life and therefore be preventable.

The limitation of medical theory to the "biology of the individual" also handicaps consideration of the role of genetic factors in disease. Frequently, naive interpretations are placed on the relative contributions of nature and nurture to disease processes. Epidemiological studies, say on ischaemic heart disease, are carried out on populations with an industrial way of life which is implicitly assumed to be normal, and on the basis of the findings a certain weight is accorded to the influence of heredity on the disease. The fact that these inherited characteristics may only become relevant to the aetiology of the condition under stresses that are, in evolutionary terms, novel—and that it is therefore the interaction between the stresses and the inherited variation in body build that is important—is often not acknowledged (72).

The third factor contributing to the dominance of the engineering approach within modern medicine was the rise of the germ theory of disease. It identified discrete, specific, and external causal agents for disease processes which were usually thought of as acute and short-lived. The theory gave support to the idea of specific therapies and failed to emphasise the importance of general resistance to infection. By contrast one could now describe the preindustrial situation with respect to infection (on the basis of McKeown's analysis) as one of chronic predisposition to infection caused by poor nutrition and environmental conditions. Thus the appropriate model for infectious disease need not, as is often suggested, be fundamentally different from that for the degenerative diseases. A fatal infection, like the occlusion of a coronary artery, is often a terminal event to which the individual involved is strongly predisposed by his social experience.

The germ theory also coincided with a high point in the view that progress was to be secured by the mechanical domination of nature. The response to the problem of infection was not thought of principally in terms of the strengthening of the natural forces of defence—for example, improved nutrition and population control. Even the preventive implications were taken up in what were literally engineering terms. Primitive man, it was imagined, lived amongst his own filth. Modern man, by means of sewers, piped water, and antiseptics would cleanse himself of germs.

The fourth group of historical influences on the rise of the engineering approach are professional and institutional ones. Rosenberg has recorded how the American medical profession in the middle of the last century hitched its fortune to the rising star of science (73). The germ theory of disease came just in time to save the faltering public prestige of doctors. Class interest was also important in suppressing an alternative approach. While the well-to-do physicians proffered their clinical skills to the rich, it was social and preventive medicine that was needed most urgently for the poor. Unfortunately, the prestigious physicians dominated the teaching hospitals and medical education and, therefore, the theoretical and practical development of public health and preventive medicine received little encouragement.

This account of the technical side of modern medicine may now be summarised. The engineering approach to the improvement of health has been dominant over an alternative approach which would emphasise the importance of way-of-life factors in disease. Curative medicine has not been very successful in reducing the impact of diseases of maladaptation. While it may be argued that the current strategy still offers the most hope—especially as significant changes in the pattern of life may seem unlikely—the nature of the underlying disease processes involved makes it improbable that curative interventions will be very successful. Nor can there be any guarantee that industrial populations have already exhausted the possibilities in respect to diseases of maladaptation. If technological advances continue to be pursued and implemented with little regard for their impact on man's biology there may well be an additional twenty-first century equivalent of the current epidemic of ischaemic heart disease.

It is therefore concluded that the problem of diminishing returns is a real one. It results from the nature of the contemporary disease burden and the limited front on which medical effort has been concentrated. These technical considerations cannot, however, explain modern medicine's considerable cultural momentum. To do so it will be necessary to explore the relationship between medicine's technical and nontechnical sides.

The Nontechnical Side of Medicine

Medical institutions can be identified by their purpose—they mediate between man and his vulnerability to disease. It is clear that medical cultures differ from one another as radically as do the total cultures of which they are a part. Further, differing medical cultures have a certain internal consistency—that is, the way in which any individual copes with disease is largely socially determined.

Magical medicine is widely regarded as the most primitive element of medical culture. But how is magic to be interpreted? Western rationalism has placed great emphasis on the importance of gaining as accurate a picture as possible of the objective world. Within this approach it is the logical and empirical content of a belief, rather than its function within the mental lives of individuals, which is considered important. Thus magic involves a set of very stupid beliefs from which there is nothing to learn. An alternative and more fruitful approach is to focus on the function of magical beliefs and practices. Levi-Strauss has shown that this is, in fact, what the practitioners of magic do (74). If the members of such a community are presented with empirical evidence which is inconsistent with their magical beliefs, they do not deny the evidence, but the evidence does not weaken their faith in magic. Belief in magic, then, is not critically dependent upon the empirical status of magical propositions. For primitive man, magic helps to impose order on the universe, to reduce ambiguities, and to neutralise and reduce perceived threats and actual misfortunes (75). Communities that are constantly exposed to natural forces that may appear to be random and beyond man's control need means of coping with their incomprehension and vulnerability. Magic is an active response to that need.

Religion and medicine were closely associated in Europe until relatively recent times. In the medieval period, it was the religious orders that maintained the hospitals and infirmaries; this association has continued in some institutions to the present day. Religious interpretations were placed upon illness and relief from suffering was sought in the healing rites of the church. The central theme in the theistic response to man's vulnerability to disease and suffering is resignation to the will of God. Belief in an afterlife helps the sufferer to minimize the cruelties of this earthly realm.

It is worth noting that there was also a fatalistic character to nonreligious interpretations of illness during the medieval period. The movement of the heavenly bodies was widely believed to be responsible for epidemics and for individual episodes of illness. If the social reinforcement of resignation to misfortune is the functional core of religious medicine, then this fatalistic core can be seen to be common also to nontheistic mysticism, such as Buddhism, and even to some atheist philosophies, such as Stoicism.

The emotive mainspring for much of the social response to disease lies in man's capacity for compassion. There are few who are not distressed by the suffering of a fellow creature. Unfortunately, there is another side to the emotive response to the sick: They may be perceived as an unwanted reminder of the vulnerability of the healthy to diseases that they dread, and so evoke apprehension and disquiet. This applies particularly to those whose behaviour is bizarre and unpredictable (the insane) and to those who are physically deformed or mentally handicapped. In these instances, social mediation may well work against the interests of the sick individual—as for example, when they are incarcerated in long-stay hospitals to relieve others of the disquiet that their presence creates. As such incarceration often has an adverse effect on the patient's health (76,77,78), the usual justification—that it was necessary for the effective treatment of the patient's condition—deserves to be treated skeptically.

So far, four modes of mediation between man and his vulnerability to disease have been identified—magic, religion, compassion, and rejection. Together they may be regarded as constituting the nontechnical or helping-to-cope side of medicine. By none of these means is the natural history of disease processes within individuals predictably and specifically changed for the better. That has been the achievement of the fifth mode—the technical mastery of disease. All medical cultures can be regarded as being made up of these five elements (79). For some centuries in the West, the technical mode of response has become increasingly manifest. There has been a progressive increase in the understanding of the structure and function of the human body and, to some extent, of the nature of disease processes within it. Disease has been described in increasingly scientific terms. But it needs emphasising that until very recently indeed, doctors could do little to alter the natural course of events (23). Thus the response to disease came to be described in technical terms well before the technical capacity to master disease became significant. The vocabulary and activities changed, but the functional content of doctor-patient interaction remained that of the helping-to-cope side of medicine.

In recent decades, and especially since World War II, scientific medical technology of an engineering kind has gained overwhelming dominance in the mediation between industrial man and disease. The situation of the sick is increasingly defined in scientific terms and, by this means, ambiguities and uncertainties are reduced. Major crises are responded to in a confident and surehanded manner. The victim of a heart attack is taken to an intensive cardiac care unit; the victim of a car accident, to an accident and emergency unit; the cancer patient "has to go to hospital for an operation." And the minor illnesses too: For upper respiratory infections, there are antibiotics; for depression and anxiety, psychoactive drugs.

The technical response to disease pervades the whole of contemporary medical culture—the organisation of medical care, the education of doctors, and the character of doctor-patient interaction. The costs of this style of medicine are not limited to its considerable and rapidly rising resource demands. It concentrates the medical effort in the large acute hospitals while the ordinary citizen finds access to primary care ever more difficult. It concentrates resources on patients with technically interesting conditions while the insane, the handicapped, and the elderly are frequently left to live out their lives in overcrowded and unpleasant conditions. Medical education detours doctors from the areas of greatest need by emphasising technical challenges rather than moral ones. Concentration on the technical (biological) problem deflects attention from the emotional and existential significance of disease.

And yet, in spite of deficiencies of this kind, discontent with health services does not usually lead to criticism of the basic characteristics of contemporary medicine. The system is strongly legitimised. This position is strengthened by medicine's consonance with the wider culture of which it is a part. Its technical aspects are themselves consonant with the general pattern of interaction between industrial man and his environment. So too is the idea of progress. Progress is seen to be the simple sum of what are taken to be its component parts. Thus, if the hospital treatment of heart attack really did show a significant, if marginal, improvement over treatment at home, this would be regarded as progress. An increase from, say, 50 to 70 percent in patients surviving 5 years after treatment for cancer would be regarded as further evidence of medical progress. So also in economic life: a + b cars per thousand population is better than a cars; x + y television sets better than x, and so on. But in terms of real human welfare, neither whole is the simple sum of parts as these. There is as little reason for believing that the health of the population is being significantly improved as there is for believing that the material conditions for human life are becoming more favourable.

The original paradox remains: Enthusiasm for the system has outpaced its concrete achievements and its indirect costs tend to be underplayed. Despite the evidence to the contrary, it is widely believed by both patients and their doctors that industrial populations owe their higher health standards to scientific medicine, that such medical technology as currently exists is largely effective in coping with the tasks it faces, and that it offers great promise for the future. To unravel this paradox it is helpful to explore further the complex and subtle relationship between the truly technical, the apparently technical, and the nontechnical elements of modern medicine. This will be done by focusing on the nature of the interaction between the sick and the purveyors of high technology medicine in two typical cases—first, the hospital treatment of heart attack and, second, the treatment of upper respiratory infections with antibiotics.

A heart attack is one of the gravest threats that faces middle-aged men of the industrial world. The sure-handedness of the technical response to this problem and its elaboration in coronary care units has already been noted. This technical response seems both impressive and credible. And yet, as noted earlier, there is no convincing evidence that this energetic intervention secures any more favourable an outcome than simple treatment at home.

What is notable in all this is the preoccupation with an engineering style of response and the reluctance to compare outcome with that from a low technology (home treatment) response. The scientific testing of this high technology response was widely regarded as unethical until the publication in August 1971 of the study by Mathers and others (69) which failed to show any benefit from it. Despite this, specialists have been willing to encourage massive expenditure on intensive cardiac care. Some of this expenditure would almost certainly have secured much greater reductions in mortality if it had been used to persuade people to change those elements in their way of life (such as smoking and overeating) which increase their risk of heart disease. (Skeptics see 80.)

The development of coronary care units has far outpaced what would have been justified in terms of a rational programme to reduce the toll from ischaemic heart disease. It has a momentum which is almost separate from considerations as rational as this. How different, *functionally*, are the activities involved from the rituals of the magicians of old? Both are active responses to forces threatening well-being. In neither case is there much enthusiasm amongst the operators for the empirical testing of the effectiveness of their treatment.

One of the recurrent annoyances of urban life is upper respiratory infections which frequently cause one to feel miserable. Patients, therefore, expect their doctor to "do something." Now most of these infections are viral and nearly all doctors, if questioned at a scientific meeting, would admit both that antibiotics are ineffective in altering the course of viral infections and that they should not be used indiscriminately. Yet the prescription of antibiotics is now widely expected by patients when they go to their doctor with an upper respiratory infection—and most doctors oblige.

The argument therefore is that the almost exclusive concentration, within modern medical culture, on the technical mastery of disease is more apparent than real. For in addition to countering the challenges to human well-being on the biological level, this technology is also being used to cope with the emotional and existential challenges that disease involves. The problem of disease cannot be reduced to the purely technical one of prevention and correction of biological malfunctioning. Nor is it sufficient just to add on the dimensions of emotion or of symptomatology. For in addition to the distress that disease causes directly and to such emotional distress as is itself regarded as a disease, there is the threat that disease poses to the individual's sense of his own integrity and well-being. This existential challenge, in the ultimate, is the threat of oblivion.

At this point it is desirable to clarify, in the terms of this analysis, the nature of symptomatic treatment. Such treatment may serve to counter disease on all three levels: First, there are medical interventions which relieve symptoms by means of specific and predictable physiological effects. The use of aspirin in a muscular sprain is a good example. Second, there are nonspecific but nonetheless physiological responses that cannot be predicted from the known properties of the drug. This is frequently referred to as a placebo effect and may be observed, for example, in the effect of dummy tablets in lowering blood pressure or relieving tension and anxiety. Third, there are those doctor-patient interactions which do not alter the observable course of events but which both parties nevertheless feel to be worthwhile. By means of explanation, ritual, and symbol, such interventions are serving principally to counter the existential threat. The patient's situation is defined, ambiguity is reduced and reassurance—as doctors frequently call it—results. Psychotherapy and much prescribing behaviour would appear to serve this objective.

In this attempt to explore the interrelation of the technical and nontechnical aspects of modern medicine, two sets of distinctions have been drawn: First, five different modes of mediation between man and disease have been identified—magic, religion, compassion for the suffering, rejection of the abnormal, and the technical mastery of disease. The first four of these may be taken as constituting the nontechnical or helping-to-cope side of medicine. Second, it has been argued that disease challenges well-being on three main levels—biological, emotional, and existential. Clearly, these two sets of factors are interrelated. Thus, the technical mastery of disease is serving to reduce biological malfunctioning. Further, the helping-to-cope side of medicine principally serves to reduce the emotional and existential challenge. But the essence of this argument is to point out that these interrelationships are not simple or self-evident. And most important of all, that which appears to be about the technical mastery of disease is not necessarily serving merely to counter biological challenges to well-being. To an increasing extent medical technology is serving as a mask for non-technical functions. It carries a large symbolic load. The more attention within medicine is focused on the technical mastery of disease, the larger become the symbolic and nontechnical functions of that technology. This process has been intensified by the decline of theistic relgion.

The Future of Medicine

It has been suggested that the character of a medical culture is largely determined by the character of the total culture and that the medical beliefs and behaviour of individuals are largely socially determined. It would be wrong, however, to ignore the possibility for change. For one thing, current developments do not always fulfill past expectations. Thus strains are created, both in the sphere of practice and the sphere of theory. The old ways of seeing the world are fractured and through the cracks the real world becomes more visible. The scope of human freedom expands. Within the wider sphere of productive life, as indeed within medicine, the most serious emerging strains derive from industrial man's relation to the natural world.

It is clear that the increase in human numbers and the increase in material consumption per capita must reach limits in a finite world. This is not a problem that will go away if it is ignored, and an increasing awareness of it is likely to lead to a fundamental reassessment of the wider constraints on human action. As ecology is central to health, it would be surprising if such a reassessment did not also involve reexamination of the assumptions underlying modern medicine. In any case, medicine is facing its own crisis of diminishing returns.

How then might medicine respond to these emerging strains? In which direction will thinking need to develop if it is to reorient itself within these newly recognised constraints? Because the technical side of medicine involves fewer conceptual problems, it will be considered first. The problem is to identify those means of increasing biological well-being that are not dependent on measures (such as continued economic growth) which are likely to aggravate the wider ecological problem. This will almost certainly involve a switch away from the increase in highly technical clinical interventions towards an emphasis on the importance of way-of-life factors in disease. For medical theory to meet this challenge it will need to broaden its scientific base. Lessons relevant to the improvement of health will need to be learned from human evolution; from the study of the health consequences of the transition from hunting and gathering to agriculture and from agriculture to industry; from historical demography and the debate about the regulation of numbers in animal populations. The health aspects of the relationship between human communities and their environments need much more detailed study. There is a need for good comprehensive epidemiological studies on groups with widely differing ways of life. The critical importance of an understanding of health and disease in hunter-gatherers deserves urgent recognition—especially because many groups are being subject to rapid acculturation (20).

It would be unrealistic however to expect all doctors to be expert in comprehending biological phenomena at both an individual level and a population level. The principal concern of the clinician will continue to be the treatment of the sick. It is understandable that clinicians, in their day-to-day practice, should take for granted the usual way of life of the community and judge the significance of behavioural factors in individual illness against that background. But if the burden of the maladaptation diseases is to be reduced by changing those elements of our way of life that are most to blame (and this is the most effective strategy currently available for these diseases) then clinicians need to have a much more sophisticated understanding of the relationships between behaviour and disease. Human population biology is essential to that understanding.

The greatest theoretical challenge within contemporary medicine lies with those responsible for the health of communities—specialists in public health or community medicine. Such specialists cannot afford to take any way of life for granted. They will need a comprehensive understanding of the experience of disease in different human communities with differing ways of life—that is, they should be experts in the biology of human populations. Unfortunately, there is, as yet, little recognition of the need to develop the theoretical basis of community medicine in this way.

When health problems are perceived differently, they may be responded to differently. For example, despite health propaganda efforts that have been very modest in comparison to the promotional activities of the tobacco interests, tobacco consumption per adult British male had fallen by 1971/2 to its lowest level since 1916 (80). Anti-smoking propaganda does seem to be having an effect—given its low intensity it would have been unreasonable to expect more. The current rates of decline in tobacco consumption are likely to prevent several thousand premature deaths each year (80). Their impact on health is therefore of an order of magnitude that bears comparison to major hospital-based activities.

Much of the impact of diseases of maladaptation may be reducible by changes in our way of life that are not too onerous. Habits can be changed. It is relatively easy to increase the amount of high residue food in the diet and, although we've become accustomed to helping ourselves to more and more sugar and salt, it is possible to wean oneself back down to more modest intakes without loss in the palatability of food. If a reduction in the intake of saturated fats is shown to reduce the risk of heart disease, then the substitution of polyunsaturated margarine for butter and the avoidance of fatty meat need be no great hardship. Avoiding obesity and keeping fit both have their own immediate rewards as well as the long-term one of improved health. The fundamental task is to change thinking about disease and what can be done about it. Given that, significant further gains in health may well be possible. In Victorian times there was a happy synergism between the germ theory of disease and the wider puritan culture which led to the successful war against the germs. That battle has been largely won. Is it too much to expect a similar future interaction between specific advice on changing health-damaging habits and a wider culture which is increasingly sensitive to the need for man to treat the natural world with respect?

None of this is meant to imply that the improvement of biological well-being should take automatic precedence over other human goals. Individuals and the wider community may well choose to pay a biological price for the achievement of competing objectives. But such choices should be both deliberate and well informed. At the moment, they are usually neither.

A switch in strategies away from complex, technological hospital medicine may have a major impact on the nontechnical side of medicine. The placing of deliberate constraints on the further development and deployment of such technology would seem to deny its potential for the alleviation of human suffering. One line of defence—especially against the existential challenge of illness—would be weakened. Such a change would, however, make possible other major gains on the nontechnical side. With a more realistic assessment of the capabilities of medical technology, there might be less of a tendency to interpret the problem of illness in purely technical terms. The emotional and existential aspects of its challenge to well-being could be given more open recognition. It has often been argued that a more balanced response to illness is more effective. By being more sensitive to the patient's situation, doctors are likely to obtain better information about the problem, provide more relevant advice and treatment, and secure more cooperation.

Little has been said so far in this chapter about the very large categories of people whose illnesses and disabilities have not been (often could not have been) prevented and who cannot be easily restored to health—those with congenital and acquired handicaps, the mentally ill, the chronic sick, and the disabled elderly. This is because the argument has been principally concerned with the major forces at work in the evolution of contemporary medical culture. Meeting the needs of these handicapped groups for humane care and rehabilitation has not been a major objective in practice (81,82). Resources and energy have been directed elsewhere—to the high technology, short–stay hospitals; to the patients with interesting conditions for whom something (i.e., a technical something) could be done. The needs of the handicapped comprise a large and growing proportion of the work load of the health services. Within a more balanced medical culture, there would be less need to translate their frequently nontechnical needs into technical ones. The challenge that they pose to the compassion of the healthy could be confronted and responded to more directly. And the resources to improve their lot can only be made available by carefully constraining the further development of expensive high-technology medicine. There is, in fact, a growing recognition that the care function of health services is in direct competition for resources with the cure function and that, hitherto, cure has had more than its fair share (83).

One of the most important preconditions for improving the care of the mentally ill is an increased tolerance on the part of the normal for bizarre and unpredictable behaviour. Given such tolerance the need for institutionalisation and its attendant harm to the patient is reduced. Currently, it is often felt necessary to represent this essentially ethical problem as a technical one—to try and make mental illness respectable by insisting that it is just like other illness and needs treatment just the same. The problem would benefit from a more direct and honest confrontation.

Conclusion

In much discussion of the current state of medicine the broader concept of medical culture is often accepted as a given. This acceptance confers an unnecessary aura of inevitability to current ideas about how to improve health and about the relationship between the technical and nontechnical aspects of medicine. Medicine is a product of man and can be as he chooses to make it. It is, in any case, possible to argue that there have always been two conflicting approaches within medicine itself—one emphasising the potency of clinical intervention, the other the importance of way-of-life factors.

Medicine may be expected to come under increasing pressure from the wider culture, which is in turn likely to change as a result of increasing confrontation with material and biological constraints on human action. With a rising proportion of illness evidently man-made and with increasing restrictions on the further increase of resource consumption for medical care, medicine seems bound to move in another, holistic direction.

If it does, biological well-being may be expected to benefit. Emotional problems in relation to illness may be increasingly respected. But the sense of exposure of the existential threat that disease represents may, by contrast, be heightened. It will be more difficult to say such things as "Don't worry, doctor. By the time I get lung cancer they'll have a cure for it." Faith in the effectiveness of society's defences against death might be weakened. With less confidence in his ability to master nature, man will have to learn to live more openly with his vulnerability to forces he cannot control and with the frailty of individual human existence. Man's domination of nature has been the central impetus of modern industrial culture. Further pursuit of this within the already industrialised countries is likely to be self-defeating and could well be disastrous. Could it be that man will return instead to the development of his inner life?

Mary Douglas has characterised the primitive world view as one which interprets the universe in terms of human needs (75). The belief that expansionary economics and technical advance will solve the most pressing human problems often contains the unsupported assumption that the material and biological worlds will help sustain the drama of human expansion—by supplying virtually unlimited raw materials and energy sources, by absorbing pollutants, and by allowing the constraints implicit in man's biological constitution to be easily transcended. Such thinking might be considered to be interpreting the universe on the basis of human needs—as being primitive. Rather, the thinking of modern man should be directed towards identifying his best available options in a universe indifferent to his welfare, but sensitive to his insults.

References

1. Department of health and social security. *Digest of health statistics, 1970*. H. M. S. O., 1971. Table 3.2.
2. Central Statistical Office. *Annual Abstract of Statistics* for 1952 and 1970.
3. Popov, G. A. *Principles of health planning in the U.S.S.R.* Public Health Paper No. 43, World Health Organisation, Geneva, 1971. Figure 5.
4. Rice, D. P., and Cooper, B. S. National health expenditures, 1929–70. *Social Security Bulletin*, U.S. Department of Health, Education and Welfare, January 1971. Table 1.
5. Klarman, H. E., Rice, D. P., Cooper, B. S., and Stettler, H. L. *Sources of increase in selected medical care expenditures, 1929–1969*. U.S. Department of Health, Education and Welfare, Social Security Administration, Office of Research and Statistics, Staff Paper No. 4, 1970, Table 2.
6. Life expectancies from Office of Population, Censuses and Surveys, *Registrar-General's statistical review for England and Wales for the year 1970*, Part II, Tables Population, H. M. S. O., London, 1972, Table B2. Infant mortality rates from the same source, Part I Tables Medical, Table 3. N. H. S. expenditure for the United Kingdom by calendar years from Office of Health Economics, Information Sheet No. 15, December 1971. Expenditure standardised using consumer price index from Central Statistical Office, *National Income and Expenditure*, 1971, H. M. S. O., London, 1971, Table 16. As costs within the health service increase more rapidly than consumer prices generally, the graph will over-state the true rise in real expenditure—perhaps by 20 to 30 percent.
7. Central Statistical Office (United Kingdom), *Annual Abstract of Statistics*, 1938–1950, 1950, 1969 (for life expectancy).

8. Office of Population, Censuses and Surveys, *Registrar-General's statistical review of England and Wales for the year 1969*, Part II. (For mean age at marriage.)

9. U.S. Department of Health, Education and Welfare. Leading components of upturn in mortality for men, United States 1952–67. *Vital and Health Statistics*, Series 20, No. 11, September 1971, Tables 1 and 2.

10. de Hass, J. H. Geographical pathology of the major killing disorders. Cancer and cardiovascular disease. In *Health of mankind*, G. Wolstenholme and M. O'Connor, eds., Churchill, London: Ciba Foundation 100th Symposium, 1968.

11. *The Registrar-General's Decennial Supplement, England and Wales, 1961*, Occupational Mortality Tables, H. M. S. O., 1971. Tables D4 to D8 and Diagram 2.

12. Central Statistical Office (United Kingdom), *Social Trends*, No. 2, 1971. Table 58.

13. Morris, J. N. *Uses of epidemiology*, 2nd ed. Edinburgh: Livingstone, 1964, p. 8.

14. Morris, J. N. Ibid., p. 11.

15. Department of Health and Social Security. *On the state of the public health, the annual report of the Chief Medical Officer . . . for the year 1970*, H. M. S. O., London, 1971. Table II.7.

16. Rendel, J. M. The time scale of genetic change. In *The impact of civilisation on the biology of man*, S. V. Boyden, ed., Canberra: Australian National University Press, 1970, 27–47.

17. Birdsell, J. B. Some predictions for the Pleistocene based on equilibrium systems among recent hunter-gatherers. In *Man the hunter*, I. De Vore and R. B. Lee, eds., Chicago: Aldine, 1968, 229–240, and the following discussion, 241–249.

18. Fenner, F. The effects of changing social organisation on the infectious diseases of man. In *The impact of civilisation on the biology of man*, S. V. Boyden, ed., Canberra: Australian National University Press, 1970, 48–76.

19. Barnes, F. The biology of pre-Neolithic man. In *The impact of civilisation on the biology of man*, S. V. Boyden, ed., Canberra: Australian National University Press, 1970, 1–26.

20. Dunn, F. L. Epidemiological factors: Health and disease in hunter-gatherers. In *Man the hunter*, I. De Vore and R. B. Lee, eds., Chicago: Aldine, 1968, 221–228.

21. Brothwell, D. R. Dietary variation and the biology of earlier human populations. In *The domestication and exploitation of plants and animals*, P. Ucko and G. Dimbleby, eds., London: Weidenfeld and Nicholson, 1969.

22. McKeown, T. *Medicine in modern society*, London: Allen and Unwin, 1965, 21–58.

23. McKeown, T. A historical appraisal of the medical task. In *Medical history and medical care*, G. McLachlan and T. McKeown, eds., London: Oxford University Press for the Nuffield Provincial Hospitals Trust, 1971, p. 36.

24. Banks, J. A. Family planning and birth control in Victorian times. Paper read at second annual conference of the Society for the Social History of Medicine, Leicester University, July 1972. Abstract in Bulletin No. 8 (September 1972) of the Society for the Social History of Medicine (183 Euston Road, London).

25. Razzell, P. E. Population change in eighteenth century England: A re-appraisal. *Economic History Review*, XVIII, 1965.

26. Kuller, L., and Reisler, D. M. An explanation for variations in distribution of stroke and arteriosclerotic heart disease among populations and racial groups. *American Journal of Epidemiology*, 1971, 93, 1–9.

27. Casley-Smith, J. R. Blood pressures in Australian aborigines. *Medical Journal of Australia*, 1959, 1, 627–633.

28. Abbie, A. A. and Schroder, J. Blood pressures in Arnhem Land aborigines. *Medical Journal of Australia*, 1960, 2, 493–496.

29. Schwartz, C. J., and Casley-Smith, J. R. Serum cholesterol levels in atherosclerotic subjects and the Australian aborigines. *Medical Journal of Australia*, 1958, 2, 84–86.

30. Schwartz, C. J., et al. Serum cholesterol and phospholipid levels of Australian aborigines. *Austral. J. Exp. Biol. Med. Sci.*, 1957, 35, 449–456.

31. Polunin, I. The medical natural history of Malayan aborigines. *Medical Journal of Malaya*, 1953, 8, 62–167.

32. Kaminer, B., and Lutz, W. P. W. Blood pressure in bushmen of the Kalahari Desert. *Circulation*, 1960, XXII, Part 2, 289–295.

33. Bronte-Stewart, B., et al. The health and nutritional status of the Kung bushmen of South West Africa. *South African Journal of Laboratory and Clinical Medicine*, 1960, 6, 187–216.

34. Truswell, A. S., and Hansen, J. E. L. Serum lipids in bushmen. *Lancet*, 1968, 2 684.

35. Tobias, P. V. The peoples of Africa south of the Sahara. In *Biology of human adaptability*, P. T. Baker and J. S. Weiner, eds., Oxford: Clarendon Press, 1966.

36. Barnicot, N. A., et al. Blood pressure and serum cholesterol in the Hadza of Tanzania. *Human Biology*, 1972, 44, 87–116.

37. Mann, G. V., et al. Cardiovascular disease in African pygmies; a survey of the health status, lipids and diet of pygmies in Congo. *Journal of Chronic Disease*, 1962, 15 341–371.

38. Neel, J. V., et al. Studies on the Xavante Indians of the Brazilian Mato Grosso. *Human Genetics*, 1964, 16, 52–140.

39. Hugh-Jones, P., et al. Medical studies among the Indians of the Upper Xingu. *British Journal of Hospital Medicine*, March 1972, 317–334.

40. Lowenstein, F. W. Blood pressure in relation to age and sex in the tropics and sub-tropics. *Lancet*, 1961, 1, 389–392.

41. Jones, R. J., ed. *Atherosclerosis: Proceedings of the Second International Symposium*, New York: Springer-Verlag, 1970.

42. Rose, G. Epidemiology of ischaemic heart disease. *British Journal of Hospital Medicine*, March 1972, 285–288.

43. Tejada, C., et al. Distribution of coronary and aortic atherosclerosis by geographic location, race and sex. *Laboratory Investigation*, 1968, 18, 5.

44. Stamler, J., Stamler, R., and Pollman, T. N., eds. *The epidemiology of hypertension*, New York: Grune and Stratton, 1967.

45. Kean, B. H., and Hammill, J. F. Anthropopathology of arterial tension. *Archives of Internal Medicine*, 1949, 83, 355.

46. Becker, B. J. P. Cardiovascular disease in the Bantu and Coloured races of South Africa. *South African Journal of Medical Science*, 1946, 11, 1–34 and 107–120.

47. Shaper, A. G., Wright, D. H., and Kyobe, J. Blood pressure and body build in three nomadic tribes of Northern Kenya. *East African Medical Journal*, 1969, 46, 273–281.

48. General Register Office. *The Registrar General's quarterly return for England and Wales*, Quarter ended 30th June, 1969, H. M. S. O., London, 1969, Appendix B.

49. Department of Health and Social Security. *Digest of Health Statistics for England and Wales*, 1971, H. M. S. O., London, 1971, Table 11.3.

50. Office of Health Economics. *The costs of medical care*, London (162 Regent Street), 1964, Table A. Twenty-five percent of the hospital costs of "mental, psychoneurotic and personality disorders" have been allocated to the mentally handicapped and transferred to category 4 in Table 2.

51. Royal College of General Practitioners. *The present state and future needs of general practice*, 2nd ed., London (14 Prince's Gate S.W.7), May 1970, Table XIX.

52. Department of Health and Social Security. *Digest of Health Statistics for England and*

Wales, 1971, H. M. S. O., London, 1971, Tables 11.6, 9.2, 9.7, 9.9. The maternity beds rate has been recalculated per one million females. Mental handicap inpatients have been divided into male and female in the same proportions as admissions (Table 9.9).

53. Royal College of Physicians of London. *Smoking and health now.* London: Pitman Medical, 1971.

54. Doll, R. The geographical distribution of cancer. *British Journal of Cancer*, 1969, *XXIII*, 1–8.

55. Burkitt, D. P. Epidemiology of cancer of the colon and rectum. *Cancer*, 1971, 28, 3–13.

56. Burkitt, D. P. The aetiology of appendicitis. *British Journal of Surgery*, 1971, 58, 695.

57. Painter, N. S., and Burkitt, D. P. Diverticular disease of the colon: A deficiency disease of western civilisation. *British Medical Journal*, 1971, 2, 450–454.

58. Doll, R., and Kinlen, L. Epidemiology as an aid to determining the causes of cancer. Cancer Research Campaign (2 Carlton House Terrace, London SW1Y 5AR), *49th Annual Report*, 1971, 42–46.

59. Quoted in Department of Health and Social Security, *On the state of the public health, the annual report of the Chief Medical Officer . . . for the year 1970*, London, H. M. S. O., 1971, p. 5.

60. Royal College of Physicians of London. *Air pollution and health.* London: Pitman Medical, 1970.

61. Boyden, S. V. The human organism in a changing environment. In *Man in his environment*, R. T. Appleyard, ed., Perth: University of Western Australia Press, 1970, 1–20.

62. West, K. M., and Kalbfleisch, J. M. Influence of nutritional factors on prevalence of diabetes. *Diabetes*, 1971, 20, 99–108.

63. Mekky, S., Schilling, R. S. F., and Walford, J. Varicose veins in women cotton workers. An epidemiological study in England and Egypt. *British Medical Journal*, 1969, 2, 591–595. (Reviews other epidemiological studies.)

64. Levi, L., ed. *Society, stress and disease: The psychosocial environment and psychosomatic diseases.* London: Oxford University Press, 1971.

65. Mims, C. Stress in relation to the process of civilisation. In *The impact of civilisation on the biology of man*, S. V. Boyden, ed. Canberra: Australian National University Press, 1970, 167–189.

66. Syme, S. L., Hyman, M. M., and Enterline, P. E. Some social and cultural factors associated with the occurrence of coronary heart disease. *Journal of Chronic Diseases*, 1964, *17*, 277–289; Syme, S. L., Borhani, N. O., and Beuchley, R. W. Cultural mobility and coronary heart disease in an urban area. *American Journal of Epidemiology*, 1966, 82, 334–346.

67. Personal communication, C. Bagley, member of Research Team, Courtauld Research Unit, Kings College Hospital, London.

68. Holland, W. W. Clinicians and the use of medical resources. *The Hospital* (London), July 1971, 236–239.

69. Mather, H. G., et al. Acute myocardial infarction: Home and hospital treatment. *British Medical Journal*, 1971, 3, 334–338.

70. Crombie, A. C. The future of biology: The history of a program. *Federation Proceedings*, 1966, *25*, 1448–1453.

71. Bailey, H., and Love, M. *A short practice of surgery.* London: H. K. Lewis and Co., 14th ed. 1968, 918–924 and 1014–1021.

72. See for example: Sonksen, P. H. Aetiology and epidemiology of diabetes. *British Journal*

of Hospital Medicine, February 1972, 151–156; Kannel, W. B., Castelli, W. P., McNamara, P. M., and Sorlie, P. Some factors affecting morbidity and mortality in hypertension, the Frammington study. *Milbank Memorial Fund Quarterly*, XLVII, 3, Part 2, 1969, 116–142.

73. Rosenberg, C. E. The medical profession, medical practice, and the history of medicine. In *Modern methods in the history of medicine*, E. Clarke, ed., London: The Athlone Press of the University of London, 1971, 22–35.

74. Levi-Strauss, C. The sorcerer and his magic. In *Magic, witchcraft, and curing*, J. Middleton, ed., New York: Natural History Press, 1967.

75. Douglas, M. *Purity and danger*. Harmondsworth: Penguin, 1970.

76. Barton, R. *Institutional neurosis*. Bristol: John Wright, 1966.

77. Lieberman, M. A. Relationship of mortality rates to entrance to a home for the aged. *Geriatrics*, October 1961, 515–519.

78. Aldrich, C. K., and Mendkoff, E. Relocation of the aged and disabled: A mortality study. *Journal of the American Geriatric Society*, March 1963, 185–194.

79. I have derived this analytic model from that used by Mark Field. To his four types of "societal response" I have added "rejection." See: Field, M. The health care system of industrial society: The disappearance of the general practitioner and some implications. In *Human aspects of biomedical engineering*. E. Mendelson, J. Swazey, and I. Taviss, eds., Cambridge: Harvard University Press, 1971, 156–180.

80. It is often suggested that health education has little effect. However tobacco consumption has recently been falling at around 5 percent per year (*The Times*, 1/12/1972). The Chief Medical Officer of the Department of Health and Social Security has estimated that there are approximately 100,000 premature deaths due to smoking in the United Kingdom each year (Department of Health and Social Security. *On the state of the public health; The annual report of the Chief Medical Officer . . . for the year 1969*, H. M. S. O., London, 1970, p. 9). As the health damage from smoking is roughly proportional to the quantity of tobacco consumed (Royal College of Physicians of London. In Smoking and health now. London: Pitman Medical, 1971), the current decline may be saving around 5000 premature deaths each year. And this is the result of a small-scale campaign. The Health Education Council spent £120,000 on its smoking and health campaign in 1970–71 (The Health Education Council, United Kingdom, *Accounts, 31st March, 1972*, Appendix IV. Meddlesex House, Ealing Road, Wembley). By contrast the tobacco industry spent £52 million on sales promotion in 1968 (Royal College of Physicians of London. *Smoking and health now*. London: Pitman Medical, 1971).

81. Mead, T. W. Medicine and population. *Public Health* (London), 1968, LXXXII, 100–110.

82. Department of Health and Social Security, Information Division, Intelligence Section. *National Health Service Notes*, 13 (figures for 1949–50) and Department of Health and Social Security. *Digest of health statistics for England and Wales, 1971*, H. M. S. O., 1971, Table 2.3 (figures for 1969–70).

83. See for example, McKeown, T. *Medicine in modern society*. London: Allen and Unwin, 1965, 104–142; Cochrane, A. L. *Effectiveness and efficiency, random reflections on health services*. London: Oxford University Press for the Nuffield Provincial Hospitals Trust, 1972, 70–77.

3

Hypertension as a Disease of Modern Society

Joseph Eyer

Defining Hypertension

Hypertension is defined medically as elevation of blood pressure above a given level, for instance for 140/95 measure commonly used now in community screening. It is also defined as elevation more than a certain amount above the average blood pressure level for the population of a given age. This latter criterion defines a young person as hypertensive at 140/90, but a 70-year-old only at 170/110 (1).

If we define hypertension, not in terms of an arbitrary criterion, but in terms of its consequences as a disease, a very different definition emerges. Hypertension increases the risks of heart attack, stroke, and kidney damage. About 50 per cent of modern men die of causes of death in one way or another related to elevated blood pressure, by this definition. Prospective studies of representative samples of the American population show that people who maintain their blood pressure around 100/60 throughout their life-span have the lowest death risks. Below this value, people experience problems with fainting and consequences of circulatory deficiency. For each increment of blood pressure above 100/60, there is a corresponding increase in death risks from heart attack, stroke, and kidney damage. It is clear that we ought to define hypertension as blood pressure above 100/60, if we use death risks to define the problem (2–4).

By this definition, most of the American population is hypertensive. This fact has led many practicing doctors to reject our reasoning. They argue that something this widespread in the population cannot be considered a disease, since it is rather the normal state of affairs; and, that were such a criterion used the medical system would be totally overloaded in treating a disease for which it has only just recently discovered any effective means of cure. Since the major curative agents are drugs, it

SOURCE: *International Journal of Health Services* 5 (1975): 539–58. Copyright © 1975, Baywood Publishing Company, Inc. Reprinted by permission.

is not surprising to find that the drug companies, on the other hand, are among the strongest advocates of the low criterion for hypertension. (See in particular Merck, Sharpe and Dohme's advertisements in medical journals in recent years.)

Cross-cultural epidemiology of normal blood pressure and associated pathology reinforces our definition of hypertension. Undisrupted hunter-gatherers have low blood pressure, constant through the life-span. Where studies have been done, they have indicated low atherosclerosis among the population, based on autopsy at a given age, as well as a lack of other consequences of elevated blood pressure. Undisrupted hunter-gathers are the most primitive social form of humanity, probably the form into which we evolved genetically, the form in which 94 per cent of all humans that have ever lived existed. Though over 99 per cent of the span of existence of the human species has been in hunter-gatherer form, the rise of settled agriculture, class societies (civilization), and particularly modern society, have confined today's hunter-gatherers to extremely marginal environments, such as the desert; today these peoples constitute a small fraction of total world population (2, Chap. 5; 5–17).

Disrupted peasant or pastoral societies, such as the West African tribes from which the American Negro slaves were derived, have average blood pressures which start slightly higher and increase progressively with age at the moderate rate (18–26). Among these populations, it is common to find elevated blood pressure associated with kidney damage, but in these cases the causal relation is opposite to the one characteristic of peoples in modern developed countries. Among peoples in underdeveloped countries, kidney damage most often is the product of infectious disease, such as tuberculosis, and hypertension is a consequence of kidney damage, not its cause (17, 27). In these populations atherosclerosis detected on autopsy at a given age is uncommon, despite the fact that many of these groups consume diets as high in saturated fat and cholesterol as the American diet (2, Chap. 5; 17). Where reliable mortality statistics are available for such populations in underdeveloped countries, the death rates for hypertension-associated disorders, particularly coronary heart disease, are two- to threefold lower than the rates characteristic of developed countries (2, Chap. 5; 28).

The highest average blood pressures, rising most rapidly with age, are found in two social categories: in both urban and rural areas in developed countries, and among populations in less-developed societies which have evolved under especially oppressive conditions, e.g. the Caribbean and South American black former slave areas, or the South African black urban areas (7, 8, 27, 29–44). These are also the societies with the highest death rates for hypertension-related disorders. Diet appears to play a role in *distributing* the deaths into one or another category in this whole system of diseases. Thus in Japan, whose citizens consume relatively little saturated fat and cholesterol, hypertension itself, stroke, and kidney damage are much higher than in America or Finland, but coronary heart disease is lower. In the latter countries, where dietary intake of atherogenic compounds is high, death rates from stroke and hypertension are relatively low, but death rates from coronary heart disease are high (2, 45).

It is hard to look at these data, which have been carefully studied and certified for accuracy for over 20 years, without concluding that they imply a criterion for hypertension identical to the implication of prospective studies within the United States. In a word, the normal state of modern populations is hypertensive, while that of undisrupted primitive societies is not.

Physiology of Essential Hypertension

Why this difference? A survey of the hypothesized causes of hypertension sheds light on this social differential. Medical science divides hypertension into two broad varieties; types of elevated pressure for which specific cause can be found, and all the rest, termed essential hypertension, for which causation has not yet been fully worked out. Among the populations of present-day developed countries, essential hypertension comprises about 90 percent of all hypertension. The remaining 10 per cent is attributed to pituitary or adrenal tumors, which can affect hormones such as noradrenalin that elevate blood pressure via constricting the arterioles; or to conditions that result in decreased blood flow through the kidneys, such as kidney damage from tuberculosis or glomerulonephritis (2,46).

Just as hypertension associated with infectious kidney damage is today a major cause of elevated blood pressure in disrupted underdeveloped countries on the brink of economic development, this was probably also the major type of hypertension during the 19th century among populations of present-day developed countries due to the great rise of tuberculosis and other infectious diseases in early modern development prior to the introduction of public health measures (47). Essential hypertension has increased recently in developed countries as a proportion of total hypertension, as tuberculosis death rates have declined. Although the older historical statistics for death rates from circulatory and kidney disorders in populations of developed countries are subject to many interpretations, it is reasonable to infer from the social cross-sections that, since total hypertension is greater in more-developed countries than in less-developed ones, essential hypertension in particular has increased rapidly with recent modern development.

Quite a bit is known about the physiology of essential hypertension. Young essential hypertensives show elevated blood levels of adrenalin, which has its major cardiovascular effects in an increase of heart rate and output; and of noradrenalin, which has its major effects on peripheral resistance via constriction of the arterioles. Older hypertensives show an elevation of noradrenalin alone. Correspondingly, younger hypertensives show both increased cardiac output and increased peripheral resistance, while older hypertensives have normal or lowered heart output and greatly increased peripheral resistance (46, 48–51). The pattern of constriction of the arterioles involved in increased resistance is that characteristic of chronic stress: vasoconstriction to the gut, kidney, and skin; and relative vasodilation to the muscles (52). This patterned vasoconstriction could be maintained directly by noradrenalin, a hormone secreted in increased amounts in stress, or by the excitation of the sympathetic nervous system, which regulates the arterioles and is activated in stress. This physiology clearly implies that essential hypertension is a disease caused by stress.

Further support for a stress hypothesis emerges from the experience with treatment of essential hypertension. Many different kinds of relaxation techniques are effective in reducing the blood pressure of essential hypertensives. These techniques are most effective with young hypertensives, less so with older ones. Where the follow-up studies have been done, it is found that when the hypertensive leaves the special program environment that reinforces relaxation, and returns to the normal social network of his life, his blood pressure rises back to previous levels. (For an example of one type of relaxation technique, see reference 53.) This latter finding suggests that the social environment has a profound influence on the level of blood pressure in essential hypertensives, a point we will develop in detail later.

The fact that relaxation techniques are more effective with younger than older essential hypertensives suggests that there are certain irreversible changes which accompany the development of the disease. Folkow and Neill (46) have summarized much of the literature in this area. What starts in adolescence as a typical physiological stress response is reinforced by muscular thickening of the arterioles in the circulatory branches subject to vasoconstriction. This results in elevated blood pressure even at normal amounts of sympathetic activation and noradrenalin secretion, since the muscles are more strongly reactive to a given nervous or hormonal stimulus, and since the additional thickness constricts the vessel's internal diameter somewhat.

Drug treatment of essential hypertension confirms the stress hypothesis. Drugs are usually administered only in the phase of sustained elevated pressure after age 30. The major categories used are powerful tranquillizers, specific vasodilators, and diuretics (54). That tranquillizers are the most effective antihypertensive drugs in terms of pressure reduction obviously supports the stress-tension hypothesis of the disease. The use of vasodilators is evidently related to the mechanisms we have sketched, and it is interesting to note here that many of the so-called specific vasodilators are also general relaxants.

Concerning the final category of drugs, the diuretics, there is disagreement concerning mode of action. In the short term, they appear to operate by decreasing blood volume via increased elimination of body fluid through the kidneys, sometimes as water alone, in other cases by eliminating both salt and water. The decrease of blood volume, all other things being equal, results in decreased blood pressure. This effect lasts only a few weeks, however; plasma volume, total body sodium, and cardiac output all return to previous levels after this time. The sustained depression of blood pressure that nevertheless occurs appears to be due to a gradual decrease in peripheral resistance from the action of these drugs on the arteriole walls. While it is clear that this vasodilation occurs, its mechanism is not understood (54).

All of the drug mechanisms clearly complement a stress hypothesis for essential hypertension. However, the major American schools of essential hypertension choose to lay emphasis on the possible role of the kidney, and this emphasis also appears prominently in popular literature (55). While the temporary effect of diuretics seems to support this role, the long-term effectiveness does not. Recall also that essential hypertension is defined by eliminating other possible causative disorders, particularly of detectable kidney damage or gross alteration of glands affecting the kidneys.

However, the kidneys may well be *secondarily* involved in essential hypertension of stress origins. Both aldosterone (the adrenal hormone causing salt and water retention by the kidney) and ADH (the pituitary hormone causing water retention) are elevated as an integral part of the stress response (56). The juxtaglomerular apparatus in the kidney, which secretes renin, a hormone which speeds aldosterone release, is activated by sympathetic neurons. Also, the juxtaglomerular apparatus will be activated by anything that reduces kidney blood flow, e.g. vasoconstriction in the arterioles leading into the kidney, such as occurs in stress (57). All of these responses are adaptive as part of a short-term·arousal response to a threatening situation, in which there may be blood loss or loss of salt and water through the sweat with strenuous physical exertion. These facts also illuminate Laragh's finding of a significant subgroup of essential hypertensives with elevated renin, as well as excess fluid retention in another large subgroup (58, 59).

Salt Consumption and Hypertension

Reading the literature from some of the advocates of kidney and salt mechanisms for essential hypertension, one would think that the major function of aldosterone is to cause inordinate body retention of salt whenever this becomes plentifully available in the diet (55, 60, 61). This unfortunate mishap in mammalian body design must then be treated by drastic solium restriction in the diet and administration of diuretics. In fact, aldosterone's primary body function is to regulate solium and potassium ion concentrations within rather narrow limits defined by the optimal levels for the function of nerve and muscle cells (57). Aldosterone is secreted or withheld directly in response to blood levels of sodium and potassium flowing past the adrenal cells. When sodium concentrations rise above the optimal levels, aldosterone secretion drops; and vice versa disturbed by stress responses or other pathology, the concentration· of salt is normally regulated within narrow limits, and increased salt intake is quickly matched by increased salt excretion through the kidneys. Even large doses of salt produce only moderate, transient blood pressure elevations in humans (62).

An increased salt load will be retained, however, if the baseline level of aldosterone is reset upward, as occurs in chronic stress. Reexamining the evidence that has been selected to support the salt-consumption theory of hypertension, it becomes plain that it supports even more a stress/salt-consumption mechanism for blood pressure elevation. When additional evidence, not ordinarily noticed by the advocates of this theory, is brought to bear, however, the relation between salt consumption and blood pressure levels begins to appear more tenuous.

While dietary salt intake by and large increases with modern social development, paralleling the increase of blood pressure trends, there are many examples of societies whose populations salt their food heavily but do not show elevated blood pressure trends. Perhaps the most striking example is the Kung bushmen, who salt their food heavily (63) and have blood pressures constant at low levels throughout their life-span (15). This result would be expected if these groups were also under little social stress, as we shall argue in the section on social stress origins of hypertension.

Widening the view of the epidemiological data a little more, there are many examples of populations under stress which have higher blood pressures than other groups in the same area under less stress, despite similar salt-consumption levels (31, 32, 36, 37). There are also groups widely differing in salt intake with similar blood pressure distributions (16, 30, 31). Looking at all of the available data, the relation between salt-consumption levels and hypertension is much weaker than the advocates of the theory would have us believe (64).

Our stress/salt-consumption hypothesis is also supported by experimental results with normal laboratory rats (62, 65). These rats are typically strangers grouped in a cage for the purpose of experimentation. Male rats show a much greater stress response than do females to such grouping, whatever the density; this is accompanied by an initial period of fighting followed by formation of a dominance hierarchy (65, 66). The process of stranger grouping itself produces blood pressure elevations in rodents (67). In many of the salt-consumption experiments, only males showed the expected elevation of blood pressure with increased dietary salt intake, a finding consistent with diet-stress interaction.

The relative quantitative contribution of stress and diet-stress interaction in the genesis of modern hypertension is not completely determinable from presently available evidence. However, it has been shown that the effect of massive sodium restriction in the diet of modern hypertensives is only a moderate decline in blood pressure (68). Dietary modification is rightly viewed as secondary to drug treatment in the conventional management of essential hypertension (54). These facts imply that salt-consumption level is not responsible for the majority of blood pressure elevation in essential hypertensives. Even for that part in which increased salt retention from the diet does play a role, a reexamination of the evidence suggests a stress mechanism as the cause of the retention.

Genetic Theories of Hypertension

Among many practicing doctors it is taken as an unquestionable article of faith that essential hypertension is primarily an inherited disorder. This belief is renewed with every family history review on an incoming patient. Aside from the problems of selective recall and suggestion, that are as important in doctors' interviews as in any other kind of retrospective research, quantitative analysis of the inheritance of hypertension does not support this medical prejudice.

Just as the risk of pathology goes up with each increase of blood pressure above 100/60, so also, hypertensives grade evenly into the distribution of pressures for the rest of the population (69–73). There is no easily isolable "hump" at the high end of the distribution, as there is for mongoloid idiocy, for instance, on the IQ distribution curves. This result suggests that hypertension is not inherited as a simple Mendelian trait with fixed phenotypic expression.

The trait must, then, be inherited in a more complex fashion, for which polygenic models, or single gene models with variable penetrance, have been proposed (71). The study of such models is most advanced by the quantitative examination of relatives of differing degrees to the identified hypertensive, including identical and fraternal twins (74–76). As a result of this kind of study, an estimate has been made of the relative contributions of heredity and environment to the phenotypes seen in a large population. This estimate, called the heritability, is about 0.2 for hypertension, which roughly signifies that 20 per cent of the variation in phenotypes in a population can be accounted for by heredity of some sort, the rest by environmental influences or genetic-environment interactions. This percentage is much lower than the corresponding figure for height or hair color and certainly does not support the assertion that inheritance is the *primary* factor in hypertension (72).

For the data we have been reviewing, it would really not matter if hypertension had a much higher heritability and a more respectable pattern of genetic transmission. Tuberculosis, for instance, is 30 per cent heritable by the same criteria, and yet no one today treats tuberculosis as a genetic disorder. The tripling of tuberculosis death rates which occurred in early modern development before the introduction of public health measures was due to large scale deterioration of the environment, including housing, nutrition, and food processing. The reduction of tuberculosis in modern countries to less than one-fiftieth its former height during the 20th century was achieved by a reversal of these conditions, as well as the introduction of pasteurization, dairy herd inspection, quarantine and sanatorium treatment, and modern drugs (47). It is *changes* of this kind that the genetic argument must address.

In particular, the genetic argument must account for the increase in the frequency of hypertension, from less than 5 per cent to over 40 per cent of the population affected, which parallels modernization in the social cross-sections we have discussed. This change from a low to a high blood pressure trend can occur in a population in less than 20 years, as in the migration of Atlas Jews to Israel, or Easter Islanders to the South American mainland (13, 77). The longest period over which this change can have occurred is less than 200 years, since developed societies did not exist before 200 years ago.

The empirical evidence on rates of genetic change in human populations indicates that, even with strong positive selection pressures, a fivefold increase in population gene frequency to 40 per cent of the population requires time spans of 1000 years or more (78). This is an order of magnitude longer than the time spans we are considering; so even with strong positive selection pressure, population genetic change can have made only a very minor contribution to the rise of essential hypertension with modern society. However, the character in question seriously increases mortality risks, and there is evidence that hypertensives also have reduced fertility (79). Hence the frequency of this gene in the population must be decreasing.

Despite this probable decrease in population frequency, there might be an increase of hypertensive phenotypes on a genetic basis because, with changing environmental conditions, the expression of the predisposition to hypertension changes. This predisposition in premodern populations might have been expressed as a particular susceptibility to infectious disease in infancy and childhood; with the lowering of infectious mortality in these age groups with modern public health advances, these genetic defectives now survive long past childhood to develop other premature pathology, for instance hypertension, in adult life (80). Fatal counterexamples for this form of argument appear in the data from premodern populations undergoing public health advance, which show equal proportional reductions in death rates across all age groups. As the children experiencing low mortality under these social conditions reach adulthood, they do not show elevated pathology from other causes (81). Additional counterexamples come from the historical urban and rural vital data for developed countries before public health advance. Urban death rates here were two to three times higher than rural, across all age groups, for both infectious and noninfectious causes (82). The populations that experienced low mortality in infancy (rural undeveloped) again show low mortality at older ages. It is only developed populations which show the peculiar combination of reduced death rates in infancy and childhood with relatively elevated older age death rates, and this only after public health advance; prior to this change, the populations most heavily selected against in youth are the ones with highest adult pathology as well. These data clearly imply that the social change of modernization overrides any shift in expression of the predisposition to hypertension which may have occurred with public health measures.

So far we have established that the genetic component in modern hypertension is small. Changes of the frequency of this predisposition in the population cannot account for observed differences in the prevalence of hypertension. Changes in the expression of this predisposition, whatever its frequency, also cannot account for the observed data. Therefore a genetic factor in essential hypertension, though clearly definable, plays a minor role in causation. The same conclusion emerges from an examination of the data for negroes and whites.

The inheritance of hypertension is often invoked to account for the higher average blood pressure levels, and the higher frequency of hypertension, among American blacks, compared to whites. However, the average blood pressure trends of blacks in the social groups from which the slaves were drawn, largely in West Africa, are the intermediate, lower blood pressure trends characteristic of disrupted peasants or pastoralists (18, 19). Other African blacks, not demonstrably related to the American, have constant low blood pressures to old age (9, 15). The majority of the world's blacks show blood pressure trends considerably below the white levels in developed countries.

Thus, the elevation of blood pressure among black Americans above that of whites may be of environmental origin. A way of approaching this question is to find whites in socioeconomic circumstances similar to those of blacks, and compare blood pressures of the two groups. This kind of study has proved very difficult to do, since it is hard to find whites who suffer similar social contradictions, such as stigmatization. However, a large study recently completed in Detroit has approximated this matching (83). The major finding is that matched blacks and whites have similar blood pressures. From these data we can conclude that if a genetic factor makes a contribution to the difference in blood pressure between blacks and whites in America, the contribution is rather small.

Other Factors and Hypertension

Extensive review of the salt theory and the genetic theory is of great importance because they are the basis of the popular education carried on routinely by doctors in treating hypertensives. Other environmental factors, some of which are correlated with modern development, have also been implicated in hypertension. Ones associated with modern development include obesity, tobacco use, coffee consumption, and changes in the diet other than salt. A noncorrelated variable is the composition of drinking water, specifically calcium and magnesium content.

In the case of obesity, the evidence suggests that only populations of disrupted or modernized societies show the positive correlation between weight at a given age and blood pressure (9, 10), while members of undisrupted primitive societies show no relation between weight and blood pressure (9, 15). This is what one would expect if both obesity and blood pressure were the independent products of some other variable, such as social stress, which was present in disrupted or developed societies, but not in isolated primitive societies. Shah's review (64) demonstrates that the other factors mentioned have no simple relationship to blood pressure in the epidemiological studies. While this does not mean that they have no effect at all, it does signify that these effects are small and that the causal relationships are hard to disentangle.

Social Stress Causes of Essential Hypertension

We have already cited the data indicating that increasing modern development of a population is accompanied by increasing average blood pressure trends and increasing prevalence of hypertension. Modernization is, of course, a complex, multifaceted social and material transformation. Many studies have been done to try to isolate which particular facets are associated with blood pressure elevation. Literacy, for instance, does not appear to be associated with elevated blood pressure across this social comparison (11).

While this kind of comparative study is still in its infancy, it will clearly be of major importance in the design of future social systems which will have the advantages of modern technical and productive power, but will not suffer the disadvantages evident in pathologies such as hypertension. Broadly speaking, such disadvantages fall into two large spheres of life: the disruption of social communities, and the rise of hierarchically controlled, time-pressured work. Simon Kuznets' *Modern Economic Growth* (84) and other standard socioeconomic histories make it plain that these stressful features are essential, not accidental, to the modernization process.

The basic move in modernization is the wresting of control over social resources, including raw materials, tools, and labor, from the village communities and craft organizations that previously organized work activity, and placing this control in the hands of a new ruling class, either private or state capitalists, who direct the accumulation of material productive power by society. This transfer of power entails the destruction of the settled rural kin-based extended family and village community, through migration to the city, and the rise of a nuclear family unit, stripped of its unnecessary kin relations and traditional work patterns, delegating socialization and work training to an extracommunal educational system. Such units are capable of migrating wherever the chances of profitability or policy dictate that labor demand will grow or decline.

People who are uprooted from stable communities, thrust into hostile, competitive urban environments in which their normal social institutions and reaction patterns make no sense, experience great elevations of blood pressure associated with this loss of control over the communal aspects of life (13, 35, 40, 77, 85–87). Adoption of social forms which more or less fit in the new environment (such as the nuclear family, fewer children (35)) reduces blood pressure somewhat from this peak, but not nearly back to levels comparable to those in the stable rural social form.

Migration continues in modern society at a much higher rate than in premodern societies, as technical change, uneven patterns of material development, and class struggle over share of the social product produce constant shifts in the profitability pattern. The reason why these migrations are also associated with blood pressure increases may be a large change in the nature of migration, as well as its rate, from premodern to modern society. In premodern social organizations, migration typically occurs in a noncompetitive context. For instance, in hunter-gatherers, it is a means of helping resolve social disputes within a local group. Migration is easy since there is little property to carry along, and the group to which one migrates is usually part of the extended kin or marriage alliance system. Finally, since such groups live amidst resources sufficient to fulfil their culturally determined needs, migrants in particular are not brought into antagonistic competion with the people in the group to which they migrate (88). Resource competition within a hierarchical system of opportunities with apparent overall scarcity of desirable goods is, however, the situation confronted by every modern migrant.

Modernization is also characterized by increased breakdown of the nuclear family itself, through separation and divorce. In general, people in modern society who have the fewest close relations and feel most alien from potential intimates have the highest blood pressure (40, 87), a fact in particular true of the divorced and separated compared with those with stable marriages (79).

Mass unemployment is also a modern phenomenon. In the historical statistics, urban rates of unemployment have remained fairly constant over development, while rural rates have risen with the creation of an agricultural labor market; since the population as a whole is urbanized at the same time, the national unemployment rate rises. These data are put into higher relief by the fact that unemployment as we understand it does not exist in premodern social formations. For us, even with unemployment compensation and welfare, unemployment means a substantial reduction in income and disruption of normal social relationships, especially in the partial community on the job, and the one remaining outpost of intimate community, the nuclear family. In premodern societies, when there is less work to do or less social product available, people generally relax and share what they have within the kin network and local community. People who undergo unemployment in the modern economy show a rise of blood pressure which lasts from the initial uncertainty about their future until they are settled into a new job (89).

The continual development of new technology and work organization also sets off modern society from previous social forms. Combined with the accompanying specialization and hierarchical division of labor, this development necessitates multiple work role adjustments during the life-span, and this in turn means that a higher proportion of people experience a lack of fit between their skills and preparation and the work position they find themselves in. To use the language of sociology, modern society is characterized by elevated rates of status incongruity (90).

This incongruity tends to be cumulative with age, both at work and in the community, so that old people in modern society, rather than accumulating wisdom from long social experience, become confused and demoralized, out of date. Within the developed economy, people who do not have correct qualifications for their job, or who experience conflicting demands within the job, have higher blood pressures than those who do not (40, 91).

The rate of technical and organizational change, the degree of unemployment, and the amount of migration are all intimately tied into the competition between the rulers of economic units for shares of social surplus and thus social power. When this competition occurs between modern states it frequently results in war, involving universal military service and mass mobilization of both troops and civilians in a total war effort. In recent centuries, this kind of mass mobilization is associated with the rise of the new model national states after the French Revolution, though of course previous civilizations have suffered the same phenomenon during their periods of warring states (92). Among societal types, the frequency and intensity of war is lowest in hunter-gatherers (93, 94). The experience of being in a modern army, whether in combat (95) or merely in training (9), is associated with comparatively elevated blood pressure.

The early period of development of a modern economy has often been characterized by a resurrection of slavery within capitalist market forms, or the special oppression of parts of the peasantry (96–98). Social groups subject to special oppression or disruption within developed societies show relatively greater blood pressure levels than those not subject to these conditions. The blacks in the western hemisphere who trace their origins from enslavement through rural sharecropping to urban slums show the highest average blood pressure trends yet studied (7, 8, 27, 29–44). This is true whether one studies the urban slums (83), or the oppressed rural areas (29, 38, 44). Comparable white groups (e.g. the white small farmers in Georgia (38), or the matched whites in Detroit (83)) show similar blood pressure levels.

However, the relationship between social class and hypertension is complex. Comparing city dwellers within a modern economy with rural inhabitants not yet extensively affected by development, we find that higher income, higher education, and skilled and professional work are associated with higher blood pressure (9, 14, 99). On the other hand, the specially oppressed groups within the modern economy have even higher blood pressure, despite their very low income, education, and so forth, especially in the rural areas (29, 44). The time-pressured, externally controlled, punishment reinforced character of work which we will show produces relative blood pressure elevation is an experience shared by blue- and white-collar workers alike. Thus, in the American economy, in which all social sectors have experienced the impact of development, there is no relation between the economic level of the population and rates of death from hypertension (36) or between family income and blood pressure, as shown in a national sample survey (100).

The same analysis applies to urban-rural comparisons. Early in the development process, blood pressure differentials between urban and rural areas are marked (9, 35). When development has extensively affected the rural areas, they show blood pressure trends as high as those in urban areas (29, 36, 44). Needless to say, this means that in modern populations, blood pressure trends are not correlated with population density (36).

The breakup of the rural community and craft guilds makes possible perhaps the most basic feature of modernization, a large increase in time-pressured work. This increase appears whether we study time awareness and time ordering of life (101), the socialization of children to believe that work achievement is the most important value, rather than communal intimacy (102), the adult belief that hard work is the supreme moral value (103), or more concretely, the lengthening of the proportion of the year spent working (104) or the lifetime economic work output of an individual (84).

Lennart Levi and his coworkers (105) have demonstrated that piecework pressure greatly increases noradrenalin and blood pressure; and that sorting ball bearings of closely similar size under time pressure increases blood pressure and blood levels of noradrenalin, free fatty acids, triglycerides, and cholesterol. Tax accountants working under deadline pressure show large increases of serum cholesterol and decreases of blood clotting time (106). Russek and Zohman (107) found that work pressure (long hours, two jobs) was a better predictor of heart attacks in young men than the standard risk factors.

Friedman and Rosenman (108, 109) have identified a behavior pattern which is highly associated with elevated blood pressure and particularly heart attack risks. This "coronary-prone behavior pattern" involves extremes of competitiveness in work, constant posing of new tasks and challenges, fast work pace and sense of time pressure, inability to enjoy the fruits of achievement, and inability to relax either at work or in intimate relationships. In their large controlled prospective study, the coronary-prone behavior pattern overlapped highly with other risk factors, such as smoking. In addition, it predicted the overwhelming majority of heart attacks that occurred, while the standard risks predicted only a minority. The difference in heart attack risk between the coronary-prone and the opposite behavior type (easygoing, sociable) is two- to fivefold, depending on age.

The pattern of emergence of elevated blood pressure with age in modern society suggests that, although early socialization undoubtedly contributes to the development of this behavior pattern, it must be backed up by the structure of adult work situations to have pathological consequences. Blood pressure trends in modern society and primitive tribes are similar until adolescence (5–17). Beyond this age, the modern curves rise sharply and continuously while the primitive remain flat. Likewise, the average blood pressure of whites and blacks is similar before adolescence, diverging only beyond this point (110–113).

A similar conclusion can be drawn from the typical life cycle development of a hypertensive (46). Very few hypertensives had elevated blood pressure before adolescence; however, after about age 30, people who are then hypertensive will mostly remain so for the rest of their life-span (114). Between ages 15 and 30, the person goes through the prehypertensive phase, in which blood pressure is sometimes normal, sometimes very much elevated (115–120). As far as these elevations are understood, they seem to correspond to major life cycle crisis points, involving military service, labor market entry, conflicts around integration into a job or career, migration, unemployment, and family formation and breakdown—all social processes which occur at peak frequency in the population at ages 15–30 (121). Beyond age 30, these sources of elevated blood pressure are replaced by the steady experience of work pressure and conflicting job demands that we have reviewed. The stresses of work may thus be responsible, along with the irreversible physiological changes such as vascular thickening, for the continued rise of blood pressure with age in modern populations.

The cluster of social stresses we have mentioned is not an exhaustive list of possible sources of stress in modern society; they are only the ones studied so far. People do rate breakup of intimate relationships, migration, and unemployment, as well as job pressure as among the most subjectively stressful of experiences (122). The situations studied, however, are weighted toward ones which affect men more than women, since a greater proportion of men work. Yet in undisrupted hunter-gatherer societies both men and women have low blood pressure through the life-span (9, 15). In modern society, between men and women on the average there is very little difference in blood pressure trends—both rise rapidly with age (5). This fact points to the necessity of studying, for instance, the boredom and social isolation of the modern housewife as a possible factor in blood pressure elevation for women.

While this list of social stressors certainly does not exhaust all the characteristics of modern societies, it clearly includes an important core shared by many different nations which have undergone development, including both private market and state planned economies. In the latter, the role of unemployment is replaced by the authority of the party and the occasional use of military repression, but this is clearly not an essential difference. The fact that hypertension-associated death rates are at similar levels in Eastern and Western Europe, or in the Soviet Union and the United States, indicates that the similarities are more important than the differences between these social structures, as far as stresses which produce elevation of blood pressure are concerned.

The Possibility of Adaptation to Social Stress

These data imply that major social changes are necessary to prevent modern hypertension. These changes seem to lie in the area of substantial increases in the communal control people can exercise over work, neighborhood and intimate life, and a corresponding decrease in the control over these areas by the ruling class. It is not clear that this shift would mean the abolition of modern worldwide technological organization and power, although there would certainly be major redefinitions of the nature of production and productivity, and major reorganization of lifetime work patterns.

This obvious conclusion is avoided by many investigators of social stress and blood pressure elevation (123). These people carry out a characteristic set of mental reclassifications which allows them to see a possibility of lowering blood pressure while society remains the same. Continual breakdown of community and the increase of alienating, time-pressured work are abstracted to the "necessity to make continual behavioral readjustments." If a way could be found to increase people's ability to make such readjustments, the stressful effects of change could perhaps be reduced.

One suggested method is the use of regularly scheduled relaxation-meditation periods, in which the mind is cleared of the convoluted pressing worries (53). While this method has been shown to lower blood pressure significantly, the method of presentation of the data begs the question. Most people are not in a position to relax more, as is evident from the fact that only a minority of people entering transcendental meditation programs become consistent meditators and experience the physiological benefits.

One needs to recall the experience of college students in the last decade in the United States. In the mid-sixties, everything seemed possible to them, and personal self-liberation became the order of the day. As the labor market for college graduates has steadily deteriorated, the students have gotten their noses back to the grindstone. While it is true that many students who make it into medical school could have worked less as undergraduates, this perception is difficult for any individual to realize before reaching the goal, especially in a society which systematically rewards overwork and increasingly threatens failure to the larger and larger numbers of marginal students. After 20 years of fairly low unemployment, the same situation is now confronting most people in American society.

Given these realities, the exhortation to relax is likely to be effective only for that minority which has the social space in which to maneuver. For this reason, Friedman and Rosenman, in their popular book (108), direct most of their suggestions about how not to be coronary-prone to professional and managerial people. Similarly, the creativity-increasing benefits of transcendental meditation have only been demonstrated for people high in the work hierarchy, not for the majority of workers. As business failures and reorganizations increase, and as the universities consider abolishing tenure in their financial predicament, even people in these strata are likely to see less room for maneuvering and experience more pressure to fill up time with work.

The exhortation to relax could then become blaming the victim, a widespread stigmatization process in modern society, which only increases stress. One could laugh at the spectacle of well-paid mental health workers telling people to relax and lose out, were it not such a grim, all-pervasive phenomenon.

Another line of approach involves cultural relativism. According to this view, there is nothing intrinsic to cooperative, communal relations among human beings which has universal value; neither is it a value to control one's destiny in intimate and work life. Different social forms have different values, and the only problem is one of transition between social forms. Scotch's treatment of factors associated with hypertension in the rural and urban Zulu falls into this category (11, 35).

This idea stumbles on several difficult facts. First, the forms of modern life are continually changing, even within each generation, so there is no possibility to adopt stably a given new system of values. Second, this suggestion is not new, and has been at the core of educational efforts associated with modernization. What is the emphasis on reason and abstraction, on present abstention and future planning, on an ideology of individualism, but the major attempt at creating a stable value-system for modern society? While people who detach themselves from traditional communal feelings and values, and become more flexible in decision making through reasonable abstraction, probably suffer less stress from having their intimate lives disrupted and their work dictated in nature and pace, than those who do not, nevertheless these people experience significant chronic stress. Grossly speaking, one should expect that the oldest and most highly developed modern countries should show an actual reduction of average blood pressure trends below those developing more recently, but this is nowhere in evidence.

We can term this kind of adaptation the individualistic-purposive-involved adaptation to modern society. There is another kind of adaptation which has been tried on a widespread basis historically in the highly disrupted and oppressive periods of a civilization, which can be termed the Buddhist solution. Transcendental meditation has its origins in this kind of adaptation. Defeated by the accumulated contradictions of one's social nexus, the person withdraws from the world and its attractions, and thus its pains. This step is a prelude to seeing reality in a new way, in which all cultural values, all relationships, all power, everything, including death, are equally meaningful or meaningless.

The meaninglessness of these things preserves one's ability to avoid pain. The meaningfulness of these things is conceived as uniformly pacific and pleasurable. Disharmony and exploitation in actual social life are transmuted, for instance, into universal harmony; unnecessary early death from preventable causes into a feature of harmony with which one can have only compassion. In the Zen variant of these ideas, playful participation in any part of the world is not only possible, but recommended.

It is interesting that the social area (India, Southeast Asia (124–128)) in which these ideals have permeated the population most widely have among the lowest average blood pressure trends for premodern agricultural class societies. Other societies in this same culture area (Taiwan (129); Japan (130, 131)) which have experienced modernization, however, have the characteristic elevated blood pressure trends of modern society. The effect of the Buddhist solution under modern social conditions is thus likely to be marginal.

All of these suggested methods of adaptation have as their goal to reduce the reaction of internal stress physiology to social disruption and oppression. Modern science has by and large pursued the same objective by chemical means. While genetic and dietary explanations of hypertension play a large role in the popular mythology of blood pressure, doctors in fact use drugs to deal with the effects of stress, as we have demonstrated. If Nirvana can be attained with a pill, who needs esoteric training methods which take years to master?

We can conceive of drug therapies as having two broad stages of effectiveness. In the first, an attempt is made to counter in detail all of the primary and secondary physiological changes resulting from stress which lead to pathology: Thus, vasodilators are prescribed for stress vasoconstriction, renin inhibitors for deranged renovascular function, and so forth. To be effective, these drugs would have to be appropriately administered to the population. For instance, the vasodilators would be given to a majority of the population starting in adolescence, so as to avoid the damaging effects of the large blood pressure fluctuations of the prehypertensive phase, which begin the positive feedback processes in later pathology.

But even under this phase of drug modification of society one could object that the persons will still experience suffering, anxiety, depression and anger, and the other manifestations of oppression and social disruption subjectively, since these drugs only alter the final peripheral expressions of stress, not its central organization. This objection leads naturally to the second phase, the development of drugs capable of altering the function of stress response systems in the central nervous system. The tranquillizers and antidepressants currently in use are rather primitive attempts at this kind of technology.

The success of this strategy would be a transformation of human values more basic than any which has occurred on a wide scale in all previous history. In Toynbee's terms, we are in the "Time of Troubles" of our civilization, a social phase which, in history, has always evoked a massive disaffection from the dominant values and social forms, a disaffection ultimately leading to the breakup of the civilization and the birth of a new one on different social premises (92). This disaffection has always taken the form of a reassertion of the autonomy of inimate human communities from powerful, disruptive hierarchies, whether it appeared in religious or revolutionary form. What the enthusiasts of technological solutions to stress reactions propose is to eliminate this sociohistorical dynamic through an alteration in the basic nature of man.

The technology that is sought is nothing other than the soma of Huxley's *Brave New World*, by which the population is transformed into so many happy alphas, betas, gammas, and deltas, each carrying out his hierarchically assigned tasks. People thus modified can be endlessly uprooted, overworked, made useless, conformed to any necessary intimacy, or, in a more rational scheme, simply maintained as part of the world's total capital equipment in proportion to their usefulness. The coherence of such a world obviously depends upon a solidified consensus among its rulers, something that does not yet exist in our present world. Once such a consensus is achieved, however, one oppressive hierarchy and one particular culture will be capable of endlessly extending itself, playing out far into the future the themes of western capitalist society.

But are we not impossibly distant from this future? The presently available anti-stress drugs by and large do not work any better than placebos, and have serious deleterious side effects. Psychosurgery is in its infancy, and is likewise relatively ineffective and damaging. But among the antihypertensives, there is a clear progression toward greater effectiveness and lesser side effects over time. Thus the veratrum alkaloids and rauwolfia derivatives, which can produce respiratory arrest, severe nausea and vomiting, or depression, are replaced by drugs like methyldopa (somnolence, constipation, and cramps) and the benzothiadiazides (elevate plasma uric acid and cause disorders of the blood elements).

It is also true that the majority of patients put on antihypertensive medication fail to take it frequently enough to obtain the benefits, perhaps because of the side effects. This difficulty is also present, however, even for drugs without serious side effects, and illustrates the great difficulty of programming in even small changes in behavior, much less big increases in daily relaxation.

But should we be using or rejecting these drugs solely on the grounds of effectiveness, which has been demonstrated, and side effects, which may improve? Should we be involved in arguments about trading off hypertension for depression or blood dyscrasias, when the only effect of such argument given our present social structure is to stimulate the allocation of more millions to find a better antistress technology? Should we maintain that the technological strategy must flop because no sufficiently powerful means of behavior modification have yet been found to guarantee its widespread application?

Rather, we are confronted with a political choice, a choice which goes down to the very foundations of modern western medicine. Down one path, doctors and the mass media will propagate the myth of the genetic and dietary origins of hypertension, while in fact dealing with the effects of stress with their medications. Technological solutions to pathology created by social disruption and oppression will then appear as fortunate gifts from the gods of science to a confused and bewildered but thankful common man. Down this path, doctors and researchers become more and more a priesthood reinforcing the position of a dominant minority. This is ultimately a social dead end, however glorious and respectable its permanence.

We need to recall that, compared to the massive disruption of their "Time of Troubles," the unified world empires of the past have imposed peace; that they have executed vast accomplishments in urban public health; and that they have by and large pursued a tolerant ideological policy and have sought practical adjustment of social contradictions whenever possible. These achievements have never been sufficient to overcome the fundamental disadvantage of such a society, the rigidity and lack of social creativity in the ruling class.

The other path looks toward aiding people to take control over the fundamental determinants of their own lives in an egalitarian community. This in many ways is a new historical and social project, especially when one contemplates not going backward to primitive social forms but preserving worldwide technical and organizational integration at the same time. That this path is as yet open-ended, and that we can see only a few steps into its density does not lessen its attractiveness. We must always keep in mind that the alternatives are continued suffering or the withdrawal from basic human values in order to adapt to a particular social hierarchy. The repulsiveness of these choices must make the path toward cooperation and equality worthy of intelligent effort and action.

Note Added in Proof—The leading figure of the salt-consumption school of essential hypertension, Lewis Dahl, along with Richard Friedman, has just published an article entitled "The Effect of Chronic Conflict on Blood Pressure of Rats with a Genetic Susceptibility to Experimental Hypertension" (Friedman and Dahl, *Psychosomatic Medicine*, 37(5): 402–416, 1975). The authors execute four major achievements in this article, all of them moves toward the stress/salt-consumption hypothesis of hypertension suggested in my review.

First, Friedman and Dahl demonstrate that the kind of chronic stress that I showed to be possibly causative of hypertension in humans is reproducible in an animal-experimental paradigm, and produces large, sustained elevations of blood pressure. They also review the other relevant animal experimental literature demonstrating this point. The critical variable emergent in this literature is the ability of the animal to control punishing or disruptive stimuli.

Second, the sustained hypertension developed in their animals persisted only so long as the reinforcement paradigm was present, a finding parallel to our own for the role of social environment in sustained hypertension in humans.

Third, the blood pressure response of the hypertension-susceptible strains was much larger than that of strains not susceptible on a genetic basis. This larger sensitivity was mediated by a hyperresponsiveness of the arterioles of the susceptible strains to the vasopressor agents, noradrenalin and renin. These observations are similar to the finding in humans that people with highly labile blood pressure, due to great vascular reactivity, are at high risk of subsequent development of sustained hypertension.

Fourth, and most significant for a one-factor salt-consumption theory, is the fact that the basis of the ease with which these animals develop hypertension under non-stressed conditions in response to high-salt diets is a genetic alteration resulting in basal blood levels of aldosterone and other mineralocorticoids over twice as high as that found in nonsusceptible strains. This finding is not typical for humans who are not under stress, and genetic inheritance plays a minor role in human essential hypertension, as I have demonstrated.

However, the major group of human essential hypertensives do have elevated renin, with consequent elevations of aldosterone and salt retention from high-salt diet. Since this group also has elevated noradrenalin and other stress hormones, there is good reason to believe that the renin elevation is due to chronic stress as well, rather than to a genetic alteration, as in the susceptible rodent strains. This possibility is explicitly pursued by Friedman and Dahl in their Discussion, citing the relevant physiological literature demonstrating the role of stress and sympathetic activation in elevating blood levels of renin.

References

1. Moser, M., and Goldman, A. *Hypertensive Vascular Disease—Diagnosis and Treatment.* J. B. Lippincott, Philadelphia, 1967.
2. Stamler, J. *Lectures in Preventive Cardiology.* Grune and Stratton, New York, 1968.
3. Moriyama, I. M., Krueger, D., and Stamler, J. *Cardiovascular Diseases in the United States.* Harvard University Press, Cambridge, Mass., 1971.
4. Kannel, W., Wolf, P., Verter, J., and McNamara, P. Epidemiologic assessment of the role of blood pressure in stroke: The Framingham study. *JAMA* 214: 301, 1970.
5. Epstein, F., and Eckoff, R. The epidemiology of high blood pressure—Geographic distributions and etiological factors. In *The Epidemiology of Hypertension*, edited by J. Stamler, R. Stamler, and T. Pullman, p. 155. Grune and Stratton, New York, 1967.
6. Bays, R., and Scrimshaw, N. Facts and fallacies regarding the blood pressure of different regional and racial groups. *Circulation* 8:655, 1953.

7. Shaper, A., and Williams, A. Cardiovascular disorders at an African hospital in Uganda. *Trans. R. Soc. Trop. Med. Hyg.* 54: 12, 1960.
8. Shaper, A., and Shaper, L. Analysis of medical admissions to Mulago Hospital. *East Afr. Med. J.* 35: 648, 1958.
9. Shaper, A. Blood pressure studies in East Africa. In *The Epidemiology of Hypertension*, edited by J. Stamler, R. Stamler, and T. Pullman. Grune and Stratton, New York, 1967.
10. Miall, W. The epidemiology of essential hypertension. In *W.H.O.—Czechoslovak Cardiological Society Symposium on the Pathogenesis of Essential Hypertension*, edited by J. Cort, V. Fencl, Z. Hejl, and J. Jirka, Macmillan, New York, 1962.
11. Scotch, N., and Geiger, H. The epidemiology of essential hypertension—A review with special attention to psychologic and sociocultural factors. *J. Chronic Dis.* 16: 1151, 1963.
12. Henry, J., and Cassel, J. Psychosocial factors in essential hypertension: Recent epidemiologic and animal experimental evidence. *Am. J. Epidemiol.* 90: 171, 1969.
13. Cruz-Coke, R., Etcheverry, R., and Nagel, R. Influence of migration on blood pressure of Easter Islanders. *Lancet* 1: 697, 1964.
14. Maddocks, J. The influence of standard of living on blood pressure in Fiji. *Circulation* 24: 1220, 1961.
15. Kaminer, B., and Lutz, W. Blood pressure in the bushmen of the Kalahari Desert. *Circulation* 22: 289, 1960.
16. Whyte, H. Body fat and blood pressure of natives in New Guinea: Reflections on essential hypertension. *Australian Annals of Medicine* 7: 36, 1958.
17. White, P. Hypertension and atherosclerosis in the Congo and in the Gabon. In *The Epidemiology of Hypertension*, edited by J. Stamler, R. Stamler, and T. Pullman, Grune and Stratton, New York, 1967.
18. Abrahams, D., Alele, C., and Barnard, G. The systemic blood pressure in a rural West African community. *West Afr. Med. J.* 9: 45, 1960.
19. Moser, M. Harris, M. Pugatch, O., Ferber, A., and Gordon, D. Epidemiology of hypertension. II. Studies of blood pressure in Liberia. *Am. J. Cardiol.* 10: 424, 1962.
20. Dawber, T., Kannel, W., Kagan, A. Donabedian, R., McNamara, P., and Pearson, G. Environmental factors in hypertension. In *The Epidemiology of Hypertension*, edited by J. Stamler, R. Stamler, and T. Pullman, Grune and Stratton, New York, 1967.
21. Donnison, C. Blood pressure in the African native. *Lancet* 1: 6, 1929.
22. Heimann, L., Strachan, A., and Heimann, S. Cardiac disease among South African non-Europeans. *Br. Med. J.* 1: 344, 1929.
23. Jex-Blake, A. High blood pressure. *East Afr. Med. J.* 10: 286, 1934.
24. Vint, F. Post-mortem findings in the natives of Kenya. *East Afr. Med. J.* 13: 332, 1937.
25. Williams, A. Blood pressure of Africans. *East Afr. Med. J.* 18: 109, 1941.
26. Williams, A. Heart disease in a native population of Uganda: Hypertensive heart disease. *East Afr. Med. J.* 21: 328, 1944.
27. Taylor, C. The racial distribution of nephritis and hypertension in Panama. *Am. J. Pathol.* 21: 1031, 1945.
28. Puffer, R., and Griffith, G. *Patterns of Urban Mortality.* Pan American Health Organization, New York, 1967.
29. Miall, W., Kass, E., Ling, J., and Stuart, K. Factors influencing arterial pressure in the general population in Jamaica. *Br. Med. J.* 2: 497, 1962.

30. Schneckloth, R., Stuart, K., Corcoran, A., and Moon, F. Arterial pressure and hypertensive disease in a West Indian negro population. *Am. Heart J.* 63: 607, 1962.

31. Johnson, B., and Remington, R. A sampling study of blood pressure in white and negro residents of Nassau, Bahamas. *J. Chronic Dis.* 13: 39, 1961.

32. Moser, M. Epidemiology of hypertension with particular reference to the Bahamas. I. Preliminary report of blood pressures and a review of possible etiological factors. *Am. J. Cardiol.* 4: 727, 1959.

33. Kean, B. Blood pressure studies on West Indians and Panamanians living on the Isthmus of Panama. *Arch. Intern. Med.* 68: 466, 1941.

34. Marvin, H., and Smith, E. Hypertensive cardiovascular disease in Panamanians and West Indians. *Military Surgeon* 91: 529, 1942.

35. Scotch, N. Sociocultural factors in the epidemiology of Zulu hypertension. *Am. J. Public Health* 53: 1205, 1963.

36. Rose, R. The distribution of mortality from hypertension within the United States. *J. Chronic Dis.* 15: 1017, 1962.

37. Comstock, G. An epidemiologic study of blood pressure levels in a biracial community in the southern United States. *American Journal of Hygiene* 65: 271, 1957.

38. McDonough, J., Garrison, G., and Hames, C. Blood pressure and hypertensive disease among negroes and whites in Evans County, Georgia. In *The epidemiology of Hypertension*, edited by J. Stamler, R. Stamler, and T. Pullman, Grune and Stratton, New York, 1967.

39. Boyle, E. Griffey, W., Nichaman, M., and Talbert, C. An epidemiologic study of hypertension among racial groups of Charleston County, South Carolina. In *The Epidemiology of Hypertension*, edited by J. Stamler, R. Stamler, and T. Pullman. Grune and Stratton, New York, 1967.

40. Stamler, J., Stamler, R., Berkson, D., Lindberg, H., Miller, W., and Collette, P. Socioeconomic factors in the epidemiology of hypertensive disease. In *The Epidemiology of Hypertension*, edited by J. Stamler, R. Stamler, and T. Pullman. Grune and Stratton, New York, 1967.

41. Adams, J. Some racial differences in blood pressures and morbidity in groups of white and colored workmen. *Am. J. Med. Sci.* 184: 342, 1932.

42. Goldstein, M. Longevity and health status of whites and nonwhites in the United States. *J. Natl. Med. Assoc.* 46: 83, 1954.

43. Lennard, H., and Glock, C. Studies in hypertension: Differences in distribution of hypertension in negroes and whites: An appraisal. *J. Chronic Dis.* 5: 186, 1957.

44. Langford, H., Watson, R., and Douglas, B. Factors affecting blood pressure in population groups. *Trans. Assoc. Am. Physicians* 81: 135, 1968.

45. Fejfar, Z., Burgess, A., and Kagan, A. Arterial hypertension and ischemic heart disease: Comparison in epidemiological studies. *Proceedings of the World Health Organization*, Geneva, 1963.

46. Folkow, B., and Neill, E. *Circulation*. Oxford University Press, New York, 1971.

47. Rosen, G. *A History of Public Health*. MD Publications, New York, 1958.

48. Eich, R., Cuddy, R., and Smulyan, H. Hemodynamics in labile hypertension. *Circulation* 34: 299, 1966.

49. Frolich, E., Tarazi, R., and Dustan, H. Reexamination of the hemodynamics of hypertension. *Am. J. Med. Sci.* 257: 9, 1969.

50. Louis, W., Doyle, A., and Anavekar, S. Plasma norepinephrine levels in essential hypertension. *New Engl. J. Med.* 288: 599, 1973.

51. Shanberg, S., Stone, R., Kirschner, N., Gunnells, J., and Robinson, R. Plasma

dopamine β hydroxylase: A possible aid in the study and evaluation of hypertension. *Science* 183: 523, 1974.

52. Brod, J., Fencl, V., and Hejl, Z. General and regional hemodynamic pattern underlying essential hypertension. *Clin. Sci.* 23: 339, 1962.
53. Wallace, R. *The Physiological Effects of Transcendental Meditation.* Students International Meditation Society, Los Angeles, 1970.
54. Page, L., and Sidd, J. Medical management of primary hypertension. *N. Engl. J. Med.* 287: 960, 1018, and 1074 (three parts), 1972.
55. Conquering the quiet killer. *Time,* Jan. 13, 1975.
56. Mason, J. Organization of psychoendocrine mechanisms. *Psychosom. Med.* 30(5): whole issue, 1968.
57. Ganong, W. *Review of Medical Physiology,* Ed. 6, p. 286. Lange Medical Publications, Los Altos, 1973.
58. Laragh, J. Evaluation and care of hypertensive patient. *Am. J. Med.* 52: 565, 1972.
59. Laragh, J. Vasoconstriction-volume analysis for understanding and treating hypertension: The use of renin and aldosterone profiles. *Am. J. Med.* 55: 261, 1973.
60. Meneely, G., and Dahl, L. Electrolytes in hypertension: The effects of sodium chloride: The evidence from animal and human studies. *Med. Clin. North Am.* 45: 271, 1961.
61. Dahl, L. Salt intake and salt need. *N. Engl. J. Med.* 258: 1152 and 1205, 1958.
62. Dahl, L. Possible role of salt intake in the development of essential hypertension. In *Essential Hypertension,* edited by K. Bock and P. Cottier, p. 53. Springer-Verlag, Berlin, 1960.
63. Thomas, E. *The Harmless People.* Vintage, New York, 1959.
64. Shah, V. Environmental factors and hypertension. In *The Epidemiology of Hypertension,* edited by J. Stamler, R. Stamler, and T. Pullman. Grune and Stratton, New York, 1967.
65. Barnett, S. *The Rat: A study in Behavior.* Aldine, Chicago, 1963.
66. Barnett, S. Social stress. *Viewpoints in Biology* 3: 170, 1964.
67. Henry, J. Meehan, J., and Stephen, P. The use of psychosocial stimuli to induce prolonged systolic hypertension in mice. *Psychosom. Med.* 29: 408, 1967.
68. Corcoran, A., Tayler, R., and Page, I. Controlled observations on the effect of low sodium dietotherapy in essential hypertension. *Circulation* 3: 1, 1951.
69. Pickering, G. *High Blood Pressure.* Churchill, London, 1968.
70. Pickering, G. The inheritance of arterial pressure. In *The Epidemiology of Hypertension,* edited by J. Stamler, R. Stamler, and T. Pullman. Grune and Stratton, New York, 1967.
71. Pickering, G. Hyperpiesis: High blood pressure without evident cause: Essential hypertension. *Br. Med. J.* 2: 959, 1965.
72. Pickering, G. The inheritance of arterial pressure. In *Epidemiology,* edited by J. Pemberton. Oxford University Press, London, 1963.
73. Hamilton, M., Pickering, G., and Roberts, J. The aetiology of essential hypertension. 4. The role of inheritance. *Clin. Sci.* 13: 273, 1954.
74. Miall, W., Heneage, P., and Khosla, T. Factors influencing the degree of resemblance in arterial pressure of close relatives. *Clin. Sci.* 33: 271, 1967.
75. Vander Molen, R., Brewer, G., and Honeyman, M. A study of hypertension in twins. *Am. Heart J.* 79: 454, 1970.
76. Strickberger, M. *Genetics,* p. 181. Macmillan, New York, 1968.

77. Dreyfuss, F., Hamosh, P., Adam, Y., and Kallner, B. Coronary heart disease and hypertension among Jews immigrated to Israel from the Atlas Mountains region of North Africa. *Am. Heart J.* 62: 470, 1961.

78. Cavalli-Sforza, L., and Bodmer, W. *Genetics of Human Populations.* W. H. Freeman, San Francisco, 1971.

79. *Mortality from Selected Causes by Marital Status.* U. S. National Center for Health Statistics, Vital and Health Statistics, Series 20, 8a, 8b, 1972.

80. Glazier, W. The task of medicine. *Sci. Am.* 228(4): 13, 1973.

81. United Nations. *Demographic Yearbooks, 1946–1972.*

82. Dublin, L., and Lotka, J. *Length of Life.* Ronald Press, New York, 1936.

83. Harburg, E., Erfurt, J., Haunstein, L., Chape, C., Schull, W., and Schork, M. Socio-ecological stress, suppressed hostility, skin color, and black-white male blood pressures: Detroit. *Psychosom. Med.* 35: 276, 1973.

84. Kuznets, S. *Modern Economic Growth.* Yale University Press, New Haven, 1966.

85. Cruz-Coke, R. Environmental influences and arterial blood pressure. *Lancet* 2: 885, 1960.

86. Syme, S., Hyman, M., and Enterline, P. Some social and cultural factors associated with the occurrence of coronary heart disease. *J. Chronic Dis.* 17: 277, 1964.

87. Gampel, M., Slome, C., and Scotch, N. Urbanization and hypertension among Zulu adults. *J. Chronic Dis.* 15: 67, 1962.

88. Lee, R., and DeVore, I. *Man The Hunter.* Aldine, Chicago, 1968.

89. Kasl, S., and Cobb, S. Blood pressure changes in men undergoing job loss: A preliminary report. *Psychosom. Med.* 32: 19, 1970.

90. Dodge, S., and Martin, W. *Social Stress and Chronic Illness: Mortality Patterns in Industrial Society.* University of Notre Dame Press, London, 1970.

91. Christenson, W., and Hinkle, L. Differences in illness and prognostic signs in two groups of young men. *JAMA* 177: 247, 1961.

92. Toynbee, A. *A Study of History.* Oxford University Press, New York, 1946 and 1957.

93. Quincy, W. *A Study of War.* University of Chicago Press, Chicago, 1939.

94. Sorokin, P. *Contemporary Sociological Theories.* Harper and Row, New York, 1928.

95. Graham, J. High blood pressure after battle. *Lancet* 248: 239, 1945.

96. Williams, E. *Capitalism and Slavery.* G. P. Putnam & Sons, New York, 1966.

97. Wolf, E. *Peasant Wars of the Twentieth Century.* Harper and Row, New York, 1969.

98. Moore, B. *Social Origins of Dictatorship and Democracy.* Beacon Press, Boston, 1966.

99. Miall, W., and Oldham, P. Factors influencing arterial blood pressure in the general population. *Clin. Sci.* 17: 409, 1958.

100. Gordon, T., and Devine, B. Hypertension and Hypertensive Heart Disease in Adults. U. S. National Center for Health Statistics, Vital and Health Statistics, Series 11, No. 13, 1966.

101. Mumford, L. *Technics and Civilization.* Harcourt, Brace, New York, 1934.

102. McClelland, D. *The Achieving Society.* Free Press, New York, 1961.

103. Weber, M. *The Protestant Ethic and the Spirit of Capitalism.* Scribners, New York, 1958.

104. Mandel, E. *Marxist Economic Theory*, Vol. 1, p. 135. Monthly Review Press, New York, 1968.

105. Levi, L. *Stress and Distress in Response to Psychosocial Stimuli.* Pergamon Press, New York, 1972.

106. Friedman, M., Rosenman, R., and Carroll, V. Changes in serum cholesterol and

blood clotting time in men subjected to cyclic variation of occupational stress. *Circulation* 17: 852, 1958.

107. Russek, H., and Zohman, B. Relative significance of heredity, diet and occupational stress in coronary heart disease of young adults. *Am. J. Med. Sci.* 235: 266, 1958.

108. Friedman, M., and Rosenman, R. *Type A Behavior and Your Heart.* Knopf, New York, 1974.

4

Risk Factor Intervention for Health Maintenance

Lester Breslow

Nature and Identification of Risk Factors

With the growing prominence on the health scene of certain chronic diseases such as lung cancer, cirrhosis of the liver, and coronary heart disease, various efforts have been undertaken to ascertain and deal with the factors responsible. One direction is to seek discovery of the biologic mechanisms of disease, for example, how an arteriosclerotic plaque develops in the wall of a coronary artery.

Another, and now highly promising, direction is to approach the problem from the epidemiological standpoint. That effort takes the form of trying to identify the characteristics of individuals that are statistically associated with an increased frequency of a disease and mortality from it; and then trying to deal with the characteristics so as to reduce the likelihood of the disease and its effects. One set of factors associated with these diseases includes personal habits, such as cigarette smoking, sedentary life, and excessive alcohol consumption. Another set consists of actual bodily changes not yet sufficient to classify an individual as having a particular disease but recognized as precursors: physiological characteristics, such as hypertension; biochemical characteristics, such as high serum cholesterol; anatomical characteristics such as cervical dysplasia; and genetic characteristics, such as trisomy 21 (Down's syndrome). Together, these two kinds of characteristics—certain common habits of people and certain bodily changes associated with increased frequency of disease and its consequences—have become known as risk factors.

Knowledge of these risk factors has accumulated rapidly during recent decades. Thoracic surgeons in the late 1930's recognized that their lung cancer patients commonly smoked cigarettes. Subsequently confirmed by many careful epidemiological investigations and summarized in the 1964 Surgeon General's

SOURCE: *Science* 200 (26 May 1978): 908–12. Copyright © 1978 by the American Association for the Advancement of Science. Reprinted by permission of the publisher and the author.

Report (1), the association between cigarette smoking and several forms of cancer, coronary heart disease, and chronic lung disease has now been well established.

While cigarette smoking was being identified and gradually accepted as a factor in lung cancer and several other important diseases, investigators noted a comparable relationship between high intake of saturated fat, high blood cholesterol, and coronary heart disease (2). Again, these studies began with fairly gross observations of the association, but continued on into prospective epidemiological studies that quantified the relationships (3).

More-or-less systematic identification, measurement, and assessment of risk factors for coronary heart disease, the leading cause of mortality in the industrialized nations, has progressed, with attention to hypertension, sedentary living, obesity, electrocardiographic (EKG) abnormalities, personality factors, family history, and diabetes, as well as cigarette smoking and high blood cholesterol (4). The most extensive study has been that in Framingham, Massachusetts, from which the probability of having cardiovascular disease according to specified characteristics has been derived (Table 1) (5). A 30-fold range exists. Approaching the problem from the standpoint of generic health, rather than individual diseases, investigators at the Human Population Laboratory, Alameda County, California, have identified exercise, no cigarette smoking, 7 to 8 hours of sleep, moderate or no use of alcohol, and regular and moderate eating as positively associated with physical health and negatively associated with mortality from all causes (6).

TABLE 1. (5). Probability per 1000 of Having Cardiovascular Disease within 8 Years According to Specified Characteristics in a 45-Year-Old Man. Framingham Study: 18-Year Follow-Up.

Glucose intolerance	Cholesterol	Systolic blood pressure (mm-Hg)							
		Does not smoke cigarettes				*Smokes cigarettes*			
		105	135	165	195	105	135	165	195
No left ventricular hypertrophy by electrocardiogram									
Absent	185	22	35	54	84	38	59	91	138
	235	35	54	84	129	59	91	139	205
	285	55	85	129	192	92	139	206	293
	335	85	130	193	277	140	207	295	401
Present	185	39	61	95	143	67	102	154	226
	235	62	95	144	212	103	155	227	320
	285	96	145	213	303	156	228	321	431
	335	145	214	304	411	229	323	433	550
Left ventricular hypertrophy by electrocardiogram									
Absent	185	60	93	141	208	101	152	223	315
	235	93	142	209	297	153	224	316	425
	285	142	210	298	405	225	317	426	543
	335	211	300	406	523	318	428	545	657
Present	185	105	158	231	324	170	246	344	456
	235	158	232	325	436	247	345	457	574
	285	232	327	437	554	346	459	576	685
	335	328	438	556	667	460	577	686	778

The present situation regarding risk factors, including the potential for intervention, is somewhat analogous to the situation that existed when polluted water became known as a causative factor of enteric infections such as cholera and typhoid, before their etiology and pathogenesis were demonstrated bacteriologically.

Epidemiology of Risk Factors

Before discussing the matter of intervention, however, it may be useful to consider briefly the epidemiology of risk factors themselves—that is, their distribution in the population, their temporal distribution, and what influences their occurrence. Understanding the epidemiology of risk factors per se, as well as the diseases to which they are related, may enhance the possibilities of successful intervention.

For example, the health and nutrition examination survey conducted by the U.S. National Center for Health Statistics between 1971 and 1974 disclosed that 23 million adults, 18.1 percent of the population aged 18 to 74, had hypertension (7). The prevalence varied considerably in different segments of the population (Table 2). The survey also disclosed factors associated with that distribution and the extent to which persons were taking antihypertensive medication. Only slightly more than one-third of all hypertensive adults between 18 and 74 had used medication for the condition during the previous 6 months, and 60 percent of these had blood pressures of 160/95 (mm-HG) or above at the time of examination. The survey also revealed the extent of salt restriction and efforts to control obesity as means of coping with hypertension.

A common notion about cigarette smokers is that they rarely can or will quit the habit. If true, that notion should lead those concerned with cigarette-induced health damage to abandon efforts to keep people from smoking cigarettes and to try other means of coping with the problem. In fact, more than 33 million Americans had actually stopped smoking cigarettes by 1976—almost double the number of former smokers in 1964, when the Surgeon General's report (1) was issued (8).

In 1964, 53 percent of all American men were cigarette smokers; by 1975 the proportion had dropped to 39 percent (9). Furthermore, the decline has been greater among younger men with more education. For example, among males up to age 30 years in Alameda County, California (a community fairly typical de-

TABLE 2. (7). Percentage of Examinees 18 to 74 Years of Age with Hypertension, by Race, Sex, and Type of Hypertension. Data are from the United States, 1971–1974.

Types of hypertension	White		Black	
	Male	Female	Male	Female
Definite	18.5	15.7	27.8	28.6
Severe*	4.9	3.4	11.2	11.1
Borderline†	21.9	15.7	17.6	14.3

*Severe: ≥ 105 mm-Hg diastolic pressure.   †Borderline: 140 to 160 mm-Hg systolic or 90 to 95 mm-Hg diastolic pressure.

mographically of the U. S. population), during the period 1965 to 1974, cigarette smoking dropped from 79 percent to 74 percent for those who had not completed high school; 65 percent to 60 percent for those who had completed high school only; and 33 percent to 20 percent for those who had completed college or more education (*10*). There has also been some drop in cigarette smoking among women.

Serum cholesterol concentration is probably the most thoroughly studied and documented risk factor for coronary heart disease. Deliberate efforts to control hypercholesterolemia have included diet, exercise, and drugs. For example, reducing the total calories derived from fat in the typical American male diet from 40 to 45 percent to 20 to 30 percent, altering the ratio of saturated to unsaturated fats from the typical 2:1 or 3:1 to 1:1, reducing daily cholesterol intake, and reducing total caloric intake if the subject is overweight "generally have been successful in lowering serum cholesterol over sustained periods of time" (*4*), p. 519). In The Anticoronary Club study in New York, the serum cholesterol fell an average of 30 milligrams per deciliter in the first year of dieting by free-living middle-aged men and persisted for more than 7 years in subjects maintaining the diet (*11*).

Concept and Methods of Risk Factor Intervention

Important risk factors are thus being identified and data are being accumulated to indicate that it is feasible to control risk factors. One risk factor—for example, cigarette smoking—may be involved in more than one disease entity; one disease—for example, coronary heart disease—may have more than one risk factor.

Until recent years, medicine has focused largely on diseases themselves. Now we are beginning to understand better the natural history of important chronic diseases and the two major possibilities of intervening in their natural history so as to avoid the diseases, reduce their mortality rates, or both.

One possibility is to identify the pathological process early in the affected individual and intervene in some way to stop the process at that point. Thus, screening with the Papanicolaou smear, determining blood pressure, and other means may detect those persons in the population, even without signs or symptoms, who are developing a disease. Intervention at such points, known as secondary prevention (to indicate that while the disease process is under way, its further development can be prevented), is increasingly effective.

Even better, of course, is primary prevention, avoiding those factors that initiate and promote the disease process. Thus, the vast majority of lung cancer and much coronary heart disease can be prevented by avoiding cigarette smoking.

Hence, risk factor intervention as an approach to chronic disease control consists of two elements: (i) identifying and quantifying the relationship of certain personal characteristics—largely habits associated with diet, use of cigarettes, alcohol consumption, exercise, and the like—and dealing with them to avoid the disease process altogether (primary prevention) and (ii) identifying the disease process in its early stages and taking steps to avoid progression of the disease (secondary prevention).

The effectiveness of this strategy depends upon (i) the means available for and the extent of the search for the risk factors in the population and (ii) the means available for controlling the various risk factors and the extent of their proper application. The potential for effective risk factor intervention varies considerably among different diseases and different social situations.

Even though the possibilities seem great, much remains to be learned concerning the extent of the potential and how it may be achieved. In general, three methods of intervention have been tried.

(1) The first consists of approaching individual persons (as in a physician's practice or mass screening in a population), identifying their risk factors, and then taking steps to reduce the risk factors found. That is the so-called "medical model."

(2) Mass education has been undertaken to change health habits through schools and public media among others. Widespread transmission of information about risk factors and other ways of influencing health-related behavior have apparently already had some impact, as in the case of cigarette smoking.

(3) Some efforts have been made to alter the products actually used by people. For example, low-fat milk and soft margarine are now more readily available.

These three means of dealing with the problem are now being intensively explored: personal health services, educational measures, and environmental measures. While these three may be separated for the purposes of analysis, they are in fact often closely related in any particular social situation.

Risk Factor Intervention Trials

So promising did the strategy of risk factor intervention appear by the early 1970's that several investigators in different parts of the world initiated large-scale trials. Three of the major trials were directed at cigarette smoking, high serum cholesterol, and hypertension, the factors most consistently identified as prominent in the risk for coronary heart disease.

Multiple Risk Factor Intervention Trial (MRFIT). The MRFIT responded to the recommendations of the Inter-Society Commission for Heart Disease Resources in 1970 (12) and the following year by the National Heart and Lung Institute (NHLI) task force on arteriosclerosis (13). The NHLI thereupon initiated a study cooperatively with 20 centers (14).

> The primary objective was to determine whether for a group of men at high risk of death from coronary heart disease, a special intervention program which is directed simultaneously toward three risk variables will result in a significant reduction in mortality from coronary heart disease. . . . A second objective is to determine the effect . . . on coronary heart disease incidence (either non-fatal myocardial infarction or coronary heart disease death), cardiovascular mortality, and total mortality (death from any cause). . . . Specific goals [for] risk factor modification [included] (i) a 10 percent reduction from baseline in serum cholesterol; (ii) a 10 percent reduction from baseline in diastolic blood pressure; and (iii) a 20, 30, or 40 percent net reduction in amount of cigarette smoking for heavy, moderate, or light cigarette smokers, respectively (15. p. 12).

The first operational step was to select the individuals at high risk upon whom intervention efforts would be focused. Out of 370,599 persons recruited for initial screening, the participating centers finally selected 12,866 individuals as meeting the criteria for admission to the study: age, 35 to 57 years; increased risk of death from coronary heart disease on the basis of the Framingham risk score, which embraced elevated serum cholesterol, elevated diastolic blood pressure, and cigarette smoking; no pre-existing definite clinical coronary heart disease or other specified causes for exclusion; and willingness to commit themselves to a 6-year intervention program (*16*). Fifty percent were randomly allocated to their usual source of medical care, and the participating centers enrolled the other 50 percent in a special intervention program.

The special intervention program began with a series of ten intensive group sessions emphasizing "factual education, selected principles from the disciplines of behavior modification and group dynamics, and the use of group process to facilitate change in a supportive atmosphere . . . applied to nutrition, smoking and treatment of hypertension" (*15*, p. 14). Those persons who achieve their goals of risk-factor reduction then begin maintenance programs; the unsuccessful ones are referred to more individualized, extended intervention programs.

The only results available from the MRFIT program are the findings from the initial screening: an average serum cholesterol of 157.3 mg/dl, average diastolic blood pressure of 99.2 millimeters of mercury, and an average of 21.62 cigarettes per day with 63.7 percent reporting smoking one or more cigarettes per day. There were essentially no differences between special intervention and usual care groups.

The MRFIT program has been under way too short a time to permit the compiling of findings pertinent to the objectives. From a self-assessment thus far,

> It is clear that a large, complex, multicenter trial such as this can survive phases of planning, controversy and compromise, and enter operations successfully. . . . The response from the mass media and the public has been generally gratifying. . . . The response from the medical profession has also been decidely favorable and helpful; [and] while it is too early even to speculate on the results, it would appear that this expensive undertaking has had an auspicious start (*14*, pp. 826–827).

The Stanford Heart Disease Prevention Program. A field experiment in three northern California towns, the Stanford heart disease prevention program has focused on the same three risk factors for cardiovascular disease as those in the MRFIT program. It has been mainly a campaign directed toward the total community, with some effort directed toward high-risk individuals (*17, 18*).

The goal was to develop and evaluate methods "to influence the adult population at large to change their living habits in ways that could reduce their risk of premature heart attack and stroke" (*18*, p. 102). Combining biomedical expertise with that of the social sciences, "the family-community model, rather than the medical-center model, was chosen because a community would be able to provide the milieu in which a consensus of support and mutual help could develop and become an essential and integral part of the behavioral change program" (*18*, p. 101).

Three roughly comparable communities in northern California, each with populations of 12,000 to 15,000, were selected for the study. All three communities were surveyed for base-line data. One was then kept as a control. A multimedia campaign in the other two communities extended over a period of 2 years; in one of them certain high-risk subjects identified in the base-line survey received additional face-to-face intensive instruction.

The intitial survey included a behavioral interview and a medical examination of a sample of persons 35 to 59 years of age in all three communities. The survey covered relevant knowledge of and attitudes toward risk-related behavior related to diet, weight, smoking, and exercise. Incorporated into the medical examination were measures included in the Framingham risk score (19).

In the two (noncontrol) communities, the Stanford program in 1972 launched a mass-media campaign incorporating materials to teach specific behavioral skills as well as to impart information and affect attitudes regarding risk-related behavior. The campaign included television and radio "spots" and hour-long programming, weekly newspaper columns, newspaper advertisements and stories, billboards, posters, and printed material mailed to participants. In one of the two communities a random sample of individuals in the top quartile of risk were recruited into intensive face-to-face instruction.

Two subsequent annual surveys showed favorable changes both in the physical variables constituting the risk score and in pertinent knowledge and behavior. Improvement in knowledge after two years in the control community was 6 percent; in the two communities where the campaign had been conducted there was 26 to 41 percent improvement, and among those receiving intensive instruction, 54 percent (18).

Saturated fat and cholesterol consumption declined 20 to 40 percent over the 2-year period in the campaign communities, a substantially greater drop than in the control community. The drop was especially large among high-risk men who received intensive instruction. Mean changes in serum cholesterol were highly correlated with the self-reported changes in dietary behavior (20).

Cigarette smoking likewise declined to a greater extent among total community participants in the campaign communities, 7 to 24 percent, compared with the control community, where the drop was only 2.5 percent at the end of year 2. Among those who received intensive instruction, the decrease in cigarette smoking was 42 percent (18).

In the control community, the risk for coronary heart disease actually increased more than 5 percent during the 2-year period of the study, but the risk in the communities where the campaign had been conducted declined 15 to 20 percent among the total participants. Again the decline was greater in the intensive-instruction high-risk group, 30 percent.

Thus the Stanford heart disease prevention program has demonstrated that a community-focused multimedia campaign over a 2-year period can substantially improve not only knowledge of risk factors for cardiovascular disease but also favorably influence behavior and risk scores. Intensive instruction of individuals identified as having a high risk score augmented the effect in that group.

The North Karelia Project. North Karelia, a county of eastern Finland with a population of approximately 180,000, nearly 70 percent in rural areas where the main occupations are farming and forestry, has an extremely high rate of coronary heart disease—perhaps the highest for any geographic area in the world (21).

Reacting to that health situation, local and national governmental representatives of the people petitioned the national government to take action. As a result the North Karelia project, a community program for the control of cardiovascular diseases, was established in 1972. The University of Kuopio assumed responsibility for the project with support from the national government in the amount of approximately $250,000 annually—less than $1.50 per capita per year. That has been essentially the "cost" of the project, the additional resources used beyond those already present in North Karelia.

The main objective was to decrease cardiovascular disease mortality and morbidity among the population of North Karelia—especially among the middle-aged male population. Intermediate objectives were to reduce the same three cardiovascular risk factors as those in the Stanford and MRFIT projects and to promote the early diagnosis, treatment, and rehabilitation of cardiovascular patients. A national objective was to provide tested field methods for nationwide use in connection with the control of cardiovascular disease and other health problems (22).

Leaders in the project decided early (i) to mount a comprehensive campaign against risk factors in the entire population of the area, not to "enroll' test subjects; (ii) to focus on just three risk factors: cigarette smoking, serum cholesterol level, and hypertension (since obesity and physical exercise were not problems in the area); (iii) to integrate the project into the existing service structure and social organization of the area; and (iv) to maintain observation of a similar nearby county as a reference (control) population.

A random-sample base-line survey of the North Karelia population 25 to 59 years of age in 1972 revealed that among males 54 percent were currently smoking cigarettes; the mean serum cholesterol was 269 milligrams per 100 milliliters, and 21 percent had a blood pressure of 160/90 (mm-Hg) or above (24). Myocardial infarction, hypertension, and stroke registers confirmed the extremely high incidence of these conditions.

The strategy in the comprehensive 6-year phased program was mainly to enlist widespread participation of the people of the region and their organizations and institutions. Activities include (i) providing public health information, through heavy use of television, radio, newspapers andother means; (ii) training personnel in health agencies, schools, and local organizations for community leadership in the project; (iii) organizing health and other public services for maximum participation; (iv) introducing environmental changes, such as restricting smoking cigarettes and encouraging low-fat dairy products; and (v) providing patient information services—for example, hypertension, stroke, and myocardial infarction registries.

Subprograms were aimed at each of the three risk factors. New laws banned cigarette smoking in public buildings and public vehicles; media carried advertisements against it; and special efforts were directed against cigarette smoking among teachers, health personnel, and persons at high risk. Dietary changes to reduce total fat consumption included introducing low-fat milk and margarine, incorporating mushrooms (as a fat replacement) into the popular sausage, and increasing the use of vegetables generally. Persons found to have hypertension in a countywide screening program were placed on therapy and followed by public health nurses. Coronary care units and ambulance services were established or improved.

Findings at the end of 4 1/2 years indicated good cooperation by the people; a decline in cigarette smoking among middle-aged males (from 54 percent of the population smoking to 43 percent); an increase in the use of low-fat milk by from 17 to 50 percent of the population; an increase from 3 to 11 percent of the male population under hypertensive therapy, and among females from 9 to 13 percent; and a decrease in systolic blood pressure of 10 mm-Hg or more among 53 percent of the 1799 persons on the hypertension register, with 40 percent showing a decrease of 10 mm-Hg in diastolic blood pressure. Results have also included a considerable decline in the annual incidence of strokes: from 3.6 per 1000 males in 1972 to 1.9 in 1975 and from 2.8 per 1000 females to 1.8 (21). Myocardial infarction rates slightly declined.

> The programme in North Karelia will continue after the initial 5-year period, and a follow-up of [cardiovascular disease (CVD)] and CVD-risk indicators is organized to assess the longer term changes. In the meantime many of the experiences are already being planned for application nationwide [in Finland] (23, p. 1).

The three projects described exemplify efforts undertaken during the 1970's to reduce cardiovascular and other major diseases by attacking risk factors. Others include (i) the American Health Foundation's "Know Your Body" program among several thousand 10- to 15-year-old school children in New York City, which screens for and attempts to reduce elevated serum cholesterol, high blood pressure, cigarette smoking, obesity, and other risk factors (24); (ii) a program in Switzerland supported by the Swiss National Science Foundation to mobilize community resources to reduce cardiovascular disease risk factors in two communities with 10,000 to 20,000 inhabitants each, compared with two kept as controls (25); and (iii) the health hazard appraisal program developed at the Indianapolis Methodist Hospital (26).

Discussion

Efforts to cope with the major fatal diseases of the 20th century in the industrially advanced nations, especially the cardiovascular diseases and cancer, have evolved mainly into a two-pronged strategy. One element, primary prevention, is to identify and reduce the causative factors so as to avoid the occurrence of the diseases, for example, by controlling cigarette smoking. The other element, secondary prevention, is to identify precursor bodily changes or initial stages of disease and avoid the progression of disease by early therapy, for example, by finding and treating asymptomatic hypertension.

At present, several large-scale trials of this strategy, known as risk factor intervention, are under way in the United States and Europe. The general aim is to test the feasibility of reducing (i) the risk factors, an intermediate objective; and (ii) the diseases and mortality from them, the ultimate objective.

Two main tactics are sometimes combined in practice. One approach is to identify those individuals who are at high risk—for example, cigarette smokers with hypertension and high serum cholesterol—and to focus intensive efforts on such persons. This may be called the medical model because it directs medical and related attention to selected individuals, as in medicine generally. The other tactic aims educational and environmental measures toward a whole community, seeking to improve the health-related behavior of a population and thus reduce its risk factors. This may be called the community model because the focus is on the entire community, not just on selected individuals who are at particularly high risk. The MRFIT program clearly follows the medical model, whereas both the Stanford and North Karelia programs are essentially of the community-model type but incorporate the medical as well. None of the projects is designed to evaluate the relative effectiveness of community and medical approaches, although the Stanford project includes that possibility to a limited extent.

Some evidence already indicates that the Stanford and North Karelia projects have been at least partially successful in reducing certain risk factors for cardiovascular disease, although meticulous comparison with the control communities remains to be done. In North Karelia the sharp decline in incidence of strokes is impressive, and the suggestion of decline in death from myocardial infarction is promising; but careful evaluation must await comparison with experience in the reference county.

Interpreting results of the specific programs is confounded by the present general trend toward a decline in risk factors such as cigarette smoking and hypertension in "control" groups or communities, probably due to general public and medical efforts-to reduce risk factors apart from the large-scale programs.

The cost-effectiveness of the North Karelia project, funded at about $1.50 per capita target population annually, is likely to be vastly greater than the programs in the United States, for which much larger expenditures are being made. The cost advantage of the North Karelia project may be due both to the deliberate program tactic of comprehensively involving the community infrastructure and to the greater feasibility of that tactic in Finnish than in American society. Individuals, organizations, and community institutions appear more oriented toward the public good in Finland than in the United States.

It must also be noted that in North Karelia the level of risk was higher at the start than in the Stanford or MRFIT original populations (even though North Karelia is not a highly industrialized community) so that improvement there may potentially be more dramatic.

The Stanford project was well designed to test intervention on risk factors themselves but not the ultimate criteria of disease occurrence and mortality. There is, of course, substantial evidence from many studies that reducing certain risk factors, such as cigarette smoking and hypertension, does favorably influence disease incidence and mortality.

The MRFIT program has not yet produced data permitting the evaluation of results. If successful in reaching its objectives, it could have considerable influence on American medical practice. Interpreting data from the project, however, will have to take into account the fact that those identified as at high risk and therefore offered intervention constitute only a minority of the persons in the population who will suffer cardiovascular disease. For example, from the Framingham variables, ten percent of the asymptomatic population can be identified (and the MRFIT program did approximately that) "in whom 25 percent of the coronary heart disease, 40 percent of the occlusive peripheral arterial disease and 50 percent of the strokes and congestive heart failure will evolve" (5, p. 269). Thus, 75 percent of the coronary heart disease in the population would not be specifically targeted by the MRFIT program. Interpretation of MRFIT data will also have to include attention to the fact that only a portion of the high-risk eligible individuals actually participated in the intervention program. Evaluation should embrace the entire high-risk group, not just those who accepted the intervention efforts.

From the MRFIT, Stanford, North Karelia, and other current risk factor intervention studies, it seems likely that significant new data on how to control the major diseases of modern times will emerge. The evidence thus far suggests that intervention will prove successful. If it does, efforts to prevent disease and maintain health will probably focus increasingly on risk factors rather than, as now, on diseases themselves. Collaboration between epidemiologists and biomedical scientists concerned with physiological, chemical, anatomical, immunological, behavioral, and genetic aspects of human functioning may point the way to health improvement in the future. That would shift the focus away from the clinical entities that have occupied medicine so largely since the days of Thomas Sydenham (1624–1689) and toward risk factors. It is these factors that now largely predict and apparently determine the extent of chronic disease and premature death; they should receive higher priority in health efforts than the diseases themselves.

References

1. U. S. Department of Health, Education, and Welfare, *Smoking and Health Report of the Advisory Committee to the Surgeon General of the Public Health Service* (Government Printing Office, Washington, D. C., 1964).
2. A. Keys, *J. Chron. Dis.* 4, 364 (1956).
3. ———, H. L. Taylor, H. Blackburn, J. Brozek, J. T. Anderson, E. Simonson, *Circulation* 28, 381 (1963); A. Kagan, W. B. Kannel, T. R. Dawber, N. Revotskie, *Ann. Intern. Med.* 55, 33 (1964); J. M. Chapman, and F. J. Massey, *J. Chron. Dis.* 17, 933 (1964).
4. D. W. Simborg, *J. Chron. Dis.* 22, 515 (1970).
5. W. B. Kannel, *Am. J. Cardiol.* 37, 269 (1976).
6. For a review, see L. Breslow, *Int. J. Epidemiol.* 1, 347 (1972).
7. U. S. Department of Health, Education, and Welfare, *Health—United States 1976–1977* [HEW Publ. (HRA) 77–1232, Government Printing Office, Washington, D. C. 1977].
8. D. Horn, *Current Needs for Dealing with Cigarette Smoking*, Statement made to the Commission on Smoking Policy of the American Cancer Society, Los Angeles, 22 March 1977.
9. National Clearinghouse for Smoking and Health, *Focal Points* (Center for Disease Control, Atlanta, 1977).
10. L. Breslow, unpublished data.
11. G. Christakis, S. H. Rinzler, M. Archer, E. Maslansky, *Public Health Rep.* 80, 64 (1966).
12. Inter-Society Commission for Heart Disease Resources, *Circulation* 42, 55 (1970).

13. Report by the National Heart and Lung Institute Task Force on Arteriosclerosis [HEW Publ. (NIH) 72–137, Government Printing Office, Washington, D. C., 1971].
14. Multiple Risk Factor Intervention Trial Group, *J. Am. Med. Assoc.* **235**, 825 (1976).
15. U. S. Department of Health, Education, and Welfare, *Multiple Risk Factor Intervention Trial, June 30, 1975, to July 1, 1976* [HEW Publ. (NIH) 77–1211, Government Printing Office, Washington, D. C., 1977].
16. Multiple Risk Factor Intervention Trial Group, *J. Chronic Dis.* **30**, 261 (1977).
17. J. W. Farquhar *et al.*, *Lancet* **1977-I**, 1192 (1977).
18. N. Maccoby, J. W. Farquhar, P. D. Wood, J. Alexander, *J. Commun. Health* **3**, 100 (Winter 1977).
19. J. Truett, J. Cornfield, W. Kannel, *J. Chronic Dis.* **20**, 511 (1967).
20. M. P. Stern, J. W. Farquhar, N. Maccoby, S. H. Russell *Circulation* **54**, 826 (1976).
21. P. Puska, J. Tuomilehto, J. Salonen, *Pract. Cardiol.* **4**, 94.
22. K. Koskela, P. Puska, J. Tuomilehto, *Int. J. Health Educ.* **21**, 59 (1976).
23. P. Puska, paper presented at the Conference on Prevention, Institute of Medicine, Washington, D. C., 16 February 1978.
24. C. L. Williams, C. B. Arnold, E. L. Wynder, *Prev. Med.* **6**, 344 (1977).
25. B. Junod and F. Gutzwiller, *Med. Soc. Prev.* **22**, 157 (1977).
26. J. H. Hall, L. C. Robbins, N. B. Gesner, *Postgrad. Med.* **51**, 114 (1972).

II

Identification of Disease in Populations and in Clinical Settings

In reading 5, White and his colleagues review surveys of illness in populations in both the United States and Britain in order to make estimates of the flow of patients from the community to varying types of medical facility. Although technical in its presentation, the article provides an important epidemiological framework for examining various problems in medical sociology. The authors estimate, for example, that in any given month a large proportion of the population has some illness. This work, in conjunction with other studies, provided the basis for appreciating that illness is not a rare event, but one that occurs with high prevalence in community populations. Moreover, the authors estimate that only one in three persons who report an illness ever appears at a doctor's office. What differentiates those who do and those who do not? As the introduction to this book noted, such differences are not adequately explained by the severity or complexity of illness. Thus the study of these differences constitutes a field of inquiry—the field of illness behavior. Further, the authors make estimates on hospitalization, referral to other physicians, and referral to teaching hospitals. In each case the processes of referral and selection are problematic, requiring detailed behavioral study.

Many biological, psychological, social, and cultural factors affect the distribution of disease and death in populations. In reading 6, Waldron takes up just one of these issues, examining why women live longer than men. She does this by going beyond overall mortality, examining the ratio of male to female deaths for varying types of disease. Her analysis makes a persuasive case for the argument that much of the sex difference is explainable by social and cultural factors that shape the ways in which men and women behave in our society.

The next three readings focus more specifically on concepts of health and disease and on the types of model physicians use to categorize patients who have varying problems.

Reading 7, a classic paper by the late Sir Aubrey Lewis, analyzes the extent to which health and disease are social concepts. Lewis basically presents the conventional medical view that the definition of disease is a way of thinking about pathology, and the models of medical diagnosis used are not based on social judgments but rather on symptoms and signs of disturbed bodily functioning. Although Lewis was sensitive to the impact of social and cultural factors on disease and on the work of the doctor, he believed that an adequate model of disease must be based on clinical signs and not on social judgments. This is easily said, but Lewis's article indicates the difficulty in making this distinction clearly, particularly in the case of psychiatric conditions.

It might be useful here to say something more about the logic of the medical disease model, in order to assist the student in understanding the background and assumptive world from which Lewis comes. Patients come to doctors with many kinds of symptom, complaint, and problem. If the doctor is to be helpful, he must have some mental set for classifying, thinking about, and dealing with the great variety of symptoms and signs demonstrated by sick patients. Medical diagnoses are ways of giving order to disorderly observations and information. In attempting to ascertain the patient's problem, the physician seeks to find interrelated signs and symptoms that imply some underlying disorder. When this cluster of symptoms fits a certain pattern that the doctor recognizes on the basis of his training and experience, it may be given an identifying label, such as tuberculosis, emphysema, multiple sclerosis, or a streptococcal infection of the throat. Once the physician has identified the condition, he often knows a great deal because then he can draw on a large body of medical science and clinical investigation concerning that condition. Having properly named the condition, for example, the physician may then know the cause, the course, and the appropriate treatment for that patient. What he actually knows in any individual instance will depend on the status of existing medical knowledge. The diagnosis thus often opens for the physician a large fund of knowledge from which he can proceed in assisting the patient. This is why a correct diagnosis is so important. If the patient has tuberculosis but the physician misdiagnoses him as having emphysema, the physician draws from the wrong fund of knowledge.

Readings 7–9 all relate to diagnosis applied to psychiatric problems, which constitute a particularly difficult issue. Although the medical diagnostic model should be as applicable to psychiatric conditions as to any other, the funds of knowledge relating to these conditions tend to be more uncertain, thus providing the physician with less information about the condition. This uncertainty has resulted in much debate as to whether psychiatric conditions are diseases, whether the disease concept is useful in psychiatry, and whether mental illness is a myth.

All definitions of illness are arbitrary. The reflect social opinions as to what aspects of functioning are desirable and undesirable. In general, we tend to see bodily states that cause pain and discomfort, or that shorten life, as diseases, but this is a matter of social judgment and not a matter of science. If we wished, we could call people with large ears, big noses, and red hair diseased, but we see no point in doing so. Thus the issue of whether psychiatric conditions are diseases or not is a nonquestion. It makes no sense. The only reasonable question is whether it is useful or not useful to adopt a disease model in dealing with psychiatric conditions, and what the costs and gains of doing so are. As the reader is probably well aware, such behavioral patterns as alcoholism and homosexuality have been labeled in various ways. Whether or not they have been called diseases depends more on the social agendas of those defining the issues than on scientific knowledge.

Lewis comes to the problem of definition of health and disease with this intellectual background, and it is not surprising that he concludes that disease must be defined on the basis of independent evidence of pathological functioning such as delusions, hallucinations, and disturbed thinking, and not on the basis of social definitions. What Lewis does not tell us clearly is how we know what is pathological. Is this not also to some extent a social judgment?

In reading 8, David Rosenhan presents a somewhat different picture of psychiatric diagnosis based on his study of pseudopatients who presented themselves at various psychiatric hospitals complaining of hearing voices that said "empty," "hollow," and "thud." Rosenhan describes in vivid detail what happened to these patients and the diagnoses and treatments they received. He concludes that we cannot distinguish sanity from insanity, and he has become, along with Thomas Szasz, Ronald Laing, and Thomas Scheff, one of the major proponents of the campaign against the use of disease model in psychiatry. This selection is followed by a critique of Rosenhan's work by Rober Spitzer, a well-known research psychiatrist at Columbia University's College of Physicians and Surgeons. In reading 9, Spitzer analyzes the report on pseudopatients and maintains that it is irrelevant to the issue of the validity of psychiatric diagnosis. He indicates that all Rosenhan has shown is the unremarkable finding that people who start out with the idea of trying to fool a psychiatrist by simulating symptoms can successfully do so, at least for a time. He notes that medical patients can do so also, and some do. The vivid example of a patient who swallows blood and comes to the emergency room vomiting blood is suggested. No doubt such a patient would be suspected of having a bleeding ulcer and not of having swallowed blood to deceive the physician. In any case, readers can examine both Rosenhan's argument and those of his critic and try to come to their own views.

Although I am inclined to side with Spitzer's logic in this debate, some of Rosenhan's observations are important. Although I do not believe that he demonstrated adequately the point he set out to show about the validity of psychiatric diagnosis, he does demonstrate that the diagnostic process in psychiatry is often sloppy; that patients are hospitalized too readily when they may not need hospital care; that once they are in the hospital the observation of patients is too slow and too casual; that the assumption that the patient is ill guides the response to the patient; and that patients are frequently overtreated with dangerous drugs that may not be necessary. Thus his article says more about current practice in psychiatry and some of the sloppiness characterizing the work of psychiatrists in the hospitals involved than about the potential value of a medical diagnostic model in psychiatry. These are not unimportant issues, however, and they deserve serious scrutiny.

5

The Ecology of Medical Care

Kerr L. White, T. Franklin Williams,
and Bernard G. Greenberg

Current discussions about medical care appear largely concerned with two questions: Is the burgeoning harvest of new knowledge fostered by immense public investment in medical research being delivered effectively to the consumers? Is the available quantity, quality and distribution of contemporary medical care optimum in the opinion of the consumers? In addition, it may be asked: Whose responsibility is it to examine these questions and provide data upon which sound judgments and effective programs can be based?

The traditional indexes of the public's health, such as mortality and morbidity rates, are useful for defining patterns of ill-health and demographic characteristics of populations who experience specific diseases. They are of limited value in describing actions taken by individual patients and physicians about disease and other unclassified manifestations of ill-health. It is the collective impact of these actions that largely determines the demand for and utilization of medical-care resources. To assess the adequacy of the resources, it may be as important to ask questions about medical-care decisions, and to relate the data to clearly defined populations and health facilities, as it is to ask questions about mortality and morbidity for other purposes. In the context of medical care the patient may be a more relevant primary unit of observation than the disease, the visit or the admission. The natural history of the patient's medical care may be a more appropriate concern than the natural history of his disease. Similarly, data for short periods (weeks or months) may be more useful than data for longer periods (a year or more) for relating potential needs and demands to medical-care resources.

Little is known about the process by which persons, perceiving some disturbance in their sense of well-being or health, decide to seek help. Nor is much known about their sources of help,[1] or about the second and third stages of decision making

SOURCE: *New England Journal of Medicine* 265 (1961): 885–92. Reprinted by permission.

at which patients and their health advisors, whether physicians, pharmacists or faith healers, seek or advise help and consultations from other medical-care resources. The available data suggest that patients control the decision-making process with respect not only to seeking but also to accepting and using medical care to a substantial extent.[2,3] Each practitioner or administrator sees a biased sample of medical-care problems presented to him; rarely has any individual, specialty or institution a broad appreciation of the ecology of medical care that enables unique and frequently isolated contributions to be seen in relation to those of others and to the over-all needs of the community.[4]

The dimensions of these relations may be described quantitatively by estimation of the proportions of defined populations who, within the relatively short period of one month, are "sick," consult a physician, are referred by him to another physician, are hospitalized or are sent to a university medical center. Such information could be a helpful prelude to further studies of the processes by which patients move from level to level up and down the hierarchy of medical-care resources, and of the best ways in which to relate these resources to one another.

Available Data

Reliable data that can be related to defined groups are available from several sources; although not strictly comparable, because of differences in time, place and criteria, they appear adequate for the present purpose and may reflect, not too inaccurately, the dimensions of certain medical-care problems. Only adults sixteen years of age and over (fifteen and over, for certain data) will be considered, first because the data lend themselves most readily to consideration of the adult population, and secondly because most decisions about children's medical care are customarily made by their parents or guardians. A month has been taken as the unit of time, since it is probably a more realistic period than a year for evaluating decisions affecting the prompt and adequate delivery of medical care. This short time has the additional advantage that surveys asking respondents to recall experiences during the previous month or two are apt to be less influenced by memory than those based on longer recall periods.

In a population of 1000 adults (sixteen years of age and over) with an age distribution comparable to those found currently in the United States and England, it would be important to know the number who consider themselves to have been "sick" or "ill" during a month. For the present purpose, "The Survey of Sickness"[5] reports useful data for a continuing representative population sample of England and Wales over a ten-year period. The "sickness rate," as defined in this survey, is "the number of people (sixteen years of age and over) per 100 interviewed reporting some illness or injury in a month regardless of when they began to be ill"; uncomplicated pregnancies are excluded, and the rate cannot exceed 100. It does not reflect the number of illnesses, injuries or diagnoses during a month, the extent of disability or incapacity or the patient's position on the gradient from "perfect" health to terminal illness. It is a monthly "sick-person" prevalence rate. It does reflect individual, subjective perception and definition of ill-health, the initial responses that lead to decisions affecting the qualitative and quantitative demand for and utilization of medical-care resources. Since potential "patients" themselves usually define this primary unit of illness for purposes of medical care, the findings from such a survey will differ from those based on screening procedures or medical examinations. Physicians, depending upon their education, experiences, interests, facilities and the cultures in which they work, may define "illness" differently from their patients or from those who never consult physicians. In a medical sense, there is probably under-reporting in the English sickness survey of occult congenital anomalies, of asymptomatic sequelae of chronic diseases and of latent, incipient or minimal illnesses of many kinds, particularly mental illnesses.

Data from this survey for a four-year period (1946–47 to 1949–50) show variations in the mean monthly sickness rates with age, sex and season between extremes of 51 and 89 per 100 adults (sixteen years of age and over), as shown in Table 1. The annual mean monthly rates are rather constant at about 68, suggesting that in a broad-based population survey, 68 adults out of every 100, in an average month, will experience at least one episode of ill-health or injury that they can recall at the end of that month.

This rate may be compared with those calculated from the reports of the Committee on the Costs of Medical Care.[6] In this study, based on a broad, representative sample of the white population of the United States in 1928–31, an illness is defined more rigidly than in the English survey, as "any symptom, disorder, or affection

TABLE 1. Mean Monthly Sickness Rates (Persons Sick per Month), According to Sex, Age and Quarter, per 100 Adults (Sixteen Years of Age and Over) Interviewed, July, 1946, to June, 1950.[*]

Yr. & Quarter (1946–1950)	16–44 Yr. of Age		45–64 Yr. of Age		65 Yr. of Age & Over		All Ages (16 & Over)		
	Men	Women	Men	Women	Men	Women	Men	Women	All Persons (annual means)
1946 July–Sept.	54	64	65	80	76	85	60	72	
Oct.–Dec.	61	71	72	81	81	88	67	76	68
1947 Jan.–Mar.	60	68	68	78	79	86	65	73	
Apr.–June	52	61	61	76	76	86	58	69	
July–Sept.	51	59	62	74	73	84	57	67	
Oct.–Dec.	59	69	67	78	79	88	64	74	66
1948 Jan.–Mar.	55	65	67	75	79	85	62	71	
Apr.–June	52	62	61	74	73	83	58	69	
July–Sept.	51	62	62	76	75	84	58	70	
Oct.–Dec.	60	70	70	81	79	88	66	76	69
1949 Jan.–Mar.	62	73	70	81	82	89	67	78	
Apr.–June	56	67	66	79	78	87	62	73	
July–Sept.	51	63	64	76	74	85	58	71	
Oct.–Dec.	61	70	68	80	76	87	65	76	68
1950 Jan.–Mar.	60	69	70	79	79	88	66	75	
Apr.–June	55	66	66	77	80	88	62	73	
Mean monthly rates	56	66	66	78	77	81	62	73	68

[*]Adapted from Tables 2 & 3 of Logan & Brooke.[5]

which persisted for one or more days or for which medical service was received or medicine purchased," and it includes "the results of both disease and injury." The data are influenced by the informant's (usually the housewife) concept of illness and her memory over periods of two to four months between the interviewer's visits. Annual rates for adults ill or injured one or more times per year vary between 41 and 65 per 100 adults (fifteen years of age and over). Mean monthly sickness rates would probably be lower than the over-all annual rate of 49 (Table 2), but use of critieria for defining "sickness' comparable to those employed in the English survey would probably increase the rates materially.

From these two surveys, it seems reasonable to conclude that the mean monthly sickness rate is unlikely to be as low as 50 or to be more than 75 per 100 adults. During an average month, in a population of 1000 adults (sixteen years of age and over), bearing in mind contemporary preoccupation with health, one may estimate that as many as 750 will experience what they recognize as injuries or illnesses.

From this population that experiences "sickness" in the course of a month, a proportion will consult physicians; a few who are not ill will do the same. The rate at which sick persons in the community consult physicians also is available from "The Survey of Sickness" in England and Wales.[7] Table 3 shows the mean numbers and rates of medical consultations per month in 1947 per 100 adults (sixteen years of age and over) who were "sick" as defined above. Only 23 per cent of all adults reporting at least one illness or injury during a month consulted a physician at least once; there are no differences in sex and slight differences in age. Expressed in relation to the base population of 100 adults, the mean monthly medical-consultation rate becomes $23/100 \times 75$, or 17 per 100 adults (sixteen years of age and over).

Data from the current United States National Health Survey[8] are also helpful in this regard, although the sampling period for the relevant published data covers only three months (July to September, 1957) in contrast to the English sickness survey, which covers one year and therefore reflects seasonal fluctuations. Monthly Medical-Consultation Rates calculated from the published data vary from 13 to 26, with an over-all monthly rate of 19 adult patients (fifteen years of age and over)

TABLE 2. Annual Sickness Rates (Persons Sick One or More Times per Year) from All Causes, According to Sex and Age, per 100 Adults (Fifteen Years of Age and Over) among 8758 Canvassed White Families (22,561 Adults) in 18 States during Twelve Consecutive Months, 1928–31.*

15–44 Yr. of Age		45–64 Yr. of Age		65 Yr. of Age & Over	
Men	Women	Men	Women	Men	Women
41	55	44	57	55	65

All Ages (15 & Over)		
Men	Women	All Persons
42	56	49

*Adapted from Table 4 of Collins.[6]

TABLE 3. Mean Monthly Medical Consultation Rates (Persons Consulting a Physician), According to Sex and Age, per 100 "Sick" Adults (Sixteen Years of Age and Over) Who Suffered from any Illness or Injury, 1947.*

Mean No. of Medical Consultations/Mo.	16–64 Yr. of Age		65 Yr. of Age & Over		All Ages (16 & Over), All Persons
	Men	Women	Men	Women	
0	77	78	72	73	77
1	9	9	12	12	10
2	5	5	7	6	5
3	3	2	2	2	2
4	3	3	5	4	3
5–9	2	2	1	2	2
10 or more	1	1	1	1	1
Mean	23	22	28	27	23

*Adapted from Stocks.[7]

consulting at least once per 100 adults (Table 4). In the English sickness survey,[5] the July-September quarter has lower mean monthly medical-consultation rates than the other quarters. In the United States National Health Survey data,[9] the physician visit rates per person during a two-year period tend to be lower in the July-September quarters than in the other three quarters for less than half the adult age-sex classifications reported.

The circumstances under which the English data were collected tend to diminish the under-reporting of persons consulting a physician each month, but the United States National Health Survey data could be more substantially biased in this respect. A preliminary study, comparing data from records of the Health Insurance Plan of Greater New York with those from the National Health Survey household interviews, suggests that the latter could under-report the number of persons consulting a physician during a two-week period by as much as a third.[10]

Considering the available data, as well as possible sources of bias, it seems reasonable to estimate the mean monthly medical-consultation rate at about 25 patients per 100 adult population. In an average month, in a population of 1000 adults (sixteen years of age and over) it may be expected that about 250 adults will

TABLE 4. Monthly Medical Consultation Rates (Persons Consulting a Physician), According to Sex and Age, per 100 Adults (Fifteen Years of Age and Over) Who had Visited a Physician in the Month before Interview, July–September, 1957.*

15–44 Yr. of Age		45–64 Yr. of Age		65 Yr. of Age & Over	
Men	Women	Men	Women	Men	Women
13	26	14	21	21	26

All Ages (15 & Over)		
Men	Women	All Persons
14	23	19

*Adapted from Table 17, U.S. National Health Survey.[8]

TABLE 5. Monthly Hospitalization Rates (Patients Reporting Hospitalization), According to Sex and Age, per 100 Adults (Fifteen Years of Age and Over) in "Short-Stay" Hospitals, 1957–58 and 1959.

Age Group	Annual Episodes of Hospitalization*	Correction Factor for Under-Reporting & to Reduce Episodes to Persons Hospitalized†	Persons Hospitalized/Yr.‡	Persons Hospitalized/Mo.§	Base Population*	Monthly Hospitalization Rates¶
15–44 yr. of age:						
Men	2,018	0.34	1,332	111	31,686	0.35
Women	6,751	0.34	4,456	371	35,064	1.06
45–64 yr. of age:						
Men	1,670	0.43	952	79	16,739	0.47
Women	1,743	0.43	993	83	17,731	0.47
65 yr. of age & over:						
Men	810	0.55	365	31	6,642	0.47
Women	944	0.54	435	36	7,871	0.46
All ages (15 & over):						
Men	4,498	0.41	2,649	221	55,067	0.40
Women	9,438	0.38	5,884	490	60,666	0.81
All persons	13,936	0.39	8,533	711	115,733	0.61

* Adapted from Table 1, U.S. National Health Survey.[11] † Based on respondents' age-specific percentages for under-reporting of hospitalization episodes, Table 3, and calculated age-specific ratios of hospitalization episodes to patients hospitalized/yr., Table 1, U.S. National Health Survey.[12] ‡ Annual episodes − correction factor × annual episodes. § Persons hospitalized/yr. ÷ 12. ¶ Persons hospitalized/mo. ÷ base population × 100.

consult a physician at least once. It is this population that is at risk of hospitalization, referral to another physician or referral to a university medical center.

The United States National Health Survey[11] has published annual rates based on household interviews for patients discharged from short-stay hospitals (including those with obstetric beds)—that is, those in which most patients stay for less than thirty days. From these annual rates, corrected both for under-reporting by respondents and to reflect patients hospitalized, rather than episodes of hospitalization, rates per 100 adults (fifteen years of age and over) may be estimated[12] (Table 5). Rates by age and sex groups vary between 0.35 and 1.06, with an over-all rate of 0.61. Younger women admitted for delivery or related problems are reflected in the 1.06 rate; there are no differences in the rates for men and women in the other broad age groups.

More accurate mean monthly rates can be calculated from data developed by Forsyth and Logan[13] for a defined population served by the Barrow and Furness Group of Hospitals in England, a group that includes among its 9 hospitals, 2 for the "chronic sick" and 4 with obstetric beds. The monthly hospitalization rates for adults (sixteen years of age and over) during a period of twelve months vary between 0.59 and 0.77 per 100 adults, with a mean monthly hospitalization rate based on the twelve-month period of 0.70 (Table 6).

Further data are available from three samples of New York City residents.[14] The "eight-week" hospitalization rate for all ages varies between 1.4 and 1.7 per 100 persons, and it can be estimated that the monthly rate would be about 0.80 or less per 100 adults (Table 7).

Rates derived from the three studies cited are remarkably similar (0.61, 0.70 and 0.80), and allowing for possible under-reporting[10] in connection with the New York

TABLE 6. Monthly Hospitalization Rates (Patients Recommended for Admission) per 100 Adults (Sixteen Years of Age and Over) in the Barrow and Furness Group of Hospitals, 1957.*

Month	Patients 16 Yr. of Age & Over Recommended for Hospitalization	
	Number	*Rate*
Jan.	595	0.66
Feb.	656	0.73
Mar.	656	0.73
Apr.	690	0.77
May	677	0.75
June	586	0.65
July	602	0.67
Aug.	567	0.63
Sept.	659	0.73
Oct.	675	0.75
Nov.	534	0.59
Dec.	646	0.72
Means	628	0.70

Population at risk (16 yr. of age & over) in area served by Barrow & Furness Group of Hospitals (1951 census), 89,400.

*Adapted from Part II, Page 79, & Appendix III, Forsyth & Logan.[13]

TABLE 7. Hospitalization Rates (Persons Hospitalized) per 100 Persons (All Ages) for New York City, 1952.*

Bases of Study	8-Wk. Hospital-ization Rates	Monthly Hospi-talization Rates†
Health Insurance Plan enrollees	1.4	0.70
New York City sample:		
Total	1.6	0.80
Insured	1.7	0.85
Uninsured	1.6	0.80

*Adapted from report by Committee for Special Research Project in Health Insurance Plan of Greater New York.[14]   †8-wk. rates ÷ 2.

study, it appears that the mean monthly hospitalization rate is unlikely to exceed a level of about 0.90 per 100 adults (sixteen years of age and over). In a population of 1000 adults (sixteen years of age and over) it may be estimated that, in an average month, about 9 will be hospitalized.

Monthly prevalence rates for referral of patients from one physician to another are even more difficult to obtain. Many patients in the United States receive primary, continuing medical care from a specialist; some may visit several specialists concurrently. Frequently, patients "refer" themselves, and in general, patients appear to control the referral process about half the time.[3] In a stratified random sample of North Carolina general practitioners, 91 physicians (97 per cent return rate) recorded their patient visits for one week; these one-week samples were spread over the period July, 1953, to June, 1954.[15] The 91 general practitioners reported 11,765 visits of adult patients (sixteen years of age and over), or a mean of 129 adult patient visits per one-week sample. Since patient visits over a period of one week are likely to approximate closely patients seen, a mean of 250 adult patients seen per two-week period seems a reasonable estimate. In a second stratified random sample of the same population of North Carolina general practitioners, 93 physicians (87 per cent return rate) reported 460 adult patients (sixteen years of age and over) referred to other physicians (excluding university medical centers) during two-week sampling periods spread from August, 1957, to February, 1959.[16, 17] The mean number of adult patients referred was 4.94, or about 5 patients referred per two-week period. The mean monthly patient-referral rate to other physicians for North Carolina general practitioners may be estimated as follows: 5/250 × 100, or 2 patients, are referred per 100 adult patients seen, and since other estimates suggest that, on the average, 250 adults per 1000 consult a physician at least once a month, approximately 5 adult patients are referred per 1000 adult population (sixteen years of age and over) per month.

Other published referral data[18-22] do not permit calculation of rates for short periods (such as a month) for patients referred, in contrast to rates for numbers of referrals. The risks of a given patient being referred to either another physician or a university medical center increase the longer he is under the care of a given physician. Annual patient-referral rates, like annual patient-hospitalization rates, will be higher than monthly rates, but the latter probably more accurately reflect the decision-making process as it affects current utilization of medical-care resources.

The final court of appeal, both for investigation of obscure medical problems and for specialized treatments, and one of the central sources of new medical knowledge and personnel, is the university medical center or teaching hospital. The composition of the patient population seen in each medical center will depend on the ecology of medical care in the region in which it is located, the demographic characteristics of the community it serves, and its own acceptance and admission policies. There may be wide differences between adjacent medical centers, between regions and between countries, but since in theory, and frequently in practice, such centers constitute the apices of referral hierarchies, it should be helpful to estimate the over-all proportion of sick persons in the community referred to them by physicians. Where primary, continuing medical care (in contrast to episodic or consultant care) is provided by university hospitals to groups of patients, or where a large proportion of self-referred patients are accepted, the compositions of the patient populations seen may differ materially from those seen at centers accepting predominantly physician-referred patients.

From the two North Carolina studies, it is possible to estimate the referral rate of general practitioners to the three university medical centers serving that state and its population of over 4,000,000 persons. The 93 North Carolina general practitioners surveyed,[16, 17] as discussed above, referred 96 adult patients (sixteen years of age and over) to the three university medical centers during two-week sampling periods in 1957–59, with a mean of about 1 patient per two-week period. The mean monthly university medical-center patient-referral rate of North Carolina general practitioners may be estimated as follows: $1/250 \times 100$, or 0.4 patients, are referred per 100 adult patients seen, and since other estimates suggest that, on the average, 250 adults consult a physician at least once a month, approximately 1 adult patient is referred to a university medical center per 1000 adult population (sixteen years of age and over) per month.

"Hard" data on the "natural history of medical care" are in short supply. Studies such as those described only suggest the broad dimensions of relative utilization for several important medical-care resources. In summary, it appears that within an average month in Great Britain or the United States, for every 1000 adults (sixteen years of age and over) in the population, about 750 will experience what they recognize and recall as an episode of illness or injury. Two hundred and fifty of the 750 will consult a physician at least once during that month. Nine of the 250 will be hospitalized, 5 will be referred to another physician, and 1 will be sent to a university medical center within that month. Expressed in other terms, 0.75 of the adult population experience sickness each month, 0.25 consult a physician, 0.009 are hospitalized, 0.005 are referred to another physician, and 0.001 are referred to a university medical center. In an average month, 0.009/0.75, or 0.012 of the "sick" adults in the community, are seen on hospital wards, and 0.001/0.75, or 0.004, are seen at university medical centers. These relations are shown in Figure 1.

Discussion

The relations reflected in the data presented are subject to wide variations. All the surveys referred to were conducted carefully, but the rates are only approximate.

FIGURE 1. Monthly Prevalence Estimates of Illness in the Community and the Roles of Physicians, Hospitals and University Medical Centers in the Provision of Medical Care (Adults Sixteen Years of Age and Over).

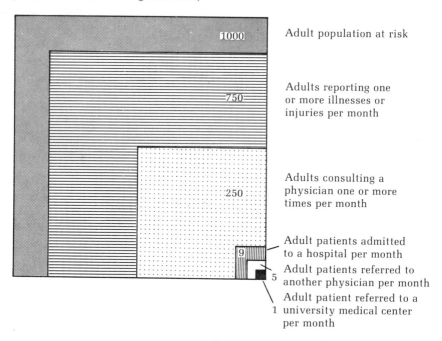

Precise sampling methods were used in all the studies, but sampling fluctuations should be considered before any confidence limits can be placed around these estimates. Sampling errors are probably small in comparison to other sources of discrepancy, and although these are discussed in connection with the original studies, no effort has been made to deal with them here. The characteristics of the populations at risk, the health resources available and the decisions made about health problems by individuals, physicians and community leaders all affect both the way in which health facilities and manpower are deployed and the characteristics, quality and quantity of medical care available to a particular society, but the broad relations and the orders of magnitude of the differences depicted in Figure 1 probably reflect the patterns of medical care in the United States and Great Britain with reasonable accuracy.

Appreciation of these relations helps to bring the contributions made by advances in the medical sciences into better perspective in the over-all view of society's health. Medical science does not make its contributions in a vacuum, and the absolute value of these to society may be substantially modified by other factors that have received relatively little attention as yet and may impose critical limitations to the attainment of better health.

Medical-care research is concerned with the problems of assessing needs and of delivering medical care; more specifically, it is concerned with problems of implementing the advances achieved by medical science. Its concerns are not the characteristics, prevalence and mechanisms of disease, but the social, psychologic, cultural, economic, informational, administrative and organizational factors that inhibit and facilitate access to and delivery of the best contemporary health care to individuals and communities. It is concerned with the identification and measurement of medical-care needs, demands and resources, and the evaluation of the qualitative and quantitative aspects of programs, personnel, services and facilities, and their utilization in the provision of preventive, diagnostic and therapeutic care and rehabilitation. It is as concerned with the health of those who do not use medical-care resources as with the health of those who do. In essence, it is concerned with medicine as a social institution.

Much more needs to be known about patients' thresholds for perceiving, acknowledging and describing their own disordered function and behavior. What factors govern the patients' assumption or rejection of the "sick" role, or the "patient" role? More needs to be known about patients' sources of help in understanding and coping with their health problems. How do patients select their physicians, and physicians their patients? Under what circumstances do physicians refer patients to other physicians and to medical centers? What kinds of patients, problems and diseases are seen at different health facilities? Do the "right" patients get to the "right" facilities at the "right" time? More specifically, do the 500 "sick" people per month who do not consult physicians enjoy better health than those who do? Are the 5 patients per 1000 referred each month those most in need of consultation? What factors determine which person in every thousand adults will be referred to a university medical center each month? Are these processes in the best interests of all patients? Are they best for medical education?

For many years, it was an unchallenged assumption that physicians always knew what was best for the people's health. Whatever the origins of this authoritarian assumption, it presumably was transmitted by the medical schools as part of the "image" of the physician. Serious questions can be raised about the nature of the average medical student's experience, and perhaps that of some of his clinical teachers, with the substantive problems of health and disease in the community. In general, this experience must be both limited and unusually biased if, in a month, only 0.0013 of the "sick" adults (or even ten times this), in a community are referred to university medical centers. The size of the sample is of much less importance than the fact that, on the average, it is preselected twice. Under such circumstances, it would be difficult, if not impossible, for those at medical centers, without special efforts, to obtain valid impressions of the over-all health problems of the community. Medical, nursing and other students of the health professions cannot fail to receive unrealistic impressions of medicine's task in contemporary Western society, to say nothing of its task in developing countries.

The present arrangements for *delivering* medical care to the consumers in the United States (or any other Western country for that matter) owe relatively little to data, ideas or proposals developed in university medical centers. Over the years, individual physicians and groups have concerned themselves with the profession's social responsibilities, but with rare exceptions the substantive problems of medical care have not been a continuing concern of either schools of medicine or schools of public health. It is one of the purposes of this communication to suggest that it is now time for schools of medicine, schools of public health and teaching hospitals to address themselves to the urgent need for medical-care research and education. It is now time for the health professions, and particularly for faculty members with clinical interests, to join their colleagues from the other disciplines, and to accord to medical-care research and teaching the same priority they have accorded research in the fundamental mechanisms of pathologic processes. Investigation and teaching directed at improved understanding of the ecology of medical care and ways of favorably modifying it eventually should reduce the time lag between developments in the laboratory and delivery to the consumers of new knowledge accruing from the vast sums of money that the latter are currently paying for disease-oriented research.

Summary and Conclusions

Data from medical-care studies in the United States and Great Britain suggest that in a population of 1000 adults (sixteen years of age and over), in an average month 750 will experience an episode of illness, 250 of these will consult a physician, 9 will be hospitalized, 5 will be referred to another physician, and 1 will be referred to a university medical center. The latter sees biased samples of 0.0013 of the "sick" adults and 0.004 of the patients in the community, from which students of the health professions must get an unrealistic concept of medicine's task in both Western and developing countries.

Medical-care research is defined, and the need for according it equal priority with research on disease mechanisms is discussed. Recognizing medicine as a social institution, in addition to disease as a cellular aberration, the objective of medical-care research is reduction of the time lag between advances in the laboratory and measurable improvement in the health of a society's members.

Acknowledgment

Supported in part by a research grant (W-74) from the Division of Hospital and Medical Facilities, United States Public Health Service.

References

1. Koos, E. L., *The Health of Regionville: What the people thought and did about it.* 177 pp. New York: Columbia, 1954.
2. Freidson, E. Organization of medical practice and patient behavior. *Am. J. Pub. Health* 51:43–52, 1961.
3. Williams, T. F., et al. Patient referral to university clinic: patterns in rural state. *Am. J. Pub. Health* 50:1493–1507, 1960.
4. Horder, J., and Horder, E. Illness in general practice. *Practitioner* 173:177–187, 1954.
5. Great Britain, General Register Office. Logan, W. P. D., and Brooke, E. M. *The Survey of Sickness, 1943–1952.* 80 pp. London: Her Majesty's Stationery Office, 1957. (*Studies on Medical and Population Subjects,* No. 12.)
6. Collins, S. D. Cases and days of illness among males and females, with special reference to confinement to bed, based on 9,000 families visited periodically for 12 months, 1928–31. *Pub. Health Rep.* 55:47–93, 1940.

7. Great Britain, General Register Office. Stocks, P. *Sickness in the Population of England and Wales in 1944–1947.* 51 pp. London: His Majesty's Stationery Office, 1949. (*Studies on Medical and Population Subjects,* No. 2.)
8. United States National Health Survey. *Preliminary Report on Volume of Physician Visits, United States, July-Sept. 1957.* 25 pp. Washington, D. C.: Public Health Service, 1958.
9. Idem. *Volume of Physician Visits, United States, July 1957-June 1959: Statistics on volume of physician visits by place of visit, type of service, age, sex, residence, region, race, income and education: Based on data collected in household interviews during July, 1957-June, 1959.* 52 pp. Washington, D. C., Public Health Service, 1960.
10. Idem. *Health Interview Responses Compared with Medical Records: Study of illness and hospitalization experience among health plan enrollees as reported in household interviews, in comparison with information recorded by physicians and hospitals.* 74 pp. Washington, D. C.: Public Health Service, 1961.
11. Idem. *Hospitalization: Patients discharged from short-stay hospitals, United States, July 1957-June 1958.* 40 pp. Washington, D. C. Public Health Service, 1958.
12. Idem. *Reporting of Hospitalization in the Health Interview Study: Methodological study of several factors affecting reporting of hospital episodes.* 71 pp. Washington, D. C.: Public Health Service, 1961.
13. Forsyth, G., and Logan, R. F. L. *The Demand for Medical Care: A study of the case-load in the Barrow and Furness Group of Hospitals.* 153 pp. London: Oxford, 1960. (*Nuffield Provincial Hospitals Trust Publication.*)
14. *Health and Medical Care in New York City: A report by the Committee for the Special Research Project in the Health Insurance Plan of Greater New York.* 275 pp. Cambridge, Massachusetts: Harvard (Commonwealth Fund), 1957.
15. Peterson, A. L., Andrews, L. P., Spain, R. S., and Greenberg, B. G. Analytical study of North Carolina general practice, 1953–1954. *J. M. Educ.* 31 (12):1–165, Part 2, 1956.
16. Andrews, L. P., et al. Study of patterns of patient referral to medical clinic in rural state: methodology. *Am. J. Pub. Health* 49:634–643, 1959.
17. Williams, T. F., White, K. L., Fleming, W. L., and Greenberg, B. G. Referral process in medical care and university clinic's role. *J. M. Educ.* 36:899–907, 1961.
18. Fry, J. Why patients go to hospitals, study of usage. *Brit. M. J.* 2:1322–1327, 1959.
19. Hopkins, P. Referrals in general practice. *Brit. M. J.* 2:873–877, 1956.
20. Great Britain, General Register Office. *General Practitioners' Records: An analysis of the clinical records of some general practices during the period April, 1952 to March, 1954.* 88 pp. London: Her Majesty's Stationery Office, 1955. (*Studies on Population and Medical Subjects,* No. 9.)
21. Idem. Logan, W. P. D. *General Practitioners' Records: An analysis of clinical records of eight practices during the period April, 1951 to March, 1952.* 140 pp. London: Her Majesty's Stationery Office, 1953. (*Studies on Medical and Population Subjects,* No. 7.)
22. Taubenhaus, L. J. Study of one rural practice, 1953. *GP* 12:97–102, 1955.

6

Why Do Women Live Longer Than Men?

Ingrid Waldron

The sex differential in mortality has increased strikingly over the past half century in the U.S. In 1920, the life expectancy for women was 56, only two years longer than that for men.[1] By 1970, women's life expectancy was 75, almost eight years longer than men's.[2] In 1920, male death rates were no more than 30 percent higher than female death rates at any age. By 1970, male death rates exceeded female death rates by as much as 180 percent for 15–24-year-olds and 110 percent for 55–64-year-olds.

Among young adults the excess of mortality for males is due primarily to accidents.[3] At older ages, cardiovascular-renal diseases make the largest contribution to higher mortality among men. Rising male mortality for these causes of death and for lung cancer has been a major component of the increase in the sex differential in mortality.[4] These trends were due in part to the sizable increase in cigarette smoking by men during the first third of the twentieth century.[5,6] Another substantial component of the increase in the sex differential in mortality has been the decline in maternal mortality and uterine cancer due to improvements in medical care. These data suggest that a wide variety of cultural factors, including the automobile use, cigarette smoking and health care, contributes to the contemporary sex differential in mortality.

Further evidence of the importance of cultural factors is provided by international comparisons, which show that higher male death rates, although common, have not been universal. In many countries female death rates have exceeded male death rates at ages between one and forty, and in some cases at older ages as well.[7] Higher mortality among females has been observed most frequently in nonindustrial countries.

SOURCE: *Journal of Human Stress* 2, no. 1 (March 1976): 2–13. Copyright © 1976 by Opinion Publications, Inc. Reprinted by permission of the publisher and the author.

The sex differential in mortality also varies for different groups within the United States. For example, the excess of male mortality is lowest among married adults, it is 10 percent greater among single and widowed adults, and it is 50 percent greater among divorced adults (data from[8]). The excess of mortality for males who are not married is particularly large for causes like cirrhosis of the liver which are strongly influenced by behavior, and for diseases like tuberculosis in which health habits and care play an important role. Gove[9] has argued that the major reasons why the sex mortality differential is higher among males who are not married is that men do not adjust as well as women do to being unmarried, and that men derive greater advantages from being married, both in care received and in psychological well-being.

Genetic factors apparently also contribute to higher male mortality, although the evidence for this is not as strong as commonly has been believed. Males have higher mortality than females in many different species, and this has been cited as evidence for a genetic contribution to the higher mortality of men.[10] However, although higher male mortality is widespread among insects, other Arthropoda and fishes,[10] higher female mortality appears to be just as common as higher male mortality among our closer relatives, the birds and mammals,[10-12] Among humans, higher female mortality is also common at certain ages, as described above. However, it is striking that, wherever statistics are available, males have had higher mortality during the first year of life.[7] Males also have been found to have higher fetal mortality in most studies,[13] although fetal mortality during late pregnancy is as high for females as for males in pairs of twins of opposite sex,[14] in multiple births of triplets or more,[15] and in a few geographical places, for example, Scotland.[16] Male mortality is higher for many different causes of death (see Table 1). Several authors[10,17] have inferred from these observations that genetically determined metabolic differences may contribute to the higher mortality of males.

Another study which has been cited widely as evidence of the importance of genetic factors is Madigan's[18] comparison of life expectancy for Roman Catholic Sisters and Brothers in teaching Orders. Madigan found that the differential in life expectancy between Sisters and Brothers has been almost as large as the differential between women and men in the general population, even though the Sisters and Brothers had more similar adult roles. However, the higher mortality of the Brothers cannot be attributed solely to genetic causes, since the Brothers smoked and drank more than the Sisters and probably were socialized differently as children, and each of these differences would contribute to higher male mortality (as discussed in detail below).

This earlier work suggests that both cultural and genetic factors contribute to the longer life expectancy of women.[19-21] Therefore, we have considered both cultural and genetic factors in our analysis of the specific causes of the sex differential in mortality in the Contemporary U.S.

Our analysis is based on the identification of the causes of death which make a large contribution to the sex differential in mortality in the United States. Table 2 lists the seven causes of death which were responsible for at least 1 percent of all deaths in the U.S. in 1967, and for which male mortality exceeded female mortality by at least 100 percent. For each of these causes of death we considered all the major factors believed to contribute to its etiology and selected for analysis those factors which appeared to be relevant to the sex difference in mortality.

Behavioral factors emerge as important determinants of the sex differential for each of the causes of death listed in Table 2. The importance of these factors is obvious in the case of accidents and suicide, and also for the respiratory diseases, which largely are due to smoking,[22] as well as for cirrhosis of the liver, which is related to alcohol consumption.[23] These causes of death with clear behavioral components are responsible for one-third of the excess of male mortality, and arteriosclerotic heart disease is responsible for an additional 40 percent of the excess

TABLE 1. Sex Mortality Ratios for All Major Causes of Death, U.S., 1967*

Ratio of Male to Female Death Rates	Cause of Death	Male Death Rate	Female Death Rate†
		(Deaths per 100,000 population)	
5.9	Malignant neoplasm of respiratory system, not specified as secondary	50.1	8.5
4.9	Other bronchopulmonic disease (71% emphysema)	24.4	5.0
2.8	Motor vehicle accidents	39.4	14.2
2.7	Suicide	15.7	5.8
2.4	Other accidents	41.1	17.4
2.0	Cirrhosis of liver	18.5	9.1
2.0	Arteriosclerotic heart disease, including coronary disease	357.0	175.6
1.8	Symptoms, senility and ill-defined conditions	14.9	8.3
1.7	Pneumonia, except of newborn	32.3	19.5
1.6	Other diseases of heart	17.9	11.1
1.6	Other diseases of circulatory system	18.2	11.1
1.5	Malignant neoplasm of digestive organs and peritoneum, not specified as secondary	53.0	36.2
1.4	All other diseases (residual)	32.4	22.4
1.4	Malignant neoplasm of other and unspecified sites	20.5	14.7
1.4	Birth injuries, postnatal asphyxia, and atelectasis	11.9	8.4
1.4	Certain diseases of early infancy	29.2	21.6
1.3	Other diseases peculiar to early infancy, and immaturity, unqualified	15.3	11.7
1.3	Nonrheumatic chronic endocarditis and other myocardial degeneration	26.8	20.5
1.2	General arteriosclerosis	17.2	14.8
1.2	Vascular lesions affecting central nervous system	96.3	83.3
1.0	Hypertensive heart disease	22.3	22.2
0.89	Malignant neoplasm of genital organs	17.9	20.1
0.89	Diabetes mellitus	14.9	16.8
0.008	Malignant neoplasm of breast	0.2	24.6
1.6	All Causes	1081.7	657.0

The causes of death with the highest sex mortality ratios all have major behavioral components (calculated from data in [98]).

*All causes of death were included, except those responsible for less than 1 percent of the deaths (for example, homicide).   †Female death rates have been age-adjusted to the male age distribution (see Table 2).

TABLE 2. Major Causes of Higher Mortality in Men

Ratio of Male to Female Death Rates	Cause of Death	Male Death Rate	Female Death Rate*
		(Deaths per 100,000 Population)	
5.9	Malignant neoplasm of respiratory system, not specified as secondary	50.1	8.5
4.9	Other bronchopulmonic disease (71% emphysema)	24.4	5.0
2.8	Motor vehicle accidents	39.4	14.2
2.7	Suicide	15.7	5.8
2.4	Other accidents	41.1	17.4
2.0	Cirrhosis of liver	18.5	9.1
2.0	Arteriosclerotic heart disease, including coronary disease	357.0	175.6
1.6	All causes	1081.7	657.0

This table lists all causes of death which had a sex mortality ratio of 2.0 or more and were responsible for at least 1 percent of all deaths in the U.S. in 1967. These causes of death are responsible for three-quarters of the sex differential in mortality. (Calculated from data in [98]).

*Female death rates have been age-adjusted using the age-specific death rates for females and the age distribution for males to calculate the death rate which would be expected for a population of females that had the same age distribution as the male population. Thus the male and female death rates are directly comparable and are not affected by the higher proportion of females at older ages.

deaths among males. The data presented in the next section suggest that men have higher death rates for arteriosclerotic heart disease in large part because they smoke cigarettes more and because they more often develop the aggressive, competitive Coronary Prone Behavior Pattern.

Arteriosclerotic Heart Disease

Death rates for arteriosclerotic heart disease, which is primarily coronary heart disease (CHD), are twice as high for men as for women (Table 3). Cigarette smoking is associated with an elevation of CHD death rates ranging from 100 percent or more among middle-aged adults to 20 percent at the oldest ages.[24] The elevated risk of CHD among smokers is probably due in part to the correlation between smoking and other risk factors (such as the Coronary Prone Behavior Pattern discussed below), but it is almost certainly also a direct consequence of the pharmacological effects of smoking.[22] A rough quantitative estimate of the contribution of smoking habits to the sex differential in CHD death rates can be obtained by comparing the sex differential among nonsmokers to the sex differential for the general population (Table 3). The contribution of cigarette smoking appears to be substantial, particularly for adults under age 65. Among middle-aged adults who have never smoked regularly, the CHD mortality for men exceeds that for women by 350 percent, while for the total sample (including smokers) men's CHD mortality exceeds women's by 650 perent.

A variety of evidence suggests that another important cause of higher rates of coronary heart disease in men may be their involvement in paid jobs and in

TABLE 3. Comparison of Sex Mortality Ratios for Nonsmokers and for Total Population

Cause of Death	Ratio of Male to Female Death Rates	
	For Those Who Never Smoked Regularly	For the Total Sample
Coronary Heart Disease		
Ages 45–54	4.5	7.5
55–64	3.3	4.4
65–74	2.1	2.4
Lung Cancer		
Ages 45–64	1.6	7.3
65–79	1.4	9.4
Emphysema		
Ages 45–64	4.0	11.7
65–79	2.2	7.3
All Causes of Death		
Ages 45–54	1.3	2.2
55–64	1.7	2.5
65–74	1.6	2.0

(Calculated from data in [24]. Figures for lung cancer and emphysema are approximate due to incomplete published data.)

aggressive, competitive roles, in contrast to the greater orientation of women toward family and less competitive, more supportive roles. For example, several studies have found that among men the risk of coronary heart disease is higher for those who have worked many hours overtime or who have held two jobs simultaneously.[25] Also, in a projective test, men who subsequently developed CHD were more likely to locate their stories in a "socioprofessional" setting and not in a family or recreational setting.[26]

A more specific formulation of the proposed hypothesis can be derived from studies of a "Coronary Prone Behavior Pattern." A person shows the Coronary Prone Behavior Pattern if he or she is work-oriented, ambitious, aggressive, competitive, hurried, impatient and preoccupied with deadlines.[27] Large prospective studies have shown that men who display this Coronary Prone Behavior Pattern are twice as likely as other men to develop or die of coronary heart disease.[27,28] Smaller retrospective studies[29-31] also have established that women who have coronary heart disease are more likely to display the Coronary Prone Behavior Pattern than controls.

Behavior pattern may make a larger contribution to the risk of coronary heart disease than does sex *per se.* Table 4 shows the prevalence of clinical CHD for samples of men[32] and women[31] who have clear Coronary Prone Behavior Pattern (called Type A in these studies) or clear Type B (the opposite of Type A). These data must be interpreted with caution since the samples were small and were not obtained by systematic or even strictly comparable methods. Nevertheless, it is striking that Type B men had the same low prevalence of CHD as did Type B women. This suggests that men who adopt a less competitive and rushed style of life are just as likely to avoid CHD as comparable women. At older ages, Type A men and women had the same high prevalence of CHD. The only category in which women had substantially lower rates of CHD was the younger Type A's, but even in this age range Type A women had more CHD than Type B men.

These data suggest the hypothesis that men have more coronary heart disease than women in part because the Type A or Coronary Prone Behavior Pattern is more prevalent among men. In a large sample of employed adults women were slightly less Type A than men (Shekelle, personal communication). Housewives may be even less Tape A than employed women,[31] and about half of adult women are housewives.[33] Aggressiveness and competitiveness are two key components of the Coronary Prone Behavior Pattern. Maccoby and Jacklin (in their review of nearly 2000 studies of sex differences in behavior[34]) conclude that, on the average, males are more aggressive and competitive than females.

Why do males develop more aggressiveness and competitiveness—more of the Coronary Prone Behavior Pattern—than females? Genetic factors make some contribution to the sex differences in aggressiveness,[34] but the extent of aggressiveness among males varies enormously, depending on child-rearing and cultural conditions.[35] Sex differences in competitiveness are fostered by parents and schools who push boys to achieve in the occupational world and girls to seek success in the family sphere.[34, 36-38] Occupational achievement apparently requires competitiveness, since in our society there are seldom as many jobs (particularly rewarding, high status jobs) as there are people who want and can do them.[39,40] In the family sphere, on the other hand, warmth and love are believed to be much more appropriate and aggressive competitiveness much less appropriate than in the business world.[37] Evidence that cultural pressures and expectations do have a substantial influence on the development of the Coronary Prone Behavior Pattern comes from the observation that this Behavior Pattern rarely develops in the social environment of many nonindustrial societies.[27,35]

Thus, a variety of evidence suggests that cultural and socioeconomic pressures

TABLE 4. Relation of Clinical Coronary Heart Disease to Age, Sex and Behavior Pattern

Sex and Age Group	Percent with Clinical Coronary Heart Disease (Sample Size)	
	Type A Behavior Pattern	*Type B* Behavior Pattern
Premenopausal Females	10% (82)	3% (110)
Men less than 50 years old	24% (61)	3% (67)
Postmenopausal Females	37% (43)	9% (22)
Men more than 50 years old	41% (22)	6% (17)

The Type A Behavior Pattern is the competitive, aggressive, impatient Coronary Prone Behavior Pattern, and Type B is its opposite. For these samples, the prevalence of clinical coronary heart disease among Type B men is as low as the prevalence among Type B women and is substantially lower than the prevalence among Type A women. Although interpretations must be made with caution because systematic sampling methods were not used, these data suggest the hypothesis that more men than women die of coronary heart disease in part because more men develop the Type A or Coronary Prone Behavior Pattern. (Data from [31] and [32].)

related to the role of men in our society push them to develop the Coronary Prone Behavior Pattern, and that this makes a major contribution to men's higher risk of coronary heart disease. Many aspects of this hypothesis need further testing; some of this testing has been started.

Although smoking and the Coronary Prone Behavior Pattern appear to be the most important behavioral factors contributing to the sex differential in arteriosclerotic heart disease, other behavioral differences also may play a role. For example, women attend church more often than men do,[41] and frequent church attenders of both sexes have a substantially lower death rate from arteriosclerotic heart disease, at least in one Protestant community studied.[41] Extrapolating the risk differential nationally leads to a prediction that men's death rates for arteriosclerotic heart disease would be 7 percent higher, based on sex differences in church attendance and exclusive of related differences in smoking.

Bengtsson and co-workers[30] reach conclusions similar to ours in their study of sex differential in coronary heart disease is provided by the wide cross-cultural variation They conclude that men's higher rates of CHD are related to their higher rates of smoking and drinking alcohol, higher aggression and achievement scores, and greater self-reported stress. These authors believe that additional factors also contribute to the observed sex differences in CHD.

Further evidence for the substantial contribution of cultural factors to the sex differential in coronary heart disease is provided by the wide cross-cultural variation in the size of this differential. In some countries the sex differential is much smaller than in the U.S.[17,43] For example, in 1960 in Greece and Hungary, arteriosclerotic heart disease mortality was only 30 percent higher for males than for females.[44] The age trend of the male excess also varies widely, with a peak at premenopausal ages in the U.S. and many European countries but a peak at postmenopausal ages in Japan and Colombia (data from[44]). On the other hand, men do have higher arteriosclerotic heart disease death rates in all countries studied, and this suggests that genetic factors also contribute to the sex differential.

Sex Hormones and CHD

Most previous discussions of the sex differential in coronary heart disease have focused primary attention on the hypothesis that this sex differential is a result of the physiological effects of the sex hormones. The evidence for this hypothesis is suggestive, but it is ambiguous and inconsistent. Castration of men apparently does not reduce deaths due to cardiovascular disease,[45] and castration of older men does not seem to reduce atherosclerosis.[46] The data of Gertler and White[47] suggest that androgen levels of male coronary patients do not differ from androgen levels in a control group. Thus male hormones do not appear to increase the risk of coronary heart disease.

Do female hormones lower the risk of coronary heart disease? Several studies have found that oophorectomy of young women is associated with increased atherosclerosis and CHD[43,48–51] but other studies have not found a relationship.[43,52,53] One investigation with negative findings is particularly interesting because women with a simple hysterectomy were used as the control group, and the prevalence of arteriosclerotic heart disease was as high for these women with only their uterus removed as it was for women whose ovaries had been removed.[52] For both groups the prevalence of arteriosclerotic heart disease was higher than the prevalence for the general female population. Since there appears to be no physiological reason why the simple removal of the uterus should lead to increased coronary heart disease,[52,54] this observation suggests that hysterectomy may be associated with behavioral characteristics, such as cigarette smoking, or psychological characteristics, such as anxiety and neuroticism,[55] which in turn are associated with elevated risk of coronary heart disease.[56] This speculation is particularly plausible since many hysterectomies are elective (for purposes of sterilization) or unnecessary. (The rate of hysterectomies has been reduced by two-thirds as a result of the initiation of either a medical audit or a requirement for consultation.[57]) These considerations are of particular importance for the interpretation of the correlates of oophorectomy since many of the oophorectomies in the studies cited were performed in association with hysterectomies.

Thus, if we tentatively accept the weight of evidence as indicating that oophorectomy of young women is associated with increased atherosclerosis and coronary heart disease, we still are left with the question of whether this increase is due to the removal of female hormones or to some behavioral or psychological characteristic of women who undergo these operations. Studies of the effect of replacement therapy are the ideal method for resolving such questions, but in this case such studies have yielded conflicting results. One investigation of estrogen therapy in castrated women found a decreased prevalence of arteriosclerotic cardiovascular disease,[51] and another found trends suggesting a reduced prevalence of electrocardiographic abnormalities.[58] However, a third study found no effect on death rates or prevalence of CHD.[52] Furthermore, most studies of estrogen therapy in men have found an *increased* risk of recurrence of myocardial infarction,[43,59-62] although in two studies, some treatment groups appeared to have a reduced risk.[43,59] The use of oral contraceptives apparently is associated with an increased risk of myocardial infarction, and the estrogen component is suspected as the cause.[63,64] The effects of estrogen therapy on the risk of coronary heart disease appear to vary with dosage, type of estrogen, and type of patient.

The failure of estrogen therapy to produce a consistent decrease in CHD is not surprising in view of the fact that estrogens have biological effects which tend to *increase* the risk of CHD as well as effects that tend to lower the risk. Evidence for this conclusion is presented in the following paragraphs, which summarize the effects of sex hormones on risk factors for CHD. The data must be interpreted with caution, since some of the studies used synthetic hormones or doses higher than normal physiological levels. Only studies of humans have been cited, with one exception as noted.

Important risk factors for CHD include high levels of serum cholesterol, β-lipoproteins, probably triglycerides, pre-β-lipoproteins and possibly also chylomicrons.[65-67] In some studies, but not all, oophorectomy of young women is associated with elevated serum cholesterol.[58,68,69] Estrogen therapy generally causes a decrease in serum cholesterol and β-lipoproteins.[58,70-72] In contrast estrogens cause an increase in serum triglycerides and pre-β-lipoproteins[43,70-73] Androgens generally cause an increase in β-lipoproteins and a decrease in serum triglycerides, pre-β-lipoproteins and chylomicrons; they have variable effects on serum cholesterol levels.[43,71] Progestogens in general have little or no effect on serum lipids and lipoproteins, although sometimes they produce a small decrease in serum triglycerides.[71,73].

Female sex hormones enhance thrombotic processes. Oral contraceptives (probably the estrogenic component) cause increased platelet reactivity, increases in various coagulation factors[74] and fibrotic vascular lesions.[75] In consequence, women who use oral contraceptives have an increased risk of death due to myocardial infarction,[63,64] cerebral thrombosis, deep vein thrombosis and pulmonary embolism.[76,77] High doses of estrogen given to men produce increased rates of pulmonary embolism and thrombophlebitis[62,70] and cerebral thrombosis.[61] We did not find data on the effects of male hormones on thrombosis.

The use of oral contraceptives results in higher blood pressures, higher angiotensinogen, plasma renin activity and aldosterone levels.[78,79] Experiments with rats suggest that female hormones may enhance vasoconstriction due to sympathetic activity, which also could lead to elevated blood pressures in females.[80-82] However, there is some doubt whether natural female hormones cause elevated blood pressures, since oophorectomy or early menopause has been found to be associated with no significant change[52,69,83] or a slight fall[30] in systolic blood pressure and no significant change[30,52] or a slight rise[69] in diastolic blood pressure. Male hormones may cause elevated blood pressures, since testosterone elevates hematocrit,[43] and higher hematocrits are associated with higher blood pressures, possibly due to the increase in viscosity of the blood.[84] However, testosterone in male castrates apparently produces only small changes in blood pressure.[10] The average systolic blood pressure of women is lower than that of men until an age which varies between 30 and 50, depending on the sample; at older ages men have lower systolic blood pressures.[69,85] Sex differences in diastolic blood pressure show somewhat similar trends but are much smaller and more variable. This pattern gives no clear evidence for differential effects of sex hormones and can as easily be attributed to psychogenic effects on blood pressure.[86]

Respiratory Diseases and Smoking

For "malignant neoplasm of the respiratory system" (primarily lung cancer), men's death rates are six times higher than women's. For "other bronchopulmonic diseases" (primarily emphysema), men's death rates are five times higher than women's. These mortality ratios are higher than for any other major cause of death (Table 2). Men have higher mortality for these diseases primarily because men smoke more and cigarette smoking is the major cause of both lung cancer and emphysema.[6,22] If men and women who have never smoked regularly are compared, the sex mortality ratios for lung cancer and emphysema are drastically reduced (Table 3). These data suggest that cigarette smoking is the primary cause of men's excess lung cancer and emphysema mortality.

Comparing those who have ever smoked cigarettes to nonsmokers of the same sex, lung cancer death rates are elevated ninefold for men, but only twofold for women. Similarly, emphysema death rates are elevated sevenfold among men smokers, but only fivefold for women smokers. The elevation of death rates is less for women smokers than for men in large part because women smokers inhale less, smoke fewer cigarettes and less of each cigarette and, in the past, women have begun smoking at older ages.[22,24] In addition, industrial hazards aggravate the effects of cigarette smoking for many men (as discussed below).

The total pathological effect of smoking, particularly the elevation of coronary heart disease, lung cancer and emphysema, makes a major contribution to the sex differential in total death rates. For middle-aged adults who never have smoked regularly, men's mortality exceeds women's by only 30 percent, compared to a male excess of 120 percent for the total sample (Table 3). For older nonsmokers, men's mortality exceeds women's by 60–70 percent, compared to 100–150 percent for the total sample. Retherford[5] (in a similar analysis which was published while this manuscript was in the final stages of preparation) estimates that as much as half of the sex differential in life expectancy from the ages of 37 to 87 may be due to the effects of higher rates of cigarette smoking in men.

Why do more men than women smoke? Smoking by women was strongly discouraged by the social mores of the early twentieth century. The conventions of that period continue to influence the smoking patterns of people who were teenagers at that time, since relatively few people begin smoking cigarettes after age 20. As a consequence, the sex differential in cigarette smoking is largest for older people who were over 60 in 1970 and who thus were teenagers before 1930.[87] Many other social and motivational factors have been shown to influence cigarette smoking.[88,89] Among these, the factor which probably contributes most to the sex differential in smoking is the strong component of rebelliousness which cigarette smoking has had for many teenagers. In general, girls tend to be less rebellious and more conforming to adult standards, probably in part because parents and teachers of school-aged children allow boys more independence and expect girls to be more obedient.[34,90–92] Girls' lesser rebelliousness is probably one reason why, until very recently, fewer teenage girls than boys had begun smoking.

Although cigarette smoking is the major cause of the higher rates of lung cancer in men, industrial carcinogens also make a substantial contribution. Men who work with asbestos have up to eight times higher a risk of (bronchogenic) lung cancer than other men.[93] This elevated risk affects primarily cigarette smokers. Asbestos is widely used in construction and insulation materials, and about one man in 100 is now or has been exposed to asbestos dust at his work.[94] Thus, asbestos may be responsible for one in 20 male lung cancer deaths in this country. Metallic dusts and fumes elevate lung cancer risk between 20 percent and 130 percent for various categories of metal workers.[95] About one man in 30 works or has worked in such an occupation.[96] Thus, metallic dusts and fumes may be responsible for one in 50 male lung cancer deaths. Taken together, the established and suspected industrial carcinogens appear to be a factor in roughly one out of every 10 male lung cancer deaths.[95,97]

Acknowledgments and Note

The author is happy to thank Joseph Eyer, Jean Gerth, Deborah Heebner, and Kimberly Schmidt for their help in finding useful materials. She is grateful to many friends and colleagues, particularly C. D. Jenkins, for their helpful comments on an earlier version of the manuscript.

This is part I of a two-part article. Part II, written with Susan Johnston, appeared in the *Journal of Human Stress* 2, no. 2 (June 1976): 19–30.

References

1. Keyfitz, N., and W. Flieger, *World Population—An Analysis of Vital Data*. University of Chicago Press, Chicago, 1968.
2. United States Department of Health, Education and Welfare, Public Health Service. *Vital Statistics of the United States, 1970, Vol. II-Mortality*. Government Printing Office, Washington, D. C., 1974.
3. Yerushalmy, J. "Factors in Human Longevity," *Amer. J. Public Health*, Vol. 53, 1963, pp. 148–162.
4. Enterline, P. E. "Causes of Death Responsible for Recent Increases in Sex Mortality Differentials in the United States," *Milbank Mem. Fund Q.*, Vol. 39, 1961, pp. 312–338.
5. Retherford, R. D. *The Changing Sex Differential in Mortality*. Studies in Population and Urban Demography #1. Greenwood Press, Westport, Conn., 1975.
6. Burbank, F. "U. S. Lung Cancer Death Rates Begin to Rise Proportionately More Rapidly for Females than for Males: A Dose-Response Effect?" *J. Chron. Dis.*, Vol. 25, 1972, pp. 473–479.
7. Stolnitz, G. J. "A Century of International Mortality Trends: II," *Population Studies*, Vol. 10, 1956, pp. 17–42.
8. United States Department of Health, Education and Welfare, National Center for Health Statistics. *Mortality from Selected Causes by Marital Status: U. S. Vital and Health Statistics*. Series 20, Nos. 8a and 8b. Government Printing Office, Washington, D. C., 1963.
9. Gove, W. R. "Sex, Marital Status, and Mortality." *Amer. J. Sociol.* Vol. 79, 1973, pp. 45–67.
10. Hamilton, J. B. "The Role of Testicular Secretions as Indicated by the Effects of Castration in Man and by Studies of Pathological Conditions and the Short Life Span Associated with Maleness," *Recent Prog. Horm. Res.*, Vol. 3, 1948, pp. 257–322.
11. Ricklefs, R. E. "Fecundity, Mortality and Avian Demography," *Breeding Biology of Birds*, D. S. Farner, ed., pp. 370–390. National Academy of Science, Washington, 1973.
12. Caughley, G. "Mortality Patterns in Mammals," *Ecology*, Vol. 47, 1966, pp. 906–918.
13. Tricomi, V., O. Serr, and C. Solish. "The Ratio of Male to Female Embryos as Determined by the Sex Chromatin," *Am. J. Obstet, Gynecol.*, Vol. 79, 1960, pp. 504–509.
14. Donaldson, R. S., and S. G. Kohl, "Perinatal Mortality in Twins by Sex," *Am. J. Public Health*, Vol. 55, 1965, pp. 1411–1418.
15. Hammoud, E. I. "Studies in Fetal and Infant Mortality," *Am. J. Public Health*, Vol. 55, 1965, pp. 1152–1163.
16. Teitelbaum, M. S. "Male and Female Components of Perinatal Mortality: International Trends, 1901–63," *Demography*, Vol. 8, 1971, pp. 541–548.

17. Scheinfeld, A. "The Mortality of Men and Women," *Sci. Am.*, Vol. 198, Feb., 1958, pp. 22–27.
18. Madigan, F. C. "Are Sex Mortality Differentials Biologically Caused?", *Milbank Mem. Fund Q.*, Vol. 35, 1957, pp. 202–223.
19. Sowder, W. T., J. O. Bond, E. H. Williams, Jr., and E. L. Flemming. *Man to Man Talk about Women . . . and Men.* Florida State Board of Health, Monograph Series No. 10, Jacksonville, 1966.
20. Potts, D. M. "Which is the Weaker Sex?", *J. Biosoc. Sci.*, Suppl. 2, 1970, pp. 147–157.
21. "Sex Differentials in Mortality," *Stat. Bull. Metropol. Life Ins. Co.*, August, 1974, pp. 2–5.
22. Report of the Royal College of Physicians, *Smoking and Health Now.* Pitman Medical and Scientific Publ., London, 1971.
23. Lelbach, W. K. "Organic Pathology Related to Volume and Pattern of Alcohol Use," *Research Advances in Alcohol and Drug Programs*, Vol. I, 1974, pp. 93–198.
24. Hammond, E. C. "Smoking in Relation to the Death Rates of One Million Men and Women," *Natl. Cancer Inst Monogr.*, Vol. 19, 1966, pp. 127–204.
25. Jenkins, C. D. "The Coronary-Prone Personality," *Psychological Aspects of Myocardial Infarction and Coronary Care*, W. D. Gentry and R. B. Williams, eds., pp. 5–23. V. Mosby, St. Louis, 1975.
26. Bonami, M., and B. Rime. "Approche Exploratoire de la Personalité Pre-Coronarienne par Analyse Standardisée de Données Projectives Thematiques," *J. Psychosom. Res.*, Vol. 16, 1972, pp. 103–113.
27. Rosenman, R. H. "The Role of Behavior Patterns and Neurogenic Factors in the Pathogenesis of Coronary Heart Disease," *Stress and the Heart*, R. S. Eliot, ed., pp. 123–141. Futura Publ., Mount Kisco, N. Y., 1974.
28. Rosenman, R. H., R. J. Brand, C. D. Jenkins, et al. "Coronary Heart Disease in the Western Collaborative Group Study," *J.A.M.A.*, Vol. 233, 1975, pp. 872–877.
29. Kenigsberg, D., S. J. Zyzanski, C. D. Jenkins, et al. "The Coronary-Prone Behavior Pattern in Hospitalized Patients With and Without Coronary Heart Disease," *Psychosom, Med.*, Vol. 36, 1974, pp. 344–351.
30. Bengtsson, C. "Ischaemic Heart Disease in Women," *Acta Med. Scand.*, Suppl. 549, 1973, pp. 1–128.
31. Rosenman, R. H., and M. Friedman. "Association of Specific Behavior Pattern in Women with Blood and Cardiovascular Findings," *Circulation*, Vol. 24, 1961, pp. 1173–1184.
32. Friedman, M., and R. H. Rosenman. "Association of Specific Overt Behavior Pattern with Blood and Cardiovascular Findings," *J.A.M.A.*, Vol. 169, 1959, pp. 1286–1296.
33. U. S. Department of Labor, Bureau of Labor Statistics, *Employment and Earnings*, Vol. 19, 1973, p. 30.
34. Maccoby, E. E., and C. N. Jacklin. *The Psychology of Sex Differences.* Stanford University Press, Stanford, 1974.
35. Dentan, R. K. *The Semai-A Nonviolent People of Malaya.* Holt, Rinehart and Winston, New York, 1968.
36. Saario, T. N., C. N. Jacklin, and C. K. Tittle. "Sex Role Stereotyping in the Public Schools," *Harvard Educational Review*, Vol. 43, 1973, pp. 386–416.
37. Bart, P. "Why Women See the Future Differently from Men," *Learning for Tomorrow: The Role of the Future in Education*, A. Toffler, ed., pp. 33–55. Random House, New York, 1972.
38. U'Ren, M. B. "The Image of Woman in Textbooks," *Woman in Sexist Society.* V.

Gornick, and B. K. Moran, eds., pp. 318–328. New American Library, New York, 1971.

39. Chinoy, E. *The Automobile Worker and the American Dream.* Doubleday & Co., New York, 1955.

40. Report of a Special Task Force to the Secretary of Health, Education and Welfare. *Work in America* MIT Press, Cambridge, 1973.

41. "U. S. Churchgoing 40% in '71 Poll," *New York Times*, January 9, 1972, p. 59.

42. Comstock, G. W., and K. B. Partridge. "Church Attendance and Health," *J. Chronic Dis.*, Vol. 25, 1972, pp. 665–672.

43. Furman, R. H. "Endocrine Factors in Atherogenesis," *Atherosclerosis*, F. G. Schettler, and G. S. Boyd, eds., pp. 375–409. Elsevier Publ., Amsterdam, 1969.

44. Segi, M., M. Kurihara, and Y. Tsukahara. *Mortality for Selected Causes in 30 Countires (1950–1961).* Kosei Tokei Kyokai, Tokyo, 1966.

45. Hamilton, J. B., and G. E. Mestler. "Mortality and Survival: Comparison of Eunuchs with Intact Men and Women in a Mentally Retarded Population," *J. Gerontol.* Vol. 24, 1969, pp. 395–411.

46. London, W. T., S. E. Rosenberg, J. W. Draper, and T. P. Almy. "The Effect of Estrogens on Atherosclerosis," *Ann Intern. Med.*, Vol. 55, 1961, pp. 63–69.

47. Gertler, M. M., and P. D. White, *Coronary Heart Disease in Young Adults.* Harvard University Press, Cambridge, 1954.

48. Berkson, D. M., J. Stamler, and D. B. Cohen. "Ovarian Function and Coronary Atherosclerosis," *Clin. Obstet. Gynecol.* Vol. 7, 1964, pp. 504–530.

49. Ask-Upmark, E. "Life and Death Without Ovaries," *Acta Med. Scand.*, Vol. 172, 1962, pp. 129–135.

50. Parrish, H., C. A. Carr, D. G. Hall, and T. M. King. "Time Interval from Castration in Premenopausal Women to Development of Excessive Coronary Atherosclerosis," *Amer. J. Obstet. Gynecol.*, Vol. 99, 1967, pp. 155–162.

51. Higano, N., R. W. Robinson, and W. D. Cohen. "Increased Incidence of Cardiovascular Disease in Castrated Women," *N. Engl. J. Med.*, Vol. 268, 1963, pp. 1123–1125.

52. Ritterband, A. B., L. A. Jaffe, P. M. Densen, et al. "Gonadal Function and the Development of Coronary Heart Disease," *Circulation*, Vol. 27, 1963, pp. 237–251.

53. Williams, T. J., and E. R. Novak. "Effect of Castration and Hysterectomy on the Female Cardiovascular System," *Geriatrics*, Vol. 18, 1963, 852–859.

54. Beavis, E. L. G., J. B. Brown, and M. A. Smith. "Ovarian Function after Hysterectomy with Conservation of the Ovaries in Premenopausal Women," *J. Obstet. Gynaecol. Br. Commonw.*, Vol. 76, 1969, pp. 969–978.

55. Barker, M. G. "Psychiatric Illness after Hysterectomy," *Br. Med. J.*, Vol. 2, 1968, pp. 91–95.

56. Jenkins, C. D. "Psychologic and Social Precursors of Coronary Disease, Part I," *N. Engl. J. Med.*, Vol. 284, 1971, pp. 244–255.

57. Bunker, J. P. "Surgical Manpower—A Comparison of Operations and Surgeons in the United States and in England and Wales," *N. Engl. J. Med.*, Vol. 282, 1970, pp. 135–144.

58. Davis, M. E., R. J. Jones, and C. Jarolim. "Long-term Estrogen Substitution and Atherosclerosis," *Am. J. Obstet. Gynecol.*, Vol. 82, 1961, pp. 1003–1018.

59. Stamler, J., M. M. Gest, and J. P. Turner. "The Status of Hormonal Therapy for the Primary and Secondary Prevention of Atherosclerotic Coronary Heart Disease," *Prog. Cardiovasc. Dis.*, Vol. 6, 1963, pp. 220–235.

60. Veterans Administration Cooperative Urological Research Group. "Treatment and Survival of Patients with Cancer of the Prostate," *Surgery, Gynecol. and Obstet.*, Vol. 124, 1967, pp. 1011–1017.

61. Blackard, C. E., R. P. Doe, G. T. Mellinger, and D. P. Byar. "Incidence of Cardiovascular Disease and Death in Patients Receiving Diethylstilbestrol for Carcinoma of the Prostate," *Cancer*, Vol. 26, pp. 249–256.

62. Coronary Drug Project Research Group, "The Coronary Drug Project-Initial Findings Leading to Modifications of its Research Protocol," *J.A.M.A.* Vol. 214, 1970, pp. 1303–1313.

63. Mann, J. I., M. P. Vessey, M. Thorogood, and R. Doll. "Myocardial Infarction in Young Women with Special Reference to Oral Contraceptive Practice," *Br. Med. J.*, Vol. 2, 1975, pp. 241–245.

64. Mann, J. I., and W. H. W. Inman. "Oral Contraceptives and Death from Myocardial Infarction," *Br. Med. J.*, Vol. 2, 1975, pp. 245–248.

65. Rosenman, R. H., M. Friedman, R. Straus, C. D. Jenkins, S. J. Zyzanski, and M. Wurm. "Coronary Heart Disease in the Western Collaborative Group Study: A Follow-up Experience of 4 1/2 Years," *J. Chronic Dis.*, Vol. 23, 1970, pp. 173–190.

66. Carlson, L. A., and L. E. Bottiger. "Ischaemic Heart-Disease in Relation to Fasting Values of Plasma Triglycerides and Cholesterol," *Lancet*, Vol. 1, 1972, pp. 865–868.

67. Zilversmit, D. B. "A Proposal Linking Atherogenesis to the Interaction of Endothelial Lipoprotein Lipase with Triglyceride-rich Lipoproteins," *Circ. Res.*, Vol. 33, 1973, pp. 633–638.

68. Tydskrif, S.-A. M. "Cholesterol, Coronary Heart Disease and Oestrogens," *S. Afr. Med. J.*, Vol. 45, 1971, pp. 359–361.

69. Weiss, N. S. "Relationship of Menopause to Serum Cholesterol and Arterial Blood Pressure: The United States' Health Examination Survey of Adults," *Amer. J. Epidemiol.*, Vol. 96, 1972, pp. 237–241.

70. Coronary Drug Project Research Group. "The Coronary Drug Project—Findings Leading to Discontinuation of the 2.5-mg/day Estrogen Group," *J.A.M.A.*, Vol. 226, 1973, pp. 652–657.

71. Furman, R. H. "Gonadal Steroid Effects on Serum Lipids," *Metabolic Effects of Gonadal Hormones and Contraceptive Steriods*, H. A. Salhanick, D. M. Kipnis, and R. L. Vande Wiele, eds., pp. 247–264. Plenum Press, New York 1969.

72. Alfin-Slater, R. B., and L. Aftergood. "Lipids and the Pill," *Lipids*, Vol. 6, 1971, pp. 693–705.

73. Glueck, C. J. and R. Fallat. "Gonadal Hormones and Triglycerides," *Proc. R. Soc. Med.*, Vol. 67, 1974, pp. 667–669.

74. Dugdale, M., and A. T. Masi. "Hormonal Contraception and Thromboembolic Disease: Effects of the Oral Contraceptives on Hemostatic Mechanisms," *J. Chron. Dis.*, Vol. 23, 1971, pp. 775–790.

75. Irey, N. S., W. C. Manion, and H. B. Taylor. "Vascular Lesions in Women Taking Oral Contraceptives," *Arch. Pathol.*, Vol. 39, 1970, pp. 1–8.

76. Vessey, M. P. "Thromboembolism, Cancer and Oral Contraceptives," *Clin. Obstet. Gynecol.*, Vol. 17, 1974, pp. 65–78.

77. Stolley, P. D., J. A. Tonascia, M. S. Tockman, et al. "Thrombosis with Low-Estrogen Oral Contraceptives," *Amer. J. Epidemiol.*, Vol. 102, 1975, pp. 197–208.

78. Fregly, M. J., and M. S. Fregly, eds., *Oral Contraceptives and High Blood Pressure*. Dolphin Press, Gainesville, Fla., 1974.

79. Fisch, I. R., S. H. Freedman, and A. V. Myatt. "Oral Contraceptives, Pregnancy, and Blood Pressure," *J.A.M.A.*, Vol. 222, 1972, pp. 1507–1510.

80. Altura, B. N. "Sex as a Factor Influencing the Responsiveness of Arterioles to Catecholamines," *Eur. J. Pharmacol.*, Vol. 20, 1972, pp. 261–265.

81. Green, R. D., J. W. Miller. "Catecholamine Concentrations: Changes in Plasma of Rats During Estrous Cycle and Pregnancy," *Science*, Vol. 151, 1966, pp. 825–826.

82. Weil-Malherbe, J. "The Adrenergic Amines of Human Blood," *Lancet 1*, 1953, pp. 974-977.
83. Kannel, W. B., and P. Sorlie. "Hypertension in Framingham," In Manuscript.
84. Kannel, W. B., T. R. Dawber. "Hypertensive Cardiovascular Disease: The Framingham Study," *Hypertension: Mechanisms and Management*, C. Onesti, K. E. Kim, and J. H. Moyer, eds., pp. 93-110. Grune and Stratton, 1973.
85. McDonough, J. R., G. E. Garrison, and C. G. Hames. "Blood Pressure and Hypertensive Disease Among Negroes and Whites," *Ann. Intern. Med.*, Vol. 61, 1964, pp. 208-228.
86. Benson, H., and M. C. Gutmann. "The Relation of Environmental Factors to Systemic Arterial Hypertension," *Stress and the Heart*, R. S. Eliot, ed., pp. 13-31. Futura Publ. Co. Mount Kisco, New York, 1974.
87. United States Department of Health, Education and Welfare, Public Health Service, National Clearinghouse for Smoking and Health. *Adult Use of Tobacco-1970*. U. S. Government Printing Office, Washington, D. C., 1973.
88. Borgatta, E. F., and R. R. Evans. "Social and Psychological Concomitants of Smoking Behavior and Its Change Among University Freshmen," *Smoking, Health and Behavior*, E. F. Borgatta and R. R. Evans, eds., pp. 206-219. Aldine Publ., Chicago, 1968.
89. Mausner, B., E. S. Platt, with assistance of J. S. Mausner, *Smoking: A Behavioral Analysis*. Pergamon Press, New York, 1971.
90. Fischer, J. L., and A. F. Fischer. "The New Englanders of Orchardtown," *Six Cultures-Studies of Child-Rearing*, B. B. Whiting, ed., John Wiley and Sons, New York, 1963.
91. Hoffman, L. W. "Early Childhood Experiences and Women's Achievement Motives," *J. Social Issues*, Vol. 28, 1972, pp. 129-155.
92. Levitin, T. E., and J. D. Chananie. "Responses of Female Primary School Teachers to Sex-typed Behaviors in Male and Female Children," *Child Dev.*, Vol. 43, 1972, pp. 1309-1316.
93. Selikoff, I. J., E. C. Hammond, and J. Churg. "Asbestos Exposure, Smoking, and Neoplasia," *J.A.M.A.*, Vol. 204, 1968, pp. 104-110.
94. Stellman, J. M., and S. M. Daum. *Work is Dangerous to Your Health*. Vintage Books, New York, 1973.
95. Hueper, W. C. "Occupational and Environmental Cancers of the Respiratory System," *Recent Results Cancer Res.*, Vol. 3, 1966, pp. 1-130.
96. U. S. Department of Commerce, Social and Economic Statistics Administration. *Subject Reports. Final Report PC(2)-7A. Occupational Characteristics*. Government Printing Office, Washington, D. C., 1973.
97. Breslow, L., L. Hoaglin, G. Rasmussen, and H. K. Abrams, "Occupations and Cigarette Smoking as Factors in Lung Cancer," *Amer. J. Pub. Health*, Vol. 44, 1954, pp. 171-181.
98. United States Department of Health, Education and Welfare, Public Health Service. *Vital Statistics of the United States, 1967, Vol. II—Mortality*. Government Printing Office, Washington, D. C., 1969.

7

Health as a Social Concept

Aubrey Lewis

The social implications of health and disease are very great, but they are obscured by uncertainty as to what these two terms refer to, or, more correctly, how to know when health is or is not present in individuals. It is particularly in respect of mental health that this doubt comes up; but the same essential uncertainty prevails also about physical health. So soon as we pass from obvious good health, or obvious disease, into the penumbra where the dubious cases lie (such as the congenital deformities, the symptomless lesions and so on), we see that the concept of health needs to be clarified: and we realize that it is hardly to be defined without reference to the material and the social environment within which each individual lives.

If my theme were the social causes and the social consequences of disease, or if it were the social conditions propitious to the maintenance of health, my task, though not easy, might be easier than the one I have chosen. A great deal of factual knowledge exists on these matters—they lend themselves to lively speculation, they can be illustrated by telling clinical instances, and there is less danger of an expositor losing himself in a tangle of intersecting paths.

Such studies commonly presuppose that we already know what health is, and can always distinguish it from disease. But we cannot safely operate with ambiguous words and concepts, such as health and disease now are. If we are determining the needs that must be met in the National Health Service, we must first estimate the prevalence of disease; yet for mental disease, in all its forms, this is at present impossible, largely because we are unsure what is to be included. Similarly we cannot agree on the duration of illnesses and on the efficacy of treatment because we have no accepted criteria of recovered health: this may sound extravagant, but there is abundant evidence that it is so.

SOURCE: *British Journal of Sociology* 2, no. 4 (1953): 109–24. Copyright © 1953 by Routledge & Kegan Paul Ltd., London, England. Reprinted by permission.

I shall therefore be dealing to-night largely with a problem of definition. I shall not be considering how the forms of illness are classified and defined, that is, I shall say nothing of the principles and criteria of diagnosis, but shall examine only the criteria of health in general. And although the matter demands theoretical discussion, the purpose is a practical one—to apply the criteria, whatever they may turn out to be, to the enumeration of sick people and healthy ones; to the selection of healthy people for various social opportunities and obligations; and to the further study of the social conditions of health and disease. Since this is the practical aim, there is no harm in accepting certain working assumptions, such as that dualist language in unavoidable here, and that the fictions, health and disease, serve a useful intellectual purpose, though we know they refer merely to uplands and lowlands in a continuously graded and terraced country.

When people say, in joke or seriously, that surely we are all a little mad, or that it is the neurotic people who contribute most to the arts and keep the world moving, or that crime should be treated as a disease and prisons turned into hospitals, they are implying, I think, that there is a social concept of health, no less important than the traditional concept which had until lately been taken for granted. The modern dilemma has been stated in an extreme form by Erich Fromm:

> The term normal or healthy can be defined in two ways. Firstly, from the standpoint of functioning society, one can call a person normal or healthy if he is able to fulfil the social role he is to take in that given society—if he is able to participate in the reproduction of society. Secondly (or alternatively), from the standpoint of the individual, we look upon health or normality as the optimum of growth and happiness of the individual.

There is high sanction for the prima facie assumption that health is partly a social concept, for it is explicit in the definition adopted by the World Health Organization five years ago. The opening passage of that body's international charter says that "health is a state of complete physical, mental and social well-being".

A proposition could hardly be more comprehensive than that, or more meaningless. But to condemn it because it is meaningless is to ignore the history and complexity of the idea behind it. In describing health as a state of perfection, such as was enjoyed perhaps by archangels and by Adam before the Fall, the charter-writers of W. H. O. were reverting to an ancient formula of unattainable wholeness of body, mind and soul, realized in the Golden Age but long since forfeited.

The workaday conception of health can best be examined in connection with the physical artivities of the body. I shall therefore begin by considering the concept of physical illness, and its possible social component. Then I shall pass to the much more difficult field of mental illness, and see whether adaptation to the social environment is a criterion of mental health, or whether other criteria—notably disturbance of psychological functions—are the only essential and useful ones. After that I shall consider sexual perversions, psychopathic personality and suicide, to see whether social deviation spells mental illness, and I shall point out that illness cannot be defined as that which doctors treat. After a brief review of some awkward consequences of an ill-defined concept of health, I shall conclude by suggesting that we should keep social well-being conceptually distinct from health so that their inter-relations can be better observed and analysed.

Now, if the various organs work well enough not to draw attention to themselves, and their owner is free from pain or discomfort, he usually supposes that he is in good health. The criterion is then a subjective one. But if he avails himself of the mass X-ray service and in consequence learned that his lung shows strong evidence of tuberculous disease, he ceases to consider that he is in good health: the criterion he now adopts is an extraneous one, viz. the assertion of a physician who relies on objective or pathological data. It is evident that the physician's criteria of physical health are not the same as the patient's, and that, in practice, it is the presence of disease that can be recognized, not the presence of health. There are no positive indications of health which can be relied upon, and we consider everyone healthy who is free from any evidence of disease or infirmity.

The constitution of the World Health Organization, however, which I have already quoted, roundly asserts the opposite: the whole passage runs: "Health is a state of complete physical mental and social well-being and not merely the absence of disease or infirmity." That idealistic statement seems to forget that the abstractions health and disease do not represent distinct states but rather areas in a continuum. Where health ends and disease begins is arbitrary, but health cannot be restricted to a narrow area at one extreme.

How difficult, if not impossible, it would be to recognize disease, or health, as an absolute is illustrated in Health Surveys. Most western countries have realized that mortality statistics do not afford sufficient basis for planning health services and detecting trends in the form and incidence of disease. Morbidity statistics are therefore required, to provide the data about all illnesses that had hitherto been available only for the notifiable diseases. Material for such statistics can be drawn from various sources: from the general practitioners; from the hospitals; and from health insurance records. As soon as the matter was looked at, it was seen that quite divergent figures would be derived, according to which of these sources was drawn upon. What the patient counted as illness would not always come within the ken of the practitioner, nor be always conceded by him to be illness; and similar difficulties would arise in using statistics derived from hospital in-patient records and from insurance certificates, which are concerned with special sections of the population or special groups of illnesses. Any conclusions about the prevalence of health and disease in the population must therefore be qualified by a statement of how the primary data were obtained.

The criteria of physical illness and health depend upon: first, the patient's account of how and what he feels, i.e. upon subjective statements; secondly, manifest signs of satisfactory or impaired function and structure; and thirdly, occult signs of such adequacy or impairment, detected by special instruments and procedures.

Each of these presupposes a norm. But since they are not identical norms, they must be considered in turn. The patient will report some change in what he has come to regard as his normal state of well-being—a state which may allow for a fairly wide range of variation or on the other hand may be a narrow and fixed mode, according to his temperament, constitution and experience. The quality of the change he has noticed will also determine whether he disregards it (which is much the same as regarding it as healthy) or construes it as a symptom of illness: pain, for example, may be treated differently from fatigue. The norm of bodily perceptions, roughly related to the external or internal stimuli which might be supposed to evoke them, is supplied by every man for himself. There is not, and cannot be, any convention about this norm, which is built up from past, incommunicable experience. To evaluate a report of any departure from it, one must guess something about the man who makes the report: about his habits, the demands he makes of his body, the attention he pays it, and the language he uses to describe its sensations. What a patient tells about his symptoms, and what he concludes about his health are therefore data which will be used by the physician only after a further process of interpretation which may transmute them and yield a different conclusion from the patient's.

The physician is of course trained to relate signs of disturbed function and structure to the norm. His personal experience and the accumulated experience of others are at his disposal. For some organs he has much fuller and more exact information at his disposal than for others: he can, for example, with much more confidence judge the state of the heart than that of the liver. But for each organ and system he has a body of knowledge about the range of normal function and the evidences of normal structure, so that equally well-trained physicians would agree about whether a particular system is working normally (which, in this context, is the same as being healthy). I do not want to overstate this: there can be much difference of opinion in difficult cases or regarding organs difficult to assess as to their functional and structural integrity: but on the whole the criteria are well known and become sharper with every advance in physiology, biochemistry, pathology and anthropometry.

I have spoken of organs and systems: but these are, of course, strictly, artificial abstractions from the total living organism. Perhaps the most important functions of the organism are those that effect a balance and unitary working of the separate systems, ensuring that a change in one is compensated for or reinforced by an appropriate change in another. When this regulatory or intergrating function is disturbed, illness is certain. As Professor Ryle put it: "The term 'health' as affecting the individual, should embrace (in addition to those of sensory wellbeing and structural integrity) ideas of balance and adaptability; these in turn reflect the co-ordinated activity of component parts each functioning within its normal range." The physician therefore must concern himself not only with the evidence of normal structure and function in parts of the body, but in its total working. If the internal milieu, as it has been called, of the body is not kept constant, the physician must detect this; but for the purpose he cannot use structural changes (which will be late consequences of disturbed integration, or local causes of it); instead he must rely on estimates of the total performance of the patient, as well as on the performance of separate parts of him, isolated for convenience as organs or systems: all should be working in responsive harmony. A great many pathologists and physicians have sought to make this the touchstone of health, which they define, or rather sum up, as "a state of physiological and psychological equilibrium", whereas they view disease as the organism's reaction to a disturbance of its inner equilibrium.

At this point we are again adrift, away from objective, well-studied norms. The adequate performance of the body working as a whole is highly individual; the range of variability in the human species is wide: performance is not the same in different races, in different climates, at different ages, in the two sexes, under innumerable conditions of past and present environment. And no instruments of precision, no application of recent discoveries in chemistry or physics can remove the difficulty. In short, for the most important of bodily functions, that which regulates the working of the whole, norms are so wide in range, or need to be so extensively hedged around with qualifying conditions that in clinical practice the physician must take the patient pretty much as supplying his own norm of total performance or behaviour, and proceed by rough and ready appraisal of whether there has been any departure from this, when due allowance has been made for the environment in which the patient has been living.

So, even in regard to physical illness, we cannot disregard total behaviour, which is a psychological concept, and the environment, which, so far as it consists of human beings and their institutions, includes a social concept. When we go on to mental illness, we may be inclined to think that the human environment is all-important, or even that the concept of "mental illness" is essentially a social, rather than a clinical or pathological one.

In general discussion it is customary to assume a monistic standpoint and to infer a physical aspect to all mental health and illness, just as we infer a psychological aspect to all physical illness; but in practice the limits set to our observations and knowledge compel us to talk a dualist language. I am therefore accepting as much distinction between physical illness—or health—and mental illness (or health) as between the subject matter of physiology and of psychology.

Mental health, ideally, might be a state of perfect equipoise in an unstable system. It has been described by some as a state in which one's potential capacities are fully realized. But unless some capacities are characterized as morbid and excluded from the generalization, this is absurd. We all have deplorable potentialities as well as desirable ones. It is hardly necessary to dwell on the emptiness of an ideal notion of mental health, perfect and unattainable. The serviceable criterion commonly employed to define mental health is the absence of mental illness. This shifts the difficulty, and slightly lessens it.

What then is mental illness? Can it be recognized, as physical disease often is, by the qualitatively altered function of some part of the total, by disturbance of thinking, for example, or disturbance of perception? This is possible: we very frequently recognize a man to be mentally ill because he has delusions or hallucinations. But not always, for if the disturbance of part-functions is without influence on his conduct, or falls within certain categories which we regard as "normal", we do not infer "mental illness" from their presence. Thus in their *Phantasms of the Living* Myers, Podmore and Gurney devoted a chapter to the hallucinations of the sane. The procedure is then semantically confused: we have a class of perceptions judged abnormal on statistical grounds, which can be assessed as normal by certain value-judgments. The confusion is manifest in the discriminatory use made of certain signs of disturbed thinking: if a man expresses an irrational belief, e.g. that he has been bewitched, we do not call it a delusion, a sign of disease, unless we are satisfied that the manner in which he came by it is morbid. This would not necessarily be the case if he had been brought up among people who believed in witchcraft, whereas if he is an ordinary twentieth-century Londoner who has arrived at such a conviction through highly individual, devious, suspicion-laden mental processes, we call the belief abnormal and the man who holds it unhealthy.

Two criteria have apparently been applied, then, to changes in function: a psychopathological one paying regard to the process, and a statistical one paying regard to the frequency of its occurrence.

When the psychopathological criterion is looked at, it shows its kinship with the pathological criterion applied in evaluating physical diseases. Unless the phenomenon to which it is applied is gross, it can be used only by experts: just as the decision whether a tumour is malignant requires a highly trained judge, so does the decision whether a queer belief or a turn of mood is due to a pathological process. "Pathological", however, often has elusively vague referents. Most commonly the highly trained judge equates it with "unbalanced", i.e. lacking in stable internal and external adjustment.

The body and the mind have remarkable powers of internal adjustment: compensating, balancing and checking. In the body these adjustments may result in extraordinary departures from the conventional structure of parts—hypertrophy of one kidney, for example, to take over the work of the other when this has been destroyed or removed. In the mind, where ignorance of anatomical substrate and other factors make it harder to delimit functions with confidence, the adjustments are more subtle and elusive, but every system of psychopathology has to pay much attention to the internal devices whereby a working unit is maintained. The psychoanalytic system is, of course, in the main an elaborate metaphorical account of how these checks, compensations and balances may be supposed to work in order to keep mental activity integrated and healthy, and how they can, in certain circumstances, get out of hand and defeat their object. That integration is never wholly attained, is a sad truth. "The basis of much frustration and many conflicts is in this universal circumstance, that no man ever fuses all his self-reactions into a single, unambiguous, coherent whole." But this imperfection can be overstressed. In healthy individuals a regulatory function is at work which keeps the organism internally adjusted and ready to meet changing external conditions. We have arrived at the same point as we reached in considering physical disease: there must be adjustment of functions within the organism, keeping its internal milieu steady: there must be adaptation of this integrated organism to its surroundings so that it remains unharmed, in spite of changing conditions.

"Adjustment" and "adaptation" are words often used as though their meaning were unequivocal. They deserve closer examination. Adequacy of adaptation is to-day the chief yardstick of mental health, for many people. The Education Authorities provide special schools for "maladjusted children". What is meant by adaptation, or adjustment, and how failure in it may be detected, is clearly important.

In the last few years the "general adaptation syndrome" has had a vigorous run in purporting to explain how phenomena of physical disease are produced in response to stress. Here adaptation is considered as a biological phenomenon; men respond to stresses with "adaptive" patterns of reaction that are conservative and protective. They may be designed to provide extra fuel and energy for vital parts of the organism, or to defend some threatened part:

The organism may sacrifice at such times some functions or capacities for the sake of promoting others that are most important to meet the adverse situation. Although there is a degree of specialization, in the sense that one or other protective arrangement is dominant, discrimination is not exact. In a threatened man it is common to find a variety of protective reactions, some of which are extremely pertinent, others less so and still others minimally effective.

So far indeed may the reactions be from pertinence or effectiveness that they are noxious to the individual. In other words, there is no dividing line between the protective mechanisms of adaptation and the same mechanisms when they are harmful: the notion of "adaptation" is then stretched to cover all the responses of the organism to external stress, irrespective of whether these are to be classified as healthy or morbid. Although the multitudinous writers on the subject are not as a rule explicit, it is, I think, plain that they take the same standpoint as McIver when he writes:

> Fresh air will stimulate our lungs and poisonous gas will destroy them; physically the one is no less an adaptation than the other. . . . Nature everywhere makes demands whatever the conditions are . . . whether in the eyes of men they are favourable or unfavourable, good or evil, this unconditional physical adaptation remains with all its compulsion. . . . Purely physical adjustment is always ongoing, is never "maladjustment".

Such a view of adaptation cannot be sustained when social adaptation is in question. Here value judgments must be made, and adaptation is distinguished from maladaptation according as a particular valued state is favoured or jeopardized. Social adaptation, by itself, is therefore rather an empty term: it must be qualified by an indication of the state desired. Consequently mental health cannot be equated with good social adaptation, as many have proposed, without risk of tautology: the valued and desired state which adaptation is to attain or maintain may itself turn out to be health.

According to the most widely used of current textbooks, psychiatry is concerned with "the study of the individual as a psycho-biological organism perpetually called upon to adapt to a social environment", but unfortunately we have not an agreed touchstone for his success or failure in this inescapable exercise. Failure in it, moreover, need not betoken mental illness. One can be sociopathic without being psychopathic.

Although social disapproval has obviously played a large part in deciding what shall be called social maladaptation, and is its main feature in current psychiatric usage, it cannot be accepted as a satisfactory criterion, varying as it does according to the group of people who express the disapproval. It is necessary to describe behaviour in terms that specify the social situation in time and place, but perilous if we must describe the behaviour further in terms of who approves it, before it can be held to show good social adaptation. It is true that behaviour indicative of social maladaptation will very often be disapproved by almost the whole of society, but there will also be forms of social maladaptation which enjoy social approval, at any rate for a time or by a section of society. Where then can we find a less shifting barrier between success and failure in social adaptation of the individual? Until we have this we are hardly in a position to examine whether such maladaptation bespeaks disease, or delinquency, or (passing from medicine and law to theology) sin.

Social maladaptation of the individual is not total, any more than malfunction of the physical body can be total: different social relations will be variously affected. But like physical malfunction, social maladaptation in any one regard may have some effect upon all that individual's social relations. It is therefore permissible, but sometimes lax, usage to consider social maladaptation as taking restricted forms, such as are seen in alcoholics or in religious fanatics.

It might be urged that the most useful criterion of whether an individual is socially maladjusted is non-conformity—non-conformity to the institutions, the mores, the verbal and other customs prevailing in his society. Social maladaptation of this sort could, of course, be a good and admired thing. It is at present usual to express it in terms of social role. A person is maladapted when his own version of his social role is not in conformity with society's version: and in so far as each person has many social roles, it is the dominant role, or those which have precedence in the daily organization of his activities, that are important here. Conflict can easily arise. Cultural lag, clashes, transitions during phases of development (as at puberty) and involuntary changes of social status will clearly favour conflicts over a man's own conception of his social role and that which society fastens upon him, and will so lead to non-conforming behaviour. Such behaviour can, of course, betoken mental illness.

One thoughtful student of the problem, Edwin Lemert, believes that the psychopathic variety of social deviation is characterized by symbolic distortion of the attitude to one's self and one's social role ("symbolic" here referring to the product of emotional and cognitive activities, which are mostly covert): "The 'me' of the self (the reflective part of the symbolic process) no longer approximates within normal limits the socially objective estimates and designations of the person's role and status." The observable aspect of this in behaviour appears as "abnormal variation in the amount and form of self-expression". Although Lemert contends that this formula covers "practically all of what is called 'neurotic' and 'psychotic' behaviour", it seems to me to be applicable mainly to some forms of insanity and near-insanity, and to be too vague to serve for differentiating psychopathic from other forms of social maladaptation. Similar objections may be made against other sociological attempts to state the denotative characteristics of mental illness. They do not stand on their social legs, but are propped by medical struts and stays.

Let us revert then to the traditional medical criteria already mentioned. They are threefold: (1) the patient feels ill—a general, subjective datum; (2) he has disordered function of some part of him—a restricted objective datum; (3) he has symptoms which conform to a recognizable clinical pattern—a typological datum. Social criteria play no part except in so far as disturbance in capacity to meet social demands, e.g. ability to work, may provoke the question: is this man ill? Difficult cases can be cited, it is true: for example, the typhoid carrier who feels well and has no reduction of capacity but who can infect others and may, because of this social consideration, be segregated and treated as though he were himself ill, perhaps even be constrained to have his gall-bladder removed. Yet I do not think anyone regards such a man as actually ill, since he does not satisfy any of the three criteria I have just listed—he has no subjective malaise, no demonstrable disorder of function, no familiar clinical symptoms and signs.

These traditional criteria were applied long before our current modes of thought about the origin and nature of disease had been developed. They accompanied the animistic notions of disease which prevailed for many centuries before systematic study of causes and of morbid anatomy was undertaken; pathological studies of disease were a comparatively late outcome of technical advances in microscopy, physiology and chemistry. For most people, over long stretches of time, ill-health has meant feeling ill, suffering pain or incapacity, and going in danger of death or mutilation. Whether this state could be traced to some structural change in the cells of the body did not enter into consideration in deciding whether a man was healthy or ill. Nevertheless, when, as in insanity, the unusual state affected the patient's whole conduct and not the activity or well-being of a limited part of his body, it was by no means invariably held that this was illness; the old animistic conceptions of disease were invoked—demoniacal possession, witchcraft, and so on. There were, however, always physicians who regarded these too as forms of ill-health. Why did they do so? What principle led them to bring insanity and physical disease under one heading, while leaving crime, for example, apart? The common feature was, surely, the evident disturbance of part-functions as well as of general efficiency. In physical disease this needs no demonstration: in mental disorders it is shown by the occurrence of, say, disturbed thinking as in delusions, or disturbed perceptions, as in hallucinations, or disturbed emotional state, as in anxiety neurosis or melancholia. Deviant, maladapted, non-conformist behaviour is pathological if it is accompanied by a manifest disturbance of some such functions. It is true, as I have already said, that functions are an artificial construct, and that disorder in any particular function will be commonly accompanied by less conspicuous disorder in many other functions—just as in the body. But, for illness to be inferred, disorder of function must be detectable at a discrete or differentiated level that is hardly conceivable when mental activity as a whole is taken as the irreducible datum. If non-conformity can be detected only in total behaviour, while all the particular psychological functions seem unimpaired, health will be presumed, not illness.

The disputes about the relative merits of structural psychology and functional psychology, coming after the excesses of faculty psychology, justify a wary approach to the listing of mental functions. There is, however, at present general agreement about the importance of the following:—perception, learning, thinking, remembering, feeling, emotion, motivation. The main objection might be that the list is not exhaustive. However, these fall into the traditional divisions—cognitive, affective, and conative; and each of them can be subdivided into many varieties, according to the fullness of the data provided by psychology or by clinical psychiatry. Motivation is the least satisfying and probably the most important: under it needs or drives, conflicts and social responses fail to be considered. As P. T. Young has pointed out, in regard to the great diversity of methods used in studying emotion and motivation, the difficulty lies in the extreme complexity of the processes and their basic significance for understanding conduct. A list of functions, such as that just given, is provisional: the history of psychology underlines that it must be so for the present. Physiological functions likewise are subject to revision. The fuller our exact knowledge of functions, the more definite our conclusion that there is a disorder of one or several, constituting illness. It is possible now, as may be seen in a textbook like that of Landis and Bolles, to classify the phenomena of mental illness in terms of disordered function.

There are some forms of socially deviant behaviour which raise nice problems—sexual perversions, for example, such as homosexuality or exhibitionism. To settle whether sexual perversions are necessarily pathological, in the light of the suggested criterion of illness, would require closer and more extensive consideration than is here possible of the place of sexual needs and activities among mental functions. In the psychoanalysts' strictures on Kinsey's findings the wide difference can be seen between a statistical criterion of what should be included within the norm of sexual function and a value-criterion of this.

The crucial difficulty arises with psychopathic personality. Every textbook of psychiatry discusses this abnormality, but almost always ambiguously because the authors do not make clear why it should be regarded as an illness. Though no definition of the term has received general assent as far as I know, the following description, taken from Norwood East, indicates what sort of person it is generally understood to cover: "A person who although not insane, psychoneurotic or mentally defective, is persistently unable to adapt himself to social requirements on account of quantitative peculiarities of impulse, temperament and character which may require specialized medical and rehabilitative treatment. . . ."

The category evidently embraces a particular group of people whose socially deviant behaviour arises from some non-cognitive psychological deviation. Furthermore, the condition may call for medical treatment; but as this is not an invariable requirement we may neglect it here.

Peculiarities of character and temperament are not acceptable indications of illness: they are, of course, very common in the general population, and it is hardly justifiable to classify all people who exhibit them as psychopathic. There remains the quantitative abnormality of impulse: this is prominent in medico-legal discussions of the matter, possibly because it is so often urged as a medical explanation for lessened responsibility in crimes of violence, especially murder. But impulse is, psychologically, an imprecise and somewhat old-fashioned term. With the dethronement of Will in modern psychology, it is not easy to specify abnormalities of conative function in terms of impulse, and it is certainly impossible to measure them.

It would seem, then, that until the category is further defined and shown to be characterized by specified abnormality of psychological functions, it will not be possible to consider those who fall within it to be unhealthy, however deviant their social behaviour.

Although social danger is a common feature of insanity, as of much physical illness also (e.g. the infectious diseases—smallpox, veneral disease and the like), the social harm is a contingent, not a necessary feature: in its absence, the condition is still an illness because of the changes in the individual. The truth is that though the social effects of disease, like the social causes, are extremely important, it is impossible to decide from them whether a condition is healthy or morbid.

The concept of disease, then—and of health—has physiological and psychological components, but no essential social ones. In examining it we cannot ignore social considerations, because they may be needed for the assessment of physiological and psychological adequacy, but we are not bound to consider whether behaviour is social deviant: though illness may lead to such behaviour, there are many forms of social deviation which are not illness, many forms of illness which are not social deviation.

It is necessary at this point to draw a distinction between illness and what doctors treat. If the view were taken that everyone who goes to the doctor and receives treatment is ill, we would have a simple operational criterion, but its defects are obvious: it will fluctuate enormously from place to place and from time to time, it will depend on an attitude by the patient towards his doctor, and it will certainly fail to include many people whom, by any common-sense standard, one must call ill.

Moreover it must be remembered that the doctor is not necessarily acting outside his proper scope if he attends to people who are not ill. Congenital defects of bodily structure and function (e.g. malformations and benign metalbolic anomalies) are not strictly illnesses but they are the concern of doctors. Pregnancy and childbirth, after all, are not illnesses either. Extension of the doctor's province has gone very far in psychiatry. The psychiatrist learns a great deal about normal and abnormal psychology which is relevant to the treatment, or the prevention, of some non-pathological states that are socially deviant. He is nowadays often, and quite properly, asked to investigate and treat disturbances of behaviour in children which can hardly be included within any warranted conception of illness (though of course they may be the prelude to illness). He may likewise investigate or treat criminals, drug addicts, prostitutes and sexual perverts. It may be that there is no form of social deviation in an individual which psychiatrists will not claim to treat or prevent—the pretensions of some psychiatrists are extreme. That time has not come, fortunately. Nevertheless it is clear that psychiatrists, and other doctors, look after plenty of people who are not ill: and conversely that there are many sick people who think as Montaigne did and would hold it absurd to commit themselves to the mercy and government of the doctors—at any rate for a nervous illness. Psychiatrists in our day are much exposed to strictures and suspicions like those which Montaigne expressed against the doctors of the sixteenth century.

Suicide illustrates the problem in deciding between social deviation and illness. No one disputes that suicide is often an outcome or symptom of illness; no one, I think, disputes that it can be the act of a mentally healthy person. If it occurs in a society which sanctions suicide in given circumstances, as ours does, and if the circumstances of the act are the approved ones, it is assumed that the act does not bespeak mental illness nor, of course, social deviation. That is, socially approved behaviour is not usually reviewed to see if it evinces mental illness; and in such a case, suicide is regarded like marriage, or any other isolated but decisive act of choice which is socially approved. But even in a society which does not disapprove of suicide, the act may be a sign of mental illness; and it may be suspected to be such for two reasons: because of the circumstances in which it occurs, and because of the disorder of psychological functions which the person displays, apart from his suicidal behaviour. When the circumstances indicate that the act is not in conformity with the social roles which the person is required to enact, this is not sufficient to denote illness, though it excites inquiry into the matter. The decision about illness must be made in the light of a further inquisition, into psychological functions. If these are found disordered, then the suicidal act may be assumed to have been also an evidence of mental illness—but even this would not be true unless the suicidal act fitted into the total pattern of disordered function which the person displayed. A person may be mentally ill, yet his suicide may be extrinsic to this, or represent, so to speak, a normal and even healthy response to the situation in which he finds himself. It may seem absurd to talk of suicide as in any circumstances a healthy response, but it is absurd only if one holds to the opinion that biological adaptation is the true and final criterion of health. By any biological standard the suicide of a person who has not reproduced is surely a supreme instance of maladaptation.

The psychoanalytical concepts of mental health and illness call for special consideration. Though there is no unanimity among psychoanalysts on the matter, they concentrate on inner psychological criteria, and some of the terms they use for definition would make it impossible to tell whether an individual is mentally healthy unless he has been psychoanalysed or his behaviour interpreted on psychoanalytic lines: the criteria, in short, are technical psychoanalytical ones. It is also common for psychoanalysts to describe mental health in loose general language: thus Karl Menninger says: "Let us define mental health as the adjustment of human beings to the world and to each other with a maximum of effectiveness and happiness." A more serious effort to grapple with the problem has been made by Ernest Jones. He lists three features of the normal or healthy mind: first, the "internal freedom" of feelings of friendliness and affection towards others; secondly, mental efficiency, i.e. "the fullest use of the given individual's powers and talents"; and finally, happiness which is "probably the most important of the three"—a combination of the capacity for enjoyment with self-content. These criteria are approximately those which he applies to a practical matter—viz. determining whether, and when, treatment has been successful: "The analytical success betokens the highest degree of the favourable results I described just now when speaking of the therapeutic criteria. One may then expect a confident serenity, a freedom from anxiety, a control over the full resources of the personality that can be obtained in no other way than by the most complete analysis possible." Such language leaves room for honest but absurdly wide differences of opinion between a psychoanalyst and another person—say a psychiatrist, a general practitioner, or a relative of the patient—about whether a psychoanalysed patient, or indeed anybody at all, is mentally healthy. Yet this is no remote and theoretical matter. Partly because it has not been settled we are still without exact information about the comparative effects of psychoanalysis and other methods of psychotherapy, or of the indications that a successful outcome will ensue from psychoanalytical treatment of a particular patient. Yet a Health Service which promises adequate treatment to the whole population is in an awkward position when a demand that much more psychoanalytic therapy be provided is refused on the ground that such treatment is costly and its efficacy open to doubt. Every psychiatrist has seen patients who, he is told, have recovered after treatment of their mental disorder but who seem to him still ill. It is not a problem that affects only the assessment of psychoanalytic treatment: it comes up quite as often after physical methods of psychiatric treatment, like leucotomy.

The inherent difficulty of the concept of mental health is underlined when we find the psychoanalyst, so expert in the microscopy of mental happenings, unable to dispense with equivocal and cloudy terms in stating his criteria of recovery.

Another psychoanalyst, Lawrence Kubie, has looked more closely than most into the social implications of health. Beginning with the assertion that "psychoanalysis is uncompromising in its concept of mental health", he goes on to say that the analyst is not "content to use conformity to the cultural mores of any time or place as his criterion of normality"...

> nor does the difference between normal and neurotic conduct depend upon the degree to which an act contributes either to the welfare of society or to its destruction, or on whether the behaviour is extravagant and fantastic or orderly and sedate. Certainly from the point of view of society all of these are important attributes of human behaviour; but they are neither constant nor explanatory as a basis for the distinction between the normal and the neurotic process.... The critical difference lies not in the act, nor in its setting, but in the psychological mechanisms which determine the act.... What passes for normality in our world to-day is not in any fundamental sense normal. It is rather the unstable equilibrium between conscious and unconscious phenomena.... The activities which result may not be peculiar or strange in themselves. They may be socially acceptable and even valuable; and they may meet all the demands of conscience....

but they are residues of the unresolved neurotic problems of childhood, they are the "veiled and universal neurotic component of 'normal' human nature". He concludes that on pragmatic grounds we may call any act normal if conscious processes predominate in it; he holds that every act is the product of biological forces and superimposed conscious, preconscious and unconscious psychological forces, all of which bear the imprint of many social pressures and are in a state of continuous unstable equilibrium. This is another way of looking at the efficiency of certain functions. But the functions are those which psychoanalysts emphasize in their account of mental organization. They are difficult functions to consider outside the psychoanalytical frame of reference, and the concept embodying them accordingly difficult to apply to the recognition of health and disease.

To deny a social content in the idea of health in no sense implies denying it a social context. Anthropologists and social psychologists have arrayed overpowering evidence showing how highly dependent we must be on knowledge of the social and cultural background when we would appraise conduct and the efficiency of psychological functions. No practising psychiatrist can be unmindful of this, and it is needless to cite the standard examples—Kwakinth and Shasta, Crow Indians and Ekoi, Yakuts and Dobuans—in order to underline it.

But in our own society the prevailing confusion about the quality and nature of health has begotten some dangerous errors. Thus during the last war many people assumed that a man who had neurotic illness would be less capable in social relations and work than a healthy man. A rather similar assumption is often made about would-be University students, and about entrants into a wide variety of careers and jobs. But the evidence for this is not conclusive, and much of what purports to be evidence is vitiated by the use of a concept of neurotic illness which takes account of occupational or social inadequacy, and a concept of occupational inadequacy which is much influenced by considerations of health. Unless the criteria of ill-health are independent and clear, it is difficult or unsafe to use data based on them for purposes of selection.

In the investigations of the Research Unit with which I have been connected this problem has come up in many forms. When we were trying to find out what influence a neurotically sick worker might have on others, and how his own output was affected by his health, it was necessary to have means for detecting such illness in men who were not under a doctor's care and were not complaining: should one attach any weight to occasional bouts of drinking, or frequent absences from work, or the way a man got at loggerheads with other people at the factory and with his wife or family. Hitherto such social data have often been given a pathological value. This may account for some divergent figures. Thus Russell Fraser, and later Morris Markowe, found that about 10 per cent of light engineering workers had suffered from definite neurotic illness, and a further 20 per cent from minor forms of neurosis, during a period of six months; whereas Lemkau found a much lower prevalence rate in a much less selected population. The prevalence rate of psychopathic personality in an American city (Baltimore) was 13 per 10,000 in 1933, but in 1936 it had fallen to 5.2 per 10,000: it seems highly probable that social considerations may have entered to a large extent into this ostensibly medical census. Indeed, the main American investigator in the Baltimore inquiry says that

> in 1933, early in the depression years, there was a tendency for the sources on which the survey was dependent to interpret inability to earn a satisfactory living as an evidence of psychopathic personality. By 1936 the seriousness of the depression had become more clearly recognized, familiarity with unemployment had made it less a mark of defective character, and consequently the diagnosis of psychopathic personality was more rarely used.

And he adds that in the last war the incidence of psychopathic personality among men examined for military service in the United States was eight per 1,000: rejections from military service for this reason accounted for more than a quarter of all rejections because of mental disease. Social considerations weighed very heavily in deciding whether these men were healthy, or ill, and the confusion of social deviation with illness may explain away the improbable fluctuation in prevalence of a supposedly constitutional disorder. In the more recent work of the M.R.C. Unit I referred to, an effort is being made to keep the estimation of mental health clear of direct occupational and other social considerations. This is especially necessary in the investigations made by the Unit into the employability of high-grade mental defectives. Mental defect has two characteristics—a deficiency in intelligence and a disorder of personality. The latter tends to be judged largely by social criteria, since the social consequences are so important, legally and administratively. The incidence of high-grade defect in the general community may therefore seem to fluctuate from place to place. The social findings have to be kept as distinct as possible from the psychological and pathological findings, in order to avoid getting spuriously high correlations between morbidity and social adjustment.

The curious implications of using a social criterion for health and illness are apparent when a whole society is characterized as unhealthy. So long as this is a literary usage, there can be no objection, but it has been seriously formulated and close analogies have been drawn between a sick society and a sick individual. If failure to conform to one's social role is a requirement of illness, a given society can only satisfy it, I suppose, if there is some larger community or world-polity within which the individual society takes the wrong road, or if, at the other extreme, the social role of a given society is that assigned to it by its individual members acting collectively. It is fairly clear that only by a bold metaphor can a society be called healthy or sick. There are plenty of other and more suitable terms we can use to praise a society or to indicate that it is disorganized.

If I now try to pull together my argument, it is this. Health is a single concept: it is not possible to set up essentially different criteria for physical health and mental health. We commonly assume a break between health and ill-health, for which there is no counterpart in the phenomena but which we cannot yet replace by a continuum because we lack means of measuring some of the necessary dimensions. Besides subjective feelings and degree of total efficiency, the criterion of health is adequate performance of functions, physiological and psychological. So far as we cannot designate formal, major functions of the human organism and lack means for judging whether they work efficiently, we are handicapped in recognizing health and illness in a reliable and valid way. The physiological functions can be thus designated and judged far more satisfactorily than the psychological. We can therefore usually tell whether an individual is physically healthy, but we cannot tell with the same confidence and consensus of many observers, whether he is mentally healthy. Though our estimate of the efficiency with which functions work must take account of the social environment which supplies stimuli and satisfies needs, the criteria of health are not primarily social: it is misconceived to equate ill-health with social deviation or maladjustment. If we avoid this error, we shall find it easier to study the relation between health and social well-being and so, one may hope, learn how to further both.

8

On Being Sane
in Insane Places

D. L. Rosenhan

If sanity and insanity exist, how shall we know them?

The question is neither capricious nor itself insane. However much we may be personally convinced that we can tell the normal from the abnormal, the evidence is simply not compelling. It is commonplace, for example, to read about murder trials wherein eminent psychiatrists for the defense are contradicted by equally eminent psychiatrists for the prosecution on the matter of the defendant's sanity. More generally, there are a great deal of conflicting data on the reliability, utility, and meaning of such terms as "sanity," "insanity," "mental illness," and "schizophrenia" (1). Finally, as early as 1934, Benedict suggested that normality and abnormality are not universal (2). What is viewed as normal in one culture may be seen as quite aberrant in another. Thus, notions of normality and abnormality may not be quite as accurate as people believe they are.

To raise questions regarding normality and abnormality is in no way to question the fact that some behaviors are deviant or odd. Murder is deviant. So, too, are hallucinations. Nor does raising such questions deny the existence of the personal anguish that is often associated with "mental illness." Anxiety and depression exist. Psychological suffering exists. But normality and abnormality, sanity and insanity, and the diagnoses that flow from them may be less substantive than many believe them to be.

At its heart, the question of whether the sane can be distinguished from the insane (and whether degrees of insanity can be distinguished from each other) is a simple matter: do the salient characteristics that lead to diagnoses reside in the patients themselves or in the environments and contexts in which observers find them? From Bleuler, through Kretchmer, through the formulators of the recently

SOURCE: *Science* 179 (19 January 1973): 250–58. Copyright © 1973 by the American Association for the Advancement of Science. Reprinted by permission.

revised *Diagnostic and Statistical Manual* of the American Psychiatric Association, the belief has been strong that patients present symptoms, that those symptoms can be categorized, and, implicitly, that the sane are distinguishable from the insane. More recently, however, this belief has been questioned. Based in part on theoretical and anthropological considerations, but also on philosophical, legal, and therapeutic ones, the view has grown that psychological categorization of mental illness is useless at best and downright harmful, misleading, and pejorative at worst. Psychiatric diagnoses, in this view, are in the minds of the observers and are not valid summaries of characteristics displayed by the observed (3–5).

Gains can be made in deciding which of these is more nearly accurate by getting normal people (that is, people who do not have, and have never suffered, symptoms of serious psychiatric disorders) admitted to psychiatric hospitals and then determining whether they were discovered to be sane and, if so, how. If the sanity of such pseudopatients were always detected, there would be prima facie evidence that a sane individual can be distinguished from the insane context in which he is found. Normality (and presumably abnormality) is distinct enough that it can be recognized wherever it occurs, for it is carried within the person. If, on the other hand, the sanity of the pseudopatients were never discovered, serious difficulties would arise for those who support traditional modes of psychiatric diagnosis. Given that the hospital staff was not incompetent, that the pseudopatient had been behaving as sanely as he had been outside of the hospital, and that it had never been previously suggested that he belonged in a psychiatric hospital, such an unlikely outcome would support the view that psychiatric diagnosis betrays little about the patient but much about the environment in which an observer finds him.

This article describes such an experiment. Eight sane people gained secret admission to 12 different hospitals (6). Their diagnostic experiences constitute the data of the first part of this article; the remainder is devoted to a description of their experiences in psychiatric institutions. Too few psychiatrists and psychologists, even those who have worked in such hospitals, know what the experience is like. They rarely talk about it with former patients, perhaps because they distrust information coming from the previously insane. Those who have worked in psychiatric hospitals are likely to have adapted so thoroughly to the settings that they are insensitive to the impact of that experience. And while there have been occasional reports of researchers who submitted themselves to psychiatric hospitalization (7), these researchers have commonly remained in the hospitals for short periods of time, often with the knowledge of the hospital staff. It is difficult to know the extent to which they were treated like patients or like research colleagues. Nevertheless, their reports about the inside of the psychiatric hospital have been valuable. This article extends those efforts.

Pseudopatients and Their Settings

The eight pseudopatients were a varied group. One was a psychology graduate student in his 20's. The remaining seven were older and "established." Among them were three psychologists, a pediatrician, a psychiatrist, a painter, and a housewife. Three pseudopatients were women, five were men. All of them employed pseudonyms, lest their alleged diagnoses embarrass them later. Those who were in mental health professions alleged another occupation in order to avoid the special attentions that might be accorded by staff, as a matter of courtesy or caution, to ailing colleagues (8). With the exception of myself (I was the first pseudopatient and my presence was known to the hospital administrator and chief psychologist and, so far as I can tell, to them alone), the presence of pseudopatients and the nature of the research program was not known to the hospital staffs (9).

The settings were similarly varied. In order to generalize the findings, admission into a variety of hospitals was sought. The 12 hospitals in the sample were located in five different states on the East and West coasts. Some were old and shabby, some were quite new. Some were research-oriented, others not. Some had good staff-patient ratios, others were quite understaffed. Only one was a strictly private hospital. All of the others were supported by state or federal funds or, in one instance, by university funds.

After calling the hospital for an appointment, the pseudopatient arrived at the admissions office complaining that he had been hearing voices. Asked what the voices said, he replied that they were often unclear, but as far as he could tell they said "empty," "hollow," and "thud." The voices were unfamiliar and were of the same sex as the pseudopatient. The choice of these symptoms was occasioned by their apparent similarity to existential symptoms. Such symptoms are alleged to arise from painful concerns about the perceived meaninglessness of one's life. It is as if the hallucinating person were saying, "My life is empty and hollow." The choice of these symptoms was also determined by the *absence* of a single report of existential psychoses in the literature.

Beyond alleging the symptoms and falsifying name, vocation, and employment, no further alterations of person, history, or circumstances were made. The significant events of the pseudopatient's life history were presented as they had actually occurred. Relationships with parents and siblings, with spouse and children, with people at work and in school, consistent with the aforementioned exceptions, were described as they were or had been. Frustrations and upsets were described along with joys and satisfactions. These facts are important to remember. If anything, they strongly biased the subsequent results in favor of detecting sanity, since none of their histories or current behaviors were seriously pathological in any way.

Immediately upon admission to the psychiatric ward, the pseudopatient ceased simulating *any* symptoms of abnormality. In some cases, there was a brief period of mild nervousness and anxiety, since none of the pseudopatients really believed that they would be admitted so easily. Indeed, their shared fear was that they would be immediately exposed as frauds and greatly embarrassed. Moreover, many of them had never visited a psychiatric ward; even those who had, nevertheless had some genuine fears about what might happen to them. Their nervousness, then, was quite appropriate to the novelty of the hospital setting, and it abated rapidly.

Apart from that short-lived nervousness, the pseudopatient behaved on the ward as he "normally" behaved. The pseudopatient spoke to patients and staff as he might ordinarily. Because there is uncommonly little to do on a psychiatric ward, he attempted to engage others in conversation. When asked by staff how he was feeling, he indicated that he was fine, that he no longer experienced symptoms. He responded to instructions from attendants, to calls for medication (which was not swallowed), and to dining-hall instructions. Beyond such activities as were available to him on the admissions ward, he spent his time writing down his observations about the ward, its patients, and the staff. Initially these notes were written "secretly," but as it soon became clear that no one much cared, they were subsequently written on standard tablets of paper in such public places as the dayroom. No secret was made of these activities.

The pseudopatient, very much as a true psychiatric patient, entered a hospital with no foreknowledge of when he would be discharged. Each was told that he would have to get out by his own devices, essentially by convincing the staff that he was sane. The psychological stresses associated with hospitalization were considerable, and all but one of the pseudopatients desired to be discharged almost immediately after being admitted. They were, therefore, motivated not only to behave sanely, but to be paragons of cooperation. That their behavior was in no way disruptive is confirmed by nursing reports, which have been obtained on most of the patients. These reports uniformly indicate that the patients were "friendly," "cooperative," and "exhibited no abnormal indications."

The Normal Are Not Detectably Sane

Despite their public "show" of sanity, the pseudopatients were never detected. Admitted, except in one case, with a diagnosis of schizophrenia (*10*), each was discharged with a diagnosis of schizophrenia "in remission." The label "in remission" should in no way be dismissed as a formality, for at no time during any hospitalization had any question been raised about any pseudopatient's simulation. Nor are there any indications in the hospital records that the pseudopatient's status was suspect. Rather, the evidence is strong that, once labeled schizophrenic, the pseudopatient was stuck with that label. If the pseudopatient was to be discharged, he must naturally be "in remission"; but he was not sane, nor, in the institution's view, had he ever been sane.

The uniform failure to recognize sanity cannot be attributed to the quality of the hospitals, for, although there were considerable variations among them, several are considered excellent. Nor can it be alleged that there was simply not enough time to observe the pseudopatients. Length of hospitalization ranged from 7 to 52 days, with an average of 19 days. The pseudopatients were not, in fact, carefully observed, but this failure clearly speaks more to traditions within psychiatric hospitals than to lack of opportunity.

Finally, it cannot be said that the failure to recognize the pseudopatients' sanity was due to the fact that they were not behaving sanely. While there was clearly some tension present in all of them, their daily visitors could detect no serious behavioral consequences—nor, indeed, could other patients. It was quite common for the patients to "detect" the pseudopatients' sanity. During the first three hospitalizations, when accurate counts were kept, 35 of a total of 118 patients on the admissions ward voiced their suspicions, some vigorously. "You're not crazy. You're a journalist, or a professor [referring to the continual note-taking]. You're checking up on the hospital." While most of the patients were reassured by the pseudopatient's insistence that he had been sick before he came in but was fine now, some continued to believe that the pseudopatient was sane throughout his hospitalization (11). The fact that the patients often recognized normality when staff did not raises important questions.

Failure to detect sanity during the course of hospitalization may be due to the fact that physicians operate with a strong bias toward what statisticians call the type 2 error (5). This is to say that physicians are more inclined to call a healthy person sick (a false positive, type 2) than a sick person healthy (a false negative, type 1). The reasons for this are not hard to find: it is clearly more dangerous to misdiagnose illness than health. Better to err on the side of caution, to suspect illness even among the healthy.

But what holds for medicine does not hold equally well for psychiatry. Medical illnesses, while unfortunate, are not commonly pejorative. Psychiatric diagnoses, on the contrary, carry with them personal, legal, and social stigmas (12). It was therefore important to see whether the tendency toward diagnosing the sane insane could be reversed. The following experiment was arranged at a research and teaching hospital whose staff had heard these findings but doubted that such an error could occur in their hospital. The staff was informed that at some time during the following 3 months, one or more pseudopatients would attempt to be admitted into the psychiatric hospital. Each staff member was asked to rate each patient who presented himself at admissions or on the ward according to the likelihood that the patient was a pseudopatient. A 10-point scale was used, with a 1 and 2 reflecting high confidence that the patient was a pseudopatient.

Judgments were obtained on 193 patients who were admitted for psychiatric treatment. All staff who had had sustained contact with or primary responsibility for the patient—attendants, nurses, psychiatrists, physicians, and psychologists—were asked to make judgments. Forty-one patients were alleged, with high confidence, to be pseudopatients by at least one member of the staff. Twenty-three were considered suspect by at least one psychiatrist. Nineteen were suspected by one psychiatrist *and* one other staff member. Actually, no genuine pseudopatient (at least from my group) presented himself during this period.

The experiment is instructive. It indicates that the tendency to designate sane people as insane can be reversed when the stakes (in this case, prestige and diagnostic acumen) are high. But what can be said of the 19 people who were suspected of being "sane" by one psychiatrist and another staff member? Were these people truly "sane," or was it rather the case that in the course of avoiding the type 2 error the staff tended to make more errors of the first sort—calling the crazy "sane"? There is no way of knowing. But one thing is certain: any diagnostic process that lends itself so readily to massive errors of this sort cannot be a very reliable one.

The Stickiness of Psychodiagnostic Labels

Beyond the tendency to call the healthy sick—a tendency that accounts better for diagnostic behavior on admission than it does for such behavior after a lengthy period of exposure—the data speak to the massive role of labeling in psychiatric assessment. Having once been labeled schizophrenic, there is nothing the pseudopatient can do to overcome the tag. The tag profoundly colors others' perceptions of him and his behavior.

From one viewpoint, these data are hardly surprising, for it has long been known that elements are given meaning by the context in which they occur. Gestalt psychology made this point vigorously, and Asch (*13*) demonstrated that there are "central" personality traits (such as "warm" versus "cold") which are so powerful that they markedly color the meaning of other information in forming an impression of a given personality (*14*). "Insane," "schizophrenic," "manic-depressive," and "crazy" are probably among the most powerful of such central traits. Once a person is designated abnormal, all of his other behaviors and characteristics are colored by that label. Indeed, that label is so powerful that many of the pseudopatients' normal behaviors were overlooked entirely or profoundly misinterpreted. Some examples may clarify this issue.

Earlier I indicated that there were no changes in the pseudopatient's personal history and current status beyond those of name, employment, and, where necessary, vocation. Otherwise, a veridical description of personal history and circumstances was offered. Those circumstances were not psychotic. How were they made consonant with the diagnosis of psychosis? Or were those diagnoses modified in such a way as to bring them into accord with the circumstances of the pseudopatient's life, as described by him?

As far as I can determine, diagnoses were in no way affected by the relative health of the circumstances of a pseudopatient's life. Rather, the reverse occurred: the perception of his circumstances was shaped entirely by the diagnosis. A clear example of such translation is found in the case of a pseudopatient who had had a close relationship with his mother but was rather remote from his father during his early childhood. During adolescence and beyond, however, his father became a close friend, while his relationship with his mother cooled. His present relationship with his wife was characteristically close and warm. Apart from occasional angry exchanges, friction was minimal. The children had rarely been spanked. Surely there is nothing especially pathological about such a history. Indeed, many readers may see a similar pattern in their own experiences, with no markedly deleterious consequences. Observe, however, how such a history was translated in the psychopathological context, this from the case summary prepared after the patient was discharged.

> This white 39-year-old male... manifests a long history of considerable ambivalence in close relationships, which begins in early childhood. A warm relationship with his mother cools during his adolescence. A distant relationship to his father is described as becoming very intense. Affective stability is absent. His attempts to control emotionality with his wife and children are punctuated by angry outbursts and, in the case of the children, spankings. And while he says that he has several good friends, one senses considerable ambivalence embedded in those relationships also....

The facts of the case were unintentionally distorted by the staff to achieve consistency with a popular theory of the dynamics of a schizophrenic reaction (*15*). Nothing of an ambivalent nature had been described in relations with parents, spouse, or friends. To the extent that ambivalence could be inferred, it was probably not greater than is found in all human relationships. It is true the pseudopatient's relationships with his parents changed over time, but in the ordinary context that would hardly be remarkable—indeed, it might very well be expected. Clearly, the meaning ascribed to his verbalizations (that is, ambivalence, affective instability) was determined by the diagnosis: schizophrenia. An entirely different meaning would have been ascribed if it were know that the man was "normal."

All pseudopatients took extensive notes publicly. Under ordinary circumstances, such behavior would have raised questions in the minds of observers, as, in fact, it did among patients. Indeed, it seemed so certain that the notes would elicit suspicion that elaborate precautions were taken to remove them from the ward each day. But the precautions proved needless. The closest any staff member came to questioning these notes occurred when one pseudopatient asked his physician what kind of medication he was receiving and began to write down the response. "You needn't write it," he was told gently. "If you have trouble remembering, just ask me again."

If no questions were asked of the pseudopatients, how was their writing interpreted? Nursing records for three patients indicate that the writing was seen as an aspect of their pathological behavior. "Patient engages in writing behavior" was the daily nursing comment on one of the pseudopatients who was never questioned about his writing. Given that the patient is in the hospital, he must be psychologically disturbed. And given that he is disturbed, continuous writing must be a behavioral manifestation of that disturbance, perhaps a subset of the compulsive behaviors that are sometimes correlated with schizophrenia.

One tacit characteristic of psychiatric diagnosis is that it locates the sources of aberration within the individual and only rarely within the complex of stimuli that surrounds him. Consequently, behaviors that are stimulated by the environment are commonly misattributed to the patient's disorder. For example, one kindly nurse found a pseudopatient pacing the long hospital corridors. "Nervous, Mr. X?" she asked. "No, bored," he said.

The notes kept by pseudopatients are full of patient behaviors that were misinterpreted by well-intentioned staff. Often enough, a patient would go "berserk" because he had, wittingly or unwittingly, been mistreated by, say, an attendant. A nurse coming upon the scene would rarely inquire even cursorily into the environmental stimuli of the patient's behavior. Rather, she assumed that his upset derived from his pathology, not from his present interactions with other staff members. Occasionally, the staff might assume that the patient's family (especially when they had recently visited) or other patients had stimulated the outburst. But never were the staff found to assume that one of themselves or the structure of the hospital had anything to do with a patient's behavior. One psychiatrist pointed to a group of patients who were sitting outside the cafeteria entrance half an hour before lunchtime. To a group of young residents he indicated that such behavior was characteristic of the oral-acquisitive nature of the syndrome. It seemed not to occur to him that there were very few things to anticipate in a psychiatric hospital besides eating.

A psychiatric label has a life and an influence of its own. Once the impression has been formed that the patient is schizophrenic, the expectation is that he will continue to be schizophrenic. When a sufficient amount of time has passed, during which the patient has done nothing bizarre, he is considered to be in remission and available for discharge. But the label endures beyond discharge, with the uncon-firmed expectation that he will behave as a schizophrenic again. Such labels, conferred by mental health professionals, are as influential on the patient as they are on his relatives and friends, and it should not surprise anyone that the diagnosis acts on all of them as a self-fulfilling prophecy. Eventually, the patient himself accepts the diagnosis, with all of its surplus meanings and expectations, and behaves accord-ingly (5).

The inferences to be made from these matters are quite simple. Much as Zigler and Phillips have demonstrated that there is enormous overlap in the symptoms presented by patients who have been variously diagnosed (16), so there is enormous overlap in the behaviors of the sane and the insane. The sane are not "sane" all of the time. We lose our tempers "for no good reason." We are occasionally depressed or anxious, again for no good reason. And we may find it difficult to get along with one or another person—again for no reason that we can specify. Similarly, the insane are not always insane. Indeed, it was the impression of the pseudopatients while living with them that they were sane for long periods of time—that the bizarre behaviors upon which their diagnoses were allegedly predicated constituted only a small fraction of their total behavior. If it makes no sense to label ourselves perma-nently depressed on the basis of an occasional depression, then it takes better evidence than is presently available to label all patients insane or schizophrenic on the basis of bizarre behaviors or cognitions. It seems more useful, as Mischel (17) has pointed out, to limit our discussions to *behaviors*, the stimuli that provoke them, and their correlates.

It is not known why powerful impressions of personality traits, such as "crazy" or "insane," arise. Conceivably, when the origins of and stimuli that give rise to a behavior are remote or unknown, or when the behavior strikes us as immutable, trait labels regarding the *behaver* arise. When, on the other hand, the origins and stimuli are known and available, discourse is limited to the behavior itself. Thus, I may hallucinate because I am sleeping, or I may hallucinate because I have in-gested a peculiar drug. These are termed sleep-induced hallucinations, or dreams, and drug-induced hallucinations, respectively. But when the stimuli to my halluci-nations are unknown, that is called craziness, or schizophrenia—as if that inference were somehow as illuminating as the others.

The Experience of Psychiatric Hospitalization

The term "mental illness" is of recent origin. It was coined by people who were humane in their inclinations and who wanted very much to raise the station of (and the public's sympathies toward) the psychologically disturbed from that of witches and "crazies" to one that was akin to the physically ill. And they were at least partially successful, for the treatment of the mentally ill *has* improved considerably over the years. But while treatment has improved, it is doubtful that people really regard the mentally ill in the same way that they view the physically ill. A broken leg is something one recovers from, but mental illness allegedly endures forever (18). A broken leg does not threaten the observer, but a crazy schizophrenic? There is by now a host of evidence that attitudes toward the mentally ill are characterized by fear, hostility, aloofness, suspicion, and dread (19). The mentally ill are society's lepers.

That such attitudes infect the general population is perhaps not surprising, only upsetting. But that they affect the professionals—attendants, nurses, physicians, psychologists, and social workers—who treat and deal with the mentally ill is more disconcerting, both because such attitudes are self-evidently pernicious and because they are unwitting. Most mental health professionals would insist that they are sympathetic toward the mentally ill, that they are neither avoidant nor hostile. But it is more likely that an exquisite ambivalence characterizes their relations with psychiatric patients, such that their avowed impulses are only part of their entire attitude. Negative attitudes are there too and can easily be detected. Such attitudes should not surprise us. They are the natural offspring of the labels patients wear and the places in which they are found.

Consider the structure of the typical psychiatric hospital. Staff and patients are strictly segregated. Staff have their own living space, including their dining facilities, bathrooms, and assembly places. The glass quarters that contain the professional staff, which the pseudopatients came to call "the cage," sit out on every dayroom. The staff emerge primarily for caretaking purposes—to give medication, to conduct a therapy or group meeting, to instruct or reprimand a patient. Otherwise, staff keep to themselves, almost as if the disorder that afflicts their charges is somehow catching.

So much is patient-staff segregation the rule that, for four public hospitals in which an attempt was made to measure the degree to which staff and patients mingle, it was necessary to use "time out of the staff cage" as the operational measure. While it was not the case that all time spent out of the cage was spent mingling with patients (attendants, for example, would occasionally emerge to watch television in the dayroom), it was the only way in which one could gather reliable data on time for measuring.

The average amount of time spent by attendants outside of the cage was 11.3 percent (range, 3 to 52 percent). This figure does not represent only time spent mingling with patients, but also includes time spent on such chores as folding laundry, supervising patients while they shave, directing ward clean-up, and sending patients to off-ward activities. It was the relatively rare attendant who spent time talking with patients or playing games with them. It proved impossible to obtain a "percent mingling time" for nurses, since the amount of time they spent out of the cage was too brief. Rather, we counted instances of emergence from the cage. On the average, daytime nurses emerged from the cage 11.5 times per shift, including instances when they left the ward entirely (range, 4 to 39 times). Late afternoon and night nurses were even less available, emerging on the average 9.4 times per shift (range, 4 to 41 times). Data on early morning nurses, who arrived usually after midnight and departed at 8 a.m., are not available because patients were asleep during most of this period.

Physicians, especially psychiatrists, were even less available. They were rarely seen on the wards. Quite commonly, they would be seen only when they arrived and departed, with the remaining time being spent in their offices or in the cage. On the average, physicians emerged on the ward 6.7 times per day (range, 1 to 17 times). It proved difficult to make an accurate estimate in this regard, since physicians often maintained hours that allowed them to come and go at different times.

The hierarchical organization of the psychiatric hospital has been commented on before (20), but the latent meaning of that kind of organization is worth noting again. Those with the most power have least to do with patients, and those with the least power are most involved with them. Recall, however, that the acquisition of role-appropriate behaviors occurs mainly through the observation of others, with the most powerful having the most influence. Consequently, it is understandable that attendants not only spend more time with patients than do any other members of the staff—that is required by their station in the hierarchy—but also, insofar as they learn from their superiors' behavior, spend as little time with patients as they can. Attendants are seen mainly in the cage, which is where the models, the action, and the power are.

I turn now to a different set of studies, these dealing with staff response to patient-initiated contact. It has long been known that the amount of time a person spends with you can be an index of your significance to him. If he initiates and maintains eye contact, there is reason to believe that he is considering your requests and needs. If he pauses to chat or actually stops and talks, there is added reason to infer that he is individuating you. In four hospitals, the pseudopatient approached the staff member with a request which took the following form: "Pardon me, Mr. [or Dr. or Mrs.] X, could you tell me when I will be eligible for grounds privileges?" (or "... when I will be presented at the staff meeting?" or "... when I am likely to be discharged?"). While the content of the question varied according to the appropriateness of the target and the pseudopatient's (apparent) current needs the form was always a courteous and relevant request for information. Care was taken never to approach a particular member of the staff more than once a day, lest the staff member become suspicious or irritated. In examining these data, remember that the behavior of the pseudopatients was neither bizarre nor disruptive. One could indeed engage in good conversation with them.

The data for these experiments are shown in Table 1, separately for physicians (column 1) and for nurses and attendants (column 2). Minor differences between these four institutions were overwhelmed by the degree to which staff avoided continuing contacts that patients had initiated. By far, their most common response consisted of either a brief response to the question, offered while they were "on the move" and with head averted, or no response at all.

The encounter frequently took the following bizarre form: (pseudopatient) "Pardon me, Dr. X. Could you tell me when I am eligible for grounds privileges?" (physician) "Good morning, Dave. How are you today?" (Moves off without waiting for a response.)

It is instructive to compare these data with data recently obtained at Stanford University. It has been alleged that large and eminent universities are characterized by faculty who are so busy that they have no time for students. For this comparison,

TABLE 1. Self-Initiated Contact by Pseudopatients with Psychiatrists and Nurses and Attendants, Compared to Contact with Other Groups

| Contact | Psychiatric hospitals | | University campus (nonmedical) | University medical center | | |
| | | | | Physicians | | |
	(1) Psychiatrists	(2) Nurses and attendants	(3) Faculty	(4) "Looking for a psychiatrist"	(5) "Looking for an internist"	(6) No additional comment
Responses						
Moves on, head averted (%)	71	88	0	0	0	0
Makes eye contact (%)	23	10	0	11	0	0
Pauses and chats (%)	2	2	0	11	0	10
Stops and talks (%)	4	0.5	100	78	100	90
Mean number of questions answered (out of 6)	*	*	6	3.8	4.8	4.5
Respondents (No.)	13	47	14	18	15	10
Attempts (No.)	185	1283	14	18	15	10

*Not applicable.

a young lady approached individual faculty members who seemed to be walking purposefully to some meeting or teaching engagement and asked them the following six questions.

1. "Pardon me, could you direct me to Encina Hall?" (at the medical school: " . . . to the Clinical Research Center?").
2. "Do you know where Fish Annex is?" (there is no Fish Annex at Stanford).
3. "Do you teach here?"
4. "How does one apply for admission to the college?" (at the medical school: " . . . to the medical school?").
5. "Is it difficult to get in?"
6. "Is there financial aid?"

Without exception, as can be seen in Table 1 (column 3), all of the questions were answered. No matter how rushed they were, all respondents not only maintained eye contact, but stopped to talk. Indeed, many of the respondents went out of their way to direct or take the questioner to the office she was seeking, to try to locate "Fish Annex," or to discuss with her the possibilities of being admitted to the university.

Similar data, also shown in Table 1 (column 4, 5, and 6), were obtained in the hospital. Here too, the young lady came prepared with six questions. After the first question, however, she remarked to 18 of her respondents (column 4), "I'm looking for a psychiatrist," and to 15 others (column 5), "I'm looking for an internist." Ten other respondents received no inserted comment (column 6). The general degree of cooperative responses is considerably higher for these university groups than it was for pseudopatients in psychiatric hospitals. Even so, differences are apparent within the medical school setting. Once having indicated that she was looking for a psychiatrist, the degree of cooperation elicited was less than when she sought an internist.

Powerlessness and Depersonalization

Eye contact and verbal contact reflect concern and individuation; their absence, avoidance and depersonalization. The data I have presented do not do justice to the rich daily encounters that grew up around matters of depersonalization and avoidance. I have records of patients who were beaten by staff for the sin of having initiated verbal contact. During my own experience, for example, one patient was beaten in the presence of other patients for having approached an attendant and told him, "I like you." Occasionally, punishment meted out to patients for misdemeanors seemed so excessive that it could not be justified by the most radical interpretations of psychiatric canon. Nevertheless, they appeared to go unquestioned. Tempers were often short. A patient who had not heard a call for medication would be roundly excoriated, and the morning attendants would often wake patients with, "Come on, you m_____f_____s, out of bed!"

Neither anecdotal nor "hard" data can convey the overwhelming sense of powerlessness which invades the individual as he is continually exposed to the depersonalization of the psychiatric hospital. It hardly matters *which* psychiatric hospital—the excellent public ones and the very plush private hospital were better than the rural and shabby ones in this regard, but, again, the features that psychiatric hospitals had in common overwhelmed by far their apparent differences.

Powerlessness was evident everywhere. The patient is deprived of many of his legal rights by dint of his psychiatric commitment (21). He is shorn of credibility by virtue of his psychiatric label. His freedom of movement is restricted. He cannot initiate contact with the staff, but may only respond to such overtures as they make. Personal privacy is minimal. Patient quarters and possessions can be entered and examined by any staff member, for whatever reason. His personal history and anguish is available to any staff member (often including the "grey lady" and "candy striper" volunteer) who chooses to read his folder, regardless of their therapeutic relationship to him. His personal hygiene and waste evacuation are often monitored. The water closets may have no doors.

At times, depersonalization reached such proportions that pseudopatients had the sense that they were invisible, or at least unworthy of account. Upon being admitted, I and other pseudopatients took the initial physical examinations in a semipublic room, where staff members went about their own business as if we were not there.

On the ward, attendants delivered verbal and occasionally serious physical abuse to patients in the presence of other observing patients, some of whom (the pseudopatients) were writing it all down. Abusive behavior, on the other hand, terminated quite abruptly when other staff members were known to be coming. Staff are credible witnesses. Patients are not.

A nurse unbuttoned her uniform to adjust her brassiere in the presence of an entire ward of viewing men. One did not have the sense that she was being seductive. Rather, she didn't notice us. A group of staff persons might point to a patient in the dayroom and discuss him animatedly, as if he were not there.

One illuminating instance of depersonalization and invisibility occurred with regard to medications. All told, the pseudopatients were administered nearly 2100 pills, including Elavil, Stelazine, Compazine, and Thorazine, to name but a few. (That such a variety of medications should have been administered to patients presenting identical symptoms is itself worthy of note.) Only two were swallowed. The rest were either pocketed or deposited in the toilet. The pseudopatients were not alone in this. Although I have no precise records on how many patients rejected their medications, the pseudopatients frequently found the medications of other patients in the toilet before they deposited their own. As long as they were cooperative, their behavior and the pseudopatients' own in this matter, as in other important matters, went unnoticed throughout.

Reactions to such depersonalization among pseudopatients were intense. Although they had come to the hospital as participant observers and were fully aware that they did not "belong," they nevertheless found themselves caught up in and fighting the process of depersonalization. Some examples: a graduate student in psychology asked his wife to bring his textbooks to the hospital so he could "catch up on his homework"—this despite the elaborate precautions taken to conceal his professional association. The same student, who had trained for quite some time to get into the hospital, and who had looked forward to the experience, "remembered" some drag races that he had wanted to see on the weekend and insisted that he be discharged by that time. Another pseudopatient attempted a romance with a nurse. Subsequently, he informed the staff that he was applying for admission to graduate school in psychology and was very likely to be admitted, since a graduate professor was one of his regular hospital visitors. The same person began to engage in psychotherapy with other patients—all of this as a way of becoming a person in an impersonal environment.

The Sources of Depersonalization

What are the origins of depersonalization? I have already mentioned two. First are attitudes held by all of us toward the mentally ill—including those who treat them—attitudes characterized by fear, distrust, and horrible expectations on the one hand, and benevolent intentions on the other. Our ambivalence leads, in this instance as in others, to avoidance.

Second, and not entirely separate, the hierarchical structure of the psychiatric hospital facilitates depersonalization. Those who are at the top have least to do with patients, and their behavior inspires the rest of the staff. Average daily contact with psychiatrists, psychologists, residents, and physicians combined ranged from 3.9 to 25.1 minutes, with an overall mean of 6.8 (six pseudopatients over a total of 129 days of hospitalization). Included in this average are time spent in the admissions interview, ward meetings in the presence of a senior staff member, group and individual psychotherapy contacts, case presentation conferences, and discharge meetings. Clearly, patients do not spend much time in interpersonal contact with doctoral staff. And doctoral staff serve as models for nurses and attendants.

There are probably other sources. Psychiatric installations are presently in serious financial straits. Staff shortages are pervasive, staff time at a premium. Something has to give, and that something is patient contact. Yet, while financial stresses are realities, too much can be made of them. I have the impression that the psychological forces that result in depersonalization are much stronger than the fiscal ones and that the addition of more staff would not correspondingly improve patient care in this regard. The incidence of staff meetings and the enormous amount of record-keeping on patients, for example, have not been as substantially reduced as has patient contact. Priorities exist, even during hard times. Patient contact is not a significant priority in the traditional psychiatric hospital, and fiscal pressures do not account for this. Avoidance and depersonalization may.

Heavy reliance upon psychotropic medication tacitly contributes to depersonalization by convincing staff that treatment is indeed being conducted and that further patient contact may not be necessary. Even here, however, caution needs to be exercised in understanding the role of psychotropic drugs. If patients were powerful rather than powerless, if they were viewed as interesting individuals rather than diagnostic entities, if they were socially significant rather than social lepers, if their anguish truly and wholly compelled our sympathies and concerns, would we not *seek* contact with them, despite the availability of medications? Perhaps for the pleasure of it all?

The Consequences of Labeling and Depersonalization

Whenever the ratio of what is known to what needs to be known approaches zero, we tend to invent "knowledge" and assume that we understand more than we actually do. We seem unable to acknowledge that we simply don't know. The needs for diagnosis and remediation of behavioral and emotional problems are enormous. But rather than acknowledge that we are just embarking on understanding, we continue to label patients "schizophrenic," "manic-depressive," and "insane," as if in those words we had captured the essence of understanding. The facts of the matter are that we have known for a long time that diagnoses are often not useful or reliable, but we have nevertheless continued to use them. We now know that we cannot distinguish insanity from sanity. It is depressing to consider how that information will be used.

Not merely depressing, but frightening. How many people. one wonders, are sane but not recognized as such in our psychiatric institutions? How many have been needlessly stripped of their privileges of citizenship, from the right to vote and drive to that of handling their own accounts? How many have feigned insanity in order to avoid the criminal consequences of their behavior, and, conversely, how many would rather stand trial than live interminably in a psychiatric hospital—but are wrongly thought to be mentally ill? How many have been stigmatized by well-intentioned, but nevertheless erroneous, diagnoses? On the last point, recall again that a "type 2 error" in psychiatric diagnosis does not have the same consequences it does in medical diagnosis. A diagnosis of cancer that has been found to be in error is cause for celebration. But psychiatric diagnoses are rarely found to be in error. The label sticks, a mark of inadequacy forever.

Finally, how many patients might be "sane" outside the psychiatric hospital but seem insane in it—not because craziness resides in them, as it were, but because they are responding to a bizarre setting, one that may be unique to institutions which harbor nether people? Goffman (4) calls the process of socialization to such institutions "mortification"—an apt metaphor that includes the processes of depersonalization that have been described here. And while it is impossible to know whether the pseudopatients' responses to these processes are characteristic of all inamtes—they were, after all, not real patients—it is difficult to believe that these processes of socialization to a psychiatric hospital provide useful attitudes or habits of response for living in the "real world."

Summary and Conclusions

It is clear that we cannot distinguish the sane from the insane in psychiatric hospitals. The hospital itself imposes a special environment in which the meanings of behavior can easily be misunderstood. The consequences to patients hospitalized in such an environment—the powerlessness, depersonalization, segregation, mortification, and self-labeling—seem undoubtedly countertherapeutic.

I do not, even now, understand this problem well enough to perceive solutions. But two matters seem to have some promise. The first concerns the proliferation of community mental health facilities, of crisis intervention centers, of the human potential movement, and of behavior therapies that, for all of their own problems, tend to avoid psychiatric labels, to focus on specific problems and behaviors, and to retain the individual in a relatively non-pejorative environment. Clearly, to the extent that we refrain from sending the distressed to insane places, our impressions of them are less likely to be distorted. (The risk of distorted perceptions, it seems to me, is always present, since we are much more sensitive to an individual's behaviors and verbalizations than we are to the subtle contextual stimuli that often promote them. At issue here is a matter of magnitude. And, as I have shown, the magnitude of distortion is exceedingly high in the extreme context that is a psychiatric hospital.)

The second matter that might prove promising speaks to the need to increase the sensitivity of mental health workers and researchers to the *Catch 22* position of psychiatric patients. Simply reading materials in this area will be of help to some such workers and researchers. For others, directly experiencing the impact of psychiatric hospitalization will be of enormous use. Clearly, further research into the social psychology of such total institutions will both facilitate treatment and deepen understanding.

I and the other pseudopatients in the psychiatric setting had distinctly negative reactions. We do not pretend to describe the subjective experiences of true patients. Theirs may be different from ours, particularly with the passage of time and the necessary process of adaptation to one's environment. But we can and do speak to the relatively more objective indices of treatment within the hospital. It could be a mistake, and a very unfortunate one, to consider that what happened to us derived from malice or stupidity on the part of the staff. Quite the contrary, our overwhelming impression of them was of people who really cared, who were committed and who were uncommonly intelligent. Where they failed, as they sometimes did painfully, it would be more accurate to attribute those failures to the environment in which they, too, found themselves than to personal callousness. Their perceptions and behavior were controlled by the situation, rather than being motivated by a malicious disposition. In a more benign environment, one that was less attached to global diagnosis, their behaviors and judgments might have been more benign and effective.

References and Notes

1. P. Ash, *J. Abnorm. Soc. Psychol.* 44, 272 (1949); A. T. Beck, *Amer. J. Psychiat.* 119, 210 (1962); A. T. Boisen, *Psychiatry* 2, 233 (1938); N. Kreitman, *J. Ment. Sci.* 107, 876 (1961); N. Kreitman, P. Sainsbury, J. Morrisey, J. Towers, J. Scrivener, *ibid.*, p. 887; H. O. Schmitt and C. P. Fonda, *J. Abnorm. Soc. Psychol.* 52, 262 (1956); W. Seeman, *J. Nerv. Ment. Dis.* 118, 541 (1953). For an analysis of these artifacts and summaries of the disputes, see J. Zubin, *Annu. Rev. Psychol.* 18, 373 (1967); L. Phillips and J. G. Draguns, *ibid.* 22, 447 (1971).
2. R. Benedict, *J. Gen. Psychol.* 10, 59 (1934).
3. See in this regard H. Becker, *Outsiders: Studies in the Sociology of Deviance* (Free Press, New York, 1963); B. M. Braginsky, D. D. Braginsky, K. Ring, *Methods of Madness: The Mental Hospital as a Last Resort* (Holt, Rinehart & Winston, New York, 1969); G. M. Crocetti and P. V. Lemkau, *Amer. Sociol. Rev.* 30, 577 (1965); E. Goffman, *Behavior* ·

in Public Places (Free Press, New York, 1964); R. D. Laing, *The Divided Self: A Study of Sanity and Madness* (Quadrangle, Chicago, 1960); D. L. Phillips, *Amer. Sociol. Rev.* 28, 963 (1963); T. R. Sarbin, *Psychol. Today* 6, 18 (1972); E. Schur, *Amer. J. Sociol.* 75, 309 (1969); T. Szasz, *Law, Liberty and Psychiatry* (Macmillan, New York, 1963); *The Myth of Mental Illness: Foundations of a Theory of Mental Illness* (Hoeber-Harper, New York, 1963). For a critique of some of these views, see W. R. Gove, *Amer. Sociol. Rev.* 35, 873 (1970).

4. E. Goffman, *Asylums* (Doubleday, Garden City, N. Y., 1961).

5. T. J. Scheff, *Being Mentally Ill: A Sociological Theory* (Aldine, Chicago, 1966).

6. Data from a ninth pseudopatient are not incorporated in this report because, although his sanity went undetected, he falsified aspects of his personal history, including his marital status and parental relationships. His experimental behaviors therefore were not identical to those of the other pseudopatients.

7. A. Barry, *Bellevue Is a State of Mind* (Harcourt Brace Jovanovich, New York, 1971); I. Belknap, *Human Problems of a State Mental Hospital* (McGraw-Hill, New York, 1956); W. Caudill, F. C. Redlich, H. R. Gilmore, E. B. Brody, *Amer. J. Orthopsychiat.* 22, 314 (1952); A. R. Goldman, R. H. Bohr, T. A. Steinberg, *Prof. Psychol.* 1, 427 (1970); unauthored, *Roche Report* 1 (No. 13), 8 (1971).

8. Beyond the personal difficulties that the pseudopatient is likely to experience in the hospital, there are legal and social ones that, combined, require considerable attention before entry. For example, once admitted to a psychiatric institution, it is difficult, if not impossible, to be discharged on short notice, state law to the contrary notwithstanding. I was not sensitive to these difficulties at the outset of the project, nor to the personal and situational emergencies that can arise, but later a writ of habeas corpus was prepared for each of the entering pseudopatients and an attorney was kept "on call" during every hospitalization. I am grateful to John Kaplan and Robert Bartels for legal advice and assistance in these matters.

9. However distasteful such concealment is, it was a necessary first step to examining these questions. Without concealment, there would have been no way to know how valid these experiences were; nor was there any way of knowing whether whatever detections occurred were a tribute to the diagnostic acumen of the staff or to the hospital's rumor network. Obviously, since my concerns are general ones that cut across individual hospitals and staffs, I have respected their anonymity and have eliminated clues that might lead to their identification.

10. Interestingly, of the 12 admissions, 11 were diagnosed as schizophrenic and one, with the identical symptomatology, as manic-depressive psychosis. This diagnosis has a more favorable prognosis, and it was given by the only private hospital in our sample. On the relations between social class and psychiatric diagnosis, see A. deB. Hollingshead and F. C. Redlich, *Social Class and Mental Illness: A Community Study* (Wiley, New York, 1958).

11. It is possible, of course, that patients have quite broad latitudes in diagnosis and therefore are inclined to call many people sane, even those whose behavior is patently aberrant. However, although we have no hard data on this matter, it was our distinct impression that this was not the case. In many instances, patients not only singled us out for attention, but came to imitate our behaviors and styles.

12. J. Cumming and E. Cumming, *Community Ment. Health* 1, 135 (1965); A. Farina and K. Ring, *J. Abnorm. Psychol.* 70, 47 (1965); H. E. Freeman and O. G. Simmons, *The Mental Patient Comes Home* (Wiley, New York, 1963); W. J. Johannsen, *Ment. Hygiene* 53, 218 (1969); A. S. Linsky, *Soc. Psychiat.* 5, 166 (1970).

13. S. E. Asch, *J. Abnorm. Soc. Psychol.* 41, 258 (1946); *Social Psychology* (Prentice-Hall, New York, 1952).
14. See also I. N. Mensh and J. Wishner, *J. Personality* 16, 188 (1947); J. Wishner, *Psychol. Rev.* 67, 96 (1960); J. S. Bruner and R. Tagiuri, in *Handbook of Social Psychology*, G. Lindzey. Ed. (Addison-Wesley, Cambridge, Mass., 1954), vol. 2, pp. 634–654; J. S. Bruner, D. Shapiro, R. Tagiuri, in *Person Perception and Interpersonal Behavior.* R. Tagiuri and L. Petrullo, Eds. (Standford Univ. Press, Stanford, Calif., 1958), pp. 277–288.
15. For an example of a similar self-fulfilling prophecy, in this instance dealing with the "central" trait of intelligence, se R. Rosenthal and L. Jacobson, *Pygmalion in the Classroom* (Holt, Rinehart & Winston, New York, 1968).
16. E. Zigler and L. Phillips, *J. Abnorm. Soc. Psychol.* 63, 69 (1961). See also R. K. Freudenberg and J. P. Robertson, *A.M.A. Arch. Neurol. Psychiatr.* 76, 14 (1956).
17. W. Mischel, *Personality and Assessment* (Wiley, New York, 1968).
18. The most recent and unfortunate instance of this tenet is that of Senator Thomas Eagleton.
19. T. R. Sarbin and J. C. Mancuso, *J. Clin. Consult. Psychol.* 35, 159 (1970); T. R. Sarbin, *ibid.* 31, 447 (1967); J. C. Nunnally, Jr., *Popular Conceptions of Mental Health* (Holt, Rinehart & Winston, New York, 1961).
20. A. H. Stanton and M. S. Schwartz, *The Mental Hospital: A Study of Institutional Participation in Psychiatric Illness and Treatment* (Basic, New York, 1954).
21. D. B. Wexler and S. E. Scoville, *Ariz. Law Rev.* 13, 1 (1971).
22. I thank W. Mischel, E. Orne, and M. S. Rosenhan for comments on an earlier draft of this manuscript.

9

More on Pseudoscience
in Science and the
Case for Psychiatric Diagnosis

Robert L. Spitzer

In January 1973, *Science*, the official journal of the Association for the Advancement of Science, reported a small study with a catchy title—"On Being Sane in Insane Places."[1] This was no ordinary study that merely added further knowledge to our understanding of psychiatric disorders; this study challenged basic psychiatric concepts and practices. If the author, D. L. Rosenhan, a professor of psychology and law, is correct, the results clearly show that psychiatrists are unable to distinguish the "sane" from the "insane" in psychiatric hospitals, and that the traditional psychiatric classification of mental disorders is unreliable, invalid, and harmful to the welfare of patients.

Partly because of the prestige of the journal in which it first appeared, and more importantly, because it said something that many were delighted to hear, the study was widely acclaimed in the popular news media (*New York Times*, Jan 20, 1974; *Saturday Review of Science*, March 1, 1973, pp. 55–56; *Newsweek*, Jan 29, 1973, p. 46). As a consequence, this single study is probably better known to the lay public than any other study in the area of psychiatry in the last decade.

Although the study has been attacked by many mental health professionals,[2-9] most articles that refer to the study have accepted its conclusions and implications.[10-24] Furthermore, two editorials in *The Journal of the Americal Medical Association* were devoted to an endorsement of the study's findings.[13-14]

The study has probably had its greatest impact in the field of psychology. Of 31 recently published psychology textbooks, 15 cite Rosenhan's article. Fully 12 of these texts[25-36] present the results uncritically with only five[27,35,37-39] even acknowledging controversy over the study's conclusions. Only three[37,39] question

SOURCE: *Archives of General Psychiatry* 33 (April 1976): 459–70. This is an expanded version of an article that originally appeared in the *Journal of Abnormal Psychology* 84 (1975): 442–52. Copyright © 1975 by the American Psychological Association. Reprinted by permission of the publisher and the author.

its results. The implication is clear: large numbers of undergraduate and graduate psychology students are being taught to accept the conclusions of this study.

Although there have been references to Rosenhan's study in articles appearing in well-known psychiatric journals, none has presented a thorough critique of this study. Such a critique would be useful, not only for what it tells us about Rosenhan's remarkable study, but also for clarifying some of the fundamental issues regarding psychiatric diagnosis. This article is such an attempt, and presents an elaboration of my contribution to a symposium that appeared in *The Journal of Abnormal Psychology,*[40-45] which was devoted to exploring the strengths and weaknesses of the Rosenhan study. In addition, this article includes a critique of Rosenhan's contribution to the symposium, an article entitled, "The Contextual Nature of Psychiatric Diagnosis,[43]" in which he responded to the critiques provided by the participants in the symposium.

Rosenhan stated the basic issue in his original article as follows:

> Do the salient characteristics that lead to diagnoses reside in the patients themselves or in the environments and contexts in which observers find them? From Bleuler, through Kretchmer, through the formulators of the recently revised *Diagnostic and Statistical Manual* of the American Psychiatric Association, the belief has been strong that patients present symptoms, that those symptoms can be categorized, and, implicitly, that the sane are distinguishable from the insane. More recently, however, this belief has been questioned. Based in part on theoretical and anthropological considerations, but also on philosophical, legal and therapeutic ones, the view has grown that psychological categorization of mental illness is useless at best and downright harmful, misleading, and pejorative at worst. Psychiatric diagnoses, in this view, are in the minds of the observers and are not valid summaries of characteristics displayed by the observed.[1(p 25 l)]

Rosenhan proposed that an adequate method to study this question was for normal people who had never had symptoms of serious psychiatric disorders to be admitted to psychiatric hospitals "and then determining whether they were discovered to be sane." Therefore, eight "sane" people, or "pseudopatients," gained admission to 12 different hospitals, each with a single complaint of hearing voices. On admission to the psychiatric ward, each pseudopatient ceased simulating any symptoms of abnormality.

The diagnostic results were as follows:

> Admitted, except in one case, with a diagnosis of schizophrenia, each was discharged with a diagnosis of schizophrenia "in remission." The label "in remission" should in no way be dismissed as a formality, for at no time during any hospitalization had any question been raised about any pseudopatient's simulation."[1(p252)]

(It should be noted that while preparing my original critique, personal communication with Rosenhan indicated that "in remission" referred to use of that term or one of its equivalents, such as "recovered" or "no longer ill," and that it also applied to the one patient who was given the diagnosis of manic-depressive psychosis. Thus, *all* of the patients were apparently discharged "in remission." However, in his 1975 article,[43] he notes that only eight of the patients were discharged "in remission" and that one was noted as "asymptomatic" and three as "improved."The discrepancy between the 1973 and 1975 articles is puzzling but does not substantially alter my interpretation of the results.)

Rosenhan concluded, "It is clear that we cannot distinguish the sane from the insane in psychiatric hospitals."[1p257] According to him, what is needed is the avoidance of "global diagnosis" as exemplified by such diagnoses as schizophrenia or manic-depressive psychosis, and attention should be directed instead to "behaviors, the stimuli that provoke them, and their correlates."

The Central Question

One hardly knows where to begin. Let us first acknowledge the potential importance of the study's central research question. Surely, if psychiatric diagnoses are, to quote Rosenhan, "only in the minds of the observers," and do not reflect any characteristics inherent in the patient, then they obviously can be of no use in helping patients. (It is remarkable that the original article, which was concerned with the validity of psychiatric diagnosis, did not contain a single sentence about the intended purposes of psychiatric diagnosis—more of this later.) However, the study immediately becomes hopelessly confused when Rosenhan suggests that his research question can be answered by studying whether or not the "sanity" of pseudopatients in a mental hospital can be discovered. Rosenhan, a professor of law and psychology, knows that the terms "sane" and "insane" are legal, not psychiatric, concepts. He knows that no psychiatrist makes a *diagnosis* of "sanity" or "insanity," and that the true meaning of these terms, which varies from state to state, involves the inability to distinguish right from wrong—an issue that is totally irrelevant to this study.

Detecting the Sanity of a Pseudopatient

However, if we are forced to use the terms "insane" (to mean showing signs of serious mental disturbance) and "sane" (the absence of such signs), then clearly there are three possible meanings to the concept of "detecting the sanity" of a pseudopatient who feigns mental illness on entry to a hospital but then acts "normal" throughout his hospital stay. The first is the recognition, *when he is first seen,* that the pseudopatient is feigning insanity as he attempts to gain admission to the hospital. This would be detecting sanity in a sane person simulating insanity. The second would be the recognition, *after* having observed him acting normally during his hospitalization, that the pseudopatient was initially feigning insanity. This would be detecting that the currently sane person never was insane. Finally, the third possible meaning would be the recognition, *during hospitalization,* that the pseudopatient, though initially appearing to be "insane," was no longer showing signs of psychiatric disturbance.

These elementary distinctions of "detecting sanity in the insane" are crucial to properly interpreting the results of Rosenhan's study. The reader is misled by Rosenhan's implication that the first two meanings of detecting the sanity of the pseudopatients, which involve determing the pseudopatient to be a fraud, are at all relevant to the central research question. Further, the true results of his study are obscured because they fail to support the conclusion when the third meaning of detecting sanity is considered, that is, a recognition that after their admissions as "insane," the pseudopatients were not psychiatrically disturbed while in the hospital.

Let us examine these three possible meanings of detecting the sanity of the pseudopatient, their logical relation to the central question of the study, the actual results obtained, and the validity of Rosenhan's conclusions.

The Patient Is No Longer "Insane"

We begin with the third meaning of detecting sanity. It is obvious that if the psychiatrists judged the pseudopatients as seriously disturbed while they acted "normal" in the hospital, this would be strong evidence that their assessments were being influenced by the context in which they were making their examination rather than the actual behavior of the patient. This, after all, is the central research question. (I suspect that many readers will agree with Hunter, who, in a letter to *Science*, pointed out:

> The pseudopatients did *not* behave normally in the hospital. Had their behavior been normal, they would have walked to the nurses' station and said, "Look, I am a normal person who tried to see if I could get into the hospital by behaving in a crazy way or saying crazy things. It worked and I was admitted to the hospital, but now I would like to be discharged from the hopsital.[46])

What were the results? According to Rosenhan, all of the patients were diagnosed at discharge as being "in remission." The meaning of "in remission" is obvious: it means without signs of illness. Thus, the psychiatrists apparently recognized that the pseudopatients were, to use Rosenhan's term, "sane." (This would apply to all of the 12 pseudopatients according to the 1973 article and to eight of them according to the 1975 article.) However, lest the reader appreciate the significance of these findings, Rosenhan gives a completely incorrect interpretation: "If the pseudopatient was to be discharged, he must naturally be 'in remission'; but he was not sane, nor, in the institution's view, had he ever been sane."[1p252] Rosenhan's implication is clear—the patient was diagnosed "in remission" not because the psychiatrist correctly assessed the patient's hospital behavior, but only because the patient had to be discharged. Is this interpretation warranted?

I am sure that most readers who are not familiar with the details of psychiatric diagnostic practice assume from Rosenhan's account that it is common for schizophrenic patients to be diagnosed "in remission" when discharged from a hospital; as a matter of fact, this is extremely unusual. The reason is two-fold. First of all, patients with a diagnosis of schizophrenia are rarely completely asymptomatic at discharge. Second, the discharge diagnosis frequently records the diagnostic conditions associated with the *admission* to the hospital without any reference to the condition of the patient at discharge.

Rosenhan does not report any data concerning the discharge diagnoses of the real schizophrenic patients in the 12 hospitals used in his study. However, I can report on the frequency of a discharge diagnosis of schizophrenia "in remission" at my hospital, the New York State Psychiatric Institute, a research, teaching, and community hospital where diagnoses are made in a routine fashion, undoubtedly no differently from the 12 hospitals of Rosenhan's study. I examined the official book that the record room uses to record discharge diagnoses and their statistical codes for all patients. Of more than 300 patients discharged in the year prior to September 1974 with a diagnosis of schizophrenia, not one was diagnosed "in remission." It is only possible to *code* a diagnosis of "in remission" by adding a fifth digit (5) to the four-digit code number for the subtype of schizophrenia (eg, paranoid schizophrenia is coded as 295.3, but paranoid schizophrenia "in remission" is coded as 295.35). I realize, however, that a psychiatrist might *intend* to make a discharge diagnosis of "in remission" but fail to use the fifth digit, so that the official recording of the diagnosis would not reflect his full assessment. I therefore had research assistants read the discharge summaries of the last 100 patients whose discharge was schizophrenia to see how often the terms "in remission," "recovered," "no longer ill," or "asymptomatic" were used, even if not recorded with the fifth digit in the code number. The result was that only one patient, who was diagnosed paranoid schizophrenia, was described in the summary as being "in remission" at discharge. The fifth digit code was not used.

To substantiate my view that the practice at my hospital of rarely giving a discharge diagnosis of schizophrenia "in remission" is not unique, I had a research assistant call the record room librarians of 12 psychiatric hospitals, chosen "catch-as-catch-can." (Rosenhan explains his refusal to identify the 12 hospitals used in his study on the basis of his concern with issues of confidentiality and the potential for ad hominem attack. However, this makes it impossible for anyone at those hospitals or elsewhere to corroborate or challenge his account of how the pseudopatients acted and how they were perceived.) The 12 hospitals used in my ministudy were the following: Long Island Jewish-Hillside Medical Center, New York; Massachusetts General Hospital, Massachusetts; St. Elizabeths' Hospital, Washington, DC; McLean Hospital, Massachusetts; UCLA, Neuropsychiatric Institute, California; Meyer-Manhattan Hospital (Manhattan State), New York; Vermont State Hospital; Medical College of Virginia; Emory University Hospital; Georgia; High Point Hospital, New York; Hudson River State Hospital, New York; and New York Hospital-Cornell Medical Center, Westchester Division. The record room librarians were told that we were interested in knowing their estimate of how often, at their hospitals, schizophrenics were discharged "in remission" (or "no longer ill" or "asymptomatic"). The results were that 11 of the 12 hospitals indicated that the term was either never used or, at most, was used for only a handful of patients in a year. The remaining hospital (a private one) estimated that the term was used in roughly 7% of the discharge diagnoses.

This leaves us with the conclusion that the pseudopatients were given a discharge diagnosis (All 12 of them? Eight of them?) that is rarely given to real patients with an admission diagnosis of schizophrenia. Therefore, the diagnoses given to the pseudopatients *were* a function of the patients' behaviors and not of the setting (psychiatric hospital) in which the diagnoses were made. In fact, a moment's reflection may cause many a reader familiar with usual diagnostic practice to marvel that so many psychiatrists acted so rationally as to use at discharge precisely the same diagnostic category, "in remission," that is rarely used with real patients. In any case, the data as reported by Rosenhan contradict his conclusions.

It is not only in his discharge diagnosis that the psychiatrist had an opportunity to assess the patient's true condition incorrectly. In the admission mental status examination, during a progress note or in his discharge note, that psychiatrist could have described any of the pseudopatients as "still psychotic," "probably still hallucinating but denies it now," "loose associations," or "inappropriate affect." Because Rosenhan had access to all of this material, his failure to report such judgments of continuing serious psychopathology, either in the original study or in his 1975 symposium article,[43] strongly suggests that they were never made.

All pseudopatients took extensive notes publicly to record data on staff and patient behavior. Rosenhan claimed that the nursing records indicated that "the writing was seen as an aspect of their pathological behavior."[K(p 253)] The only datum presented to support this claim is that the daily nursing comment on one of the pseudopatients was "patient engages in writing behavior." Because nursing notes frequently and intentionally comment on nonpathological activities that a patient engages in so that other staff members have some knowledge of how the patient spends his time, this particular nursing note in no way supports Rosenhan's thesis. Once again, the *failure* to provide data regarding instances where normal hospital behavior was categorized as pathological is remarkable. The closest that Rosenhan comes to providing such data is his report of an instance where a kindly nurse asked if a pseudopatient, who was pacing the long hospital corridors because of boredom, was "nervous." It was, after all, a question and not a final judgment.

Let us know examine the other two meanings of detecting sanity in the pseudopatients, that is, the recognition that the pseudopatient was a fraud either when he sought admission to the hospital or during his hospital stay, and the relationship of those meanings to the central research question.

Detecting "Sanity" before Admission

Whether or not psychiatrists are able to detect individuals who feign psychiatric symptoms is an interesting question, but it is clearly of no relevance to the issue of whether or not the salient characteristics that lead to diagnoses reside in the patient's behavior or in the minds of the observers. After all, a psychiatrist who believes a pseudopatient who feigns a symptom *is* responding to the pseudopatient's *behavior*. Rosenhan does not blame the psychiatrist for believing the pseudopatient's fake symptom of hallucinations. He blames him for making the diagnosis of schizophrenia. He states:

> The issue is not . . . that the psychiatrist believed him. . . . Neither is it whether the pseudopatient should have been admitted to the psychiatric hospital in the first place. . . . The issue is the diagnostic leap that was made between the single presenting symptom, hallucinations, and the diagnosis, schizophrenia (or, in one case, manic-depressive psychosis). . . . Had the pseudopatients been diagnosed "hallucinating" there would have been no further need to examine the diagnostic issue. The diagnosis of hallucinations implies only that: no more. The presence of hallucinations does not itself define the presence of "schizophrenia." And schizophrenia may or may not include hallucinations.[47(pp 366, 367)]

Let us see. Unfortunately, as judged by many of the letters to *Science* commenting on the study,[6] many readers, including psychiatrists, accepted Rosenhan's thesis that it was irrational for the psychiatrists to have made an initial diagnosis of schizophrenia *as the most likely condition* on the basis of a single symptom. In my judgment, these readers were wrong. Their acceptance of Rosenhan's thesis was aided by the content of the pseudopatients' auditory hallucinations, which were voices that said "empty," "hollow," and "thud." According to Rosenhan, these symptoms were chosen because of "their apparent similarity to existential symptoms [and] the *absence* of a single report of existential psychoses in the literature."[1(p251)] The implication is that if the *content* of specific symptoms has never been reported in the literature, then a psychiatrist should somehow know that the *symptom* has no diagnostic significance. This is absurd. Recently I saw a patient who kept hearing a voice that said, "It's OK. It's OK." I know of no such report in the literature. So what? I agree with Rosenhan that there has never been a report of an "existential psychosis." However, the diagnoses made were schizophrenia and manic-depressive psychosis, not existential psychosis. (I am reminded of a game that was played when I was a kid. "I can prove that you are not here." "How?" "Are you in Chicago?" "No." "Then you must be in some other place. If you are in some other place then you can't be here.")

Differential Diagnosis of Auditory Hallucinations

Rosenhan is entitled to believe that psychiatric diagnoses are of no use and therefore should not have been given to the pseudopatients. However, it makes no sense for him to claim that *within* a diagnostic framework it was irrational to consider schizophrenia seriously as the most likely condition *without* his presenting a consideration of the differential diagnosis. Let me briefly give what I think is a reasonable differential diagnosis, based on the initial clinical picture of the pseudopatient when he applied for admission to the hospital.

Rosenhan says that "beyond alleging the symptoms and falsifying name, vocation, and employment, no further alterations of person, history, or circumstances were made."[1(p251)] However, the clinical picture clearly includes not only the symptom (auditory hallucinations) but also the desire to enter a psychiatric hospital, from which it is reasonable to conclude that the symptom is a source of significant distress. (In fact, in his 1975 symposium article Rosenhan acknowledges that the pseudopatients reported that "the hallucinations troubled them greatly at the outset."[43(p471)] This, plus the knowledge that the auditory hallucinations were reported to be of three weeks' duration (D. L. Rosenhan, oral communication), establishes the hallucinations as significant symptoms of psychopathology as distinguished from so-called "pseudohallucination" (hallucinations while falling asleep or awakening from sleep, or intense imagination with the voices heard from inside of the head).

Auditory hallucinations can occur in several kinds of mental disorders. The absence of a history of alcohol, drug abuse, or some other toxin, the absence of any signs of physical illness (such as high fever), the absence of evidence of distractibility, impairment in concentration, memory or orientation, and negative results from a neurological examination all make an organic psychosis extremely unlikely. The absence of a recent precipitating stress rules out a transient situational disturbance of psychotic intensity or (to use a nonofficial category) hysterical psychosis. The absence of a profound disturbance in mood rules out an affective psychosis (we are not given the mental status findings for the patient who was diagnosed manic-depressive psychosis).

What about simulating mental illness? Psychiatrists know that occasionally an individual who has something to gain from being admitted to a psychiatric hospital will exaggerate or even feign psychiatric symptoms. This is a genuine diagnostic problem that psychiatrists and other physicians occasionally confront and is called "malingering." However, there was certainly no reason to believe that any of the pseudopatients had anything to gain from being admitted to a psychiatric hospital except relief from their alleged complaint, and therefore there was no reason to suspect that the illness was feigned. What possible diagnoses are left in the classification of mental disorders now used in this country for a patient with a presenting symptom of hallucinations, with the previously considered conditions having been ruled out? There is only one—schizophrenia!

Admittedly, there is a hitch to a definitive diagnosis of schizophrenia. Almost invariably there *are* other signs of the disorder present, such as poor premorbid adjustment, affective blunting, delusions, or signs of thought disorder. I would hope that if I had been one of the 12 psychiatrists presented with such a patient, I would have been struck by the lack of other signs of the disorder, but I am rather sure that having no reason to doubt the authenticity of the patient's claim of auditory hallucinations, I also would have been fooled into noting schizophrenia as *the most likely* diagnosis.

What does Rosenhan really mean when he objects to the diagnosis of schizophrenia because it was based on a "single symptom"? Does he believe that there are real patients with the single symptoms of auditory hallucinations who are misdiagnosed as schizophrenic when they actually have some other condition? If so, what is the nature of that condition? Is Rosenhan's point that the psychiatrists should have used "diagnosis deferred," a category that is available but rarely used? I would have no argument with this conclusion. Furthermore, if he had presented data from real patients indicating how often patients are erroneously diagnosed on the basis of inadequate information and what the consequences are, it would have been a real contribution.

Until now, I have assumed that the pseudopatients presented only one symptom of psychiatric disorder. Actually, we know very little about how the pseudopatients presented themselves. What did the pseudopatients say when asked, as most must have been, what effect the hallucinations were having on their lives? Did any of the pseudopatients depart from the protocol (which called for describing only one symptom), perhaps in an effort to justify admission to the hospital? (It occurred to me that the best way to shed light on this question would be to read the original admission notes to determine just how the psychiatrist described the present illnesses of pseudopatients. Communication with Rosenhan indicated that he has this material. I have made several requests for him to send me copies, with deletion of all information that could possibly identify the particular hospitals that were involved. To summarize a lengthy correspondence, he has indicated that editing this material is more difficult that I would judge and that he would be glad to supply the material after he has completed analyzing it for a book he is preparing.)

Detecting Sanity after Admission

Let us now examine the relationship to the central research question of the last meaning of detecting sanity in the pseudopatients, namely, the psychiatrist's recognition, *after* observing the pseudopatient act normally during his hospitalization, that he was initially feigning insanity. If a diagnostic condition were known to be always chronic and unremitting, it would be irrational not to question the original diagnosis if a patient were later found to be asymptomatic. As applied to this study, if the concept of schizophrenia did not admit the possibility of recovery, then failure to question the original diagnosis when the pseudopatients were no longer overtly ill would be relevant to the central research question. It would be an example of the context of the hospital environment influencing the psychiatrist's diagnostic decision. However, neither any psychiatric textbook nor the American Psychiatric Association's *Diagnostic and Statistical Manual of Mental Disorders*[48] suggests that mental illnesses endure forever. Oddly enough, it is Rosenhan who, without any reference to the psychiatric literature, says, "A broken leg is something one recovers from, but mental illness allegedly endures forever."[1(p254)] Who, other than Rosenhan, alleges it?

Rosenhan should know that although some American psychiatrists restrict the label of schizophrenia to mean chronic or process schizophrenia, most American psychiatrists include an acute subtype from which there is often remission. The *Diagnostic and Statistical Manual* in describing the subtype, "acute schizophrenic episode," states that "in many cases the patient recovers within weeks."[48]

A similar straw man is created when Rosenhan says:

> The insane are not always insane . . . the bizarre behaviors upon which their [the pseudo-patients'] diagnoses were allegedly predicated constituted only a small fraction of their total behavior. If it makes no sense to label ourselves permanently depressed on the basis of an occasional depression, then it takes better evidence than is presently available to label all patients insane or schizophrenic on the basis of bizarre behaviors or cognitions.[1(p254)]

Who ever said that the behaviors that indicate schizophrenia or any other diagnostic category comprise the totality of a patient's behavior? A diagnosis of schizophrenia does not mean that *all* of the patient's behavior is schizophrenic, any more than a diagnosis of carcinoma of the liver means that all of the patient's body is diseased. (While discussing the pitfalls of generalizing, how about Rosenhan's conclusion that "It is clear that we cannot distinguish the sane from the insane in psychiatric hospitals,"[1(p257)] which is based on a sample size of eight pseudopatients admitted to 12 hospitals!)

Does Rosenhan at least score a point by demonstrating that, although the professional staff never considered the possibility that the pseudopatient was a fraud, this possibility was often considered by other patients? Perhaps, but I am not so sure. Let us not forget that all of the pseudopatients "took extensive notes publicly." Obviously, this was highly unusual patient behavior and Rosenhan's quote from a suspicious patient suggests the importance it had in focusing the other patients' attention on the pseudopatients: "You're not crazy. You're a journalist, or a professor [referring to the continual note-taking]. You're checking up on the hospital."[1(p252)]

Rosenhan presents ample evidence, which I find no reason to dispute, that the professional staff spent little time actually with the pseudopatients. The note-taking may easily have been overlooked, and therefore the staff developed no suspicion that the pseudopatients had simulated illness to gain entry into the hospital. The note-taking, in which all of the pseudopatients engaged, may well have been *the* cue that alerted the patients to the possibility that the pseudopatients were there under false pretenses. However, I would predict that a pseudopatient on a ward of patients with mixed diagnostic conditions would have no difficulty in masquerading convincingly as a true patient to both staff and patients if he did nothing unusual to draw attention to himself.

Rosenhan presents one way in which the diagnosis did affect the psychiatrist's preception of the patient's circumstances—historical facts of the case were often distorted by the staff to achieve consistency with psychodynamic theories. Here, for the first time, I believe Rosenhan has hit the mark. What he described happens all the time and often makes attendance at clinical case conferences extremely painful, especially for those with logical minds and research orientations. Although his observation is correct, it would seem to be more a consequence of individuals attempting to rearrange facts to comply with an unproven etiological theory than a consequence of diagnostic labeling. One could easily imagine a similar process occurring when a weak-minded, behaviorally oriented clinician attempts to rewrite the patient's history to account for "hallucinations reinforced by attention paid to patient by family members when patient complains of hearing voices." Such is the human condition.

One final finding requires comment. In order to determine whether "the tendency toward diagnosing the sane insane could be reversed," the staff of a research and teaching hospital was informed that at some time during the following three months, one or more pseudopatients would attempt to be admitted. No such attempt was actually made. Yet approximately 10% of 193 real patients were suspected by two or more staff members (we are not told how many made judgments) to be pseudopatients. Rosenhan concluded, "Any diagnostic process that lends itself so readily to massive errors of this sort cannot be a very reliable one."[1(p252)] My conclusion is that this experimental design practically assures only one outcome. (Did the hospital director, or whoever it was that agreed to participate in this ministudy, really believe that the design was relevant to some serious research question?)

Elementary Principles of Reliability of Classification

Some very important principles that are relevant to the design of Rosenhan's study are taught in elementary psychology courses and should not be forgotten. One of them is that a measurement or classification procedure is not reliable or unreliable *in itself* but only in its application to a specific population. There *are* serious problems with the reliability of psychiatric diagnoses as they are applied to the population to which psychiatric diagnoses are *ordinarily* given. However, I fail to see, and Rosenhan does not even attempt to show, how the reliability of psychiatric diagnoses applied to a population of individuals seeking help is at all relevant to the reliability of psychiatric diagnoses applied to a population of pseudopatients (or one including the threat of pseudopatients). The two populations are just not the same. Kety has expressed it dramatically:

> If I were to drink a quart of blood and, concealing what I had done, come to the emergency room of any hospital vomiting blood, the behavior of the staff would be quite predictable. If they labeled and treated me as having a bleeding peptic ulcer, I doubt that I could argue convincingly that medical science does not know how to diagnose that condition.[3(p959)]

(I have no doubt that if the condition known as "pseudopatient" ever assumed epidemic proportions among admissions to psychiatric hospitals, psychiatrists would in time become adept at identifying them, though at what risk to real patients I do not know.)

Attitudes toward the "Insane"

The latter part of Rosenhan's study[1] deals with the experience of psychiatric hospitalization. The staff and the patients were strictly segregated. The professional staff, especially the psychiatrists, were not available and were rarely seen. When the staff was asked for information "their most common response consisted of either a brief response to the question, offered while they were 'on the move' and with head averted, or no response at all."[1(p255)] "Attendants delivered verbal and occasionally serious physical abuse to patients in the presence of other observing patients."[1(p256)] One attendant awakened patients with "Come on you m-----f-----s, out of bed!"[1(p256)] "One patient was beaten in the presence of other patients for having approached an attendant and told him, 'I like you.'"[1(p256)]

Because some of the hopsitals participated in residency training programs and are described as "research oriented," I do find it hard to believe that the conditions were quite as bad as depicted. Perhaps they were. But how are we then to understand Rosenhan when in the summary to his original article he says:

> It could be a mistake, and a very unfortunate one, to consider that what happened to us derived from malice or stupidity on the part of the staff. Quite the contrary, our overwhelming impression of them was of people who really cared, who were committed and who were uncommonly intelligent.[1(p257)]

Surely what he described, including the verbal and physical abuse given to patients, is hardly what most people would regard as the behavior of people who "really cared" and were "uncommonly intelligent."

There is an obvious reason for the discrepancy between the actual behavior of the staff that Rosenhan describes and his exoneration of them for any responsibility for "malice" or "stupidity." To direct attention to any shortcomings on the part of the staff would detract attention from the real culprit, namely, diagnostic labels. Thus, Rosenhan asserts, without a shred of evidence from his study, that "Negative attitudes [toward psychiatric patients] . . . are the natural offspring of the labels patients wear and the places in which they are found."[1(p254)] Nonsense! This makes as much sense as asserting that the attitude of the public toward cancer is the natural offspring of the label "cancer" without considering the attitude of the public to any of the *features* of neoplastic disease.

In recent years, large numbers of chronic psychiatric patients, many of them chronic schizophrenic and geriatric patients with organic brain syndromes, have been discharged from state hospitals and placed in communities that have no facilities to deal with them. The affected communities are up in arms not primarily because they are mental patients labeled with psychiatric diagnoses (because the majority are not recognized as expatients) but because the *behavior* of some of them is sometimes incomprehensible, deviant, strange, and annoying. In a similar fashion, in a study of psychiatric labeling and the rehabilitation of former psychiatric inpatients, Schwartz and colleagues[49] found that an expatient's level of impairment (his behavior) was far more important in determining whether or not he was rejected by the community than knowledge that the individual was receiving psychiatric treatment (and therefore was labeled mentally ill).

Rosenhan never considers the possibility that the negative attitude toward patients with psychiatric diagnostic labels might at least have *something* to do with the attitude of people toward the very behaviors that might be the basis for the diagnostic labels. For example, he says:

> The stigmatizing effects of psychiatric labels are so well known empirically and experientially (how might you feel if your colleagues believed you were a paranoid schizophrenic?) that it is hard to understand how or why those effects could be denied.[50(p1647)]

Does Rosenhan think the answer to his hypothetical question would be any different if put solely in behavioral terms without a diagnostic label—"how might you feel if your colleagues believed that you had an unshakeable but utterly false conviction that everybody was out to harm you"?

It is informative to consult the references[51–53] that Rosenhan[1] cited as offering data that "a psychiatric diagnosis is harmful." My interpretation of these data is that they merely show that the general public in a variety of ways ascribes a negative valuation to behavior that has been identified as mental illness. It is hard to see how the public would have a more positive attitude toward individuals with behavioral diagnoses unless you could convince the public that what was wrong with these individuals had nothing to do with mental illness. Merely changing the name of the type of mental illness will not eliminate the negative attitude. That is why the attempt every few decades to change the name of the condition given to individuals whose behavior is negatively evaluated by the public, with the hope of thereby changing the attitude towards such individuals, is largely doomed to fail. Recall how "psychopath" became "sociopath" and more recently "antisocial personality." Recall how the "sexual perversions" became "sexual deviations," which might become (according to a recommendation of the Task Force on Nomenclature and Statistics, Subcommittee on Sexual Disorders) "sexual object and situation disorders." As soon as everyone finds out what the new terms really mean, the basic attitude toward individuals with these conditions reappears.

Rosenhan does not propose the "mental illness as myth" notion, although why he does not is a mystery, since it clearly is consistent with his basic hypothesis that diagnoses are in the minds of the observers and not the behavior of the patients. Furthermore, the only way to avoid the stigma of the mental illness diagnoses that Rosenhan decries would be to do away with the concept of mental illness itself. Can this be done? In a fascinating study of psychiatric labeling among Eskimos, Jorubas, and other divergent groups, J. M. Murphy, PhD (unpublished data), noted the following:

> Explicit labels for insanity appear to exist in most groups. The labels refer to beliefs, feelings, and actions which are thought to emanate from the mind or inner state of an individual; they cause such persons to seek the aid of healers; and they bear strong resemblance to what we call schizophrenia. Of signal importance is the fact that the labels for insanity do not refer to one specific attribute but to a pattern of several interlinked phenomena. Despite wide variation in culture, a pattern composed of hallucinations, delusions, disorientations, and behavioral aberrations appears to identify the idea of "losing one's mind" almost everywhere even though the content of these behaviors is colored by cultural beliefs.

The implication is clear—mental illness is a label for phenomena that apparently exist in all cutures. Efforts to avoid the negative attitudes toward the phenomena by eliminating the label are misdirected. The most effective way of improving attitudes toward mental illness (as toward "cancer" or any other frightening illness) is to develop treatments that work and then convey this information to the public.

The Uses of Diagnosis

Rosenhan believes that the pseudopatients should have been diagnosed as having hallucinations of unknown origin. It is not clear what he thinks the diagnosis should have been if the pseudopatients had been sufficiently trained to talk, at times, incoherently, and had complained of difficulty in thinking clearly, lack of emotion, and that their thoughts were being broadcast so that strangers knew what they were thinking. Is Rosenhan perhaps suggesting multiple diagnoses of hallucinations, difficulty in thinking clearly, lack of emotion, and incoherent speech, all of unknown origin?

It is no secret that we lack a full understanding of such conditions as schizophrenia and manic-depressive illness, but are we quite as ignorant as Rosenhan would have us believe? Do we not know, for example, that hallucinations, in the context just described, are symptomatic of a different condition than are hallucinations of voices accusing the patient of sin, when associated with depressed affect, diurnal mood variation, loss of appetite, and insomnia? What about hallucinations of God's voice issuing commandments, associated with euphoric affect, psychomotor excitement, and accelerated and disconnected speech? Is this not also an entirely different condition?

There is a *purpose* to psychiatric diagnosis.[54] It enables mental health professionals to *communicate* with each other about the subject matter of their concern, *comprehend* the pathological processes involved in psychiatric illness, and *control* psychiatric disorders. Control consists of the ability to predict outcome, prevent the disorder from developing, and treat it once it has developed. Any serious discussion of the validity of psychiatric diagnosis or suggestions for alternative systems of classifying psychological disturbance must address itself to these purposes of psychiatric diagnosis.

In terms of its ability to accomplish these purposes, I would say that psychiatric diagnosis is moderately effective as a shorthand way of communicating the presence of constellations of signs and symptoms that tend to cluster together and is woefully inadequate in helping us understand the pathological processes of psychiatric disorders; however, it does offer considerable help in the control of many mental disorders. Control is possible because psychiatric diagnosis often yields information of value in predicting the likely course of illness (eg, an early recovery, chronicity, or recurrent episodes) and because for many mental disorders (particularly the severe ones), it is useful in suggesting the best available treatment.

Let us return to the three different clinical conditions that I described, each of which had auditory hallucinations as one of its manifestations. The reader with any familiarity with psychopathology will have no difficulty in identifying the three hypothetical conditions as schizophrenia, psychotic depression, and mania. Anyone familiar with the literature on psychiatric treatment will know that there are numerous well-controlled studies[55] indicating the superiority of the major tranquilizers for the treatment schizophrenia, electroconvulsive therapy for the treatment of recurrent unipolar depression and, more recently, lithium carbonate for the treatment of mania. Furthermore, there is convincing evidence that these three conditions, each of which is often accompanied by hallucinations, are influenced by separate genetic factors. As Kety[3] said, "If schizophrenia is a myth, it is a myth with a strong genetic component."

Should psychiatric diagnosis be abandoned for a purely descriptive system that focuses on simple phenotypic behaviors *before* it has been demonstrated that such an approach is more useful as a guide to successful treatment or for understanding the role of genetic factors? I think not. It is of interest that examination of the behavior therapy literature, which is full of theoretical attacks on the usefulness of psychiatric diagnosis, does not indicate that it has been abandoned in actual practice by behaviorally oriented therapists. The traditional diagnostic categories of anxiety neurosis, phobia, anorexia nervosa, obsessive-compulsive disorder, schizophrenia, and depression and sexual dysfunction to name but a few, are apparently alive and well, and presumably responding to specific behaviorally oriented therapies. (I have a vision. Traditional psychiatric diagnosis *has* long been forgotten. At a conference on behavioral classification, a keen research investigator proposes that the category "hallucinations of unknown cause" be subdivided into three different groups based on associated symptoms. The first group is characterized by depressed affect, diurnal mood variation, and so on, the second group by euphoric mood, psychomotor excitement, etc.

If psychiatric diagnosis is not quite as bad as Rosenhan would have us believe, that does not mean that is is all that good. What *is* the reliability of psychiatric diagnosis? A review of the major studies of the reliability of psychiatric diagnosis prior to 1972 revealed:

Reliability appears to be only satisfactory for three categories: mental deficiency, organic brain syndrome... and alcoholism. The level of reliability is no better than fair for psychosis and schizophrenia and is poor for the remaining categories.[56]

So be it. But where did Rosenhan get the idea that psychiatry is the only medical specialty that is plagued by inaccurate diagnosis? Studies have shown serious unreliability in the diagnosis of pulmonary disorders,[57] in the interpretation of electrocardiograms,[58] in the interpretation of roentgenograms,[59, 60] and in the certification of causes of death.[61] A review of diagnostic unreliability in other branches of physical medicine is given by Garland[62] and the problem of the vagueness of medical criteria for diagnosis is thoroughly discussed by Feinstein.[63] The poor reliability of medical diagnosis, even when assisted by objective laboratory tests, does not mean that medical diagnosis is of no value. So it is with psychiatric diagnosis.

Recognition of the serious problems of the reliability of psychiatric diagnosis has resulted in a new approach to psychiatric diagnosis—the use of specific inclusion and exclusion criteria, as in contrast to the usually vague and ill-defined general descriptions found in the psychiatric literature and in the standard psychiatric glossary of the American Psychiatric Association. This approach was started by the St. Louis group associated with the Department of Psychiatry of Washington University[64] and has been further developed by my co-workers and myself[65] as a set of criteria for a selected group of functional psychiatric disorders, called the Research Diagnostic Criteria (RDC). The Table shows the specific criteria for a diagnosis of schizophrenia from the latest version of the RDC.

Reliability studies utilizing the RDC with case record material (from which all cues as to diagnosis and treatment were removed), as well as with live patients, indicate high reliability for all of the major categories and reliability coefficients

TABLE Diagnostic Criteria for Schizophrenia from the Research Diagnostic Criteria*

A. At least two of the following are required for definite and one for probable diagnosis:
  1. thought broadcasting, insertion, or withdrawal (as defined in this manual)
  2. delusions of control, other bizarre delusions, or multiple delusions (as defined in this manual), of any duration as long as definitely present
  3. delusions other than presecutory or jealousy, lasting at least one week
  4. delusions of any type if accompanied by hallucinations of any type for at least one week
  5. auditory hallucinations in which either a voice keeps up a running commentary on the patient's behavior or thoughts as they occur, or two or more voices converse with each other
  6. nonaffective verbal hallucinations spoken to the subject (as defined in this manual)
  7. hallucinations of any type throughout the day for several days or intermittently for at least one month

B. A period of illness lasting at least two weeks

C. At no time during the active period of illness being considered did the patient meet the criteria for either probable or definite manic or depressive syndrome (criteria A and B under Major Depressive or Manic Disorders) to such a degree that it was a prominent part of the illness

*For what it is worth, the pseudopatient would have been diagnosed as "probable" schizophrenia using these criteria because of A6. In an oral communication, Rosenhan said that when the pseudopatients were asked how frequently the hallucinations occurred, they said "I don't know." Therefore, criterion A7 is not met.

generally higher than have ever been reported.[66] It is therefore clear that the reliability of psychiatric diagnosis can be greatly increased by the use of specific criteria. (The interjudge reliability [chance corrected agreement, kappa] for the diagnosis of schizophrenia, using an earlier version of the RDC criteria with 68 psychiatric inpatients at the New York State Psychiatric Institute, was .88, which is a thoroughly respectable level of reliability.) It is very likely that the next edition of the American Psychiatric Association's *Diagnostic and Statistical Manual* will contain similar specific criteria.

There are other problems with current psychiatric diagnosis. The recent controversy over whether or not homosexuality per se should be considered a mental disorder highlighted the lack of agreement within the psychiatric profession as to the definition of a mental disorder. (It is difficult to determine at twilight whether it is day or night, but we have no such difficulty at midnight or noon. So too, our difficulty in defining the precise border of mental disorder and nonmental disorder in no way indicates the lack of utility of the concepts involved.) To the extent that our profession defines mental disorder as any significant deviation from the "good life" or "optimal human functioning," we will needlessly label many individuals as ill who are in no distress, function reasonably well, and hurt no one. This is a utopian conception of mental health that subjects the profession to the accusation that the sole function of the concept of mental disorder is social control and the pejorative labeling of all forms of social deviance. It is for this reason that we have proposed a more circumscribed definition,[54] but the criteria for this definition now appear to me to have incorrectly omitted certain, but by no means all, forms of antisocial behavior.

There are serious problems of validity. Many of the traditional diagnostic categories, such as some of the subtypes of schizophrenia and of major affective illness, and several of the personality disorders, have not been demonstrated to be distinct conditions or to be useful for prognosis or treatment assignment. In addition, despite considerable evidence supporting the distinctness of such conditions as schizophrenia and manic-depressive illness, the boundaries separating these conditions from other conditions are certainly not clear. Finally, the categories of the traditional psychiatric nomenclature are of least value when applied to the large numbers of outpatients who are not seriously ill. This may be a result of our greater ease in classifying conditions, such as the organic mental disorders and the psychoses, where the manifestations of the illness are qualitatively different from normal functioning. (For example, hallucinations are not part of normal functioning.) In contrast, with the personality disorders, we are dealing with quantitative variations in the intensity and pervasiveness of ubiquitous traits. (For example, some degree of suspiciousness or histrionic behavior is part of normal functioning.)

Rosenhan's Response to Critiques of His Study

In his recent symposium article, "The Contextual Nature of Psychiatric Diagnosis," Rosenhan[43] responded to the critiques offered by me and by the other participants. My impending exhaustion, and I suspect, that of most readers who have gotten this far with my article, suggests the need for a *limited* critique of Rosenhan's article, which is as fascinating for what it omits as for what it says.

Let us start with the former. The interested reader can decide for himself which of the specific critiques of Rosenhan's original study that I presented in the earlier part of this article are telling and therefore worthy of a response from Rosenhan, and which his article neglected to discuss. I believe they are numerous.

What is most significant is his omission of any discussion of the crucial issue of how diagnostic labels given to pseudopatients with unusual complaints are at all relevant to the problems of the psychiatric diagnosis of real patients. There is also no discussion of the criticism that the concept of schizophrenia does not exclude the possibility of recovery, so there was no reason why the admission diagnosis of schizophrenia should have been revised merely because of normal behavior while in the hospital.

There is a most remarkable response to my demonstration that the pseudopatients were given an unusual diagnosis at discharge, "in remission," thus proving that the diagnoses given to the pseudopatients were a function of their behavior and not of the setting. Rosenhan states:

> Spitzer (1975) points out that the designation "in remission" is exceedingly rare. It occurs in only a handful of cases in the hospitals he surveyed, and my own cursory investigations that were stimulated by his confirm these observations. His data are intrinsically interesting, as well as interesting for the meaning they have for this particular study. How shall they be understood?
>
> Once again we return to the influence of context on psychiatric perception. Consider two people who show no evidence of psychopathology. One is called sane and the other is called paranoid schizophrenic, in remission. Are both characterizations synonymous? Of course not. Would it matter to you if on one occasion you were designated normal, and on the other you were call psychotic, in remission, with both designations arising from the identical behavior? Of course it would matter. The perception of an asymptomatic status implies little by itself. It is the context in which that perception is embedded that tells the significant story.[43(p468)]

Amazing! Of course "in remission" is not the same as "normal," but neither are the behaviors that are the basis for such categorization. The individual labeled "in remission" has the same behavior as the individual labeled "normal" only for one period of observation (current examination). He has a different history. The individual who has recoved (partially or completely) from an episode of schizophrenia has a probability of recurrence that far exceeds the probability for individuals who have never had such an episode of illness.[67] There is also evidence that maintenance phenothiazine treatment is effective in decreasing the probability of recurrence of schizophrenic episode.[55] Therefore, if I, or a member of my family, had in fact recently recovered from an episode of schizophrenic illness and were currently asymptomatic, I would *prefer* a diagnosis of schizophrenia in remission to a diagnosis of "normal," since it would suggest that a particular kind of treatment might well be indicated. That, after all, is one of the purposes of diagnosis. The same argument would apply with even greater force to the justification of the category "in remission" for individuals who have had recurrent episodes of depressive or manic illness or both and who at a particular examination are asymptomatic. Without the concept of affective disorder in remission, how could one justify the use of lithium carbonate as a prophylactic agent?

The justification of the category "in remission" for certain psychiatric disorders that tend to be chronic and recurrent in no way minimizes the difficulty in providing specific guidelines as to when use of this category is appropriate. Just as it would make no sense to use this category after all episodes of psychiatric illness regardless of type or duration of asymptomatic status, so it makes no sense to argue on logical grounds that it should never be used.

Rosenhan apparently believes he has discovered a scandal regarding the process by which the official nomenclature of the American Psychiatric Association is developed and adopted. He states:

> Unlike most medical diagnoses, which can be validated in numerous ways, psychiatric diagnoses are maintained by consensus alone. This is not commonly known to either the consumer or the mental health profession. Spitzer and Wilson[54] clarify the matter:
>
> > In 1965 the American Psychiatric Association... assigned its Committee on Nomenclature and Statistics... the task of preparing for the APA a new diagnostic manual of disorders... A draft of the new manual, DSM II, was circulated in 1967 to 120 psychiatrists known to have special interests in the area of diagnosis and was revised on the basis of their criticisms and suggestions. After further study it was adopted by the APA in 1967, and published and officially accepted throughout the country in 1968.[43(p464)]

Does Rosenhan believe that it is only the psychiatric portion of the medical nomenclature that is decided on by a committee? (I am haunted by visions. The scene is Geneva, Switzerland, the offices of the World Health Organization. A senior official is overheard talking to a new employee who has recently joined his unit. "In order to keep on schedule, this would be a good time for you to go up to the mountain and bring down the stones that have the latest revision of the ICD [International Classification of Diseases] for the ninth edition. I wonder if He will make many changes?" The junior official, demonstrating his ignorance, asks, "Does He give us the entire medical classification that way?" The senior official replies: "Of course not. We only get the nonpsychiatric part that way. In order for us to get the psychiatric classification we have to have a committee that gets together and votes on the changes. It's all very messy and thank God it's only a small part of the entire medical classification.")

Classifications are all man-made, and either some single person or a group of individuals decides what they shall be. When a committee to develop a psychiatric classification functions, it can act, like any committee, wisely or foolishly. A committee acts foolishly if it has no clear understanding of the purposes of the classification it is developing and if it merely perpetuated traditional nosologic distinctions that are based on theoretical assumptions not supported by data. A committee acts wisely if it understands the multiple purposes of psychiatric classification, if it makes a serious effort to consider the data that have accumulated regarding such issues as the internal consistency of the phenomenology, differential response to treatment, outcome, familial pattern and genetic loading, and the understanding of basic psychopathological and physiological processes. A committee acts wisely if it consults with experts in the various areas under consideration and if draft proposals of the classification are subjected to public scrutiny.

Let us return again to Rosenhan's statement that "Unlike most medical diagnoses, which can be validated in numerous ways, psychiatric diagnoses are maintained by consensus alone."[43(p464)] Here Rosenhan is confusing the validation of the medical examination with the validation of a medical diagnosis. The distinction is subtle but important for understanding the true differences between psychiatric and nonpsychiatric medical diagnoses.

The validity of a procedure or concept is determined by how useful it is for the particular purposes for which it is intended. Consider the medical examination. The purpose is to make a correct diagnosis. Let us assume that a physician, during the course of a medical examination, determines on the basis of the patterning and course of symptoms and the physical examination that the most likely diagnosis is diabetes. The use of a laboratory procedure such as a glucose tolerance test can then validate the *examination* that led to the diagnosis of diabetes. The laboratory procedure, however, does not in any way validate the diagnostic category of diabetes. The validity of diabetes as a diagnosis is a function of the ability of physicians to understand and treat patients who have medical problems that are categorized as either diabetes or not diabetes. This is a function of our understanding of the illness, its course and associated features, and the availability of specific treatments. As greater understanding of the pathophysiology of diabetes and as more effective methods for treating diabetes are developed, the validity of the diagnostic category of diabetes increases.

Now let us consider the psychiatric examination. Its purpose is to make the correct psychiatric diagnosis. It is true that except for the organic brain disorders, we have no laboratory procedures that can be used to validate the psychiatric *examination*. That does not mean, as Rosenhan suggests, that we have no procedures for validating psychiatric diagnoses other than consensus. The procedures for validating psychiatric diagnoses do not differ in principle from those used to validate nonpsychiatric medical diagnoses. They consist of studies that indicate the extent to which knowledge of *membership* in a given diagnostic category provides useful information, not already contained in the defining characteristics of the diagnostic category. Reference has already been made to studies indicating the specificity of various forms of somatic treatment and separate genetic factors for several of the major psychiatric diagnostic categories. These studies, as well as other studies dealing with some of the other purposes of psychiatric diagnosis, *are* the procedures by which psychiatric diagnoses are validated.

Rosenhan's Suggestions for the Future

Rosenhan[43] concludes his response to the critiques of his study with a section entitled "The Future." It begins as follows: "It is natural to infer that what I have written here argues against categorization of all kinds. But that is not the case. I have been careful to direct attention to the present system of diagnosis, the DSM-II [*Diagnostic and Statistical Manual of Mental* Disorders[48]]."[43(p472)] Only DSM II and not the general utility of psychiatric diagnosis? What about the following statements in the original article[1]?

> Psychiatric diagnoses, in this view, are in the minds of the observers and are not valid summaries of characteristics displayed by the observed . . . It seems more useful . . . to limit our discussions to behaviors, the stimuli that provoke them, and their correlates . . . Rather than acknowledge that we are just embarking on understanding, we continue to label patients "schizophrenic," "manic-depressive," and "insane," as if in those words we had captured the essence of understanding.[43(pp251,254,257)]

What about the following statement in the same article, in which Rosenhan claims to be discussing the DSM II only?

> Indeed, at present, my own preference runs to omitting diagnoses entirely, for it is far better from a scientific and treatment point of view to acknowledge ignorance than to mystify it with diagnoses that are unreliable, overly broad, and pejoratively connotative.[43(p467)]

Rosenhan continues:

> Nothing that is said here is intended to deprive the researcher of his classificatory system. He cannot proceed without it, but as long as his diagnostic data remain in his file until they are fully validated, they can do patients and treatment no harm.[43(p473)]

What in the world is a "fully validated" diagnostic system? What is the clinician, who has to do the best he can with what information is currently available, to do as he waits for the appearance of the "fully validated" classification? Rosenhan ignores the historical fact that classification in medicine has always been preceded by clinicians using *imperfect* systems that have been improved on the basis of clinical and research experience.

(Hang on reader. We are almost finished.) Rosenhan again states:

> What might we require of new diagnostic systems before they are published and officially accepted? . . . We should ask that coefficients of agreements between diagnosticians in a variety of settings *commonly* reach or exceed .90. That figure, which is associated with a bit more than 80% of the variance in diagnosis, is a liberal one in terms of the possible consequences of misdiagnosis and the reversibility of the diagnoses. The full reasoning behind that figure takes us away from the central thrust of this paper, but interested readers can confirm it for themselves in Cronbach, Gleser, Harinder, and Nageswari [68], and Cronbach and Gleser [69].[43(p473)]

First of all, the coefficients of agreement, such as the kappa index to which Rosenhan previously referred, unlike product moment correlations, are already in units of the proportion of subject variance and do not need to be squared.[70,71] Thus, a kappa of .8 means that 80% of the variance is associated with true subject variability.

The more important error is Rosenhan's justification of an entirely arbitrary requirement of a given level of interrater agreement by citing a tradition in psychometrics, which makes an assumption that cannot be made in psychiatric diagnosis. Rosenhan's reference to the two excellent psychometric textbooks discusses the desirability of avoiding decisions when the likelihood of an error exceeds .05 or .10. What about situations when a decision cannot be avoided, which is the general rule when a patient is examined psychiatrically? Let us take the example of a decision regarding suicidal behavior (which admittedly is not a diagnosis but illustrates the issues well). Interrater agreement regarding suicidal potential is undoubtedly much below .8. Does that mean that a clinician should never make a management decision based on his best judgment? Obviously, he must—to avoid making a decision is itself a decision. The facts are that despite our difficulty in reliably making medical judgments regarding diagnostic categories in psychiatry and the rest of medicine, patients must be treated and that treatment must follow from the decision of the clinician as to what he thinks is wrong with the patient. And that is what a diagnosis is.

Finally, Rosenhan concludes:

> We should require that the proven untility of such a system exceed its liabilities for patients. Understand the issue. Syphilis and cancer both have negative social and emotional overtones. But the treatments that exist for them presumably exceed the personal liabilities associated with the diagnosis.[43p472]

The implications of this are staggering! Is Rosenhan suggesting that prior to the development of effective treatments for syphilis and cancer, he would have decried the use of these diagnostic labels? Should we eliminate the diagnoses of antisocial personality, drug abuse, and alcoholism until we have treatments for these conditions whose benefits exceed the potential liabilities associated with the diagnosis? How do we study the effectiveness of treatments for these conditions if we are enjoined from using the diagnostic categories until we have effective treatments for them?

I have not dealt at all with the myriad ways in which psychiatric diagnostic labels can be and are misused and hurt patients rather than help them. This is a problem requiring serious research that Rosenhan unfortunately does not help illuminate. However, whatever the solutions to that problem, the available evidence that psychiatric diagnostic labels are *inherently* harmful to patients is scant indeed. Their misuse is not sufficient reason to abandon their use; when properly used, they have been shown to be of considerable value.

Acknowledgments

Jean Endicott, PhD, Joseph Fleiss, PhD, Joseph Zubin, PhD, Janet Forman, MSW, Karen Greene, MA, and Rose Bender assisted with the preparation of this article.

Note

This article is a revision of one that appeared in *The Journal of Abnormal Psychology* (84:442–452, 1975).

References

1. Rosenhan DL: On being sane in insane places. *Science* 179:250–258, 1973.
2. Dimond RE: Popular opinion is not empirical data. *Clin Soc Work J* 2:264–270, 1974.

3. Kety SS: From rationalization to reason. *Am J Psychiatry* 131:957–963, 1974.
4. Rifkin A, Klein DF, Quitkin F, et al: Sane: Insane. *JAMA* 224:1646–1647, 1973.
5. Klein DF, Rifkin A, Quitkin FM: Sane: Insane. *JAMA* 226:1569, 1973.
6. Fleischman PR, Israel JV, Burr WA, et al: Psychiatric Diagnosis. *Science* 180:356–365, 1973.
7. Pattison EM: Social criticism and scientific responsibility. *J Am Sci Affil* 26:110–114, 1974.
8. Rabichow HG, Pharis ME: Rosenhan was wrong: The staff was lousy. *Clin Soc Work J* 2:271–278, 1974.
9. Shectman F: On being misinformed by misleading arguments. *Bull Menninger Clin* 37:523–525, 1973.
10. Abrahamson D: Procedure re-examined. *Lancet* 1:1153–1155, 1974.
11. Arthur RJ: Social psychiatry: An overview. *Am J Psychiatry* 130:841–849, 1973.
12. Burdsal C, Greenberg G, Timpe R: The relationship of marihuana usage to personality and motivational factors. *J Psychol* 85:45–51, 1973.
13. Sane: Insane, editorial. *JAMA* 223:1272, 1973.
14. Insane: Sane, editorial. *JAMA* 223:1381, 1973.
15. Glaser FB: Medical ethnocentrism and the treatment of addiction. *Int J Offender Ther Comp Crimino* 18:13–27, 1974.
16. Hoekstra A: Concerning science and society. *Clin Soc Work J* 2:299–306, 1974.
17. Kane RA: Look to the record. *Soc Work* 19:412–419, 1974.
18. Levy CS: On sane social workers in insane places. *Clin Soc Work J* 2:257–263, 1974.
19. Mark VH: A psychosurgeon's case *for* psychosurgery. *Psychol Today* 8:28ff, 1974.
20. Morse N: Some problems with insane institutions. *Clin Soc Work J* 2:291–298, 1974.
21. Oran D: Judges and psychiatrists lock up too many people. *Psychol Today* 7:20ff, 1973.
22. Perry TL, Hansen S. Tischler B, et al: Unrecognized adult phenylketonuria. *N Engl J Med* 289:395–398, 1973.
23. Scheff TJ: The labelling theory of mental illness. *Am Sociol Rev* 39:444–452, 1974.
24. Walden T, Singer G, Thomet W: Students as clients: The other side of the desk. *Clin Soc Work J* 2:279–290, 1974.
25. Daves WF: *Textbook of General Psychology.* New York, Thomas Y Crowell Co, 1975.
26. Davison G, Neale JM: *Abnormal Psychology—An Experimental Clinical Approach.* New York, John Wiley & Sons Inc, 1974.
27. Haber R, Fried A: *An Introduction to Psychology.* New York, Holt Rinehart & Winston Inc, 1975.
28. Hilgard E, Atkinson R, Atkinson R: *Introduction to Psychology,* ed 6. New York, Harcourt Brace Jovanovich Inc, 1975.
29. Kleinmuntz B: *Essentials of Abnormal Psychology.* New York, Harper & Row Publishers Inc, 1974.
30. Krech D, Crutchfield R, Livson N: *Elements of Psychology,* ed 3. New York, Alfred A. Knopf Inc, 1974.
31. London P: *Beginning Psychology.* Homewood, Ill, Dorsey Press Inc. 1975.
32. McMahon FB: *Psychology: The Hybrid Science,* ed 2. Englewood Cliffs, NJ, Prentice-Hall Inc, 1974.
33. Rubinstein J: *The Study of Psychology.* Guilford, Conn, Dushkin Publishing Group Inc, 1975.
34. Ullman L, Krasner L: *A Psychological Approach to Abnormal Behavior,* ed 2. Englewood Cliffs, NJ, Prentice-Hall Inc, 1975.
35. Wrightsman L, Sanford F: *Psychology: A Scientific Study of Human Behavior,* ed 4. Monterey, Cal, Brooks/Cole Publishing Co, 1975.

36. Zimbardo P, Ruch F: *Psychology and Life*, ed 9. Glenview, Ill, Scott Foresman & Co, 1975.

37. Brown R, Herrnstein R: *Psychology*. Boston, Little Brown & Co, 1975.

38. Kimble G, Garmezy N, Zigler E: *Principles of General Psychology*, ed 4. New York, Ronald Press Co, 1974.

39. Lindzey G, Hall C, Thompson R: *Psychology*. New York, Worth Publishers Inc, 1975.

40. Crown S: On being sane in insane places: A comment from England. *J Abnorm Psychol* 84:453–455, 1975.

41. Farber IE: Sane and insane: Constructions and misconstructions. *J Abnorm Psychol* 84:589–620, 1975.

42. Millon T: Reflections on Rosenhan's "On being sane in insane places." *J Abnorm Psychol* 84:456–461, 1975.

43. Rosenhan DL: The contextual nature of psychiatric diagnosis. *J Abnorm Psychol* 84:462–474, 1975.

44. Spitzer RL: On pseudoscience in science, logic in remission, and psychiatric diagnosis: A critique of Rosenhan's "On being sane in insane places." *J Abnorm Psychol* 84:442–452, 1975.

45. Weiner B: On being sane in insane places: A process (attributional) analysis and critique. *J Abnorm Psychol* 84:433–441, 1975.

46. Hunter FM: Psychiatric diagnosis. *Science* 180:361, 1973.

47. Rosenhan DL: Psychiatric diagnosis. *Science* 180:365–369, 1973.

48. *Diagnostic and Statistical Manual of Mental Disorders*, ed 2. Washington DC, American Psychiatric Association, 1968.

49. Schwartz CC, Myers JK, Astrachan BM: Psychiatric labeling and the rehabilitation of the mental patient: Implications of research findings for mental health policy. *Arch Gen Psychiatry* 31:329–334, 1974.

50. Rosenhan DL: *Sane: Insane*. JAMA 224:1646–1647, 1973.

51. Nunnally JC Jr: *Popular Conceptions of Mental Health*. New York, Holt Rinehart & Winston Inc, 1961.

52. Sarbin TR: On the futility of the proposition that some people be labelled "mentally ill." *J Consult Clin Psychol* 31:447, 1967.

53. Sarbin TR, Mancuso JC: Failure of a moral enterprise: Attitudes of the public toward mental illness. *J Consult Clin Psychol* 35:159–173, 1970.

54. Spitzer RL, Wilson PT: Nosology and the official psychiatric nomenclature, in Freedman A, Kaplan H, Sadock B (eds): *Comprehensive Textbook of Psychiatry*. Baltimore, Williams & Wilkins Co, 1975, pp 826–845.

55. Klein D, Davis J: *Diagnosis and Drug Treatment of Psychiatric Disorders*. Baltimore, Williams & Wilkins Co, 1969.

56. Spitzer RL, Fleiss JL: A reanalysis of the reliability of psychiatric diagnosis. *Br J Psychiatry* 125:341–347, 1974.

57. Fletcher A: Clinical judgment of pulmonary emphysema—an experimental study. *Proc R Soc Med* 45:577–584, 1952.

58. Davies LG: Observer variation in reports on electrocardiograms. *Br Heart J* 20:153–161, 1958.

59. Cochrane AL, Garland LH: Observer error in interpretation of chest films: International investigation. *Lancet* 2:505–509, 1952.

60. Yerushalmy J: Statistical problems in assessing methods of medical diagnosis, with special reference to x-ray techniques. *Public Health Rep* 62:1432–1449, 1947.

61. Markush RE, Schaaf WE, Seigel DG: The influence of the death certifier on the results of epidemiologic studies. *J Natl Med Assoc* 59:105–113, 1967.

62. Garland LH: The problem of observer error. *Bull NY Acad Med* 36:570–584, 1960.
63. Feinstein A: *Clinical Judgment.* Baltimore, Williams & Wilkins Co, 1967.
64. Feighner JP, Robins E, Guze SB, et al: Diagnostic criteria for use in psychiatric re-search. *Arch Gen Psychiatry* 26:57–63, 1972.
65. Spitzer RL, Endicott J, Robins E: *Research Diagnostic Criteria (RDC).* New York, Biometrics Research, New York State Department of Mental Hygiene, 1974.
66. Spitzer RL, Endicott J, Robins E, et al: Preliminary report of the reliability of Research Diagnostic Criteria applied to psychiatric case records, in Sudilofsky A, Beer B, Gershon S (eds): *Prediction in Psychopharmacology.* New York, Raven Press, 1975, pp 1–47.
67. Gunderson JG, Autry JH, Mosher LR, et al: Special report: Schizophrenia, 1974. *Schizophrenia Bull* 9:15–54, 1974.
68. Cronbach LJ, Gleser GC, Harinder N, et al: *The Dependability of Behavioral Mea-surements: Theory of Generalizability for Scores and Profiles.* New York, John Wiley & Sons Inc, 1972.
69. Cronbach LJ, Gleser GC: Interpretation of reliability and validity coefficients: Remarks on a paper by Lord. *J Educ Psychol* 50:230–237, 1959.
70. Fleiss JL, Cohen J: The equivalence of weighted kappa and the intraclass correlation coefficient as measures of reliability. *Educ Psychol Meas* 33:613–619, 1973.
71. Fleiss JL: Measuring agreement between two judges on the presence or absence of a trait. *Biometrics* 31:651–659, 1975.

III

Reactions to Health and Illness and to Social Aspects of Disease

Medical sociologists have studied people's definitions and reactions to illness perhaps more than almost any other issue. Indeed, such study has been the building block of one of the major intellectual perspectives in medical sociology and the sociology of deviance—labeling theory. Labeling theory has many contributors, but most important was the early work by Edwin Lemert in his book *Social Pathology* (New York: McGraw Hill, 1951), which developed the basic intellectual approach.

In the mental-health area, the expansion of this perspective that was most influential was the work of Thomas Scheff. Reading 10 presents in outline form the foundations of his position. Scheff later expanded this work in an influential book entitled *Being Mentally Ill* (Chicago: Aldine, 1966), but the paper reprinted here states the basic theory. Scheff's argument about the importance of labeling in the generation of mentally disordered behavior stimulated much interest and research, and attracted strong proponents and opponents. An extensive research literature has developed around issues Scheff discusses, and this theoretical perspective has been particularly appealing to those sociologists who like to believe that most things of importance are caused by social structure, and not biology. In my judgment, Scheff offers a useful and powerful perspective for studying and understanding the *course* of mental disorders, but he has not been substantiated to any significant extent in his hypotheses about *causes*.

In reading 11, Lee Robins takes one area, alcoholism, and critically examines the assumptions of labeling theory against what is presently known. This is a devastating critique of the labeling position, at least as it relates to alcoholism. Robins speculates about the areas in which labeling theory may have more or less explanatory power, and remains open to the usefulness of the perspective despite her critical appraisal.

In reading 12, I review what is generally known about the way patients come to perceive symptoms and the factors that influence their reactions. Using recent developments in attribution theory in social psychology, I suggest some new ways in which we can look at patients' presentations of their complaints and how they might be more effectively managed by the physician. *Medical Sociology*, 2d ed., contains a much more extensive discussion of illness behavior (pp. 249–89) than is possible here, and the reader who wishes a more general introduction to the area may wish to review that discussion.

The next four readings all deal with studies of social and psychological determinants of illness. These papers are simply samples from a large literature that is attempting to map the ways in which sociocultural and psychosocial factors affect the occurrence of illness. In reading 13, Lawrence Hinkle, a professor of medicine at the Cornell Medical School and a long-term student of stress, reviews his program of research extending over many years on social change and health. Reading 14 is an intriguing study by Meyer and Haggerty in which they took throat cultures on children, relating the occurrence of streptococcal infections to stresses in the family. This study again illustrates the complexity of illness. Although some children who had the streptococci in their throats never became ill, others did. The challenge is to discover why. Meyer and Haggerty suggest that family stress may contribute to explaining this difference. Reading 15, by David Jenkins, reviews evidence on the possible role of psychosocial factors in coronary heart disease. Jenkins presents growing evidence of a link between a behavior pattern called Type A and the occurrence of coronary disease. This pattern of behavior is characterized by an intense striving for achievement, competitiveness, impatience, and time urgency. The findings in this area have been sufficiently provocative to interest many scientists in trying to understand these behaviors and their link to heart disease. In reading 16, Bruce Dohrenwend reviews a large number of studies on social status and psychological disorder, addressing the issue of social selection versus social causation discussed in my introduction. As will become clear, working out the relative influence of these two processes is not easy, and Dohrenwend suggests a strategy that he has adopted to try to do so in the case of psychological disorder.

10

The Role of the Mentally Ill
and the Dynamics of Mental Disorder

A Research Framework

Thomas J. Scheff

Although the last two decades have seen a vast increase in the number of studies of functional mental disorder, there is as yet no substantial, verified body of knowledge in this area. A quotation from a recent symposium on schizophrenia summarizes the present situation:

> During the past decade, the problems of chronic schizophrenia have claimed the energy of workers in many fields. Despite significant contributions which reflect continuing progress, *we have yet to learn to ask ourselves the right questions.* [1]

Many investigators apparently agree; systematic studies have not only failed to provide answers to the problem of causation, but there is considerable feeling that the problem itself has not been formulated correctly.

One frequently noted deficiency in psychiatric formulations of the problem is the failure to incorporate social processes into the dynamics of mental disorder. Although the importance of these processes is increasingly recognized by psychiatrists, the conceptual models used in formulating research questions are basically concerned with individual rather than social systems. Genetic, biochemical, and psychological investigations seek different causal agents, but utilize similar models: dynamic systems which are located within the individual. In these investigations, social processes tend to be relegated to a subsidiary role, because the model focuses attention on individual differences, rather than on the social system in which the individuals are involved.

Recently a number of writers have sought to develop an approach which would give more emphasis to social processes. Lemert, Erikson, Goffman, and Szasz have notably contributed to this approach. [2] Lemert, particularly, by rejecting the more conventional concern with the origins of mental deviance, and stressing instead the

SOURCE: *Sociometry* 26 (1963): 436–53. Copyright © 1963 by the American Sociological Association. Reprinted by permission of the publisher and the author.

potential importance of the societal reaction in stabilizing deviance, focuses primarily on mechanisms of social control. The work of all of these authors suggests reasearch avenues which are analytically separable from questions of individual systems and point, therefore, to a theory which would incorporate social processes.

The purpose of the present paper is to contribute to the formulation of such a theory by stating a set of nine propositions which make up basic assumptions for a social system model of mental disorder. This set is largely derived from the work of the authors listed above, all but two of the propositions (#4 and #5) being suggested, with varying degrees of explicitness, in the cited references. By stating these propositions explicitly, this paper attempts to facilitate testing of basic assumptions, all of which are empirically unverified, or only partly verified. By stating these assumptions in terms of standard sociological concepts, this paper attempts to show the relevance to studies of mental disorder of findings from diverse areas of social science, such as race relations and prestige suggestion. This paper also delineates three problems which are crucial for a sociological theory of mental disorder: what are the conditions in a culture under which diverse kinds of deviance become stable and uniform; to what extent, in different phases of careers of mental patients, are symptoms of mental illness the result of conforming behavior; is there a general set of contingencies which lead to the definition of deviant behavior as a manifestation of mental illness? Finally, this paper attempts to formulate special conceptual tools to deal with these problems, which are directly linked to sociological theory. The social institution of insanity, residual deviance, the social role of the mentally ill, and the bifurcation of the societal reaction into the alternative reactions of denial and labeling, are examples of such conceptual tools.

These conceptual tools are utilized to construct a theory of mental disorder in which psychiatric symptoms are considered to be violations of social norms, and stable "mental illness" to be a social role. The validity of this theory depends upon verification of the nine propositions listed below in future studies, and should, therefore, be applied with caution, and with appreciation for its limitations. One such limitation is that the theory attempts to account for a much narrower class of phenomena than is usually found under the rubric of mental disorder; the discussion that follows will be focused exclusively on stable or recurring mental disorder, and does not explain the causes of single deviant episodes. A second major limitation is that the theory probably distorts the phenomena under discussion. Just as the individual system models under-stress social processes, the model presented here probably exaggerates their importance. The social system model "holds constant" individual differences, in order to articulate the relationship between society and mental disorder. Ultimately, a framework which encompassed both individual and social systems would be desirable. Given the present state of knowledge, however, this framework may prove useful by providing an explicit contrast to the more conventional medical and psychological approaches, and thus assisting in the formulation of sociological studies of mental disorder.

The Symptoms of "Mental Illness" as Residually Deviant Behavior

One source of immediate embarrassment to any social theory of "mental illness" is that the terms used in referring to these phenomena in our society prejudge the issue. The medical metaphor "mental illness" suggests a determinate process which occurs within the individual: the unfolding and development of disease. It is convenient, therefore, to drop terms derived from the disease metaphor in favor of a standard sociological concept, deviant behavior, which signifies behavior that violates a social norm in a given society.

If the symptoms of mental illness are to be construed as violations of social norms, it is necessary to specify the type of norms involved. Most norm violations do not cause the violator to be labeled as mentally ill, but as ill-mannered, ignorant, sinful, criminal, or perhaps just harried, depending on the type of norm involved. There are innumerable norms, however, over which consensus is so complete that the members of a group appear to take them for granted. A host of such norms surround even the simplest conversation: a person engaged in conversation is expected to face toward his partner, rather than directly away from him; if his gaze is toward the partner, he is expected to look toward his eyes, rather than, say, toward his forehead; to stand at a proper conversational distance, neither one inch away nor across the room, and so on. A person who regularly violated these expectations probably would not be thought to be merely ill-bred, but as strange, bizarre, and frightening, because his behavior violates the assumptive world of the group, the world that is construed to be the only one that is natural, decent, and possible.

The culture of the group provides a vocabulary of terms for categorizing many norm violations: crime, perversion, drunkenness, and bad manners are familiar examples. Each of these terms is derived from the type of norm broken, and ultimately, from the type of behavior involved. After exhausting these categories, however, there is always a résidue of the most diverse kinds of violations, for which the culture provides no explicit label. For example, although there is great cultural variation in what is defined as decent or real, each culture tends to reify its definition of decency and reality, and so provide no way of handling violations of its expectations in these areas. The typical norm governing decency or reality, therefore, literally "goes without saying" and its violation is unthinkable for most of its members. For the convenience of the society in construing those instances of unnamable deviance which are called to its attention, these violations may be lumped together into a residual category: witchcraft, spirit possession, or, in our own society, mental illness. In this paper, the diverse kinds of deviation for which our society provides no explicit label, and which, therefore, sometimes lead to the labeling of the violator as mentally ill, will be considered to be technically *residual deviance*.

The Origins, Prevalence and Course of Residual Deviance

The first proposition concerns the origins of residual deviance. 1. **Residual deviance arises from fundamentally diverse sources.** It has been demonstrated that some types of mental disorder are the result of organic causes. It appears likely, therefore, that there are genetic, biochemical or physiological origins for residual deviance. It also appears that residual deviance can arise from individual psychological pecularities and from differences in upbringing and training. Residual deviance can also probably be produced by various kinds of external stress: the sustained fear and hardship of combat, and deprivation of food, sleep, and even sensory experience.[3]

Residual deviance, finally, can be a volitional act of innovation or defiance. The kinds of behavior deemed typical of mental illness, such as hallucinations, delusions, depression, and mania, can all arise from these diverse sources.

The second proposition concerns the prevalence of residual deviance which is analogous to the "total" or "true" prevalence of mental disorder (in contrast to the "treated" prevalence). **2. Relative to the rate of treated mental illness, the rate of unrecorded residual deviance is extremely high.** There is evidence that grossly deviant behavior is often not noticed or, if it is noticed, it is rationalized as eccentricity. Apparently, many persons who are extremely withdrawn, or who "fly off the handle" for extended periods of time, who imagine fantastic events, or who hear voices or see visions, are not labeled as insane either by themselves or others.[4] Their deviance, rather, is unrecognized, ignored, or rationalized. This pattern of inattention and rationalization will be called "denial."[5]

In addition to the kind of evidence cited above there are a number of epidemiological studies of total prevalence. There are numerous problems in interpreting the results of these studies; the major difficulty is that the definition of mental disorder is different in each study, as are the methods used to screen cases. These studies represent, however, the best available information and can be used to estimate total prevalence.

A convenient summary of findings is presented in Plunkett and Gordon.[6] This source compares the methods and populations used in eleven field studies, and lists rates of total prevalence (in percentages) as 1.7, 3.6, 4.5, 4.7, 5.3, 6.1, 10.9, 13.8, 23.2, 23.3, and 33.3.

How do these total rates compare with the rates of treated mental disorder? One of the studies cited by Plunkett and Gordon, the Baltimore study reported by Pasamanick, is useful in this regard since it includes both treated and untreated rates.[7] As compared with the untreated rate of 10.9 per cent, the rate of treatment in state, VA, and private hospitals of Baltimore residents was .5 per cent.[8] That is, for every mental patient there were approximately 20 untreated cases located by the survey. It is possible that the treated rate is too low, however, since patients treated by private physicians were not included. Judging from another study, the New Haven study of treated prevalence, the number of patients treated in private practice is small compared to those hospitalized: over 70 per cent of the patients located in that study were hospitalized even though extensive case-finding techniques were employed. The over-all prevalence in the New Haven study was reported as .8 per cent, which is in good agreement with my estimate of .7 per cent for the Baltimore study.[9] If we accept .8 per cent as an estimate of the upper limit of treated prevalence for the Pasamanick study, the ratio of treated to untreated cases is 1/14. That is, for every treated patient we should expect to find 14 untreated cases in the community.

One interpretation of this finding is that the untreated patients in the community represent those cases with less severe disorders, while those patients with severe impairments all fall into the treated group. Some of the findings in the Pasamanick study point in this direction. Of the untreated patients, about half are classified as psychoneurotic. Of the psychoneurotics, in turn, about half again are classified as suffering from minimal impairment. At least a fourth of the untreated group, then, involved very mild disorders.[10]

The evidence from the group diagnosed as psychotic does not support ʌnis interpretation, however. Almost all of the cases diagnosed as psychotic were judged to involve severe impairment, yet half of the diagnoses of psychosis occurred in the untreated gruoup. In other words, according to this study there were as many untreated as treated cases of psychoses.[11]

On the basis of the high total prevalence rates cited above and other evidence, it seems plausible that residual deviant behavior is usually transitory, which is the substance of the third proposition. **3. Most residual deviance is "denied" and is transitory.** The high rates of total prevalence suggest that most residual deviancy is unrecognized or rationalized away. For this type of deviance, which is amorphous and uncrystallized, Lemert uses the term "primary deviation."[12] Balint describes similar behavior as "the unorganized phase of illness."[13] Although Balint assumes that patients in this phase ultimately "settle down" to an "organized illness," other outcomes are possible. A person in this stage may "organize" his deviance in other than illness terms, e.g., as eccentricity or genius, or the deviant acts may terminate when situational stress is removed.

The experience of battlefield psychiatrists can be interpreted to support the hypothesis that residual deviance is usually transistory. Glass reports that combat neurosis is often self-terminating if the soldier is kept with his unit and given only the most superficial medical attention.[14] Descriptions of child behavior can be interpreted in the same way. According to these reports, most children go through periods in which at least several of the following kinds of deviance may occur: temper tantrums, head banging, scratching, pinching, biting, fantasy playmates or pets, illusory physical complaints, and fears of sounds, shapes, colors, persons, animals, darkness, weather, ghosts, and so on.[15] In the vast majority of instances, however, these behavior patterns do not become stable.

If residual deviance is highly prevalent among ostensibly "normal" persons and is usually transitory, as suggested by the last two propositions, what accounts for the small percentage of residual deviants who go on to deviant careers? To put the question another way, under what conditions is residual deviance stabilized? The conventional hypothesis is that the answer lies in the deviant himself. The hypothesis suggested here is that the most important single factor (but not the only factor) in the stabilization of residual deviance is the societal reaction. Residual deviance may be stabilized if it is defined to be evidence of mental illness, and/or the deviant is placed in a deviant status, and begins to play the role of the mentally ill. In order to avoid the implication that mental disorder is merely role-playing and pretence, it is first necessary to discuss the social institution of insanity.

Social Control: Individual and Social Systems of Behavior

In *The Myth of Mental Illness*, Szasz proposes that mental disorder be viewed within the framework of "the game-playing model of human behavior." He then describes hysteria, schizophrenia, and other mental disorders as the "impersonation" of sick persons by those whose "real" problem concerns "problems of living." Although Szaz states that role-playing by mental patients may not be completely or even mostly voluntary, the implication is that mental disorder be viewed as a strategy chosen by the individual as a way of obtaining help from others. Thus, the term "impersonation" suggests calculated and deliberate shamming by the patient. In his comparisons of hysteria, malingering, and cheating, although he notes differences between these behavior patterns, he suggests that these differences may be mostly a matter of whose point of view is taken in describing the behavior.

The present paper also uses the role-playing model to analyze mental disorder, but places more emphasis on the involuntary aspects of role-playing than Szasz, who tends to treat role-playing as an individual system of behavior. In many social psychological discussions, however, role-playing is considered as a part of a social system. The individual plays his role by articulating his behavior with the cues and actions of other persons involved in the transaction. The proper performance of a role is dependent on having a cooperative audience. This proposition may also be reversed: having an audience which acts toward the individual in a uniform way may lead the actor to play the expected role even if he is not particularly interested in doing so. The "baby of the family" may come to find this role obnoxious, but the uniform pattern of cues and actions which confronts him in the family may lock in with his own vocabulary of responses so that it is inconvenient and difficult for him not to play the part expected of him. To the degree that alternative roles are closed off, the proffered role may come to be the only way the individual can cope with the situation.

One of Szasz's very apt formulations touches upon the social systemic aspects of role-playing. He draws an analogy between the role of the mentally ill and the "type-casting" of actors.[16] Some actors get a reputation for playing one type of role, and find it difficult to obtain other roles. Although they may be displeased, they may also come to incorporate aspects of the type-cast role into their self-conceptions, and ultimately into their behavior. Findings in several social psychological studies suggest that an individual's role behavior may be shaped by the kinds of "deference" that he regularly receives from others.[17]

One aspect of the voluntariness of role-playing is the extent to which the actor believes in the part he is playing. Although a role may be played cynically, with no belief, or completely sincerely, with whole-hearted belief, many roles are played on the basis of an intricate mixture of belief and disbelief. During the course of a study of a large public mental hospital, several patients told the author in confidence about their cynical use of their symptoms—to frighten new personnel, to escape from unpleasant work details, and so on. Yet these *same* patients, at other times, appear to have been sincere in their symptomatic behavior. Apparently it was sometimes difficult for them to tell whether they were playing the role or the role was playing them. Certain types of symptomatology are quite interesting in this connection. In simulation of previous psychotic states, and in the behavior pattern known to psychiatrists as the Ganser syndrome, it is apparently almost impossible for the observer to separate feigning of symptoms from involuntary acts with any degree of certainty.[18] In accordance with what has been said so far, the difficulty is probably that the patient is just as confused by his own behavior as is the observer.

This discussion suggests that a stable role performance may arise when the actor's role imagery locks in with the type of "deference" which he regularly receives. An extreme example of this process may be taken from anthropological and medical reports concerning the "dead role," as in deaths attributed to "bone-pointing."

Death from bone-pointing appears to arise from the conjunction of two fundamental processes which characterize all social behavior. First, all individuals continually orient themselves by means of responses which are perceived in social interaction: the individual's identity and continuity of experience are dependent on these cues.[19] Secondly, the individual has his own vocabulary of expectations, which may in a particular situation either agree with or be in conflict with the sanctions to which he is exposed. Entry into a role may be complete when this role is part of the individual's expectations, and when these expectations are reaffirmed in social interaction. In the following pages this principle will be applied to the problem of the causation of mental disorder.

What are the beliefs and practices that constitute the social institution of insanity?[20] And how do they figure in the development of mental disorder? Two propositions concerning beliefs about mental disorder in the general public will now be considered.

4. Stereotyped imagery of mental disorder is learned in early childhood. Although there are no substantiating studies in this area, scattered observations lead the author to conclude that children learn a considerable amount of imagery concerning deviance very early, and that much of the imagery comes from their peers rather than from adults. The literal meaning of "crazy," a term now used in a wide variety of contexts, is probably grasped by children during the first years of elementary school. Since adults are often vague and evasive in their responses to questions in this area, an aura of mystery surrounds it. In this socialization the grossest sterotypes which are heir to childhood fears, e.g., of the "boogie man," survive. These conclusions are quite speculative, of course, and need to be investigated systematically, possibly with techniques similar to those used in studies of the early learning of racial sterotypes.

Assuming, however, that this hypothesis is sound, what effect does early learning have on the shared conceptions of insanity held in the community? There is much fallacious material learned in early childhood which is later discarded when more adequate information replaces it. This question leads to hypothesis No. 5. **5. The stereotypes of insanity are continually reaffirmed, inadvertently, in ordinary social interaction.**

Although many adults become acquainted with medical concepts of mental illness, the traditional stereotypes are not discarded, but continue to exist alongside the medical conceptions, because the stereotypes receive almost continual support from the mass media and in ordinary social discourse. In newspapers, it is a common practice to mention that a rapist or a murderer was once a mental patient. This negative information, however, is seldom offset by positive reports. An item like the following is almost inconceivable:

> Mrs. Ralph Jones, an ex-mental patient, was elected president of the Fairview Home and Garden Society in their meeting last Thursday.

Because of highly biased reporting, the reader is free to make the unwarranted inference that murder and rape occur more frequently among ex-mental patients than among the population at large. Actually, it has been demonstrated that the incidence of crimes of violence, or of any crime, is much lower among ex-mental patients than among the general population.[21] Yet, this is not the picture presented to the public.

Reaffirmation of the stereotype of insanity occurs not only in the mass media, but also in ordinary conversation, in jokes, anecdotes, and even in conventional phrases. Such phrases as "Are you crazy?", or "It would be a madhouse," "It's driving me out of my mind," or "It's driving me distracted," and hundred of others occur frequently in informal conversations. In this usage insanity itself is seldom the topic of conversation; the phrases are so much a part of ordinary language that only the person who considers each word carefully can eliminate them from his speech. Through verbal usages the stereotypes of insanity are a relatively permanent part of the social structure.

In a recent study Nunnally demonstrated that reaffirmation of stereotypes occurs in the mass media. In a systematic and extensive content analysis of television, radio, newspapers and magazines, including "confession" magazines, they found an image of mental disorder presented which was overwhelmingly stereotyped.

> . . . media presentations emphasized the bizarre symptoms of the mentally ill. For example, information relating to Factor I (the conception that mentally ill persons look and act different from "normal" people) was recorded 89 times. Of these, 88 affirmed the factor, that is, indicated or suggested that people with mental-health problems "look and act different": only one item denied Factor I. In television dramas, for example, the afflicted person often enters the scene staring glassy-eyed, with his mouth widely ajar, mumbling incoherent phrases or laughing uncontrollably. Even in what would be considered the milder disorders, neurotic phobias and obsessions, the afflicted person is presented as having bizarre facial expressions and actions.[22]

Denial and Labeling

According to the analysis presented here, the traditional stereotypes of mental disorder are solidly entrenched in the population because they are learned early in childhood and are continuously reaffirmed in the mass media and in everyday conversation. How do these beliefs function in the processes leading to mental disorder? This question will be considered by first referring to the earlier discussion of the societal reaction to residual deviance.

It was stated that the usual reaction to residual deviance is denial, and that in these cases most residual deviance is transitory. The societal reaction to deviance is not always denial, however. In a small proportion of cases the reaction goes the other way, exaggerating and at times distorting the extent and degree of deviation. This pattern of exaggeration, which we will call "labeling," has been noted by Garfinkel in his discussion of the "degradation" of officially recognized criminals.[23] Goffman makes a similar point in his description of the "discrediting" of mental patients.[24] Apparently under some conditions the societal reaction to deviance is to seek out signs of abnormality in the deviant's history to show that he was always essentially a deviant.

The contrasting social reactions of denial and labeling provide a means of answering two fundamental questions. If deviance arises from diverse sources—physical, psychological, and situational—how does the uniformity of behavior that is associated with insanity develop? Secondly, if deviance is usually transitory, how does it become stabilized in those patients who became chronically deviant? To summarize, what are the sources of uniformity and stability of deviant behavior?

In the approach taken here the answer to this question is based on hypotheses Nos. 4 and 5, that the role imagery of insanity is learned early in childhood, and is reaffirmed in social interaction. In a crisis, when the deviance of an individual becomes a public issue, the traditional stereotype of insanity becomes the guiding imagery for action, both for those reacting to the deviant and, at times, for the deviant himself. When societal agents and persons around the deviant react to him uniformly in terms of the traditional stereotypes of insanity, his amorphous and unstructured deviant behavior tends to crystallize in conformity to these expectations, thus becoming similar to the behavior of other deviants classified as mentally ill, and stable over time. The process of becoming uniform and stable is completed when the traditional imagery becomes a part of the deviant's orientation for guiding his own behavior.

The idea that cultural stereotypes may stabilize primary deviance, and tend to produce uniformity in symptoms, is supported by cross-cultural studies of mental disorder. Although some observers insist there are underlying similarities, most agree that there are enormous differences in the manifest symptoms of stable mental disorder *between* societies, and great similarity *within* societies.[25]

These considerations suggest that the labeling process is a crucial contingency in most careers of residual deviance. Thus Glass, who observed that neuropsychiatric casualties may not become mentally ill if they are kept with their unit, goes on to say that military experience with psychotherapy has been disappointing. Soldiers who are removed from their unit to a hospital, he states, often go on to become chronically impaired.[26] That is, their deviance is stabilized by the labeling process, which is implicit in their removal and hospitalization. A similar interpretation can be made by comparing the observations of childhood disorders among Mexican-Americans with those of "Anglo" children. Childhood disorders such as *susto* (an illness believed to result from fright) sometimes have damaging outcomes in Mexican-American children.[27] Yet the deviant behavior involved is very similar to that which seems to have high incidence among Anglo children, with permanent impairment virtually never occurring. Apparently through cues from his elders the Mexican-American child, behaving initially much like his Anglo counterpart, learns to enter the sick role, at times with serious consequences.[28]

Acceptance of the Deviant Role

From this point of view, then, most mental disorder can be considered to be a social role. This social role complements and reflects the status of the insane in the social structure. It is through the social processes which maintain the status of the insane that the varied deviancies from which mental disorder arises are made uniform and stable. The stabilization and uniformization of residual deviance are completed when the deviant accepts the role of the insane as the framework within which he organizes his own behavior. Three hypotheses are stated below which suggest some of the processes which cause the deviant to accept such a stigmatized role.

6. **Labeled deviants may be rewarded for playing the stereotyped deviant role.** Ordinarily patients who display "insight" are rewarded by psychiatrists and other personnel. That is, patients who manage to find evidence of "their illness" in their past and present behavior, confirming the medical and societal diagnosis, receive benefits. This pattern of behavior is a special case of a more general pattern that has been called the "apostolic function" by Balint, in which the physician and others inadvertently cause the patient to display symptoms of the illness the physician thinks the patient has.[29] Not only physicians but other hospital personnel and even other patients, reward the deviant for conforming to the stereotypes.[30]

7. **Labeled deviants are punished when they attempt the return to conventional roles.** The second process operative is the systematic blockage of entry to nondeviant roles once the label has been publicly applied. Thus the ex-mental patient, although he is urged to rehabilitate himself in the community, usually finds himself discriminated against in seeking to return to his old status, and on trying to find a new one in the occupational, marital, social, and other spheres.[31] Thus, to a degree, the labeled deviant is rewarded for deviating, and punished for attempting to conform.

8. **In the crisis occurring when a primary deviant is publicly labeled, the deviant is highly suggestible, and may accept the proffered role of the insane as the only alternative.** When gross deviancy is publicly recognized and made an issue, the primary deviant may be profoundly confused, anxious, and ashamed. In this crisis it seems reasonable to assume that the deviant will be suggestible to the cues that he gets from the reactions of others toward him.[32] But those around him are also in a crisis; the incomprehensible nature of the deviance, and the seeming need for immediate action lead them to take collective action against the deviant on the basis of the attitude which all share—the traditional stereotypes of insanity. The deviant is sensitive to the cues provided by these others and begins to think of himself in terms of the stereotyped role of insanity, which is part of his own role vocabulary also, since he, like those reacting to him, learned it early in childhood. In this situation his behavior may begin to follow the pattern suggested by his own stereotypes and the reactions of others. That is, when a primary deviant organizes his behavior within the framework of mental disorder, and when his organization is validated by others, particularly prestigeful others such as physicians, he is "hooked" and will proceed on a career of chronic deviance.

The role of suggestion is noted by Warner in his description of bone-pointing magic:

> The effect of (the suggestion of the entire community on the victim) is obviously drastic. An analogous situation in our society is hard to imagine. If all a man's near kin, his father, mother, brothers and sisters, wife, children, business associates, friends and all the other members of the society, should suddenly withdraw themselves because of some dramatic circumstance, refusing to take any attitude but one of taboo . . . and then perform over him a sacred ceremony . . . the enormous suggestive power of this movement . . . of the community after it has had its attitudes (toward the victim) crystallized can be somewhat understood by ourselves.[33]

If we substitute for black magic the taboo that usually accompanies mental disorder, and consider a commitment proceeding or even mental hospital admission as a sacred ceremony, the similarity between Warner's description and the typical events in the development of mental disorder is considerable.

The last three propositions suggest that once a person has been placed in a deviant status there are rewards for conforming to the deviant role, and punishments for not conforming to the deviant role. This is not to imply, however, that the symptomatic behavior of persons occupying a deviant status is always a manifestation of conforming behavior. To explain this point, some discussion of the process of self-control in "normals" is necessary.

In a recent discussion of the process of self-control, Shibutani notes that self-control is not automatic, but is an intricate and delicately balanced process, sustainable only under propitious circumstances.[34] He points out that fatigue, the reaction to narcotics, excessive excitement or tension (such as is generated in mobs), or a number of other conditions interfere with self-control; conversely, conditions which produce normal bodily states, and deliberative processes such as symbolization and imaginative rehearsal before action, facilitate it.

One might argue that a crucially important aspect of imaginative rehearsal is the image of himself that the actor projects into his future action. Certainly in American society, the cultural image of the "normal" adult is that of a person endowed with self-control ("willpower," "back-bone," "strength of character," etc.). For the person who sees himself as endowed with the trait of self-control, self-control is facilitated, since he can imagine himself enduring stress during his imaginative rehearsal, and also while under actual stress.

For a person who has acquired an image of himself as lacking the ability to control his own actions, the process of self-control is likely to break down under stress. Such a person may feel that he has reached his "breaking-point" under circumstances which would be endured by a person with a "normal" self-conception. This is to say, a greater lack of self-control than can be explained by stress tends to appear in those roles for which the culture transmits imagery which emphasizes lack of self-control. In American society such imagery is transmitted for the roles of the very young and very old, drunkards and drug addicts, gamblers, and the mentally ill.

Thus, the social role of the mentally ill has a different significance at different phases of residual deviance. When labeling first occurs, it merely gives a name to primary deviation which has other roots. When (and if) the primary deviance becomes an issue, and is not ignored or rationalized away, labeling may create a social type, a pattern of "symptomatic" behavior in conformity with the stereotyped expectations of others. Finally, to the extent that the deviant role becomes a part of the deviant's self-conception, his ability to control his own behavior may be impaired under stress, resulting in episodes of compulsive behavior.

The preceding eight hypotheses form the basis for the final causal hypothesis. 9. **Among residual deviants, labeling is the single most important cause of careers of residual deviance.** This hypothesis assumes that most residual deviance, if it does not become the basis for entry into the sick role, will not lead to a deviant career. Most deviant careers, according to this point of view, arise out of career contingencies, and are therefore not directly connected with the origins of the initial deviance.[35] Although there are a wide variety of contingencies which lead to labeling rather than denial, these contingencies can be usefully classified in terms of the nature of the deviant behavior, the person who commits the deviant acts, and the community in which the deviance occurs. Other things being equal, the severity of the societal reaction to deviance is a function of, first, the degree, amount, and visibility of the deviant behavior; second, the power of the deviant, and the social distance between the deviant and the agents of social control; and finally, the tolerance level of the community, and the availability in the culture of the community of alternative nondeviant roles.[36] Particularly crucial for future research is the importance of the first two contingencies (the amount and degree of deviance), which are characteristics of the deviant, relative to the remaining five contingencies, which are characteristics of the social system.[37] To the extent that these five factors are found empirically to be independent determinants of labeling and denial, the status of the mental patient can be considered a partly ascribed rather than a completely achieved status. The dynamics of treated mental illness could then be profitably studied quite apart from the individual dynamics of mental disorder.

Conclusion

This paper has presented a sociological theory of the causation of stable mental disorder. Since the evidence advanced in support of the theory was scattered and fragmentary, it can only be suggested as a stimulus to further discussion and research. Among the areas pointed out for further investigation are field studies of the prevalence and duration of residual deviance; investigations of stereotypes of mental disorder in children, the mass media, and adult conversations; studies of the rewarding of stereotyped deviation, blockage of return to conventional roles, and of the suggestibility of primary deviants in crises. The final causal hypothesis suggests studies of the conditions under which denial and labeling of residual deviation occur. The variables which might effect the societal reaction concern the nature of the deviance, the deviant himself, and the community in which the deviation occurs. Although many of the hypotheses suggested are largely unverified, they suggest avenues for investigating mental disorder different than those that are usually followed, and the rudiments of a general theory of deviant behavior.

Acknowledgments

This project was supported in part by the Graduate Research Committee of the University of Wisconsin. The help of many persons, too numerous to list here, who criticized earlier drafts is gratefully acknowledged.

References and Notes

1. Nathanial S. Apter, "Our Growing Restlessness with Problems of Chronic Schizophrenia," in Lawrence Appleby, et al., Chronic Schizophrenia, Glencoe, Ill.: Free Press, 1958.
2. Edwin M. Lemert, Social Pathology, New York: McGraw-Hill, 1951; Kai T. Erikson, "Patient Role and Social Uncertainty—A Dilemma of the Mentally Ill," Psychiatry, 20 (August, 1957), pp. 263–274; Erving Goffman, Asylums, New York: Doubleday-Anchor, 1961; Thomas S. Szasz, The Myth of Mental Illness, New York: Hoeber-Harper, 1961.

3. Philip Solomon, *et al.* (eds.), *Sensory Deprivation*, Cambridge: Harvard, 1961; E. L. Bliss, *et al.*, "Studies of Sleep Deprivation—Relationship to Schizophrenia," *A.M.A. Archives of Neurology and Psychiatry*, 81 (March, 1959), pp. 348–359.

4. See, for example, John A. Clausen and Marian R. Yarrow, "Paths to the Mental Hospital," *Journal of Social Issues*, 11 (December, 1955), pp. 25–32; August B. Hollingshead and Frederick C. Redlich, *Social Class and Mental Illness*, New York: Wiley, 1958, pp. 172–176; and Elaine Cumming and John Cumming, *Closed Ranks*, Cambridge: Harvard, 1957, pp. 92–103.

5. The term "denial" is used in the same sense as in Cumming and Cumming, *ibid.*, Chap. VII.

6. Richard J. Plunkett and John E. Gordon, *Epidemiology and Mental Illness*, New York: Basic Books, 1960.

7. Benjamin Pasamanick, "A Survey of Mental Disease in an Urban Population, IV, An Approach to Total Prevalence Rates," *Archives of General Psychiatry*, 5 (August, 1961), pp. 151–155.

8. *Ibid.*, p. 153.

9. Hollingshead and Redlich, *op. cit.*, p. 199.

10. Pasamanick, *op. cit.*, pp. 153–154.

11. *Ibid.*

12. Lemert, *op. cit.*, Chap. 4.

13. Michael Balint, *The Doctor, His Patient, and the Illness*, New York: International Universities Press, 1957, p. 18.

14. Albert J. Glass, "Psychotherapy in the Combat Zone," in *Symposium on Stress*, Washington, D.C.: Army Medical Service Graduate School, 1953. Cf. Abraham Kardiner and H. Spiegel, *War Stress and Neurotic Illness*, New York: Hoeber, 1947, Chaps. III–IV.

15. Frances L. Ilg and Louise B. Ames, *Child Behavior*, New York: Dell, 1960, pp. 138–188.

16. Szasz, *op. cit.*, p. 252. For discussion of type-casting see Orrin E. Klapp, *Heroes, Villains and Fools*, Englewood Cliffs, New Jersey: Prentice-Hall, 1962, pp. 5–8 and *passim*.

17. Cf. Zena S. Blau, "Changes in Status and Age Identification," *American Sociological Review*, 21 (April, 1956), pp. 198–203; James Benjamins, "Changes in Performance in Relation to Influences upon Self-Conceptualization," *Journal of Abnormal and Social Psychology*, 45 (July, 1950), pp. 473–480; Albert Ellis, "The Sexual Psychology of Human Hermaphrodites," *Psychosomatic Medicine*, 7 (March, 1945), pp. 108–125; S. Liberman, "The effect of Changes in Roles on the Attitudes of Role Occupants," *Human Relations*, 9 (1956), pp. 385–402. For a review of experimental evidence, see John H. Mann, "Experimental Evaluations of Role Playing," *Psychological Bulletin*, 53 (May, 1956), pp. 227–234. For an interesting demonstration of the inter-relations between the symptoms of patients on the same ward, see Sheppard G. Kellam and J. B. Chassan, "Social Context and Symptom Fluctuation," *Psychiatry*, 25 (November, 1962), pp. 370–381.

18. Leo Sadow and Alvin Suslick, "Simulation of a Previous Psychotic State," *A.M.A. Archives of General Psychiatry*, 4 (May, 1961), pp. 452–458.

19. Generalizing from experimental findings, Blake and Mouton make this statement about the processes of conformity, resistance to influence, and conversion to a new role: ". . . an individual requires a stable framework, including salient and firm reference points, in order to orient himself and to regulate his interactions with others. This framework consists of external and internal anchorages available to the individual whether he is aware of them or not. With an acceptable framework he can resist giving or accepting

information that is inconsistent with that framework or that requires him to relinquish it. In the absence of a stable framework he actively seeks to establish one through his own strivings by making use of significant and relevant information provided within the context of interaction. *By controlling the amount and kind of information available for orientation, he can be led to embrace conforming attitudes which are entirely foreign to his earlier ways of thinking."* Robert R. Blake and Jane S. Mouton, "Conformity, Resistance and Conversion," in *Conformity and Deviation*, Irwin A. Berg and Bernard M. Bass (eds.), New York: Harper, 1961, pp. 1–2. For a recent and striking demonstration of the effect on social communication in defining internal stimuli, see Stanley Schachter and Jerome E. Singer, "Cognitive, Social, and Physiological Determinants of Emotional State," *Psychological Review*, 69 (September, 1962), pp. 379–399.

20. The Cummings describe the social institution of insanity (the "patterned response" to deviance) in terms of denial, isolation, and insulation. Cumming and Cumming, *loc. cit.*

21. Henry Brill and Benjamin Malzberg, "Statistical Report Based on the Arrest Record of 5354 Male Ex-patients Released from New York State Mental Hospitals During the Period 1946–48," mimeographed document available from the authors; L. H. Cohen and H. Freeman, "How Dangerous to the Community are State Hospital Patients?", *Connecticut State Medical Journal*, 9 (September, 1945), pp. 697–701.

22. Jum C. Nunnally, Jr., *Popular Conceptions of Mental Health*, New York: Holt, Rinehart and Winston, 1961, p. 74.

23. Harold Garfinkel, "Conditions of Successful Degradation Ceremonies," *American Journal of Sociology*, 61 (March, 1956), pp. 420–424.

24. Goffman, "The Moral Career of the Mental Patient," in *Asylums, op. cit.*, pp. 125–171.

25. P. M. Yap, "Mental Diseases Peculiar to Certain Cultures: A Survey of Comparative Psychiatry," *Journal of Mental Science*, 97 (April, 1951), pp. 313–327; Paul E. Benedict and Irving Jacks, "Mental Illness in Primitive Societies," *Psychiatry*, 17 (November, 1954), pp. 377–389.

26. Glass, *op. cit.*

27. Lyle Saunders, *Cultural Differences and Medical Care*, New York: Russell Sage, 1954, p. 142.

28. For discussion, with many illustrative cases, of the process in which persons play the "dead role" and subsequently die, see Charles C. Herbert, "Life-influencing Interactions," in *The Physiology of Emotions*, Alexander Simon, *et al.*, eds., New York: Charles C. Thomas, 1961.

29. Balint, *op. cit.*, pp. 215–239. Cf. Thomas J. Scheff, "Decision Rules, Types of Error and Their Consequences in Medical Diagnosis," *Behavioral Science*, 8 (April, 1963), pp. 97–107.

30. William Caudill, F. C. Redlich, H. R. Gilmore, and E. B. Brody, "Social Structure and the Interaction Processes on a Psychiatric Ward," *American Journal of Orthopsychiatry*, 22 (April, 1952), pp. 314–334.

31. Lemert, *op. cit.*, provides an extensive discussion of this process under the heading of "Limitation of Participation," pp. 434–440.

32. This proposition receives support from Erikson's observations: Kai T. Erikson, *loc. cit.*

33. W. Lloyd Warner, *A Black Civilization*, rev. ed., New York: Harper, 1958, p. 242.

34. T. Shibutani, *Society and Personality*, Englewood Cliffs, N. J.: Prentice-Hall, 1961, Chapter 6, "Consciousness and Voluntary Conduct."

35. It should be noted, however, that these contingencies are causal only because they become part of a dynamic system: the reciprocal and cumulative inter-relation between

the deviant's behavior and the societal reaction. For example, the more the deviant enters the role of the mentally ill, the more he is defined by others as mentally ill; but the more he is defined as mentally ill, the more fully he enters the role, and so on. By representing this theory in the form of a flow chart, Walter Buckley pointed out that there are numerous such feedback loops implied here. For an explicit treatment of feedback, see Edwin M. Lemert, "Paranoia and the Dynamics of Exclusion," *Sociometry*, 25 (March, 1962), pp. 2–20.

36. *Cf.* Lemert, *op. cit.*, pp. 51–53, 55–68; Goffman, "The Moral Career of the Mental Patient," in *Asylums, op. cit.*, pp. 134–135; David Mechanic, "Some Factors in Identifying and Defining Mental Illness," *Mental Hygiene*, 46 (January, 1962), pp. 66–74; for a list of similar factors in the reaction to physical illness, see Earl L. Koos, *The Health of Regionville*, New York: Columbia University Press, 1954, pp. 30–38.

37. *Cf.* Thomas J. Scheff, "Psychiatric and Social Contingencies in the Release of Mental Patients in a Midwestern State," forthcoming; Simon Dinitz, Mark Lefton, Shirley Angrist, and Benjamin Pasamanick, "Psychiatric and Social Attributes as Predictors of Case Outcome in Mental Hospitalization," *Social Problems*, 8 (Spring, 1961), pp. 322–328.

11

Alcoholism and Labelling Theory

Lee N. Robins

It is difficult either to support or refute labelling theory by appeal to empirical data because the theory has not been put into refutable form by its proponents. Nor can we soon expect them to do so or agree with others' attempts to do so, since the proponents of labelling theory tend to be just those sociologists most suspicious of the validity of "hard" data. They could scarcely feel otherwise, because the essential point made by labelling theory is that so-called "objective" records (i.e., data created by police or hospitals) are *not* objective representations of the behaviors they purport to refer to. Their contention is that even information collected by interview is distorted, since after having been labelled by official agencies, the labelled individual reinterprets his or her prelabelling behavioral history as deviant and acts in accordance with the label thereafter. In short, labelling theorists believe that deviance in a society is largely the product of attempts to measure or record it. Like Archimedes, who realized he would have to stand outside the earth if he were to move it, the sociologist accepting labelling theory has nowhere to stand from which he or she can observe the "natural" rates against which the size of the distortion in official rates and rates based on interviews can be measured, to estimate the impact of labelling.

I do not really believe that the attempt to test labelling theory empirically is that hopeless. At any rate, we shall try to see whether what is known about alcoholism is consistent with what labelling theory would suggest. If it is not, our doubts about labelling theory will be increased. If results are consistent with what labelling theory would lead us to expect, its plausibility will be increased, although its correctness will still not be demonstrated.

SOURCE: Walter R. Gove, ed., *The Labelling of Deviance: Evaluating a Perspective* (Beverly Hills/ London: Sage Publications, Inc., 1975), pp. 21–33. Copyright © 1975 by Sage Publications, Inc. Reprinted by permission of the publisher and the author.

My own research experience has led me to have much more confidence in empirical data than have labelling theorists. Distortions undoubtedly do occur, perhaps as a result of labelling and certainly as a result of biases in likelihood of detection and recording as well as of measurement error. I have nevertheless been greatly impressed with the sturdiness of findings in the field of deviance, no matter what the bias of the investigator, how careless the methodology, what were the indices used, or how varied the social setting in which the research was done. Studies of predictors of deviant behavior have produced consistent results for forty years (from Healey and Bronner, 1926 to Wolfgang, 1972), in various countries (Sweden, the United States, Norway, Germany, Australia, and England, for example), and by authors with very different etiological theories and methods. Results compiled by social workers, criminologists, psychologists, educators, sociologists, psychiatrists—both Freudian and anti-Freudian—have agreed, whether their empirical data base was vital statistics, police records, school records, interviews, or anonymous questionnaires.

Both the predictors and their relative importance appear reasonably consistent from study to study. The best predictor of any specific later deviant act seems always to be early deviant behavior, and the specific *nature* of that earlier deviant behavior seems uniformly to be rather unimportant. Being a late adolescent or young adult male and having parents with a history of deviance—again, the specific nature of that deviance is not important—are the next best predictors of later deviance. Family history continues to be a potent predictor even when the child does not live with the affected parent. Social group memberships predict deviance, too, but they follow as a poor third. Being urban, poor, and/or undereducated, and in ethnic groups of low social status (black in the United States, Irish in the United Kingdom) are strong predictors only if family history and the person's own prior behavior are not held constant—for the latter variables tend to be highly correlated with social group membership.

These well-replicated findings have made me suspect that labelling theory is either incorrect or at least not a powerful explanatory theory for the continuation of deviance for several reasons.

(1) Since the social and personal predictors of deviance are as clear-cut when unlabelled behavior (covert illegal behavior, for instance) is studied as when labelled behavior is studied (as long as some estimate of frequency or severity is used for the unlabelled behavior to parallel the fact that arrests and other official labels almost always occur after repeated occasions of deviance). Labelling is clearly not a *necessary* intervening variable between social and personal history and later deviance.

(2) Labelling would not seem to have the irreversible effects on later behavior claimed for it. All common forms of deviance (drug use, theft, drinking, sexual promiscuity, fighting) seem to drop off with age, whether or not they have been labelled and whether or not their being labelled eventuated in intervention in the form of treatment or punishment. This dropping off of deviance with aging argues against labelling theory, because the number of times one has been labelled in a lifetime can only increase, not decrease, over time. If deviant labels produce enduring increases in the labelled behavior, one would expect increasing liabilities to deviance with age as the experiences of being labelled accumulate, instead of the

actual self-limited period of risk for deviance, terminating for most people in middle age.

(3) Labelling theory argues that labels encourage the very behavior specified in the label. That is, one steals because one is labelled a thief; one acts "crazy" because one is designated psychotic. But in fact, labels for one kind of deviance frequently prognosticate different types of deviance as well or better than they do the continuation of the same type. Young girls caught stealing are less likely to be adult thieves than they are to be adult suicide attempters, sexually promiscuous, or alcoholic (Robins, 1966). Since these particular associations between childhood and adult behaviors are not generally known, it is unlikely that labelling a girl thief would give her the self-image of a suicide attempter. To attribute the powerful carryover between childhood deviance of one type and adult deviance of very different types to the effects of labelling, the symbolic meaning of the label would have to be a very general one indeed: "You're bad and that means you will continue to be bad in any way that becomes fashionable later." How else can labelling theory explain that young men expelled from school in the rural South, who had never thought of using heroin before they were sent to Vietnam in the Army, had a high risk of getting addicted to heroin if they experimented with it there (Robins, 1974)?

(4) The fact that the importance of the parents' deviance as a predictor was undiminished when the child did not live with or know about his or her parents means the parents' influence must be something *other* than the label which being their child provided. Indeed, the evidence for genetic or perinatal factors in schizophrenia, crime, and alcoholism may be more substantial at this moment than is evidence not only for labelling theory but for any type of social causation.

These consistent findings with respect to predictors of deviance do not negate a possible effect of labelling in addition, but they do suggest that labelling is not the sole explanation, and perhaps not a very important one.

This brief overview of generalizations from empirical studies of predictors of deviance indicates why I did not anticipate finding very compelling evidence for labelling theory as an explanation for the intractability of alcoholism. There is, after all, a large body of research on alcoholism that shows its predictors follow much the same patterns that I have outlined above for deviance in general. Alcoholism, like other forms of deviance, is better predicted by early antisocial behavior of a nonspecific type than by any social characteristic (Cahalan and Room, 1974). It is largely confined to males in late adolescence and early adulthood (Cahalan, 1970: 42), although medical complications appear late in its course. It runs in families, and recent research has shown that biological parents appear potent influences even when the child is given up for adoption at an early age (Goodwin et al., 1973, 1974). The social correlates of alcoholism are being poor, male, undereducated, and in low-status ethnic groups (black, Indian, Spanish-American) (Cahalan, 1970), although in addition there appears a special vulnerability among Irish and perhaps Scandinavian and other groups of north European origin. These correlates are found equally reliably in official statistics of hospitals (Zax et al., 1967; Rosenblatt et al., 1971) and police (Zax et al., 1964), in area surveys that include "unlabelled" problem drinkers, and in randomly collected blood alcohol levels that cannot reflect either official labelling or self-labelling (Wechsler et al., 1970).

It is not surprising that patterns for deviance in general also hold for alcoholism, since alcoholics have elevated rates of every common form of socially disapproved behavior (fighting, poor work history, theft, marital instability, geographical mobility). Conversely, histories of problem drinking can be elicited from large portions of individuals who come to public attention for each of these forms of deviance.

Thus, any difficulties with labelling theory that apply to other forms of antisocial behavior apply equally well to alcoholism. In addition, there are some further findings specific to alcoholism that increase our doubts that labelling theory is a powerful explanation for the maintenance of problem drinking.

(1) The most common labeller of the alcoholic is a member of his own family. Studies of social problems associated with heavy drinking (Cahalan and Room, 1974; Robins et al., 1968) consistently show that family complaint is the most common problem associated with drinking and that it tends to occur before problem drinking is detected by employers, police, or doctors. The risk of being labelled a problem drinker seems proportional to the social distance between the labeller and the alcoholic, decreasing from family to friends and neighbors, to employer, to police, to doctor. While labelling theory does not clearly indicate who is to be the first labeller if there are multiple stages in the labelling process, the prototypic examples are the delinquent, first labelled by the judge; and the psychotic, first labelled by the psychiatrist. The first labeller of the problem drinker is not such an outside authority whose right to label may be relatively exempt from challenge, but is rather someone who shares the alcoholic's own view of drinking and of his own behavior, and whose opinion is based on no special expertise. Thus, the power of the first label to modify future behavior and to change the drinker's self-image might be expected to be considerably less than the power of a label such as "delinquent" or "psychotic."

(2) There is typically a long delay between the onset of heavy drinking and the first application of a label, even by close relatives. In a recently completed study of 219 men aged 46 to 64, selected from patients in an acute psychiatric hospital, a medical clinic, job applicants to a casual labor office, and enrollees in a union-sponsored health maintenance organization, we found 78 who had regularly drunk more than a fifth of whiskey a day, almost all of whom had been labelled as alcoholics at some point in their lives (Robins and West, n.d.). Asking the age at which they first became heavy drinkers (defined as seven or more drinks at least one evening per week) and the age at which a member of their families first complained about their drinking yielded a median interval between the two of over eleven years. Apparently families do not typically rush to stigmatize their members as heavy drinkers. And, more importantly for questioning labelling theory, excessive drinking seems to persist for many years without benefit of the experience of having been labelled. The labelling theorists argue that occasional deviance will disappear spontaneously if it is not entrenched by labelling. Drinking heavily seems to provide sufficient reinforcement of its own so that this is not the case.

(3) There is bountiful evidence that, rather than being overeager to label, official agencies aid and abet the denial of alcoholism. Careful questioning of patients on medical wards (Barchha et al., 1968) shows very high rates of problem drinking,

particularly among young and middle-aged males. Hospitalization of men this age should be expected to raise their doctors' suspicions about their drinking histories, because they are not yet in the age range when nondrinkers are likely to develop serious medical problems. Yet there is rarely a mention of their drinking habits in the medical record. Alcoholism was also found to be a frequently missed diagnosis among emergency room patients unless they fulfilled the stereotype of the "Bowery bum" or had no medical or surgical problem that could serve as an alternative diagnosis (Blane et al., 1963). Death certificates grossly underreport alcoholism as a cause of death (Nicoll and Bellows, 1934; Puffer and Griffith, 1967), even when doctors admit in interview that they knew it to be the cause. Doctors explain that they avoid recording the deceased's alcoholism to spare the family embarrassment. Even police records fail to note how frequently men engaged in assault or breaking and entering are intoxicated, although interviews with these men show that they themselves often attribute their arrests to their drunkenness (Robins et al., 1968). The failure of doctors and police to recognize and report alcoholism probably grows out of conflicts in their own beliefs as to whether alcoholism is a disease or a characterological failing. Mulford and Miller (1961) found that doctors as well as the general public often hold both viewpoints simultaneously, leading to remarkably inconsistent and conflicting answers to a set of related questions. For instance, they state that alcoholism is a disease, but when given a case history of an alcoholic, reject the idea that the man described to them is sick; or if they do call him "sick," when asked where he should go to get help, they do not recommend medical care. Because doctors share the view that alcoholism is a disgrace, they avoid labelling "respectable" people. Judges, on the other hand, may be reluctant to use the label because it might excuse the crime on psychiatric grounds.

When there is so much denial of alcoholism in persons with long histories of excessive drinking, it is not clear how to interpret the fact that some groups do indeed have a greater likelihood of being labelled alcoholics than others. As we noted, the unemployed emergency room patient is more likely to be so diagnosed than is an equally addicted man with a job. Labelling theory would argue that the powerless, unemployed individual is more subject to premature labelling—i.e., to labelling on the basis of only occasional or sporadic problems. Another plausible interpretation is that neither the weak nor the powerful are prematurely labelled, and that the powerful are able to defer appropriate labelling even longer than the less powerful. Thus, in the case of alcoholism, the finding of differences between groups in their likelihood to be labelled might be evidence for a theory of the denial and normalization of deviance rather than for labelling theory.

(4) Frequent and heavy use of alcohol produces a physiological addiction that makes the heavy use of alcohol self-perpetuating. After physiological addiction occurs. motivation to continue drinking becomes independent of any social factors or attitudes that may have explained the original excessive drinking. Evidence for this comes from animal experimentation (Ellis and Pick, 1971; Essig and Lam, 1971; Freund, 1971) which shows that all animals can, like man, develop alcohol dependence, as indicated by life-threatening withdrawal symptoms when the daily dose of alcohol is abruptly terminated, and from demonstrations of the development of tolerance in animals and human beings, which accounts for alcoholic's ability to

behave normally after ingesting amounts of alcohol that would make a nontolerant individual comatose. Thus it is difficult to argue, as labelling theory does, that labelling accounts for maintenance of the deviant behavior. While labelling could conceivably play a role in perpetuating heavy drinking long enough to produce initial addiction, once physiological addiction takes place heavy drinking will tend to continue whether or not the individual has been labelled.

(5) When labelling of alcoholics is carried out by doctors, treatment is usually recommended. According to the medical view, treatment should reduce subsequent heavy drinking, while according to labelling theory, identification as an alcoholic should tend to increase it. Actually, evidence for the effectiveness of treatment is modest (Pokorny et al., 1968), but on the other hand, there are no studies showing an *increase* in the risk of drinking heavily as a result of referral for treatment. Alcoholics Anonymous, which is generally believed, despite a lack of well-controlled studies, to have a higher success rate than most alternative treatments, actively tries to persuade its members to internalize the label of "alcoholic," to announce that label publicly, and to view it as permanent. They teach that alcoholism is an inborn "allergy" to alcohol from which no recovery is possible, so that while drinking may be arrested, the condition exists to the grave. Thus, the alcoholic is never cured, but, by total abstinence and that alone, he can be spared the social and medical consequences of his disease. (Incidentally, there is no evidence for *this* theory and some evidence against it. A fair number of ex-alcoholics do return to moderate social drinking [Pattison et al., 1968].) Whether the "allergy" theory is right or wrong, if Alcoholics Anonymous does have as good or better a success rate than other therapies, their instruction to internalize the alcoholic label must not increase the danger of perpetuating heavy drinking.

A very small study of labelled and unlabelled untreated problem drinkers (Kendell and Staton, 1966) suggests that whether an alcoholic is labelled or unlabelled makes no difference in his outcome. The seven men they regarded as not alcoholic despite their appearance at an alcohol treatment center had outcomes at follow-up as poor as the untreated men they labelled as alcoholic—one had committed suicide and three had serious social problems as a result of drinking.

(6) The label of alcoholism applies to persons who drink heavily only if they have social or medical problems as a result. Indeed, heavy drinking without problems is something for a man to be proud of in a considerable segment of our society, although it is a necessary precursor of alcoholism. Labelling theory argues that membership in powerless social categories increases the risk of being labelled as deviant. Certainly powerless groups (lower-class, disadvantaged ethnic groups) are more frequently labelled alcoholic. However, when we restrict the population of interest to those at risk of alcoholism because they are heavy drinkers, we find that the poor and ethnic minorities have no more alcoholism than others (Robins et al., 1962; Cahalan and Room, 1974). In other words, the association between social characteristics and alcoholism seems to depend largely on the fact that there are disproportionate numbers of *nonlabelled* heavy drinkers with these characteristics. *Among* heavy drinkers, it is early deviance, not social characteristics, that predicts alcoholism. This same finding also appears to hold for heroin addiction. In our follow-up of Vietnam veterans (Robins, 1974), demographic variables predicted

drug experimentation, but did not predict which soldiers who experimented with drugs would become addicted to them. On the other hand, a history of prior deviance did predict addiction, once exposed. These data suggest that a more appropriate version of labelling theory might be that a prior label as deviant for any reason increases the risk of being relabelled as a deviant of a different type.

(7) Labelling theory argues that once an individual is labelled, the label becomes a permanent identification which resists removal even when the behavior ends. Whether labelling theory is correct or incorrect, one would expect some delay in the reversal of labels after the cessation of problem drinking, since the prudent observer would require sufficient elapsed time to demonstrate that the former alcoholic can really drink moderately again. Labelling theory seems to claim that the delay is unreasonably long. However, in a recent study referred to above (Robins and West, n.d.), families that had previously objected to the drinking of men who had at some point drunk more than a fifth a day usually no longer felt that their drinking was a problem if the men had not been heavy drinkers in the past year. Seventeen of the seventy-eight formerly extremely heavy drinkers whose families had complained reported that they had not done any heavy drinking in the current year. Of these only three (seventeen percent) said the family still thought that they drank too much. Among those who had continued to drink heavily, seventy-five percent reported the family continued to object. Thus, the label of excessive drinker does seem to be reversible in response to a termination of excessive drinking. Labelling by family members seems to be at least as susceptible to reversal as is "scientific" diagnosis by doctors, who usually insist on a three-year remission before they consider an alcoholic probably cured.

(8) There is one aspect of the labelling hypothesis of alcoholism with respect to which we have been able to muster no empirical evidence: that the label becomes a "master label"—i.e., that it colors the responses to a man in areas in which his drinking is irrelevant. How would one test this proposition for alcoholism? One could imagine doing so and proving the existence of a master label with respect to homosexuality, since sexual behavior affects only a circumscribed part of an individual's life. The male homosexual's life as public citizen, employee, son, and brother may be quite within normal limits. When a homosexual is deprived of his political freedom or his right to employment, clearly the label has affected how he is treated in irrelevant areas and must be interpreted as a "master label." But what areas of a male alcoholic's life are similarly segregated from his drinking? Drinking affects mood, participation in voluntary organizations, interpersonal relationships, work performance, health, ability to talk, walk, and make love. Without being able to delineate roles to which alcoholism is clearly irrelevant, it is impossible to support or negate the hypothesis that alcoholism becomes a master label.

In sum, we do have evidence that the process of labelling in alcoholism is rather different from that imagined by the labelling hypothesis. The alcoholic is likely to be first labelled by a member of his own social circle, not by some official. And even that label occurs only after many years of showing behavior that warrants the label of alcoholism, thus suggesting that labelling is seldom premature. In fact, the alcoholic's liability to premature labelling seems rather less than the likelihood that his identity as an alcoholic will be denied long after evidence for problem behavior is clearly available. His deviant behavior appears to be self-sustaining over many years, even when unlabelled, in part because it produces physical dependence. While we do not know for certain whether labelling improves or decreases the chances of recovery, evidence would seem to indicate that internalization of the label may actually help to improve the chances rather than lowering them. At any rate, there certainly is no evidence that being labelled an alcoholic encourages excessive drinking. Nor is there evidence that the label of alcoholic is irreversible when improvement in drinking behavior does take place, as it frequently does in middle age.

This picture of the course of alcoholism seems far from the model envisioned by the labelling theorists. Indeed, alcoholics seem a much less likely group to support such a hypothesis than do other types of deviants. Why does the public not rush to label the alcoholic as it does the homosexual, for instance? We may speculate that the reason that some types of deviance fail to fit the labelling model lies in the fact that they represent behavior that is not disjunctive with normative behavior, but is only an exaggeration of that behavior. In our society, drinking is not only accepted, but to a certain extent rewarded. This is particularly true for young males, who seem to be the group most likely to drink heavily. Thus, the difference between an alcoholic and a "normal" heavy drinker is quantitative, not qualitative, depending on the frequency of intoxication and the degree to which that intoxication interferes with role performance. Because there is no sharp breaking point, a decision that the limits of social drinking have been crossed tends to be deferred until the criteria have been met beyond any doubt.

Are there other forms of deviance that are exaggerations of acceptable behavior and to which this same pattern of deferral rather than premature labelling apply? It might be fruitful to consider religious fanaticism and obesity as possible examples. Both are excesses of behavior that is sometimes accepted when used moderately. The deferral of judgment when differences are quantitative rather than qualitative might also help to explain our "softness" on white-collar crime, which often seems to be only an extension of sharp business practices.

In contrast, society rushes to stigmatize deviance seen as qualitatively different from normal behavior. Male homosexuality is a good example here. Because all sexually tinged contacts between males are taboo, the mildest of "passes" is sufficient to bring about a label of homosexual, even in the absence of evidence of genital contact. Once labeled, the victim may be forced into homsexuality because others will not accept him, thus fulfilling the prediction of labelling theory. And, until very recently, the label of homosexual was extraordinarily hard to lose, and certainly became a master label in the sense that it was treated as relevant in many areas in which it really was not. If the critical issue is the perception of deviance as qualitatively rather than quantitatively different from normal behavior, we might expect to find labelling theory more nearly supported for alcoholism in abstinence cultures than in urban America. Where abstincence is required, there is no continuum between approved drinking and alcoholism. In such cultures, there may be a tendency to label a man as alcoholic the first time he is found drunk, and that label might "drive him to drink" if "nice" people will no longer associate with him. At least there is some supporting evidence for this view: In the Bible Belt and among students from abstinent subcultures there are many abstainers and some problem drinkers, but relatively few moderate drinkers (Cahalan and Room, 1974; Globetti, 1967; Skolnick, 1958), a situation which could occur if labelling forced moderate drinkers into excessive drinking. (I personally hold what I consider a more parsimonious view of the reason for this pattern: when drinking is proscribed, everyone who can abstain does, leaving the drinking portion of the population to the problem drinkers.)

This paper has examined empirical evidence that alcoholism might fit the model suggested by labelling theory and found that model wanting. It has suggested one criterion that deviant behavior might need to comply with if the model is to fit the data: that the behavior in question be seen as qualitatively different from normative behavior. This is not to suggest that labelling theory is an appropriate model for all deviance that is seen as qualitatively different. As the other members of this group pursue its appropriateness for various kinds of deviance, they may still find that the labelling theory falls short for these as well. But at least when the deviant behavior is alcoholism and there is a continuum of accepted drinking behavior, societal reaction seems more characteristically denial than premature labelling.

Acknowledgments

This work was supported by Research Grants DA 01120, MH-18864, AA-00209, RSA 36,598, and Contract HSM-42-72-75.

References

Bailey, M. B., P. W. Haberman, and H. Alksne
  1965 "The epidemiology of alcoholism in an urban residential area." Quarterly Journal of Studies on Alcohol 26, 1: 19–40.
Barchha, R., M. A. Stewart, and S. B. Guze
  1968 "The prevalence of alcoholism among general hospital ward patients." American Journal of Psychiatry 125, 5: 681–684.
Blane, H. T., W. F. Overton, Jr., and M. E. Chafetz
  1963 "Social factors in the diagnosis of alcoholism: 1. Characteristics of the patient." Quarterly Journal of Studies on Alcohol 24, 4: 640–663.
Calahan, D.
  1970 Problem Drinkers. San Francisco: Jossey-Bass.
  ———— and R. Room
  1974 Problem Drinking Among American Men. Monograph of the Rutgers Center of Alcohol Studies, New Brunswick, New Jersey.
Ellis, F. W. and J. R. Pick
  1971 "Ethanol intoxication and dependence in Rhesus monkeys." In N. K. Mello and J. H. Mendelson (eds.) Recent Advances in Studies in Alcoholism. Publication (HSM) 71-9045. Washington, D.C.: Government Printing Office.
Essig, C. F. and R. C. Lam
  1971 "The alcohol abstinence syndrome in dogs and its treatment with phenobarbital." In N. K. Mello and J. H. Mendelson (eds.) Recent Advances in Studies in Alcoholism. Publication (HSM) 71-9045. Washington, D.C.: Government Printing Office.

Freund, G.
    1971 "Alcohol, barbiturate, and bromide withdrawal in mice." In N. K. Mello and J. H. Mendelson (eds.) Recent Advances in Studies of Alcoholism. Publication (HSM) 71-9045. Washington, D.C.: Government Printing Office.
Globetti, G.
    1967 "A comparative study of white and Negro teenage drinking in two Mississippi counties." Phylon 28: 131–138.
Goodwin, D. W., F. Schulsinger, L. Hermansen, S. B. Guze, and G. Winokur
    1973 "Alcohol problems in adoptees raised apart from alcoholic biological parents." Archives of General Psychiatry 28: 238–243.
Goodwin, D. W., F. Schulsinger, N. Moller, et al.
    1974 "Drinking problems in adopted and nonadopted sons of alcoholics." Archives of General Psychiatry 31 (August): 164–169.
Healy, W. and A. F. Bronner
    1926 Delinquents and Criminals: Their Making and Unmaking. New York: Macmillan.
Kendall, R. E. and M. C. Staton
    1966 "The fate of untreated alcoholics." Quarterly Journal of Studies on Alcohol 27, 1:30–41.
Mulford, H. A. and D. E. Miller
    1961 "Public definitions of the alcoholic." Quarterly Journal of Studies on Alcohol 22, 2: 312–320.
Nicoll, M. Jr. and M. T. Bellows
    1934 "Effect of a confidential inquiry on the recorded mortality from syphillis and alcoholism." American Journal of Public Health 24, 8: 813–820.
Pattison, E. M., E. B. Headley, G. C. Gleser, and L. A. Gottschalk
    1968 "Abstinence and normal drinking." Quarterly Journal of Studies on Alcohol 29, 3: 610–633.
Pokorny, A. D., B. A. Miller, and S. E. Cleveland
    1968 "Response to treatment of alcoholism: a follow-up study." Quarterly Journal of Studies on Alcohol 29: 364–381.
Puffer, R. and G. W. Griffith
    1967 "Patterns of urban mortality." Pan American Health Organization Scientific Publication 151, September.
Robins, L. N.
    1966 Deviant Children Grown Up. Baltimore: Williams & Wilkins. (Reprinted in 1974 by Robert E. Krieger, Huntington, New York.)
    1974 "The Vietnam drug user returns." Special Action Office Monograph, Series A, Number 2, May.
_____ and P. A. West
    n.d. "Correlates of suicidal behavior and ideas in middle-aged black and white men." Unpublished manuscript.
Robins, L. N., W. M. Bates, and P. O'Neal
    1962 "Adult drinking patterns of former problem children." In D. J. Pittman and C. R. Snyder (eds.) Society, Culture and Drinking Patterns. New York: John Wiley.
Robins, L. N., G. E. Murphy, and M. B. Breckenridge
    1968 "Drinking behavior in young urban Negro men." Quarterly Journal of Studies on Alcohol 29, 3: 657–684.
Rosenblatt, S. M., M. M. Gross, M. Broman, E. Lewis, and B. Malenowski
    1971 "Patients admitted for treatment of alcohol withdrawal syndromes: an epidemiological study." Quarterly Journal of Studies on Alcohol 32 (March): 104–115.

Skolnick, J. H.
  1958 "Religious affiliation and drinking behavior." Quarterly Journal of Studies on Alcohol 19, 3: 452–470.
Wechsler, H., H. W. Demone, Jr., D. Thum, and E. H. Kasey
  1970 "Religious-ethnic differences in alcohol consumption." Journal of Health and Social Behavior 11 (March): 21–29.
Wolfgang, M. E., R. M. Figlio, and T. Sellin
  1972 Delinquency in a Birth Cohort. Chicago: University of Chicago Press.
Zax, M., E. A. Gardner, and W. T. Hart
  1964 "Public intoxication in Rochester: a survey of individuals charged during 1961." Quarterly Journal of Studies on Alcohol 25, 4: 669–678.
  1967 "A survey of the prevalence of alcoholism in Monroe County, New York, 1961." Quarterly Journal of Studies on Alcohol 28, 2: 316–327.

12

Social Psychologic Factors Affecting the Presentation of Bodily Complaints

David Mechanic

Patients often recognize symptoms for which they seek medical assistance, but on the basis of a history and physical and laboratory examination, the physician cannot obtain evidence to account for or justify the patients' complaints.[1] Such patients conform in part to Gillespie's concept of hypochondria, which he viewed as "a persistent preoccupation with the bodily health, out of proportion to any existing justification and with a conviction of disease."[2] There is considerable disagreement, however, on the appropriate formal definition of hypochondria,[3] and it may be incorrect to apply the same designation to profound and persistent hypochondrical syndromes associated with psychiatric illness and the type of hypochondriasis commonly seen in general practice.

Perceptions of Symptoms

Estimates derived from British and American morbidity surveys indicate that three of four persons have symptoms in any given month for which they take some definable action such as use of medication, bed rest, consulting a physician and limiting activity.[4] In addition, persons experience many other symptoms, which they regard as trivial and which they ignore. Investigators believe that it is pointless to attempt to measure symptoms that do not receive some type of treatment or special attention since they occur commonly and have too little impact to be reported accurately in household surveys.[5,6] Yet such symptoms overlap appreciably with typical presenting complaints among patients seeking medical care.[7]

The major task of this paper is to suggest how normal attribution processes develop in the definition of symptoms. As an intitial formulation, it appears that persons tend to notice bodily sensations when they depart from more ordinary feelings. Each person tends to appraise new bodily perceptions against prior experience and his anticipations based on the experiences of others and on general

SOURCE: *New England Journal of Medicine* 286 (25 May 1972): 1132–39. Reprinted by permission.

knowledge. Many symptoms occur so commonly throughout life that they become part of ordinary expectations and are experienced as normal variations. Other experiences, such as a young girl's first menstruation, might be extremely frightening if prior social learning has not occurred, but would ordinarily be accepted as normal if it had. In analyzing responses to more unusual symptoms it is instructive to examine situations in which normal attribution processes become disrupted as a consequence of special kinds of learning, and in this regard hypochondriasis among medical students is an interesting example.

The Case of the Medical Student

It has frequently been observed that medical students experience symptom complexes that they ascribe to some pathologic process. This syndrome appears to have high prevalence—approximately 70 per cent.[8,9] Factors contributing to the development of this syndrome usually include social stress and anxiety, bodily symptoms and detailed but incomplete information on a disease involving symptoms similar to the bodily indications perceived by the student. Hunter, Lohrenz and Schwartzman describe the process as follows:

> The following constellation of factors occur regularly. The student is under internal or external stress, such as guilt, fear of examinations and the like. He notices in himself some innocuous physiological or psychological dysfunction, e.g., extrasystoles, forgetfulness. He attaches to this an undeserved importance of a fearful kind usually modeled after some patient he has seen, clinical anecdote he has heard, or a member of his family who has been ill.[9]

It is not clear from such descriptions to what extent each of the components—stress, bodily symptoms and external cues—is necessary to the process and what specific role each plays. Since both stress and bodily symptoms are extremely common among students in general—and the phenomenon in question does not appear to occur so dramatically or with equal prevalence among them—it seems reasonable to suspect that the medical student's access to more detailed medical information contributes greatly to the attribution process.

An experiment by Schachter and Singer[10] helps explain how information affects emotional response. Subjects were told that the experimenters were interested in the effects of a vitamin compound called Suproxin (a nonexistent substance) on their vision, and these subjects were given an injection. Each subject was then asked to wait, while the drug took effect, in a room with another student who appeared to be a subject who had received the same injection, but who was really a confederate of the experimenter.

The injection received was epinephrine bitartrate (adrenaline), whereas subjects in control groups recieved a saline solution (the placebo). Some of the subjects who received epinephrine were told to anticipate heart pounding, hand tremor and a warm and flushed face; this group was correctly informed. A second group receiving epinephrine was given no information about what to expect; this group was called the ignorant group. A third group receiving epinephrine was incorrectly informed that their feet would feel numb, that they would have itching sensations, and that they would get a slight headache; this group was called the misinformed group. While the subject was waiting for the "experiment" to begin, the confederate of the experimenter went into a scheduled act in which he slowly worked himself into a "euphoric" state playing imaginary basketball, flying paper airplanes, hula-hooping, and so on. During this period the subject was observed behind a one-way window, and his behavior was rated in terms of relevant categories. Later, he was asked to report as well his subjective feelings. Three additional groups were studied in a variation of the same situation: another epinephrine informed group; an epinephrine ignorant group; and a placebo group. In this second situation the confederate simulated anger instead of euphoria. Thus, it is possible to assess the influences of epinephrine, the various expectations subjects are given for their bodily experiences, and the different environmental cues (i.e., an angry or euphoric confederate.)

Subjects who received an injection of epinephrine and who had no correct or appropriate explanation of the side effects that they experienced (particularly the epinephrine misinformed group) were most affected in their behavior and feeling states by the cues provided by the student confederate. The nature of the emotion—whether anger or euphoria—was influenced by the behavior of the confederate. Schachter and Singer believe that emotion involves a two-stage process requiring physiologic arousal and a definition of it. They maintain that the same internal state can be labeled in a variety of ways, resulting in different emotional reactions. External influences on definitions of internal states are particularly important when persons lack an appropriate explanation of what they are experiencing.

With the use of the Schachter-Singer formulation, "medical students' disease" can be characterized as follows. Medical school exposes students to continuing stress resulting from the rapid pace, examinations, anxieties in dealing with new clinical experiences and the like. Students, thus, are emotionally aroused with some frequency, and like others in the population, they experience a high prevalence of transient symptoms. The exposure to specific knowledge about disease provides the student with a new framework for identifying and giving meaning to previously neglected bodily feelings. Diffuse and ambiguous symptoms regarded as normal in the past may be reconceptualized within the context of newly acquired knowledge of disease. Existing social stress may heighten bodily sensations through autonomic activiation, making the student more aware of his bodily state, and motivating him to account for what he is experiencing. The new information that the student may have about possible disease and the similarity between the symptoms of a particular condition and his own symptoms establishes a link that he would have more difficulty making if he were less informed. Moreover, the student—in the process of acquiring new medical information—may begin to pay greater attention to his own bodily experiences and may also attempt to imagine how certain symptoms feel. This tendency to give attention to bodily feelings may assist the development of the syndrome.

Woods, Natterson and Silverman[8] found that, contrary to usual belief, "medical students' disease" was not an isolated experience linked to a particular aspect of medical training, but occurred with relatively equal frequency throughout the four years of medical school. Thus, the syndrome's occurrence may depend on the coincidental existence of student arousal, the presence of particular bodily feelings, and cues acquired from new information about disease that seems relevant to existing symptoms.

Hunter, Lohrenz and Schwartzman,[9] on the basis of their study, conclude that symptom choice is influenced by "a variety of accidental, historical and learning factors, in which the mechanism of identification plays a major role." Yet there appears to be a variety of factors that may increase the probability of the occurrence of the syndrome, and it is important to inquire under what conditions concern about illness in contrast to alternative definitions will become manifest. The normal person may have a variety of symptoms without experiencing a fear of illness. Many investigators of hypochondriacal patients note that reported symptoms tend to be diffuse and may change from one occasion to another. Such patients often report numerous complaints referring to a variety of organ systems, or they report non-localized symptoms: insomnia, itching, dizziness, weakness, lack of energy, pain all over, nausea, and the like.[11-13] Kenyon,[14] in reviewing 512 patient case records at the Bethlem Royal and Maudsley hospitals, found that the head and neck, abdomen and chest were the regions of the body most frequently affected, and that the most typical complaints were headache and gastrointestinal and musculoskeletal symptoms. Striking features of almost all descriptions of hypochondriacal patients, particularly in early stages, are the lack of specificity of complaint and similarity to frequently occurring symptoms in normal populations. Moreover, many of the complaints tend to be of symptoms that commonly occur under stress and that epidemiologic studies show to have very high prevalence in ordinary community populations.[15,16] The common occurrence of such symptoms and their diffuseness establish conditions under which widely varying attributions may reasonably occur. Incorrect attributions may occur as well in existing organic disease because of the diffuseness of symptoms, referred pain, particular characteristics of the patient or some combination of these factors.

It is noteworthy that "medical students' disease" terminates readily and within a relatively short time. Woods and his colleagues report that the syndrome sometimes disappears spontaneously, but more often through further study of the illness or by direct or covert consultation with an instructor or physician. They suggest that it is "reassurance" that limits the condition, but the term is exceedingly vague and has a variety of meanings. Most reports in the literature concerning more persistent hypochondria suggest that such patients are not easily reassured, and thus it would be useful to have more specific understanding of the mechanism by which "medical students' disease" is short-circuited.

One way in which the medical student discovers errors in attribution is through further understanding of diagnostics. As he learns more about the disease, he may discover that the attribution he made does not really fit or that a great variety of symptoms that commonly occur may be characteristic of the clinical picture. Another possibility is that the stress in the student's life that is fluctuating subsides with some relief in his anxiety, and his awareness of his symptoms may decline. How the incorrect attribution comes to be corrected has never been studied, but possibly the student's growing knowledge of symptomatology sharpens his judgment about his own complaints. If clear knowledge is indeed necessary to disconfirm the attribution adequately, the syndrome should be more persistent when knowledge is disputed and uncertain. In this light it is of interest that "medical students' disease" of a psychiatric character appears to be less transient and more chronic than such syndromes that develop around fears of physical illness.[8] In the psychiatric area it is more difficult to separate the attribution from the entity to which the attribution is made.

Another issue concerns the origins of the initial attribution of illness. The conclusion reached by Hunter, Lohrenz and Schwartzman[9] that identification plays a major part has already been noted, and this appears to be the most generally accepted psychiatric point of view. The concept of identification as used by the authors in this respect is more descriptive than explanatory, and it encompasses the observation often made that the patient will frequently focus on a disease that affected a loved one. An examination of cases described in the literature suggests that the localization and definition of the complaint may depend on idiosyncrasies or may be fortuitous. Ladee[3] reports the ovservation of Orbán concerning a veterinary surgeon who felt a pain in the right lower part of his abdomen. Apparently, he feared an incipient bowel obstruction rather than appendicitis, and Ladee explains that appendicitis is rare among cattle whereas ileus is frequent. Felix Brown,[17] in a thoughtful review of 41 cases of hypochondria, notes the important influence of topical suggestions. Many commentators have also observed how frequently symptoms of a particular kind follow publicity given to the illness or death of a well known personality or a dramatic mass-media demonstration concerning some disease.

It appears that the concept of identification may be too diffuse and imprecise in encompassing such varied phenomena as the association between mother and child, audience and public figure, and the occurrence of a stomach pain and seeing a movie concerning a person with stomach cancer. An alternative perspective from which to analyze such influences would involve consideration of factors affecting the perception of personal vulnerability.

Perceptions of Personal Vulnerability

Although persons may vary widely in their sense of invulnerability—which appears to be linked with their levels of self-esteem—psychologic survival generally depends on the ability of people to protect themselves from anxieties and fears involving low-risk occurrences to which all persons are exposed or dangers that they are powerless to prevent.[18,19] Feelings of invulnerability are threatened under circumstances of greatly increased risk such as combat and new and difficult experiences, but even under these conditions, persons generally manage to maintain a relatively strong sense of invulnerability through various psychologic defense processes and coping actions. However, a "near-miss" can dramatically undermine one's sense of invulnerability and may lead to extreme anxiety and fear reactions. The death of a close friend or coworker in combat,[20] being involved in an automobile accident in which others are killed or suffer bodily injury, and learning that someone who is defined as having comparable ability to oneself has failed an important examination that one is intending to take[21] serve to threaten the sense of security.

Basic to the undermining of a sense of invulnerability are social comparison processes. It is much less difficult to explain injury to people of unlike characteristics without threat to oneself in that one can attribute the injury to aspects of the person that are different from one's own. When such persons are more like oneself—in terms of age, sex, life style or routine—it is much more difficult not to perceive oneself at risk, and personal intimacy or physical proximity similarly increases feelings of vulnerability.

Various studies suggest that self-esteem is an intervening variable between situation and response. Although the role of self-esteem is not fully clear, one possibility is that persons with high self-esteem see themselves as more capable of dealing with threatening situations and, thus, are less vulnerable.[22] The awareness that one is able to cope and that one has had success in the past in dealing with adversity insulates the person from anxiety.[23] This concept of the self-esteem effect appears most reasonable in cases in which coping ability can affect the situation and realistically reduce threat; it is not so obvious that self-esteem reduces a sense of threat of impending illness, although many writers on hypochondria note specifically that low self-esteem is associated with this syndrome. A sense of confidence may generalize to situations even when it is not particularly realistic, or may lead persons to focus less on bodily indications. This is clearly an area for more focused inquiry.

Some symptoms present in a fashion that makes them difficult to ignore, and many symptoms are sufficiently impressive in their occurrence or sufficiently disruptive of normal functioning so that variation in response is relatively limited. Moreover, many symptoms occur so as not to allow alternative attributions readily. Hypochondria developing around a fear that one has a fractured leg or an extremely high fever is not found ordinarily; indeed, the response to such symptoms is not mediated in any influential way by social and cultural variables. But when symptoms are more diffuse, variation in response is more likely to occur.

In sum, it has been maintained that most ordinarily occurring symptoms are considered normal or explained in conventional frameworks, as when muscle aches are attributed to unaccustomed physical activity or indigestion to overeating. When such ordinary symptoms occur concomitantly with emotional arousal, and when they are not easily explained within conventional and commonly available understandings, external cues become important in defining the character and importance of such bodily feelings. Such cues may be fortuitous, or they may be the consequence of prior experience, cultural learning or personal need for secondary gain. The manner in which sociocultural and psychologic contexts condition attributional responses requires further examination.

Social and Cultural Influences on Response to Symptoms

From very young ages children more or less learn to respond to various symptoms and feelings in terms of reactions of others to their behavior and social expectations in general. As children begin to mature, clear age and sex patterns become apparent, and the children become clearly differentiated in the manner in which they respond to pain. their risk-taking activities, and their readiness to express their apprehensions and hurts.[24] Learning influences the tendency of males as compared with females to take more risks, to seek medical care less readily, and to be less expressive about illness and appear more stoical.

The role of cultural differences in identification and response to illness has been described nicely by Zborowski[25] and has been amplified in a variety of other studies.[26] Zborowski, in studying reactions to pain in a New York City hospital among various ethnic groups, noted that whereas Jewish and Italian patients responded to pain in an emotional fashion, "Old Americans" were more stoical and "objective," and Irish more frequently denied pain. He also noted a difference in the attitude underlying Italian and Jewish concern about pain; although the Italian patients primarily sought relief from pain and were relatively satisfied when such relief was obtained, the Jewish patients appeared to be concerned mainly with the meaning of their pain and the consequences of pain for their future health and welfare. Thus, different attributional processes appeared to form the basis of these manifest similarities. Zborowski reported that Italian patients seemed relieved when they were given medication for pain, and their complaining ceased. In contrast, Jewish patients were reluctant to accept medication and appeared to have greater concern with the implications of their pain experience for their future health.

Other studies have similarly found that ethnic groups differentially report symptoms and seek medical assistance for them, and vary in the extent to which they are willing to accept psychologic interpretations of their complaints.[27,28] It is unclear whether the ethnic differences, noted in the literature, are a result of the fact that children with particular prior experiences and upbringing come to have more objective symptoms, interpret the same symptoms differently, express their concerns and seek help with greater willingness, or use a different vocabulary for expressing distress. Such distinctions are important.

Responses to Perceived Illness and Vocabularies of Distress

It is apparent that social learning will affect the vocabularies persons use to define their complaints and their orientations to seeking various kinds of care. It is reasonable to expect that persons from origins where the expression of symptoms and seeking help is permissible and encouraged will be more likely to do so, particularly under stressful circumstances. In contrast, in cultural contexts where complaining is discouraged, persons experiencing distress may seek a variety of alternative means for dealing with their difficulties. Zborowski, in describing the "Old American" family, stressed the tendency of the mother to teach the child to take pain "like a man," not to be a sissy and not to cry. Such training, according to Zborowski, does not discourage use of the doctor, but it implies that such use will be based on physical needs rather than on emotional concerns. One might, therefore, anticipate that persons with such backgrounds might be reluctant to express psychologic distress directly, but might express such distress through the presentation of physical complaints. Kerekhoff and Back,[29] in a study of the diffusion of a hysterical illness among female employees of a Southern mill alleged to be caused by an unknown insect, found that the prevalence of the condition was high among women under strain who could not admit they had a problem and who did not know how to cope with it.

Pauline Bart,[30] in comparing women who entered a neurology service, but who were discharged with psychiatric diagnoses, with women entering a psychiatric service of the same hospital, found them to be less educated, more rural, of lower socio-economic status, and less likely to be Jewish than those who came directly to a psychiatric service. Bart suggests that these two groups of women were differentiated by their vocabularies of discomfort, which affected the manner in which they presented themselves. She also observed that 52 per cent of the psychiatric patients on the neurology service had had a hysterectomy as compared with only 21 per cent on the psychiatric service. The findings suggest that such patients may be expressing psychologic distress through physical attributions and, thus, expose themselves to a variety of unnecessary medical procedures.

Most of the understanding of the patient's conplaint comes from observation of that part of the process that brings the patient into contact with the physician. It should be clear that this tends to focus on only a segment of the entire sample and excludes patients with comparable problems who do not seek assistance. Various analysts of the medical consultation, such as Balint,[31] note that the symptoms that the patient presents are frequently of no special consequence, but serve to establish a legitimate relation between patient and doctor. He maintains that the presentation of somatic complaints often masks an underlying emotional problem that is frequently the major reason the patient has sought help. Certainly, a complaint of illness may be one way of seeking reassurance and support through a recognized and socially acceptable relation when it is difficult for the patient to present the underlying problem in an undisguised form without displaying weaknesses and vulnerabilities contrary to expected and learned behavior patterns. The emphasis that Balint places on the symptom as a front for underlying emotional distress, although characteristic of some patients, neglects the fact that many patients who are more receptive to psychologic vocabularies may also be viewed as hypochondriacal.

The response to bodily indications may also depend on the social acceptability of certain types of complaints, and even the nature and site of the complaint, according to Balint, is a matter frequently negotiated between patient and physician. Harold Wolff[32] has also noted that minor pains from certain parts of the body may be more frequent because they are culturally more acceptable and because they bring greater sympathetic response. Hes,[33] in a study of hypochondriac patients referred to a psychiatric outpatient clinic, noted the inhibition of emotional expression as a result of culturally determined taboos on complaining about one's fate and a culturally determined excessive use of bodily language. He found these conditions particularly characteristic of Oriental Jewish women, who made up a major proportion of his patients with hypochondria.

Mechanic and Volkart[34] examined the influence of stress and inclination tò use medical facilities among 600 male students at a major university. Stress (as measured by indexes of loneliness and nervousness) and inclination to use medical facilities (as measured by anticipated behavior given hypothetical illness situations) were clearly related to the use of a college health service during a one-year period. Among students with high stress and a high inclination to use medical facilities 73 per cent were frequent users of medical facilities (three or more times during the year), but among the low-inclination-low-stress group, only 30 per cent were frequent users of such services. Among those of high inclination, "stress" was an important influence in bringing people to the physician. Seventy-three per cent of persons experiencing high stress used facilities frequently, although only 46 per cent did so among those with low stress.[35] A similar trend was observed among those who were less inclined to seek advice from a doctor, but the relation between stress and actually seeking advice was substantially smaller and not statistically significant. These data support the interpretation that stress leads to an attempt to cope; those who are receptive to the patient role tend to adopt this particular mode of coping more frequently than those who are not so receptive. The previous discussion also suggests that when stress helps initiate a medical contact, the contact may be presented through a vocabulary of physical symptoms that frequently impress the physician as trivial or unimportant. A very similar study was carried out with comparable results among British women using two general-practice panels within the English National Health Service.[36]

The impression emerging from these studies is that there are at least two major patterns of behavior that physicians tend to regard as hypochondriacal. The first consists of patients who have a high inclination to use medical facilities and willingness to use a vocabulary of psychologic distress, openly complaining of unhappiness, frustration and dissatisfaction.[37] The more common and difficult patient to deal with is one who has a high receptivity to medical care but who lacks a vocabulary of psychologic distress. Such patients tend to present the doctor with a variety of diffuse physical complaints for which he can find no clear-cut explanation, but he cannot be sure that they do not indeed suffer from some physical disorder that he has failed to diagnose.

Patients who express psychologic distress through a physical language tend to be uneducated or to come from cultural groups where the expression of emotional distress is inhibited. Such patients frequently face serious life difficulties and social stress, but the subculture within which they function does not allow legitimate expression of their suffering nor are others attentive to their pleas for support when they are made. Because of their experiences these patients frequently feel, sometimes consciously but more frequently on a level of less than full awareness, that expression of their difficulties is a sign of weakness and will be deprecated. They thus dwell on bodily complaints, some that are ever present, and others that are concomitant with their experience of emotional distress. These patients are often elderly, lonely and insecure, and they may be inactive enough to have time to dwell on their difficulties. When such patients seek out physicians they may use their physical symptoms and complaints as a plea for help.

Effects of Emotional Distress on Symptoms

It has been suggested at various points that emotional arousal appears to heighten the experience of symptoms, and in this regard the literature on reactions to pain is noteworthy. Beecher[38] has reported the failure of 15 different research groups to establish any dependable effects of even large doses of morphine on pain of experimental origin in man. He has found it necessary to distinguish between pain as an original sensation and pain as a psychic reaction. As Beecher notes, one of the difficulties with most forms of laboratory pain is that they minimize the psychic reaction, which has an essential role in pain associated with illness. For example, in a comparative study he found that civilian patients undergoing surgery reported strikingly more frequent and severe pain than wounded soldiers with greater tissue trauma. He observed that such variations resulted from varying subjective definitions, and concluded that there is no simple, direct relation between the wound per se and the pain experienced.

A variety of reports both of an anthropologic nature and in the experimental literature indicate how a person's definition of a painful experience conditions how much pain he is willing to tolerate and what he will endure without protest. In experimental situations persons can be given instructions and incentives to endure severe pain stimulation.[39,40,41] Here it is difficult to separate what people may feel from their willingness to control expression patterns, but many such reports suggest that when there is strong positive motivation, people will undergo extraordinary pain without complaint. Also, if intensely involved in some pattern of behavior, they may not become immediately aware of severe body trauma.[42]

The reactive component in illness has long been recognized as an important aspect not only in defining the condition but also in the patient's response to treatment and in the course of the illness. Imboden and his colleagues have studied prolonged convalescence in chronic brucellosis and influenza, in which they argue that emotional stress concomitant with the course of the illness may become intermingled with symptoms of the illness in such a way that the end point of the illness becomes confused with continuing emotional distress.[43,44] They note that symptoms of emotional distress may be attributed to the physical illness well beyond the normal course of the infection, which may serve to maintain the patient's self-concept.

The studies on prolonged convalescence suggest some of the conditions under which misattribution may occur. For example, the course of influenza and brucellosis is likely to leave the patient fatigued, with a lack of energy and interest, weakness and a variety of other somatic symptoms. These symptoms may also accompany depression and other emotional distress. The similarity in the symptoms makes it reasonable for the patient to attribute these symptoms after the illness to the persistence of the illness. The similarity that makes the errors of attribution more likely also makes it difficult for the physician to determine when the symptoms are a product of an emotional problem and when they are complications of the physical illness. Thus, the physician may unwittingly reinforce the patient's confusion.

The manner in which physicians may come to reinforce particular patient tendencies is suggested by a variety of reports.[45,46] Zola,[45] for example, on the basis of a study of patients for whom no medical disease was found, suggests that the patient's cultural background influenced how he presented his symptoms and, thus, how the doctor evaluated them. Although the ethnic groups studied did not differ in the extent of their life difficulties, Italians, who are more emotional in the presentation of symptoms and give more attention and expression to pain and distress, were more likely to be evaluated as suffering from a psychogenic condition.

Treating the Chronic Complainer—Correcting Errors in Attribution

In a classic paper, Felix Brown[17] defined bodily complaints in five ways: partly on a physiologic or somatic level, associated with anxiety; symbolic of something else;

consistent with mood disturbance, usually depression; by substitution or conversion of an affect, usually anxiety, with more or less elimination of the affect; and with more or less conscious purpose for the patient—purposive hypochondriasis.

The first three groups are most typical of the chronic complainer seen in ordinary medical practice. Ordinarily, it is believed that doctors must provide general reassurance, which relieves the patient's level of distress, but if the implications of some of the theoretical statements made earlier are followed, it should become clear why reassurance alone may not be the most effective approach. Frequently, the interpretation that the patient has made of his symptoms is a provisional and vague definition, and, as Balint indicates, this attribution is readily changed by the physician's suggestions. The physician may be able to alleviate the patient's distress to the extent that he can provide the patient with benign interpretations of his distress that are credible and to the extent to which he can reassure him and bolster his esteem and sense of mastery. To provide general reassurance alone may have no effect on the patient's perspective relevant to the meaning of his symptoms, although it may contribute to the alleviation of anxiety. Providing alternative attributions is difficult because they not only must relieve anxiety but also must be culturally and psychologically acceptable to the patient as well. For example, if the patient has learned that a psychologic expression of distress is unacceptable, such an interpretation by the physician may be of little use to the patient, may exacerbate his anxiety, and may disrupt the relation between doctor and patient.

The suggestion that the attribution the doctor provides must be credible means that it must be consistent with what the patient is experiencing and likely to experience in the future. If not, it may serve to arouse the patient's anxiety further and will not be taken seriously. Some evidence on this matter comes from a study by Rickels and his colleagues[47,48] on the effects of placebos. Suggestibility is an important factor in the medical situation, and placebos have been found to alleviate distress in a wide range of medical disorders.[26] Rickels and his colleagues, however, found that patients with prolonged experience with anxiety and the use of tranquilizing drugs do poorly when treated by placebos, and many suffer a worsening of their anxiety state. Patients who are attuned to their inner feelings and have had experiences with psychoactive drugs do not experience placebos as credible. The impact of the suggestion effect is hardly equal to the patients' past experiences of true relief of their symptoms with tranquilizers, and the failure of the placebo to reduce their anxieties to the level they expect may alarm them and make them think that they are more upset than usual.

Such an interpretation is offered by Storms and Nisbett[49] in a study of insomniac subjects. These subjects were given placebos to take before going to bed; some were told that the pill would increase their arousal, and others that it would decrease it. The former reported that they got to sleep more quickly than previously, whereas the latter reported that they took longer to get to sleep than before. Storms and Nisbett believe that the subjects who thought that their arousal was due to the pill felt less upset and could fall asleep more easily, but those who continued to feel arousal despite the fact that the pill was to reduce their arousal defined themselves as particularly upset. Although caution is required in generalizing to clinical situations, such studies illustrate how the efficacy of the doctor's interpretations of his patient's problem will depend on the extent to which they are credible in terms of the patient's experiences and the extent to which he anticipates the patient's reactions to symptoms and treatment.

The adequacy of the doctor's management of the patient is also likely to depend on the kinds of expectations and instructions he provides the patient in preparation for what lies ahead. Whether doctors say anything or not, patients will anticipate and acquire expectations of the course of their condition, how they expect to feel, what is likely to happen and the like. To the extent that the patient is not instructed, his expectations may be highly contrary to what is likely to occur, and this discrepancy may alarm the patient and disrupt his management. Various experimental studies suggest that very modest instruction and information have an important effect on patient outcomes,[50,51] and on facilitating preventive health actions.[22]

Egbert and his colleagues,[50] for example, selected a random group of patients undergoing surgery and gave them simple information, encouragement and instruction concerning the impending operation and means of alleviating postoperative pain. The researchers, however, were not involved in the medical care of the patients studied, and they did not participate in decisions concerning them. An independent evaluation of the postoperative period and the length of stay of patients in the experimental and control groups showed that communication and instruction had an important beneficial effect.

In a similar experimental study by Skipper and Leonard,[54] children admitted to a hospital for tonsillectomy were randomized into experimental and control groups. In the experimental group patients and their mothers were admitted to the hospital by a specially trained nurse, who attempted to create an atmosphere that would facilitate the communication of information to the mother and increase her freedom to verbalize her anxieties. Mothers were told what routine events to expect and when they were likely to occur, including the actual time schedule for the operation. The investigators found that the emotional support reduced the mothers' stress and changed their definition of the hospital situation, which in turn had a beneficial effect on their children. Children in the experimental group experienced smaller changes in blood pressure, temperature and other physiologic measures; they were less likely to suffer from postoperative emesis and made a better adaptation to the hospital, and they made a more rapid recovery after hospitalization, displaying fewer fears, less crying, and less disturbed sleep than children in the control group.

In sum, credible instructions provided in a sympathetic and supportive way that help people avoid attributional errors and that avoid new reasons for anxiety might be more helpful to the complaining patient than blanket reassurances that provide no alternative framework for understanding his symptoms. Reassurance that does not take into account the patient's assessment of the threat that he faces might serve only to mystify him and to undermine his confidence in his physician. The literature contains frequent reports not only of patients with hypochondria who went from one doctor to another but also of repeated cases in which the patient appeared to get gratification in disconfirming the doctor's appraisal. Therapeutic approaches that facilitate the patient's coping efforts may be particularly useful with these difficult patients.

Acknowledgment

Supported in part by Public Health Services grant 5 RO1 MH 14835, National Institute of Mental Health.

References

1. Gardner EA: Emotional disorders in medical practice. Ann Intern Med 73:651–653, 1970
2. Gillespie RD: Hypochondria: its definition, nosology and psychopathology. Guys Hosp Rep 8:408–460, 1928
3. Ladee GA: Hypochondriacal Syndromes. Amsterdam. Elsevier Publishing Company, 1966
4. White KL, Williams TF, Greenberg BG: The ecology of medical care. N Engl J Med 265:885–892, 1961
5. United States National Center for Health Statistics. Health Survey Procedure: Concepts, questionnaire development, and definitions in the health interview survey (PHS Publication No 1000, Series 1, no 2). Washington, DC, Government Printing Office. May 1964. p 4
6. Mooney HW: Methodology in Two California Health Surveys, San Jose (1952) and statewide (1954–55). (PHS Monograph No 70) Washington, DC. Government Printing Office, 1963
7. Mechanic D, Newton M: Some problems in the analysis of morbidity data. J Chronic Dis 18:569–580, 1965
8. Woods SM, Natterson J, Silverman J: Medical students' disease: hypochondriasis in medical education. J Med Educ 41:785–790, 1966
9. Hunter RCA, Lohrenz JG, Schwartzman AE: Nosophobia and hypochondriasis in medical students. J Nerv Ment Dis 139:147–152, 1964
10. Schacter S, Singer JE: Cognitive, social and physiological determinants of emotional state. Psychol Rev 69:379–399, 1962
11. Katzenelbogen S: Hypochondriacal complaints with special reference to personality and environment. Am J Psychiatry 98:815–822, 1942
12. Greenberg HP: Hypochondriasis. Med J Aust 1 (18):673–677, 1960
13. Robins E, Purtell JJ, Cohen ME: "Hysteria" in men: a study of 38 patients so diagnosed and 194 control subjects. N Engl J Med 246:677–685, 1952
14. Kenyon FE: Hypochondriasis: a clinical study. Br J Psychiatry 110:478–488, 1964
15. Srole L, Langner TS, Michael ST, et al: Mental Health in the Metropolis: The Midtown Manhattan study, New York, McGraw-Hill Book Company, 1962
16. Leighton DC, Harding JS, Macklin DB, et al: The Character of Danger: Psychiatric symptoms in selected communities. New York, Basic Books, 1963
17. Brown F: The bodily complaint: a study of hypochondriasis. J Ment Sci 82:295–359, 1936
18. Janis IL: Air War and Emotional Stress: Psychological studies of bombing and civilian defense. New York, McGraw-Hill Book Company, 1951
19. Wolfenstein M: Disaster: A psychological essay. New York, Free Press, 1957
20. Grinker RR, Spiegel JP: Men Under Stress. Philadelphia, Blakiston Publishing Company, 1945
21. Mechanic D: Students Under Stress: A study in the social psychology of adaptation. New York, Free Press, 1962

22. Leventhal H: Findings and theory in the study of fear communications. Adv Exp Soc Psychol 5:119–186, 1970

23. Lazarus RS: Psychological Stress and the Coping Process. New York, McGraw-Hill Book Company, 1966

24. Mechanic D: The influence of mothers on their children's health attitudes and behavior. Pediatrics 33:444–453, 1964

25. Zborowski M: Cultural components in responses to pain. J Soc Issues 8 (4):16–30, 1952

26. Mechanic D: Medical Sociology: A selective view. New York, Free Press, 1968

27. *Idem*: Religion, religiosity, and illness behavior: the special case of the Jews. Hum Organ 22:202–208, 1963

28. Fink R, Shapiro S, Goldensohn SS, et al: The "filter-down" process to psychotherapy in a group practice medical care program. Am J Public Health 59:245–260, 1969

29. Kerckhoff AC, Back KW: The June Bug: A study of hysterical contagion. New York, Appleton-Century-Crofts, 1968

30. Bart PB: Social structure and vocabularies of discomfort: what happened to female hysteria? J Health Soc Behav 9:188–193, 1968

31. Balint M: The Doctor, his Patient and the Illness. New York, International Universities Press, 1957

32. Wolff HG: Headache and Other Head Pain. Second edition. New York, Oxford University Press, 1963

33. Hes JP: Hypochondriacal complaints in Jewish psychiatric patients. Isr Ann Psychiatry 6:134–142, 1968

34. Mechanic D, Volkart EH: Stress, illness behavior, and the sick role. Am Sociol Rev 26:51–58, 1961

35. Mechanic D: Some implications of illness behavior for medical sampling. N Engl J Med 269:244–247, 1963

36. Mechanic D, Jackson D: Stress, Illness Behavior, and the Use of General Practitioner Services: A study of British women (mimeographed). Madison, Department of Sociology, University of Wisconsin

37. Kadushin C: Individual decisions to undertake psychotherapy. Adm Sci Q 3:379–411, 1958

38. Beecher HK: Measurement of Subjective Responses: quantitative effects of drugs. New York, Oxford University Press, 1959

39. Lambert WE, Libman E, Poser EG: The effect of increased salience of a membership group on pain tolerance. J Pers 28:350–357, 1960

40. Ross L, Rodin J, Zimbardo PG: Toward an attribution therapy: the reduction of fear through induced cognitive-emotional misattribution. J Pers Soc Psychol 12:279–288, 1969

41. Blitz B, Dinnerstein AJ: Role of attentional focus in pain perception: manipulation of response to noxious stimulation by instructions. J Abnorm Psychol 77:42–45, 1971

42. Walters A: Psychogenic regional pain alias hysterical pain. Brain 84:1–18, 1961

43. Imboden JB, Canter A, Cluff LE, et al: Brucellosis, III. Psychologic aspects of delayed convalescence. Arch Intern Med 103:406–414, 1959

44. Imboden JB, Canter A, Cluff I.: Symptomatic recovery from medical disorders: influence of psychological factors. JAMA 178:1182–1184, 1961

45. Zola IK: Problems of communication, diagnosis, and patient care: the interplay of patient, physician and clinic organization. J Med Educ 38:829–838, 1963

46. Brodman K, Mittelmann B, Wechsler D, et al: The relation of personality disturbances to duration of convalescence from acute respiratory infections. Psychosom Med 9:37–44, 1947

47. Rickels K, Downing RW: Drug- and placebo-treated neurotic outpatients: pretreatment levels of manifest anxiety, clinical improvement, and side reactions. Arch Gen Psychiatry 16:369–372, 1967
48. Rickels K, Lipman R, Raab E: Previous medication, duration of illness and placebo response. J Nerv Ment Dis 142:548–554, 1966
49. Storms MD, Nisbett RE: Insomnia and the attribution process. J Pers Soc Psychol 16:319–328, 1970
50. Egbert LD, Battit GE, Welch CE, et al: Reduction of postoperative pain by encouragement and instruction of patients: a study of doctor-patient rapport. N Engl J Med 270:825–827, 1964
51. Skipper JK Jr, Leonard RC: Children, stress, and hospitalization: a field experiment. J Health Soc Behav 9:275–287, 1968

13

The Effect of Exposure to Culture Change, Social Change, and Changes in Interpersonal Relationships on Health

Lawrence E. Hinkle, Jr.

This chapter is a summary of some findings from studies that have been carried out by the Division of Human Ecology at Cornell University Medical College and by the Human Ecology Study Program which preceded it. These investigations were directed at the question of how the health of people is affected by changes in their cultural or social milieu or by changes in their interpersonal relationships. They began in 1952 and have continued to the present. All of them have been collaborative efforts, involving the parallel activities of physicians, psychiatrists, epidemiologists, psychologists, sociologists, anthropologists, and in some instances political scientists. In each investigation the representatives of the various disciplines have applied their own methods and concepts to the subject matter and the findings have been interrelated as the study proceeded. The investigators involved in each study were different; the names of the participants are listed in the bibliography as coauthors of the papers which described the research in which they took part.

Since physicians first began to observe and describe illness, they have been aware that occurrences which affect the supply of food, the character of the diet, the exposure of people to infectious or toxic agents or to opportunities for injury profoundly influence the amount and kind of illness that they experience. From the earliest times, War, Famine, and Pestilence have been three of the Four Horsemen of the Apocalypse. In the last few centuries less dramatic phenomena, such as technological changes and changes in general economic conditions, have been recognized as influencing patterns of illness. More recently there has been much concern about the effects that may be produced by rapid culture change, social dislocation, and changes in interpersonal relations. It has been recognized that each

SOURCE: Barbara S. Dohrenwend and Bruce P. Dohrenwend, *Stressful Life Events* (New York: Wiley, 1974), pp. 9–44. Copyright © 1974 by John Wiley & Sons, Inc. Reprinted by permission of John Wiley & Sons, Inc.

of these phenomena may be associated with changes in diet and habits, changes in physical activity, and changes in the opportunity for exposure to infection, toxic agents, or trauma; but beyond this there has been a special concern about whether the effects of such changes may be mediated directly by the central nervous system through its influence on the internal biochemical and physiological processes of the individual.

By the end of the decade of the 1940s, it was appreciated that changes in the relation of people to their social group, and in their relation to other people of importance in their lives, might represent stimuli sufficient to cause the central nervous system to initiate physiological reactions that could influence the course of disease. By then, experimental evidence indicated that the mediation of such neurally initiated reactions could be by way of the glands of internal secretion as well as by the effects of the autonomic and voluntary nervous systems (Cannon, 1929; Selye, 1946; Wolff, Wolf, & Hare, 1950). Although the precise details of the processes of this mediation were not yet clear, the evidence already uncovered made it apparent that probably any biochemical process within the cell could be influenced in some manner and to some degree by the central nervous system. Therefore it seemed evident that there would probably be no aspect of human growth, development, or disease that would in theory be immune to the influence of the effect of a man's relation to his social and interpersonal environment. Subsequent experimental investigations over the course of the 1950s and 1960s have filled in many details of the mechanisms involved and have strongly supported the conclusion suggested by the evidence that was available in 1949 (Hinkle, 1969).

During the same period a great deal was learned about the fundamental features of the higher functions of the central nervous system that are relevant to such neurally initiated organic reaction patterns (Hinkle, 1968, 1973). It became quite clear that the substrate for the operations of the nervous system is "information" in the technical sense. With the organs of special sense acting as "sensors," the nervous system acquires information from the environment, evaluates this against "memory" using a combination of innate and acquired programmatic processes, and elaborates highly organized patterns of response designed to serve the biological needs of the organism. The process is communicative in nature, and the response of the organism is to the biological meaning to the information that it has acquired (Hinkle, 1973). One might say therefore that from a physiological point of view a man may be expected to react to the "meaning" of information he obtains from his social environment and not necessarily to the "objective" features of it that are discernible by others.

However, to postulate that a man's relation to his social environment, and especially to the important people in his life, may have an important influence on his health is not to say that it actually does so. The relative importance of such relationships as determinants of health and the effect of social change, culture change, and changes in interpersonal relations on the patterns of health of members of human populations must be determined by the direct observation of the effect of such variables on humans. It was an attempt to learn more about this that led us to the study of the effects of the social environment on human populations and induced me to organize, with Dr. Harold Wolff, The Human Ecology Study Program at

Cornell University Medical College in 1954. Dr. Wolff and I used the term "human ecology," which was then unfamiliar to the general public, in its literal sense to mean the study of the relationships between men and their environment, our specific interest being the effect of these relationships on human health.

Studies of Groups of Similar People in Relatively Unchanging Environments

Our initial investigations were directed at two population groups whose members shared a very similar and stable social environment (Hinkle & Plummer, 1952; Hinkle & Wolff, 1958). The first of these was a group of career telephone operators in New York City (Hinkle & Plummer, 1952; Hinkle, Plummer, Metraux, Richter, Gittinger, Thetford, Ostfeld, Kane, Goldberg, Mitchell, Leichter, Pinsky, Goebel, Bross, & Wolff, 1957; Hinkle & Wolf, 1958). This was essentially a population of steadily employed semiskilled working women. Most of the women in this population originated from "blue-collar" families and had, on the average, a grammar school or part of a high school education. When they married, their husbands were likely to be steadily employed blue-collar workers. Generally they became telephone operators at the age of 17 or 18. The great majority of those who started in this employment dropped out after a few months or several years, but approximately 10% continued to work as telephone operators for 20 years or more. During this time they were covered by a sickness benefit program which enabled them to afford an average level of medical care for members of the community in which they lived. It also provided detailed and continuous records of all of their episodes of illness and all of their days of sickness absences throughout their careers. They were examined initially at the time of their employment, and most of them were examined from

FIGURE 1. Distribution of 226 American working men by episodes of disabling illness during 20 years, age 20 to 40. (Data from records.)

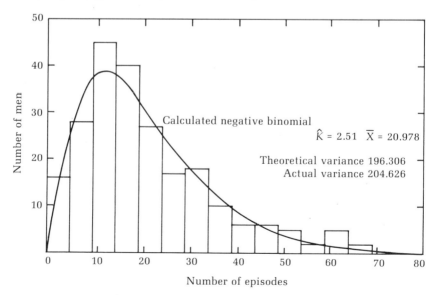

FIGURE 2. Episodes of illness versus syndromes of 116 American working men during 20 years, age 20 to 40.

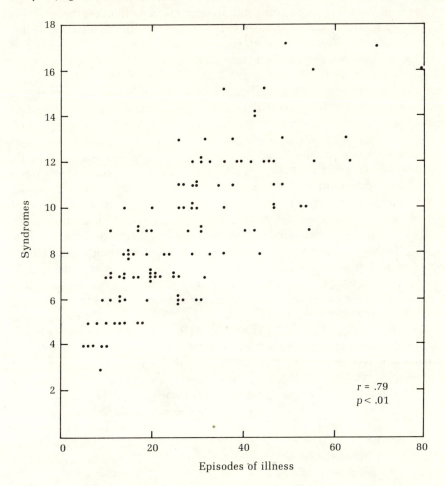

time to time after that for any one of a number of reasons. Any illness lasting a few days was covered by a physician's report, and often by a report from a hospital or from an attending physician as well as by diagnostic examinations carried out in the company's medical department. One could therefore obtain quite complete records of the number of days of illness and the number of episodes of sickness disability experienced by these women as well as information about the nature and the cause of the illnesses and the injuries that they had incurred.

For the purposes of our investigation we selected all of the 1327 telephone operators who were employed in one "division" of the company in eastern Manhattan (Hinkle & Plummer, 1952). Within this group there were 336 who had been employed continuously for more than 20 years. We investigated the frequency and the kinds of illness that each of these women had experienced over a 20-year period from her mid-twenties to her mid-forties. When the distribution of illness within the group had been determined, we selected the 20 women who had had the greatest number of days of sickness disability during the 20-year period and the 20 women who had had the smallest number of days of sickness disability. We examined each of these women in detail and we interviewed each at length.

We use a similar procedure to study 1527 blue-collar workmen who represented all of the men employed as installers, repairmen, and skilled workmen concerned with inside telephone equipment who were on the payroll of a similar division of the company on January 1, 1953 (Hinkle, Pinsky, Bross, & Plummer, 1956). These men also came from blue-collar families. On the average they were somewhat better educated than the women, having all or part of a high school education. They had been employed at a somewhat later age, in their early twenties. Approximately 90% of them had remained on the payroll from the time of their initial employment. The same kinds of medical and attendance records were available for these men. By a random sampling procedure we selected 226 with 20 or more years of service and studied their illnesses over a 20-year period from their mid-twenties to their mid-forties. After rank ordering the men in this sample according to the total number of days of disability during the observation period, we designated for intensive study the 20 men with the greatest number of diabilities and the 20 men with the smallest.

Since the findings from these two populations of men and women were similar, they may be summarized together. Within each of these groups of similar people who had been employed in a similar occupation in the same city over a similar period of life, there had been a marked difference in the amount of illness experienced by the individual members (Hinkle et al., 1956; Hinkle, Plummer, et al., 1957; Hinkle & Plummer, 1952; Hinkle & Wolff, 1957, 1958). Illness was not distributed within the group in the manner that one would have expected it to be if episodes of illness were independent events and every person had an equal risk of becoming ill. We found that episodes of illness were distributed in a manner that could be explained only on the assumption that some people had a much greater likelihood of having an illness than others. The theoretical distributions that fitted the data best were those based on such an assumption. The negative binomial distribution, which is based on the assumption of a chi-square distribution of risk, fitted the observations reasonably well, whereas the Poisson distribution, which is based on the assumption of equal risk, did not.

At one end of the distribution curve there were men and women who had no days of sickness disability and no episodes of disabling illness during a 20-year period. There were many men and women who had fewer than five days of sickness absence and only one or two episodes of disabling illness each year. At the other end of the distribution there were men and women whose total period of sickness disability during the 20 years, from age 20 to 40, amounted to more than 1000 days, or almost three calendar years. Some of these people had had approximately 100 episodes of disabling illness during this time. There was a strong positive correlation between the number of days of sickness disability that a person had experienced, the number of episodes of disabling illness that he had experienced, and the number of different kinds of illnesses he had experienced. The people with the greater amount of disability had had more disease syndromes, more of their organ systems primarily involved in disease, and diseases arising from a greater number of apparent causes. Those with more sickness disability had had more brief illnesses of minor conse-

TABLE 1. An "Ill" American Working Woman; Illnesses Experienced from Age 16 to Age 51

"Body System"	Syndrome	Episodes of Disability
Respiratory system	Influenza	1
	Pertussis	1
	Minor upper respiratory infections (approx.)	44
	Severe tonsillitis	2
Gastrointestinal system	Cholecystitis and cholelithiasis	2
	Diaphragmatic hernia	5
	Duodenal diverticulum	0
	Postoperative biliary symptoms	4
	Mucous colitis	4
	Infectious gastroenteritis (chronic, nondisabling constipation, low abdominal pain, "gas," and nausea, present for many years)	3
Cardiovascular system	Essential hypertension	0
Genital system	Myomata of uterus	0
	Dysmenorrhea (chronic)	0
	Postmenopausal flushes, severe	1
Urinary system	Pyelonephritis	1
	Cystitis	1
Blood	Hypochromic anemia	0
Musculoskeletal system	"Low back pain"	4
	Osteoarthritis	1
Head	Vascular headaches (nondisabling headaches occurred about once a month)	2
Ears	Otitis media	2
	Ménière's syndrome	1
Eyes	Conjunctivitis	1
Teeth	Dental caries (total extractions)	3
Skin	Urticaria	2
	Cellulitis	1
Breast	Fibroma	1
Metabolic	Obesity	
Mood, thought, behavior	Moderately severe depressions	3
	Anxiety-tension states (symptoms of anxiety, tension, depression chronically present)	5
Accidents	Contusions	8
	Lacerations	3
	Sprains	1
Operations	Cholecystectomy	
	Hysterectomy and oophorectomy	
	Excision of fibroma of breast	
	Total dental extractions	

Summary

Total days disabled	1041
Disabling episodes of illness	95
"Major" illnesses	9
Disabling disturbances of mood, thought, and behavior	8
"Body systems" involved	15
Accidents	12
Operations	4

TABLE 2. A "Healthy" American Working Man; Illnesses Experienced to Age 59

Birth and early development	Normal
Illnesses experienced before age 12	"Very few colds"
	"Few childhood diseases"
	"Mild"
Estimated days of disability before age 12	<12
Illnesses experienced, age 12–24	One minor laceration
	"Maybe a few colds"

Illnesses by Record and History, Age 24–59		
"Organ System"	Syndrome	Episodes
Respiratory	Minor upper respiratory infections	9
Gastrointestinal	Acute gastroenteritis	2
	Hemorrhoid	1
Genitourinary	Varicocele	1
Skin	Furuncle	1
Eyes	Hyperopia	1
Teeth	Caries	1
Accidents	Minor contusions and lacerations	5
Mood, thought, and behavior	Anxiety, acute	1

Summary	
Total days disabled, 35 years	7
Total episodes of illness	22
"Major" episodes	0
Disabling episodes	5
Episodes of disturbance of mood, thought, and behavior	1
"Organ systems" involved	8
Operations	0

quences and also more prolonged and life-endangering illnesses. The coefficients of correlation between these different aspects of illness (Spearman's rho) was of the order of $+.4$ to $+.6$ in most instances and was significant at the 1% level or beyond.

The direct examination of the most frequently disabled members of these populations confirmed that they were sick people in almost every respect. Table 1 is an example of the medical history of a frequently disabled woman, and Table 2 presents the medical history of a "healthy man."

The illnesses that occurred among the members of these populations generally were not isolated during a few years of the observation period. They tended to occur from time to time throughout the entire 20-year period. If a person had few episodes of illness, these were likely to be scattered over the 20 years rather than being located within 1 or 2 years. If a person had many episodes of illness, he also was likely to have had some episodes in almost every year of the 20 years. This finding was so consistent that the amount of illness experienced by a subject during one 5-year period could be used to predict the frequency of his illness during the next 15- or 20-year period.

In spite of the overall constancy of patterns of illness, the frequency of the illness experienced by each individual did fluctuate to some extent. Men and women with higher levels of disability did have some years in which they experienced a great many episodes of illness and other years in which they experienced fewer episodes. During periods in which they had many episodes of illness, these illnesses included both "minor" and "major" illness, illnesses involving several organ systems, and illnesses arising from several different primary causes. We referred to these as "clusters of illness." This "clustering" phenomenon was also seen among people who had a moderate level of disability and a moderate frequency of illness and those who had relatively little disability and a low frequency of illness. Those with moderate levels of illness had clusters of moderate size, and those with low levels of illness had clusters of small size; in each instance the clusters contained illnesses of several kinds and of several apparent causes, and sometimes they contained major illness as well as minor illness.

In summary, we observed that within these two populations, made up of similar people engaged in similar activities in a similar environment over a similar period of life, each individual tended to have his own mean level of frequency of episodes of illness and of sickness disability over a 20-year period, around which his observed episodes of illness fluctuated from year to year. To explain this observation one could set up a null hypothesis that the variations in illness were simply random fluctuations around a mean arising from the interaction of many factors. By the statistical analyses of these data alone, we were not able to establish that the null hypothesis is not correct. The explanation for the apparent clustering of illness therefore might simply be the random fluctuation of the many factors that determine the occurrence of any given episode of illness. One does not necessarily have to postulate that the clustering phenomenon has any special significance in any given instance. However, it is also possible that each cluster represents a response of the individual to significant changes in his environment.

FIGURE 3. Number of episodes of disabling illness experienced by 226 American working men versus number of years of the 20-year observation period during which the informant experienced a disabling illness. (Data from records.)

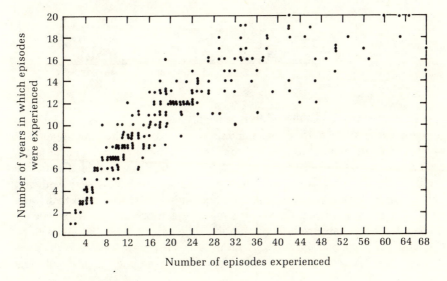

FIGURE 4. Number of episodes of illness occurring annually in each of five frequently ill American men. The "observation period" begins at time of employment (age 15 to 24 years) and continues to the mid-forties. Major disabling illnesses are in black; minor disabling illnesses are hatched; nondisabling illnesses are in white.

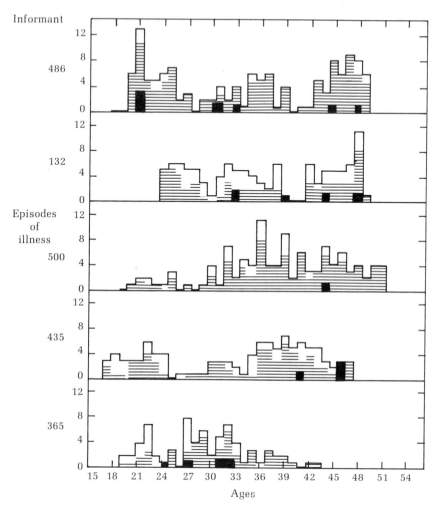

We found that the healthy subjects generally were people whose social backgrounds, personal aspirations, and interests coincided with the circumstances in which they found themselves, whereas this often was not the case among those who were frequently ill (Hinkle, 1959; Hinkle, Christenson, Kane, Ostfeld, Thetford, & Wolff, 1958). In other words, the "healthy" telephone operators were women of blue-collar backgrounds, with grammar school educations, who liked their work, found it easy and satisfying, liked their families and associates, and were generally content and comfortable with their lot in life. This was often not the case with the frequently ill telephone operators. A number of these were women of disparate backgrounds—for example, women of white-collar background who had had a high school or even part of a college education—and many of them were working at this job not because they liked it but from necessity. They often described it as confining or boring. For various reasons these women were unhappy with their lot in life, with their families, their associates, and their communities. However, we observed that there were some members of the frequently ill group who did not express dissatisfaction with important aspects of their lives, and conversely there were a considerable number of women in the healthy group whose life histories were full of deprivation and difficulties, and whose social backgrounds and aspirations did not show a close fit with their present life situation. We made similar observations within the group of men.

The longitudinal and retrospective life histories obtained from the frequently ill and the moderately ill usually suggested that a cluster of illness coincided with a period when the individual was experiencing many demands and frustrations arising from his social environment or his interpersonal relations. These histories suggested that significant changes in the relations of ill people to their social group and in their

FIGURE 5. Number of episodes of illness occurring annually in each of eight American men with a moderate frequency of illness.

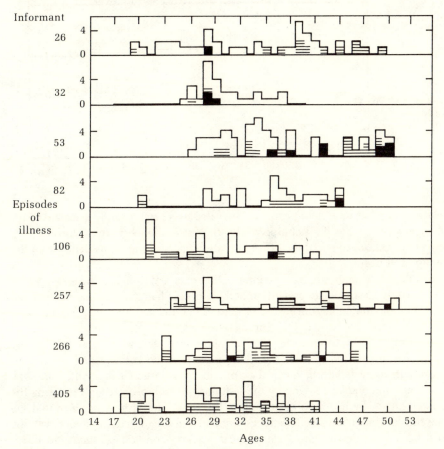

FIGURE 6. Number of episodes of illness occurring annually in each of eight American men with a low frequency of illness.

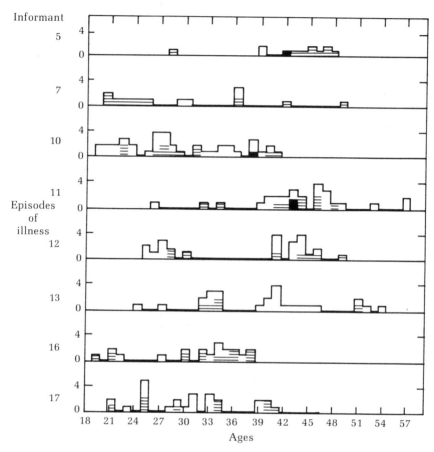

relations to other important people in their lives were significantly associated with changes in their health. Retrospectively, the association between "stressful" life situations "perceived" as "difficult" or "unsatisfying" was quite consistent within the group of ill people.

On the other hand, some of the information obtained from the "healthy people" indicated that a significant proportion of these people had encountered many social demands and difficulties during the observation period and had endured important changes in their lives and in their interpersonal relations without developing illness. For example, one of the "healthiest" telephone operators was a woman who had been an effective and well-liked worker throughout the entire period of her employment. As evidenced by medical examinations and interviews, by the testimony of friends and employees, and by the testimony of unbroken records covering the entire period, she had been healthy all of this time. Her history indicated that she was the daughter of an alcoholic longshoreman and a teenaged immigrant girl. She had been born into a household of great poverty, constant conflict, and much turmoil. Four of her nine siblings had died in infancy of infection and apparent malnutrition. When she was 3 years of age her father had deserted his family. When she was 5 years of age she had been placed in an orphanage by community action because her mother was neglecting her and had been adjudged unfit to raise her. She had had a barren childhood in orphanages. When she was 13 she had been put out to work as a servant. At the age of 16 she had left the place at which she was working and had lived, as she put it, "all around the town" with another teenage girl. During this time she had had a number of casual sexual attachments and many jobs. When she had obtained her present job as a telephone operator she was 23 years old. At the age of 27 she had married a chronically ill, neurotic plumber's helper, whom she had had to support thereafter. They had no children. He had

FIGURE 7. Two "clusters" of illness of American working men—one between ages 18 and 24; the other between ages 32 and 40.

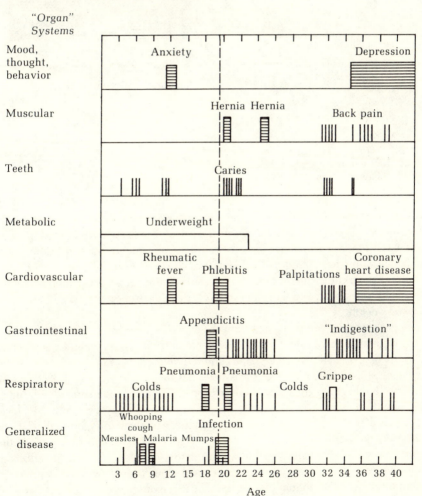

FIGURE 8. The relation between life situations and clusters of illness of the American working man. The major disabling illnesses are in black; minor disabling illnesses are hatched; nondisabling illnesses are white. (This figure is reprinted with the permission of the author from L. E. Hinkle, Jr., and H. G. Wolff. Ecological investigations of the relationship between illness, life experience, and the social environment. *Annals of Internal Medicine*, 1958, **49**, 1373–1388.)

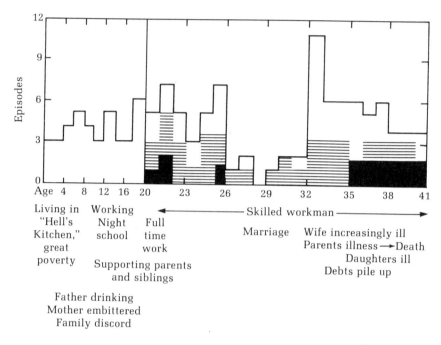

died in her arms of a massive gastric hemorrhage when she was 44 years old. Thereafter she lived alone as a widow. At the age of 54, when we examined her and interviewed her, we found her to be a well-liked and highly respected employee. She had had only two episodes of sickness disability in 31 years. The only significant illnesses that we could uncover on extensive questioning and examination had been a few colds. However, she said she did have a few days of "nervousness" after her husband's death.

Similar examples could be cited from the experiences of the men as well as those of the women. It was evident that some people in these groups could be exposed to major social deprivations and demands and to major changes in their interpersonal relations without becoming ill. It was true that the life histories described by the "healthy" tended to be more benign that those described by the frequently ill, but at least one-third of the "most healthy people" in both groups were found to have experienced major deprivations or major changes in their interpersonal relations during the course of their lives. Interviews suggested that a frequent feature of the personalities of such healthy people was a relative "insulation" from the effects of such changes—a capacity to experience social change, and personal deprivation without a profound emotional or psychological response.

Studies of Groups of People Exposed to
Major Changes in Their Social Environment

For our next group of investigations we sought subjects who had been exposed to major social and cultural changes and who had experienced separations from their families and communities and major personal dislocations. The first such group that we investigated was made up of Chinese-born graduate students and technical and professional people living in New York City in the early 1950s (Hinkle, Plummer et al., 1957; Hinkle & Wolff, 1957, 1958; Hinkle, Gittinger, Goldberger, Metraux, Ostfeld, Richter, & Wolff, 1957). The members of this group had all been reared in China, in the Chinese cultural milieu. Most of them were the sons or daughters of upper-class Chinese who had been adherents of the Chinese Nationalist Government of Chiang Kai-shek. Most of them had been born between 1910 and 1930. During the course of their lives they had been exposed to the effects of the disruption of the old Chinese culture, the rapid change in Chinese society, the social upheavals, and the geographic dislocation which characterized the first half of the twentieth century in China. Many of them had had personal experience with wars, revolutions, new customs, and technological changes in their homelands. In China they had recieved, or had been in the process of receiving, a modern Western college education, and in this context they had had to make a personal adaptation to features of two dissimilar cultures.

With few exceptions, they had to come to the United States in the period after World Ward II, between 1946 and 1949, in pursuit of further educational or professional training, leaving their families behind and planning on returning to careers in China. They had been unable, or unwilling, to return to China after the Chinese Communist accession to power in 1948–49. Stranded in the United States, most of them had since been in a situation of uncertainity, without assurance of their future status, their occupations, or their careers, and often with no knowledge of the fate of their families, friends, and possessions in China. They were therefore a group who had experienced many major changes in their lives and who had had to make many major adaptations to new social relationships.

When our investigation was initiated in the fall of 1954, there were several thousand such Chinese in the United States. The 100 that we selected for our study were obtained from a list of these people in the New York City area. Our sample was intended to cover the major variables of age, background, intellectual and professional interests within this population. Participants were recruited by a widely respected member of this Chinese group, who selected their names from various lists that were available. He asked those selected to participate in a study that was designed to investigate the personal experiences and problems of adjustment of the members of this group. He told them that they would not be paid for their participation, but that they would receive $25 to cover their expenses during the day that they were with us. Since most of the members of this group were highly interested in making their problems and difficulties better known, and many were, in addition, in financial straits, we were informed that very few of those designated were unwilling to participate. Health was not one of the variables that was considered in the selection of participants and the recruiter was not himself aware that the health of those recruited was one of our major interests. We did not detect any evidence of a major "health bias" in the sample during the course of the examination, but the possibility that there was some bias in relation to health cannot be excluded.

Most of the participants were in their twenties or thirties at the same time that we saw them. Medical information was obtained from them by means of a systematic medical history and by examinations carried out by a physician. Each member of the group was also studied with a number of psychological tests, with interviews with psychiatrists, and with interviews with an anthropologist. There were 69 men and 31 women among them.

Of the men, 60 were more than 32 years of age. The distribution of illness among these men during the 20-year period from age 12 to 32 was studied in the same way that we had studied the distribution of illness in the two groups of American working people. This distribution exhibited the same features that we had observed in the two American groups. A small proportion of the group had experienced the greater proportion of the sickness disability and of the episodes of illness. Episodes of illness were distributed within the group in a manner which indicated that some members had a much greater likelihood of experiencing an episode than others. The data rather closely fitted a negative binomial distribution. Those who had had the greatest number of illnesses had the greatest variety of illnesses involving a greater number of their organ systems and a greater number of possible etiological agents. The frequently ill people had had many illnesses throughout the 20-year observation period, whereas the healthy had had few or none. The clustering of illness episodes was less apparent among these Chinese, although it could be seen among the more ill members of the group. It was felt that the retrospective or recall nature of the medical data might have tended to obscure this phenomenon because of the difficulty in recalling relatively minor illnesses and the time of their occurrence.

All of these Chinese had been exposed to culture change, to major social dislocations, and to disruptions of some of their important interpersonal relationships. Since most of them were of upper-class origin, they had been more protected from the physical aspects of the Chinese environment than one would have expected had they been poor, but some of the experiences that they had encountered during wars, revolutions, and other disruptions of their lives had probably provided them with more opportunity for exposure to infectious disease and trauma than one might have expected in a similar group of middle-upper-class Americans. These two factors may have accounted for the relatively greater average frequency of major evidences of disease among the Chinese than among the Americans at a similar age.

Among these Chinese, as among the Americans, there were some who had experienced remarkably little illness during the period from age 12 to 32. An example is a man who was the son of a successful Nationalist officer. Because of civil warfare he had been sent, at the age of 3 with his mother, to live with his grandparents in a rural village. From that time to the age of 10 he had been reared in a traditional Chinese village setting with all that this implied in terms of sanitation and opportunity for infection. He then rejoined his father's household and was sent to modern Chinese primary schools and "middle schools." During World War II he continued his education at Chung-king with great difficulty, experiencing many bombings and much privation and fatigue. Later in the war he left China and accompanied his father to Europe. There, without friends, and in a cultural setting quite strange to him, he entered a medical school, which he attended for three years. In the late 1940s he was taken by his father to the United States and was left alone while his father returned to China. He had tried to get into an American medical school but had failed. After that he made no further attempt to attain an education or to find a job. He lived on the money his father had left with him until this gave out. In the meantime, the Nationalist government on the Chinese mainland collapsed. His father was imprisoned, some of his funds were cut off, and he lost all contact with his relatives in China. Shortly after that his last few thousand dollars were stolen from him. He then moved to another American city and finally obtained a fulltime job of a routine nature in a field entirely unrelated to medicine. He found this work dull, but he continued to do it out of necessity. At the time that we saw him, he was living alone in a strange city with no relatives and with few associates of his own background. Throughout all of this he had remained essentially healthy.

Both the psychiatrists and the psychologists who participated in the Chinese study commented upon the apparent "emotional insulation" of the more healthy members of the Chinese group. Major "life changes," which they had expected to create profound emotional reactions in these people, seemed to have rather little effect on them.

We next studied a group of people who were in the midst of a major social and geographic dislocation at the time that we saw them: the refugees from the Hungarian revolution of 1956 (Hinkle, 1956; Hinkle, Kane, Christenson, & Wolff, 1959). In the early summer of 1956 the Hungarian political and social situation had seemed to these people to be much as it had been during the previous 10 years. For most of our future subjects, life then had the rather monotonous and gray flavor of a society in which a state-run economy and a rigid bureaucracy provided an adequate but meager living for most people at the cost of many annoying shortages, delays, and inconveniences, and much perceived limitation of individual initiative. In August and early September of that year an unexpected series of political events led to an uprising in which many young people of the cities, many workers, and a good many soldiers took a leading role. As a result of this uprising the state police and the ruling regime were temporarily overthrown. For several weeks it appeared as if a new and more liberal government would be established; but then an intervention by the Russian army restored the original party group to control. During the period of the revolution, and for some time after the Russian intervention, the border between Hungary and Austria was open. Many people who had been out of sympathy with the Communist state took the opportunity to flee as soon as this opportunity appeared. Others, including many who participated in the revolution, found it necessary to flee for their own safety when the revolution was crushed. By November 1956, approximately 60,000 Hungarians were refugees in Austria. During November and December some 30,000 of them were flown to the United States in a massive airlift. These Hungarians, who had been going about their daily lives in their accustomed manner in July 1956, found themselves in January 1957 to be refugees in a foreign country, in the meantime having passed through a period of profound disturbances of their usual daily routine, a major social upheaval, and a long journey to a new society and a new culture, in which they were separated from their families and from most of the important social groups and interpersonal relationships that they had previously enjoyed.

In the period from December 1956 to June 1957, we studied a group of these people. The demographic characteristics of the population of Hungarian refugees were not specifically known at that time, and it was not possible to draw a probability sample from the group. Therefore we used a procedure like that which we had used with the Chinese. We designated a group of informants who represented the major demographic segments of the refugee population as we knew them and who appeared to be more or less representative of the group from which they were taken. The 69 subjects included students, professionals, teachers and other intellectuals, skilled and semiskilled workers, and young people between the ages of 15 and 25 from the large cities. The procedures used to study these people included a careful and extensive chronological life history, a detailed history of all illnesses, medical examinations, interviews with sociologists, psychologists, and a cultural anthropologist, and a series of psychological tests. The whole investigation required two days of each subject's time.

We found that during the previous 10 years, the rate at which these Hungarians had experienced episodes of illness of many types, both physical and psychological, was higher than that which we had seen in any other comparable group including the Chinese. These people also expressed a profound degree of insecurity and frustration about the social environment in which they had been living. The personal historical evidence suggested that when these people had had difficulty in making a satisfactory adaptation to their social environment in the past, and most notably during the periods when they felt insecure, frustrated, or threatened, they had had an increased number of episodes of many varieties of illness. This again had been especially true of those who had been frequently ill.

On the other hand, the physical dislocation and the social, emotional, and psychological changes that they had experienced during the revolution and subsequent flight had been accompanied by an improvement in their general health and well-being in most instances. In spite of the difficulties they had encountered, there was an element of pleasurable excitement and anticipation—in some instances amounting almost to a euphoria—in their attitude toward their recent and present experiences. When each person's medical condition during the six months of recent acute change was compared with his own previous medical history, the majority of these people were found to have experienced a period of relative or absolute well-being during the period of their acute dislocation in the months before we saw them.

Among these Hungarians, as among the members of the groups that we studied previously, we found that individuals differed markedly in their general susceptibility to illness. Those having the greatest number of episodes had experienced more types of illness involving more of their organ systems, falling into more "causal" categories. The frequently ill people also had experienced a greater number of disturbances of mood, thought, and behavior.

There were some members of this group who had lived through remarkably diverse and demanding life situations, including significant changes in their social position, their physical environment, and their family relationships, with very little illness. There were others who had experienced many illnesses in settings which appeared to be much more benign. Such differences in susceptibility to illness appeared to be dependent in part on the physical characteristics of the individual, including both his genetically determined susceptibilities to disease and his previous experience with the infectious, traumatic, toxic, and other damaging agents from the physical environment which had helped to create the various kinds of illness that he had experienced. In this, as in the other investigations, there was also evidence from the personality studies which indicated that those who had experienced the greater amount of illness had, in general, perceived their environment as more threatening, challenging, demanding, and frustrating than the healthier people. The more healthy members of the group tended to describe their life situations in a much more benign manner, even though these experiences "objectively," in the eyes of the examiner, seemed to be very like the experiences of the frequently ill.

During the period from 1954 to 1956 we had the opportunity to observe a third group of people who had experienced extreme degrees of social dislocation and deprivation, threat and insecurity, often in a setting of extreme physical hardship. This opportunity was provided by a review of the experience of American prisoners of war in North Korea at the time of the Korean conflict, and by a review of the methods that were used by the state police systems of Eastern European countries, and in China, for the arrest and interrogation of people suspected of political crimes, for their subsequent preparation for trial, and the process of their "reeducation" during their imprisonment (Hinkle, 1961; Hinkle & Wolff, 1956). This was not a study of a population sample but an opportunity to review data from many sources and to see and study in detail some people who had experienced these procedures or had helped to carry them out.

The evidence from all sources indicated that the sudden arrest of a person suspected of a political crime and his total isolation and systematic interrogation in a setting of great fear and uncertainty predictably produced, in many subjects, serious signs of disorganization of the highest integrative functions of the brain, accompanied by confusion, pliability, and suggestibility, sleep disturbance, and evidence of disturbances of various bodily functions. The effect of this procedure could be greatly enhanced if it was accompanied by the deliberate manipulation of the subjects' position or activity, his food and fluic intake, his sleep cycle, the temperature of his surroundings, or painful or damaging physical harassment.

The psychological effects of these procedures were not dependent on the manipulation of the physical environment of the prisoner or the infliction of pain or injury. A substantial disorganization might occur quite in the absence of any of these, provided the total social isolation and the other features of the interrogation procedure were carried out. On the other hand, the physical manipulation of the subject or of his environment, if sufficiently intense and prolonged, had certain unavoidable physiological consequences, whereas the manipulation of the social and psychological milieu, taken alone, did not necessarily have such consequences. Subjects who were familiar with the procedures of the state police, who had experienced social isolation and interrogation before, and who felt fairly secure about what could and could not be done to them under the circumstances might endure the interrogation process with all of the isolation and threat that accompanied it indefinitely without adverse effect (Bone, 1957).

Prospective Investigations of the Relation between Discrete and Definable Life Changes and Specific Manifestations of Illness

Our next investigations were aimed at obtaining information by the use of ongoing "prospective" observations of carefully defined population groups under circumstances in which both the manifestations of illness and the nature of the change in social relationships or interpersonal relationships could be defined in advance and observed as the events occurred. The first of these efforts was aimed at the short-term observation of factors affecting the occurrence of acute episodes of illness (Hinkle, Christenson, Benjamin, Kane, Plummer, & Wolff, 1961). We undertook to study the common cold and acute gastroenteritis, illnesses that take the form of discrete episodes and occur with great frequency in the general population of the United States.

To study these phenomena we designated at random 24 telephone operators from a group of 737 who worked in close proximity with each other in two large air conditioned rooms of a building on East 56th Street in New York City. Since they were associated with each other closely and traveled to work in winter on crowded public buses and subways, there was good reason to believe that all of these women would have a widespread exposure to any of the 70 or more viruses that were then known to cause the common cold syndrome and might be prevalent in the community. Having designated our subjects, we persuaded them to be examined and to allow us to observe them at weekly intervals, while photographing their nasal mucus membranes, observing the redness, engorgement, and secretion in their noses and throats, obtaining bacterial cultures and throat washings for viral agents, and obtaining serum samples for antibody determinations once a month.

Each subject kept a diary of her symptoms and of her important activities during the week. At each weekly visit this was reviewed with her. The 24 women were observed for six months throughout the winter of 1959–1960, from mid-October to mid-April.

At the time of the first examination we found the same skewed distribution of illness among the women in this sample that we observed in other population groups. Records indicated that during the 10 years prior to our study a small proportion of these women had had a great many illnesses of many varieties and that a much larger proportion of them had had few or no illnesses. This distribution applied to respiratory illnesses as well as to other kinds of illness. During the six-month observation period all of the women were closely exposed to each other and to the other women in the building. Presumably they had equal exposure to the respiratory pathogens that were present in the community at large. In spite of this, respiratory illnesses were not randomly distributed among them. Past experience with respiratory illness predicted present and observed experience to an unexpected degree. Those women who had had a great many respiratory illnesses in the past had several respiratory illnesses during the observation period, and most of those who had had few such illnesses in the past had few episodes of illness during the observation period. The same held for episodes of acute gastroenteritis.

When an epidemic of the A2 or "Asian" strain of influenza virus appeared in the city during the winter, it caused a marked increase in the number of respiratory illnesses among all the women who worked in the building. The women in our study group experienced an increased frequency of illness at the same time. A number of those who had had many respiratory illnesses in the past came down with acute florid episodes of pneumonia or of the common cold syndrome. Those who had had fewer illnesses in the past developed colds or gastroenteritis and some others had minor symptoms; some developed antibodies indicating that they had been infected by the virus but had no evidence of illness at all.

The events and situations that these women encountered during the course of the winter were, for the most part, the mundane and various changes in interpersonal relations and in ordinary activities that people usually encounter during their daily lives: minor conflicts with other members of their families, disputes with landlords, breakdowns of plumbing or electrical appliances, or a "crisis" when the dog had puppies on the living room rug. Occasionally there was a sickness, a death in the family, or, conversely, a vacation trip or a happy Christmas reunion. From the reports of the women given at the time of these events, it appeared that those which

TABLE 3. Response to Infection with Asian Strain of Influenza Virus

	Disabling Respiratory Illnesses		Illness Observed			
Informant	Previous Five Years	Observation Period	Serological Evidence of Infection	Disabling Episodes	Episodes Not Disabling	No Episodes
3F	CCCCCCCCCCCFFGG	CFF				
4F	CCCCCCCCCCCGGGG	FG				
15F	CCCCCCCCFGGGGGG	CF				
14F	CCCCCFFGGG	CFF	•	F		
13F	CCCCCGGGG	CCCG				
1F	CCCCFGG	C				
10F	CCCFGGG	CFF	•	F		
12F	CCCGGG	GG	•	G		
17F	CCFFGG					
2F	CCCG		•		C	
16F	CCFG					
19F	CCCG	C	•	C		
20F	CCCF	C	•	C		
44F	CFGG		•		C	
47F	CCCF		•			0
40F	CFG	CG	•	G		
45F	CCF		•			0
7F	F	C				
9F	G		•			0
21F	C					
11F						
22F						
23F						
24F			•		C	

C = common cold.　　F = influenza.　　G = gastroenteritis.

caused sadness or weeping or periods of sexual excitement (either of which might cause an increase in the engorgement and secretion of the nasal mucosa) were likely to be followed by an acute respiratory illness, provided an adequate exposure to a viral agent occurred at the same time. Other kinds of pleasurable excitement and arousal, like that created by the preparation for a long-anticipated winter vacation, also seemed to set the stage for the occurrence of an acute respiratory illness. However, the number of instances of these phenomena was too small to allow one to draw any firm conclusions from the data.

It was clearly desirable to study a larger population over a longer period of time, to have a large proportion of the members of this population systematically exposed to clearly definable and potentially major changes in social and interpersonal relations, and to have a clearly identifiable major illness as the dependent variable. Therefore we turned to the population of 270,000 men employed by the Bell System throughout the continental United States. These men, mostly of northern and western European stock, in the age range of 20 to 65, are employed in a limited number of highly specifiable jobs. Almost all of them are career employees who enter this system in their early twenties. Most of them continue in its employment until they retire or die. They are covered by a uniform system of sickness and retirement benefits, and records of their health, attendance, and occupational experiences are maintained in a standard manner throughout the system.

The Bell System employs men of two sorts: 250,000 of its male employees have all or part of a high school education. The great majority of these men enter the system as semiskilled blue-collar workers and soon become skilled craftsmen who install, repair, or maintain telephone equipment; but some of them enter as white-collar clerical employees. As nonmanagement employees, they earned up to $8000 a year at the same time that our study began. Approximately half of these "no-college" men become foremen or other first-line supervisors before they retire, and a great many of them become second level supervisors. Only a relatively small proportion attain the highest levels of management, but the number from which they are drawn is so great and the system is so large that 321 men, or approximately one-fifth, of all the managers and executives of level five and above were of no-college background in 1963. These managers and executives earned from $33,000 to more than $45,000 per year at that time, and they presided over organizations of considerable technical complexity, employing thousands of men, and capitalized at many millions of dollars. By the commonly accepted criteria for American social class, men who have attained such managerial or executive positions have attained upper-middle-class or upper-class status.

The remaining 20,000 employees of the Bell System are recruited as young men who have recently graduated from college after four years of education beyond secondary school. They are hired by the System with the expectation that they will become managers, but with no guarantee that they will do so. These college men start out in nonmanagement jobs alongside the no-college workmen as trainees. Within a few years most of them have attained the first level of management. From this point on the System makes no formal distinction between them and the no-college men. College and no-college men compete for the same managerial jobs. At least half of the college men ultimately attain the third level of management, and a disproportionate number of them become senior managers and executives. As a result, they constitute four-fifths of the upper level managers of the Bell System.

The Bell System population thus can be used to study men of two different social backgrounds who are engaged in similar occupations throughout the nation. Some men from each background are upwardly and geographically mobile, whereas others are not. This system also keeps records of the causes of death and the sickness absences of all men in the employee group. One of the most clearly definable major causes of death and disability in this system is coronary heart disease. Death rates and attack rates for coronary heart disease among these men are comparable to those for all American men. It is therefore possible to investigate the extent to which the experiences of mobile men might influence the incidence and prevalence of coronary heart disease among them, as well as to estimate what effect the social class backgrounds and present social categories of men might have on their likelihood of developing this disease.

Our first effort in this direction was the investigation of the relation between certain highly specific occupational experiences and the occurrence of coronary heart disease in an age cohort of men selected from a typical Bell System company (Hinkle, Benjamin, Christenson, & Ullmann, 1966; Lehman, Schulman, & Hinkle, 1967). For this purpose we selected the New Jersey Bell Telephone Company, which is near the median for all companies in the industry in size, in rural-urban distribution, in the age of its employees, and in the proportion of those on the payroll who are men. The cohort was selected by obtaining a complete payroll from the company for January 1, 1935, and designating all men on this list who had been born between January 1, 1902, and December 31, 1908, and had been hired between January 1, 1923, and December 31, 1930. Of the 1160 men so designated, 274 were college men and 886 were no-college men. On January 1, 1935, the median age of the men in this cohort was 30 years. With perhaps one or two exceptions, every man in the group could be considered to be "at risk" for the development of clinical coronary heart disease at that time. We were able to trace 1152 of these men from 1935 to 1965, that is, from age 30 to age 60, and to determine who among them had died from coronary heart disease during this period.

From occupational records we were able to abstract data on nine categories of experience bearing on the organizational and social mobility of these men: the highest rank attained, the number of promotions, the number of job changes, the number of different job titles, the number of demotions, the number of company departments served in, the number of work location changes, the number of transfers to other companies in the industry, and the line-staff managerial experience. The basic unit of measurement was the number of changes that had occurred per unit time. To determine the possible relationship between these indicators of organizational mobility and death due to coronary heart disease, the mobility experience of those who died from this disease before age 60 was compared with the experience of otherwise similar men in the cohort who had equivalent lengths of exposure within the company. The details of this matching procedure were described elsewhere (Hinkle, et al., 1966). Each man who died of coronary heart disease was matched with a man who died of another cause and whose age at death and year of death was closest to that of the coronary man. He was also matched to another man who survived and the survivor's experience over the same period of years was compared with that of the man who died. The "matched trios" were contrasted in terms of the nine dimensions of organizational mobility discussed above.

A "principal components analysis" was used in the study of the data. Two factors were isolated which accounted for approximately 60% of the observed variation in mobility. The first, or mobility factor, was made up of five highly intercorrelated dimensions: final level attained, number of promotions, number of job changes, number of job titles, and line-staff experience. The second, or immobility factor, was composed of four dimensions: number of demotions, number of job changes, number of job location changes, and number of job title changes. This accounted for about 15% of the variation.

Two hypotheses were tested: (1) Those who died from coronary heart disease had experienced a greater amount of organizational mobility than either the men who died from other causes or the survivors; (2) Those who died from coronary heart disease had experienced a greater amount of immobility than either those who died from other causes or survivors. Neither of these hypotheses was substantiated. The mobility and the immobility scores of the men who died from coronary heart disease were not significantly different from the scores of those who died of other causes or from the scores of those who survived. When the three groups of men were compared on each dimension of experience singly, the findings were the same. In no case had the coronary men had mobility experiences significantly different from the experiences of men who died of other causes or of those who survived.

The relation between the development of coronary heart disease and exposure to organizational, social, and geographic mobility, and to the "life experiences" and changes in interpersonal relationships which accompany these, was also investigated by prospective study of the entire Bell System population of 270,000 men (Hinkle, Whitney, Lehman, Dunn, Benjamin, King, Plakun, & Flehinger, 1968; Hinkle, 1972).

In 1961 arrangements were made so that the clinical data on each new illness and death of a man in the System that was reported under Rubric 420 of the seventh edition of the *International Classification of Diseases** was investigated and reviewed by a company physician according to a prearranged schedule, and these data were reported each quarter to our staff. Elaborate arrangements were made to assure the accuracy and completeness of the reporting and the uniform classification of the episodes (Hinkle et al., 1968). For five years, from January 1, 1962, to December 31, 1966, all events of coronary heart disease that occurred in the System were analyzed. There were 4306 first events (new cases) and 1839 deaths.

When specific attack rates and death rates for men in various categories were computed, the data indicated that the most upwardly mobile men, those men without college education who had risen to the highest managerial and executive

---

*Rubrick 420, Seventh Edition of International Classification of Diseases: *Arteriosclerotic Heart Disease, Including Coronary Disease.* Included under this Rubric are coronary occlusion, coronary insufficiency, and angina pectoris, as well as other manifestations of coronary heart disease.

levels of the organization, had coronary attack rates no higher than those of men of the same age and length of service who had remained as workmen and foremen. Even men who had come into the system without a college education and who had obtained a college education by going to school at night, while at the same time rising to become managers before the age of 40, had overall attack rates no higher than other men—although there was a suggestion that they may have experienced a small excess of new events and death during the period when they were age 30 to 40, at a time when they were actually going to college and working nights as well as days.

Certain categories of occupational experience which could be clearly identified and were generally regarded as highly demanding for those exposed to them were studied in more detail. The effect of promotion to a higher level of responsibility was studied by examining the coronary attack rates among managers in relation to the amount of time that had passed since they were last promoted. It was found that men who had been promoted to new responsibilities within the past year had had no higher attack rates than those who had been promoted less recently. The effect of transfer from one department to another, which is regarded as requiring a major adaptation for many men, was also not associated with an increase in the attack rate. The effect of transfer from one company to another, which was looked upon as probably the most demanding sort of occupational experience that one might encounter, since it required the transfer of families to new locations, and the uprooting of family and community relationships, as well as changes in working relationships and new responsibilities, was studied also. It was found that this was not associated with any increase in the coronary attack rate.

Studies Now in Progress

Since 1962 we have been following prospectively 838 men between the ages of 40 and 65 (Hinkle, 1972; 1973). Each of these men was examined intensively at the time of entry into the study, and each has been followed carefully at intervals since that time. Of these men, 301 were a stratified sample selected from the cohort of men in the New Jersey Bell Telephone Company described in the preceding section. Another 127 men were in their late thirties and early forties designated from other companies in the Bell System in other parts of the country. The most recent 400 are men from 21 industries and 3 labor unions in the New York metropolitan area. The social categories of these men range from lower blue-collar, unskilled workmen to upper white-collar executives and professional men. The medical data include intensive diagnostic procedures to determine the presence of evidence of coronary heart disease, hypertensive disease, pulmonary disease, and such metabolic abnormalities as diabetes mellitus, gout, and hyperlipidemia as well as complex efforts to determine the abnormalities of the cardiac conduction system which may be involved in the phenomenon of sudden death. Social and psychological data have been obtained by interview schedules developed by our sociological associates and carried out by them. Psychological testing has been carried out through the use of large batteries of standard, clinical, psychological tests of a paper-pencil variety, administered by the psychological associates. In all groups, data on daily activities and events were obtained from round-of-life schedules, from employment records, and from questionnaire-guided interviews at frequent intervals.

The observations of the people in these groups up to the present indicate the following:

1. New cases of coronary heart disease rarely if ever occur except among men who have some combination of hyperlipidemia, abnormalities of carbohydrate metabolism, hypertension, cigarette smoking, and a family history of this disease. In many instances these people also have preexisting evidence of arteriosclerosis in other vessels.

2. Unexpected sudden death rarely if ever occurs to men who do not have preexisting evidence of coronary heart disease, hypertensive heart disease, pulmonary disease with cardiac involvement, or alcoholism, especially if they are heavy cigarette smokers.

3. The life experiences of people who develop new events of coronary heart disease and of those who die suddenly are quite similar to the life experiences of their matched controls who do not develop the disease or die.

4. Acute events of coronary heart disease and sudden death often occur in a setting of hard work, difficult interpersonal relations, and fatigue. They often are precipitated by activities such as arguments or emotional upsets, unexpected exertion, or sexual intercourse. These activities do appear to precipitate acute events of myocardial infarction in people with preexisting metabolic abnormalities, atherosclerosis, hypertension, or heart disease, and they seem to precipitate fatal events in people with preexisting serious heart disease: but when people are without evidence of predisposing factors or cardiovascular disease, such activities seem to have no untoward consequences.

Conclusions and Comments

The observations that I have described suggest several conclusions. The first conclusion is that in populations of similar people who share similar experiences over comparable periods of one or two decades, between the ages of 10 and 50, there will be a few people who have a great many episodes of disabling illness and days of disability, some who have a moderate number, many who have very little, and some who have none. The manifestations of illness will be distributed among the members of these populations in a manner which indicates that some people have a much greater risk of becoming ill than others. The people at greatest risk will have more days of disability, more episodes of disability, more kinds of illness (more "disease syndromes"), involving more organ systems, attributable to a greater variety of causal agents, and including more major and life-endangering illnesses as well as more minor and transient episodes. The patterns of illness created by differences in risk are likely to continue over periods as long as 20 years or more, with the frequently ill continuing to have much illness and the less frequently ill continuing to be relatively healthy.

The explanations for these phenomena appear to arise partly from the biological characteristics of "illness" and partly from arbitrary and empirical procedures that are used to define and classify the manifestations of illness. Diseases or disease syndromes, as these are commonly defined medically, are not discrete and independent entities. Some diseases such as coronary heart disease are manifestations of other diseases such as generalized arteriosclerosis. Some acute illnesses such as congestive heart failure may be manifestations of any one of a number of diseases. The occurrence of an episode of one disease increases the likelihood that episodes of other diseases will occur. Thus obesity increases the likelihood that latent diabetes mellitus will become manifest; the presence of diabetes mellitus increases the likelihood that infections of the urinary tract will occur; infections of the urinary tract increase the likelihood that serious kidney disease will occur; kidney disease increases the likelihood that hypertension will occur; hypertension increases the likelihood that coronary heart disease will occur; and so on. Thus the presence of one disease may imply the presence of other diseases and beget yet other diseases.

The classification of diseases by their organ system of primary occurrence is an arbitrary and convenient way of grouping diseases, but is artificial. Few if any disease processes are confined to only one organ system. Diabetes mellitus, for example, which is commonly classified as a disease of the metabolic system, is a biochemical disorder that involves cells in every part of the body and produces major manifestations in the kidneys, the blood vessels, the peripheral nerves, the eyes, and the gastrointestinal tract. The result of this arbitrary method of classification is that anyone who has many syndromes, or episodes of illness, will almost by definition have manifestations of illness that involve many organ systems, and the number of organ systems will increase as the number of episodes of illness increases.

The division of diseases according to their primary cause is also arbitrary and artificial. Every disease has more than one cause. Diabetes mellitus is a genetic disease in the sense that the capacity to have it is based upon a genetic susceptibility; however, it is also a dietary disease because often it does not become manifest unless the subject becomes obese, and its manifestations may disappear if the total calories and the carbohydrates in the diet are restricted. Diabetes is also a degenerative disease in the sense that it often becomes manifest only as old age approaches, and with increasing age more and more people show evidence of its presence. It is not an infectious disease, but it increases the likelihood that infections will occur. It is not a disorder of mood, thought, or behavior, but it may first appear in the setting of a depressive illness and may become very much worse in people who are upset by profound interpersonal conflict, and so on. People who have many episodes of illness are thus likely to have illnesses of many apparent primary causes.

The occurrence of minor and transient episodes of illness increases the likelihood that major and life-endangering episodes of illness will occur. The common cold, for example, is a minor and transient episode of illness. A person may experience several hundred colds in his life without any adverse effect. However, when people have colds, they are distinctly more likely to develop major and potentially life-endangering illnesses such as bronchial pneumonia, lobar pneumonia, asthma, or congestive heart failure. Even a very benign condition such as a migraine headache carries a small but real increase in the risk of having a stroke.

Finally, many people have congenital, or acquired, predispositions to have disorders of one or another of their organ systems—for example, a propensity for hyper-function of the nasorespiratory mucosa, with repeated episodes of vasomotor rhinitis, "allergic" rhinitis, profuse and prolonged colds, and bronchitis, or even bronchial pneumonia. Others have comparable phenomena involving their gas-trointestinal tracts, skin, or other organ systems.

The second conclusion that may be drawn is that when people have preexisting susceptibilities to illness, or have established patterns of illness, the frequency of their illnesses and the number and kind are likely to change when there are signifi-cant changes in their social or interpersonal relationships.

The apparent reasons for this have been mentioned several times. Changes in significant social or interpersonal relationships are very often accompanied by changes in habits, changes in patterns of activity, changes in the intake of food and medication, and changes in exposure to potential sources of infection or trauma. They are also frequently associated with changes in mood and with physiological changes directly mediated by the central nervous system. Any or all of these might affect the frequency or severity of illness.

Our observations also lead to the conclusion that some people live through major changes in social relationships, major deprivations and dislocations, and major changes in interpersonal relations and exhibit little if any overt evidence of illness. This phenomenon appears to have two explanations. First, some of these people do not appear to have the preexisting patterns of illness or the necessary physical factors of susceptibility which render them vulnerable to the occurrence of illness. Acute changes in social or interpersonal reationships are much more likely to be accom-panied by acute episodes of illness when subjects have preexisting and well-estblished susceptibilities to illness for other reasons. Apparently the physiological concomitants of adaptations to social and interpersonal change are of such mag-nitude that they may easily precipitate illness among people in whom illnesses are already quite likely to occur, but they do not readily precipitate illness in others who have no special preexisting susceptibilities.

Moreover, some people who remain free from illness in the face of major life changes appear to have psychological characteristics which help to "insulate" them from the effects of some of their life experiences. The anthropologists, psychiatrists, psychologists, sociologists, and physicians who were involved in our various studies of American working people, of Chinese, of Hungarians, and of political prisoners were very different, yet they all commented on the fact that the healthiest members of our samples often showed little psychological reaction to events and situations which caused profound reactions in other members of the group. The loss of a husband or wife, the separation from one's family, the isolation from one's friends, community, or country, the frustration of apparently important desires, or the failure to attain apparently important goals produced no profound or lasting reac-tion. They seemed to have a shallow attachment to people, goals, or groups, and they readily shifted to other relationships when established relationships were dis-rupted. There was an almost "sociopathic" flavor to some of them. Others endured prolonged deprivations, boredom, or sustained hard work without obvious adverse effects.

Many of these people displayed a distinct awareness of their own limitations and their physiological needs. They behaved as if their own well-being were one of their primary concerns. They avoided situations that would make demands on them if they felt they could not, or did not want to meet these demands. An employed man or woman might refuse a promotion because he did not want the increased responsibility, refuse a transfer because it was "too much trouble," or refuse to work overtime because it might be too tiring—despite the fact that each of these changes might have increased his income, increased his prestige, or increased his opportunity to get ahead in his occupation. As family members, such people might refuse to take the responsibility for an aged or ill parent or sibling, giving as an explanation a statement implying that it would be "too much for me." If such a person learned that family members or relatives in a foreign country were in need, or were being oppressed, he might give little evidence of concern about this, and he might explain, if asked, that he saw no reason to worry about it since there was nothing he could do about it. If it was the lot in life of such a person to be poor, or to live alone, he seemed to feel no need to be unhappy about this or to rebel against it. Such psychological characteristics, and the attitudes that accompanied them, appear to play a role in the "immunity" of some people to the effects of deprivation and change.

A fourth conclusion is that the effect of a social change, or a change in interpersonal relations, on the health of an individual cannot be defined solely by the nature of the change itself. The effect depends on the physical and psychological characteristics of the person who is exposed to the change and on the circumstances under which it is encountered.

This has been observed in every population that we studied. The explanation appears to lie in the many biological, social, and psychological phenomena that we have been discussing. Changes that have been associated with important fluctuations of the health of some people in each group have had little or no effect on the health of others. Exposure to profound and sustained culture change, social change, and change in interpersonal relations of the type that was seen among the Chinese was not necessarily associated with any manifestations that could be described as illness. Acute major dislocations of the type experienced by the Hungarians did not necessarily produce illness. Even the profound social isolation, insecurity, threats, demands, and deprivations that were thrust upon political prisoners and prisoners of war did not always produce major adverse physiological or psychological reactions if they were not accompanied by physical injury or serious manipulation of the physical environment. Systematic occupational and social changes in the American populations have not produced major episodes of illness, except among those who were especially susceptible.

Our findings point to the following general conclusions:

1. Exposure to culture change, social change, and change in interpersonal relations may lead to a significant change in health if (*a*) a person has preexisting illness or susceptibility to illness, and he perceives the change as important to him, or (*b*) there is a significant change in his activities, habits, ingestants, exposure to disease-causing agents, or in the physical characteristics of his environment.

2. Exposure to culture change, social change, and change in interpersonal relations may lead to *no* significant change in health if (*a*) a person has no significant preexisting illness or susceptibility to illness, or if he does not perceive the change as important to him, and (*b*) there is no significant change in his activities, habits, ingestants, exposure to disease-causing agents, or in the physical characteristics of his environment.

3. If a culture change, social change, or change in interpersonal relations is not associated with a significant change in the activities, habits, ingestants, exposure to disease-causing agents, or in the physical characteristics of the environment of a person, then its effect upon his health cannot be defined solely by its nature, its magnitude, its acuteness or chronicity, or its apparent importance in the eyes of others.

Acknowledgment

This research was supported in part by grants from the Russell Sage Institute of Pathology.

References

Bone, E. *Seven Years Solitary*. New York: Harcourt, Brace, 1957.

Cannon, W. B. *Bodily Changes in Pain, Hunger, Fear and Rage, An Account of Recent Research into the Function of Emotional Excitement*, Second Edition. New York: D. Appleton and Company, 1929.

Hinkle, L. E., Jr. The concept of "stress" in the biological and social sciences. Invited paper before the Third International Conference on Social Science and Medicine, August 14–18, 1972, Elsinore, Denmark. To be published in *Science and Medicine*.

Hinkle, L. E., Jr. The effects of "social" and "behavioral" aspects of the environment on human health. Background document prepared for NIEHS Task Force on Research Planning in the Environmental Health Sciences. Deposited in the National Library of Medicine. (Copies available on request to: National Library of Medicine, 8600 Rockville Pike, Bethesda, Md. 20014.)

Hinkle, L. E., Jr. An estimate of the effects of "stress" on the incidence and prevalence of coronary heart disease in a large industrial population in the United States. *Proceedings of the II Congress of the International Society on Thrombosis and Haemostasis, July 13, 1971, Oslo, Norway*. Stuttgart, Germany: F. K. Shattaur Verlag, 1972.

Hinkle, L. E., Jr. Motivations of the individuals who took part in the uprising. In *Second Seminar on the Hungarian Revolution of October, 1956*. Forest Hills, N.Y.: Society for the Investigation of Human Ecology, 1958.

Hinkle, L. E., Jr. Physical health, mental health, and the social environment: Some characteristics of healthy and unhealthy people. In R. H. Ojemann (Ed.), *Recent Contributions of Biological and Psychological Investigations to Preventative Psychiatry*. Iowa City: State University of Iowa, 1959.

Hinkle, L. E., Jr. The physiological state of the interrogation subject as it affects brain function. In A. D. Biderman & H. Zimmer (Eds.), *The Manipulation of Human Behavior*. New York: John Wiley & Sons, 1961.

Hinkle, L. E., Jr. Relating biochemical, physiological and psychological disorders to the social environment. *Archives of Environmental Health*, 1968, 16, 77–82.

Hinkle, L. E., Jr. A study of the precursors of acute and fatal coronary heart disease. Public

Annual Report, Cornell University Medical College, NHLI 70-2069, February 1, 1972. Copies available from National Technical Information Services (NTIS), Springfield, Va.

Hinkle, L. E., Jr. A study of the precursors of acute and fatal coronary heart disease. Public Annual Report, Cornell University Medical College, NHLI 70-2069, February 1, 1973. Copies available from National Technical Information Services (NTIS), Springfield, Va.

Hinkle, L. E., Jr., Benjamin, B., Christenson, W. N., & Ullman, D. S. Coronary heart disease: The thirty-year experience of 1,160 men. *AMA Archives of Environmental Health*, 1966, **13**, 312–321.

Hinkle, L. E., Jr., Christenson, W. N., Benjamin, B., Kane, F. D., Plummer, N., & Wolff, H. G. The occurrence of illness among 24 "normal" women: Evidences of differences in susceptibility to acute respiratory and gastrointestinal syndromes. With the Collaboration of Morris Schaefer, M.D. and Daniel Widelock, Ph.D. of the Department of Health of New York City. Unpublished. Presented before the American College of Physicians, Annual Scientific Meeting, Miami Beach, May 10, 1961.

Hinkle, L. E., Jr., Christenson, W. N., Kane, F. D., Ostfeld, A., Thetford, W. N. & Wolff, H. G. An investigation of the relation between life experience, personality characteristics, and general susceptibility to illness. *Psychosomatic Medicine*, 1958, **20**, 278–295.

Hinkle, L. E., Jr., Gittinger, J. W., Goldberger, L., Ostfeld, A., Metraux, R., Richter, P., & Wolff, H. G. Studies in human ecology: Factors covering the adaptation of Chinese unable to return to China. In *Experimental Psychopathology*. New York: Grune & Stratton, 1957.

Hinkle, L. E., Jr., Kane, F. D., Christenson, W. N., & Wolff, H. G. Hungarian refugees: Life experiences and features influencing participation in the revolution and subsequent flight. *American Journal of Psychiatry*, 1959, **116**, 16–19.

Hinkle, L. E. Jr., Pinsky, R. H., Bross, I. D. J., & Plummer, N. The distribution of sickness disability in a homogeneous group of "healthy adult men." *American Journal of Hygiene*, 1956, **64**, 220–242.

Hinkle, L E., Jr., & Plummer, N. Life stress and industrial absenteeism in one segment of a working population. *Industrial Medicine and Surgery*, 1952, **21**, 363–375.

Hinkle, L. E., Jr., Plummer, N., Metraux, R., Richter, P., Gittinger, J. W., Thetford, W. N., Ostfeld, A. M., Kane, F. D., Goldberger, L., Mitchell, W. E., Leichter, H., Pinsky, R., Goebel, D., Bross, I. D. J., & Wolff, H. G. Studies in human ecology, factors relevant to the occurrence of bodily illness and disturbances in mood, thought, and behavior in three homogeneous population groups. *American Journal of Psychiatry*, 1957, **114**, 212–220.

Hinkle, L. E., Jr., Whitney, L. H., Lehman, E. W., Dunn, J., Benjamin, B., King, R., Plakun, A., & Flehinger, B. Occupation, education and coronary heart disease. *Science*, 1968, **161**, 238–246.

Hinkle, L. E., Jr., & Wolff, H. G. Communist interrogation and indoctrination of "enemies of the state." Analysis of methods used by the Communist state police (a special report). *Archives of Neurology & Psychiatry*, 1956, **76**, 115–174.

Hinkle, L. E., Jr. & Wolff, H. G. Ecologic investigations of the relationship between illness, life experiences and the social environment. *Annals of Internal Medicine*, 1958, **49**, 1373–1388.

Hinkle, L. E., Jr., & Wolff, H. G. Health and social environment: Experimental investigations. In A. H. Leighton, J. A. Clausen, & R. N. Wilson (Eds.), *Explorations in Social Psychiatry*. New York: Basic Books, 1957.

Hinkle, L. E., Jr. & Wolff, H. G. The methods of interrogation and indoctrination used by the Communist state police. *Bulletin of the New York Academy of Medicine*, 1957, **33**, 600–615.

Lehman, E. W., Schulman, J., & Hinkle, L. E., Jr. Coronary deaths and organizational mobility: The 30-year experience of 1,160 men. *Archives of Environmental Health*, 1967, 15, 455–461.

Selye, H. The general adaptation syndrome and the diseases of adaptation. *Journal of Clinical Endocrinology*, 1946, 6, 117–230.

Wolff, H. G., Wolf, S. G., and Hare, C. C. (Eds.) *Life Stress and Bodily Disease*. Baltimore: The Williams and Wilkens Company, 1950.

14

Streptococcal Infections in Families

Factors Altering Individual Susceptibility

Roger J. Meyer and Robert J. Haggerty,
with technical assistance of
Nancy Lombardi and Robert Perkins

There is little precise data to explain why one person becomes ill with an infecting agent and another not. Stress, in the form of immersion in cold water, many years ago, by Pasteur,[1] was shown to increase the susceptibility of chickens to anthrax. In humans such experimental data is difficult to obtain, but it is clear that for many common infections (such as those with beta hemolytic streptococci) commensalism, or peaceful-coextence between this organism and its human host, is the rule, while disease is the exception. Cornfeld *et al.*[2,3] found that as many as 29.8% of well school children harbored this agent, but Mozziconacci *et al.*[4] showed that the risk of being colonized by streptococci was not a random one, for in some individuals the rate was higher than expected. Despite intimate exposure between husbands and wives, both rarely carry the same organism at the same time.[5]

Once an individual is colonized with streptococci, his risk of developing illness varies, widely, being reported as high as 43%[6] to as low as 20%.[2] Breese and Disney,[7] Brimblecombe *et al.*,[8] and others have also shown that susceptible individuals vary in their rate of acquisition and illness when exposed to other persons carrying hemolytic streptococci.

The present study was designed to study some of the factors responsible for this variability in individual susceptibility to beta hemolytic streptococcal acquisition and illness.

Methods

Sixteen lower-middle class families, comprising 100 persons who were being followed in a comprehensive family health care program, were systematically investi-

SOURCE: *Pediatrics* 29 (April 1962): 539–49. Copyright © 1962 American Academy of Pediatrics. Reprinted by permission of the publisher and the authors.

TABLE I. Beta-streptococcal Infections in Families:* Factors Studied

Host	Agent
Age	Colony count
Sex	Group-type
Family history	
Antibody response	
Tonsillectomy	

Environmental Factors	
Season	Sleeping arrangements
Weather	Acute stress
Housing	Chronic stress
Family size	Therapy

*100 persons, 16 families, 12 months.

gated for a 12-month period from April, 1960, through March, 1961. They were selected if they had two or more children and would co-operate in the study. All but one family had at least one child of school age. In the hope of obtaining wide variation in the rates of infection, two groups of eight families each were chosen on the basis of their previous history of frequent or infrequent respiratory infections.

Throat cultures were made on all family members every 3 weeks and at times of acute illness, by vigorous swabbing of both tonsils or tonsillar fossae. These swabs were promptly inoculated on the suface of 5% defibrinated horse-blood agar plates, and a stab was made through the streaked material to study hemolysin production by subsurface colony growth. After incubation at 37°C for 18 to 24 hours, representative beta-hemolytic colonies were isolated in pure subculture at 5% defibrinated sheepblood agar, and identified by Gram-stained smear, grouped by the bacitracin disk method[9] and grouped and typed by Lancefield's method.[10] Specific typing sera against 39 different serologic types were supplied by the Communicable Disease Center of the United States Public Health Service at Chamblee, Georgia. Sera for anti-streptolysin 0 titers were drawn approximately every 4 months and measured by standard methods.[11] A difference of 2 dilution increments was considered a significant increase.

Acquisition was defined as the detection of a new type of Group A beta-hemolytic streptococcus or the reappearance of the same type after at least 8 weeks with negative cultures. *Streptococcal illness* was defined as the appearance, in association with a positive culture for beta-hemolytic streptococcus, of one or more of the following: a red, sore throat with or without exudate or cervical adenopathy; coryza; epistaxis; moderate or marked pharyngeal exudate; cough; otitis media; and scarlatina-form rash.

Diagnosis and treatment of respiratory infections deemed serious enough by the parents to warrant a call to their physician were carried out as usual by the family's assigned pediatric house officer or medical student under the supervision of the authors. Diagnoses were made on the basis of anatomic findings, symptoms, or both, and conformed to the usually accepted diagnostic terms.

Serial interviews were conducted by the authors with the families about past and current medical and social factors that might influence the incidence of illness; each family kept, in addition, a diary of illness, therapy, and life events. Since this was an exploratory study, attempts were made to record many factors considered by other authors or by the families to be responsible for the development of infections, with the goal of a detailed study of a few families for fruitful leads, rather than a definitive study of only a few variables. The independent variables recorded with streptococcal acquisition and illness rates, prolonged carrier states (defines as over one month), and antistreptolysin O titer rises. Table I indicates the dependent variables studied, grouped under host, agent, and environmental categories.

Results

Of the 1,639 cultures obtained, 248 (20.6%) were positive for beta-hemolytic streptococci (Table II), 22.4% of which did not belong to Group A. Twenty-four per cent of *all* recorded illnesses in the families were associated with an isolation of beta-hemolytic streptococci, but 52.5% of all acquisitions were not associated with any illness. The over-all streptococcal illness rate was 0.9 per person year.

Agent Factors

Surprisingly, no significant differences were found between illness rates associated with the acquisition of Group A as compared to non-Group A streptococci (Table III), nor with the various specific types of Group A streptococci. Of the Group A strains nontypable ones were isolated 99 times (40%), A-1 and A-12 31 times each (each 12%); types 4, 5, 13, and 28 accounted for all the others (48%) seen. Persons with greater numbers of streptococci on a blood agar plate also were no more likely to be ill than those who had small numbers of colonies (Table IV).

While quantitation of the number of colonies per blood agar plate is not an infallible method of determining the number of organisms in patients, carefully standardized techniques of swabbing, culturing, and reading by the same experienced technician were carried out to minimize these variations.

This lack of correlation between illness and the two agent factors—streptococcal group and type, and number of colonies—may have been because most of the illnesses recorded were not caused by the streptococci isolated.

The low rate of antistreptolysin O increase observed following beta-hemolytic

TABLE II. Beta-streptococcal Infections in Families*

Age (yr)	Persons (no.)	Person-months	Cultures (no.)	Positive Cultures (no.)	Positive Cultures per Person-month
<2	16	192	228	11	0.057
2–5	28	360	563	98	0.272
2–15	22	252	386	99	0.392
16+	34	396	462	40	0.103
	100	1,200	1,639	248	0.206

*12 months, 16 families.

TABLE III. Beta-hemolytic-streptococcal Infections in Families: Relation of Illness to Streptococcal Group

| | Cultures | | | | Acquisitions | | | |
| | Ill | | Not Ill | | Ill | | Not Ill | |
Group	No.	%	No.	%	No.	%	No.	%
A	68	34.4	129	65.6	48	43.2	63	56.8
Non-A	21	36.8	36	63.2	8	38.0	13	62.0

streptococcal acquisitions (28%) may be partially explained by the predominance of younger patients less likely to develop antibodies in response to streptococcal infection; a number of young children sustained quite elevated titers during the study, however. Another factor may be that the interval between samples was prolonged, although Rantz et al. [12] reported persistence of elevated titers over a considerable period of time, varying with age, reinfection and other factors. The relatively high rate of reinfection in the present study tends to diminish the disadvantage of the prolonged interval between antistreptolysin 0 titers, despite the desirability of a shorter interval. Even in those illnesses in association with beta-hemolytic streptococci and followed by antistreptolysin O increase, there was no significant difference between antibody increase associated with non-Group A (21.9%) and Group A (29.0%) strains. When more than half the colonies in the original agar plate were streptococci, 38% of these patients had a subsequent antibody increase, while only 21% with plates with under 50% streptococci developed such an increase (p less than 0.01).

Thus, differences in the group and type of streptococci, and the number of colonies isolated, while undoubtedly of some importance in the pathogenesis of illness, did not seem to play a crucial role in determining acquisition, illness rates, or immune response. Increased predominance of streptococci on culture was associated with a significantly higher frequency of antibody increases, but neither were consistent indicators of clinical disease.

TABLE IV. Beta-streptococcal Infections in Families: Relation of Number of Colonies to Illness

| | Positive Cultures (%) | |
Quantity of Colonies	Ill	Not Ill
<25%	23.5	27.6
25–50%	42.4	38.3
>50%	28.2	31.1
Unknown	5.9	2.9
	100.0	99.9

TABLE V. Beta-streptococcal Infections in Families*

Age (yr)	Persons in Study (no.)	Persons with Positive Culture during Year (no.)	Individual Beta-streptococcal Acquisitions	
			Total Number	*With Illness*
<2	16	7	9	4
2–5	28	26	53	31
6–15	22	20	48	25
16+	34	19	29	13
Individuals	100	72	139	73
Total Family Episodes	—	—	47	33

*All 16 families were positive at some time during the 12 months observation.

Host Factors

Age was certainly one important factor responsible for differences in colonization rates, with school children having the highest, 2-to-5-year-olds the second highest, adults the next, and infants under 2 years old the lowest rates of acquisition (Table II). Once colonized, the chance of an individual becoming ill varied little between different age groups (Table V), but the type of illness was quite different in these different age groups (Table VI), a point clearly documented by Rantz *et al.*[13] and others. In spite of these differences in the symptoms and signs of infection, there was little difference in severity by age.

Only 28% of all streptococcal acquisitions were followed by an anti-streptolysin O elevation. This was far more likely to occur after an illness (49%) than after an asymptomatic colonization (16%), and it occurred more frequently in school-age groups than in either younger children or adults (although the numbers for each group are too small to permit significance testing).

There was no significant association of streptococcal illness or antibody increase with sex, family history of repeated respiratory infections, strong personal allergic

TABLE VI. Beta-streptococcal Infections in Families

Age (yr)	Persons (no.)	Illness Rates per Person-year (associated with beta-streptococci)			
		Undifferentiated Upper Respiratory	*Pharyngitis & Tonsillitis*	*Otitis Media*	*All Other*
<2	16	1.68 (0.31)	0.31 (0)	0.69 (0.18)	0.56 (0)
2–5	28	2.52 (0.53)	0.68 (0.43)	0.43 (0.14)	1.80 (0.14)
6–15	22	2.18 (0.81)	0.46 (0.27)	0.05 (0)	1.41 (0.31)
16+	34	0.97 (0.17)	0.56 (0.24)	0 (0)	0.76 (0.12)

*Beta streptococcal illness rate per person-year, 0.9; 24.1% of all illness associated with beta streptococci; 52.5% of all acquisitions not associated with illness.

history, or the presence or absence of tonsils. There was a slightly higher chronic carrier rate among individuals still possessing their tonsils. Mothers were more likely to become colonized and ill than fathers.

Environmental Factors

Physical Environment. The largest number of cultures positive for beta-hemolytic streptococci occurred in March and April, but a great deal of variation in both colonization and illness was observed from month to month, with several other months almost equalling the spring months. The late summer and fall months were characterized by the isolation of a much higher proportion of non-Group A strains, however. In spite of this general correlation with the seasons, no consistent relation of colonization or illness rates to specific weather characteristics could be determined; no relation could be found between the rates of streptococcal acquisition or illness and humidity, temperature level and change, or type or amoung of precipitation. Housing was generally adequate for all these families, and there was no correlation between acquisition or illness rates and number of rooms, type of heating, or type of house.

Surprisingly, there was also no consistent relation between family size and number of acquisitions or illness. For example, the greatest number of individual acquisitions occurred in a family of only two children, while another family with seven children had one of the lowest rates. All families had about the same potential contact with streptococci, as judged by the number of school age children, the degree of neighborhood crowding, and other types of non-home contacts, including the fathers' working environment.

Family sleeping patterns appeared to be the only physical factor related to acquisition or illness; when one family member acquired a beta-hemolytic streptococcus he was twice as likely to spread it to another family member occupying the same bedroom as to the other family members sleeping in separate rooms.

FIGURE 1. Acute life stress and streptococcal infection.

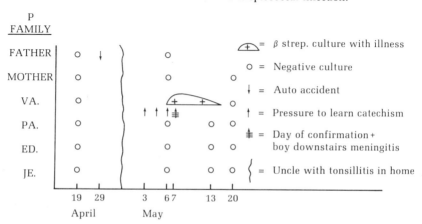

TABLE VII. Respiratory Infections in Families: Relation to Acute Stress

Type Episode	Episodes of Acute Stress (no.)		Infections	
	Two Weeks Before	*Two Weeks After*	*Total Number*	*Associated with Stress (%)*
Beta-strep illness	17	3	56	35.7
Beta-strep acquisitions without illness	12	3	76	19.5
Non-strep respiratory infections	17	4	201	10.5
	46	10	333	17.0

Human Environment. Throughout the year parents frequently commented on the relation of acute family crises to the onset of illness. Figure 1 illustrates such an example in a family who otherwise had no streptococcal acquisitions during the entire year. As far as can be determined, exposure of all family members to beta-hemolytic streptococcus occurred on May 1, but only the child who was subjected to increasing pressure during the week to learn her catechism before confirmation, became colonized and ill. This was not an isolated coincidence; similar circumstances were seen in other families. By means of the interview and diaries, life events that disrupted family or personal life and caused excess anxiety, and other evidences of disorganization were independently recorded.

About one quarter of the streptococcal acquisitions and illnesses followed such acute family crises, and there was an even clearer relation between both acquisitions and illness and these acute crises when the period 2 weeks before and 2 weeks after acquisitions or illness was compared. Table VII documents this relation and shows that streptococcal acquisition and illness, as well as non-streptococcal respiratory infectoins, were about four times as likely to be preceded as to be followed by acute stress. While this difference is statistically quite significant, the causal role and the precise mechanisms are far from clear. The types of acute crises seen in the 29

TABLE VIII. Acute Family Stress and Respiratory Infections

Type of Stress	Episodes (no.)
Loss of family member	6
Death of grandmother (3)	
Serious illness in family	3
Pneumonia, amputation, nephritis	
Minor illness: serious implications	6
Broken leg, birth, breast lump removal	
Family crisis: non-medical	8
Aunt divorced, burned out, confirmation, father lost job, all tired and wet	
Non-family crisis: impact on members	4
Witness to violent death	
Multiple family stresses	2
Total	29

TABLE IX. Respiratory Infections in Families: Chronic Family Stress Rating Scale

Family Function	Scale		
	Smoothly Functioning	→	Disorganized
External relations	0	→	4
Arrangement for outside activity			
Ability to use non-family members in emergency			
Ability to use community resources			
Network of relations-friends and neighbors			
Relation to legal institutions			
Internal relations	0	→	4
Child-rearing values consistent with children's needs			
Parental and family responsibility for each other			
Realistic care of ill member			
Parents' relations to each other			
Emotional adjustment of family members			
Medical care	0	→	4
Plan for preventive services			
Realistic ability to detect and seek help for individual ills			
Capacity to relate to medical resources			
History of handling of previous medical stresses			
Environmental and economic	0	→	4
Suitability and organization of home			
Income adequacy-cost in parents' energy			
Ability to meet medical and other needs			
Total	0	→	16

episodes occurring in the 2 weeks before acquisition of streptococci are listed in Table VIII. Exposure of children to wet and cold often occurred during the study but was rarely associated with such acquisitions unless fatigue was also present.

An equally useful dependent variable was the level of chronic stress found in each family. The level of chronic stress was determined by a rating scale based upon four general indices of family functioning as judged independently by two observers (physician and bacteriology technician) and occasionally by other members of the health team (Table IX). This rating scale was designed to measure family functioning as described by Bell and Vogel[14] and others. Total scores could range from 0 to 16, with higher numbers indicating greater degrees of disorganization and chronic stress.

When all four independent variables (acquisition rates, prolonged carrier states, streptococcal illness rates, and antistreptolysin O responses) were compared, there is a definite increase of all these variables as chronic stress scores increased (Fig. 2). Table X indicates the number of streptococcal acquisitions followed by an increase of antibodies in the low compared to the moderate and high stress families. After an acquisition of streptococci, antistreptolysin 0 increases were seen in only 21% of the patients in the low-stress families, compared to 49% of those patients in the moderate-high stress families, a statistically significant difference (p = 0.01).

As part of the initial interview with these families, they were asked which of their children was most likely to become ill. All had a ready answer, sometimes modify-

FIGURE 2. Beta-streptococcal infections in families—relation to chronic stress. The dotted line represents a visual mean for each of the independent variables.

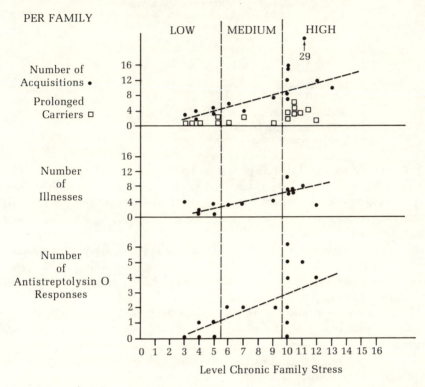

Level Chronic Family Stress

ing this by saying that although one was more likely to become ill, another was more likely to become seriously ill if he became sick at all. It is interesting that the parents were able to predict correctly which child was more likely to become ill in 11 of the 16 families.

Therapy

Adequate penicillin therapy for streptococcal infections has been shown to eradicate the organism[15,16] and also to suppress antibody responses[17,18] in the majority

TABLE X. Beta-streptococcal Infections in Families*

	Antistreptolysin O Response†			
	Episodes Group A Acquisition			
Level of Chronic Family Stress	ASO Rise	No Rise	Total	No Strep Acquisitions
Low	3	11	14	19
Moderate-high	34	36	70	9

*100 persons, 16 families, 12 months.   †Two or more tubes.   (p<0.05.)

TABLE XI. Beta-streptococcal Infections in Families*

Therapy	Antistreptolysin O Response† to Separate Acquisitions		
	Rise	No Rise	Total
Penicillin	11	33	44
No therapy	22	12	34
	33	45	78

*100 persons, 16 families, 12 months.
†Two or more tubes.

of instances. As seen in Table XI patients adequately treated with penicillin were less likely to have an antibody increase following acquisition of a beta-hemolytic streptococcus than those not treated. A larger number of patients would be required before antibody response could be correlated significantly with the time therapy was begun, however.

Adequate treatment was followed by reappearance of the same type of streptococcus in a few families, confirming previous reports.[17] In three families these recurrences ceased only after prolonged carrier states had been allowed to exist until anti-streptolysin O rises occurred.

Thirty per cent of acquisitions treated with penicillin were followed by the appearance of penicillin resistant staphylococci in the throat, compared to only 19% in those patients who received no therapy. In two patients the presence of these penicillinase-producing organisms was associated with failure of penicillin treatment to eradicate the streptococcus.

Comment

It is clear that there are few solid data to explain why one child becomes sick or colonized, while another does not, with such a common organism as the beta-hemolytic streptococcus. From the clinician's point of view it has become exceedingly difficult to decide who should be treated, a paradoxical situation since there are few other infections for which such safe and effective therapy is available. The clinical diagnosis of streptococcal infection cannot be expected to be much better than 75% correct[19] even if "syndromes of symptoms and signs" are used[20] rather than single findings. On the other hand, streptococci are so often found in healthy children that their presence in children with acute respiratory infections does not, per se, indicate a significant streptococcal infection. Thus throat cultures, while helpful, cannot be used alone to decide which person requires therapy. Since therapy does not reduce the duration of acute symptoms[21] or lower the carrier rate in schools,[2,22] there are only two general reasons to treat streptococcal disease: (1) the presence of suppurative complications, or (2) the risk of non-suppurative complications. The patient with suppurative complications presents only a minor problem; all would agree that he must be treated. But not until more satisfactory criteria are available for deciding who is most likely to develop the non-suppurative complications can more rational treatment be given. The fact that adequate penicillin therapy will reduce the antistreptolysin O response to a given infection has been shown before[17, 18] and is confirmed in our data. Such treatment for illness does not depress the individual's eventual production of antibodies, which may well be the response to a large number of asymptomatic infections ultimately giving rise to antibody responses, as shown by Breese *et al.*[23] Although type-specific streptococcal immunity does not prevent colonization, it does inhibit type-specific illness, which bears out the importance of such acquired immunity.[24] If, as seems likely, it is useful for an individual to develop antibodies, the least risk of non-suppurative complications probably follows such asymptomatic infections. Thus, in general, carrier states may be left untreated with very little risk.

Indeed, in occasional patients penicillin therapy seems to exert an adverse influence either by supressing the formation of protective antibody or by promoting the growth of penicillinase producing staphylococci that may interfere with the action of penicillin against streptococci.

The purpose of this investigation was to study the factors that predispose to respiratory infections, with the ultimate hope that one might gain some clinically useful data as to which individuals in family groups would be more likely to acquire such infections. The agent factors investigated did not yield much useful information; neither group, type nor number of colonies were very reliable indicators of who had significant infection. Although only Group A streptococci are generally credited with responsibility for non-suppurative complications, Packer *et al.*[25] also reported that non-Group A organisms were capable of producing illness and antibody response.

Age was an important factor in host susceptibility to streptococcal illness. (School-aged children were most susceptible, followed by 2-to-5-year-olds.) Weather played only a minor seasonal role, for while infection increased during the late winter and spring, precise types of weather or weather changes could not be shown to be associated with higher rates of infection in this small study group, as had previously been shown for influenza.[26] Close contact with other family members ill with proven streptococcal disease, particularly through sharing a bedroom, increased the likelihood of significant disease.

When acute life stress or chronic family disorganization is considered in addition to these other factors, there seems to be an additional criterion for selecting the more susceptible individual or family. Not only are higher acquisition and illness rates associated with acute and chronic stress situations, but also the proportion of persons in whom there is a significant rise of anti-streptolysin O following the acquisition of streptococci increases with increasing stress. While this does not prove that such persons are more likely to have non-suppurative complications— only a very large study could show this—it does suggest that this may be one explanation for the well-known increased risk of rheumatic fever among lower socioeconomic groups.[27, 28] It remains to be determined whether stress is higher or significantly different in lower socioeconomic groups.

Certain emotional states have been shown to be associated with the onset of certain illnesses[29] and with the occurrence of beta-hemolytic streptococcal colonization.[30] Neither the precise emotional states that might predispose to increased rates of infection, nor the pathophysiologic mechanisms by which such changes could be mediated are known.

Stress is generally credited with increasing the output of adrenal corticosteroids, but beyond isolated examples in patients with tuberculosis[31,32] and varicella,[33] few data exist to support such a mehanism as being responsible for increased risk in acute infections. While a great many studies have been performed in animals in an attempt to elucidate some of these factors responsible for resistance and susceptibility[34-39] it is difficult to translate these findings to man. Studies aimed at linking changes in the host's internal environment as measured by hormones, antibodies and leukocytes, with external environmental changes of weather, housing, nutrition, family living, fatigue, medical therapy, and life stress are clearly the next step. Only in this way can meaningful relations with sound therapeutic and preventive implications be found. From our data it seems likely that no one cause will be found, for beta-hemolytic streptococcal infections seem to be another example of "multiple causation" of disease.

Summary

Sixteen lower-middle-class families, comprising 100 persons, were intensively studied for one year, with systematic throat cultures for beta-hemolytic streptococci, periodic measurements of antistreptolysin O titer, and clinical evaluation of all illnesses; the results of those observations were compared to certain dependent variables of host, agent, and environment. The factors that seemed to play an important part in determining whether a given person acquired a streptococcus, became ill with this acquisition, or developed a subsequent increase in antistreptolysin O were age, season, closeness of contact with an infected person as measured by sleeping arrangements, acute or chronic family stress, and penicillin treatment. No relationship was found between streptococcal episodes and the number or type of streptococci present, sex of the patient, the presence or absence of tonsils, an allergic history, changes in weather, type of housing, or family size. Further evidence for the multiple causation of beta-hemolytic streptococcal disease has been obtained, although the mechanisms through which these factors exert their influence are not clear.

Acknowledgments

Supported by grants from the Barnstable Chapter of the Massachusetts Heart Association and the Commonwealth Fund. Dr. Meyer's research was supported by Grant 2M-6420 from the National Institute of Mental Health.

The authors wish to express their appreciation for the professional advice of Dr. Benedict Massell in carrying out this study, and to the families whose co-operation made the study possible.

References

1. Pasteur, L., Joubert, J., and Chamberland: Le charbon des poules. Compt. Rend. Acad. Sci., 87:47, 1878 (Cited by Perla, D., and Marmorston, J., in Natural Resistance and Clinical Medicine, Boston, Little, Brown & Co., 1941).

2. Cornfeld, D., and Hubbard, J. P.: A four-year study of the occurrence of beta-hemolytic streptococci in 64 school children. New Engl. J. Med., 264:211, 1961.
3. Cornfeld, D., *et al.*: Epidemiologic studies of streptococcal infection in school children. Amer. J. Pub. Health, 51:242, 1961.
4. Mozziconacci, *et al.*: A study of group A hemolytic streptococcus carriers among school children: II. Significance of the findings. Acta Pediat., 50:33, 1961.
5. Harvey, H. S., and Dunlap, M. D.: Upper respiratory flora of husbands and wives: a comparison. New Engl. J. Med., 262:976, 1960.
6. James, W. E. S., Badger, G. F., and Dingle, J. H.: A study of illness in a group of Cleveland families: XIX. The epidemiology of the acquisition of group A streptococci and of associated illness. New Engl. J. Med., 262:687, 1960.
7. Breese, B. B., and Disney, F. A.: The spread of streptococcal infections in family groups. *Pediatrics*, 17:834, 1956.
8. Brimblecombe, F. S. W., *et al.*: Family Studies of respiratory infections. Brit. Med. J., 1:119, 1958.
9. Maxted, W. R.: The use of bacitracin for identifying group A hemolytic streptococci. J. Clin. Path., 6:224, 1953.
10. Swift, H. F., Wilson, A. T., and Lancefield, R. C.: Typing group A streptococci by micro precipitation in capillary pipettes. J. Exp. Med., 78:127, 1943.
11. Hodge, B. E., and Swife, H. F.: Varying homeolytic and constant combining capacity of streptolysins: influence on testing for antistreptolysins. (Massell, B.: Modification of this method). J. Exp. Med., 58:277, 1933.
12. Rantz, L. A., Maroney, M., and DiCaprio, J. M.: Antistreptolysin O response following hemolytic streptococcus infection in early childhood. Arch. Int. Med., 87:360, 1951.
13. Rantz, L. A., Maroney, M., and DiCaprio, J. M.: Hemolytic streptococcal infection in childhood. *Pediatrics*, 12:498, 1953.
14. Bell, N. W., and Vogel, E. F. (Editors): Introductory Essays, *in* a Modern Introduction to The Family. Glencoe, Free Press, 1960.
15. Chamovitz, R., *et al.*: Prevention of rheumatic fever by treatment of previous streptococcal infections. New Engl. J. Med., 251:466, 1954.
16. Breese, B. B., and Disney, F. A.: Penicillin in the treatment of streptococcal infections: a comparison of effectiveness of five different oral and one parenteral form. New Engl. J. Med., 259:57, 1958.
17. Brock, L. L., and Siegel, A. C.: Studies on prevention of rheumatic fever: effect of time of initiation of treatment of streptococcal infections on immune response of host. J. Clin. Invest., 32:630, 1953.
18. Lancefield, R. C.: Persistence of type specific antibodies in man following infection with group A streptococci. J. Emp. Med., 110:271, 1959.
19. Breese, B. B., and Disney, F. A.: The accuracy of diagnosis of beta streptococcal infections on clinical grounds. J. Pediat., 44:670, 1954.
20. Stillerman, M., and Bernstein, S. H.: Streptococcal pharyngitis: evaluation of clinical syndromes in diagnosis. J. Dis. Child., 101:476, 1961.
21. Brumfitt, W., O'Grady, F., and Slater, J. D. H.: Benign streptococcal sore throat. Lancet, 2:419, 1959.
22. Phibbs, B., *et al.*: The Casper Project—an enforced mass-culture streptococci control program. J. A. M. A., 166:1113, 1958.
23. Breese, B. B., Disney, F. A., and Talpey, W. B.: The prevention of type specific immunity to streptococcal infections due to the therapeutic use of penicillin. J. Dis. Child., 100:353, 1960.
24. Wannamaker, L. W., *et al.*: Studies on immunity to streptococcal infection in man. Amer. J. Dis. Child., 86:347, 1953.

25. Packer, H., Arnoult, M. B., and Spurnt, D. H.: A study of hemolytic streptococcal infections in relation to antistreptolysin O titer changes in orphange children. J. Pediat., 48:545, 1956.

26. Kingdon, K. H.: Relative humidity and airborne infections. Amer. Rev. Resp. Infect., 81:504, 1960.

27. Knownelden, J.: Mortality from rheumatic heart disease in children and young adults in England and Wales. Brit. J. Soc. Prev. Med., 3:29, 1949.

28. Quinn, R. W., and Quinn, J. P.: Mortaility due to rheumatic heart disease in the socio-economic districts of New Haven, Connecticut. Yale J. Biol. Med., 24:15, 1951.

29. Schmale, A. H., Jr.: Relationship of separation and depression to disease: a report on a hsopitalized medical population. Psychosom. Med., 20:259, 1958.

30. Kaplan, S. M., Gottshalk, L. A., and Fleming, D. E.: Modifications of oropharyngeal bacteria with changes in the psychodynamic state. Arch. Neurol. Psychiat., 78:656, 1957.

31. Lurie, M. B.: The reticuloendothelial system: cortisone and thyroid function: their relation to native resistance and to infection. Ann. N.Y. Acad. Sci., 88:83, 1960.

32. Holmes, T. H., et al.: Psychosocial and Psychophysiologic studies of tuberculosis. Psychosom. Med., 19:134, 1957.

33. Haggerty, R. J., and Eley, R. C.: Varicella and Cortisone. Pediatrics, 18:160, 1956.

34. Dubos, R. J., and Schaedler, R. W.: Nutrition and infection. J. Pediat., 55:1, 1959.

35. Evans, D. G., Miles, A. H., and Niven, J. S. F.: The enhancement of bacterial infections by adrenaline. Brit. J. Exp. Path., 29:20, 1948.

36. Hayashida, T.: Effect of pituitaryadrenocorticotropic and growth hormone on the resistance of rats infected with pasteurella pestis. J. Exp. Med., 106:127, 1957.

37. Teodoru, C. V., and Shwartzman, G.: Endocrine factors in pathogenesis of experimental poliomyelitis in hamsters: role of inoculatory and environmental stress. Proc. Soc. Exp. Biol. Med., 91:181, 1956.

38. Sprunt, D. H., and Flanigan, C. C.: The effect of malnutrition on the susceptibility of the host to viral infection. J. Exp. Med., 104:687, 1956.

39. Rasmussen, A. F., Jr., Marsh, J. T., and Brill, N. Q.: Increased susceptibility to herpes simplex in mice subjected to avoidance—learning stress or restraint. Proc. Soc. Exp. Biol. Med., 96:183, 1957.

15

Recent Evidence Supporting Psychologic and Social Risk Factors for Coronary Disease

C. David Jenkins

Stress and Life Change

Excessive overtime work, previously associated with increased risk of coronary disease, has received further support as a risk factor in the last five years. Theorell and Rahe[57] compared 62 patients with myocardial infarction in Stockholm with 109 healthy employees of a municipal agency and found that the patients had been doing much more overtime work but had lower responsibility and less supervisory activity (and hence, presumably, a greater amount of physical exertion) than the healthy controls. However, the difference in the institutional sources from which the two groups were drawn might account for many of these work-related differences. Parallel findings are described by Mertens and Segers.[42] Similarly, Theil et al.[19] reported that 13 of their 50 patients with infarction had been working more than 70 hours per week—sharply more than control subjects.

Wardwell and Bahnson[22] constructed a "total stress scale" based on the sum of nine subscales each representing one source of stress. Normal controls scored significantly higher than patient groups on total stress. For only one subscale did patients with coronary disease have a tendency ($P = 0.11$) toward higher scores. With specific exceptions noted elsewhere, this study failed to find support for the "stress hypothesis."

Many recently published studies have used summary measures of life change, particularly the Holmes and Rahe Schedule of Recent Experience.[58] Respondents check the occurrence of events requiring personal adjustment, such as loss of a job, buying a house, arguments with spouse, and many others, and the weighted values for such events are summed. Most such studies to date are flawed by lack of adequate comparison groups. Use of patients as their own controls—comparing life

SOURCE: *New England Journal of Medicine* 294 (6 May 1976): 1033–39. Reprinted by permission. N.B.: This reading is the second part of a two-part paper.

changes recalled from the six months before acute illness with those recalled from earlier periods of the patients' lives—allows the possibility that the usually greater number of life changes reported for the most recent period occurs because recent memory is more complete than distant memory.

The following findings have been reported from retrospective studies. From a list of 67 persons who experienced sudden cardiac death in Stockholm, Rahe and Lind[59] were able to interview 39 next of kin, who reported the decedents to have experienced three times the magnitude of life-change score in the last six months of life as compared to earlier periods. No control group was studied. In an innovative secondary analysis of medical charts rich in psychosocial data, Theorell extracted life-change data from the University of Oklahoma longitudinal study of patients with coronary disease directed by Dr. Stewart Wolf.[60] Rahe then scored the life-change protocols blind to other characteristics of the patients. Surviving patients had steady levels of life-change scores over two years, whereas those dying of coronary disease had peak rates of life change seven to 12 months before death, with a decrease to average levels over the last six months before death.

A study of 54 survivivors of myocardial infarctions showed a crescendo of life-change scores in the six months before the infarction, but only for the patients who had no previous history of heart disease. Those with prior heart disease had generally higher life-change scores at all previous periods covered by the interview.[57] Another retrospective study of 30 patients showed no such crescendo of life change immediately before infarction. There was considerable variability of mean life-change scores over the several years covered by the recall interview.[61]

A comparable project conducted among 279 survivors of infarction in Helsinki showed a rising rate of life change for the six months immediately before infarction.[62] Although there was no comparison group, dividing the patients into those with and without other serious illness before the index infarction revealed nearly twice as much life change in the previously ill group as in the previously well group in earlier six-month periods, but the increase in life change for the last six months characterized both groups with coronary disease. The same study showed that obtaining data about patients from their spouses generated similar average life-change scores as asking the patients themselves, but the comparison was in terms of group means and not by the more revealing method of a distribution of differences between husband-wife pairs.

A retrospective study of Swedish women with myocardial infarction and a healthy reference group from the population revealed a higher frequency of troubling social events in response to a structured interview in the former.[24]

Lundberg et al.,[63] using a matched control group in their retrospective study of life changes and myocardial infarction, found no statistically significant differences between patients with infarction and the control group when total life-change units were calculated by the standard method. They discovered, however, that when each person assigned weights reflecting his own perception of the impact of each event, the patients with infarction generated a significantly higher mean than the controls. It can be hypothesized either that more distressing life events were more likely to precede myocardial infarction or that the crisis of a coronary-disease episode sensitized patients to attach more importance to earlier life events than persons without a recent life-threatening illness. The use of a comparison group that had experienced equally serious health crises of types unlikely to be precipitated by stress might serve to test this competing hypothesis.

In a prospective test of the life-change hypothesis consisting of 6579 Swedish construction workers 41 to 61 years of age,[64] Theorell, Lind, and Flodérus found no association between elevated life-change scores and incidence of acute myocardial infarction over the ensuing 12 to 15 months. Elevated scores, however, did predict development of neuroses and certain other chronic disabling illnesses.

The totality of findings thus far generated regarding a possible association between increased rate of life changes and the timing of myocardial infarction are provocative but remain unconvincing because of the inconsistencies among them. Furthermore, the studies that are stronger methodologically are the ones with negative results. The use of matched control groups that have experienced life-threatening events similar to those of patients with myocardial infarction would eliminate some sources of possible bias of recall, but the best way to perform a definitive test of this hypothesis is through further prospective study. It is still unresolved whether life changes might raise the risk of illness by reason of depleting a person's available "adaptive energy" (the Holmes-Rahe position) or whether the mechanism might be the reactions of alarm and distress certain life changes cause (the Paykel-Uhlenhuth position). This question, too, needs sharper resolution.

Coronary-Prone Behavior Pattern

Since 1970 studies conducted at many research centers have supported earlier reports that higher risk of coronary disease is present in persons manifesting the "coronary-prone behavior pattern, Type A"—a style of behavior characterized by some or all of the following: intense striving for achievement; competitiveness; easily provoked impatience; time urgency; abruptness of gesture and speech; overcommitment to vocation or profession; and excesses of drive and hostility. It should be emphasized that this behavior pattern is not the same as "stress." It represents neither a stressful situation nor a distressed response, but rather a style of behavior with which some persons habitually respond to circumstances that arouse them. The clinical features of this pattern have been comprehensively described.[65, 66] The pattern can be reliably rated and is a deeply ingrained, enduring trait. All but one of the studies here reviewed found evidence supporting the association of at least some part of this Type A behavior pattern with incidence or prevalence of coronary disease. Table 2 lists these studies in terms of their research design and results.

Wardwell and Bahnson[22] examined matched groups of patients with myocardial infarction, other hospitalized patients and healthy community controls to test hypotheses using composite scales of items to assess each major variable. Only the Type A behavior pattern and somaticizing, previously discussed, were particularly characteristic of patients with myocardial infarction at statistically significant levels. The Type A behavior pattern was measured with a scale of 17 items administered in a structured interview. Thiel et al.[19] included six questions dealing with the behavior pattern in interviews of patients with infarction and controls. They did not present group means for the scale as a whole but found that individual items about

TABLE 2. Summary of Recently Reported Associations between the Coronary-Prone Behavior Pattern, Its Components, and Coronary Disease.*

Study	Type†	Measure of Type A Behavior			Individual Components of Type A Behavior
		Structured interview	"Activity survey"	Ad hoc approach	
Rosenman et al[67–69]	P	+			
Jenkins et al[70]	P		+		
Bonami & Rimé[54]	P			+	Achievement, job involvement
Bruhn et al[38]	P	+			
Mathews et al[71]	P	+			
G. Friedman et al[36]	P			0	
Theorell et al[64]	P			+	Hostility when slowed, added responsibility
Flodérus[35]	P			+	Time pressures, excess job responsibility
Jenkins et al[72]	M		+		
Wardwell & Bahnson[22]	RC			+	
Cohen et al[24a]	RC		+		
Stokols[73]	RC		+		
Jenkins et al[74]	RC		+		
Kenigsberg et al[75]	RC		+		
Shekelle et al[76]	RC		+		
Ganelina & Kraevsky[77]	RC			+	Ambitious, responsible, works fast
Thiel et al[19]	RC			+	Excess drive, rapid movement
Mertens & Segers[42]	RC			+	Time pressure, seeks responsibility
Theorell & Rahe[57]	RC			+	Hostility when slowed
van Dijl[78]	RC			+	Overactivity, job involvement
Bengtsson[24]	RC			+ −	
M. Friedman et al[79]	Aut	+			
Blumenthal et al[80]	Ang	+	0		
Zyzanski et al[48]	Ang		+		

*Positive findings are indicated by +. Absence of a positive indication usually represents failure to use a measure. Entry of + − indicates mixed results with regard to components of Type A behavior. Entries of 0 indicate more definitive negative results.

†Type of study design is coded as follows: P, prospective; M, mixed design involving both prospective & retrospective cases of repeat myocardial infarction; RC, retrospective with comparison groups; Aut, autopsy study with deceased control group; & Ang, angiographic studies of coronary arteries with comparison groups.

excessive drive and rapid body movements significantly discriminated the patients with infarction. The other four questions had trends in the hypothesized direction.

Friedman and his associates[79] conducted an autopsy study of cardiac disease in 64 cases of sudden deaths and 16 deaths from non-cardiovascular causes. They interviewed next-of-kin to ascertain the behavior pattern of the decedents and found a significantly higher percentage of Type A persons among those dying of coronary disease than among those dying from other causes.

A number of European studies have tested retrospectively the relation of various components of the coronary-prone pattern to coronary disease. Mertens and Segers[42] compared 48 older middle-class patients with coronary disease with 47 younger, mostly working-class patients with fractures from the same hospital. Twenty-seven variables differed significantly between the groups, relating variously to Type A behavior (works longer hours, feels time pressure, seeks responsibility, strong sense of duty), to life dissatisfaction (wants to change job, marital discord), to social and organizational activities and lack of exercise. The data seem to support the Type A, life-dissatisfaction and physical-inactivity hypotheses, but they are compromised to an unknown degree by the sociodemographic differences between clinical groups.

Theorell and Rahe[57] found that patients with myocardial infarction in Stockholm reported more hostility when slowed by others but showed no differences on expressed need to rush against time deadlines. A large prospective study of 6579 Swedish construction workers also provides support to the Type A hypothesis.[64] The investigators administered a variety of questions by means of a postal questionnaire and followed morbidity and mortaility for 12 to 15 months through health-services registries (estimated to be 99 per cent complete in Sweden).

A 10-question "discord index" was significantly associated with the incidences (in persons previously free of these conditions) of myocardial infarction, neurosis and total mortality. The "discord index" was composed of five items reflecting Type A behavior—two items on life satisfaction, two on family structure in childhood and one on number of residential changes. It appears, in the absence of specific tallies on each item, that the "discord index" may have obtained much of its predictive strength from its Type A content. Of all 46 psychosocial items collected, only four had significant univariate associations with incidence of myocardial infarction. Of eight items reflecting facets of Type A, two were statistically associated with future infarction ("recently received increased responsibility at work" and "becomes very hostile when held up in queues").

A prospective study of Swedish twins[35] found items reporting time pressures and excessive job responsibility to precede the development of angina pectoris (by self-report on the London School of Hygiene Questionnaire). Ganelina et al.,[77] in the Soviet Union, compared 30 control patients equivalent in occupations with 50 male patients with coronary disease (39 with infarction and 11 with angina pectoris). All patients with coronary disease also had coronary insufficiency. The study assigned men to three predefined personality categories. It was found that 76 per cent of the patients with coronary disease but only 23 percent of control patients were classified in the group characterized by having high ratings on strength of will, organizing abilities, ambition and acceleration of rate of work. They were not neurotic but were active, sociable, and held high social ideals. This description sounds much like the coronary-prone behavior pattern.

Van Dijl[78] constructed scales by factor-analyzing a pool of statements dealing with characteristics attributed to patients with coronary disease by prior researchers. In a cross-sectional study of 102 patiens with myocardial infarction scored higher than both of two control groups matched for age and education on scales measuring overactivity and exaggerated job involvement.

In one of the few large-scale studies of psychosocial factors associated with coronary disease in women, Bengtsson, Hallstrom and Tibblin obtained data from both patients and reference groups of women in five one-year age cohorts in Goteborg, Sweden.[24] Women with myocardial infarction scored significantly higher than the healthy reference population on aggression, marginally higher on achievement, and significantly higher on a combined index called "neurotic self-assertiveness," which included the two scores mentioned in addition to guilt feelings and defense of status.

An interesting sidelight on the relation of Type A behavior pattern to coronary disease is revealed in a socioecologic study by Appels.[81] He found highly significant correlations between nationally published mortality rates for arteriosclerotic heart disease and the rank-ordering of the prominence of achievement themes in children's storybooks from the same nations, as they had been quantified by McClelland.[82] The inference was drawn that emphasizing the achievement motive when socializing children leads to a higher prevalence of Type A behavior, and, thus, to higher risks of arteriosclerotic and coronary disease. This is merely an ecologic association, as were many of the early reports linking national diet and coronary disease. It is reported here because of its consistency with many other studies, including the one described next.

Bonami and Rimé[54] performed a prospective analysis on responses to the Van Lennep Four Picture Test as the responses were recorded in the personnel files of a large corporation. These projective tests were taken an average of 9.7 years before the emergence of clinical coronary disease in 32 men. They were compared with the stories given by 40 control subjects carefully matched for age, education, occupational level and length of time in the organization. In contrast to the controls, the men in whom coronary disease later developed showed a greater need for achievement and a greater concentration on their socioprofessional setting at the expense of attention to their family and to recreation. This is an interesting use of personnel records and "blind"-study design to perform a historical prospective study.

The Western Collaborative Group Study (WCGS) included at intake a structured interview specifically designed to measure the coronary-prone behavior pattern. Reports of the incidence of clinical coronary disease after 4.5, 6.5 and 8.5 years of surveillance have shown that men judged to possess the coronary-prone behavior pattern (Type A) at intake had 1.7 to 4.5 times the rate of new coronary heart disease as men judged to possess the converse, relaxed, easygoing pattern (Type B). The behavior pattern was judged without knowledge of other risk factors, and diagnosis of disease was made without knowledge of behavior type or risk factors. The relative risk ratio observed differs by the age group at intake and the length of follow-up observation, with younger Type A men generating higher relative risk ratios than older men.[67–69] The analysis by Brand et al.[83] applying the Framingham multiple logistic equation to WCGS incidence data suggests that inclusion of behavior Type A adds appreciably and independently to the prediction of coronary risk, particularly in higher-risk deciles as defined by traditional risk factors. This accounting for hitherto unexplained variance is responsive to the need expressed in the Keys[1] and Gordon[2] reports.

Bortner's double-blind reauditing and item-by-item rating of a matched sample of WCGS incidence cases and controls was factor-analyzed by Mathews et al.[71] Of the five factors derived, only two generated scores that were associated either with the global judgment of Type A or with the future emergence of clinical coronary disease. The factors labeled competitive drive and impatience related to both these dependent variables, implying that they are the critical components of Type A behavior. Bruhn and his colleagues employed the structured interview developed by Rosenman and Friedman[67] to assess behavior Type A and a psychiatric interview to determine the presence of the "Sisyphus reaction" (effortful striving without emotional fulfillment) in a study of recurrent fatal infarction among patients with coronary disease in Oklahoma.[38] The close similarity of the Sisyphus reaction to the Type A pattern is attested to by the observation that in this sample of 118 study subjects, seven of the 10 persons with the most extreme Sisyphus reactions were also among the 10 with the most extreme Type A patterns. Both these behaviors were significantly associated with coronary death.

Several studies have also used a self-administered, computer-scored questionnaire for determination of the coronary-prone behavior pattern (the Jenkins Activity Survey).[84] Two studies have reported the association of Type A scores derived from this test with prevalence of coronary disease. In the WCGS, 83 men with coronary disease scored significantly higher on both the Type A and Hard-Driving Scales than 524 controls.[74] In a study at the Bridgeport, Connecticut, Hospital, 48 patients with coronary disease (both men and women) scored significantly higher on these same two scales than 42 patients hospitalized with other diseases.[75]

Shekelle, Schoenberger and Stamler[76] studied prevalence of myocardial infarction in 1208 middle-aged white men who were among 4108 persons 25 to 64 years of age of both sexes and two races entering screening programs of the Chicago Heart Association. They found that the Type A score from the Activity Survey was positively associated with socioeconomic status and weakly related to cigarette smoking. Type A score was only weakly and insignificantly associated with prevalence of coronary disease when considered as an isolated variable. However, when age, serum cholesterol, diastolic blood pressure, and cigarette smoking were controlled statistically by a multiple logistic regression, the Type A score became a statistically significant correlate of coronary-disease prevalence. Its contribution to prediction, as reflected in the standardized regression coefficient, was slightly greater than that of serum cholesterol and slightly less than that of diastolic blood pressure. This study is an important example of the value of simultaneous study of biologic and psychosocial risk factors to coronary disease.

Activity Survey Type A scores were also found predictive of risk of new coronary disease in a prospective study conducted as part of the Western Collaborative Group Study. Men scoring in the top third of the Type A score distribution incurred 1.7 times the incidence of coronary disease occurring in those scoring in the lowest third (the Type B end) of the distribution.[70]

Type A scores on this test are also associated with increased risk of reinfarction among persons already having clinical coronary disease. This relation has been found in two samples drawn from the Western Collaborative Group Study[72,83] and parallels the finding of Bruhn et al.[38] discussed earlier.

Two unpublished dissertations studying patients with coronary disease in North Carolina and Hawaii respectively, both found that men with coronary disease had significantly higher mean scores[73] on the Type A Scale of the Activity Survey than comparison groups without this disease.[24a] In the Hawaiian study, however, it was found that the excess prevalence of coronary disease was occurring largely in Type A men who had previously experienced either social mobility or status incongruity.[24a]

A major study that found negative evidence concerning the Type A behavior pattern was the historical prospective analysis of the Kaiser-Permanente data.[36] A 155-item true-false inventory, which dealt largely with interpersonal problems and neurotic symptoms, had been administered to thousands of health-plan subscribers in earlier years. Two researchers familiar with the coronary-prone pattern were asked to select items from this pool that would be characteristic of Type A and Type B respondents. These items were not further studied to test their sensitivity in discriminating known Type A from Type B persons. Neither of these individually picked sets of true-false items, nor the common items selected by both raters, was predictive of the persons who incurred myocardial infarction after taking the test in this study group. In contrast to most other studies reviewed in this section, this population included both men and women over a wide age range, including persons over 70 years of age.

The scientific value of established associations between any risk factor and coronary disease is greatly strengthened when evidence can be obtained regarding the pathologic mechanism linking the associated variables. Early evidence along these lines comes from two double-blind studies conducted at about the same time in separate institutions. Ninety-six men with a variety of cardiologic diagnoses who underwent coronary angiography at Boston University School of Medicine completed self-administered questionnaires, including the Activity Survey.[48] It was not feasible to perform the behavior-type interview. Cineangiograms were replayed with stop action, and the degree of obstruction of each of four major coronary vessels was measured to the nearest millimeter. Men with two or more coronary vessels obstructed 50 per cent or more at the point of greatest involvement were found to score significantly higher than men with lesser atherosclerosis on all four scales of the Activity Survey (i.e., the Type A Scale and the three-factor analytic scales, speed and impatience, job involvement and hard driving). The differences in mean scores observed between men with different degrees of atherosclerosis exceeded in absolute size the differences previously found in Activity Survey studies of incidence and prevalence of coronary disease.

Blumenthal et al.[80] studied 142 men and women undergoing coronary angiography at Duke University Medical Center. These patients were categorized as manifesting Behavior Type A or B on the basis of the structured interview of Friedman and Rosenman. They were also administered the Activity Survey and several other questionnaires and tests. Patients found to have at least a 75 per cent narrowing of one or more coronary arteries had been blindly judged to be Type A in 82 per cent of the studies (59 of 72), whereas only 37 per cent of patients (26 of 70) with lesser arterial disease had been judged Type A ($P = 0.001$). The Type A score did not correlate significantly with angiographic judgments in but the evidence is mostly from retrospective sources (two small sample prospective exceptions are the studies of Thomas and Greenstreet[37] and Bonami and Rimé[54]). The Type A behavior pattern seems to be associated with both these manifestations of coronary disease. If angina and infarction have different psychosocial risk factors, some of the inconsistencies among studies in past years may be attributable to the different mixture of patients with angina and infarction in the respective samples. It is important that future studies build into their research design the distinction between these two presentations of coronary disease.

A substantial increase in an understanding of the mechanisms by which stress-inducing circumstances, hostility, time urgency, competitiveness and unpleasant affects influence the cardiovascular system could be obtained if these conditions could be produced in an animal model that is susceptible to atherosclerosis. The dietary hypothesis of atherosclerosis has gained much of its strength from animal experimentation, and the same result could become true for behavioral factors. Recent progress in operant conditioning technics, behavioral control of animals and the simulation of human conflict situations makes this kind of research more feasible than ever before. It would also be cost effective to add a behavioral dimension to ongoing animal studies of atherosclerosis.

Another immediate research application of psychosocial risk factors is to incorporate them in preventive field trials for coronary disease. This approach would have two advantages. It would provide an inexpensive prospective test of the strength and independence of psychosocial risk factors. It would also permit a more precise estimate of the effect of the reduction of standard risk factors upon morbidity of coronary disease by removing the contribution of psychosocial factors from the error-variance term of the statistical test.

The last five years of published studies relating psychosocial risk factors to coronary disease have reaffirmed that these variables are measurable, usually by more than one approach. In addition, the validity of the relation between certain psychosocial risk factors and coronary disease has been confirmed in both prospective and retrospective studies in a variety of different populations and by a great many research teams. Finally, a start has been made toward delineating the pathophysiologic mechanisms by which social and psychologic factors create changes in the cardiovascular system. Additional, well designed, large-scale research is needed to consolidate these findings, to resolve inconsistencies, and to integrate the epidemiologic and pathologic observations. This development could provide a better basis for deciding whether it would be feasible to design intervention studies to test whether reducing psychosocial risk factors would also reduce morbidity and mortality from coronary disease.

Acknowledgments

Supported by a research grant (HL 15399) from the National Heart and Lung Institute. I am indebted to Drs. Stephen J. Zyzanski, S. Leonard Syme, Robert M. Rose, William Insull and John C. Cassel for reviews of an earlier draft of this paper (I relied heavily on the Medical Literature Analysis and Retrieval Service [MEDLARS] of the National Library of Medicine).

References

1. Keys A, Aravanis C, Blackburn H, et al: Probability of middle-aged men developing coronary heart disease in five years. Circulation 45:815–828, 1972

2. Gordon T, Garcia-Palmieri MR, Kagan A, et al: Differences in coronary heart disease in Framingham, Honolulu and Puerto Rico. J Chronic Dis 27:329–344, 1974

3. Coronary heart disease in seven countries. Edited by A Keys. Circulation 41:Suppl 1: 1970

4. Marmot M, Winkelstein W: Epidemiologic observations on intervention trials for prevention of coronary heart disease. Am J Epidemiol 101:177–181, 1975

5. Dwyer JT, Feldman JJ, Mayer J: The social psychology of dieting. J Health Soc Behav 11:269–287, 1970

6. McDonough JR, Hames CG, Stulb SC, et al: Coronary heart disease among negroes and whites in Evans County, Georgia. J Chronic Dis 18:443–468, 1965

7. Henry JP, Cassel JC: Psychosocial factors in essential hypertension: recent epidemiologic and animal experimental evidence. Am J Epidemiol 90:171–200, 1969

8. Syme SL, Oakes TW, Friedman GD, et al: Social class and racial differences in blood pressure. Am J Public Health 64:619–620, 1974

9. Mai FMM: Personality and stress in coronary heart disease. J Psychosom Res 12:275–287, 1968

10. Christian P: Interdependenz von Umwelt und Person am Beispiel des Herzinfarktes. Psychother Psychosom 16:210–223, 1968

11. Mertens C, Segers MJ: L'influence des facteurs psychologiques dans la gènese des affections coronariennes. I. Données bibliographiques. Bull Acad R Med Belg 11:155–199, 1971

12. Jenkins CD: Psychologic and social precursors of coronary disease. N Engl J Med 284:244–255, 307–317, 1971

13. Williams AO: Coronary atherosclerosis in Nigeria. Br Heart J 33:95–100, 1971

14. Lehman EW: Social class and coronary heart disease: a sociological assessment of the medical literature. J Chronic Dis 20:381–391, 1967

15. Cassel J, Heyden S, Bartel AG, et al: Incidence of coronary heart disease by ethnic group, social class, and sex. Arch Intern Med 128:901–906, 1971

16. Sigurjonsson J: Occupational variations in mortality from ischemic heart disease. J Am Geriatr Soc 19:34–40, 1971

17. Kitagawa EM, Hauser PM: Differential Mortality in the United States: A study in socioeconomic epidemiology. Cambridge, Massachusetts, Harvard University Press, 1973

18. Croog SH, Levine S: Social status and subjective perceptions of 250 men after myocardial infarction. Public Health Rep 84:989–997, 1969

19. Thiel HG, Parker D, Bruce TA: Stress factors and the risk of myocardial infarction. J Psychosom Res 17:43–57, 1973

20. Comstock GW: Fatal arteriosclerotic heart disease, water hardness at home, and socioeconomic characteristics. Am J Epidemiol 94:1–10, 1971

21. Weiss NS: Marital status and risk factors for coronary heart disease: the United States Health Examination Survey of Adults. Br J Prev Soc Med 27:41–43, 1973

22. Wardwell WI, Bahnson CB: Behavioral variables and myocardial infarction in the Southeastern Connecticut Heart Study. J Chronic Dis 26:447–461, 1973

23. Comstock GW, Patridge KB: Church attendance and health. J Chronic Dis 25:665–672, 1972

24. Bengtsson C, Hällström T, Tibblin G: Social factors, stress experience, and personality traits in women with ischaemic heart disease, compared to a population sample of women. Acta Med Scand [Suppl] 549:82–92, 1973

24a. Cohen JB: Sociocultural change and behavior patterns in disease etiology: an epidemiologic study of coronary heart disease among Japanese Americans, Ph.D dissertation in Epidemiology, School of Public Health, University of California at Berkeley, August, 1974

25. Horan PM, Gray BH: Status inconsistency, mobility and coronary heart disease. J Health Soc Behav 15:300–310, 1974

26. Shekelle RB, Ostfeld AM, Paul O: Social status and incidence of coronary heart disease. J Chronic Dis 22:381–394, 1969

27. Bruhn JG, Wolf S, Lynn TN, et al: Social aspects of coronary heart disease in a Pennsylvania German community. Soc Sci Med 2:201–212, 1968

28. Shekelle RB: Status inconsistency, mobility and CHD: a reply to Horan & Gray. J Health Soc Behav (in press)

29. Lehr I, Messinger HB, Rosenman RH: A sociobiological approach to the study of coronary heart disease. J Chronic Dis 26:13–30, 1973

30. Medalie JH, Kahn HA, Neufeld HN, et al: Myocardial infarction over a five-year period. I. Prevalence, incidence and mortality experience. J Chronic Dis 26:63–84, 1973

31. Syme SL, Hyman MM, Enterline PE: Cultural mobility and the occurrence of coronary heart disease. J Health Hum Behav 6:178–189, 1965

32. Williams CA: The relationship of occupational change to blood pressure, serum cholesterol, a specific overt behavior pattern, and coronary heart disease. Dissertation, Department of Epidemiology, University of North Carolina at Chapel Hill, 1968

33. Kaplan BH, Cassel JC, Tyroler HA, et al: Occupational mobility and coronary heart disease. Arch Intern Med 128:938–942, 1971

34. Medalie JH, Snyder M, Groen JJ, et al: Angina pectoris among 10,000 men: 5 year incidence and univariate analysis. Am J Med 55:583–594, 1973

35. Floderus B: Psychosocial factors in relation to coronary heart disease and associated risk factors. Nord Hyg Tidskr Suppl 6: 1974

36. Friedman GD, Ury HK, Klatsky AL, et al: A psychological questionnaire predictive of myocardial infarction: results from the Kaiser-Permanente Epidemiologic Study of Myocardial Infarction. Psychosom Med 36:327–343, 1974

37. Thomas CB, Greenstreet RL: Psychobiological characteristics in youth as predictors of five disease states: suicide, mental illness, hypertension, coronary heart disease and tumor. Johns Hopkins Med J 132:16–43, 1973

38. Bruhn JG, Paredes A, Adsett CA, et al: Psychological predictors of sudden death in myocardial infarction. J Psychosom Res 18:187–191, 1974

39. Eastwood MR, Trevelyan H: Stress and coronary heart disease. J Psychosom Res 15:289–292, 1971

40. Finn F, Mulcahy R, Hickey N: The psychological profiles of coronary and cancer patients and of matched controls. Ir J Med Sci 143:176–178, 1974

41. Mayou R: The patient with angina: symptoms and disability. Postgrad Med J 49:250–254, 1973

42. Mertens C, Segers MJ: L'influence des facteurs psychologiques dans la gènese des affections coronariennes. II. Donnée experimentales. Bull Acad R Med Belg 11:201–221, 1971

43. Rimé B, Bonami M: Specificité psychosomatique et affections cardiaques coronariennes: essai de verification de la theorie de Dunbar au moyen du MMPI. J Psychosom Res 17:345–352, 1973

44. Segers MJ, Graulich P, Mertens C: Relations psycho-biocliniques dans un group de coronariens: étude preliminaire. J Psychosom Res 18:307–313, 1974

45. Kavanagh T, Shephard RJ: The immediate antecedents of myocardial infarction in active men. Can Med Assoc J 109:19–22, 1973

46. Greene WA, Goldstein S, Moss AJ: Psychosocial aspects of sudden death: a preliminary report. Arch Intern Med 129:725–731, 1972

47. Ruskin HD, Stein LL, Shelsky IM, et al: MMPI comparison between patients with coronary heart disease and their spouses together with other demographic data. Scand J Rehabil Med 2:99–104, 1970

48. Zyzanski SJ, Jenkins CD, Ryan TJ, et al: Emotions, behavior pattern and atherosclerosis. Presented at the Annual Meeting of the American Psychosomatic Society. New Orleans, March 21, 1975

49. Rose GA, Blackburn H: Cardiovascular Survey Methods. Geneva, World Health Organization, 1968, pp 172–175

50. Wolpert A, Yaryura-Tobias JA, Kertzner L: Silent myocardial infarction in a chronic psychotic population. Dis Nerv Syst 32:280–283, 1971

51. Rosenman RH, Friedman M, Jenkins CD, et al: Clinically unrecognized myocardial infarction in the Western Collaborative Group Study. Am J Cardiol 19:776–782, 1967

52. Bruhn JG, Chandler B, Wolf S: A psychological study of survivors and nonsurvivors of myocardial infarction. Psychosom Med 31:8–19, 1969

53. Croog SH, Shapiro DS, Levine S: Denial among male heart patients: an empirical study. Psychosom Med 33:385–397, 1971

54. Bonami M, Rimé B: Approche exploratoire de la personalité pre-coronarienne par analyse standardisée de données projectives thematiques. J Psychosom Res 16:103–113, 1972

55. Dongier M: Psychosomatic aspects in myocardial infarction in comparison with angina pectoris. Psychother Psychosom 23:123–131, 1974

56. Keys A, Taylor HL, Blackburn H, et al: Mortality and coronary heart disease among men studied for 23 years. Arch Intern Med 128:201–214, 1971

57. Theorell T, Rahe RH: Behavior and life satisfactions characteristic of Swedish subjects with myocardial infarction. J Chronic Dis 25:139–147, 1972

58. Holmes, TH, Rahe RH: The social readjustment rating scale. J Psychosom Res 11:213–218, 1967

59. Rahe RH, Lind E: Psychosocial factors and sudden cardiac death: a pilot study. J Psychosom Res 15:19–24, 1971

60. Theorell T, Rahe RH: Life change events, ballistocardiography and coronary death. J Hum Stress 1(3):18–24, 1975

61. Rahe RH, Paasikivi J: Psychosocial factors and myocardial infarction. II. An outpatient study in Sweden. J Psychosom Res 15:33–39, 1971

62. Rahe RH, Bennett L, Romo M, et al: Subjects' recent life changes and coronary heart disease in Finland. Am J Psychiatry 130:1222–1226, 1973

63. Lundberg U, Theorell T, Lind E: Life changes and myocardial infarction: individual differences in life change scaling. J Psychosom Res 19:27–32, 1975

64. Theorell T, Lind E, Flodérus B: The relationship of disturbing life-changes and emotions to the early development of myocardial infarction and other serious illnesses. Int J Epidemiol 4:281–293, 1975

65. Friedman M: Pathogenesis of Coronary Artery Disease. New York, McGraw-Hill Book Company, 1969, pp 75–135

66. Jenkins CD: The coronary-prone personality, Psychological Aspects of Myocardial Infarction and Coronary Care. Edited by WD Gentry, RB Williams Jr. St. Louis, The CV Mosby Company, 1975, pp 5–23

67. Rosenman RH, Friedman M, Straus R, et al: Coronary heart disease in the Western Collaborative Group Study: a follow-up experience of 4½ years. J Chronic Dis 23:173–190, 1970

68. Rosenman RH: Assessing the risk associated with behavior patterns. J Med Assoc Ga 60:31–34, 1971
69. Rosenman RH, Brand RJ, Jenkins CD, et al: Coronary heart disease in the Western Collaborative Group Study: final follow-up experience of 8½ years. JAMA 233:872–877, 1975
70. Jenkins CD, Rosenman RH, Zyzanski SJ: Prediction of clinical coronary heart disease by a test for coronary-prone behavior pattern. N Engl J Med 290:1271–1275, 1974
71. Mathews KA, Glass CD, Rosenman RH, et al: Competitive drive, pattern A and coronary heart disease: a further analysis of some data from the Western Collaborative Group Study. J Chronic Dis (in press)
72. Jenkins CD, Zyzanski SJ, Rosenman RH: Risk of new myocardial infarction in middle-aged men with manifest coronary heart disease. Circulation 53:342–347, 1976
73. Stokols JJ: Life dissatisfaction as a risk factor in coronary heart disease. PhD. dissertation in Psychology, University of North Carolina at Chapel Hill, 1973
74. Jenkins CD, Zyzanski SJ, Rosenman RH: Progress toward validation of a computer-scored test for the Type A coronary-prone behavior pattern. Psychosom Med 33:193–202, 1971
75. Kenigsberg D, Zyzanski SJ, Jenkins CD, et al: The coronary-prone behavior pattern in hospitalized patients with and without coronary heart disease. Psychosom Med 36:344–351, 1974
76. Shekelle RB, Schoenberger JA, Stamler J: Correlates of the JAS Type A behavior pattern score. J Chronic Dis (in press)
77. Ganelina IE, Kraevsky YaM: Premorbid personality peculiarities in patients with cardiac ischemia. Kardiologiia 11(2):40–45, 1971
78. van Dijl H: Activity and job-responsibility as measured by judgment behavior in myocardial infarction patients. Psychother Psychosom 24:126–128, 1974
79. Friedman M, Manwaring JH, Rosenman RH, et al: Instantaneous and sudden deaths: clinical and pathological differentiation in coronary artery disease. JAMA 225:1319–1328, 1973
80. Blumenthal JA, Kong Y, Rosenman RH, et al: Type A behavior pattern and angiographically documented coronary disease. Presented at the meeting of the American Psychosomatic Society, New Orleans, March 21, 1975
81. Appels A: Het hartinfarct een cultuurziekte. Tijdschr Soc Geneesk 50:446–448, 1972
82. McClelland DC: The Achieving Society. New York, D Van Nostrand Company, 1961
83. Brand RJ, Rosenman RH, Sholtz RI, et al: Multivariate prediction of coronary heart disease in the Western Collaborative Group Study compared to the findings of the Framingham Study. Circulation 53:348–355, 1976
84. Jenkins CD, Rosenman RH, Friedman M: Development of an objective psychological test for the determination of the coronary-prone behavior pattern in employed men. J Chronic Dis 20:371–379, 1967
85. Jenkins CD, Zyzanski SJ, Rosenman RH, et al: Association of coronary-prone behavior scores with recurrence of coronary heart disease. J Chronic Dis 24:601–611, 1971
86. Prevention of Ischemic Heart Disease: Principles and practice. Edited by W Raab. Springfield, Illinois, Charles C Thomas, 1966
87. Syme SL, Hyman MM, Enterline PE: Some social and cultural factors associated with the occurrence of coronary heart disease. J Chronic Dis 17:277–289, 1964
88. Ostfeld AM, Lebovits BZ, Shekelle RB, et al: A prospective study of the relationship between personality and coronary heart disease. J Chronic Dis 17:265–276, 1964

16

Social Status and Psychological Disorder

An Issue of Substance and an Issue of Method

Bruce P. Dohrenwend

Epidemiological studies have been held to support a variety of hypotheses about the social causation of psychological disorder. Most often, the causal role of social factors is inferred from rate differentials according to geographical location or social category. These correlations have been viewed as pointing to the etiological significance of such factors as social disorganization, social isolation, migration, acculturation and social class.[1]

There are, however, at least two major difficulties with the evidence for social causation. First, there are studies which fail to replicate the correlations on which the interpretations are based.[2] Second, the correlations themselves are open to equally plausible opposing interpretations in which social or geographical location is viewed as consequence rather than cause of psychological disorder; the assumption, as Dunham formulates it, is that social selection "... explains significant rate variations as due to the manner in which a given social system functions through time and in its functioning tends to sort and sift persons into class and community positions."[3]

From the opposing vantages of social causation and social selection, a number of well-known dilemmas of explanation have been posed. For example, with regard to high rates of disorder found in new immigrant groups, does the impact of the strange environment produce disorder, or are sick people more likely to migrate?[4] With regard to high rates of disorder found in slums, do slum conditions contribute to the development of disorder through adverse influence on slum residents, or does prior disorder contribute to the slum conditions as sick individuals "drift" into or fail to rise out of slum environments?[5] On the basis of a review of much of the evidence, Dunham has concluded that even for "the so-called functional disorders ... the

SOURCE: *American Sociological Review* 31 (1966): 14–34. Copyright © 1966 by the American Sociological Association. Reprinted by permission of the publisher and the author.

evidence is highly inconclusive for asserting with any confidence that a high rate in a given position of a social structure is a product of certain stresses, strains, and conflicts in that position."[6]

An Issue of Substance

The most consistent demographic finding reported in social psychiatric field studies is an inverse relationship between social class and psychological disorder.[7] As with others, this relationship has been interpreted on the one hand as evidence of social causation, with low status producing psychopathology; and on the other, as evidence of social selection, with pre-existing disorder determining social status. The latter interpretation is compatible with the position that genetic factors are important[8] in the etiology of disorders widely held to be of psychogenic origin.[9]

Consider by way of illustration some results from the Midtown Study in New York City.[10] In an advance over previous work on this problem, the Midtown researchers attempted to choose between social causation and social selection interpretations by investigating the impact of parental class position, a factor clearly antecedent to the current psychiatric condition of their adult respondents. Finding a significant inverse relation between their respondents' symptomatology and the socioeconomic status of their respondents' parents, the investigators suggested that environmental deprivation in childhood is a causal factor in psychiatric disorder. However, they also found that the relation between parental socioeconomic status and impairing symptoms was weaker than the relation of own socioeconomic status to impairing symptoms. Moreover, respondents rated impaired were most likely to be found among those who were downwardly mobile relative to their parents, and least likely to be found among those who were upwardly mobile. Accordingly, the Midtown researchers concluded that perhaps both social causation, in the form of childhood deprivation, and social selection, in the form of intergeneration mobility, contribute to the strong inverse relation between rates of impairing symptoms and the respondent's own socioeconomic status. Genetic predisposition could, however, with equal plausibility, be substituted for childhood deprivation in this interpretation. The dilemma of the relative importance of social causation and social selection explanations of class differences in psychiatric disorder remains.

The problem of finding a basis for assessing the relative importance of social causation vs. social selection factors in class differences in rates of disorder has proved persistent. Obstacles reside in the nature of the epidemiological surveys, each conducted at one point in time and necessarily without experimental controls. Causality is inherently difficult to demonstrate in such studies. Short of experiments involving the manipulation of social class, or possibly prospective surveys over long periods of time, is there any key to a solution? We will argue that at least one such key does potentially exist.

The history of New York City has been marked by great successive waves of new immigrant groups: the Irish and Germans in the 1840's; the Jews and Italians starting in the 1880's; the Negroes after World War I; and the Puerto Ricans after World War II. Possibly excepting (non-Jewish) Germans, the initial conditions of these new groups in the city have been those of poverty, slums and working class jobs. The Jews, the Irish and, to a lesser extent, the Italians have moved up over succeeding generations into relatively affluent and largely middle-class circumstances. In this process of assimilation, these three ethnic groups have achieved a substantial share in the wealth and power of the city.

In sharp contrast to these now relatively advantaged ethnic groups are the Negroes and Puerto Ricans—concentrated geographically in the city's slums, and occupationally in its low-paying unskilled and semi-skilled jobs. Glazer and Moynihan summarize the economic picture in the city as follows:

> ... the economy of New York... is dominated at its peak (the banks, insurance companies, utilites, big corporation offices) by white Protestants, with Irish Catholics and Jews playing somewhat smaller roles. In wholesale and retail commerce, Jews predominate. White collar workers are largely Irish and Italian if they work for big organizations, and Jewish if they work for smaller ones. The city's working class is, on its upper levels, Irish, Italian, and Jewish; on its lower levels, Negro and Puerto Rican. Other ethnic groups are found scattered everywhere, but concentrated generally in a few economic specialties. [11]

These investigators see the situation faced today by Negro and Puerto Rican New Yorkers as different from Jews, Irish, and Italians at the start of their climb. At the same time the supply of Negro and Puerto Rican labor has been increasing, industrial wages have been decreasing. Of the consequences of these trends, coupled with ethnic and racial prejudice against Negro and Puerto Rican New Yorkers, Glazer and Moynihan write:

> To a degree that cannot fail to startle anyone who encounters the reality for the first time, the overwhelming portion of both groups constitutes a submerged, exploited, and very possibly permanent proletariat. [12]

It would be consistent with the reports of an inverse relationship between social class and psychological disorder to expect relatively high rates of such disorder among New York Negroes and Puerto Ricans. [13] If such an expectation were confirmed by the facts, what would it suggest? In social selection terms, it would indicate that high rates of prior psychological disorder, probably genetically produced, are causing the low status of Negroes and Puerto Ricans in New York City. Against the background of the history and contemporary circumstances of ethnic groups in New York City, such an explanation would, however, strain credulity. It is plausible only as an explanation of high rates of disorder in the low status members of groups which, as wholes, are relatively advantaged.

Let us, then, make the plausible assumption that the downward pressure maintaining the low group status of Negro and Puerto Rican New Yorkers stems more from such social factors as society's reactions to difference in skin color and to difference in the culture of new immigrant groups than from hereditary defects of personality. Let us also assume that such downward social pressure on Jewish, Irish, and Italian New Yorkers is much less strong, since many of the social obstacles to achievement now facing Negroes and Puerto Ricans have either been removed or were never encountered by these more advantaged ethnic groups. If, therefore, we hold such indicators of class as income and education constant and find that Negroes and Puerto Ricans show higher rates of psychological disorder than their class counterparts in the more advantaged ethnic groups, this would be strong support for the social causation interpretation of class differences in rates of disorder. The reason is that increased downward social pressure would be shown to produce an increment in psychopathology over and above that produced by the lesser downward social pressure on members of more advantaged ethnic groups.

If, on the other hand, we were to find that rates of psychological disorder among Negroes and Puerto Ricans are lower than rates among their class counterparts in more advantaged ethnic groups, the implication would be that class differences in rates of disorder are due less to social causation than to social selection. The reason is that less psychological disorder among Negroes and Puerto Ricans would demonstrate that increased downward social pressure does not lead to increased psychopathology. Rather, these pressures would be seen to block upward mobility to a greater extent for psychologically healthy Negroes and Puerto Ricans than for psychologically healthy members of more advantaged ethnic groups. As a result of these social selection processes, there would be a larger "residue" of ill among the low status members of the more advantaged ethnic groups.[14]

We have, then, a major substantive issue which could turn on a simple question of fact: Namely, do Negroes and Puerto Ricans have higher or lower rates of psychological disorder than their class counterparts in more advantaged ethnic groups in New York City?

State of the Facts

What are the facts about rates of psychological disorder among Negroes and Puerto Ricans in contrast to more advantaged ethnic groups? Relatively high treatment rates at various facilities have been reported for both Negroes and Puerto Ricans.[15] It is difficult, however, to interpret the results of studies in which the circumstance of being in treatment constitutes the sole definition of disorder.[16] For example, treatment rates vary with the availability of treatment facilities and with attitudes towards their use. Either of these factors could be responsible for spurious relations between ethnicity and number of cases in treatment.

Recognition of this problem has stimulated more than twenty-five attempts to assess the prevalence of untreated as well as treated disorder in communities. The overall rates of disorder reported in these studies range from less than 1% to more than 60%.[17] Analysis of these differences shows that the factors primarily responsible for the great variability in rates are methodological, involving, e.g., thoroughness of data collection and problems of case definition.[18] Despite these overall inconsistencies, however, 14 of the 18 studies providing relevant data on social class show the highest rate in the lowest economic stratum.[19] It seems reasonable to inquire, therefore, whether they show trends on ethnic and racial comparisons.

Rates comparing Negroes and whites can be obtained from eight of these studies. As Table 1 shows, the eight divide evenly, with four showing higher rates for Negroes and four showing higher rates for whites. If it were possible to control social class in these comparisons, we would expect differences favoring whites to be decreased, and differences favoring Negroes to be increased. On their face, therefore, the results would tend to support a social selection explanation of the generally reported inverse relation between social class and psychological disorder.

TABLE 1. Rates of Psychological Disorder Reported for Whites and Negroes in Studies Including Untreated as Well as Treated Cases

Rate for Whites Higher				Rate for Negroes Higher			
Per Cent				Per Cent			
White	Negro	d	Place & Date of Study	White	Negro	d	Place & Date of Study
1.9*	1.2*	0.7	Eastern Health District, Baltimore, 1936[1]	2.2*	2.8*	0.6	Eastern Health District Baltimore, 1933[5]
7.1	5.0	2.1	Nationwide Selective Service, WW II[2]	1.8*	7.0*	5.2	Nassau County, N.Y. around 1910[6]
7.8	4.2	3.6	Williamson County, Tennessee, 1938[3]	11.1*	37.2	26.1	Boston Selective Service, WW II[7]
11.2	4.6	6.6	Eastern Health District, Baltimore, around 1952[4]	**	**	**	County in Canada, 1952[8]

*Calculated by B. S. Dohrenwend.   **Results not reported in percentages.

[1]P. Lemkau, C. Tietze, and M. Cooper, "Mental Hygiene Problems in an Urban District: Second Paper," *Mental Hygiene*, 26 (1942), pp. 100–119.

[2]L. G. Rowntree, K. H. McGill, and L. P. Hellman, "Mental and Personality Disorders in Selective Service Registrants," *Journal of American Medical Association*, 128 (1945), pp. 1084–1087.

[3]W. F. Roth and F. B. Luton, "The Mental Hygiene Program in Tennessee," *American Journal of Psychiatry*, 99 (1943), pp. 662–675.

[4]B. Pasamanick, D. W. Roberts, P. W. Lemkau, and D. B. Krueger, "A Survey of Mental Disease in an Urban Population: Prevalence by Race and Income." In B. Pasamanick (Ed.), *Epidemiology of Mental Disorder*, Washington, D.C.: American Association for the Advancement of Science, 1959, pp. 183–191.

[5]B. B. Cohen, Ruth Fairbank, and Elizabeth Greene, "Statistical Contributions from the Eastern Health District of Baltimore. III. Personality Disorder in the Eastern Health District in 1933," *Human Biology*, 11 (1939), pp. 112–129.

[6]A. J. Rosanoff, "Survey of Mental Disorders in Nassau County, New York, July–October, 1916," *Psychiatric Bulletin*, 2 (1917), pp. 109–231.

[7]R. W. Hyde and R. M. Chisholm, "The Relation of Mental Disorders to Race and Nationality, *New England Journal of Medicine*, 231 (1944), pp. 612–618.

[8]Dorothea C. Leighton, J. S. Harding, D. B. Macklin, A. M. Macmillan, and A. H. Leighton, *The Character of Danger*, New York: Basic Books, Inc., 1963.

Note, however, that three of the four studies showing higher rates for whites were done in the South; the fourth, a nationwide study of Selective Service applicants, includes the South (with about half the Negro population of the United States).[20] In contrast, three of the four studies showing higher rates for Negroes were done in the North, one of them in Canada. There is no persuasive reason for either a social selection or a social causation point of view why this should be the case.

A discussion by Pettigrew of contrasting results obtained by Negro and white interviewers in opinion polls provides a possible explanation. As he points out, for example, a 1942 Memphis poll contained the question: "Would Negroes be treated better or worse here if the Japanese conquered the U.S.A.?" When the question was asked by white interviewers, 45% of the Negroes said "worse" as compared to only 25% when the question was asked by Negro interviewers.[21] There have been similar findings in other studies.

Pettigrew emphasizes that Negroes in white America are always acting, transforming their behavior to conform to white prejudices and avoid white punishment. The resulting facade they present is often so convincing that " . . . many white

Americans have long interpreted it as proof that Negroes are happy and contented with their lot."[22] It seems possible that Negroes in the South, more repressed than in the North, would present the more undisturbed facade in investigations conducted under white auspices. If so, the results shown in Table 1 may reflect the white-oriented role behaviors of Negroes in the South rather than their psychiatric condition.

Only one published investigation of untreated disorder provides data on Puerto Ricans, and this is the Midtown Manhattan Study.[23] Although there were very few Puerto Ricans in the area of New York City studied by the Midtown researchers (only 1.2% of the total population), 27 were included in the sample of about 1600 respondents. These Puerto Ricans were psychiatrically evaluated as having the largest proportion with impairing symptoms of all the subgroups in the study.[24] The researchers compared a subsample of 252 respondents having family incomes identical with those of 18 Puerto Ricans in the lowest income bracket. They report that the proportion (31%) rated as showing impairing symptoms in the former was about half the proportion among the low income Puerto Ricans (61%).

Washington Heights, a different section of New York City and the scene of our own current research, provides opportunity for more extensive comparisons. Washington Heights contains four major ethnic groups; in order of size, these are Jewish, Negro, Irish and Puerto Rican. Our subjects consist of a probability sample of about 1000 adults from these four ethnic groups. Their ages range from 21 to 59, similar to the 20–59 age limits in the Midtown Study.[25]

Of these four main ethnic groups in Washington Heights, Negroes and Puerto Ricans are more disadvantaged socially and economically than the Jewish or the Irish. The Bureau of Labor Statistics has estimated that the cost of a "modest but adequate" level of living for a working-class family in New York City is about $5,200—excluding taxes.[26] Fifty-one per cent of the Negroes and 55 per cent of the Puerto Ricans have family incomes of less than $5,000 per year before taxes. Only 25 per cent of the Jewish and 28 per cent of the Irish are below the $5,000 figure. Outright poverty is most striking in the Negro group, where 26 per cent have incomes of under $3,000. Sixteen per cent are at this level among the Puerto Ricans, seven per cent among the Jewish and eight per cent among the Irish.

The clearest evidence of downward pressure by the larger society on Negroes and Puerto Ricans is in the relation of education to income in these groups as compared with the more advantaged Jewish and Irish. Table 2 shows that, at any given educational level other than college graduate, income in the Negro and Puerto Rican groups is well below that of their educational counterparts among the Jewish and Irish. Thus, although a person's education determines to a large degree what income he can hope to earn, a Negro or a Puerto Rican high school graduate is likely at the present time to have to settle for less than a Jewish or an Irish high school graduate.

To exploit for our problem the research potential of this situation in Washington Heights, a measure of psychological disorder is necessary. In the Midtown Study, about 120 items were used to elicit symptomatology relevant to psychiatric assessment of the respondents. Most of these items were selected from two sources: the United States Army Neuropsychiatric Screening Adjunct developed for Selective

TABLE 2. Per Cents with Family Incomes Under $5,000 per Year According to Advantaged (Jewish and Irish) vs. Disadvantaged (Negro and Puerto Rican) Ethnic Status, Controlling on Educational Level (Figures in parentheses indicate base for per cent and exclude "no answers" on Family Income or Educational Level)

Years of Formal Education	Ethnic Status	
	Advantaged (Jewish and Irish)	Disadvantaged (Negro and Puerto Rican)
7 or less	47.6 (21)	57.6 (85)
8–11	31.3 (131)	59.3* (189)
12–15	22.4 (264)	47.4* (175)
16 and over	22.4** (49)	12.5 (24)
Total Respondents	(465)	(473)

*Differs significantly at 0.05 level or better from advantaged (Jewish and Irish) counterparts according to one-tailed t-test of difference between proportions.
**Includes a number of graduate students with temporarily low incomes.

Service during World War II, and the Minnesota Multiphasic Personality Inventory. The main index of psychiatric disorder reported in Volume I of the Midtown Study was based on averaged ratings by two psychiatrists of responses to the 1,600 interviews. The interviews themselves were conducted by lay interviewers. The ratings ranged respondents on a scale from "well" through five degrees of severity of symptomatology: "mild," "moderate," "marked," "severe," and "incapacitated." Almost a quarter (23.4%) of the Midtown respondents were classified in the last three categories: marked, severe, and incapacitated. These are referred to collectively as "impaired," and are the "cases" in the Midtown Study sample.[27] Only a small minority of these "cases" had ever been in psychiatric treatment.

The Midtown researchers found that 22 symptom items from their questionnaire could be scored to provide a close approximation of the Midtown Study psychiatric ratings.[28] The items are scored either "one," indicating the presence of a symptom, or "zero," indicating its absence. Thus, theoretically, an individual's score can range from zero to 22. Most responses to the questions are in fixed alternative

TABLE 3. Symptom Score According to Income* (Per Cent) (Excluding "no answers" on Income)

Symptom Score	Income Group			
	<$3,000	$3,000– $4,999	$5,000– $7,499	$7,500 and over
4 or more	24.3	27.0	18.1	17.4
Base for %	(140)	(226)	(337)	(236)

*Chi-square = 9.39; p < 0.05.

TABLE 4. Symptom Score According to Educational Level* (Per Cent)
(Excluding "no answers" on Education)

Symptom Score	Years of Education			
	0–7	*8–11*	*12–15*	*16 or more*
4 or more	30.2	24.3	17.8	8.4
Base for %	(116)	(342)	(471)	(83)

*Chi-square = 18.99; p < 0.01.

"yes-no" or "often-sometimes-never" categories. For example, the presence of the symptom is indicated by the response "often" to the question "Are you ever bothered by nervousness? Would you say often, sometimes, or never?"

Langner, one of the Midtown researchers, describes a score of four or more on these 22 items as useful "... since it identifies only one per cent of the psychiatrically evaluated Wells, but... almost three quarters of the entire Impaired group."[29] On this evidence, it seemed useful to include these 22 items from the Midtown Study in the Washington Heights interviews.

If this 22-item index of psychological disorder shows the same *relationship* with class in the Washington Heights sample as a whole as was found in the Midtown Study with the full evaluation, we can have increased confidence that it provides a close approximation to Midtown ratings. As Table 3 shows, there is a significant inverse relationship between impairing symptoms and family income.

Table 4 shows that the relationship is even stronger with educational level. Thus, in general, the overall relationship reported for class in the Midtown Study holds for Washington Heights. What then of the crucial question about rates of psychopathology among Negroes and Puerto Ricans as against rates in more advanced subgroups?

Table 5 shows that, with income as the index of class, the Puerto Ricans have larger proportions with four or more symptoms than their counterparts in the other

TABLE 5. Per Cents with Four or More Symptoms (Per Cent) According to Family Income and Ethnicity (Figures in parentheses indicate base for per cent)

Yearly Family Income	Ethnicity			
	Jewish	*Irish*	*Negro*	*Puerto Rican*
Less than $3,000	10.5 (19)	26.7 (15)	24.4 (82)	33.3 (24)
$3,000–$4,999	30.8 (52)	20.0 (35)	16.2 (80)	42.4* (59)
$5,000–$7,499	20.5 (117)	11.1 (81)	14.0 (93)	32.6* (46)
$7,500 or more	15.3 (98)	13.7 (51)	18.8 (64)	30.4 (23)

*Differs significantly at 0.05 level or better from combined Jewish and Irish counterparts according to one-tailed t-test of difference between proportions.

TABLE 6. Per Cents with Four or More Symptoms According to Educational Level and Ethnicity (Figures in parentheses indicate base for per cent)

Years of Formal Education	Ethnicity			
	Jewish	Irish	Negro	Puerto Rican
0–7	(Too few cases) (7)	28.6 (14)	25.0 (52)	37.2 (43)
8–11	21.5 (65)	17.6 (68)	17.8 (135)	44.6* (74)
12–15	19.8 (192)	9.9 (91)	18.2 (148)	25.0 (40)
16 or more	9.1 (44)	15.4 (13)	0.0 (22)	(Too few cases) (4)

*Differs significantly at .05 level or better from combined Jewish and Irish counterparts according to one-tailed t-test of difference between proportions.

ethnic groups. Table 6 shows that the results are much the same if educational level is used as the index of class.[30]

If our comparisons involved only Puerto Ricans and members of more advantaged white groups, the results would support a social causation explanation of class differences in rates of disorder. Once again, however, we are confronted by difficulties in interpretation. As Tables 5 and 6 indicate, Negroes do not show higher rates of symptoms than Jews or Irish; this contradicts expectations from the social causation hypothesis.

There are two ways in which the results, had they been other than what they are, could have led to clear cut substantive interpretation of class differences in rates of disorder. First, the social causation hypothesis could have been confirmed, if both Negroes and Puerto Ricans showed higher rates of psychopathology with class controlled. Second, the social selection hypothesis could have been confirmed, if both Negroes and Puerto Ricans showed lower rates than their class counterparts in the advantaged groups. The actual outcome, however, appears to be neither of these: With class controlled, Puerto Ricans showed higher rates but Negroes did not. If accepted at face value, these results would leave us in an extremely unparsimonious state of theoretical affairs.

An Issue of Method

The question, of course, is whether these results should be accepted at face value. Are there problems of method that signal caution?

The problem of social desirability set toward the symptoms items. Is it possible, for example, that, like the Negro respondents to white interviewers in the Memphis poll mentioned above, the Washington Heights Negroes are playing a part they believe the white interviewers in the present study expect of them? To test this possibility, a probability subsample of 30 Negro respondents were reinterviewed on the 22 symptom items by a staff of six Negro interviewers an average of two years after the first interview. We found no difference in either the average number of symptoms reported the second time, nor in the proportion showing four symptoms or more. If, therefore, the Negroes in our Washington Heights study, two thirds of whom were born in the South, are presenting a facade which conceals their true psychiatric condition, it may well be a differently motivated facade from that which could account for the results obtained by white vs. Negro interviewers in studies of Negroes in the South.[31] An indirect clue may be contained in some results of research reported by Manis and his colleagues.[32]

These researchers attempted a cross-validation of the 22 Midtown items, using samples from patient and nonpatient populations. Finding that a group of predischarge ward patients had an average symptom score lower than two nonpatient groups consisting of college students and a cross-section of a community, the researchers argued that the result indicated a failure of the test, since "there is little or no reason to believe that the mental health of these predischarge patients is equal to or better than the nonhospitalized populations."[33] It seems likely that the predischarge ward patients, in the interests of "getting out," were less willing than the nonpatients studied to admit socially undesirable behavior. Note that the studies shown in Table 1 were all done prior to the 1954 Supreme Court decision on school desegregation. Is it possible that now, in the 1960's, Negroes who originally came to New York to improve their lot, also feel on the verge of "getting out" as movements for Negro civil rights and increased educational and economic opportunity gather momentum? And, like the predischarge ward patient, may these Negroes not also be showing conscious or unconscious resistance to admitting characteristics they judge to be socially undesirable?[34] Such an interpretation would be consistent with findings from recent studies that Northern Negroes tend more than whites to under-report hospitalization for a variety of illnesses,[35] and to state somewhat higher educational and occupational aspirations for their children than whites.[36] Whether and to what extent this interpretation is correct, however, is another question. As our further results will show, it probably implies less chaos and more order than exists for Northern Negroes under current conditions.

Questions must also be raised about the meaning of the high rates of symptoms shown by Puerto Ricans. The entire Midtown sample reported an average of 2.8 of the 22 symptom items.[37] The receiving ward patients studied by Manis et al. showed an average of 6.1 of these symptoms. Langner administered the 22 Midtown items in questionnaire interviews to a sample of 297 Mexican born residents of Mexico City.[38] Their mean score was 5.4 symptoms. Recall that a score of four or more was used as the cutting point in the analysis of data from Washington Heights reported above because this score screened the large majority of those judged impaired in the Midtown Study. Is the *average resident* of Mexico City, then, with a score of 5.4, a psychiatric case in the sense of the Midtown Study evaluations? Or is it possible that the difference between the respondents in Mexico City and in Midtown stems from a difference in normative orientation towards these symptoms? Are Puerto Ricans, with language and some other aspects of culture in common with Mexicans, showing similar differences not in amount of disorder, but rather in culturally patterned mode of expressing distress and/or culturally patterned willingness to express distress?

Consider a sample of the 22 Midtown Study items which were used to measure disorder:

Have you ever been bothered by your heart beating hard? Would you say: often, sometimes, or never?

Do your hands ever tremble enough to bother you? Would you say: often, sometimes, or never?

Would you say your appetite is poor, fair, good, or too good?

You have had periods of days, weeks or months when you couldn't take care of things because you couldn't "get going." (Yes or No)

You are bothered by acid or sour stomach several times a week. (Yes or No)

You have personal worries that get you down physically; i.e., make you physically ill. (Yes or No)

You feel somewhat apart or alone even among friends. (Yes or No)

As might be expected from a quick inspection of the examples above, most people see the characteristics called for by these items as socially undesirable. Some judgments by further subsample of 27 Jewish, Irish, Negro and Puerto Rican respondents in Washington Heights will illustrate.[39] On a scale from "one," representing "extremely undesirable," to "nine," representing "extremely desirable," the average rating given the 22 Midtown items was 3.2, with individual items ranging from 2.17 to 4.12.

To supplement these data we also collected ratings from two other groups: from a small sample of Negro males with fourth grade education and below and, if they were married, their wives—22 in all; and from 19 Puerto Rican residents of a tenement in a section of the Bronx, adjacent to Washington Heights. By adding data from these two groups to the data from the original 27, it is possible to compare the ratings made by 18 Jewish and Irish respondents (combined mean education 11.2 years) with the ratings by 26 Negroes (mean education 6.6 years) and by 24 Puerto Ricans (mean education 8.7 years).[40] A vivid difference results.

Only one item received a scale value as high as neutral (five on the scale) by any of the three groups.[41] There is, nevertheless a clear contrast between the Puerto Ricans and all the others. On 17 of the 22 items, the Puerto Ricans give a less undesirable rating than either the Jewish and Irish, or the Negroes.[42] The Negro respondents, if anything, give slightly more undesirable ratings than the Jews and Irish, exceeding them on 11 of the 22 items and tying them on three more.

The Negroes, in contrast to the Puerto Ricans, then, are close in their judgments of social desirability to the norms of the more assimilated Jewish and Irish groups. With a sensitivity to such norms developed under long-standing conditions of oppression, and heightened, perhaps, at this time of increased striving toward greater equality within the value framework of the wider society,[43] the Negroes may be more likely than the Jews or the Irish to suppress admission of symptoms they judge socially undesirable. If so, their actual rate of disorder may be much higher than the symptom measure suggests.

The Puerto Ricans, in turn, regard the characteristics described in the 22-item screening instrument as less undesirable than do members of the other ethnic groups. It seems possible that they would also be more willing than the other groups, on this account, to admit such characteristics. If so, they may actually have a much lower rate of disorder than their rate of reported symptoms would suggest. On the other hand, the reason Puerto Ricans see these symptoms as less undesirable may be because they are actually more common among Puerto Ricans. If this is so, then higher rates of reported symptoms among Puerto Ricans and their lower tendency to see these symptoms as strongly undesirable, may both indicate the same thing—higher actual rates of disorder. [44]

Investigation of these possibilities ideally requires a definition of untreated disorder independent of the symptomatology we are examining for differential susceptibility to cultural patterning. As we have no such definition for our nonpatients, no solution of this order is possible. We can, however, examine groups of Jewish, Irish, Negro and Puerto Rican psychiatric patients, all independently defined as ill by their patient status.

To this end, we asked psychiatrists at three outpatient services, in or adjacent to Washington Heights, to select patients for us to study by means of the 22-item screening instrument and other questions. [45] In order to insure rough comparability in the distribution of different types of disorder in each ethnic group, we used a quota system to secure patients of six different behavior types. [46] Table 7 shows the mean number of symptoms related to each behavior type among the 114 patients secured for this study. [47]

Our quota system provided a roughly similar distribution of the six behavior types

TABLE 7. Mean Number of Symptoms on 22-Item Screening Instrument for Psychiatric Out-Patients of Each of Six Behavior Types

Behavior Type	Mean No. of Symptoms	Total Patients
One person is very suspicious; doesn't trust anybody; and is sure that everybody is against this person.	10.4	17
A second person is very quiet; doesn't talk much to anyone; acts afraid of people; stays alone and daydreams all the time; and shows no interest in anything or anybody.	9.5	17
A third person worries a lot about little things, seems to be moody and unhappy all the time; and can't sleep nights, brooding about the past, and worrying about things that *might* go wrong.	8.6	39
A fourth person drinks too much; goes on a spree when there is money in the pocket. This person promises to stop drinking, but always goes off again.	5.3	13
A fifth person just can't leave the house without going back to see whether the gas stove was left lit or not; always goes back again just to make sure the door is locked; and is afraid to ride up and down in elevators.	8.2	26
A sixth person has been telling lies for a long time now, and stealing things. Others are very upset about these acts, but the person pays no attention to others.	7.0	2
Total	8.5	114

in each of the four ethnic groups. Thus, if similar degrees and types of disorder are expressed in similar ways by each ethnic group, we should find no ethnic differences among these patients in rates of symptoms. Table 8 shows that, as among our nonpatient cross-sections in Washington Heights, there is a generally higher rate among the Puerto Ricans. It would seem, then, that we must question high rates of such symptoms *per se* as indicators of high rates of psychological disorder in the nonpatient cross-sections. This would be true regardless of whether the high rate was due to cultural differences in willingness to admit such symptoms when they are present, or to cultural differences in mode of expressing distress.[48] If the latter is the case, of course, another problem is raised—the problem of the representativeness of the sample of symptom items.

The problem of bias in sampling symptom items. The Midtown researchers report that they attempted to include a sample of "... such symptoms as would demonstrably represent the most salient and *generalized* indicators of mental pathology."[49] Descriptively, these were said to consist "... principally of the psychophysiologic manifestations and those tapping anxiety, depression, and inadequacy dimensions."[50] Also included were items "... bearing particularly on... phobic reactions, and mood."[51]

The Midtown researchers also suggest, however, that the full battery of items on which their psychiatric evaluation was based, and perhaps especially the derivative 22-item screening instrument, tend to miss certain types of disorder such as alcoholism, sociopathic traits, and the early stages of paranoid schizophrenia.[52] It seems reasonable to consider the possibility, therefore, that symptoms associated with these disorders may be more prominent among New York's Negroes and

TABLE 8. Mean Number of Symptoms on the 22-Item Screening Instrument Among Jewish, Irish, Negro and Puerto Rican Psychiatric Out-Patients According to Behavior Type

Behavior Types	Ethnicity			
	Jewish	Irish	Negro	Puerto Rican
Suspicious, etc.	11.0	8.0	9.8	14.0
	(3)	(3)	(8)	(3)
Quiet, afraid, etc.	6.7	5.7	10.1	14.3
	(3)	(3)	(8)	(3)
Worry, moody, unhappy, etc.	7.9	5.4	8.4	11.9
	(10)	(7)	(12)	(10)
Drinks too much, etc	3.0	6.3	5.2	5.0
	(1)	(3)	(8)	(1)
Checks stove, afraid of elevator, etc.	5.7	8.2	6.0	13.0
	(6)	(4)	(9)	(7)
Lies, steals, etc.	...	...	7.0	...
	(—)	(—)	(2)	(—)
Total	7.4	6.6	7.9	12.5*
Total Cases	(23)	(20)	(47)	(24)

*Differs significantly at the 0.05 level or better (two-tailed t-tests) from Jewish mean, Irish mean, and Negro mean.

TABLE 9. Possible Indications of Alcoholism According to Ethnicity and Education

Problems with Drinking	Not High School Graduate				High School Graduate or More*			
	Jewish	Irish	Negro	Puerto Rican	Jewish	Irish	Negro	Puerto Rican
	%	%	%	%	%	%	%	%
Both:								
a. Trouble with health and work and	....	....	....	8.0	....	....	....	7.7
b. Arguments with family								
Either								
a. or b.	11.1	19.8	19.8	20.0	5.3	14.3	26.7	38.5
Neither								
a. nor b.	88.9	81.2	81.2	72.0	94.7	85.7	73.3	53.8
Total %	100.0	100.0	100.0	100.0	100.0	100.0	100.0	100.0
Total Respondents	(9)	(16)	(16)	(25)	(38)	(14)	(15)	(13)

*A one-tailed t-test indicates (p < 0.05) that the combined higher-educated Jewish and Irish have larger proportions with neither a. nor b. than the combined higher-educated Negroes and Puerto Ricans.

Puerto Ricans than among its white groups of predominantly European ancestry, even with class controlled.[53]

With one of its purposes to provide a preliminary check on this possibility, a follow-up study was conducted of a small subsample of Jewish, Irish, Negro and Puerto Rican respondents in Washington Heights—151 in all.[54] In these re-interviews, items designed to provide clues to paranoid tendencies, sociopathic tendencies, and alcoholism were included.

There were two items bearing on alcoholism: "I have not had trouble with my health or my work because of drinking." "I have had arguments with my family because of my drinking." These were answered either "true" or "false," with the first (and slightly more likely to elicit problems) keyed "false," and the second keyed "true."[55] Table 9 shows that there is a greater tendency for combined Negroes and Puerto Ricans of higher educational level to report drinking problems than the Jews or the Irish at higher educational levels. But the similarity of the advantaged and disadvantaged ethnic groups at lower educational levels, and the tendency of less-educated Negroes and Puerto Ricans to report fewer drinking problems than higher-educated Negroes and Puerto Ricans is puzzling from either a social causation or a social selection point of view.

With regard to sociopathic tendencies, six items were included. From most to least likely to be answered in the sociopathic direction they are:[56]

I think most people would not lie to get ahead. (Keyed "false.")
It is all right to get around the law if you don't actually break it. (Keyed "true.")
I don't blame anyone for trying to grab everything he can get in this world. (Keyed "true.")
I think most people are honest more for other reasons than for fear of being caught. (Keyed "false.")

Most respectable people in my neighborhood would not object to the kind of people I've gone around with. (Keyed "false.")

I can easily make people afraid of me and sometimes do just for the fun of it. (Keyed "true.")

Responses to all but the first of these six items conform to the Guttman scale pattern, thus providing a cumulative scale score of from zero to five "sociopathic" responses.[57] Table 10 shows that, if we disregard the 9 Jews of low education, these indications of possible sociopathic tendencies are most pronounced among Negroes and Puerto Ricans of low education. Moreover, there is a tendency for the Negroes and Puerto Ricans at higher educational levels to have higher scores than educational counterparts among the Jews and Irish. These results, then, taken at face value, tend to support the social causation hypothesis.

Six items were also provided to index possible paranoid tendencies. These in order of greatest "popularity" of the possible paranoid alternative, are:[58]

I do not tend to be on my guard with people who are somewhat more friendly than I had expected. (Keyed "false.")

My way of doing things is apt to be misunderstood by others. (Keyed "true.")

Behind my back people say all kinds of things about me. (Keyed "true.")

I have no enemies who really wish to harm me. (Keyed "false.")

I feel it is safer to trust nobody. (Keyed "true.")

I do not believe I am being plotted against. (Keyed "false.")

Although the responses fall short of meeting the criteria for a Guttman scale, we have scored them as in the case of the sociopathic items above.[59] The evidence of possible paranoid tendencies appears strongest, as Table 11 shows, in the low educated Negro and Puerto Rican groups. Among the higher educated respondents, Negroes and Puerto Ricans tend to have higher scores than the Jews and the Irish.

TABLE 10. Possible Indications of Sociopathy According to Ethnicity and Education* (per cent)

Number of "Sociopathic" Responses (0–5)	Not High School Graduate				High School Graduate or More			
	Jewish	Irish	Negro	Puerto Rican	Jewish	Irish	Negro	Puerto Rican
0	....	25.0	....	8.0	34.2	42.9	33.3	23.0
1	33.3	43.7	31.2	40.0	26.3	50.0	13.3	38.4
2	44.4	31.2	31.2	28.0	34.2	....	46.7	30.8
3	22.2	....	31.2	20.0	5.3	7.1	6.7	7.7
4	....	....	6.2	4.0	....	....	....	....
5	....	....	....	....	....	....	....	....
Total %	99.9	99.9	99.8	100.0	100.0	100.0	100.0	99.9
Total Respondents	(9)	(16)	(16)	(25)	(38)	(14)	(15)	(13)

*In comparisons of proportions scoring zero, one-tailed t-tests indicate that combined Negroes and Puerto Ricans of lower educational level differ significantly ($p < 0.05$ or better) from combined higher-educated Negroes and Puerto Ricans and from combined higher-educated Jews and Irish.

TABLE 11. Possible Indications of Paranoid Tendencies According to Ethnicity and Education* (per cent)

Number of "Paranoid" Responses (0–6)	Not High School Graduate				High School Graduate or More			
	Jewish	Irish	Negro	Puerto Rican	Jewish	Irish	Negro	Puerto Rican
0	22.2	50.0	12.5	8.0	50.0	35.7	46.7	46.1
1	55.5	25.0	18.7	40.0	21.1	35.7	20.0	7.7
2	22.2	12.5	31.2	28.0	18.4	21.4	13.3	23.0
3	....	....	31.2	16.0	10.5	7.1	20.0	15.4
4	....	12.5	6.3	8.0	....	....	....	7.7
5–6	....	....	....	....	....	....	....	....
Total %	99.9	100.0	99.9	100.0	100.0	99.9	100.0	99.9
Total Respondents	(9)	(16)	(16)	(25)	(38)	(14)	(15)	(13)

*In comparisons of proportions scoring zero, one-tailed t-tests indicate that combined Negroes and Puerto Ricans of lower educational level differ significantly ($p < 0.05$ or better) from: combined Negroes and Puerto Ricans with higher educational levels; combined Jewish and Irish of lower educational level; and combined Jewish and Irish of higher educational level.

Thus we have here results which, on their face, are the most consistent so far with a social causation explanation.

The measures of possible sociopathic and possible paranoid tendencies involved in these results show little relation to the 22 Midtown-item score. This suggests that the Midtown items may grossly underrepresent psychological symptomatology, especially among lower educated Negroes and Puerto Rican respondents.[60]

The problem of acquiescence response style. Again, however, questions must be raised about accepting these results at face value. Recall that the possibly paranoid items did not scale and that, on a random basis, three of the six items were keyed "true," the other three "false." It is necessary to inquire whether tendencies to "yeasay" (agree) or "naysay" (disagree) regardless of item content may have constituted a competing dimension that both generated scale errors and distorted the substantive results.[61]

To investigate this problem of acquiescence response style, separate scores ranging from zero to three were constructed for the "true" and "false" keyed items respectively. To the extent that yeasaying or naysaying occurred, we would expect little correlation between the two indices. We find that there is a significant ($p < 0.05$) positive correlation of 0.33 for the higher-educated respondents. For the lower-educated respondents, however, the correlation is not only insignificant, but negative (−0.03). This negative correlation is most pronounced in the Negro group where it reaches -0.32.[62] Thus, we must reckon with yeasaying or naysaying response styles in interpreting the results which, so far, are most consistent with a social causation point of view.

Table 12 shows that we would have to alter our interpretation if we relied on an index made up of the false-keyed paranoid items. Most important is the difference

TABLE 12. Comparisons of "True" and "False" Keyed Indices of Possible Paranoid Tendencies According to Ethnicity and Education (per cent)

Number of "True" vs. "False" Keyed "Paranoid" Responses	Not High School Graduate				High School Graduate or More			
	Jewish	Irish	Negro	Puerto Rican	Jewish	Irish	Negro	Puerto Rican
"True" Keyed (0–3)								
0	56.6	68.8	25.0	44.0	52.6	71.4	60.0	61.5
1	44.4	25.0	31.3	32.0	36.8	14.3	26.7	30.8
2	. . . .	6.3	18.8	24.0	10.5	14.3	13.3	7.7
3	. . . .	. . . .	25.0	. . . .	. . . .	. . . .	. . . .	. . . .
Total per cent	100.0	100.1	100.1	100.0	99.9	100.0	100.0	100.0
Total Respondents	(9)	(16)	(16)	(25)	(38)	(14)	(15)	(13)
"False" Keyed (0–3)								
0	44.4	62.5	56.3	32.0	76.3	42.9	60.0	53.8
1	55.6	18.8	31.3	44.0	15.8	57.1	33.3	23.1
2	. . . .	12.5	12.5	20.0	7.9	. . . .	. . . .	7.7
3	. . . .	6.3	. . . .	4.0	. . . .	. . . .	6.7	15.4
Total per cent	100.0	100.0	100.1	100.0	100.0	100.0	100.0	100.0
Total Respondents	(9)	(16)	(16)	(25)	(38)	(14)	(15)	(13)

among the lower educated Negroes depending on how the items are keyed. For them, there appears to be a clear tendency toward yeasaying.[63]

The problem of psychological symptoms as indicators of psychological disorder. It would seem, then, that further work in this field can ignore the problem of response bias only at its peril. Would control of response bias in itself, however, provide adequate measures of psychological disorder? This is doubtful.

If a tendency to agree to items regardless of their content on the part of lower educated Negroes were the whole story of their higher scores on our measure of possible paranoid tendency,[64] why, then, did such a response style not produce similar high scores on the 22 Midtown items which were uncontrolled for acquiescence? For 11 of these 22 items, a "yes" response was scored as indicating pathology. The response alternatives for most of the others were "often, sometimes, or never" and might also be susceptible to yeasaying or naysaying tendencies (see the examples given above).

Earlier, it was noted that the 22 Midtown screening items were rated for degree of social desirability by small samples of Jewish, Irish, Negro and Puerto Rican respondents. Puerto Ricans, it will be remembered, tended to see these items as less undesirable than did Jews and Irish. In contrast Negroes, if anything, saw the items as more undesirable than did Jews and Irish. These same respondents also rated the present items on alcoholism, sociopathic, and paranoid tendencies. Like the 22 Midtown items, these items tend to fall on the undesirable side of the scale. This time, however, the picture is somewhat different for the Negroes. Compared to the combined Jews and Irish, the Negroes see four of the five sociopathic items, four of the six paranoid items, and one of the two alcoholic items as less socially undesirable.[65] The results are similar for the Puerto Ricans, but more pronounced, because they tend to see the sociopathic items as even less undesirable than the Negroes.

It seems possible and even likely, therefore, that acquiescence styles among the lower-educated Negroes do not operate independently of judgments of the social desirability of the content involved.[66] Differences in the appraisal of social desirability may account in part, at least, for our symptom results. So again we must consider the two alternative possibilities raised by the social desirability factor, this time for Negroes as well as Puerto Ricans: Are Negroes and Puerto Ricans simply more willing than the Jews and the Irish to admit problems with projected anger, and anti-social beliefs and behaviors because they judge such things as less undesirable? Or are these less undesirable ratings themselves a function of the greater prevalence of such beliefs and behaviors in the Negro and Puerto Rican groups?

It seems unlikely that normatively induced variation in willingness to admit paranoid and sociopathic tendencies is the whole story. On these grounds, the Puerto Ricans who see four of the five sociopathic items as less undesirable than do the Negroes should also show stronger tendencies to admit such things than the Negroes. As can be seen by glancing again at Table 10, this is not the case. If anything, the Puerto Ricans score lower than the Negroes on this index of sociopathic tendencies.[67]

Let us assume, then, at least for purposes of argument, that Tables 10 and 11 portray actual differences in beliefs and behavior between Jews and Irish on the one hand, and Negroes and Puerto Ricans on the other.[68] If so, would there be any reason to believe that these differences in responses to possibly sociopathic, and possibly paranoid, symptom items are compelling evidence of the presence of these types of psychological disorder? It appears to be true that our patient sample is more likely to give paranoid responses to these items than our non-patient sample; moreover, the patients who were judged to show paranoidlike behavior by their psychiatrists are more likely to give the paranoid types of responses to these items than are the other patients.[69] It is possible that interviews with individuals who have known sociopathic histories would reveal that they also will describe themselves in terms of the sociopathic items. Should the high rates of similar responses in our low educated Negro and Puerto Rican community samples, then, be taken as evidence of the high frequency of such disorders in these groups?

M. J. Field has pointed out that, in Ghana, where nobody looks twice at a lorry announcing in big letters, "Enemies all about me," or "Be afraid of people," the universality of the "normal" paranoid attitude makes it necessary to diagnose paranoid schizophrenia with great caution. She writes: "But just as, in our own society, we are able to recognize as abnormal the man from whom no reassurance can shift the groundless conviction that he has cancer, so we are able in rural Ghana to recognize the morbidly ineradicable paranoid conviction."[70] The sign of the difference between normal and abnormal she refers to as the "peculiar recalcitrant obstinacy" of the distorted outlook.[71] Is it possible that the responses of lower-class Negroes and Puerto Ricans in our Washington Heights study to the kinds of paranoid and sociopathic items described above are less evidence of personality disorder than of what Durkheim has described as "derivatives" of anomie—the currents of anger, disillusionment, discontent and so on that are held, unlike that comparative rarity, the act of suicide, to be the more prevalent responses to anomie?[72]

Attempts to codify clinical experience in the form of diagnostic nomenclatures emphasize the persistence of symptomatology indicative of pathology. Consider descriptions of the functional mental disorders in the widely used 1952 *Diagnostic and Statistical Manual* of the American Psychiatric Association. Here we read, for example, of the " . . . increase in severity of symptoms over long periods . . . " that is characteristic of the simple type of schizophrenic reaction,[73] and of the " . . . chronic and prolonged course . . ." of paranoia.[74] Lifelong studies of psycho-neurotics are said to " . . . usually present evidence of periodic or constant mal-adjustment of varying degree from early life."[75] In most instances of the person-ality disorders, including sociopathy and alcoholism, " . . . the disorder is man-ifested by a lifelong pattern of action or behavior. . . . "[76] And the symptoms of the psychophysiological autonomic and visceral disorders are held to be " . . . due to a chronic and exaggerated state of the normal physiological expression of emo-tion. . . . "[77] Thus most of the so-called functional psychiatric disorders are de-scribed as chronic in nature. They stem from a persistent defect of personality of whatever origin. It seems reasonable to assume that a source in such defect is what is meant by the term "pathology" in relation to psychological symptomatology, or by the term "disorder" in relation to personality.

The Midtown Study researchers suggest that their untreated "cases" show psychological pathology like that of psychiatric patients.[78] Yet, unlike the psychiat-ric patient, seen over a course or several courses of treatment, the untreated "case" in cross-sectional surveys such as the Midtown Study is seen at only one point in time.[79] Moreover the questions used to elicit evidence of symptomatology in the Midtown Study vary with respect to temporal reference, some calling for present problems, some being of the "have you ever" variety (see the sample questions above). Is it possible that such symptoms bear only a pseudo-resemblance to the persistent symptomatology observed in psychiatric patients?

Our subsample of 151 respondents in Washington Heights were reinterviewed an average of two years after the original interviews were conducted. Both the first and the second interviews with these respondents included the 22 Midtown items. The second interview also included some questions about objective events that might have changed the respondent's situation between the two interviews, especially occurrences related to work and physical health.

The relevant questions about intervening events were as follows:

Let's see, a Columbia University interviewer first visited your family to ask about health matters in _____ That was about _____ months ago.

Have you had any serious illness or health problems since then? (If Yes:) What is (was) the matter?

What were you doing most of the past _____ months? (For males:) Working, looking for work, or something else? (For females:) Working, looking for work, keeping house, or something else?

Has there been any change in your work or job status since the time of the first interview _____ months ago? (If Yes:) What change was that? Why did you change?

The responses to these questions were classified into the following categories of intervening events.

Unfavorable events:

1. Poor physical health of respondent; i.e., physical illness, injury, accident, etc., which seems current in negative consequences either because the respondent says so, or because it seems inherently so.
2. Poor physical health of respondent's spouse. (The large majority of the sample was made up of husbands and wives in the same household, receiving identical interviews.)
3. (For the male main earner:) Socioeconomic deterioration; i.e., demotion, business failure, unemployment, etc.
4. (For female spouses:) Socioeconomic deterioration; i.e., demotion, business failure, unemployment, etc. of male main earner.

Favorable events:

1. (For male main earners:) Socioeconomic improvement; i.e., promotion, raise, "better job," etc.
2. (For female spouses:) Socioeconomic improvement; i.e., promotion, raise, "better job," etc. for male main earner.
3. Birth of one or more children.

Unknown:

1. Events related to the above whose current consequences could not be ascertained.
2. Other events which were mentioned adventitiously; i.e., not in response to a specific question asked of all and bearing on the event.
3. No evidence of intervening event.

This classification of events was made independently by a psychiatrist and a sociologist who had no information about the respondents' psychological symptoms, ethnicity, or class background. They disagreed on 14 of the 74 events classified by either one or the other in the above event categories. None of these disagreements was over whether an event was favorable or unfavorable.

The questions included in the reinterview, of course, provide far from a complete list of the events that could have intervened between the two interviews. Nevertheless, 56 respondents were classified as currently influenced either by events judged entirely favorable or by events judged entirely unfavorable in the terms of the above categories. The direction of the changes in symptom scores on the 22 Midtown items from the first to the second interview for these respondents, as well as for respondents not so classified, are presented in Table 13.[80]

Table 13 shows that the relation between symptom changes and the quality of currently impinging events is significant.[81] Note that, since each respondent serves as his own control on response bias, such bias might diminish the magnitude of these changes, but can in no way account for the changes that occurred. The categories of favorable and unfavorable events are detailed to show that the results are not due solely to changes in physical health with which the 22-item symptom measure may be contaminated, or to socioeconomic changes which could be consequences rather than causes of the symptoms of the main earner. Thus we see, for

TABLE 13. Direction of Symptom Change According to Quality of Events Currently Impinging on Respondents at Time of Second Interview* (per cent)

| | Direction of Symptom Change | | | | |
| | | | No Change | | |
Quality of Events	Fewer Symptoms on Second Interview	More Symptoms on Second Interview	Same Number of Symptoms on Both Interviews	No Symptoms on Either Interview	Number of Respondents
Favorable (Totals 100 per cent)	41	23	13	23	31
Socioeconomic improvement:					
Main male earner—N	5	5	2	4	16
Wife of main earner—N	4	2	2	1	9
Birth of Children:					
Wife—N	2	. .	. .	. .	2
Husband—N	. .	. .	. .	2	2
Combinations of above—N	2	. .	. .	. .	2
Unfavorable (Totals 100 per cent)	16	56	25	8	25
Poor physical health of:					
Self—N	. .	7	2	. .	9
Spouse—N	2	3	3	2	10
Socioeconomic deterioration:					
Main male earner—N	1	2	. .	. .	3
Wife of main earner—N	. .	2	. .	. .	2
Combination of above—N	1	. .	. .	. .	1
Mixed** or Unknown (Totals 100 per cent)	37	31	17	15	80

*Chi-square indicates (p < 0.05) that the symptom changes according to favorable vs. unfavorable events could have occurred by chance. (Mixed or unknown events and no change excluded.)
**Four cases.

example, that symptoms tend to increase for respondents whose spouses become ill, and that wives' symptoms tend to increase or decrease with negative or positive changes respectively in their husbands' job situation. These results suggest, therefore, the importance of further investigation of the individual's contemporary situation, as distinct from his possible personality defects, in attempts to explain psychological symptomatology.[82]

Conclusion

It would seem that the major substantive issue with which we started, the issue of the relative importance of social causation vs. social selection factors in class differences in rates of psychological disorder, must yield precedence to resolution of the central unsolved problem of psychiatric epidemiology—the measurement of untreated psychological disorder. For, while the results of field studies of psychological symptomatology make it clear that there are group differences in modes of expressing distress, including some that are apparently stylistic, the studies are far from clear about the relation of these modes to the underlying psychiatric condition of individuals.

Two major questions confront further work in this field. First, what are the cultural and situational factors that lead to different modes of expressing psychological symptoms? Second, under what conditions does symptomatic expression of psychological distress become evidence of underlying personality defect?[83] When we can answer these questions, we shall be able to measure psychological disorder in different groups with some hope of resolving the crucial etiological issues.

Acknowledgments

This work has been supported in part by Grants OM-82, MH 07327-01, MH 07328-01 and MH 10328-01 from the National Institute of Mental Health, U.S. Public Health Service. It has also been supported in part by Grant U1053 from the N.Y.C. Health Research Council to the Community Population Laboratory of the School of Public Health & Administrative Medicine. For their help in facilitating interviews with psychiatric patients included in this study, I would like to thank Dr. Elizabeth B. Davis of Harlem Hospital, Dr. Roger MacKinnon and Dr. Joseph Snyder of Vanderbilt Clinic of the Columbia-Presbyterian Medical Center, and Dr. Jack Sheps of Jewish Memorial Hospital. I would also like to express my appreciation to Mr. Edwin Chin-Shong for his able assistance in analyzing the data, to Dr. John Colombotos and Dr. Gladys Egri for undertaking the classification of stressor events and providing helpful comment, and to Dr. Barbara S. Dohrenwend for useful criticism.

References and Notes

1. For a review of these interpretations and some of the studies on which they are based, see H. Warren Dunham, "Social Structures and Mental Disorders: Competing Hypotheses of Explanation," in *Causes of Mental Disorders: A Review of Epidemiological Knowledge, 1959,* New York: Milbank Memorial Fund, 1961, pp. 227–265.
2. *Ibid.;* Robert J. Kleiner and Seymour Parker, "Goal Striving, Social Status, and Mental Disorder: A Research Review," *American Sociological Review,* 28 (April, 1963), pp. 189–203; and Elliot G. Mishler and Norman A. Scotch, "Sociocultural Factors in the Epidemiology of Schizophrenia," *International Journal of Psychiatry,* 1 (April, 1965), pp. 258–305.
3. Dunham, *op. cit.,* p. 255.
4. E.g., Benjamin Malzberg, *Social and Biological Aspects of Mental Disease,* Utica, New York: State Hospital Press, 1940, Chapter 6; Ø. Ødegaard, "Emigrations and Mental Health," *Mental Hygiene,* 20 (October, 1936), pp. 546–553.
5. E.g., Robert E. L. Faris and H. Warren Dunham, *Mental Disorders in Urban Areas,* New York: Hafner, 1960, especially pp. 163–177; Dorothea C. Leighton, John S. Harding, David B. Macklin, Allister M. Macmillan, and Alexander H. Leighton, *The Character of Danger,* New York: Basic Books, 1963, especially pp. 343–346; Alexander H. Leighton, T. Adeoye Lambo, Charles C. Hughes, Dorothea C. Leighton, Jane M. Murphy, and David B. Macklin, *Psychiatric Disorder Among the Yoruba,* Ithaca, New York: Cornell University Press, 1963, especially p. 280.
6. Dunham, *op cit.,* p. 258.
7. Bruce P. Dohrenwend and Barbara S. Dohrenwend, "The Problem of Validity in Field Studies of Psychological Disorder," *Journal of Abnormal Psychology,* 70 (February, 1965), pp. 52–69.
8. Note that social selection explanations do not necessarily imply genetic or biochemical causation. Any given social selection hypothesis posits an alternative cause only to the

specific social factor, such as low class position, in the given correlation to be explained. If our original social factor of, for example, low class position, is discredited as a cause, it is possible that a social factor other than low class position has produced the disorder which has somehow been socially selected into a low status position. It is also possible, and somehow more readily credible, however, that a genetic or biochemical factor initially caused the disorder. The reason is that it is difficult to think of an alternative social factor that would explain a fact of social selection, such as downward drift, in terms of the social causation of psychological disorder.

9. See descriptions in the American Psychiatric Association Committee on Nomenclature and Statistics, *Mental Disorders: Diagnostic and Statistical Manual*, Washington, D.C.: American Psychiatric Association Mental Hospital Service, 1952.

10. Leo Srole, Thomas S. Langner, Stanley T. Michael, Marvin K. Opler, and Thomas A. C. Rennie, *Mental Health in the Metropolis*, New York: McGraw-Hill, 1962, pp. 212–213 and pp. 228–229.

11. Nathan Glazer and Daniel P. Moynihan, *Beyond the Melting Pot*, Cambridge, Mass.: M.I.T. Press, 1963, p. 5.

12. *Ibid.*, p. 299.

13. Srole, for example, makes just this prediction on the basis of the Midtown results with white, non-Puerto-Rican groups. See Srole et al., *op. cit.*, p. 365.

14. Cf. Ernest M. Gruenberg, comments on Dunham, *op cit.*, p. 269.

15. Benjamin Malzberg, *Statistical Data for the Study of Mental Disease Among Negroes in New York State, 1949–1951*, Albany, N. Y.: Research Foundation for Mental Hygiene and New York State Department of Mental Hygiene, 1959; Benjamin Malzberg, *Mental Disease Among Puerto Ricans in New York State, 1960–1961*, Albany, N. Y.: Research Foundation for Mental Hygiene, 1965.

16. E.g., Robert H. Felix and R. V. Bowers, "Mental Hygiene and Socio-environmental Factors," *Milbank Memorial Fund Quarterly*, 26 (1948), pp. 125–147; Ernest M. Gruenberg, "Problems of Data Collection and Nomenclature," in C. H. H. Branch, E. G. Beier, R. H. Anderson, and C. A. Whitmer (Eds.) *The Epidemiology of Mental Health*, Brighton, Utah; Department of Psychiatry and Psychology, University of Utah and Veterans Administration Hospital, Fort Douglas Division of Salt Lake City, Utah, 1955, 63–70.

17. Dohrenwend and Dohrenwend, *op. cit.*

18. *Ibid.*

19. *Ibid.*

20. Eli Ginzberg and Alfred S. Eichner, *The Troublesome Presence*, New York: Free Press, 1964, p. 330. See pp. 329–332 for documentation of the lower educational level and economic status of Negroes in the South as compared to Negroes in the North.

21. Thomas F. Pettigrew, *A Profile of the Negro American*, Princeton, N.J.: D. Van Nostrand, 1964, p. 50.

22. *Ibid.*, p. 50.

23. Srole et al., *op. cit.*

24. *Ibid.*, pp. 290–292.

25. A description of the probability sampling procedures for the larger sample of which these respondents are a subpart is contained in Jack Elinson and Regina Loewenstein, *Community Fact Book for Washington Heights, New York City, 1960–1961*, New York: Columbia University School of Public Health and Administrative Medicine, 1963.

26. Herman P. Miller, "New Definition of Our 'Poor'," *New York Times Magazine*, April 21, 1963.

27. Srole et al., *ob. cit.*, p. 333.

28. Thomas S. Langner, "A Twenty-two Item Screening Score of Psychiatric Symptoms Indicating Impairment," *Journal of Health and Human Behavior*, 3 (Winter, 1962), pp. 269–276.

29. *Ibid.*, p. 275.

30. No attempt was made to combine occupation, education, and income into a composite index of class because education has different implications for income according to ethnicity. Negroes and Puerto Ricans earn much less than Jews and Irish at every educational level other than college graduate (see Table 2 above).

   A check was made to see if use of mean number of symptoms and controls on sex and age would alter the results. With dichotomized variables of sex, age, and income controlled simultaneously within ethnic groups, Puerto Ricans remain consistently highest of the four ethnic groups in rate of symptoms on the large majority of comparisons (six of eight) while no coherent pattern of differences emerges among the other three ethnic groups. The result is the same when education is substituted for income in these comparisons controlled on sex and age.

31. To check on the possibility that relative deprivation was greater for the Negroes in Washington Heights born outside the South, we compared them in rate of symptoms with the Southern born. With education controlled to offset the somewhat lower educational level of the Southern born, there is no difference in rate of symptoms.

32. Jerome G. Manis, Milton J. Brawer, Chester L. Hunt, and Leonard C. Kercher, "Validating a Mental Health Scale," *American Sociological Review*, 28 (February, 1963), pp. 108–116.

33. *Ibid.*, p. 111.

34. Such a tendency to deny socially undesirable characteristics and "admit" socially desirable ones has been held to be an important determinant of responses in personality tests and inventories used usually with captive audiences such as students, patients, and prisoners. See Allen L. Edwards, *The Social Desirability Variable in Personality Assessment and Research*, New York: Dryden Press, 1957; also, for example, Douglas N. Jackson and Samuel Messick, "Response Styles on the MMPI: Comparison of Clinical and Normal Samples," *Journal of Abnormal and Social Psychology*, 65 (November, 1962), pp. 285–299.

35. U.S. Department of Health, Education, and Welfare, *Health Statistics from the U.S. National Health Survey: Reporting of Hospitalization*, (May 1961), Series D, Number 4, especially p. 10; also U.S. Department of Health, Education, and Welfare, *Health Statistics from the U.S. National Health Survey: Comparison of Hospitalization Reporting in Three Survey Procedures*, (January, 1963), Series D, Number 8, especially p. 20.

36. Richard Bloom, Martin Whiteman, and Martin Deutsch, "Race and Social Class as Separate Factors Related to Social Environment," *American Journal of Sociology*, LXX (January, 1965), pp. 471–476.

37. Thomas S. Langner, "Psychophysiological Symptoms and the Status of Women in Two Mexican Communities," in Jane M. Murphy and Alexander H. Leighton (Eds.), *Approaches to Cross-Cultural Psychiatry*, Ithaca, N. Y.: Cornell University Press, 1965, pp. 360–392.

38. *Ibid.*

39. In collecting these ratings, the procedure followed was that of Edwards, *op cit*. This sample of 27 Jewish, Irish, Negro and Puerto Rican respondents are husbands or wives who finished, well ahead of their spouses, an interview in which husbands and wives were being questioned separately but simultaneously in different parts of their apartment

by a team of interviewers. These joint interviews were conducted as a followup of a subsample of 151 respondents from families in the larger sample interviewed an average of two years earlier.

40. The ratings were self-administered after the procedure was explained by Negro interviewers to Negro respondents and by Puerto Rican interviewers to Puerto Rican respondents.

41. The scaling method used is that of equal-appearing intervals, a procedure commonly employed by Edwards in his work on the social desirability variable. *Op. cit.*

42. With one tie, a two-tailed sign test indicates that this result could have occurred by chance less than one time out of a hundred.

43. Cf. Pettigrew, *op. cit.*, pp 27–34.

44. Cf. Alfred B. Heilbrun, Jr., "Social-Learning Theory, Social Desirability, and the MMPI," *Psychological Bulletin*, 61 (May, 1964), pp. 377–387.

45. The three outpatient services are at Vanderbilt Clinic of the Columbia-Presbyterian Medical Center, Jewish Memorial Hospital, and Harlem Hospital.

46. Psychiatrists at each service were asked to sort their current patients in terms of the descriptions of behavior most and least like the patients. In this way, we hoped to avoid problems of unreliability in diagnosis while still insuring a diversity of patient types. See, for example, William A. Scott, "Research Definitions of Mental Health and Mental Illness," *Psychological Bulletin*, 55 (January, 1958), pp. 29–45. These "behavior types" are shortened adaptations of case descriptions of fictitious individuals developed by Shirley Star with psychiatric consultation for her study of public attitudes towards mental illness. As originally set forth, they were meant to illustrate paranoid schizophrenia, simple schizophrenia, anxiety neurosis, alcoholism, compulsive phobic behavior, and juvenile character disorder. The original descriptions have been used in a number of attitude studies since, and can be found, for example, in Elaine Cumming and John Cumming, *Closed Ranks*, Cambridge, Mass.: Harvard University Press, 1957.

47. The uneven n's in the various ethnic groups and among the various behavior types are due to scarcity of some of the desired types of patient at the facilities to which we had access. After a while, we concentrated on securing the rarer types of patients so as to have a roughly equal distribution of the behavior types in each ethnic group. Even so, we will have to go elsewhere to interview an appreciable number of alcoholics and sociopaths.

48. See Charles Kadushin, "Social Class and the Experience of Ill Health," *Sociological Inquiry*, 34 (Winter, 1964), pp. 67–80.

49. Srole, et al., *op. cit.*, p. 41.

50. *Ibid.*, p. 42.

51. *Ibid.*, p. 60.

52. *Ibid.*, p. 65; Langner, *op. cit.*, p. 269.

53. For vivid illustrations of possible cultural (including class subcultural) patterning of symptomatology, and perhaps even of type of disorder, see Andrew F. Henry and James F. Short, *Suicide and Homicide*, Glencoe, Ill.: Free Press, 1954; Marvin K. Opler and Jerome L. Singer, "Ethnic Differences in Behavior and Psychopathology: Italian and Irish," *International Journal of Social Psychiatry*, 2 (Summer, 1956), pp. 11–22; M. J. Field, *Search for Security*, Evanston, Ill.: Northwestern University Press, 1960; Joseph W. Eaton and Robert J. Weil, *Culture and Mental Disorders*, Glencoe, Ill.: Free Press, 1955; August B. Hollingshead and Frederick C. Redlich, *Social Class and Mental Illness*, New York: Wiley, 1958; and Thomas S. Langner and Stanley T. Michael, *Life Stress and Mental Health*, New York: Free Press of Glencoe, 1963.

54. This probability subsample was selected on the basis of ethnicity of the male head of the

household. An equal number of households was designated from each of the four main ethnic groups, and within each ethnic group, proportional allocation according to educational level of the male head was employed. Negro and Puerto Rican respondents were interviewed by Negro and Puerto Rican interviewers. Husbands and wives were interviewed separately but simultaneously in different parts of their apartments by male and female interviewers respectively. In all, 94 married couples and 26 single male household heads (214 individuals in all) were to be interviewed. Interviews were completed with the designated respondents in 69% of the households. An additional 12% had to be removed from the sample because we could not locate them, and because of verified moves out of the state, death, etc. Respondents in 19% of the households, disproportionately first-generation Irish, refused to be interviewed after repeated call-backs. In all, 71% of the designated respondents were interviewed. This gives us a rather good representation of married couples in all groups other than the Irish who were born in Ireland. It excludes a very important category among Negroes, the female household head with children but no husband present. Also, 14 of the 26 single male household heads were Negro, and we succeeded in interviewing only eight of them. These eight probably include the more stable among the single male household heads in the Negro group. This inference is based on the fact that differences between Negroes and their Jewish and Irish educational counterparts on the indices to be described are, if anything, sharper when all single males in the subsample are excluded from the analysis. The single males are retained in Tables 9, 10 and 11 in the interest of not further decreasing an already small n. If anything, the nature of the sample as a whole, with its emphasis on married couples and more stable single males, should reduce rather than accentuate differences in the variables of interest: possible alcoholism, possible sociopathy, and possible paranoid tendencies. An additional problem arises, however, from the fact that in this small sample, Negroes and Puerto Ricans have almost a monopoly on respondents who did not graduate from grammar school, while Jews have the large majority of college graduates—thus compromising our ability to control educational level. This is most important for the results shown in Tables 10 and 11. Nevertheless, when respondents with 0-7 years of education and those with college or more are omitted from Tables 10 and 11, sharp contrasts tending to support the social causation hypothesis remain.

55. These items were suggested by Margaret Bailey and Paul Haberman of the National Council on Alcoholism.

56. These items were selected on the basis of their face validity and with some changes in wording from the MMPI. We provided alternative wordings for each item so that each could have an equal chance of being keyed "true" or "false."

57. Guttman's coefficient of reproducibility for the five items that scaled is 0.905; Menzel's coefficient of scalability is 0.606. It is interesting to speculate after the fact on why the item about "lying to get ahead" did not scale. Possibly this is because it involves achievement orientation, and hence focuses to a greater extent than the other five on what may be a form of middle-class sociopathy.

58. These items were selected on the basis of their face validity and with some changes in wording from the MMPI. We provided alternative wordings for each item so that each could have an equal chance of being keyed "true" or "false."

59. Guttman's coefficient of reproducibility for the six items is 0.884 and Menzel's coefficient of scalability is 0.418, neither one acceptable. Nor can a satisfactory scale be constructed by dropping an item.

60. The Spearman rank order correlation coefficients (corrected for ties) for the 22 Midtown items score by the sociopathy scale and by the paranoid index though statistically significant at the 0.01 level, are only 0.218 and 0.249 respectively over the whole sample.

61. E.g., Arthur Couch and Kenneth Kenniston, "Yeasayers and Naysayers: Agreeing Response Set as a Personality Variable," *Journal of Abnormal and Social Psychology*, 60 (March, 1960), pp. 151–174.

62. The Spearman rank order correlation coefficients (corrected for ties) for the higher educated (high school graduates or more) in each ethnic group are: Jewish, 0.42; Irish, 0.22; Negro, 0.42; and Puerto Rican 0.39. For the lower educated (did not graduate from high school) in each ethnic group, they are: Jewish, —0.10; Irish, 0.41; Negro, —0.32; and Puerto Rican, —0.02.

63. Among the low educated Puerto Ricans, there are apparently both yeasayers and naysayers, and these appear to balance each other on the two indices.

64. A check on the distribution of scale errors in the sociopathy scale according to ethnicity and educational levels indicates that such error was not due in any important way to yeasaying or naysaying in specific ethno-educational groups. There is a tendency, not statistically significant, for the less-educated Puerto Ricans to have fewer respondents who are scale types than the other lower educated respondents. With this possible exception, error is not appreciably more frequent in any one of the eight ethno-educational groups than in any others. Overall, 62% of the respondents were scale types; the range is from 44% among the lower-educated Puerto Ricans to 69% among the lower-educated Negroes. Since three of the sociopathy scale items are keyed "true" and two are keyed "false," even roughly comparable indices cannot be built, as in the case of the six paranoid items, for still further checking. Nevertheless, the direction of relationships seems similar for an index built of the three "true" keyed items vs. an index built of the two "false" keyed items according to ethnicity and education. The fact that these five items scaled thus appears to mean that content was dominant over yeasaying or naysaying response styles in their case.

65. A one-tailed sign test indicates (p < .073) that this difference could have occurred by chance.

66. It has generally been assumed that the more ambiguous an item, the more likely it is to elicit a yeasaying or naysaying response style independent of content (see, for example, Richard Christie and Florence Lindauer, "Personality Structure," *Annual Review of Psychology*, 14 (1963), especially pp. 207–208.) It seems possible that the lower the educational level of respondents, the more ambiguous some of these items may have appeared. However, there is no apparent reason why the paranoid items should seem more ambiguous than the 22 Midtown items. To the extent that content was irrelevant as a determinant of the responses of low educated Negroes, for example, acquiescence should have led to high scores on the 22 Midtown items as well as on the paranoid index.

67. At both higher and lower educational levels, Puerto Ricans appear to have somewhat smaller proportions than Negroes with scores of two or more in Table 10.

68. In this eventuality, it is interesting to speculate on a possible real difference between the Negroes and Puerto Ricans of lower educational level. These groups, so similar on these "acting out" types of items, were vastly different on the 22 Midtown items calling more for expression of subjective suffering. Is it possible that Negroes, with a longer history of oppression, have indeed developed something like what the Negro comedian, Dick Gregory, has referred to as a "callus on the soul" that guards against the conscious experience of personal pain?

69. If we use the statistical criterion adopted by the Midtown researchers, for selecting their 22 items, chi-square tests show that three of these "paranoid" items discriminate at the 0.01 level between our patient and cross-section groups as wholes (the items are "misunderstood," "people say things behind my back," and "safer to trust no one"). Moreover, three show differences of 20% or more (in two cases twice the proportion) between the 17

patients judged by their therapists to be predominantly "suspicious, etc." and the remaining 97 patients (the items are "enemies who wish to harm me," "believe I am being plotted against," and "misunderstood"); with as few as 17 patients in the "suspicious, etc." category, however, each of these latter differences is statistically significant at only the 0.10 level using one-tailed t-tests of the difference between proportions.

70. M. J. Field, *op. cit.*, p. 296.
71. *Ibid.*, p. 296.
72. For a discussion of these derivatives, see Bruce P. Dohrenwend, "Egoism, Altruism, Anomie, and Fatalism: A Conceptual Analysis of Durkheim's Types," *American Sociological Review*, 24 (August, 1959), especially pp. 468–469.
73. Committee on Nomenclature and Statistics of the American Psychiatric Association, *op. cit.*, p. 26.
74. *Ibid.*, p. 28.
75. *Ibid.*, p. 31.
76. *Ibid.*, p. 34.
77. *Ibid.*, p. 29.
78. Srole et al., *op. cit.*, p. 333.
79. To date, the field studies attempting to estimate true prevalence of psychological disorder have provided almost no data on persistence or change in symptomatology evidenced by their respondents over time; see Dohrenwend and Dohrenwend, *op. cit.*
80. Only 13.3% of the respondents had scores of four or more symptoms on both interviews, in contrast to 20.0% on one of the two interviews.
81. See also Paul W. Haberman, "An Analysis of Re-test Scores for an Index of Psychophysiological Disturbance," *Journal of Health and Human Behavior*, in press.
82. For some possible leads along these lines, see Erich Lindemann, "Symptomatology and the Management of Acute Grief," *American Journal of Psychiatry*, 101 (September, 1944), pp. 141–148; James S. Tyhurst, "The Role of Transition States—Including Disasters—in Mental Illness," in *Symposium on Preventive and Social Psychiatry*, Washington, D.C.: United States Government Printing Office, 1957, pp. 149–169; Bruce P. Dohrenwend, "The Social Psychological Nature of Stress," *Journal of Abnormal and Social Psychology*, 62 (March, 1961), pp. 294–302; Dohrenwend and Dohrenwend, *op. cit.*; and Barbara S. Dohrenwend and Bruce P. Dohrenwend, " Stress Situations, Birth Order, and Psychological Symptoms," *Journal of Abnormal Psychology*, in press.
83. For one possible conceptualization of the problem, see Bruce P. Dohrenwend and Barbara S. Dohrenwend, *op. cit.*, especially pp. 66–67.

IV

The Macro System
of Health Care

As medical knowledge and technology have expanded and as insurance coverage and federal subsidy of medical care have increased, the problem of medical-care cost has become a paramount concern. All medical systems are seeking means to meet population expectations and needs while also containing costs. Achieving cost containment is a formidable challenge, and thus far efforts have been relatively unsuccessful. In reading 17, I take a broad view of the problem, looking at the theoretical potentialities for controlling medical-care costs by affecting both consumer and provider behavior. However successful such efforts might be, it is inevitable that medical care will have to be more strictly rationed as the potentialities of generating new costs mount. Thus I discuss various rationing alternatives, the implications of each, and what we know and do not know about them. What emerges from this discussion is that the development of successful social policy requires understanding that goes well beyond traditional economic analysis. It is necessary to study the structure of the medical-care system as a whole, and the likely effects of different types of incentive and disincentive on the behavior of both patients and professionals.

One of the problems in planning for medical care is the lack of firm knowledge of how much care is really optimal and what is truly necessary. Numerous studies suggest that the actual distribution of medical resources and the amount of medical work performed are not linked closely with known patterns of illness or mortality. This is vividly illustrated by Wennberg and Gittelsohn in reading 18, their analysis of small area variations in the state of Vermont. They identify vast differences from one area to another in the rate of hospital use, amount of surgical intervention, use of ancillary services, level of expenditure, and other important indicators. Understanding the cause of these differences is essential for sound social policy, and it is even more important to identify the impact of these large variations in the provision of medical care. As Wennberg and Gittelsohn point out, the provision of services seems more related to the location of physicians, surgeons, and facilities than to the likely need for services as indicated by such measures as the proportion of persons in the area over 65 years of age. Public policies and the way they are designed often result in increase inequalities, despite the goal of moderating differences in access to and provision of services.

The next two readings examine health care from a cross-national perspective. In reading 19, Paul Beeson, Distinguished Physician at the Veterans Administration Hospital in Seattle and formerly professor of medicine at both Yale University and Oxford University, England, presents his impressions of the differences in the way the American and English systems function. He directs particular attention to the way the English have controlled the proliferation of specialty practice, which is a problem in the American context, and the way the English have managed to retain the institution of the family practitioner. Beeson, on the basis of his personal experiences as an important medical educator in the two countries, illustrates some of the advantages of the British pattern of organization. Similarly, in reading 20, Smits and Draper direct their attention to the different ways in which the structure of American and British medicine affects opportunities to provide good medical care for the aged. The proportion of aged persons in the population is growing, and elderly people are more prone to illness and use much more medical care than younger persons. Indeed, long-term care constitutes one of the most significant future problems we will have to deal with, and Smits and Draper suggest some principles of care used by the British from which we can benefit.

17

Approaches to Controlling the Costs of Medical Care
Short-Range and Long-Range Alternatives

David Mechanic

The containment of the increasing costs of medical care has become of highest priority to government in the United States as well as in many other western nations. Medical-care spending in 1976 in the United States consumed 8.6 per cent of the Gross National Product (GNP), and all projections for the future suggest that health-care expenditures will requires increasing proportions of both the GNP and governmental budgets. There is no absolute ceiling on how much expenditure for medical care the nation can afford, but there is a great skepticism in government and elsewhere that marginal increases in the health-care budget provide adequate benefits as compared with similar investments in other sectors. With large budgetary pressures on federal, state and local governments, it is inevitable that greater energies will be given to controlling increased expenditure.

Although the concept of rationing medical care has an odious ring to many ears, rationing of care has always been the norm in the United States and elsewhere.[1] No community has ever provided all the care that its population might be willing to use, and the magnitude of consumption has reflected the manpower and facilities available, the price of services and the noneconomic barriers to care such as queues, waiting time and distance to sites of care. An important change in recent years, however, is the extent to which services are free of cost to the recipient at the point of consumption. As government and third parties cover an increasing proportion of medical-care costs, there are fewer financial inhibitions on the use of services. Thus, the marketplace as a rationing process must be replaced by consciously planned means of rationing either by government edict or through incentives or controls intended to change the behavior of health professionals.

Rationing is simply a means to apportion or distribute some good through a method of allowance. As the marketplace becomes a less important method of

SOURCE: *New England Journal of Medicine* 298 (2 February 1978): 249–54. Reprinted by permission.

allowance, the mix of cost-containment technics changes. The agenda is to understand better what a good mix is, not only from the perspective of achieving economies, but also to improve quality, enhance interactions between health professionals and patients, and to provide opportunities for trust and mutual respect. More stringent rationing must also be weighed against alternative strategies that either change the dependence of the population on the physician and its demands for more medical care, that improve the production of medical services, or that develop alternative community structures to deal with many types of problems typically treated by physicians.

Factors Affecting the Consumption of Services

A major way to reduce expenditures for medical care and the requirement for developing more facilities and personnel is to limit the needs and desires among patients for medical care. Reducing needs involves the prevention of illness or diminishing patients' psychologic dependence on the medical encounter for social support or other secondary advantages. Reducing desire for services requires changing people's views of the value of different types of medical care, making them more aware of the real costs of service in relation to the benefits received, and legitimizing alternatives for dealing with many problems that physicians increasingly deal with as the boundaries of medical care expand.

Prevention can be conceived of broadly as having three aspects. At the most global level are efforts in sectors other than health affecting the quality of the environment, standards of living, education and nutrition, employment and other social conditions relevant to health status.[2] The benefits of pollution control, for example, in relation to cost are high, and such efforts add to health status by reducing prevalence of disease as well as to the quality of living.[3] Possibilities for preventive efforts outside the medical sector are considerable, but the required policies frequently compete with economic and other social priorities and may be difficult to implement.

A second approach to prevention involves clearly identifying risk factors and structuring the environment or motivating people to minimize them. Although the examples of cigarette smoking, alcohol and drug dependence and inactivity and obesity are most frequently cited, these are complex behavioral problems that do not yield simply to exhortation or educational approaches. Often, these behaviors are deeply rooted in personality and are related to other serious problems that are intractable to change. Although there is sufficient evidence of progress in changing the population's habits to avoid excessive pessimism,[4] it is prudent to recognize the difficulty of the task, the forces working against successful change and the depths of ignorance concerning the origins of these behaviors and the ways in which they can best be modified. It may be that the greatest potential in changing health behavior is by focusing on the young before these behavioral patterns become well entrenched, but overcoming the influence of peer groups and other incentives to dangerous habits remains a formidable task.

A complementary approach is to make efforts to design living environments that reduce risk regardless of individual behavior.[5] The inflatable airbag in automobiles, fortified food and the safe cigarette are examples. Moreover, daily routine patterns of healthful behavior such as exercise[6] can be introduced into social environments in which persons spend much of their time, such as the workplace. Although technologic alternatives to changing individual behavior have been vigorously advocated, a prudent social policy would direct efforts to both behavior change and technologic alternatives. Too great an emphasis on technology alone might create disincentives for young people to develop responsible behavior relevant to their health.

Closest to the delivery of medical services are primary prevention programs such as immunization and early screening and treatment of disease and disabilities. In such areas as control of hypertension, effective diagnosis and treatment are available, but overcoming the behavioral problem of achieving continuing co-operation still constitutes a major barrier. Early detection of vision and hearing difficulties also limits later problems and costs and does not involve major behavior barriers. Appropriate treatment of common childhood ailments such as streptococcal infections and otitis media avoid damaging secondary problems that may result in the consumption of considerable services in adult life.[7] The difficulty is that beyond a limited number of instances, preventive or early care remains an untested concept, and the costs of identifying a small number of cases of asymptomatic illness early may be prohibitive.[8] To the extent that nontreatable asymptomatic disease is detected and made known to the patient, the consequences may be counterproductive because of the anxiety and worry aroused, socially induced disability or stigmatization.

Another way of reducing demand for care is to modify patients' perceptions of its value or appropriateness. There seems to be a consensus that patients have exceptionally high and unrealistic expectations of physicians and that they become too dependent on medical care. A number of studies have found that unrealistic expectations result in disappointment and less successful outcomes.[9] Although the medical profession may have contributed to such excessive expectations by exaggerating the effects of medical advances, it is in the interests of both patients and physicians to have the public better informed about the limitations of medical care as well as its benefits. The challenge is to educate the patient without encouraging further distrust of physicians and their work.

Changing expectations is an exercise in modifying the culture of medical care. This process requires changing perceptions of how particular health and illness incidents are to be handled, and such modified conceptions may involve as much adjustment for the physician as for the patient. Extreme examples are the redefinition of the appropriate way to die and the development of hospices, with many preferring a less frantic end in the company of their loved ones and sympathetic health personnel to the stupor and high technology associated with the intensive-care unit. The growth of technology has shaped services to a larger degree than patients' needs or desires or prudent expenditure patterns would justify. Third-party payment has made it possible to finance new technology without tough consideration of whether its benefits outweigh its costs. Cultural redefinitions would encourage patients to demand different ways of dealing with many problems.

As patients become better educated about the value, but also about the risks and limitations, of many medical procedures, they may be less likely to demand dangerous interventions that are unnecessary. Mothers may become less enthusiastic about tonsillectomies and routine x-ray studies, and patients with ordinary colds, weight problems and insomnia less demanding of antibiotics, amphetamines and barbiturates. Moreover, as patients become better informed, less responsible physicians will have greater difficulties in carrying out inappropriate procedures and treatments. The task is fairly subtle, and the challenge is to teach patients to question constructively and physicians to respond to such questioning appropriately and in a manner that builds on the patient's trust in the physician's competence and good intentions.

Factors Affecting the Production of Services

In recent years there has been increased attention to the training of physician assistants and nurse practitioners, to the development of health-maintenance organizations and to improved information systems and managerial practices. These may all be ways to increase efficiency in the production of services. Medical care in western countries is dependent on advanced technologies and expensive personnel. The ordinary medical encounter depends less on communication and clinical judgment and increasingly more on a battery of expensive diagnostic procedures and laboratory tests. The bias in medical care is toward what Fuchs has called the technologic imperative[10]—a tendency to take action, whatever the cost, if it offers even a slight possibility of utility. This situation increases the costs of medical care without evidence that the benefits exceed those of adopting a modest approach.

Methods of production refer to the way in which problems are handled, the time devoted to each case, the routine procedures performed and the apportionment of tasks among personnel. For example, one Kaiser plan provides a multiphasic health examination performed largely by technicians as a substitute for the more traditional annual examination performed almost exclusively by physicians. Also, clinicians and clinics may vary in the amount of time that they schedule for new and routine visits, the procedures conventionally performed with new patients and modes of dealing with routine problems. Production of services may be affected in four ways: by changing the mix of personnel involved; by changing the technologic inputs; by changing the content of the encounter; or by changing the auspices of care. For example, nurse practitioners can substitute for physicians quite successfully for certain types of care, as a variety of studies have demonstrated,[11] and many aspects of care can be transferred to nurses, physician assistants and others in a way that improves the productivity of the physician.[12] Similarly, specialists and subspecialists in primary-care settings order more procedures than family physicians and general practitioners and have longer encounters.[13] Although such production methods may involve higher quality, the benefits derived from a more intensive technical approach in ambulatory settings remain conjectural.[14] The use of laboratory and many other diagnostic and technical aids can be contained not only to reduce cost and limit iatrogenic diseases but also to improve the quality of care.[15] Shifting the auspices of care may involve considerable economies as well. Hospital-based care for a particular problem is almost always more expensive, and ambulatory hospital-based practices use more procedures than free-standing practices and thus increase the costs of care. For hospital care, studies in relation to a wide variety of conditions suggest that length of stay can be reduced without any demonstrable medical consequences.

There is a compelling need for investigation of the relation between production methods and patient outcome. Although there is an implicit bias in medical practice that more is better, alternative production methods that devote time to knowing the patient and communicating effectively may yield more valuable results than increasing the intensity of technology. When the "art of medicine" and social care are considered, the role of functional alternatives becomes more obvious.

Functional Alternatives to Existing Medical-Care Patterns

Developments in medical technology, unless of a preventive type such as immunization, tend to increase the costs of a typical medical encounter. As more is known and as more can be done, patients' expectations increase, and they demand increased coverage for medical care. To facilitate the effective use of physician resources, it is desirable to shift to other sectors to the extent possible the services that nonprofessionals and other types of professionals can provide as well and at less cost.

Although estimates vary depending on the criteria used, there is agreement from both clinical judgments and the epidemiologic evidence that much of the demand for medical care arises from conditions that physicians are powerless to change or that are simple in terms of the kinds of care required.[16] The utilization of medical care is influenced by illness behavior[17]—the varied ways in which persons identify, define and evaluate symptoms and what to do about them. Three modes of illness behavior are most relevant here. The first consists of many patients with common self-limited problems that may cause discomfort for a short time but little harm and in any case are not amenable to effective medical intervention. The second are a large variety of minor complaints that can be treated successfully but in which self-care can serve as a suitable substitute with modest self-care aids. The third, and most problematic, are the relatively large numbers of patients with mild and moderate depressions, anxiety, psychosomatic discomforts and insomnia who frequently come to physicians seeking relief of distress, support and reassurance. Epidemiologic surveys suggest that at any given time approximately one fifth of the population may be characterized in this way. Those that come to physicians may be truly suffering, but the hurried and technical stance of the physician in busy ambulatory settings may contribute little to providing the support and comfort that these patients require. The problem of care is made even more difficult because these patients did not explicitly acknowledge the nature of their discomforts, mask these problems with presentations of vague physical symptoms and often resist psychologic redefinitions of their distress.[18]

Although physicians must continue to deal with many of these problems and must do so more capably, alternatives exist through development of self-help groups, improved community networks of social support and a variety of voluntary and professional counseling and information services. To the extent that such services are developed, are defined as legitimate and avoid excessive professionalization of personnel, they are likely to reach more people at lower cost than the current medical-care structure. However, because many such problems will continue to be first recognized through the medical-care system, physicians must learn to work co-operatively with other helping services and make referrals to them. Opportunities for linking self-help and other community helping services to the mainstream of medical care will vary with the reimbursement system.

A model that is instructive is Planned Parenthood. Although the provision of contraceptive services has been seen as a medical function, and physicians continue to do a great deal in this area, many persons are not effectively reached through the medical sector. Planned Parenthood clinics, staffed largely by nonphysicians, reach many needy people, providing them with levels of assistance and instruction often unavailable from busy physicians. More time may be given to each client for careful instruction, questioning and feedback.

Care for the elderly is an area with large potential for alternative types of service. Old people inevitably have chronic illness, and the financing structure encourages a reliance on medical and particularly hospital care. Medicare has brought many benefits to old people who have serious medical problems that require and can benefit from appropriate interventions. But simple social measures that contribute to the continued participation of the elderly and to a sense of meaningful activity can often do more to promote their well-being than narrow technical interventions. Perceived health among the elderly is less positive among persons with a history of depression, who feel neglected and whose morale is low,[19] and self-ratings of health are the strongest correlate of life satisfaction among old people.[20] Medical practice has also become entirely too dependent on total institutional care for old people. Although this development is a product of other trends in the society, existing social policies do little to facilitate the encouragement of independence and continued community functioning among the old. The type of "institutionalism" characteristic of many nursing homes is destructive of human morale,[21] and such facilities should surely be the last resource.

Although this discussion is focused on theoretical options, it is prudent to remain aware that medical care is one of the largest industries, and large sectors of the population depend on it for their employment.[22] Any change in the direction of medical care must be accomplished by retraining of health workers for a variety of new functions such as helping persons to remain in community housing and to function at their highest possible level, providing homemaker services and supervising activity, exercise and recreation. Employees, through their unions, have increasingly used their political leverage to oppose the closing of institutions or the merger of services. Efforts to revise priorities will require widespread co-operation, community commitment and wise planning.

The Role of the Health Sciences

Most of the alternatives for cost containment in the long run depend on the acquisition of basic and applied knowledge that identifies causes and effective interventions in disease, that facilitates community prevention and behavior modification and that provides information on how the medical-care system is working and how its quality and efficiency can be improved. The causes of most major diseases remain unknown, and efforts are mostly ameliorative. Halfway technologies, as Lewis Thomas[23] has noted, are enormously expensive in relation to the uncertain results achieved. The future depends on improved basic knowledge that promotes primary prevention and more targeted treatments.

In the behavioral field much rhetoric is devoted to the ideas of responsibility for health and self-care. The patterns of behavior, however, that require modification are complex responses that have their roots in social and economic patterns, in values and aspirations, modes of socializing the young, peer influence and the mass media, and in many other factors that are only poorly understood. Although society seems prepared to rush ahead with large-scale programs, it seems less willing to invest in the rigorous research necessary that will give a better understanding of the behaviors that should be changed and the ways in which they might successfully be modified. The questions are numerous. To cite some examples: Is clinical depression related to patterns of learned helplessness, and can such patterns be unlearned? Can biofeedback technics be used to facilitate self-regulation of noxious physiologic states, and what long-term effect can it have on the occurrence of illness and disability? Does the modification of Type A behavior traits associated with coronary heart disease affect the occurrence of disease or its course? What types of psychologic and social management best contain disability associated with chronic disease, and how can social supports prevent secondary disability often associated with illness?

Health-services research, in contrast, focuses on the organization, financing and quality of care.[24] It deals with questions of distribution of care, access to care and outcomes. It evaluates the consequences resulting from innovations in health personnel, new technologies and modified ways of delivering care. It examines the costs and benefits of various alternatives and the manner in which new practices are adopted and implemented. It studies the effects of different patterns of remuneration on physicians and varying incentives and cost-sharing obligations on patients. In short, health-services research deals with many issues reviewed in this paper that remain problematic and require further conceptualization and inquiry.

Alternatives for Rationing Medical Care

How consumers use services, how services are produced, and the acquisition of basic understanding of disease, intervention and health-services provision are all long-term issues. Each area not only involves important gaps in knowledge and understanding but also must confront substantial political resistance. Thus, although some improvements in the areas discussed may be anticipated, it is inevitable that more direct forms of rationing will also be imposed. The stringency of such rationing will depend on the success in using the resources already invested in health care with greater efficacy and efficiency.

Rationing may be applied to affect the patient, the physician or the structure of medical-care programs. Fee-for-service and cost-sharing devices such as coinsurance and deductibles impose barriers to access and use among potential patients. Capitation payment requires physicians to make harder decisions on their allocation of time and efforts among patients. Fixed prospective budgeting similarly demands that administrators make more explicit decisions than typical concerning the provision of varying types of manpower and facilities and types of services.

Coinsurance and deductibles are intended to share costs with patients and to inhibit unnecessary use of services. They affect the behavior of the poor more than the affluent, however, and create problems of equity. Moreover, they inhibit the use of care for serious as well as trivial complaints, are costly and burdensome to administer and may encourage distortions in patterns of care to avoid the requirement of such payments. Although cost sharing may affect the use of ambulatory care and drugs, it has less certain effects on hospital utilization that involves decisions made largely by physicians. These decisions are more likely to respond to rationing than to indirect pressures through the patient.

The concept of implicit rationing refers to established limitations on the resources available to any provider of care such as fixed prospective budgets and restrictions on sites of care, hospital beds or specialty positions. These decisions are implicit because they do not specify what services should be provided or what assessments physicians should make, but achieve their effects by placing greater pressures on doctors to make hard allocation choices. Explicit rationing, in contrast, involves direct administrative decisions such as exclusion of certain types of services from insurance coverage, limitations on the availability of specific types of visits or procedures, prereview of the use of expensive procedures, concurrent utilization review, required intervals between the provision of specified services and limits on total benefits. Although physicians favor an open-ended system in which they can make whatever judgments seem medically desirable, the function of both explicit and implicit rationing is to restrict options.

Implicit, as compared with explicit, rationing is viewed as more consistent with physician autonomy and clinical responsibility. The hypothesis is that resource limitation encourages the physician to define priority of need more carefully and distinguish between services that are more or less necessary. However, because of the uncertainty of much of medical practice and the ambigous links between processes of care and outcomes, judgment by clinicians is likely to vary a great deal, reflecting training and style of practice as much as rigorous criteria of effectiveness.[25] Moreover, physicans engage in complex and subtle interactions with patients and may find it difficult to deny services demanded by more sophisticated, knowledgeable and educated patients, in contrast to those who may be more needy but also more passive and accepting of whatever they get.[26] Although it is widely assumed that eliminating economic incentives in physician decision making leads to more appropriate decisions, professionals also respond to personal needs and desires for prestige and recognition. Physicians paid on capitation devote fewer hours to patient care, refer patients to other facilities more readily and may be more inflexible and less responsive in dealing with patients.[27]

Explicit rationing involves direct control over allocative decisions. It entails judgments on budgetary allocations, on the appropriate mix between physicians and other health workers and on the relative distribution of resources among levels of primary, secondary and tertiary care. Moreover, administrators can exclude payment for procedures that are likely to yield low benefits or that are high risk in relation to benefits, or they can specify when such procedures can be performed, or by whom, through requirements for prereview or by specification of necessary credentials for eligibility for reimbursement. Although planned rationing seems like a reasonable approach, it is highly susceptible to public pressures and political influence and does not necessarily result in a fairer allocation of resources.[28] Also, although in theory allocation decisions made on an aggregate base are probably better than individual clinical judgments, data in most clinical areas are not sufficiently firm to justify detailed explicit control, and there is the further danger that those who develop guidelines and regulations become too far removed from the complex uncertainties and contingencies of practice, from the large variability that is evident among patients and from the kind of sensitivity that comes from working with clinical problems.

It has been argued that asking physicians to ration services is to violate their primary responsibility to the patient to do everything possible.[29] Although the ethic of doing everything possible is increasingly unrealistic in the face of biomedical advances,[30] explicit rationing helps shift much of the responsibility for limiting services from the physician to an impersonal third party. Although this step may reduce potential conflicts between patients and doctors, it has serious disadvantages for both. It may seriously limit the physician's professional discretion and the opportunity to respond creatively to unique aspects of the clinical situation. It removes responsibility from the patient to a more distant authority—one that will be more impervious to appeal or to persuasion.

In the forseeable future any system of national health insurance introduced will be a mix of rationing by consumer cost sharing and by implicit and explicit methods. There is relatively little firm knowledge about the effects of different methods of rationing on patients, physicians and the types of relations that evolve between them, and this is a serious question for the near future. The goal is to find a mix of technics that are responsive to patient need, that protect the best aspects of physician discretion and clinical judgment and that protect the public purse.

The choices are not easy, and any serious system of rationing will impose hardships on some. The United States is a wealthy country and is capable of providing a very high level of care. To the extent that opportunities to improve the production of services, and to affect consumer need and desire for them, are taken seriously, they will relieve some of the pressures for more forceful rationing in the future. If rationing is repugnant to health professionals, they must do what they can to contribute to progress on these other fronts.

Acknowledgment

Supported in part by the Robert Wood Johnson Foundation (Dr. Mechanic was the recipient of a John Simon Guggenheim Foundation Fellowship).

References

1. Mechanic D: The growth of medical technology and bureaucracy: implications for medical care. Milbank Mem Fund Q 55:61–78, 1977

2. McKeown T: The Role of Medicine: Dream, mirage, or nemesis? London, Nuffield Provincial Hospitals Trust, 1976
3. Lave LB, Seskin EP: Air pollution and human health. Science 169:723–733, 1970
4. Farquhar JW, Maccoby N, Wood PD, et al: Community education for cardiovascular health. Lancet 1:1192–1195, 1977
5. Robertson LD: Behavioral research and strategies in public health: a demur. Soc Sci Med 9:165–170, 1975
6. Haggerty RJ: Changing lifestyles to improve health. Prev Med 6:276–289, 1977
7. Institute of Medicine: A Strategy for Evaluating Health Services: Contrasts in health status. Vol 2. Washington DC, National Academy of Sciences, 1973
8. Screening in Medical Care: Reviewing the evidence. Edited by T McKeown. London, Oxford University Press, 1968
9. Ley P, Spelman MS: Communicating with the Patient. London, Staples Press, 1967
10. Fuchs VR: The growing demand for medical care N Engl J Med 279:190–195, 1968
11. Rabin D, Spector K: Factors that affect new practitioner performance in practice setting. Presented at the Physician Assistant/Nurse Practitioner Manpower Symposium, Airlie, Virginia, 1977
12. Reinhardt UE: Physician Productivity and the Demand for Health Manpower: An economic analysis. Cambridge, Massachusetts, Ballinger, 1975
13. Mechanic D: General medical practice: some comparisons between the work of primary care physicians in the United States and England and Wales. Med Care 10:402–420, 1972
14. Beeson PB: Some good features of the British National Health Service. J Med Educ 49:43–49, 1974
15. Brook RH, Williams KN: Evaluation of the New Mexico peer review system 1971–1973. Med Care 14:Suppl:1–122, 1976
16. White KL, Williams TF, Greenberg BG: The ecology of medical care. N Engl J Med 265:885–892, 1961
17. Mechanic D: The concept of illness behavior. J Chronic Dis 15:189–194, 1962
18. Mechanic D: Social psychologic factors affecting the presentation of bodily complaints. N Engl J Med 286:1132–1139, 1972
19. Maddox GL: Some correlates of differences in self-assessment of health status among the elderly. J Gerontol 17:180–185, 1962
20. Palmore E, Luikart C: Health and social factors related to life satisfaction. J Health Soc Behav 13:68–80, 1972
21. Townsend P: The Last Refuge: A survey of residential institutions and homes for the aged in England and Wales. London, Routledge and Kegan Paul, 1962
22. National Commission for Manpower Policy: Employment Impacts of Health Policy Developments (Special Report No. 11). Washington, DC, 1976
23. Thomas L: On the science and technology of medicine. Daedalus 106:35–46, Winter, 1977
24. President's Science Advisory Committee Panel: Improving Health Care through Research and Development. Washington, DC, Office of Science and Technology, 1972
25. Freidson E: Doctoring Together: A study of professional social control. New York, Elsevier, 1975
26. Hetherington RW, Hopkins CE, Roemer MI: Health Insurance Plans: Promise and performance. New York, Wiley-Interscience, 1975
27. Mechanic D: The Growth of Bureaucartic Medicine: An inquiry into the dynamics of patient behavior and the organization of medical care. New York, Wiley-Interscience, 1976

28. Cooper MH: Rationing Health Care. New York, Wiley, 1975
29. Fried C: Rights and health care—beyond equity and efficiency. N Engl J Med 293:241–245, 1975
30. Mechanic D: Rationing health care: public policy and the medical marketplace. Hastings Cent Rep 6:34–37, 1976

18

Small Area Variations
in Health Care Delivery

John Wennberg and Alan Gittelsohn

Recent legislation has extended planning and regulatory authority in the health field in a number of important areas. The 1972 amendments to the Social Security Act provide authority for regulating the construction of facilities and establish Professional Standard Review Organizations (PSRO's), which are accountable for setting standards and evaluating professional performance. Phase 3 of the Wage and Stabilization Act of 1970 and state insurance commissions provide authority for regulating dollar flow by controlling the price of services and the price of insurance.

Taken together, this legislation influences major factors determining how a specific health care organization performs—the expenditures it can incur, the facilities and manpower it can use, and the kind and amount of services it produces. While the immediate effects of these decisions are on an institution, there are important questions concerning their effects on the communities that receive the services: How much in the way of resources, money, manpower, and facilities is expended for the residents of the community? What cases are treated and what types of therapy employed? How do decisions made by the public sector change the situation? Answers to these questions depend on statistics that describe, on a per capita basis, the input of resources, and the production of services, and the effect of these on health status. If this information were available for the different communities of a region or state, it would be possible to appraise the impact of regulatory decisions on the equality of distribution of resources and dollars and the effectiveness of medical care services.

For technical and organizational reasons, documentation of the health care experience of populations has been restricted to large political jurisdictions such as counties, states, or nations. Studies at this level of aggregation have used indicators that support direct comparisons among areas. Relationships between the supply of

SOURCE: *Science* 182 (14 December 1973):1102–1108. Copyright © 1973 by the American Association for the Advancement of Science. Reprinted by permission.

manpower, facilities, and expenditures and the population on whose behalf these resources are expended are expressed as direct input rates—for example, the number of physicians or beds per thousand persons or per capita expenditures. The quantity of services produced or the kinds of cases treated are commonly expressed as "utilization rates." Examples of hospital utilization statistics include the number of days the residents of an area spend in hospital (called "patient days"), number of surgical procedures, and number of cases of a given diagnosis admitted—all expressed in terms of events per thousand persons at risk. These rates are commonly calculated on an annual basis and, for utilization, are often "age-adjusted" so as to remove the effect of age as an explanation of difference between regions.

With these indicators, a number of studies have shown population-based differences in use of health manpower and facilities and delivery of health services that are difficult to attribute to differences in illness rates. In Canada, hospital utilization rates tend to be as much as 50 percent higher than rates in the United States. Variations among states are large. Medicare expenditures per enrollee in 1970 were twice as high in California as in Arkansas. The number of physicians per thousand persons has been up to three times higher in some states than in others. International comparisons and studies of regions within states show that there are large differences in the rate of delivery of specific surgical procedures.[1]

In 1969, there was implemented in the state of Vermont a data system that monitors aspects of health care delivery in each of the 251 towns of the state. When the population of the state is grouped into 13 geographically distinct hospital catchment, or service, areas, variations in health care are often more apparent than they are when the population is divided into fewer, larger areas. Population rates can be used to make direct statistical comparisons between each of the 13 hospital service areas. Since the medical care in each area is delivered predominantly by local physicians, variations tend to reflect differences in the way particular individuals and groups practice medicine. The specificity of the information in Vermont's data system makes it possible to appraise the impact that decisions controlling facility construction, price of insurance, and the unit price of service have on the equality of distribution of facilities and dollars in a given population.

Our article examines the extent to which bed and manpower use, expenditures, and utilization vary among hospital service areas in Vermont. Variations in utilization appear to indicate that the effectiveness of a given level of delivery of service is uncertain. Observed variations in expenditure are evaluated in terms of lateral transfer of income among areas; these variations occur because in some areas the average price of insurance is consistently higher than the average per capita reimbursement. Past decisions of the Price Commission and the state Hill-Burton agency are reviewed. Evidence is presented that their decisions, based on institutional rather than population data, have served to increase rather than decrease inequalities among areas.

Concepts and Measures

Vermont, with a population in 1970 of 444,000, is largely rural; less than a third of its population lives in towns and villages of over 2500 persons. The state is organized administratively into 251 towns, averaging 37 square miles (1 square mile = 2.59

square kilometers) in area and ranging in population from 10 to 35,000 persons, with a median of 825. Relevant health data on these populations have been assembled from sources of data and published reports in order to develop files on hospital discharges, nursing home admissions, Medicare reimbursements, health manpower, facilities, expenditures, and mortality.[2] Several special surveys were necessary to complete data sets. At least the following data on each patient are available: age, sex, residence, length of stay in the hospital, diagnoses, procedures, and referring and attending physician and surgeon. In this article, data describing the use of medical services are based on 1969 abstracts, hospital and nursing home discharges, and home health agency encounters—except for (i) Medicare Part B, which is an estimate for 1972 based on all billings processed by the third-party carrier during January and February 1972, and (ii) a 1963 patient origin study by the Vermont State Health Department that we used to estimate 1963 hospital expenditure rates. We believe that, for each set of data used in this article, the information includes nearly the total medical care experience of the populations under study.

To study particular health care systems, we have grouped towns into hospital service areas surrounding the hospital used most frequently by the town (Table 1 and Figure 1). Residents of towns located near a hospital show a high percentage of use of the local facility. In the smaller, more rural towns located between hospitals, use tends to be divided. Service areas were set up to maintain geographic continuity.[3] Three areas contain two hospitals in the same community, while the remainder contain a single facility. Three areas with populations under 5000 have been excluded, leaving 13 available for analysis. Twelve of the 13 areas are served primarily by community hospitals, varying in bed size from 32 to 207. Area 12

TABLE 1. Admissions, by Area of Residence, and Admissions to Hospital in Area, by Residential Status, Vermont, 1969.

| Hospital service area | Population | Number | Admissions, by area of residence | | | Admissions to hospital in area | | |
| | | | Hospital | | | | | |
			Local (%)	Referral (%)	Other (%)	Number	Residents	Non-residents
1	12,301	2,669	81	12	7	2,526	85	15
2	18,762	2,798	85	13	2	2,910	82	18
3	7,960	1,271	72	11	17	1,658	55	45
4	18,057	3,060	86	7	7	3,735	71	29
5	31,187	4,469	85	6	9	5,171	74	26
6	32,886	5,637	82	16	2	5,550	83	17
7	12,175	2,595	76	18	6	2,703	73	27
8	20,170	3,676	86	10	4	3,538	89	11
9	20,624	3,454	75	14	11	3,235	80	20
10	53,389	8,553	86	10	4	8,515	87	13
11	53,002	8,544	82	14	4	7,713	91	9
12	109,750	17,423	95*		5	24,400	67	33
13	13,200	1,760	63	31	5	1,862	60	40

*Includes referral hospital, which was located within the service area.

FIGURE 1. Map of Vermont showing minor civil divisions, the Vermont town (lighter line). Darker line shows boundaries of hospital service areas. Circles represent hospitals. Areas without circles are served principally by hospitals in New Hampshire.

contains a 100-bed community hospital and a 587-bed teaching hospital, which serves both as a community hospital and as the principal referral hospital for most of the state. A university hospital in New Hampshire is the principal referral hospital for three service areas located in the eastern portion of Vermont.

Measures of health care delivery include age-adjusted utilization rates and indices of manpower, facilities, and expenditures. Estimates of manpower and facility use in a geographically defined population present technical and conceptual difficulties. Patient mobility, regionalization of specilized services, and the absence of residential qualifications for admission to facilities contribute to these difficulties. While the number of hospital beds physically situated in an area provides a rough index of supply, it does not account for hospitalization of residents outside the area or for local use by nonresidents. We have estimated the rate of input of hospital beds based on total hospital utilization by the population of each service area. Estimates are made by allocating facilities to each service area of the state in proportion to the use of these facilities by residents. For example, if 10 percent of a hospital's admissions originate in a given service area, 10 percent of its beds are assigned to that area. The sum of all hospitals' contributions to the service area provides a measure of total input of beds to that service area.[4] In effect, the procedure assigns an average cost and unit of effort to each admission.[3,4]

A similar allocation approach has been used to develop estimates of nursing home beds, hospital expenditures, medical manpower, and nonphysician hospital staff. For each physician acting as attending physician or surgeon in a hospital, one full-time equivalent (FTE) physician was allocated to the area, in proportion to the distribution of his patients' residences. The sums within specialty classes and over-all physicians for a given service area have been used as estimates of physician labor input. Active physicians in the state who did not use hospitals (fewer than 10 percent) were assigned to the hospital service area in which their practices were located. Estimates of expenditures for hospitals and nursing homes by each hospital service area were based on allocations of total reported institutional expenditures, according to frequency of admission of area residents. Medicare Part B expenditures were obtained directly from reimbursement data on the unit record claims forms.

Variations among Service Areas

Tables 2 and 3 present the ranges of variation in expenditures, input of manpower and facilities, and production of health services, measured by utilization, for the 13 hospital service areas of Vermont.

Variations in use of resources. We recorded variations in hospital bed rates and nonphysician manpower over the 13 service areas. The number of beds per 10,000 persons ranged from 34 to 59, and the number of hospital personnel per 10,000 persons from 68 to 138. Nursing home beds varied from 9 to 65, nursing home employees from 8 to 52. The input of physician effort ranged between 8 and 12 FTE physicians per 10,000 persons, with individual specialties having wider var-iations. The input of internists and general surgeons was more than twice in some areas what it was in others; pediatrician and obstetrician effort was more than ten times greater in some areas than in others.

Variations in expenditures. The estimated 1969 per capita expenditures for hos-pital services were more than twice as much in some areas as in other; for nursing some services, they were more than five times greater in one area than another. The range of reimbursements for Medicare Part B among Vermont communities is larger than that among the 50 states—and reimbursements can be up to twice as great in one state as in another.

Estimated Part B expenditures in 1972, primarily reflecting physician services, ranged between $54 and $162 per capita in the population over age 65. Greater

TABLE 2. Variation in Utilization, Facilities, Manpower, and Expenditure Rates among 13 Hospital Service Areas, Vermont, 1969.

Resource input and utilization indicators	Lowest two areas		Entire state	Highest two areas	
Utilization rates per 1000 persons					
Hospital days	1015	1027	1250	1380	1495
Hospital discharges	122	124	144	195	197
All surgical procedures	36	49	55	61	69
Respiratory disease	10	13	16	29	36
Genitourinary disease	8	9	12	15	18
Circulatory disease	12	13	17	22	25
Digestive disease	15	16	19	24	26
Nursing home admissions, age 65 and over	14	22	52	81	81
Beds per 10,000 persons					
Hospitals	34	36	42	51	59
Nursing homes	9	26	42	62	65
Personnel per 10,000 persons					
Hospital	68	76	100	119	128
Nursing home	8	23	32	51	52
FTE physicians per 10,000 persons	7.9	8.4	10.3	11.9	12.4
General practice	1.5	1.7	2.5	3.8	4.4
Internal medicine	.9	.9	1.6	1.7	2.6
Pediatrics	.1	.2	.7	1.1	1.2
Obstetrics	.1	.2	.7	1.0	1.1
General surgery	.7	.9	1.1	1.5	1.7
Expenditures per capita ($)					
Hospitals	58	63	89	92	120
Nursing homes	5	13	17	25	26
Medicare Part B, age 65 and over (1972)	54	84	127	147	162

variations are seen for specific types of Medicare services. Reimbursement for diagnostic x-ray services differed by 400 percent over service areas, electrocardiogram reimbursements by 600 percent, and total laboratory services by 700 percent.

Differences in expenditures among areas apparently are long-standing. Estimated expenditures for hospital services in 1963 correlated .82 with 1969 rates.[5] Both 1963 and 1969 hospital expenditures were related to 1972 Medicare reimbursements (4 = .79 and .75, respectively). Of Medicare reimbursements to physicians, 52 percent were for services delivered in hospitals.

Variations in utilization. Hospital discharge rates for all causes, adjusted for age composition, varied from a low of 122 to a high of 197 per 1000 persons. The Vermont rate of 144 was similar to the rate for the New England region. Age-adjusted hospital patient days per 1000 persons ranged between 1015 and 1495. Nursing home admissions rates varied from 1.3 to 10.0 and were not significantly correlated with hospital admissions or expenditures.

The variations in use of hospitals for broad classes of diagnoses and in rate of performance of surgical procedures is shown in Table 2. The annual rate at which respiratory conditions were treated in hospitals showed marked differences among areas: the lowest rate was ten admissions per 1000 persons, the highest 36. Defining surgery as procedures (excluding biopsies) generally requiring anesthesia and per-

TABLE 3. Variation in Number of Surgical Procedures Performed per 10,000 Persons for the 13 Vermont Hospital Service Areas and Comparison Populations, Vermont, 1969. (Rates adjusted to Vermont age composition.)

Surgical procedure	Lowest two areas		Entire state	Highest two areas	
Tonsillectomy	13	32	43	85	151
Appendectomy	10	15	18	27	32
Hemorrhoidectomy	2	4	6	9	10
Males					
Hernioplasty	29	38	41	47	48
Prostatectomy	11	13	20	28	38
Females					
Cholecystectomy	17	19	27	46	57
Hysterectomy	20	22	30	34	60
Mastectomy	12	14	18	28	33
Dilation and curettage	30	42	55	108	141
Varicose veins	6	7	12	24	28

formed in operating rooms, the total surgery rate varied between 360 and 689 per 10,000 persons over the 13 service areas.

The age-adjusted rates of nine frequently performed surgical procedures are exhibited in Table 3. The rates varied tremendously over the 13 service areas, the most striking example being tonsillectomy, which varied from a low of 13 to a high of 151 cases per 10,000 persons. The neighbors of the highest tonsillectomy area recorded rates of 32, 35, 38, and 39. Primary appendectomy rates ranged from 10 to 32, with a state total of 18 per 10,000 persons. Similar variations were observed in the rate of removal of prostates, gall bladders, and uteri. For each of the procedures, the differences in rates were statistically significant by chi-square tests.

The per capita number of days spent in a hospital, reflecting the combined effect of medical decisions about admissions and about length of stay, also varied widely over the Vermont service areas. Tonsillectomy days per 10,000 persons, adjusted for age, varied from 17 to a high of 314. Appendectomy days ranged from 42 to 204, prostatectomy from 65 to 524, hysterectomy from 64 to 616, and mastectomy from 21 to 198.

Evaluation of Variations

There are a number of indications that there is uncertainty concerning the value of a given level of health care delivery. This appears to apply to the aggregate of all services, as measured by expenditures, as well as to specific procedures. Expenditures for hospitalizations and for physician services under Medicare Part B show no significant correlation with age-adjusted mortality ($r = .05$ and $.01$) and perinatal mortality ($r = .08$ and $.10$). Hospitalization rates for specific admitting diagnoses and for surgical procedures are almost ten times greater in some hospital service areas as in others. Neither the medical literature nor our data provides substantial clues as to whether spending six times more for electrocardiograms or seven times more for laboratory services results in greater improvement in health for persons age 65 and over than does a lesser expenditure. Tonsillectomy provides an example of variability. Assuming that age-specific rates remain stable, there is a 19 percent probability that a child living in Vermont will have his tonsils removed by age 20. The probability recorded in the highest service area is over 66 percent, as contrasted with probabilities ranging from 16 percent to 22 percent in the five neighboring communities, which are ostensibly similar in demographic characteristics. There are no data available that would allow us to relate these variations to the prevalence of tonsilitis, but it appears that the variations are more likely to be associated with differences in beliefs among physicians concerning the indications for, and efficacy of, the procedure.

Because of lack of data on the prevalence of disease in the Vermont communities, the relationship between health needs and input of physician services cannot be measured directly. However, since a general association exists between serious illness and age, the age structure of the population should be an indicator of the relative health needs of a community. The percentage of the population 65 years of age and over varied among service areas from 8.9 to 13.4. Multiple regression analysis of the influence of community size, population structure, and income on supply of physicians shows that physicians concentrate their efforts in the more populous service areas and in those with higher per capita incomes. They tend to avoid areas with larger proportions of persons age 65 and above. The multiple correlation between rate of physician input and population size, income, and age structure was $r = .90$, a result significant at the .001 level. The simple correlations were .51, .60, and —.64, respectively. Hospital service areas with small populations have proportionately more persons age 65 and over. These data suggest a poor correspondence between physician input and population need.

Factors intrinsic to the operation of the health care system appear to be responsible for variations in performance. The results of most medical encounters are primarily dependent on medical decisions and the economic circumstances and behavior of patients seeking care. The wide variations in utilization rates between different Vermont populations suggests that provider and consumer behavior is rarely uniform, even when economic circumstances are more or less constant, as they are for Medicare enrollees. The observation that native Vermonters of similar age and income use physician services approximately one-half as often as nonnatives suggests the importance of consumer behavior.[6] Further evidence suggests that, once a patient is "in the system," the actual services he receives depend in part on provider characteristics.

The correlation between the total surgery rate and the input of physicians performing surgery is positive and significant, with $r = .64$. Table 4 presents simple correlation coefficients for three categories of physicians and selected surgical procedures ranked by complexity.[7] The supply of general surgeons is positively related to the surgery rate at all levels of surgical complexity and for nearly all types of individual procedures. Populations served by proportionately higher numbers of general practitioners performing surgery tend to have lower surgery rates for the more complex procedures and higher rates for the less complex procedures. By contrast, a higher supply of physicians who do not perform surgery, particularly

TABLE 4. Simple Correlation between Medical Manpower Rates and Rates for Surgical and Diagnostic Procedures in 13 Vermont Hospital Service Areas, 1969.

| | Physicians performing surgery | | |
Procedure	General surgeon	General practitioner	Physicians not performing surgery
Surgical			
Most complex	.54	−.25	−.19
Intermediate A	.21	−.21	−.04
Intermediate B	.68	.12	−.42
Intermediate C	.55	.16	−.39
Least complex	.48	.40	−.27
Mastectomy	.48	−.20	−.24
Hysterectomy	.39	−.21	−.34
Cholecystectomy	.48	.24	−.04
Appendectomy	.31	.14	−.28
Tonsillectomy and adenoidectomy	.46	.42	−.28
Varicose veins	.07	.31	−.16
Dilation and curettage	.08	.38	−.42
Total	.54	.19	−.44
Diagnostic			
Electrocardiogram	−.12	−.36	.41
Laboratory	−.06	−.30	.30
X-ray	−.10	−.28	.35

internists, tends to be either associated with lower surgery rates or unrelated altogether.

The ancillary, nonsurgical diagnostic procedures obtained through Medicare Part B exhibited opposite trends. Electrocardiogram, x-ray, and laboratory expenditure rates among persons age 65 and over tend to correlate positively with the supply of internists and other physicians who do not perform surgery and to be unrelated to the supply of surgeons. All three kinds of procedures were positively related to the input of hospital beds and nonsurgeons, the multiple correlations being r = .69 for x-rays, .67 for electrocardiograms, and .82 for laboratory procedures.

Variations in the health care experience of different Vermont populations may be explained more by behavioral and distributional differences than by differences in illness patterns. We are, of course, unable to state which utilization rates are "normal" or which input rate represents a better allocation of resources. For example, for a given kind of surgery or diagnostic technique, it is not clear which rate indicates that medically unnecessary procedures are being performed or that not enough is being done. An important reason for uncertainty is that few prospective studies under controlled circumstances have been performed. Because the outcome of one type of service compared to another (or to none at all) is often not known, the variation in therapeutic and diagnostic procedures observed among different Vermont communities cannot be strictly evaluated.[8] However, given the magnitude of these variations, the possibility of too much medical care and the attendant likelihood of iatrogenic illness is presumably as strong as the possibility of not enough service and unattended morbidity and mortality.

While interpretation of variations in utilization poses rather than answers questions concerning effectiveness, the data provide prima facie evidence of inequality in the input of resources. Variations in expenditure, sustained in large part through third-party payment mechanisms, pose questions of equity, since the price of insurance is not adjusted to reflect these differences. Under Medicare Part B, the enrollee and the federal treasury each contribute $68 annually (1972). The lowest per capita reimbursement in the B areas of Vermont is $54, 20 percent less than the average amount contributed by the enrollee. In contrast, the highest reimbursement in the state was $164 per capita, representing a benefit recovery that exceeded combined patient and federal contributions by more than 20 percent. A similar situation obtains for private medical and hospital insurance. Under Blue Cross-Blue Shield, premiums are established on a Vermont- and New Hampshire-wide "community rating" basis, with residents of low expenditure areas paying similar amounts for similar levels of coverage as residents of high expenditure areas.

Price Commission and Hill-Burton Decisions

A review of the decisions of the Hill-Burton and Price Commission agencies in Vermont reveals the difficulties of public regulation without the benefit of information about variations in per capita facility and manpower input, expenditures and service utilization. The information available to these agencies is based on indicators that do not describe the experience of the population receiving services from the regulated health care organizations. They cannot take into account the effect of their decision on lateral transfer or income nor appraise the value of increasing the rate of delivery of services.

The planning method used by the Hill-Burton agency in Vermont is similar to that used in most states. The formula for estimating hostpial bed need is based on manifest demand, as measured by hospital patient days (without reference to the population), and an average daily patient census equal to 80 percent of a hospital's total beds. Population coverage enters the formula only through projected growth. No account is taken of admissions of area residents to other hospitals or of services delivered to nonresident patients (which in area 12, for example, comprise over one-third of all admissions). The single underlying premise is that demand, in terms of the total number of days a hospital bed is used, constitutes need.

Application of the Hill-Burton technique is illustrated by the recommendations for more hospital beds in the state contained in the 1971 Vermont State Plan[9] (Table 5). The recommended increase bore little relation to existing bed input and service utilization. The greatest increment (44 percent) was assigned to a hospital with a bed rate of 5.9 and a patient day rate of 1495, both the highest in all 13 areas. The lowest increment (2 percent) was assigned to a hospital with a bed rate of 3.4 and a patient day rate of 1015, both the lowest in all 13 areas. The second highest increase (27 percent) was assigned to a hospital of intermediate service utilization and bed rates, but with an average daily census approaching 100 percent and a mean length of stay exceeding state average by 22 percent.

Since 1969, three hospitals in Vermont have undertaken construction projects financed under the Hill-Burton program. Assuming that the geographic distribution of patients using these facilities remains the same, the increased number of beds in

TABLE 5. Population-Based Indicators of Bed Input and Patient Days, Compared to Bed Need as Determined by Hill-Burton Planning Formula (Vermont service areas, ranked by 1969 bed input rates).

Hospital service areas*	Bed input (per 1000 persons)	Patient days (per 1000 persons)	Percent increase in bed need
1	5.9	1495	44
2	4.4	1361	5
3	4.3	1027	22
4	4.0	1292	27
5	3.7	1174	18
6	3.7	1132	8
7	3.6	1077	6
8	3.4	1015	2

*Contains only hospital service areas that are coterminous with Hill-Burton areas.

two of the hospitals will move the bed input rates in these service areas to the second and third highest positions in the state. Examination of subsequent years' data will be required to ascertain whether the increase in bed input is associated with increase in service utilization or a general drop in average daily census.

The Federal Price Commission's control of expenditures on hospitals is indirect, since it is concerned with limiting increases in prices of routine, daily hospital services and of ancillary services, including x-ray and laboratory procedures. Decisions are based on unit pricing structure and other institutional contingencies and do not take volume of services into consideration. Since the expenditure rate for a community represents the combined effects of volume and unit price, both factors must be considered. For hospital expenditures, the per capita rate may be expressed as a function of the patient day rate and the average cost per patient day. Over the 13 service areas, volume and the weighted average cost per day each accounted for nearly 40 percent of the variation in per capita hospital expenditures, with the rest attributed to differences in the amounts of ancillary services. The implication is that the two factors are of about equal importance in the determination of expenditures.

Since the inception of phase II Price Commission guidelines limiting annual increases in unit service price to under 6 percent, three Vermont hospitals have initiated requests for exceptions. The first was withdrawn voluntarily before a public hearing was held, the second was denied, and the third was approved. The hospital receiving the exception was the principal institution serving an area that ranked first in the state in hospital manpower input rate and first in patient day rate. While the average patient day charges were relatively low, the high admission rate resulted in a per capita expenditure rate that ranked second highest in the state.

Both the Hill-Burton and the Price Commission decisions have served to *increase* variations in health care in Vermont. The decisions of the Price Commission to award a selective exception to a Vermont area with high hospital manpower use and expenditure rates will probably increase the disparities among areas and increase horizontal transfer of income. The building of additional facilities in high utilization areas presumably will lead to increased utilization. Both decisions probably will result in the delivery of additional health services without evidence that additional health services are of specific value for the receiving population.

For the Medicare and Medicaid populations. PSRO's are assigned broad respon-sibility for establishing the medical necessity of current health care patterns within their particular regions. This responsibility suggests that PSRO's are the appropriate agency to come to grips with the meaning of variations in population-based utiliza-tion rates among different medical care markets. However, rational inquiry into the meaning of variations in probability of surgical removal of organs, diagnostic proce-dures, hospital admission case mix, and so forth, will often require formal testing of an hypothesis concerning the relations between health care and outcome. This is a long-range proposition and requires a high level of organization and technical attainment, which will not be easily developed. However, specifically in those instances where public decisions precede the implementation of new health care technology (for example, the installation of coronary intensive care units), it seems reasonable to tie implementation to the willingness of PSRO's to develop explicit clinical standards and perform prospective evaluations of the effect of the technol-ogy on medical outcome. This strategy could convert the essentially uncontrolled experiments in health care delivery that characterize the majority of health care efforts to a situation in which both the profession and the public can reach some certainty concerning the value of the investment.

Short of engaging in extensive evaluation of alternative levels of service, PSRO's could provide a valuable service by reviewing medical necessity through more routine methods of peer review. Population-based indicators of resource input, utilization, and mortality are particularly useful in identifying communities whose health care experience deviates from regional averages. These profiles can aid in the selection of areas for further review, when the likelihood is high that medically unnecessary care is being delivered. Further, continuous monitoring of these com-munities will identify the successes and failures of PSRO's in dealing with perfor-mance that departs from regional norms.

Summary and Conclusions

Health information about total populations is a prerequisite for sound decision-making and planning in the health care field. Experience with a population-based health data system in Vermont reveals that there are wide variations in resource input, utilization of services, and expenditures among neighboring communities. Results show prima facie inequalities in the input of resources that are associated with income transfer from areas of lower expenditure to areas of higher expenditure. Variations in utilization indicate that there is considerable uncertainty about the effectiveness of different levels of aggregate, as well as specific kinds of, health services.

Informed choices in the public regulation of the health care sector require knowl-edge of the relation between medical care systems and the population groups being served, and they should take into account the effect of regulation on equality and effectiveness. When population-based data on small areas are available, decisions to expand hospitals, currently based on institutional pressures, can take into account a community's regional ranking in regard to bed input and utilization rates. Proposals by hospitals for unit price increases and the regulation of the actuarial rate of insurance programs can be evaluated in terms of per capita expenditures and income transfer between geographically defined populations. The PSRO's can evaluate the wide variations in level of services among residents in different communities. Coordinated exercise of the authority vested in these regulatory programs may lead to explicit strategies to deal directly with inequality and uncertainty concerning the effectiveness of health care delivery. Population-based health information systems, because they can provide information on the performance of health care systems and regulatory agencies, are an important step in the development of rational public policy for health.

References and Notes

1. For example, see J. P. Bunker, *N. Engl J. Med.* 282, 135 (1970); A. M. Burgess, Jr., T. Cotton, O. L. Peterson, *ibid.* 273, 533 (1965); C. E. Lewis, *ibid.* 281, 880 (1969); L. S. Reed and W. Carr, *Soc. Sec. Bull.* 31, 12 (1968); S. Shapiro, L. Weiner, P. M. Densen, *Amer. J. Public Health* 48, 170 (1958); Department of Health, Education, and Welfare, Social Security Administration, *Reimbursement by County and State; Medicare 1970* (Government Printing Office, Washington, D.C., 1972).

2. Each data has been modified into a standard format and code system for individual physicians, diagnoses, procedures, and other key variables. Since 1969, hospital discharge abstracts have been collected for all patients discharged from the 18 short-term, voluntary hospitals in the state and for Vermont residents discharged from referral hospitals in New Hampshire and New York. Patient information from hospitals participating in the Professional Activities Study (PAS) was obtained from the Commission on Professional and Hospital Activities, Ann Arbor, Michigan. Four smaller, nonparticipating hospitals were surveyed directly by the staff. Although hospitalization of Vermonters outside these areas has not been recorded, the resultant underreporting is estimated to be less than 3 percent for all classes of admission. Nursing home admission files and home health agency files have been obtained through staff surveys of each institution and agency in the state. Medicare Part B information has been obtained from the third-party carrier responsible for reimbursement. Problems of data accuracy are bound to arise in multi-institutional studies. Despite extensive consistency checks made by PAS and by the staff, the reliability of certain items of information is primarily dependent upon the initiators of the record form. This applies particularly to diagnosis and cause of death, where the criteria are unspecified and the extent of diagnostic workup highly variable. Simple facts such as sex, age, dates, place, and procedures appear to be recorded with a reasonable degree of accuracy, based on independent reabstracting of samples of records from several institutions. An age-specific rate relates to the events in the population within a particular age category. An age-adjusted rate is the weighted average of age-specific rates within a given group. It is designed to account for differences in age structure among populations and to permit direct comparisons between areas and groups. In this article, the weights are the proportions of persons in each 5-year age group in the entire state. Since many of the occurrences under consideration are highly age-dependent, we have used age-adjusted rates whenever the relevant data were available to us.

3. In contrast to highly urbanized centers, the hospital service areas of Vermont tend to be relatively discrete and seldom overlap. Vermont residents in 1969 took place in the service area of residence. Maternity patients, patients requiring general surgery, and most patients with medical conditions that comprise the majority of admissions are

usually hospitalized in their own area. Patients with conditions requiring specialized services were more often referred to other areas. In the community hospital areas, about two-thirds of the admissions for neoplasms were treated locally and one-third treated in referral hospitals. Neoplasm was the major diagnosis in 5 percent of hospital admissions.

4. The major effect of the allocation procedure on estimated bed supply was to distribute one-third of the 587 beds of the referral hospital to the other hospital service areas in and outside of the state. In four areas, the number of allocated beds was lower than the number of resident beds, reflecting overlap at service boundaries. In none of the community hospital service areas did the allocated number of beds differ from the resident beds by more than 20 percent.

5. Significance level for simple regression coefficient with 11 degrees of freedom: r: .55 = 5 percent; .68 = 1 percent.

6. Unpublished report prepared by the Northern New England Regional Medical Program for the Connecticut Valley Health Compact, Springfield, Vermont, 1971.

7. Blendon's classification of level of difficulty of surgical procedures was used [R. J. Blendon, thesis, Johns Hopkins University (1969)].

8. Cochrane has recently summarized technical and organizational problems encountered in appraising the effectiveness and efficiency of health services. Failure to subject particular medical actions to randomized, controlled trials is, in his opinion, the major reason for uncertainty about the value of many common preventive, therapeutic, and diagnostic activities [A. L. Cochrane, *Effectiveness and Efficiency* (Nuffield Provincial Hospital Trust, London, 1972)].

9. Modified from *Vermont State Plan for Construction and Modernization of Hospital and Medical Facilities* (Vermont State Health Department, Burlington, 1971).

10. Partially supported by Public Health Service grant PHS-RM0303. We gratefully acknowledge the help of W. Gifford, R. Gillim, P. Hickcox, K. Provost, and J. Senning in the work leading to the development of this article.

19

Some Good Features of the British National Health Service

Paul B. Beeson

I was glad to be invited to speak to this audience about the British National Health Service, in which I have been working during the last eight years. I shall not be describing it as a model we should copy here; nevertheless, there are some useful lessons to be learned from it. I must acknowledge that when I moved from Yale to Oxford in 1965 I did not quite realize that a professor in one of England's old universities would have to work in conformation with the guidelines of a huge nationalized industry, but indeed that is the case; and it soon showed me some sharp contrasts with the American way of doing things. I found myself having to take more interest in the problems of medical care from a national standpoint that I had ever done before.

The British System

Let me review briefly certain essential features of the British system. Its stated goal is to provide "a comprehensive medical health service, free and open to all." It started with a bang, so to speak, because on a given day in 1948 the government took possession of all the hospitals and put virtually all the doctors on its payroll. Measures were instituted to ensure a relatively even distribution of doctors over the entire country. Every man, woman, and child was to be enrolled with a general practitioner, who would provide primary care and would arrange for specialist attention or hospital treatment as required.

Now, what is the situation after 25 years? About 50,000 doctors are active in Britain today. A relatively small proportion is engaged in industrial, military, or public health work. About half are in general practice; the other half are doing

SOURCE: *Journal of Medical Education* 14 (January 1974): 43–49. Reprinted by permission of the publisher and the author.

hospital work. In the hospitals are 15,000 junior staff, equivalent to our interns and residents, whereas only 8,000 are of the consultant grade, which includes specialists in all fields.

It is worth emphasizing that only 8,000 specialists staff all the hospitals in a country that has about one-fourth the population of the United States. Obviously, they have to be very carefully distributed. To achieve this, the country is divided into regions, each of which has its quotas. The Oxford region in which I work serves about 2,000,000 people in an area roughly 50 by 40 miles. Our quotas for a few specialties are as follows: general physicians, 46; general surgeons, 41; neurosurgeons, 3; pediatricians, 15; and psychiatrists, 70. For the nation as a whole, the numbers in certain types of specialities are as follows: general physicians, 927; general surgeons, 889; ophthalmologists, 348; pediatricians, 303; neurosurgeons, 74; obstetricians and gynecologists, 589. Compared with America, these numbers look very small indeed. To emphasize this point, note that there are only 927 general physicians for all the United Kingdom; yet by comparison Harvard's Department of Medicine alone has 500 full-time and part-time teachers, and the American College of Physicians has 24,000 members.

In Britain the distribution of posts for specialists is made on the advice of committees which appraise the current situation and try to foresee future developments. To avoid a surfeit of trainees in any one specialty, the Department of Health maintains firm control on the junior positions in the nation's hospitals. Thus it is very hard to establish a new house staff job in a popular field such as general medicine but comparatively easy to do so for certain undersubscribed specialties.

When any consultant post becomes vacant, the opening is announced in the weekly medical journals, and qualified trainees can apply for it. A local committee selects the new consultant from the applicants. It can be seen, therefore, that young British doctors are not free to choose the places in which they will practice their specialties; their options depend on the places that happen to fall vacant at the time they are nearing the end of their training.

While I am dealing with the relatively small number of specialist physicians in Britain, I should like to digress to its effect on clinical teaching in the medical schools. The size of clinical faculties in all British medical schools is fairly uniform, because the number of positions is dependent on government support in accord with national formulas, whether the salary comes via a university or the National Health Service. I have put in Table 1 the relative strengths of Oxford, Harvard, Ohio State, and the University of Washington. As we all know, the size of clinical departments in American medical schools expanded greatly during the past quarter century owing to the initiative of section heads who have secured research grants that included salaries. I realize, of course, that the scale of research is far greater in this country and that there is also a large teaching responsibility for graduates because of the greater numbers of residents and research fellows. I want only to consider this matter of size from the standpoint of undergraduate teaching. As you can see from the Oxford figures, the senior staff strength simply does not allow for much individual or small group teaching. All the full-time people carry out some service work, and the part-time people are National Health Service consultants, each with a full hospital service to maintain. Medical students are, of course,

TABLE 1. Strengths of Clinical Faculties

	Full-time	Part-time
Oxford	69	114
Harvard	840	1,129
Ohio State	400	1,006
University of Washington	520	1,000

assigned to the wards and outpatient clinics, but there is no possibility of attaining a one-to-one teacher-to-student ratio as can frequently be done in the outpatient clinic of an American school. British teachers have to place considerable reliance on such old-fashioned pedagogy as didactic lectures and textbooks. The surprising thing is that I do not find much difference in the products of the two systems. I had previously allowed myself to be persuaded that didactic lectures are a waste of time and that the more teachers one can have in the hospital the better the learning opportunity for the students. It would be an interesting experiment to give the same examination to a sample of the graduating classes of British and American schools and see how they do come out.

Now to return to the work of British doctors in the Health Service. As to the consultants, except for restrictions on choice of location, I have the impression that most are well satisfied with their jobs. Each has security and a good deal of autonomy—his own beds in the hospital, his own team of nurses and junior doctors. The patients he sees have been screened so that comparatively little of his time is spent inappropriately. His income at present ranges from $14,000 to $20,000. In addition, about one consultant in three receives a supplementary merit award, which in a few cases could bring the income up to as much as $36,000. These figures are small when contrasted with American professional incomes, but remember that there is no overhead for office expenses. Moreover, there is no compelling need to pile up capital for retirement because each will receive a government pension.

If we turn now to look at the general practitioner in Britain, we find that dispersal throughout the country is managed in a different way. The government pays each one an annual fee according to the number of patients on his list and aims to have about 2,500 patients per general practitioner. If too many GPs were to try to locate in one place, there would just not be enough income to go around.

In discussions of general practice, one has heard much about the unhappy plight of the British GP. He is described as isolated and forced to work with inadequate office equipment and staff. That did characterize the early days of the Health Service, and it was the principal reason for emigration of some thousands of British doctors. But the Department of Health has energetically set out to improve the conditions of general practice. Incomes have been brought up to a range similar to that of hospital consultants. Funds have been made available for equipping and staffing of offices. The formation of group practices has been encouraged, and many so-called health centers have been built. These are places in which small groups of general practitioners work together. Public health nurses and social workers have been provided. Laboratory services for general practitioners have been established.

Post-graduate teaching centers, now over 200 in number, have been located all over the country. These are equipped with lounges, seminar rooms, and libraries, and GPs receive payment for attendance at post-graduate instruction.

As a result of these measures, their surroundings are more suitable, their isolation has been lessened, and they have predictable hours off duty. The British general practitioner is now far happier, and the problem of emigration no longer exists. A number of them have told me they regard their jobs as more rewarding and more challenging than any in the Health Service. The good ones enjoy the continuing relation with their own group of patients and look on themselves as leaders of small community teams. While at Oxford I have seen a marked change in the career plans of our students. Right now the great majority ot them intend to become general practitioners; this includes some of the top people who could undoubtedly survive the competition for good consultant posts. Incidentally, we have made no change in our teaching and have no department of general practice. What it all seems to show is that careers in family practice can be made attractive to young doctors if the working conditions are improved and the pay is comparable with that of specialists.

How well does the British Health Service really work? There are, of course, many unsolved problems, and there are frustrations from the restrictions of any nationalized business. Nevertheless, my feeling is that the system works surprisingly well. The goal of providing a good standard of medical care for every person without private cost has been achieved, and the health service has the approval of the British people. No politician would dream of suggesting that it be supplanted by something else. I have been interested to note, too, that people belonging to all social classes use it. We see some of Oxford's most distinguished citizens on our ward services, and they accept this quite naturally. But the thing I want to stress most of all is that British doctors themselves approve of the principle of the service. Several medical friends have told me they believe Britain has the best system of medical care in the world. And, when a young doctor returns after spending a year or two training in the United States, I have learned to expect a remark like this, "Well, it was interesting and worthwhile, but I certainly am glad to get back to the NHS."

Now, while talking about good features, I am going to venture to say something about attitudes toward patient care in the teaching hospitals of the two countries. I do so with trepidation, because it entails criticism in an extremely sensitive area. Let me just preface it by saying that I am still an American, proud of many accomplishments of American medicine, and am looking forward to coming back to a new job in this country within the year. But, in general, I have come to feel that more thought is given to the comfort and welfare of the patient in a British teaching hospital. There is less drive to be absolutely thorough, and no special credit comes from solving the diagnostic puzzle in record time. Not uncommonly a patient is sent home for a rest after some uncomfortable procedure. Due to the fact that each consultant controls a small unit throughout the year, it is accepted that house staff will clear important decisions with him. Consequently, the conduct of work seems a little less venturesome, especially if a procedure carries with it risk or discomfort. I have spent a week or two as a visiting professor in this country every year since 1965 and confess that now and then I have felt uncomfortable because of the relentless drive of the diagnostic work-up. Long before 1965 I remember being nettled by the comments of some British friends that our house officers have too much freedom. In rebuttal I used to describe all the checks in our system, but I have had to modify my view on this. While I was writing this paper, I received a letter from a former registrar, who is presently working in one of America's best medical centers. Here is a paragraph:

> I have recently started teaching clinical students, which I am finding a fascinating experience. The students are remarkably keen, and by English standards work very long hours on the ward. The organization of the wards is very curious. The house staff take the attitude that every conceivable differential diagnosis has to be excluded, including all the possible tests, before a diagnosis can be reached. The patients get a pretty thin time, for not only do they have three ward rounds a day (one with the attending and two by the house staff), but they are also subjected to many unnecessary tests. It is not hard to see why medical costs are escalating so much.

In what I have just been saying, my illustrations were in the context of internal medicine, but I think they apply to other fields as well. Certainly, there are figures to show that about twice as much surgery is done in the United States as in Britain. And America seems to rush in all too rapidly with such procedures as coronary by-pass surgery. I tend to attribute these tendencies to the freedom of action that characterizes American medicine at every level of its organization. I think that some constraints may be advantageous.

A national health service has great advantage over our free-enterprise system in terms of economy and avoidance of redundancy. For example, such expensive facilities as those for hemodialysis or cardiac surgery are distributed in Britain according to a national plan and not, as so often happens here, because groups of doctors would like to be able to have these things available in their hospitals. According to HEW figures, the American health industry cost about $83 billion in 1972. The bill for the British National Health Service will be in the neighborhood of $6 billion in 1973. I do not think this vast difference can be explained by higher wages and costs of supplies in the United States.

Personal Views

Now I am going to offer some personal views that I have developed as a result of working abroad for several years. I ought first to repeat what I said at the beginning, namely that the British system would not be suitable for us. It evolved from a different background of medical practice and is tailored to the needs of a small, densely populated country which is politically far more socialistic. Despite these and other dissimilarities, I believe we can make use of their experience in our search for a better American medicine.

As I see it now, the striking thing about the American medical scene is lack of overall regulation. There is no uniform planning and no top guidance. The federal government and several states have tried a variety of schemes to influence the training of medical students and residents, but these efforts have had little effect. Many medical schools and their teaching hospitals have inaugurated programs to involve themselves more in community medicine and to encourage young doctors to go into family practice in localities where they are needed, but these have all been more or less in the nature of experiments and limited in scope. I feel that time for experimenting is short. If we are to avoid a takeover such as that which happened in Britain in 1948, we must achieve better organization.

I understand that a new top level body, the Coordinating Council on Medical Education, has been formed to take the lead in national planning. Any such agency will have to do more than issue hand-wringing statements; it will have to exert powerful pressure, for there is much intertia. A real campaign of education and persuasion will have to be directed at the medical profession if its individual members and its various organizational units are to be convinced that changes are needed. And if one central issue is to characterize that campaign, I would aim at reversing the trend to specialty practice. I would go after it with all the passion we are given to population control throughout the world. Data on specialty practice in America are given by Rousselot in the August issue of the *American Journal of Medicine.* They show that only 19 percent of America's doctors are now in family practice; And extrapolation of present trends indicates that this percentage will fall to six by 1900. Thoughtful students of medical care, such as John Knowles, William Longmire, Robert Ebert, Francis Moore, and Rosemary Stevens, have all issued warnings about the course we are on; nevertheless, our training mills seem to be running unchecked. Note, for example, the recent controversy about neurosurgery in the *New England Journal of Medicine.* This specialty is surely supersaturated in the United States today, yet there was strong objection to the suggestion that resident training be reduced. Let me remind you again how our organization of medical practice contrasts with that in Britain. There are 22,000 in family practice in the United Kingdom and 70,000 in family practice in the United States. There are 8,000 in specialist practice in the United Kingdom and 280,000 in specialist practice in the United States. Here is a country with one-fourth the population of the United States, where the current trends in health statistics are better than ours, where every person has access to a good standard of medical care, and where the total expenditure for medicine is far below ours. The striking difference is economy in the use of specialists. To me this is the most obvious reason why America has a badly distributed, excessively costly system. If we could begin to shift our ratio of specialists to primary physicians toward that of Britain, I think we would cease to hear about the need for more doctors or for training paramedical assistants. I have no doubt at all that a good family doctor can deal with the great majority of medical episodes quickly and competently. A specialist, on the other hand, feels that he must be thorough, not only because of his training but also because he has a reputation to protect. He, therefore, spends more time with each patient and orders more laboratory work. The result is a waste of doctors' time and patients' money. This not only inflates the national health bill but also creates an illusion of doctor shortage when the only real need is to have the existing doctors doing the right things. We now have board-certified internists spending more than half their time with patients who have functional complaints and board-certified pediatricians checking well babies or treating the self-limited viral infections of childhood. Good family doctors can do these as well and sometimes better.

American professors of medicine often tell me that the well trained internist is the best answer to America's need for a family physician. I cannot agree with that. Today's well trained internist is hospital-oriented and wants to practice "big" medicine. He has had little training in such important branches as pediatrics, dermatology, or nonsurgical gynecology. If we really believe that the internist is the family doctor of the future, we ought to change our system of training and strengthen links between the American College of Physicians and the Academy of General Practice. The subspecialties of internal medicine have their own organizations, anyway.

Where should we begin our efforts to achieve better balance? Undoubtedly, it should be in our medical schools and teaching hospitals. Other places will follow that lead. Unfortunately, however, American medical schools and their associated residency training programs are overwhelmingly oriented toward certification by some board or other. Resistance to change springs from the fact that present systems of resident training are traditional and convenient. Clinical teachers rely on them in every phase of their work: patient care, research, and undergraduate instruction. If American clinical professors today are like I was in 1965—and my guess is that many of them are—their main attention is on local hospital and medical school affairs and research. Although they may be somewhat troubled by criticism, they are loath to make radical changes. Many of the gestures that have recently been directed at a larger world seem to me quite inadequate. It is just not enough for a famous teaching hospital to organize a minor family practice training program by affiliation with some nearby community hospital. I feel we need to have our most respected teaching centers putting the highest priority on training programs suited to national needs. Perhaps we should try to break down some of the elaborate sectional barriers that we created during the lush 1950s and 1960s. This would not inevitably impair the quality of research or training.

Our profession is almost certainly going to have to give up a share of its traditional independence and free enterprise. Some kind of control of medical practice already exists almost everywhere else in the world. We must realize that we have a sort of monopoly on an essential service—a service that has lately become hugely expensive but still has major shortcomings. Admittedly, many of the difficulties relate to social and economic factors outside our sphere, but we must accept responsibility for excessive independence of action. I speak here of action at all levels—the house officer, the head of an academic section, the individual medical school, the certification board, the private practitioner. It would be miraculous if such an arrangement added up to a good system of health care for the country.

Some agency will have to take charge; and, of course, the federal government is the most likely one. Wouldn't it be gratifying, though, if we could exhibit the statesmanship and self-discipline to do it ourselves?

20

Care of the Aged:
An English Lesson?

Helen Smits and Peter Draper

The United States and Great Britain face a period of significant change in the delivery of health care. Many Americans have concluded that there is a "crisis" in the distribution and cost of medical care in the United States and have joined in debate about what should be done to end the crisis. The British, who are faintly surprised by and sometimes deservedly proud of the accomplishments of their 25-year-old National Health Service, have, as their next step, reorganized its basic structure. A new administration is scheduled to begin operation in April of this year.

Particularly during this changeover, it would seem wise to see whether there are any lessons to be learned from comparison of the two systems. Although some comparitive studies may take insufficient account of historical and other cultural differences, Americans can still learn much about their own complex and very variable patterns of organization by carefully comparing them with those of other countries, particularly when the comparison focuses on the way institutions influence clinical activities and the ways in which clinicians and their patients exert a reciprocal influence on institutions.

In this paper we contrast British and American experiences, with particular emphasis on those areas where Britons may offer valuable lessons to Americans. Services for the elderly have been chosen as the focus for our discussion to allow a concrete comparison of the way institutional structure and national financing affect the care of an important group of patients. By looking at the services provided for the aged, light is thrown on the ways in which the provision of a nationwide and public health service has affected the physicians' area of responsibility. The institutional structure of the National Health Service (NHS) is also considered, particularly with respect to its current reorganization. The issues of "bureaucracy" and "central

SOURCE: *Annals of Internal Medicine* 80 (1974):747–53. Copyright © 1974 by the Annals of Internal Medicine. Reprinted by permission.

control," currently under discussion in Britain, are important to American clinicians, who face the prospect of increased Federal involvement in the provision of medical care and who are concerned about the effects that involvement may have on their clinical independence.

The Health Care of a Key Group

The evolution of specialized care of the elderly in Britain since World War II has been strongly influenced by the divided administrative structure of the NHS. Three relatively independent branches have composed the bulk of British health care: the general practice services, the hospitals, and the local authority health services. Hospital services, as in the United States, have included large and growing outpatient departments in addition to the care of inpatients. British specialists have typically worked only within the hospital system, even in fields, such as pediatrics, which in the United States consist chiefly of office practice. The local authorities have provided services such as home nursing care ("district nursing"), which has been increasingly organized in close association with general practitioners (in "attachment" schemes), and have also had responsibility for public health and preventive medicine. To the American visitor, one particularly striking aspect of this arrangement has been the sharp separation between the care that the general practitioner has given at home or in his office and that given by the specialist in the hospital.

The specialty of geriatrics has developed steadily within Britain since the establishment of the NHS. It is a support service for the general practitioner that is a model of health care, centered on the patient and the overall population rather than on an organ and its diseases. The multiple medical, psychological, and social problems of elderly patients are the concern of the geriatrician. The field demands skills in rehabilitation medicine and some psychiatry, in addition to the usual skills of the internist. Furthermore, geriatricians are by necessity coordinators and collaborators who have a key place in multispecialty teams that care for the aged; they help individual nurses, social workers, occupational and physical therapists, and others to work together to provide an effective overall service. In Britain this means working with community services and the resources provided by many voluntary agencies, as well as integrating specialized care with that given by general practitioners.

All the care for the elderly in hospital beds or outpatient departments is not provided by geratricians; a patient with an uncomplicated pneumonia or myocardial infarction may still be admitted to an acute medical ward. The total number of geriatricians has increased rapidly; in England and Wales it rose from 93 consultants in 1962 to 280 in 1972.[1] Not surprisingly, there has been some debate within Britain about whether geriatrics should be a separate specialty. The consultative services of the new specialists are well used, however, and the aim is to provide one geriatrician per 100,000 total population, one for approximately 12,000 elderly patients,[2] which, with the strong interest in developing a balanced geographic distribution of specialists, should make geriatric consultation easily accessible to any general practitioner and his patients.

Geriatrics is a relatively new field, and its services and facilities are by no means evenly distributed throughout Great Britain, although steps are being taken to accomplish this, as in other specialties. Certain individual geriatricians, who have been able to persuade hospital boards and local authorities to support innovative techniques, deserve much credit for the increased interest in the field in recent years.[3] One example is the consultative geriatric clinic established by Ferguson Anderson and Nairn Cowan in collaboration with the local health authority in Rutherglen, Scotland (1). The many routine examinations done at this clinic and at others patterned after it have helped to identify those problems for which preventive medicine has real value for elderly patients, for instance, nutrition, accident prevention, and the early detection of psychiatric disorders. Other experiments in preventive care are being undertaken, such as the use of geriatric health visitors to do screening[4] (2) and encouraging general practitioners to participate in the screening procedures. Executive Councils often help general practitioners to organize their lists of patients on an age/sex basis, so that the number of patients at risk can be identified.[5] General practitioners now receive higher capitation rates of payment for elderly patients than for those under 65 years old, to provide some compensation for the greater workload in the care of the aged, especially those general practitioners who have an above average proportion of elderly patients.

"Progressive patient care," the grouping of hospitalized patients according to their medical nursing needs, has been applied to geriatric services in some parts of Britain (3). Distinctions are drawn between *initial treatment beds,* where concentreated nursing care is available; *continuation care beds,* where stress is placed on rehabilitation; *halfway house beds* for the convalescent; and *long-stay beds* for those who may require prolonged or permanent care. More important than the exact grading of beds, however, is the flexibility that the responsible geriatrician has in using the resources available to him, so that the needs of the local community are met. One use is the *holiday admission,* whereby an infirm patient is admitted to a geriatric hospital for a short stay so that the famiily may go on vacation or simply get a rest.

Another imaginative use of hospital facilities is the geriatric *day hospital,* modeled after the one established by Cosin at Oxford (4). The purpose of these centers, to which over 20,000 new patients were admitted in 1972,[6] is to provide a facility where hospital-based evaluation and treatment may be carried out without admitting the patient. Many patients in day hospitals are undergoing continued rehabilitative treatment, others are being evaluated over a period of days in a congenial setting, and still others attend primarily to give relief to the relatives who are caring for them.

At best, the members of a geriatric service give much thought to the social and environmental factors that allow old people to remain independent. Although the amount of care available for patients at home varies among different local authorities, it seems very extensive everywhere in Britain to an American physican accustomed to the problems of public health nursing in an urban setting. Besides the usual nursing and homemaker services, some remarkably humane and imaginative arrangements have been developed in some areas, such as domiciliary night nurses and *night watchers,* who sit up with ill patients so that the family may sleep.

Despite the major advances outlined above, of course many problems remain. Geriatrics as a specialty has grown in stature over the past years, but it is still relatively poorly housed, funded, and staffed. Nursing positions and house staff jobs in geriatric programs are difficult to fill in many parts of the country. The number of beds is not always adequate; such facilities as day hospitals, night watchers, and holiday admissions are increasing steadily but are not uniformly available. In addition, the teaching of geriatrics to medical students is, like the teaching of general practice, limited. Some schools, particularly in Scotland, include rotations on geriatric wards in their curricula, but many British medical students are still given a restricted view of the scope of clinical practice. The job satisfaction derived from dynamic, imaginative, and humane care of the aged is not yet part of the experience of every clinical student, which certainly has an adverse effect on recruitment to this new field. There are problems at the level of house staff education as well. For example, Wright (5) suggests that geriatric services would benefit if senior specialists (consultants) spent more time on teaching and allowed house officers to become more involved in the overall rehabilitation of patients.

The organizational division of the three branches of the NHS has had a particularly unfortunate effect in an area such as geriatrics, where coordination of the efforts of the general practitioner and the hospital service and the supportive services provided by the local authority is essential. In particular, much of the work of geriatric consultants, in dealing with the social and economic effects of chronic illness, overlaps that of the general practitioner. Although many British physicians accept the dissociation between the general practitioner and the hospitalized patient, even arguing that these physicians "don't use beds well," there is some tendency toward the integration of the general practitioner into the hospital side of geriatric care.[7] There is also a reverse move, to allow geriatricians to hold outpatient clinics in the larger health centers, bringing them where they can collaborate more closely with general practitioners. Despite progress in this area, Wright suggests that much more can be done to bring general practitioners into close alliance with other members of the geriatric team (5).

The Side Effects of Medicare

Although geriatrics is recognized as a specialty in Britain and is developing rapidly there, in the United States it barely exists. There are geriatric physicians scattered throughout the country, but the geriatrician is a rare figure at medical schools, and specific beds for geriatric care are almost nonexsitent. The overall care of the elderly is usually undertaken by internists and general practitioners, who may have had no training at all in such critical areas as rehabilitation medicine and psychiatry and who have to work with limited community health and social services.

Medicare (Title XVIII of the Social Security Act) perpetuates the existing situation. American physicians, edgy about the prospect of "government control" of their clinical activities, actually work under a degree of control by insurers, both public and private, that usually astonishes British doctors who study or experience it. The influence is subtle but pervasive and can even affect the way in which physicians and other health workers define their roles. For example, Part B of Medicare pays for doctors' fees and hospital out-patient services but specifically excludes routine physical check-ups, routine foot care, and immunizations unrelated to an injury or immediate risk of infection (6). This situation means that a consultative geriatric diagnostic clinic like Rutherglen could be established only for private, paying patients. By refusing to pay physicians for preventive medicine, Medicare actually discourages them from dealing fully with some major clinical problems. A pertinent example is the fractured femur, a condition that is epidemic among the old and that reaches staggering proportions in some subgroups, especially the oldest women. With a responsibility to provide complete care to the population at risk, many British geriatricians are involved in accident prevention; they define the risk factors that lead to falls and attempt, where possible, to reduce them. Given the cost, both emotional and financial, of healing a fracture, this seems a problem that warrants enthusiastic American interest. The specific exclusion of foot care from Medicare benefits is also surprising; British geriatricians are convinced that early treatment of foot problems prevents the development of more severe and disabling illness.

The care of hospitalized geriatric patients in the United States is similarly profoundly influenced by the type of funding supplied through Medicare. The concept of "progressive patient care" was well understood when the legislation was written, and an effort was made to provide resources that could shorten hospital stays, such as home health agencies and extended care facilities (ECFs). The usefulness of such facilities is best documented in conditions such as femoral fracture (7), but they may also provide care for patients with strokes, myocardial infarctions, and a host of other illnesses. Although cost savings have been stressed as the reason for developing convalescent facilities in the United States, more humanitarian considerations should be given equal or perhaps greater weight. A service aimed at providing good acute care is neither a pleassant nor an appropriate place for recovering from a long illness. A good convalescent facility, focused on the needs of the recuperating patient, can provide a far more cheerful, relaxed, and rehabilitative atmosphere.

The American record on providing good, generally available facilities for convalescence is poor, and there is little evidence that the situation has improved since the passage of Medicare legislation. One midwestern study of the impact of Medicare on community health resources found that "hospital administrators chose to emphasize the acute care needs of the elderly and used Medicare as a justification for expansion of acute care facilites. Comparable efforts were not made to develop extended or intermediate care facilities, rehabilitation centers and so on" (8). The per capita expenditure on health care for individuals over 65 years old confirms this finding. Between 1967 and 1970, a period of rapid increase both in costs and overall expenditure, the *percentage* of the total expenditure going to nursing homes increased by only 0.2%, from 16.07% of the total to 16.27%. During this same time, acute hospitals, already receiving the lion's share of 44% of the total in 1967, managed to increase it to 47% by 1970 (9). These figures suggest that no significant deployment of resources away from the acute hospital bed is taking place. In addition, in 1970 a Congressional study group found that improvement in the quality of extended care facilities, which was one of the aims of the original legislation, had not taken place (10).

The same midwestern study indicated that the amount of home help provided in the region had increased but that coordination among the various services was very poor. The per capita expenditure for health professionals other than physicians for the geriatric age group is still so small (9) that it is difficult to believe that home nursing and other services are adequate in many parts of the country. A study devoted exclusively to home health services in Massachusetts supports this impression (11).

The Paperwork Problem: A Bureaucracy of Fear

If one intent of the Medicare legislation was to provide less expensive—and, we believe, more humane and appropriate—alternatives to acute hospitalization, and if studies suggest that these alternatives are not available, it is important to determine the cause. One answer can be found in the restrictions on transfer from the acute hospital: "These restrictions take the form of additional physician documentation of the reasons why a patient requires skilled nursing care: diagnostic data, treatment plans, etc., all of which makes the physician wonder why he should go to the trouble of transferring the patient in the first place" (7).

This problem of paperwork, although one frequently raised by physicians in arguments against more government involvement in medical care, has not received the scholarly consideration it deserves. Physicians, nurses, and other health workers in the United States are required to justify their activities to the fiscal intermediaries in a manner that surprises foreign visitors—even foreign visitors from "socialized" systems of medical care. American physicians who equate state medicine with a snowstorm of paperwork would do well to spend a day or two with a British general practitioner or geriatrician. The British physician gives far less time to paperwork, both in absolute terms and on a per-patient basis, than does his American colleague. Records of a doctor's "list" of patients are kept by the Executive Council; a general practitioner is required to report only the changes in this list, such as births and deaths, to receive his capitation payments. The few forms that are required are principally related to X-ray and pathology investigations and to the items for which the physicians have negotiated extra payments, such as immunizations and Papanicolaou smears.

Physicians and trained nurses are expensive, and if most of them in the United States are spending a great deal of time filling out or checking forms that often repeat material already available in the medical records, then ways of reducing this part of their workload should be found. Forms may sometimes be so detailed and time-consuming that the desire to avoid completing them actually influences medical care (7). Moreover, forms convey the attitudes and values of those who designed them and who process the information contained in them. Physicians may quite justifiably feel that the government—and the insurance companies—see doctors and other health workers as needing constant monitoring and control. Actually the monitoring carried out to date has not prevented some major scandals in the disbursement of Medicare and Medicaid funds, so we may also ask whether our current system of collecting information is an *effective* way of checking on physicians' actions. Clearly, it is an extremely costly way of accounting for private and public funds.

1974 or 1984?

Paperwork, however, is just one effect of bureaucracy operating at the level of the individual doctor/patient contact. The more basic problem is not how many forms a physician signs but how health care is to be organized. Americans would do well to consider in detail the debate over the first major reorganization of the British NHS, which starts to come into effect in April. Both major political parties in England have agreed for some years now that it is necessary to integrate the three previously separate branches. The bringing together of general practitioners, public health services, and the hospitals under a single administration might be expected to have automatically beneficial effects. Nevertheless, some major objections have been raised against the current plan.

To grasp the issues in the debate, any visitor to Britain needs some historical perspective on the sharp division between the general practitioner and the hospital-based consultant. Details of this history are available in Rosemary Stevens's book, *Medical Practice in Modern England* (12); a briefer summary of the history of general practice is available in a review article by a British general practitioner, J. Tudor Hart (13). Although no simple generalization can convey the complexity of the modern situation, it is safe to say, as a first approximation, that the historical difference between general practitioners and consultants was at least partly one of social class. The professional antecedents of the general practitioners were apothecary-surgeons, relatively poor and relatively uneducated men who served for centuries as the chief source of medical care for the laboring classes. Specialist consultants, on the other hand, trace their history back to the better-educated physicians and to the academic surgeons who achieved comparable status at a later time. Although initial training in medical schools has been the same for both groups for more than a century, and there has been much social mobility in Britain during that period, echoes of the old class distinctions can be heard in the way in which general practitioners and consultants regard one another. When the NHS was instituted, the division between the two groups was so great that it was thought necessary, for practical political reasons, to preserve that division in very separate administrative structures (14). When general practitioners today express concern about an integration that might rob them of their autonomy, they are partly indicating their fear that the hospital-based consultants, with their long history of greater prestige and power, will dominate the service. In fact, the proposals for full integration of the NHS was so unattractive to the general practitioners that they exerted considerable and successful political pressure to be allowed to retain a largely separate administration. As a result, the Executive Councils (which administer their contracts) are preserved as relatively independent bodies in all but name in the new "integrated" structure (15, 16).

The details of the integration now being proposed do indeed suggest that the hospitals and hospital-based consultants—with their particular clinical attitudes—will continue to dominate. The main bodies that will control services under the Department of Health and Social Security—the Regional Health Authorities—are likely to speak for the hospitals' viewpoint, partly because most of their technical and administrative staff have had the bulk of their experience in the hospital field and partly because most of the lay people appointed to sit on the authorities have also had their previous experience with hospitals. The hospital influence can also be seen in the fact that the basic unit of organization in the new structure will be a "district." This was originally defined as a catchment area of the *district general hospital,* the basic acute hospital in British hospital planning since the midfifties; a district's population is now planned to be in the range of 200,000 to 500,000. It can reasonably be argued that the basic unit for health planning could have been a group of general practice or health center with a population of 25,000 to 50,000, a size similar to that of the American Health Maintenance Organization (HMO). The experience in both countries is that a group of this size can provide almost all the ambulatory and domiciliary services necessary for complete care of patients. Only hospital beds and some very complex diagnostic and therapeutic services will need to be provided for a larger population. When planning begins at the health center, the medical needs of the community are the first consideration; when planning begins at the hospital, then the needs of the institution and of its secondary and tertiary specialists—both medical and managerial—are very likely to assume priority.

Another reason why the consultants' point of view may dominate the new NHS is that a major contribution to planning will come from district teams, which will look at the needs of special patient groups. The elderly are likely to be one of these groups; others suggested are the mentally ill, the handicapped, and mothers and children. There is widespread suspicion, however, that hospital and consultant interests will control this planning. At least some general practitioners are certain to be on such planning teams, but the structure almost imposes an orientation to the secondary and tertiary specialist. The special problems and challenges of primary care will continue to be undervalued by the planners.

But the reorganization of the British National Health Service is interesting for another reason. It embodies a particular kind of business and governmental management that many commentators, both students of organizations and business experts, fear is inappropriate for a service such as health care (17). The present Secretary of State for Health and Social Security, Sir Keith Joseph, introduced his proposals by suggesting that they mainly differed from earlier plans put out by the previous administration in "the emphasis they place on effective management." If "effective management" simply means good organization, then who could object to this aim? What the British critics are suggesting, however, is that the particular kind of management that has been chosen is inappropraite for medical care. Members of a Royal Commission (18), writers on management in the *Financial Times* (19) and the *Times* (20), and an academic group that made the original studies of the theories used in the reorganization (21, 22) suggest that its main effect would be to increase the bureaucratic characteristics of the service. This allegation is made for several reasons, including the key principle of the reorganization, which has essentially been one of control from the top; delegation downward rather than decentralization or devolution.

From Crisis to What?

To American observers it may seem surprising that British critics should suggest that a streamlining of the administration of their health service could increase its bureaucratic characteristics. Is the NHS not synonymous with the bureaucratic organization of health care? The answer is no. The truth, as opposed to the propaganda, is that any large organization, whether government or private, can have different degrees of bureaucratic characteristics. Since the best modern health care in economically developed countries requires some kinds of organization on a large scale, it seems more sensible to pose the question, In what ways is that organization best arranged? How can local rather than bureaucratic responsibility best be encouraged?

In the United States, one particularly disturbing aspect of the current discussions of the various proposals for increased Federal involvement in health care is that very little attention is being paid to this issue. The debate focuses on costs and extent of coverage, often ignoring the very real question of whether the institutions that will administer the funds are sufficiently flexible and sensitive to provide the support needed in a field as rapidly changing and as intimately involved with human values as health. Senate Bill HR3, introduced by Senator Kennedy, has been attacked on the ground that it will create a new, monolithic Federal bureaucracy (23, 24). Yet the other major bills now pending *all* preserve the present insurance structure largely as it is, without attempting to increase the responsiveness of those fiscal organizations to either consumer or provider (25, 26). The Kennedy bill, which would encourage the mass hiring of insurance employees into the new civil service jobs, does attempt to deal with the problem of representation by establishing a Federal National Health Security Advisory Council, on which would sit representatives both of consumer and provider groups (27). This council would study the operation of the bill and advise the decision-makers on policy. Whether or not this kind of "counter-bureaucracy" is the most appropriate mechanism for consumer participation is one of the questions that should be at the center of discussions on our future health care system.

We do not mean to disparage the accomplishments of those who run the major health insurance schemes or to belittle their recent efforts at leadership. We would ask, however, exactly what kind of institutions these are. How do their bureaucracies work? Are the consumer boards effective? Do all providers of care have an equal voice? Certainly some physicians suspect that surgical specialists are favored by insurors, in comparison with, for example, their colleagues in pediatrics and psychiatry. Other lower-paid health professionals have even more of a case for contending that the existing insurance structure supports the prevailing dramatic differentials in income between doctors and other valuable members of the health team, such as podiatrists or physical therapists.

As far as the individual's needs are concerned, flexibility has not been the hallmark of the current arrangements. Consider, for example, the holiday admission. Any physician caring for elderly patients could think of a family or two who would be much helped by such a scheme. But how should doctor, family, and patient set about convincing the appropriate carrier that such a brief hospitalization is beneficial? The relentless utilization committee has its guidelines; who in the chain of command beyond the hospital even has the *right* to change the rulings? Americans may well ask themselves whether they do not already have what opponents of Sir Keith Joseph's reorganization fear for Britain: institutions that bring "to the administration of an essentially human service all the vision and imagination of the cost accountant and all the warmth and compassion of the balance sheet" (28).

One assumption, common to many of the discussions of the various new Federal proposals, is that the best way for the consumer to exert his influence is by exercising his right to choose among insurance policies or among various prepaid packages (24, 26). It is believed that such a choice will in itself give adequate consumer protection. But to make an informed choice among insurance policies necessitates the possession of many facts, to which the consumer often has no access. Such a choice also requires so much training in medical statistics that the average consumer is simply in no position to make and review annually the family decision on the best health coverage for that year. Consumers acting in groups can do better; major contributions in this area have already been made by organizations such as unions. But in a field as complex as health, "buying" a group of doctors or one kind of insurance is a very insensitive way to influence decisions. Furthermore, such influence is largely closed to those most in need—the "poor risks" and the "uninsurable." If all insurance policies exclude "custodial care," then the individual has no way to purchase for himself or his family the equivalent of a holiday admission. With hundreds of such decisions going into the design of any program of health care it is highly unlikely than an individual could, simply by choosing, have much effect on the details that may vitally affect the services available to him and his family. In fact, in such a situation, the relevant policy decisions are made by a comparatively small group of people who are effectively accountable to neither consumers nor providers.

Even when some group, such as a Health Maintenance Organization, undertakes to offer "complete" health services to a community or other population, policy decisions must be made concerning the exact composition of that complete care. Everyone would agree that a functioning HMO must provide X-rays and penicillin for its patients with pneumococcal pneumonia or orthopedists to treat those who break their legs. But, to return to one of our geriatric problems, what should they do about the fractured femur? How much money and effort should be spent on accident prevention? On immunization? On home health aides? To what extent can work opportunities in old age prevent some of the aging process and therefore decrease accidents? In the last analysis, the answers to these questions are not simply technical but involve value judgments and decisions about social priorities. In other words, they are exactly the sorts of decisions that, in a democratic society, should be discussed openly and decided by all who will be affected by them.

Genuine consumer participation is perhaps best seen as a social process that has to be learned. The growing sophistication and organization of American consumers in the field of health means that we have already taken the first major step in this learning process. Consumers, honestly represented, are not likely to let us lose sight of the fact that measurements such as "cost effectiveness" are not in themselves a sufficient basis for decision-making in health and that they may even, in some instances, be a hindrance. It is not cost effective to take good care of the elderly, any more than it is cost effective to take good care of the disabled veteran, but it is the mark of a civilized society.

Geriatrics is little if it is not a team specialty. Consultants, nurses, social workers, and occupational and physical and other therapists, families, and volunteers work together with patients to make aging a time of ability and dignity. Like some other fields of medicine, it can provide a professional and interdisciplinary way of organizing health care; with real involvement of patients and relatives in decision-making, it provides a model of a decentralized, democratic process.

In the United States much needs to be done to distribute our vast medical resources more evenly and to relieve the sick and disabled members of the public and their families of the crushing burden of the costs of health care. But we must be careful that we do not, in the name of justice, retain and even worsen a system that suits bureaucrats and financial wizards but neither the patients nor the professionals who care for them. If, instead, we base our national health care on the team concept and have the courage to open its administration to the irritant creativity and vitality of the consumer movement, we can use the billions of dollars already being spent to purchase what nearly everyone wants: a humane and effective network of care.

Acknowledgment

Grant support: Traveling Fellowship, Royal Society of Medicine Foundation, Inc.

Notes

Footnotes identified by symbols in the source have been gathered into the following numbered list.
1. Statistics Board, Department of Health and Social Security: Personal communication.
2. W. T. Thom, Scottish Home and Health Department: Personal communication.
3. A. N. Exton-Smith: Geriatrics and the National Health Service. Unpublished.
4. A health visitor is a State Registered nurse who typically has an extra year of training that stresses preventive medicine and social services.
5. W. T. Thom, Scottish Home and Health Department: Personal communication.
6. Statistics Board, Department of Health and Social Security: personal communication.
7. W. T. Thom, Scottish Home and Health Department: Personal communication.

References

1. Anderson WF, Cowan NR: A consultative health centre for older people. *Lancet* 2:239–240, 1955
2. Williamson J, Lowther CP, Gray S: The use of health visitors in preventive geriatrics. *Gerontol Clin (Basel)* 8:362–364, 1966
3. Exton-Smith AN: Progressive patient care in geriatrics. *Lancet* 1:260–262, 1962
4. Cosin LZ: The organization of a day hospital for psychiatric patients in a geriatric unit. *Proc R Soc Med* 49:237–244, 1956
5. Wright WB: Misuse of doctors in the care of the elderly. *Lancet* 2:252–253, 1973
6. Title XVIII, Social Security Act, Section 1862
7. Deabler L: Regional planning for effective services in extended care facilities. *Am J Public Health* 62:877–879, 1972
8. Coe RM, Andrews KR: Effects of Medicare on the provision of community health resources. *Ibid.*, pp. 854–856
9. Cooper BS, McGee MF: Medical care outlays for three age groups: young, intermediate and aged. *Soc Security Bull* 34:3–14, 1971
10. Staff to the Committee on Finance, United States Senate: *Medicare and Medicaid:*

Problems, Issues and Alternatives. Washington, D.C., U.S. Superintendent of Documents, 1970

11. Morris R, Harris E: Home health services in Massachusetts, 1971: their role in the care of the long-term sick. *Am J Public Health* 62:1088–1093, 1972

12. Stevens R: *Medical Practice in Modern England.* New Haven, Yale University Press, 1966, pp. 26–37

13. Hart JT: Primary care in the industrial areas of Britain. *Int J Health Service* 2:349–365, 1973

14. *See* Reference 12, pp. 95–105

15. *National Health Service Reorganization: England.* London, Her Majesty's Stationery Office, 1972

16. *Management Arrangements for the Reorganized National Health Service.* London, Her Majesty's Stationery Office, 1972

17. Battistella RM, Chester TE: Role of management in health services in Britain and the United States. *Lancet* 1:626–630, 1972

18. Crowther-Hunt L, Peacock AT: *Royal Commission on the Constitution 1969–1973,* vol. 2, *Memorandum of Dissent.* No 5460-I. London, Her Majesty's Stationery Office, 1973

19. What Sir Keith can learn from Mr. Wilson. *The Financial Times,* 23 January 1973, p. 17

20. The New NHS 'a Bureaucratic monster.' *The Times,* 1 January 1973, p. 22

21. Draper P, Smart T: *The Future of Our Health Care,* London, Department of Community Medicine, Guy's Hospital, 1972

22. Draper P, Grenholm G: The British National Health Service, in *Medical Sociology,* edited by Tuckett D. London, Tavistock, 1974

23. Patricelli R: National Health Insurance proposals: leverage for change? *Bull NY Acad Med* 48:120–129, 1972

24. Somers HM: National Health Insurance: strategy and standards. *Med Care* 10:81–87, 1972

25. Somers AR, Somers HM: The organization and financing of health care: issues and directions for the future. *Am J Orthopsychiatry* 42:119–136, 1972

26. Eilers R: National health insurance: what kind and how much. *N Engl J Med* 284: 881–886, 945–954, 1971

27. Senate Bill 3, 93rd Congress, 1st session 1973

28. *Hansard* (House of Commons), 26 March 1973, Column 947

V

The Micro System of Health Care

Understanding large structural variations and designing effective organizational programs require not only studies in the aggregate but also micro studies that reveal more intimately the way patients and health professionals behave in varying types of clinical context. In reading 21, we continue with our cross-national perspective, but focus more specifically on the role of the personal physician in the larger and increasingly complex system of medical care. George Godber, a distinguished medical administrator in the English National Health Service, presents his conception of the way the role of the personal physician will evolve as the health service itself continues to change. Reading 22 is a review by Eliot Freidson of his study of a large prepaid medical group. Freidson gives us some insight into how physicians behave differently in prepaid group settings as compared with office-based, fee-for-service practice, and he suggests a useful sociological conception for characterizing the differences between patient and colleague influences over the doctor's work and decision-making practices. Freidson elaborates on these ideas and observations in two excellent books, *Profession of Medicine* (New York: Dodd, Mead, 1970) and *Doctoring Together* (New York: Elsevier, 1975). I recommend both very highly.

Reading 23, by Jerome Frank, addresses the issue of doctor-patient relationships and examines the sources of the doctor's influence over the patient. This very successful paper was later expanded into a stimulating book, which has been reissued in a new paperback edition. The student wishing to follow up the issues raised in Frank's paper would do well to read *Persuasion and Healing*, rev. ed. (Baltimore: Johns Hopkins Press, 1974). Frank's discussion in the present volume as well as in his book helps illuminate such important outcomes as the placebo effect. We then return, in reading 24, to the work of Eliot Freidson and his analysis of the changing role and perspective of the physician in varying types of medical-group structure. Freidson illustrates the way the contractual practice characteristic of prepaid groups creates a new type of difficult patient, in addition to some other types that doctors have problems in managing. This new type of patient demands certain services as a matter of "rights." Freidson, in analyzing why doctors react as strongly as they do to such difficult patients, brings to light some of the dominant assumptions of the physician.

The last two readings in this section are reports of field experiments dealing with hospital organization and its effects on patient outcomes and interprofessional relationships. In the experiement reported in reading 25, children hospitalized for tonsillectomy were randomized into two groups, one receiving routine care, the other receiving similar care with the addition of a nurse contact who related to the mother and communicated information about the surgery and what to expect. Skipper and Leonard show quite persuasively how a modest and inexpensive interpersonal innovation can make a difference in affecting objective outcomes. In another context, I have examined some of the difficulties of implementing the findings of such studies. Students interested in this issue may wish to consult "Sociological Critics versus Institutional Elites in the Politics of Research Application," in N.J. Demerath III et al., eds., Social Policy and Sociology (New York: Academic Press, 1975), pp. 99–108. The Skipper and Leonard experiment exemplifies the possibilities of doing excellent experimental investigations in natural field situations that are ethical and informative and use objective indicators of outcome instead of subjective measures.

Finally, reading 26, a study by Charles K. Hofling and some colleagues, illustrates in a real experimental situation the authority of the physician and the deference of the nurse, to the point where the nurse fails to exercise any reasonable independent judgment. It raises profound questions about such authority and the extent to which nurses lack confidence to act on their own when the circumstances warrant it. A similar study has been performed with more heartening results (Steven Rank and Cardell Jacobson, "Hospital Nurses' Compliance with Medication Overdose Orders: A Failure to Replicate," Journal of Health and Social Behavior 18 [June 1977]: 188–93). Unlike those in the Hofling et al. experiment, most nurses in this study were unwilling to administer a medication overdose simply because it was ordered by a physician. Only two of eighteen nurses were prepared to administer the overdose. The experimenters speculate that increased self-esteem among nurses, fear of malpractice suits, and a more general erosion of authority help explain the varying results between the two experiments. In fact, both studies raise interesting and provocative issues about the appropriate definition of relationships between physicians and nurses and the structure of their roles and responsibilities.

21

The Future Place
of the Personal Physician

George E. Godber

The invitation to give this seventh Michael M. Davis Lecture came as a total
surprise. It is a privilege that could not have been more welcome to one who has
enjoyed the friendship of Dr. Davis and his family for more than twenty years and
has admired and received inspiration from his own and his son's work through that
period. This is not the place for a eulogy, but in preparation for this occasion I have
re-read "Medical Care for Tommorrow"—with us for fourteen years and still bearing an apposite title—and read for the first time the first lecture in this series in
which Dr. Davis provided what could have been texts for those who were to follow
him for many years to come. Most of us spend our time cultivating in depth some
small area in fields of personal health services or operate much more superficially,
and with understanding which must decline with the passage of years, over a much
wider area. Mine has been the second of these functions, and in Britain where the
organisation is so different from your own. Perhaps the most striking of those
differences is the extent to which we have depended in our National Health Service,
and expect to depend, upon the work of the personal physician who undertakes
primary medical care and is the means of access to the ever more complex system of
specialist service which is complementary to his work.

In his Michael Davis Lecture last year Dr. Arthur Engel described the evolution
of a system which has given Sweden one of the best health records in the world.
Over more than a century the county councils in Sweden have evolved their
hospital system and they now also administer the district medical service, which is
the nearest thing to British general practice they have. Their service is thus administratively unified but, like our own, has serious divisions in function, especially
between care in the community and the hospital and specialist services. Elsewhere

SOURCE: Michael M. Davis Lecture, Center for Health Administration Studies, Graduate School of
Business, University of Chicago, 1969. Reprinted by permission.

in Scandinavia the same division occurs and even in Denmark personal physicians work single-handed with even less contact with hospitals than in Britain. Yet the intention in these countries, as in Britain, is that the public will first seek medical care from general practitioners and will only be sent on for specialist help if the general practitioner requires it. This has been the common situation in the past throughout Western Europe, but the growth of specialisation has gradually led patients in most countries to seek specialist help direct where there is no rule to prevent it. In your country that process has gone further and faster. Dr. Davis made the point in the first lecture in this series that four-fifths of your younger graduates were training for specialties, and three years later Dr. Coggeshall said that over 85 per cent of new physicians enter specialised practice. The changing trend is not merely recent; Dr. Davis said that in 1931, three-quarters of all active physicians in the United States were general practitioners, but by 1963 60 per cent limited their practice to a specialty. By comparison, in Britain there are roughly 21 doctors in general practice to 23 in hospital work, including junior staff, and there are two principals in general practice for each established specialist in hospital.

Other Systems

In Eastern Europe planned development has gone much further. In the U.S.S.R. there is one physician for every 450 persons. Each district with a population of about 1,800 adults has a uchastok doctor to provide primary care, but he is not responsible for the care of children. In a city he will work with perhaps 20 others from a polyclinic which also has a full staff of specialists, to whom patients may go direct, and which serves a population of 50,000. Yet other specialists will treat those patients who are admitted to hospital wards, and these patients on discharge may be supervised by different physicians again. As a shift system is worked, it is hardly possible to say that a personal physician exists.

In Yugoslavia the system is nearer that of Britain; the generalists are grouped in medical centres and serve a defined population, but the specialist health centres may receive patients direct and their links with hospitals are less close than they would be in Britain.

In a country such as Brazil the doctors are concentrated in the larger towns and most of them work in a specialty. Many patients go direct to hospital in the event of serious illness, or to ambulatoria staffed by specialists for primary diagnosis and treatment if they are not acutely ill. Continuing care by a personal physician is the privilege of a very few.

In India again it is difficult to get medical care outside the large cities, and only the few have personal physicians; many with acute, possibly communicable diseases seek assistance first, and often at a late stage, from the emergency department of a hospital.

In West Africa, where the proportion of physicians to population is very small, little more than emergency diagnosis and treatment at health centres is practicable outside hospitals, which are few. Separate field programmes with mobile units for the control of some of the communicable diseases may be used. Specialist services and most of the physicians are concentrated in the largest cities; for example, a fifth of all the active physicians in Ghana work at the teaching hospital in Accra. Detached health centres amongst widely scattered rural populations can only offer straightforward emergency services, and continuing contact with the personal physician of one's own choice is, for the great majority, simply not possible.

Population-Physician Ratios

I have mentioned the developing countries to call attention to the fact that for a very large part of the world's population one of the assumptions under which we live— that the need for medical care will be satisfied in one way or another—is simply not attainable. It requires a ratio of physicians to population which a very large part of the world's population will not have within the lifetimes of most of us here. Most countries with sophisticated health services have a ratio of population to physicians of 1,000 to one or less, but in Asia and Africa the ratio may be anywhere from 10,000 to 60,000 to one. For those latter populations medical service is not even at the point from which the U.S.S.R. had to develop 50 years ago, for their ratio then was 7,000 to one. To achieve the standard that we now enjoy would require a co-ordinated, almost military, type of programme spread over many years, with a defined strategy of approach to limited objectives year by year. The lesson of Eastern Europe is that such a programme can be made to work—not that it is a suitable programme for us.

Dr. Engel last year described the logical step-by-step evolution of the Swedish health services, which had the great advantage that they already possessed a unified administration by the time the real sophistication of medical work began. One hospital system had operated over a period of more than 100 years; it led to the development of hospitals of the right size and in the right place before modern methods made concentration for efficiency essential. Competition between comparable institutions in the same place—with the waste of resources of men, equipment and money, that had bedevilled the situation in Britain and in North America—was thus avoided. No such orderly development could occur in Britain until our National Health Service was initiated almost 21 years ago. Without the radical solution of transferring the hospitals to state ownership we could not have made such progress as we have achieved in the last 20 years. The physical reconstruction has been limited by an inheritance of buildings and competing claims on resources, but at least what we have had has been applied to relief of the greatest need.

The administrative pattern of health services in any country must reflect in some degree its social organisation in other ways. The size of the country, the distribution of the population, and the pattern of central and local government all have a bearing on the way in which health services can and should be organised. The British system has been evolutionary, with occasional mutations of which the transfer of ownership of hospitals in 1948 was one. Since then development has shown interesting parallels with that of Sweden, although the system of financing is more akin to that of Eastern Europe and insurance payments play only a minor part. Its peculiar feature derives from the history and present nature of British general practice, and for a true understanding of this one must go a little farther back in history than 1948. The process has been well described by Rosemary Stevens in her book, "Medical Practice in Modern England" and the system itself by Dr. Burnet Davis in *Public Health Notes* in 1949.

British Development

The registration of doctors in Britain, and therefore the control of standards, goes back a mere 113 years. Before the Medical Act of 1856 there had been confusion as to responsibility, and conflict between the physicians (that is, the specialists in internal medicine) on the one hand and the apothecaries (forerunners of the general practitioners) on the other, with the surgeons falling somewhere in between. In the next half century that conflict ended in a fairly clear division of responsibility between specialists on the one hand and generalists on the other. It was to leave the specialists (and particularly the specialists in internal medicine) with the clearly-defined custom that they only received patients referred to them by general practitioners, and also with an assumption of superiority of which of course they were more conscious than anyone else.

Of course there were some patients who evaded this barrier at either end of the social scale, but it was not normal even for the most eminent and wealthy to consult a specialist direct. At the other end of the social scale some poor patients, especially children, might go direct to the so-called casualty departments of hospitals when acutely ill and so reach specialist care. The development of sick clubs and friendly societies toward the end of the last century, and the introduction in 1911 of a National Health Insurance scheme to provide personal physician services for employed workers, helped to crystallise this situation and also to ensure that there were general practitioners within the reach of everyone—geographically if not always financially. Except in the event of accident or other emergency, this also controlled access to hospital. Even the very poor under the old Poor Law system could go to general practitioners, appointed as district medical officers, who could provide what was called medical out-relief for the destitute.

This position was firmly established even in most of the smaller towns where the limited group of specialists having hospital appointments were also in general practice. The two functions of specialist and generalist practice were sharply distinguished. The profession itself was ambivalent about this, some thinking of rural practice away from town and hospital alike as the ideal practice, others regarding general practice linked with a hospital post as the best; but a large proportion had neither position.

Evolution of Specialties

The evolution of many of the specialties has taken place largely during this century. In addition to the physicians and surgeons there were gynaecologists and obstetricians, paediatricians, ophthalmologists, otologists and pathologists in main centres at the beginning of this century, but over most of Britain these specialties were only slowly being separated between the wars, and differentiation was not complete when the health service was introduced in 1948. The one immediate effect upon medical practice after the change in 1948 was to complete, within a matter of two years throughout the country, not only the separation between specialist and generalist but also the differentiation of the specialties. There had been many general surgeons who undertook traumatic surgery or gynaecology or even otology; there had been specialists in internal medicine who were also paediatricians or perhaps pathologists or even radiologists. The reason for this was simply financial, because hospital work had been unpaid, and private practice outside hospital or in a few special beds in hospital was the only support of specialists. Hospital patients, who were the majority, did not pay fees themselves. Once work in hospital became remunerative, appropriate staff could be appointed in the numbers required, so far as suitably trained people were available. At the same time the division between specialist and generalist was completed because very few generalists remained with hospital appointments in specialties; most of those who were fully trained in a specialty turned to the specialist side of their practice.

The National Health Service Act transferred all but a very few (mainly denominational) hospitals to state ownership. It provided for their administration through regional boards, which determined planning and policy, and through local management by committees in charge of groups serving substantial districts, instead of leaving management to some thousands of individual units. The first ten years of the hospital service were substantially devoted to organising and developing clinical services within each mixed group of hospitals, and to providing a rapid expansion of staff in the specialties. Despite lack of resources for building, and the gross inadequacies of much of the accommodation that existed, a reorganisation of function within each group and great improvement in quality of work was possible. Moreover, these changes could be brought about without the standard dependence on local resources, since the cost was met by the state. Where the need was greatest most could be done, and what building was possible could be undertaken where the need—rather than local wealth—was most manifest. But this process of change established in each hospital group a specialist team which was divided from the general practitioners in function.

Payment for service made it possible to provide the specialists that the community needed, but it also made it possible for the specialists to segregate themselves sharply from their colleagues outside the hospitals, on whom they no longer had to rely for private patient referrals. There were times when feeling in the profession that there were conflicting interests between the two groups became sharply apparent. There was indeed differentiation between them in the adjustment of their remuneration, which was only put right for the general practitioners by arbitration four years after the beginning of the service. There was, in fact, an administrative structure and a system under which a specialist service could be and was evolved; there was no such system promoting evolution in general practice, and it is most unlikely that it would have been acceptable to our individualist profession if it had been proffered in 1948.

When the Health Service was first mooted, there was much talk of health centres where family physicians could work together with those providing preventive services. It was thought that some specialist service might also have been undertaken making the centres outposts of the hospitals. In fact, when the service was introduced, about half the doctors were in some form of partnership and a few were in well organised groups but the other half, especially the majority of older doctors, were in single-handed practice. What might be thought the ideal relationship of one doctor always available to one patient was the model at the back of people's minds.

System of Payment

The system of remuneration for general practitioners that was inherited from the old health insurance was one of a capitation payment for each person at risk, with a limit of 4,000 on the individual doctor's list. Expenses were reimbursed in total, but the pay of the individual doctor was not related to the expenses he himself incurred. It was left the doctor to organise his practice as he chose, to provide himself with adequate assistants or not, and to practice single-handed or in partnership. The only limitation was that he had to have approval for the use of a paid medical assistant.

It was a system economical for government, which knew the cost it faced, but it left the doctor to provide all practice requisites and was not calculated of itself to improve the quality of practice, since a doctor could set his standard of practice facility almost as low as he chose. Because of the remarkable stability of practice populations a large list had formerly been a valuable asset which a doctor could sell on retirement, but this procedure was abolished, with financial compensation, by the National Health Service Act.

Clearly this unorganised pattern of practice could not last when the changes that were taking place in medicine itself so obviously required better organisation, and least of all could it stand comparison with the rapidly improving organisation of hospital medical work.

At the insistence of the profession, safeguards were built into the National Health Service Act against compulsion of doctors to change their methods of practice. This Act was essentially devised to make it possible for all members of the public to use the medical care which practitioners as independent contractors were prepared to provide. The physician had a duty to provide all the services needed or to see that patients were referred to other sources such as the hospital. The underlying assumption was that the doctor himself was the one fixed point of contact, but that he would prescribe drugs, usually dispensed by pharmacists, and that parallel services from dentists and optometrists could be used as required by those who needed them.

Patterns of medical practice change slowly, and the public was already familiar with the service as it was. There was therefore no great pressure for rapid change, but there was an immediate—if modest—increase in demand, because service was now free at the time of use to the women, children, and old people who had not been insured previously. However, the established usage of reference to hospitals only through general practitioners, which continued under the new system, prevented a rapidly increasing demand on specialist services. General practice bore the brunt of the immediate change.

Years of Slow Change

There have been 20 years of slow change since then—slow partly because any profession is slow to change, and partly because the financial and administrative basis of the service in its original form was not such as to promote change. General practice was simply accepted as if it were a fact of life, and because it was strong enough to carry the immediate burden the hospital service was reorganised almost under its protection.

Dr. Coggeshall three years ago said that modern medicine was really a development of the last 30 years. I think he was a little unfair to the first 35 years of this century which saw the beginnings of radiology, pathology, and cardio-respiratory physiology, but certainly the pace of the last 30 years has not only been faster than that of any earlier period but has been constantly accelerating and is still accelerating.

Most of the scientific apparatus of medicine is in hospitals. Because of the extraordinary speed and range of the expansion of scientific knowledge applied to medicine, specialisation which permits a man to be informed in depth about at least part of his subject has become accepted, despite the resistance that was still evident 20 years ago to some of the fragmentation which now goes unquestioned.

Resistance continues against the further subdivision which must still occur. There are less than 30 medical specialties in which consultant appointments are made in British hospitals now. There are 64 recognised specialties in the U.S.S.R. The figure accepted here (for instance by the Hospital Insurance Plan of New York) is somewhere in between. Yet within specialties like internal medicine or even cardiology there are sub-specialties in which individuals or individual units achieve pre-eminence. While the argument is still going on in Britain as to whether paediatric surgery or urology, for instance, should be distinguished from general surgery, or whether a consultative neurological service is needed in every hospital centre, specialties like neuroradiology, neuropathology, and clinical cardio-respiratory physiology become established in leading centres. Some techniques like those of organ transplantation are developed by specialist teams who may receive patients from clinical colleagues anywhere in the country, while there remain other fields of medicine where such progress is resisted—for instance, physical medicine, because it is said that all clinical specialists should be rehabilitation-minded, although we know very well that they are not.

In the last 20 years admissions to hospital in England and Wales have increased from 2.9 million a year to well over 5 million, despite great reductions in admissions for tuberculosis and other communicable diseases. But the greatest proportionate increase has been in services for traumatic and orthopaedic surgery, gynaecology, such regional specialties as neurosurgery, plastic surgery, and thoracic surgery, while general surgery and internal medicine show less than the average overall increase. In fact, admissions have increased almost entirely because of shortened stay, and the total of days of care in hospital each year has actually fallen.

It is specialisation which has brought more patients into ward care, and it is in supporting services such as pathology, radiology, and anaesthesiology that the greatest increases in specialist staff have occurred. Anaesthesiology is the largest specialty in Britain today and the next two are pathology and psychiatry. Psychiatry also has made great progress, with more rapid and effective treatment, so that fewer patients are retained for long-term care and there is far more outpatient and day hospital treatment. In 13 years, from 1954 to 1967 inclusive, the proportion of the population in psychiatric hospital units at one time has fallen from 3.4 per thousand to 2.7, and in some regions more than half of those inpatients are first admitted to psychiatric units in general hospitals.

I have said that specialisation will go further and mentioned some specialties which are established, but in which progress is slow. There are others like the subdivisions of pathology, clinical haematology, clinical physiology, toxicology, clinical pharmacology, and human genetics which are underdeveloped over the country as a whole; there are some special departments, mainly in teaching centres, but they cannot meet the needs of a service which sets out to provide for all what it can provide for any.

Financial Implications

The main problem of a National Health Service is this of generalisation. Once it is established that a new clinical service like cardiac surgery or a change in equipment is beyond the research and development stage—as for instance from a valve to a transistorised hearing aid in the 1950's, or maintenance haemodialysis or intensive care for acute myocardial infarction in the last five years—we must try and bring it within reach of all who need it. It is always relatively easy to get support for a research programme, but the financial implications to a universal service may be enormous. If these can be met, it can be no part of any medical ethic that a service which can meet an acknowledged need can be rationed by the patient's income alone.

Last year Dr. Engel described the way Swedish services have been deployed nationally, regionally, and locally to meet much the same demand. In Britain a few national centres exist and some of the highly specialised centres in London draw patients from far outside the metropolitan area at least in the development stage (for instance, centres for cardiac surgery in small infants, or heart valve replacement). Special centres were needed for the provision of powered artificial limbs for children with phocomelia after thalidomide. Some of the work on chemotherapy of certain forms of cancer such as chorion-epithelioma has been or is being concentrated in a few centres. Reference centres for microbiology, for poison control and for cytogenetics, special hospitals for mentally ill or subnormal criminals, centres for grossly disturbed adolescents and for control of radiation safety are other examples. Broadly, each of our 15 hospital regions is organised to provide all specialists services apart from such exceptions. Centres have been established in all regions for such specialised work as neurosurgery, cardiac surgery or radiotherapy, and from these consultative clinics are provided in many of the peripheral hospital groups. Other highly specialised investigative work can be undertaken by one or more laboratories for a whole region serving from 1.5 to 5 million people, or even for several regions in, for instance, chromosomal studies or toxicological tests. Before the precipitin tests for pregnancy we had two large centres for the whole country using the Hogben test with specially imported Xenopus toads. One centre currently produces all sera for tissue typing. Some centres are beginning to develop highly automated chemical pathological services which can serve more than one hospital group. Each hospital group provides services in all the ordinary specialties, and through it—or directly—the regional centres are accessible. Through the regional organisation hospital staff can get specialist support in any field.

Hospital Plan

All this is set out in the Hospital Plan published at the beginning of 1962, which outlined the background and future development of a building programme then already under way. A similar programme for various health and welfare community services was published a year later. Both plans referred to general practice, but neither attempted to incorporate a plan for its development, since the practitioner's status as independent contractor with the health service remained. Yet the definition that has been given to the hospital programme carries with it the logical certainty of some re-orientation of general practice. The hospital plan proposed a network of district general hospitals in every region, each supported by regional centres for some specialties to provide consultative services throughout the network. The concept of the district general hospital is similar to that of the central hospital in Sweden which Dr. Engel described last year. It incorporates provision for geriatric and psychiatric patients and envisages the disappearance of separate special hospitals, small or large. It should serve a district with a population of 150 to 250 thousand, and it is essentially an exercise in concentration and replacement. So much of our existing building is outworn and outdated, and despite all the efforts of the 1950s to provide scientific departments to support the use of these old buildings, they cannot often be made fully efficient, and should not be retained for any longer than we can help. District hospitals need the support of special centres at regional hospitals which are usually larger and may be associated with a medical school. The "teaching hospital" is often now a group of several hospitals, some for special purposes, associated with a university medical school; it is not now seen merely as a district general hospital, but every new teaching hospital we build will be a district general hospital with added educational and regional functions. A third of these district general hospitals are built, building, or in an advanced stage of planning. Many others will consist of the redevelopment or replacement on the same site of existing hospitals, and often some part of that redevelopment has already occurred. There is of course no end to a hospital building programme, but at least one can foresee the day when we reach the stage of hospital building related to planned obsolescence.

Distances Short

A typical district in Britain is far smaller in area than you would expect here. Our population is so concentrated that it is unlikely that 10 per cent would have to travel more than 10 miles to a district general hospital. Our difficult areas might involve for a few people a journey of 45 miles, and in Scotland the distance might be greater still, but compared with the distances you have to face in, say, North Dakota, that is child's play.

Our distances are so short that much consultation and investigative work can be undertaken in out-patient departments, and indeed consultative out-patient work is of an importance quite comparable to that of the work in the wards. Roughly 160 out-patient first consultations for every thousand of the population take place in a year, and including accident and emergency departments total attendances of out-patients are of the order of 45 million a year. By comparison, approximately 104 admissions per thousand of the population occur each year. Since patients only reach consultative out-patient departments on reference from general practice, it is apparent that a close partnership between generalist and specialist practice is needed. Indeed these out-patient consultations must be seen as the chief points of contact between specialist and generalist practice, with an important effect on both.

Our hospital plan is essentially a building plan. It is a programme to provide the material resources that the specialists of the country need. Yet the hospital is not primarily a building but a group of people working together on behalf of the population served. One can regard the district general hospital as the group practice centre of the specialists working in it. It is inevitable that the subdivision of hospital medicine has made the specialists more, not less, dependent on each other. If this were not so the decision to concentrate them all at a large district general hospital might well be questioned.

No patients now are the responsibility of one specialist alone. Full investigation calls for assistance from diagnostic departments, which in turn must work with the whole range of clinical specialties if their own expertise is to meet requirements. Surgery is powerless without anaesthesiology; modern therapy, either medical or surgical, involves the use of methods which require far closer observation of patients, often using increasingly complex instrumentation.

This support is only practicable in large general hospitals, and these become powerful centralised units which are in some danger of becoming too introspective. We have called the unit the district general hospital and that puts the emphasis where it should be, in that the district comes first. Hospitals as we all know are for patients, not for doctors. Therefore we must see the function of the district general hospital as that of providing a particular kind of service for the population of the district, not as an end in itself.

Partners of Medicine

The modern district general hospital not only requires a specialist medical team but also many others who are partners of medicine. Nurses have been the chief partners of medicine for almost as long as medicine has existed. Their training is more scientific—and their remuneration is higher—than ever before, but there is now a large group of other professions which are also supplementary to medicine. They have a varying degree of organisation and they range from the highest levels of physical and chemical science to electronic engineering and various technologies.

The most highly trained in these professions should clearly rank with the most senior doctors with whom they work, and we must expect that non-medical biochemists, physicists, and the like will increasingly take part in the medically orientated teams which are now responsible for medical care. The same point was made by Dr. Coggeshall in his lecture, and it has been made most forcibly in the recent report in Britain of a special committee under Sir Solly Zuckerman. There must still be a doctor responsible for the patient's care, but he commonly shares that responsibility with others. For every 10 consultants in the Health Service—that is, fully trained specialists, in our parlance—there are working in the hospitals 15 other doctors, 100 trained nurses or midwives, 170 other nursing staff, 30 scientists or technologists, and 270 other staff. In the related community services there are 20 general practitioners and 15 nursing staff. This group of professionals of all kinds makes up the Greater Medical Profession, and collectively it serves 430 patients in hospital at any one time and 53,000 people outside who need care.

Altogether the district general hospital is an extremely formidable grouping of people, with a forbidding range of skills to be faced by the prospective patient. The selection of his portal of entry is no light matter. For reasons I have already given, the patient does not have to make this selection himself; his family doctor does it for him. But that means that the generalist must himself know the citadel well enough to make the right choice. He must know which one or more of a large group of colleagues best meet his patient's needs, and that colleague or those colleagues must be prepared to help and inform him in return. Just as specialisation has made specialists dependent on one another, so has general practice become the largest specialty of all—dependent upon the hospital specialist group, but also depended upon by them.

General practitioners have direct access to radiological and pathological services in hospital, providing about a 10th of the loads of these departments, and because in this way the reports of specialists are made direct to them, few attempt such work themselves in their own practice premises. Consultative out-patient services, in which specialists are able to investigate and treat patients referred by general practitioners or refer them back with an opinion and recommendations about further treatment, are among the main activities of all hospital groups; group practices containing both generalists and specialists, such as have developed in the United States, are not needed. A specialist group is a hospital group and general practice is practice mainly outside hospital; the two share responsibility for the district and must combine to do it.

Access to Beds

Some critics of British general practice make much of the fact that few have access to hospital beds for the care of their own patients. In fact, nearly one in five has access to beds in hospital, and about one in four has part-time work for hospital authorities in some non-specialist capacity. 260,000 patients were treated by their own doctors in hospital in 1967—more than 5 per cent of all admissions and about a quarter of maternity cases. Nevertheless it is true that two-thirds of general practitioners do not have such facilities, and some, not all, of this majority do desire them. An enquiry in Wessex showed that one in eight did not. The right answer to this must be that even a service which is deliberately orientated toward home care, where this is possible, cannot always provide suitable support where the home is inadequate. At any one time about 20 patients from an average practice are in hospital. Twelve of them are in beds for the mentally ill, mentally subnormal or chronic sick; less than six are in beds for acute medical or surgical cases; only one or two are in beds for internal medicine, and only occasionally will one of these not need specialist supervision. Nevertheless it is wrong that practitioners who could assume such responsibility for even occasional ward patients cannot do so, and in some district hospitals this is arranged.

There is great rigidity in the allocation of beds to individual specialists, and a spurious prestige often attaches to the number so allocated. What is needed is greater flexibility in use of beds, not yet another allocation.

The Health Service also provides, as part of community care, nurses, midwives, and health visitors. These work with patients in their own homes, and are employed by local authorities, not by the hospitals or by general practitioners. The work of the home nurses has always been closely related to general practice, but has been arranged in the past to cover a district rather than the work of a particular doctor or group of doctors. Midwives formerly dealt independently with home confinements, calling a doctor only in case of need, but under the Health Service, since a quarter of all confinements still occur in the home, midwives now work much more closely with doctors. Here again until recently they dealt with patients from an area, rather than a practice.

Public health nurses in the past also dealt with areas and had little contact with general practice. They were based on the Well Baby Clinics, which are the responsibility of local authorities. Obviously all this work needs co-ordination with general practice and that has developed rapidly in recent years. Single-handed general practice with no co-ordination between practices and no attempt to rationalise geographical distribution is singularly ill-adapted to the needs of a community today.

Promote Group Practice

In a few places groups of general practitioners had been formed before the health service began, working in common premises and sharing ancillary help, usually in partnership. Fifteen years ago central funds to promote the provision of group practice premises were first established, since few doctors then showed any readiness to work from publicly provided health centres. Now the actual number and the proportion of single-handed practitioners is steadily declining, while the proportion of doctors in partnerships of three or more is rapidly increasing and already exceeds half the total. Under a new system of remuneration, introduced three years ago, the expenses of a practice, including ancillary help, are met largely by direct repayment, and a special allowance is paid to doctors in group practice. Almost half of all general practitioners were entitled to receive it by the end of 1968.

Fifteen years ago local authority nursing staff were first attached to two group practices, working with the doctors for their practice population instead of being responsible for an area in which many doctors might work. After 10 years of very slow progress this movement is now developing rapidly. Two years ago one in six of all health visitors was working with a practice, and one in nine of all local authority nursing staff. By now those proportions must at least have doubled, and the principle is accepted by the great majority of local authorities and doctors. In several areas all the nursing staff are now attached to practices. In a few groups also, local authority-employed social workers have been associated with practices, and Forman and Fairbairn last year reported on one such group which included five doctors, two health visitors, and a social worker, as well as a home nurse.

In 1948, 10 premises were taken over as health centres; in the next 16½ years 20 health centres were built; in the last four years 66 have been built. During 1968, 39 were opened in England and Wales, at this moment 90 are being built, and 200 more are in various stages of planning.

The implications of all this are clear. Single-handed general practice is unlikely to continue, although of course a few individualists will remain for a time. The normal pattern within a few years will be that the personal physicians will work in groups, and health visitors, nurses, and midwives will join them in those groups. I have a personal dislike of the description "attachment" normally given to this arrangement. Hospital medicine is largely a doctor/nurse partnership in which now, of course, scientists and technologists are also partners, and practice in the community ought to be a doctor/nurse partnership too. The fact that at present the nurses are employed by local authorities need be no deterrent.

Most groupings of doctors have been originally a result of personal links rather than a deliberately planned organisation of medical care for a district. In a few places, like Dartford in Kent where the doctors joined together in two sets of premises, and Skipton in Yorkshire where there were two groups, this began before the Health Service came into being. In Swindon there was for many years a large health centre for one particular occupational group. Recently, some health centre developments have deliberately provided for all doctors serving the district, and there have been examples—for instance Hyde or Cheadle Hulme near Manchester—of all the doctors in an area forming groups with the same object. It is easy to see where this trend will take us.

District Hospital

Our hospital pattern has already emerged with the District General Hospital designed to provide all specialist services for the population of a much larger district than that served by a health centre. Within this larger district common-sense, public, and professional advantage and economy all point towards planned regrouping for the personal physicians, in centres provided by themselves or by health authorities, so as to provide reasonable access for the public and simplified access for the professional staff to the hospital. With nursing staff working with the groups, preventive work in the community—including well baby clinics, antenatal care, and personal preventive measures like immunisation and special screening procedures—can obviously be best developed in such group centres. Within the groups there may be some development of special medical interests in which, too, part-time work in a specialist group in a hospital may be practicable.

But the personal physician should not need to have such a special interest in order to satisfy himself, since his own specialty of general practice will be as important as any. I do not mean that all doctors will now be arbitrarily directed into practice centres planned for them, but rather that the logic of the situation is apparent to the doctors themselves, and the group practice and health centre developments show that in large numbers they are now actively seeking such a reorganisation. Moreover, the new system of payment for general practitioners has made it possible for them to employ the needed supporting staff in their practices with little cost to themselves.

It is obvious that the progressive rearrangement of all medical practice in the district between the district general hospital on the one hand and group practice centres on the other cannot be the end of the story. General practice has become one of the special fields of medicine, admittedly the largest, but still a field of work requiring special preparation and aptitudes and no less skill. I commented earlier on the way in which specialisation in hospital work makes the specialists more, not less, dependent on each other. It makes them, as a group, even more dependent upon the personal physician working in the community.

If there were no specialists the general practitioners could provide a service for most of the illness in the community, but if there were no general practitioners, or their equivalent, the specialists would be overwhelmed. Since generalists and specialists are dependent on each other, there must be a ready communication between them, and a meeting place. The practice of using outpatient departments for investigation results, in Britain, in a hospital admission rate which is only about three-quarters of that in the United States or Sweden and only half that of Saskatchewan or the U.S.S.R. This also means that there is less participation by general practitioners in in-patient hospital work. For many years they have been less accustomed to use the hospital premises and, therefore, to meet their specialist colleagues than have their counterparts in the United States.

It is in hospital that advanced resources exist, and the contact specialists have with each other helps to keep all in touch with medical advances. The pace is such now that no one isolated from this sort of exchange can continue to practice modern medicine. But equally scientific, specialised medicine needs to keep contact with real life and human needs in a community; science is not all.

A Meeting Place

The division between specialist and generalist practice necessitates the provision of a meeting place. Moreover, there is another large group of doctors, the junior staff in hospitals, for whose further training an organised programme is essential. To meet this need, medical institutes with library and teaching facilities are now being generally provided. There are 200 such centres in existence in England and Wales, two-fifths already in especially-built premises, and organised programmes of vocational training for the younger doctors and of continuing education for all are provided in them. More academic programmes are organised on a regional basis for those training in specialties, and special refresher courses for general practitioners, which have been provided since the health service began, have been greatly increased. In 1952 one-twentieth of all general practitioners attended at least one postgraduate course, in 1968 about one-half did; altogether, over 18,000 courses were taken. Not only are expenses paid for such courses but there are now incentives in remuneration for those who take them.

There is thus emerging in Britain a functional unit upon which the organisation of health services will be based. It is the district which requires a general hospital and a group of practice centres, with a medical institute at the hospital to serve as an educational centre and meeting place for all the health professions. The public is then served by a complex, at the centre of which is the hospital as the main support of practice centres dispersed through the community. In this way general practice is supported by the specialties, and the service the community requires in any area of medicine is partly provided by each.

The sharp differentiation between practice in hospital and the community should diminish and we are now planning hospital development on the assumption that this will occur. The effect in reducing capital requirements, as well as increasing functional efficiency, can be very large. Last year the detailed plans of two new district hospitals were announced, which are to cost together about as much as one would have cost in the past. Each provides generous diagnostic and treatment facilities with the latest scientific resources for the neighbourhood, but has fewer beds than we have been accustomed to provide for the same population. By the intensive use of out-patient and day care facilities, and shortened stay in the wards for those who must be admitted, followed by care in the community, it is believed that a service of at least equal efficiency can be given with substantial economy. But this is wholly dependent upon close association between specialists and generalists and the hospital and community nursing staff. We must demonstrate that this can be successfully done, but the intent to do it amounts to no more than the logical application of best current practice where facilities now permit.

Public Health Function

I have deliberately said little about public health or social medicine or whatever name we use next, but there is a crucial function for the community physician—the heir to the Medical Officer of Health—who I think will be the man best able to help both specialists and generalists do the work the community needs—preventive and curative. Individual clinicians do not think first of community needs. Why should they? Their concern must be—as everyone of us, when a patient, hopes—with the individual under care at the moment. But individuals will only get what they need in this complicated world of medical science if competent, understanding men have organised the deployment of mutually supporting services to that end.

If the best results are to be obtained from the district general hospital group practices complex, it will be necessary to improve upon the services now provided in some hospitals in support of general practice. The first of these must be communication, in general on the educational lines already mentioned, and in particular on the prompt provision of information about individual patients. We may one day see a comprehensive individual health record file with automated access, provided it can be kept in confidence.

It will be necessary to make hospital diagnostic facilities more easily available to the general practitioner, and it may be necessary to ensure tranport for some patients to group practices, since the isolated doctor in a village is unlikely to remain.

It will no doubt be possible to put some group practice centres actually on hospital sites, but although our Royal Commission on Medical Education has suggested that health centres might be much larger, it is most unlikely that 80 to 100 doctors serving a large area will all be congregated in one place. The largest health centre we are building at the moment is for 17 doctors, but we have several for 10 or more. There is no reason why a group of 10 or more doctors should not be made up of several teams, as Draper has suggested, but, although larger groups may be practicable in thickly populated cities, there will be areas served by a group maybe of six or less.

General Practice Content

So far I have said little about the content of general practice. There are some who would dismiss it as a collection of trivia, grossly overburdened by the unreasonable demands of patients under a free Health Service. Some have lamented an alleged decline in interest or transfer of interest to hospitals. Some have suggested that in modern medicine there is far less that the general practitioner can do. There is in fact far more. It is true that we have far better control of many infections now, but they still have to be controlled, and this is done very largely by new therapies and new prophylaxis which the general practitioner uses. Much of our medicine is now concerned with the management and limitation of chronic and degenerative conditions, and this is an ideal opportunity for joint specialist/generalist work. The management of hypertension, for instance, has great potential not only for the limitation of cardiac disability but the prevention of stroke.

Medicine of the future will certainly involve more intensive search for inapparent disease. This is not likely to be by wholesale screening campaigns, but rather by selective screening by the personal physician dealing with a practice population—in the main well-known to him—and using specialist diagnostic facilities. We could well devote more effort to providing simple diagnostic apparatus for use in practice. Wonderful new machines that do every conceivable test in a matter of seconds and print our abnormal results in red at a cost of hundreds of thousands of dollars in outlay are not necessarily the most useful.

It is true that the community service could be provided on a clinic basis, with the patient simply seeing the doctor of the day; or general practice might be provided, as McKeown has suggested, in three or four sub-specialties, rather as the Russians have done. That might happen one day, but it is unlikely in Britain now; it is much more likely that we will go on trying to make general practice in its new form more efficient. Grouping of nursing staff with the practice, and provision of secretarial and other ancillary help, can greatly reduce the personal load on the doctor and give him time for things that require his skills.

I have no doubt that efficient practice organisation could be as important a contribution—as Herman Hilleboe has emphasised—to the improvement of general practice as the other steps I have described.

Better Training

I am not saying that our brand of general practice is right for everyone, only that we can with our system improve it greatly and provide what we want to have. A part of that improvement must be through better professional training for practice, at undergraduate and postgraduate level, such as the Royal Commission recommended, the Royal College of General Practitioners has long advocated, and your own specialty boards will doubtless require here. Several schemes for such training already exist, and I believe they will become general and, in effect, obligatory within the next few years.

We do not want to turn general practice into a faint carbon copy of specialist practice. The progress of specialisation in hospital will continue and the personal physician will soon be the only doctor with a truly comprehensive and continuing view of his patient's health. Shorter patient stay in hospital inevitably gives him a part in every specialist's work for his patient before and after—and perhaps during—in- or out-patient care. If there is to be a General Physician in the future—and surely the patient needs some medical guide through the scientific maze—then a general practitioner properly prepared for the role and helped to fulfill it is a possible answer. The patient's need for the future is not total care by one doctor, but timely use of the skills he needs at the moment, under the guidance of a practitioner who knows when to involve others. The ultimate object is not the organisation of medicine for the doctor's sakes but better patient care.

When we have done all this you may ask whether the effort will have gone into propping up an institution which may be dear to us but can never be as efficient as a group of specialists could be. My answer is that we have indeed looked at the alternatives, and have deliberately chosen what we are now trying to do because we believe it will be more efficient. We have, in fact, accepted the view that our separation of specialist practice into a service reached only through the personal physician will, in our context, give a more satisfying result to the patient and a more efficient use of technical resources. In fact we can have humanity and science too. It is not a universal panacea, but we believe it will work best for us, so we are setting out to give it the best opportunity we can devise.

I end with a quotation from the *New England Journal of Medicine. . . .* "Medical care is increasingly fragmented and complex, and the warmth of a long term association with a single physician has become a luxury for a few rather than the customary setting for the delivery of health care." I do not know if that is true here. I do know that it is our wish and intention that it shall not be true in Britain.

References

Coggeshall, L. T. Progress and Paradox on the Medical Scene. (Michael M. Davis Lecture, 1966). Chicago, University of Chicago, 1966.

Davis, B. M. The British National Health Service. U.S.P.H.S. Public Health Notes, Feb. 1949.

Davis, M. M. America Challenges Medicine. (Michael M. Davis Lecture, 1963). Chicago, University of Chicago, 1963.

Davis, M. M. *Medical Care for Tomorrow.* New York: Harper, 1955.

Department of Health and Social Security. Report of the Committee on Hospital Scientific and Technical Services. (Zuckerman Committee). London: H.M.S.O., 1968.

Draper, P. Community-Care Units and Inpatient Units as Alternatives to the District General Hospital. *Lancet*, London, 1967, Dec. 30, col. ii, pp. 1406–1409.

Engel, A. G. W. Planning and Spontaneity in the Development of the Swedish Health System. (Michael M. Davis Lecture, 1968). Chicago, University of Chicago, 1968.

Forman, J. A. S., and Fairburn, E. M. *Social Casework in General Practice.* London: Oxford University Press, 1968.

Francis, V., Korsch, B. M., and Morris, M. J. Gaps in Doctor-Patient Communications. *New England Medical Journal.* March 6, 1969, p. 535.

Hilleboe, H. E., and Larimore, G. W., Editors. *Preventive Medicine: Principles of Prevention in the Occurrence and Progression of Disease.* Philadelphia and London: Saunders, 1965.

McKeown, T., and Lowe, C. R. *An Introduction to Social Medicine.* Oxford: Blackwell, 1966.

Ministry of Health. *A Hospital Plan for England and Wales.* (Cmnd. 1604) London: H.M.S.O., 1962.

Ministry of Health. *Health and Welfare: The Development of Community Care Plans for the Health and Welfare Services of the Local Authorities in England and Wales.* (Cmnd. 1973) London: H.M.S.O., 1963.

Stevens, R. *Medical Practice in Modern England.* New Haven and London: Yale University Press, 1966.

Wessex Regional Hospital Board. *What Do They Really Want?* A report on a questionnaire addressed to general practitioners in the Wessex Region. Winchester: Wessex Regional Hospital Board, 1964.

22

Medical Care and the Public

Case Study of a Medical Group

Eliot Freidson

Medical practice cannot take place without submitting to the assessment of laymen who, by definition, are not equipped to do so on a scientific basis. This paradoxical condition exists because medicine is not, strictly speaking, synonymous with medical science. Medicine is the *application* of medical science, which is quite another thing. Problems of applying science vary considerably from one discipline and task to another. One significant criterion of variation lies in whether application requires the consent of the subject or not and, in addition, whether it depends upon the initiative of the subject or not.

The most successful fields of application are those in which the subject need neither consent nor take any initiative. The addition of vitamins to foods at the factory, for example, influences nutrition independently of what people may know or believe about modern medicine. Medical practice, however, may be said to deal with that very large residue of health problems which have not yet been controlled by automatic methods. Its success is contingent on the willingness of people to seek out and to co-operate with its services. This contingency creates an important source of strain, in that, in order to gain patients, the doctor may have to give up some of his control over the quality of the services he gives. Indeed, it may be said that it is particularly difficult to maintain a high quality of care in some types of medical practice.

Group practice is said to solve the problem of maintaining high standards of medical care, but is it equally successful at attracting and holding its patients? In this paper, after discussion of significant variation in medical practice, I shall report the general findings of an attempt I made to assess how patients responded to the care they got from one group practice.

SOURCE: *Annals of the American Academy of Political and Social Science* 346 (1963): 57–66. Reprinted by permission of the publisher and the author.

Types of Medical Practice

The common distinction between the general practitioner and specialist consultant points to one important variable bearing on the motivation of the people who are seeking medical services. Put somewhat oversimply, the people who use a general practitioner are less likely to be profoundly worried about their ailments than are the people who use a specialist after having seen a general practitioner. People distinguish between everyday, simple ailments and "serious" illness, between seeking relief for temporary discomforts and cure for unusually persistent pain. Thus, the nature of the patient's motivation to co-operate with the physician varies.

Furthermore, the patient's capacity to take initiative in his relation with the doctor also varies by, if nothing more, the stage of his illness. A very sick patient has not enough energy to do more than lie in bed and be worked on, nor has an anesthetized patient. The legally committed mental patient is stripped of the capacity to take any initiative that the therapists do not themselves encourage. Obviously, patients in these positions are very much like hungry people who have nothing but factory-processed foods to choose.

These observations allow us to identify the type of medical practice where the problems of the application of scientific medical knowledge are greatest, namely, practice in which the everyday ills of not-very-sick people are treated. The general practitioner obviously stands for such practice, as do, in some circumstances, the internist, pediatrician, and other specialists to whom people may go for their initial complaints. These practices all depend on the layman's own choice under conditions in which his motives to co-operate with the doctor, and the doctor's leverage over him, are not strong. They may be called patient-chosen practices.

The very survival of such practices depends on attracting choices and satisfying wants which, by definition, do not rest on a knowledgeable scientific basis. It is commonly believed and apparently true that people are prone to pick doctors of their own religion or national background, of pleasing personality, and other scientifically irrelevant criteria. Where there are enough doctors to permit choice, the doctor's success and even economic survival depend upon his conformity to such criteria.

Furthermore, it is plausible that doctors in such a position also are pressed to conform to other lay criteria bearing more directly on the medical care they give. The volume of prescriptions for the various antibiotics, steroids, and tranquilizers cannot be ascribed entirely to actual need. Doctors who depend on lay choices and referrals are subject to persistent lay demands for "wonder drugs" and other well-published modes of treatment, and, apparently, many give in.

The second type of practice, unlike the first, does not rest on patient choice. It is colleague-chosen, in that, at a stage of illness in which he is getting worried, the patient is referred to the doctor by another practitioner. Its success depends upon conforming to the criteria that guide the choice of and referral by other doctors. Unlike the patient-chosen practice, its medical accomplishments are always in the nature of the case visible to and assessed by the referring physician. Without presuming to make the picture rosier than it is—for the referring doctor in the United States does, on occasion, attempt to impose his relatively uninformed prejudices upon the specialist he refers to—it seems to follow that high standards in this type of practice are more easily encouraged and maintained.

How powerful and pervasive the impact of lay prejudices is on medical practice is unknown at present, but there is sufficient evidence to suggest that it is, at least on occasion, a significant element in patient-chosen practice. Indeed, maintaining high standards of medical care in such practices is particularly difficult. Although in them are treated illnesses which are not regarded as "serious," also treated in the early stages are illnesses which later turn out to be serious. The way early symptoms are treated may make the difference between quick cure or long, drawn-out complications. Maintaining high standards in such patient-chosen practice is, thus, of obvious importance and is a serious problem of public policy both in the United States and abroad.

Promise of Group Practice

One way in which this problem is said to be attacked is by organizing both patient-chose and colleague-chosen practices into a single unit. In the United States, this is called group practice; the organization is called a medical group. Compared to individual solo practice, the medical group is said to be advantageous to physicians in a number of ways. It is advantageous economically in that the overhead costs of practice can be shared, administration rationalized efficiently, and physician income in the early and late years of the career made more secure. It is advantageous personally in that vacations and time off are securely and predictably arranged. And it is advantageous professionally in that continuous association with colleagues may be intellectually rewarding.

This last advantage imputed to group practice is the one most important for the equality of medical care, for it implies that the physician's work is more likely to be subject to the scrutiny and pressure of his colleagues than would be the case if he were practicing alone in his own office, and the physician is thus encouraged to maintain professional standards. If this is really true, group practice is obviously important for public policy. The question is, however, whether it is true or not. General assessment of group practice is not yet possible, but we can gain some preliminary ideas from a study of one group practice on the Eastern Seaboard.[1]

Comprehensive-Care Medical Group

The medical group studied is not characteristic of medical groups in the United States, varying in two important respects. First, its physicians are employed by a hospital which operates the group. Most medical groups are owned by physicians who, being partners, control and operate the practice. Second, the medical group studied is not operated on a fee-for-service basis, as are most in the United States. Patients pay an insurance premium in return for which the group supplies almost all home, office, and hospital services they may need, at no additional charge. These two characteristics are intended to eliminate economic considerations from care, the first presuming that the salaried physician will not be tempted to render unnecessary services because he has no income to gain from them and the second that the patient will use medical services whenever he needs them without concern for their out-of-pocket cost.

By and large, the quality of medical care given by the medical group is higher than average. Some rough indication of this is provided by the fact that all physicians in it are rather well trained. Pediatricians and internists give the everyday care: both they and the other specialists are all either eligible to take specialty-board examinations or have done so and have been certified. Outside consultants have, on occasion, inspected samples of the medical records and, in general, have had high praise for the quality of the care provided by the group. Available comparative statistics indicate that many more disorders are "picked up" and treated in the group than in others. On a medical level, then, the group fulfills the promise of those who regard it as a mode of practice in which technically good care can be provided. The question remaining, however, is whether or not it also supplies the conditions which allow the effective application of scientific skill. One condition necessary for effective application is attracting and holding the patient. What does the group patient expect of the doctor, and what does he believe he gets from the medical group serving him?

Three Patient Wants

Using intensive interviews and questionnaires, it was found that the group patients seemed to desire three things from medical care.

Technical adequacy

First of all, they wanted medical care to be adequate technically. This does not mean that any of them believed a physician to lack a certain minimum competence. Rather, they wanted physicians with more than average competence.

In history-taking and physical examination, the patients looked for what they believed to be indications of care and thoroughness. They made much of the physician who "just looked at me," who did not ask about prior outbreaks of the same symptoms, and who seemed to give an perfunctory examination. The less sophisticated patient tended to use time and number as his criterion, thoroughness becoming synonymous with a time-consuming consultation and the ordering of a great many laboratory tests. More sophisticated patients were more detailed in their expectations of a wide variety of concrete examination procedures and laboratory tests.

There was considerably more complexity and variety in the way the patients assessed competence in diagnosis and therapy. In some way difficult to define precisely, the physician's diagnosis must make sense to the patient, must fit in with his own suspicions. The patient suffering pain and thoroughly convinced he is sick will not be likely to accept a doctor's outright deprecation of his symptoms. If he is not so convinced, he will be relieved by the doctor's assurances that he has nothing to worry about. In addition, when the patient expects some unpleasant mode of treatment—such as surgery—to be required for his ailment and the physician manages to avoid using it, the patient will be impressed. And these days, when "cure" is generally expected of the physician, exceptional competence is imputed by the patients to those who cure quickly and with minimum unpleasantness.

Personal interest

Second, all patients insisted that the doctor take personal interest in them. Although some appreciated a jovial familiarity and others a certain reserve, none had anything approving to say about "impersonality." All agreed that doctors express interest by being willing to talk to them. The words "curt" and "abrupt" occurred again and again as epithets describing uninterested physicians, indicative both of the importance of conversation in the consulting room and of how the appearance of consuming time indicates personal interest as well as thoroughness.

The words "mechanical" and "automatic" were also used to characterize disliked doctors, implying both a lack of personal interest and of the alertness necessary to the exercise of competence. Indeed, the patients were prone to feel that a doctor could not really practice competently unless he took personal interest in them. Interest is seen as a motive for the taking of pains. Its lack not only makes the patient feel uncomfortable as a person but also implies to him that the attention he is getting is not sufficiently well motivated to allow the proper competence to be exercised.

Accessibility

Third and finally, the patients wanted an accessible practice. To the patient who believes he is seriously ill, no expenditure of effort is too much. The physician is expected to give of his own time and energy unstintingly, responding to the patient's call instantly, without hesitation. This is what is expected of the "emergency." Furthermore, when the patient is not so strongly motivated, he wants medical care to be convenient. That is, he wants to be able to get an appointment at an hour convenient to him, even be able to see a doctor if he happens to be passing by and merely drops in. Carried to its logical extreme, he wants the physician to come to his home in order to avoid the trouble of coming to the office at all. Optimal adjustment of practice to the patient's personal life is rarely to be found, of course, save for the court physician of the past and the body physicians of the presently great and eminent, but the patients' efforts are to pull practice toward that direction.

Patient Satisfaction

Given these desires on the part of the patients, did the group practice satisfy them? Insofar as direct questions about satisfaction mean anything, we may say, yes. Almost all of the patients claimed to be completely or generally satisfied. Comparatively few complaints about the care are registered in the "patient complaint department" of the medical group. The average utilization of medical services in the group was higher than in the United States as a whole—a finding certainly reflecting the lack of economic restraints, but one which could not be expected to occur if people were gravely dissatisfied. Furthermore, almost all patients severing their connections with the group claimed they did so because they have moved out of its area of coverage rather than because of dissatisfaction. There is, thus, no doubt that, in a general way, this group practice is successful at attracting patients and holding them. But how do patients assess its virtues in relation to the practitioners they had before they used the medical group?

Examining only the responses of patients who had a regular family doctor before they went to the medical group, consistent evidence from answers to a variety of questions was found to indicate that, among those who felt there was any difference at all, those who felt a comparative lack of personal interest on the part of group doctors were considerably larger in proportion than those who felt such from their former doctors. This picture changes when we examine answers to questions bearing on competence. Most patients were not prone to impute any distinctive competence to either this group or to their former doctors, but a significant proportion were prone to feel they obtained better medical care at the group than they did from their prior doctors. Interviews suggested that the laboratory and referral resources of the group were responsible for the difference in the patients' eyes. Finally, questionnaire responses indicated that a fair proportion of the patients complained about being kept waiting more by their prior practitioner than by the group and about feeling rushed out of the doctor's office slightly more in the group than by their prior practitioner. Considerably more patients complained of the difficulty of getting house calls from their prior practitioners than from the medical group.

Clearly, the patients' experience in the medical group compares rather well with their prior experiences with solo practitioners, though some criticism is raised by the lesser personal interest they feel in the group. By and large, both in professional evaluation of the quality of medical care it provides and in patient satisfaction, we can find evidence of its fulfillment of its promise. However, this conclusion stems from examining the statistical norm which, because the medical group is by no means typical of others, does not allow generalization. It is by examining the statistically minor exceptions that we obtain an idea of the vulnerabilities, the stresses and strains implicit in the situation, and possibly more prominent in other medical groups. We begin to see that those stresses emerge when we examine instances in which patients have avoided the use of the medical group.

Why Patients Avoid the Group

In the survey of group patients, 12 per cent reported they or a member of their family had gone outside the group for an operation or obstetrical delivery and paid the expenses out of pocket. Most of the same people were among the 46 per cent reporting that, on one or more occasions, a doctor outside the medical group was used by some member of the family for nonsurgical services. In the light of our almost total ignorance of the nature of such behavior in other groups and in solo practice, we cannot use these statistics to argue comparative deficiency on the part of the medical group. However, they indubitably point to partial failure, for, if the medical group were entirely attractive, we could not have found such reported "disloyalty."

The use of outside services is associated with a number of variables. The passage of time during which an occasion for outside use may arise is itself significant; the longer the time one is a patient, the greater the likelihood that outside services will be used. The economic capacity to pay for such outside service is also obviously involved. Certain attitudes are connected with outside use, such as feeling a "clinic atmosphere" in the medical group, comparative lack of enthusiasm in evaluating the services of the group, comparatively active and critical responses to medical services in general, and attachment to the physician used before subscribing to medical group services.

The patients' own reasons for seeking outside surgical-obstetrical services stressed, in the majority of cases, preference to use the outside man because of prior familiarity with him, a reason advanced by a fairly small proportion of those using outside medical services. About half of the patients' reason for using outside medical services stressed actual dissatisfaction with the quality of the care they got in the medical group—feeling disinterest on the part of the doctor, lacking confidence in the doctor, failing to obtain persuasive diagnosis or treatment. Most of the remaining reasons—more than a third of all given—referred to house calls, appointments too far in advance, emergency needs, and other items reflecting on the accessibility of the medical group. Indeed, almost two-thirds of those who regularly used an outside doctor cited his greater accessibility to explain their utilization.

Lay versus Professional Judgment

There are, then, three basic reasons people give for their disposition to use medical services outside the medical group. Each one in its own way reflects on some difficulty in the relation of this medical service to its lay clientele. The first reflects the difficulty some patients have relying solely on professionally controlled modes of selecting consultants. The second reflects the difficulty some patients have suspending their own imperfect judgment of the practitioner's diagnosis and prescription or their response to the interest they fail to perceive. The third reflects the difficulty some patients have accepting professional assessments of their need for services.

Leaving aside the less tangible psychological aspects of healing, the patient is denied by the profession to have sufficient competence to evaluate the physician's skill. Professionally, the ideal would be to restrict choice to all those meeting adequate minimum standards established by the profession. This the medical group attempts to do, using specialty-board standards which are higher than those of law. But, in so doing, the group expects the patient to have complete confidence in both its standards and its mode of maintaining them.

Many patients are not prepared to do this, understandably seeking to introduce their own experience into the process. If a man has cured them before, he must be good. If one has never used another, and no one else one knows has ever used him, he is an unknown quantity, even if he has the qualifications necessary for being hired by the group. The tried-and-true is less uncertain than the merely professionally certified.

In the same way, personal experience of illness and cure and like-seeming experience of others are measured against professional diagnosis and prescription. Unless the patient is willing to suspend the evidence of his senses, his personal experience, and that of those close to him, this cannot be otherwise. His very sense of individuality—that the general rules may not apply to him—requires him to gauge the doctor's performance against his own experience. If his "bronchitis" was earlier "cured" by massive doses of penicillin, he finds it hard to accept the doctor's rejection of his suggestion to try it again. If a friend's "cyst" "cleared up" with injections, a woman finds it hard to accept periodic examinations before any decisions and the subsequent recommendation of surgery rather than injections.

In like manner, to feel rather bad but to accept telephone refusal of a house call or an emergency appointment because the symptoms sound like currently epidemic upper-respiratory infections for which no therapy but rest will help is to accept on faith the inclusiveness and accuracy of the doctor's diagnosis in spite of one's subjectively real discomfort. In this, as in the other cases, it is more to be wondered that so many people are willing to accept the professional than that a number do not.

Professionalism and the Group

The very professionalism of the medical group seems to prevent sympathy with such patient responses. Insofar as a medical group brings together a fair number of physicians, it increases the scale of practice. Increase in scale beyond that permitted by the economics of solo practice makes possible the very facilities that impress the patient. However, it also contributes to resistance on the part of the doctor to using the facilities the way the patient might think necessary, for, where each man individually might have several thousand patients, the group may have tens of thousands. This sheer increase in the size of the practice reduces the importance to its economic survival of any individual patient and is part of the reason why high standards can be maintained in spite of patient pressure.

Furthermore, increased scale allows a degree of efficient organization not common to solo practice, laying constraints on both patients and physicians. For example, systematic allocation of time and energy guarantees both twenty-four hour service to the patient and regular leisure hours to the physician. However, time becomes cut up into small units in advance, giving both doctor and patient little space for maneuvering. Leisurely consultations of the sort likely to convey the "taking of pains" and to tolerate conversation become difficult.

Within this framework we can also observe that the bringing together of exceptionally well-qualified men into a situation in which they sustain each other's standards and are comparatively insulated from patient pressures discourages consideration of the patient's subjective needs. The group sees as its business, first of all, the providing of medical care reinforced by high professional standards. It hires its doctors on the basis of professional qualification and reputation rather than lay reputation and only secondarily attends to their gift of dealing with patients.

Moreover, because of their view of themselves as especially well-qualified people, their sensitivity to being "prepaid" and, thus, vulnerable to "being taken advantage of" by the patient, and the general spirit of professionalism, the doctors are inclined to resent having to deal with what they believe to be trivial, for treating the trivial is boring and requires no extraordinary medical skill. Both pediatricians and internists tend to see house calls as almost entirely unnecessary, consuming time and energy which should be saved for serious cases and genuine emergencies. Their self-respect as well-trained people suffers when they are pressed to be accommodating to the patient in circumstances which their judgment declares medically unnecessary.

All things considered, traces of a certain intolerance and rigidity can be found in many of the group physicians' responses to patients, all in the name of high standards and professionalism. The attempt seems to be to leave apparently everyday illness out in limbo. Were it not for the service contract, one would expect many more patients to drop out of sight completely rather than only intermittently, as is now the case.

Professional Syndicalism

In the instance studied, as in the past, the patient has some other doctor to go to, or at least that was the contradicted assumption a doctor made when a patient of his dropped out of sight. However, as the proportion of doctors in the United States diminishes, and as group practices grow and come to include all the physicians in an area, there will cease to be any other place for the patient to go on those occasions when he questions his care. Of course, he may avoid care entirely and dose himself, he may go to a nonmedical practitioner, or he may even hang onto the group with resentment and possibly self-damaging resistance, but none of these alternatives is desirable. The only really desirable alternative is that he find sympathetic consultants in the group who are able to persuade him of the legitimacy of some of their recommendations and, in turn, can be persuaded of the necessity of accepting some of his. The feasibility of that alternative seems to depend on the direction in which group practice develops in the future.

If group practice expands to the point of absorbing solo practice, as has already occurred in parts of the West and Middle West, there is a very real danger of the development of what Richard Titmuss calls a new professional syndicalism unlikely to nurture a desirable alternative for the patient.[2] The fee-for-service system is likely to contribute to the danger, because it involves no continuous obligation to the patient and supports an unqualified take-it-or-go-elsewhere response which, in the face of there being no place else to go, can only be irresponsible. An entrepreneurial foundation for organizing practice is similarly dangerous in a monopolistic context, emphasizing as it does the efficiency necessary for a profitable volume of services. Finally, perhaps most dangerous of all are the all-too-human values of the profession itself—its desire to avoid having to deal with trivial routine and refusal to allow nonmedical practitioners to do so, its desire to brook no encroachment on its responsibility for the patient and to avoid the full consequences of that responsibility.

None of these problems is so serious as to negate the promise of group practice. There really seems to be no choice if high quality is desired. The problem to be solved is the tendency under some circumstances for the very form contributing to high professional quality also to discourage lay utilization of it. That problem is by no means insoluble. Solution, however, is unlikely to be attained by assuming that the same mechanisms under which solo practice flourished are automatically applicable to this quite different form of practice. Systematic study remains to be done, but it is clear that more critical and analytical attention to the problem is required than has thus far been given by either the supporters or detractors of group practice.

Notes

1. Details of the study can be found in Eliot Freidson, *Patients' Views of Medical Practice* (New York: Russell Sage Foundation, 1961).
2. Richard Titmuss, *Essays on 'The Welfare State'* (London: George Allen and Unwin, 1958), pp. 200–202.

23

The Dynamics of the
Psychotherapeutic Relationship

Determinants and Effects of the Therapist's Influence

Jerome D. Frank

All forms of psychotherapy, whatever their underlying theories, and whatever techniques they employ, attempt to promote beneficial changes in a patient's attitudes and symptoms through the influence of a therapist with whom the patient has a close relationship. The purpose of this paper is to review data from diverse sources bearing on the determinants and effects of the patient's emotional dependency on his psychotherapist for relief. The effects may include modifications of the patient's productions in the interview, the duration of treatment itself, and changes in the patient's attitudes and bodily states. Certain mechanisms which may transmit the therapist's expectancies to the patient will be described, and some implications of these data for research and practice will be briefly considered. The major sources of material are reports concerning brainwashing, miracle cures, experimental studies of the psychotherapeutic interview, and the placebo effect.

In general terms, all psychotherapies are concerned with using the influence of the therapist to help patients to unlearn old, maladaptive response patterns and to learn better ones, but they differ considerably in their specific goals and methods. Examples of goals are helping the patient to recover early memories, develop insight, work through transference relationships, release his spontaneity or modify his self-concept. Methods include, for example, free association, client-centered interviews, and progressive relaxation. These differences in therapeutic approach are reflected in differences in the patient's behavior and in the kinds of change resulting from treatment.

In addition to the differing effects of the psychotherapist's influence which depend on his particular orientation and method, all forms of psychotherapy seem to produce certain similar effects based on a quality common to the relationships they

SOURCE: *Psychiatry* 22 (1959): 17–39. Copyright © 1959 by the William Alanson White Psychiatric Foundation, Inc. Reprinted by special permission of the William Alanson White Psychiatric Foundation, Inc.

offer. This common feature is the patient's reliance on the therapist to relieve his distress.

This reliance, which may be forced or voluntary, arises from the interplay of environmental pressures and the patient's subjective state, the relative contribution of each differing from case to case. An example of forced reliance produced primarily by environmental pressure would be the situation of a paranoid patient, placed in a hospital against his will, who believes his incarcertaion to be unjust, but who is nevertheless forced to depend on the staff to gain his release. An example of forced reliance arising from subjective pressure would be the patient in a panic who flees to the psychiatrist for protection. More commonly, especially in office practice, the patient's dependence on the psychiatrist is voluntary and arises from the interplay of more subtle environmental and subjective factors. These lead the patient to expect relief from the psychiatrist, an expectancy which sometimes may be strong enough to justify the term *faith*.

Determinants of the Patient's Reliance on His Psychotherapist

Conditions maintaining or strengthening a patient's reliance on his psychotherapist to relieve his suffering may be conveniently grouped under four headings: the culture, the treatment situation, the therapist, and the patient.

The Culture

The beliefs of members of a culture as to what constitutes illness and its treatment are formed and supported by generally held cultural attitudes.[1] A member of a particular society can regard himself as having an emotional illness—for which the proper treatment is psychotherapy—only if his society recognizes the existence of such illnesses and sanctions psychotherapy as the appropriate treatment for them. The same symptoms which in the Middle Ages were viewed as signs of demoniacal possession to be treated by exorcism, are now regarded as manifestations of mental illness to be treated by a psychiatrist. In World War II Russian soldiers did not have psychoneuroses, which can only mean that the Russian army did not recognize the existence of such conditions. Presumably soldiers with functional complaints were regarded either as malingerers, and thus subject to disciplinary action, or as medically ill, and therefore to be treated by regular physicians. In the American army, by contrast, many commonplace reactions to the stresses of military life were initially regarded as signs of psychoneurosis. Soldiers with these complaints, therefore, often received psychotherapy, which not infrequently culminated in their discharge. Today many of these same soldiers would be promptly returned to active duty.

In mid-century America, mental illness has not fully shaken off its demonological heritage, as evidenced by the stigma still attached to it. Both psychotics and neurotics, however, are seen as suffering from bona fide illnesses, and the dominant treatment for most of the conditions subsumed under mental and emotional illness is psychotherapy. Moreover, the psychiatrist is generally regarded as the best qualified dispenser of this form of treatment, although other professional groups are challenging his right to this pre-eminence. Therefore an American today, once he has accepted the label of being mentally or emotionally ill, is culturally predisposed to expect relief from psychotherapy and to look to a psychiatrist for this relief.

The Treatment Situation

Certain situations in which psychotherapy is practiced, notably mental hospitals, to a varying degree force the patient to become dependent on the treatment staff. Even when there is no external compulsion, however, many aspects of the psychotherapeutic situation in both hospital and office supply cues which tend to impress the patient with the importance of the procedure, and also to identify psychotherapy with other healing methods. In both ways they strengthen his expectation of relief and thus his dependency on the therapist. The cues start to operate before the patient and therapist meet. Most patients reach the presence of the psychotherapist only after some preliminaries. If the patient is hospitalized, the commitment procedure heightens his sense of dependence on the hospital staff for his release. Voluntary admission procedures usually require the patient to sign a witnessed request for admission which contains a "three-day notice" clause. This impresses him with the importance of the step he is taking and underlines the staff's control over him while in the hospital. If properly conducted, the admission procedure can heighten the patient's hope of benefit from his stay and his trust in the treatment staff.

Psychiatrists working with outpatients are rightly concerned that the referral heighten the patient's favorable expectations, rather than making him feel that he is being 'brushed off—a situation which frequently occurs. One of the purposes of the intake procedure of psychiatric outpatient clinics is to predispose the patient favorably to psychotherapy. At the Phipps Clinic, for example, each new patient is first briefly interviewed by a trained nurse as a deliberate reminder that he is under medical auspices.

More commonly, patients coming to a psychiatric clinic first have one or more intake interviews with a social worker. The avowed purposes of these are to determine the patient's suitablity for psychotherapy and to prepare him for it. The patient may, however, perceive the intake process as a probationary period to determine his worthiness to receive the psychiatrist's ministrations. Thus subtly impressing him with the importance of psychotherapy heightens his susceptibility to the psychiatrist's influence. In this sense the intake procedure is analogous to the preparatory rites undergone by suppliants at faith healing shrines, with the social worker in the role of acolyte and the psychiatrist as high priest.

Once in the presence of his therapist, the patient's favorable expectancies are reinforced by the setting. Psychotherapy has developed its own trappings, to symbolize healing; like other physicians, psychotherapists display diplomas prominently, but in place of the symbols of the stethoscope, the ophthalmoscope, and the reflex hammer, they must rely on the heavily laden bookcases, the couch, the easy chair, and usually a large photograph of the leader of their particular school looking benignly but impressively down on the proceedings. In medical institutions, much of the same effect is created simply by the locale of the psychiatrists' offices, which identifies them with the healing activities of the hospital.[2]

The therapist's activities in the initial interview may also have the function, in part, of heightening the patient's favorable expectancies. Psychiatrists usually take a history, loosely following the model of a medical history, thereby reinforcing their identification with the medical profession in the patient's mind. Psychologists frequently begin by giving the patient a battery of psychological tests, their badge of special competence. Both are apt to conclude the interview by offering the patient some sort of formulation which impresses him with their ability to understand and help him.

In the early days of psychoanalysis, before the setting and procedures had achieved their symbolic power, the analyst might have found it necessary to impress the patient by other means. This is illustrated by Freud's example of the patient who failed to shut the door to the waiting room. He pointed out that this omission

> ... throws light upon the relation of this patient to the physician. He is one of the great number of those who seek authority, who want to be dazzled, intimidated. Perhaps he had inquired by telephone as to what time he had best call, he had prepared himself to come on a crowd of suppliants. ... He now enters an empty waiting room which is, moreover, most modestly furnished, and he is disappointed. He must demand reparation from the physician for the wasted respect that he has tendered him, and so he omits to close the door between the reception room and the office. ... He would also be quite unmannerly and supercilious during the consulation if his presumption were not at once restrained by a sharp reminder.[3]

In terms of this discussion, Freud interpreted the patient's behavior as expressing a lack of confidence in him as a successful healer, and sought to restore this confidence by a brusque command.

As treatment progresses, the therapist instructs the patient in certain activities which are based on a particular theory. Whatever their specific nature, all implicitly convey that the therapist knows what is wrong with the patient and that the special procedure is the treatment for it. In addition, the underlying theory supplies a frame of reference which helps the patient to make sense of behavior and feelings which had been mysterious and to learn that they are not unique, but represent important and widely shared experiences.

Thus from the moment the prospective patient approaches psychotherapy until his treatment terminates, he is confronted with cues and procedures which tend to impress him with both the importance of the procedure and its promise of relief. These heighten the therapist's potential influence over the patient and, as will be discussed below, probably have some therapeutic effects in themselves by mobilizing his favorable expectations.

The Therapist

In addition to as yet ill-defined personal characteristics, two attitudes of the therapist foster the patient's confidence in him. One is his faith in the patient's capacity to benefit from treatment, which is implied in the mere act of accepting him as a patient. The therapist's acceptance of the patient may be influenced by his own feelings. In his first publication on psychotherapy Freud wrote:

> The procedure ... presupposes ... in [the physician] ... a personal concern for the patients. ... I cannot imagine bringing myself to delve into the psychical mechanism of a

hysteria in anyone who struck me as low-minded and repellent, and who, on closer acquaintance, would not be capable of arousing human sympathy.[4]

Similar considerations make some psychotherapists unwilling to accept alcoholics or patients with antisocial character disorders for treatment. Schaffer and Myers[5] have found that middle-class clinic patients, more often than lower-class ones, are assigned to senior staff members, who presumably have first choice. They relate this to the fact that middle-class patients appear to offer better prospects for therapy because their values are closer to those of the psychiatrists. The therapist's faith in the capacities of his patient is a strong incentive to maintain that attitude of active personal participation which helps the patient to develop confidence in him.[6]

The other therapeutically potent attitude of the therapist is his confidence in his theory and method of treatment. How these enhance the therapeutic meaning of the treatment situation in the patient's eyes has been touched on above. Adherence to a definite therapeutic procedure and theory also helps to maintain the psychotherapist's confidence. As one young analyst remarked, "Even if the patient doesn't improve, you know you're doing the right thing."

In fields where there is a common body of validated knowledge and the effectiveness of treatment has been demonstrated—for example, abdominal surgery or infectious disease—the physician's confidence rests on his mastery of the pertinent knowledge and diagnostic and therapeutic techniques. In psychotherapy, which lacks such a body of information, therapists tend to rely for their emotional security on allegiance to a group which represents a particular view. This allegiance is fostered by a long period of indoctrination, as many writers have pointed out.[7] Glover, who deplores the effect of this on the research capacities of young psychoanalysts, writes:

> It is scarcely to be expected that a student who has spent some years under the artificial ... conditions of a training analysis and whose professional career depends on overcoming 'resistance' to the satisfaction of his training analyst, can be in a favorable position to defend his scientific integrity against his analyst's theories and practice. ... For according to his analyst the candidate's objections to interpretations rate as 'resistances.' In short there is a tendency inherent in the training situation to perpetuate error.[8]

The effectiveness of indoctrination in psychotherapy is suggested by replies of a group of psychotherapists—mainly Freudian, Adlerian, or Jungian in orientation—to a questionnaire distributed by Werner Wolff.[9] Seventy percent stated that they believed their particular form of therapy to be the best, a high figure considering the absence of any objective data that one form of therapy is superior to another.[10] Only 25 percent, however, professed themselves satisfied with their theoretical orientation. It is interesting that these consisted mostly of disciples of Adler and Jung. Wolff comments: "The degree of identification of each member with the leader of the group is greater in minority groups, which defend their new system against the system of the majority group."[11] Thus 45 percent, or about half of those who responded, believed their therapy to be best, not only in the absence of objective evidence but also without being sure of the soundness of the theory on which it was based. This is a striking testimonial to the faith of those therapists in their procedures.

It seems safe to conclude that training in psychotherapy tends to develop a strong allegiance in the young therapist to his therapeutic school. This contributes to his confidence in his brand of treatment, which, in turn, helps him to inspire confidence in his patients.

At this point it seems appropriate to mention that the factors so far enumerated which enhance the patient's faith in psychotherpy in the United States are remarkably similar to those reported with respect to shamanism in Indian tribes. Henri Ellenberger, for example, points out that among the Kwakiutl Indians, "to become a shaman requires a four-year program in a kind of professional school with strict rules. The shamans constitute a corporation and possess a considerable body of knowledge which they are anxious to transmit to qualified persons."[12] He mentions four factors to which the success of shamanistic cures is attributed. These are: the faith of the shamans in their own abilities, the faith of the patient in the healer's abilities, the acknowledgment of the disease by the social group, and the acceptance of the healing method by the group. Shamans do not treat all diseases, many of which are treated by natural medications or plants; but there are special diseases for which the intervention of the shaman is the only recourse.

The Patient

The extent to which a patient accepts the cues offered by the culture, the treatment situation, and his therapist as representing potential relief depends, of course, also on his own attributes. Many complex and as yet poorly understood factors influence a patient's ability to develop trust in his therapist. In a recent study of patients in a psychiatric clinic, more of those who remained in individual psychotherapy at least six months than of those who dropped out within the first month were suggestible, as measured by a sway test.[13] This study also confirmed the results of Schaffer and Myers with respect to social and educational status and remaining in treatment.[14] That is, patients whose values were such that the goals and methods of psychotherapy made sense to them were more likely to stay in treatment.

Perhaps the major personal determinant of the patient's faith in treatment is the degree of his distress. The literature is consistent in the finding that with neurotics the degree of reported distress is positively related to remaining in treatment.[15] There are at least two possible, and compatible, explanations of this. One, which is consistent with the little that is known about miracle cures, is that presumably the more wretched a person is, the greater his hunger for relief and the greater his predisposition to put faith in what is offered.[16] The other possibility is that the patient's revelation of distress is in itself a sign that he is favorably disposed to trust the therapist and therapy; that is, it may indicate a willingness on the part of the patient to emphasize aspects of himself which show his vulnerablility or weakness.

Modes of Transmission of the Therapist's Influence

That the psychotherapist influences his patients is generally accepted. Early psychotherapeutic techniques such as mesmerism, direct suggestion under hypnosis, and the moral persuasion of Dubois deliberately exploited the therapist's power. Directive forms of psychotherapy still dominate the treatment scene in their modern forms of hypnotherapy, progressive relaxation, directive counseling, and simple advice-giving. Of Wolff's respondents, most of whom, it will be remembered, were trained in the broad psychoanalytical tradition, only 27 percent said they used a strictly nondirective approach. [17]

Nevertheless, beginning with Freud's substitution of so-called free association for hynosis, the dominant trend in writings on psychotherapy has emphasized the desirability of the therpist's using more indirect methods of influence. Tte goals of treatment are expressed in more ambitious terms than the relief of the patient's distress and improvement of his functioning. He must be helped toward greater self-actualization, spontaneity, maturity, creativity, and the like. The therapist facilitates the patient's movement by empathizing with him, accepting him, colaborating with him, respecting him, and being permissive. The patient's natural tendency to be dependent on the therapist is to be combatted. The therapist is not to persuade or advise, since such activities impede the patient's growth toward emotional maturity.

This trend may spring in part from democratic values, which place a higher worth on apparently self-directed, spontaneous behavior than on that obviously caused by outside influence. [18] The swing from directive techniques also derives in part from the experience that many cures achieved through these means proved to be transitory, although whether a larger percentage of enduring results is achieved by more permissive techniques is still unknown.

I shall now review some ways in which the therapist may transmit his expectancies to the patient and so influence the latter's productions in treatment, often without the awareness of either. Data are adduced from two sources: Chinese thought reform or brainwashing, and content analyses of patients' and therapists' verbalizations in treatment.

Chinese Thought Reform

At first glance, nothing could seem more remote from psychotherapy than methods used by Chinese Communists to obtain confessions from their prisoners. The objects of psychotherapy are patients; those of thought reform, prisoners. Patients and therapists operate within the same broad cultural framework; the cultural values of interrogators and prisoners clash. The goals of psychotherapist and patient are roughly similar; those of interrogator and prisoner are diametrically opposed. In psychotherapy the welfare of the patient is uppermost; in thought reform that of the prisoner is of no account. Thought reform relies on the application of extreme force; psychotherapy typically eschews overt pressure on the patient.

Nevertheless, several psychiatrists have been impressed by certain parallels between psychotherapy and thought reform; [19] in both someone in distress must rely on someone else for relief, and in both the person in distress is required to review and reinterpret his past life in detail. Just as the study of pathological processes increases the understanding of normal ones by throwing certain of their characteristics into relief, a study of thought reform, which may be regarded as a pathological form of psychotherapy, highlights some aspects of the latter which have received inadequate attention.

Thought reform utilizes both group and individual pressures to break down the prisoner's sense of personal identity and influence him to assume a new one incorporating the attitudes and values of his captors. The victim is snatched from his usual activities and abruptly plunged into a completely hostile environment. Present miseries are compounded by threats of worse to come, with the possibility of death always present. Physical tortures are of the humiliating type, such as manacling the prisoner's hands behind his back so that he has to eat like an animal. He receives none of the respect or consideration accorded to his previous status. For example, he is allowed only a few moments to defecate and must do it in public. He is completely immersed in a group which incessantly hammers at his values and demands that he adopt theirs. The group's attitude is implacable and rigidly consistent. For example, the group assumes that the prisoner is guilty and that the enormity of his offenses justifies the harshest punishment. Therefore, any punishment he does receive is a sign of his captor's leniency. The effect of these pressures on the prisoner is strengthened by complete severance of his contact with former associates, and he receives only such distorted and fragmentary news of the outer world as fits the aims of his captors. By these means his sense of personal identity is weakened and his critical faculties are dulled, decreasing his ability to resist.

The prisoner is removed from the group only for the time he spends with an interrogator, whose task it is to obtain the prisoner's "confession" of his "crimes." Certain features of the interrogation situation are relevant to this discussion. It is characterized by rigidity in some respects, by ambiguity in others, by repetition, and by insistence on the prisoner's participation.

The rigidity lies in the interrogator's attitude of infallibility. His position is that the Communist viewpoint on every issue is the only correct one. The prisoner's guilt is axiomatic, and all his productions are judged in the light of this assumption. The interrogator indicates that he knows what the crimes are, but the prisoner must make his own confession. He is encouraged to talk or write freely about himself and his alleged crimes, but he is not told what to write. He may be punished severely, however, if his production does not accord with the desires of his interrogator. Those statements which do meet the interrogator's wishes gain approval, which reinforces them the more effectively because of the prisoner's previous apprehensiveness.[20] No matter what he confesses, it is never enough, but the hope continues to be held out to him that once he makes a proper and complete confession he will be released. The prisoner is thus placed in a perceptually ambiguous situation which compels him to scrutinize the interrogator for clues as to what is really wanted, while at the same time offering him no target against which to focus his resistance.

The participation of the prisoner in bringing about his own change of attitude is implicit in this procedure. By putting the responsibility for writing an adequate confession on him, his captors force him to commit himself to the process. Schein describes the same procedure in Korean prison camps: "It was never enough for the prisoner to listen and absorb; some kind of verbal or written response was always demanded. . . . The Chinese apparently believed that if they could once get a man to participate . . . eventually he would accept the attitudes which the participation expressed.[21]

Finally, repetition is an important component of thought reform: "One of the chief characteristics of the Chinese was their immense patience in whatever they were doing. . . . they were always willing to make their demand or assertion over and over again. Many men pointed out that most of the techniques used gained their effectiveness by being used in this repetitive way until the prisoner could no longer sustain his resistance."[22]

Under these pressures the prisoner's self-searchings produce material increasingly in line with the interrogator's desires, and eventually the victim may be unable to tell fact from fantasy. In extreme cases he accepts his fabricated confession as true. Lifton tells of a man who confessed with conviction and in detail that he had tried to attract the attention of an official representative of his country who passed by the door of his cell, only to discover later that the episode could not possibly have occurred.[23]

The world of the victim of thought reform seems a far cry from that of the mental patient, and yet the analogies are sometimes startling. Some patients are in the same state of terror and bewilderment that the Communists try to produce in their prisoners. To quote Hinkle and Wolff,

> In all [the Communist indoctrination programs] the subject is faced with pressure upon pressure and discomfort upon discomfort, and none of his attempts to deal with his situation lead to amelioration of his lot. Psychiatrists may refer to a man in such a situation as 'emotionally bankrupt.' Some of the patients who seek the help of psychiatrists are in a similar state. The pressures and convolutions of their lives have reached a point at which they can no longer deal with them, and they must have help. It is recognized that such a state of 'emotional bankruptcy' provides a good opportunity for the therapist.[24]

Furthermore, some interrogators are analogous to psychotherapists in two respects. Their contact with the prisoner is close and prolonged, and they see themselves as trying to promote the prisoner's true welfare by getting him to discard his unhealthy, outmoded values and attitudes and adopt the "healthier" ones of the Communist ideology. Under these conditions it is not surprising that intense transferences and countertransferences can develop between a prisoner and his interrogator.

As Erving Goffman has vividly pointed out, mental hospitals, in the eyes of many patients, may display some of the characteristics of the Communist prisons.[25] Patients are deprived of their usual badges of personal identity and are forced into a humiliating position of complete dependence on the treatment staff for even such small things as cigarettes. They are cut off from their contacts with the outer world and totally immersed in a different culture. They see themselves as completely in the power of the staff, whose decisions often appear to them to be arbitrary or capricious. They know that in order to get out they must satisfy the demands of the staff, but they have no clear idea as to how to do this.

Moreover, the ideology of the mental hospital is consistently and rigidly maintained. Thus all measures applied to the patient, such as transfer from an open to a locked ward, are perceived by the staff as "therapy." If the patient demurs, he is met with what Goffman calls the "institutional smirk," with its implication that "you may think that's what you want, but we know better." Although this somewhat malicious description deliberately highlights the coercive aspects of the mental hospital, the caricature is not so extreme as to be unrecognizable.

The parallels between thought reform and outpatient psychiatry, whether in clinic or private practice, are much fainter, but they can still be discerned. As with hospitalized patients, the psychiatrist's potential influence on the outpatient depends in part on the latter's expectancy of help. A few office patients turn to the psychiatrist as a last resort after having vainly tried other possible sources. Their favorable expectancy, like that of many hospitalized patients, is based on desperation. A larger group are not sure why they have come to the psychiatrist or how the latter can help them. The psychiatrist then has the task of mobilizing their favorable expectancies by convincing them that they are ill, and that the illness is best treated by psychotherapy. This is usually expressed as arousing the patient's consciousness of illness. As Kubie writes: "Without a full-hearted acknowledgment of the sense of illness a patient can go through only the motions of treatment.[26]

Moreover, he writes, "it is often necessary during an analysis to lead a patient through a sustained period of relative isolation from his usual activities and human associations."[27] It may not be entirely farfetched to read into such a statement a recognition that a patient, like the prisoner, can more easily be brought to change his ideology if he is removed from the groups which reinforce his current one.

Viewing psychotherapy in the light of thought reform calls attention to another feature which tends to enhance the therapist's influence. This is his interpretation of all of the patient's thoughts, feelings, and acts in terms of a consistent and unshakable theoretical framework. In accordance with his theory, the therapist assumes that the patient's distress is related to repressed infantile memories, parataxic distortions, or an unrealistic self-image, to take three examples. Therapy continues until the patient acknowledges these phenomena in himself and deals with them to the therapist's and hiw own satisfaction. The possibility that he has not experienced the phenomena in question or that they may be irrelevant to his illness is not entertained. Freud's handling of his discovery that patients confabulated infantile memories may serve as a prototype of this way of thinking. As he was quick to see, "this discovery... serves either to discredit the analysis which has led to such a result or to discredit the patients upon whose testimony the analysis, as well as the whole understanding of neurosis, is built up." A bleak predicament indeed, from which Freud extricates himself by a tour de force. He points out that "these phantasies possess *psychological* reality in contrast to *physical* reality," and "*in the realm of neuroses the psychological reality is the determining factor.*"[28] Therefore the fact that these infantile experiences were fantasies rather than actualitites, far from refuting his theories, actually confirms them. The Freudian theory of neurosis rests on more solid evidence than real or fabricated infantile memories, of course. The purpose of this example is to illustrate a type of thinking which is characteristic of psychotherapists and which contributes to their influence on patients.

The therapist may protect the infallibility of his theoretical orientation in subtle ways. For example, behavior of patients which does not conform to his position is apt to be characterized as "resistance," or "manipulation." Patients' criticisms can always be dismissed as based on "transference," implying that they are entirely the result of the patient's distorted perceptions. Faced with such behaviors, the therapist is admonished not to become "defensive"—that is, not to admit, even by implication, that his viewpoint requires defending.

The therapist also has ways of maintaining his faith in his theory and procedures in the face of a patient's failure to respond favorably. He may take refuge in the position that the patient broke off treatment too soon. Or he may conclude that the patient was insufficiently motivated or otherwise not suitable for treatment. Occasionally he may entertain the possibility that he applied his technique incorrectly, but failures rarely lead him to question the technique itself or the premises underlying it. In short, the vicissitudes of treatment are not permitted to shake the therapist's basic ideology.

In calling attention to the means by which psychotherapists maintain their conviction of the correctness of their theories and procedures, I imply no derogation. On the contrary, this conviction probably is partly responsible for the success of all forms of psychotherapy. I stress it here as one of the ingredients which heighten the therapist's influence on the patient.

The methods of psychotherapy, finally, are slightly analogous to those of thought reform with respect of repetition, participation, and ambiguity. In long-term psychotherapy, the patient repeatedly reviews material connected with certain issues, toward which the therapist maintains a consistent attitude. That this may tend to influence the patient in accordance with the therapist's viewpoint is consistent with what is known concerning the role of repetition in all learning.

The desirability of the patient's being an active participant or collaborator in the treatment process is universally recognized. One of the many reasons for encouraging such an attitude is that it forestalls or combats the patient's tendency to become dependent on the therapist. Yet the perspective of thought reform suggests that it may also heighten the therapist's influence in at least two ways. The more the patient's active participation can be obtained, the more he commits himself to the change which the therapist is trying to induce. Moreover, the patient has greater difficulty in mobilizing his resistance against a collaborative than a directive therapist.

It is in the ambiguity of the therapeutic situation, however, that its greatest potentiality for influence probably lies. Like the interrogators in thought reform, some psychotherapists convey to the patient that they know what is wrong with him but that he must find it out for himself in order to be helped. This is one means of enlisting his participation, but it also gives the patient an ambiguous task.[29] This ambiguity is heightened by the fact that the end-point of this process, whether it be unearthing his infantile memories, making his unconscious conscious, correcting his idealized image, or what not, is indeterminate, like that of the confession. The patient is to keep on trying until he is cured, but the criteria which will indicate that cure has been achieved are not clearly specified.

Psychotherapists have always been alert to the possibility of directly imposing their own ideas in the long-term, repetitive relationship of psychotherapy and have advocated certain attitudes to diminish this possibility. One is permissiveness; that is, the therapist leaves the patient free to use the therapeutic situation as he wishes. The perspective of thought reform suggests that, given a patient who expects the therapist to relieve his distress, the latter's permissiveness, by creating an ambiguous situation, may enhance rather than diminish his power to indoctrinate the patient. By failing to take a definite position, the therapist deprives the patient of a target against which to mobilize his opposition. Furthermore, an ambiguous situation tends to create or increase the patient's confusion, which as Cantril suggests, tends to heighten suggestibility.[30] It also makes him more anxious, therefore presumably heightening his motivation to please the therapist.[31] This motivation is enhanced by the fact that the ambiguity is in a context of threat of unfortunate consequences if the patient does not perform the task properly. In thought reform the threat of punishment for failure is direct; in psychotherpy it is indirectly conveyed by the implication that the patient's distress will not be relieved, and perhaps also by subtle hints of the therapist's disapproval or lack of interest when the patient is not "cooperating." That an ambiguous therapeutic situation may intensify the patient's search for subtle hints as to how well he is doing can be testified to by many analysands, who are acutely aware of changes in the analyst's respiration, when he lights his pipe, shifts in his chair, and so on, even when he is out of their sight.

In summary, factors similar to those in thought reform can, in greatly attenuated form, he discerned in psychotherapy, and may in part determine the strength of the psychotherapist's influence. Changes produced by such means range from mere verbal compliance which vanishes with the disappearance of the influencing agent, to genuine internalization of attitudes and values, depending on personal and situational factors still not understood.[32]

Psychotherapy as Operant Conditioning

A mechanism of transmission of influence which seems analogous to operant conditioning[33] occurs in psychotherapy, according to some experimental evidence, and probably also in thought reform. This technique, which produces extremely rapid learning in animals, consists in reinforcing by a prompt reward some spontaneous act—such as a pigeon's pecking at a target or a rat's hitting a lever with his paw. For example, when the rat hits the lever he receives a pellet of food. Analogously, in psychotherapy the patient's spontaneous behavior is his speech, and the therapist reinforces certain verbalizations by cues of approval which may be as subtle as a fleeting change of expression, or as obvious as an elaborate interpretation.

The reinforcing effect of simple signs of interest lies in the fact that, as Jurgen Ruesch says: "The driving force inherent in any form of psychotherapy is related to the patient's experience of pleasure when a message has been acknowledged. Successful communication is gratifying; it brings about a feeling of inclusion and security and leads to constructive action. Disturbed communication is frustrating; it brings about a feeling of loneliness and despair and leads to destructive action."[34]

The first experimental support of the hypothesis that verbal behavior might be subject to operant conditioning was offered by Greenspoon.[35] He had graduate students say as many words as they could in 50 minutes. He sat behind the subjects and exerted no ostensible control over them. In accordance with a preconceived plan, however, he sometimes said, "Mm-hm," and sometimes, "Huh-uh," just after the subjects used a plural noun. He also introduced other variations as controls. By statistical analysis he showed that "Mm-hm" significantly increased the number of plural nouns spoken by the subjects and "Huh-uh" significantly decreased them. These effects occurred without the subjects' knowledge that they were being influenced.

Following this lead, experimenters have begun to study the patient's productions in psychotherapy as influenced by the therapist's behavior. Only a few results have been published to date, but they confirm Greenspoon's findings. Salzinger and Pisoni used as subjects 14 female and 6 male schizophrenics newly admitted to the New York State Psychiatric Institute.[36] Each patient was interviewed for 30 minutes, once by a man and once by a woman, on two consecutive days, within one week after arrival. In each interview, for the first ten minutes the interviewer offered no reinforcement. During the next ten minutes he systematically reinforced affect statements by the patient, by simple grunts, looks of interest, and so on. During the third ten minutes, no reinforcement was offered. Affect statements were defined as those beginning with "I" or "we," followed by an expression of feeling. They found that, with both interviewers, even a ten-minute period of reinforcement significantly increased the frequency of affect statements over both the control periods. Apparently patients learn as fast as pigeons. Murray reports a content analysis of two case protocols, one of his own and one of "Herbert Bryan" published by Rogers.[37] In his patient, "defensive statements" as defined by him, and which he disapproved, fell from 140 to 9 per interview, over 17 sessions. Expressions of hostility, which he permitted—and perhaps subtly reinforced—rose from practically none to nearly 80 by the fourth interview. In Herbert Bryan's protocol, statements in categories disapproved by the therapist fell from 45 percent of the total number of statements in the second hour to 5 percent in the eighth. Statements in approved categories rose from 1 percent in the second hour to 45 percent in the seventh.

The case of Herbert Bryan has particular interest because it was offered as an example of nondirective therapy. The therapist presumably believed that he was not influencing the patient's productions, yet different raters were able to classify his interventions as implicitly approving or disapproving with a high degree of reliability. Apparently a therapist can strongly affect his patient's productions without being aware that he is doing so.

Perhaps other conventional psychotherapeutic maneuvers may also function as positive or negative stimuli for operant conditioning, thereby influencing the patient's productions in the direction of the therapist's expectancies. Silence, for example, when used to indicate lack of interest, might be a negative reinforcer, influencing the patient to desist from those verbalizations which elicit it.

An interpretation can be viewed as having both positive and negative reinforcing potential. It acts as a positive reinforcer by implicitly conveying the therapist's interest in the patient's verbalization, and, more specifically, by heightening its significance. This it does by relating the patient's statement to a larger system of thought, often with dramatic overtones, as is implied by such concepts as, for example, Oedipus complex, persona and anima, and self-actualization. On the negative side, an interpretation of a patient's behavior as resistance—for example, as an implicit indication of the therapist's disapproval—would probably act as a negative reinforcer.

Beyond their function as positive and negative reinforcers, interpretations are the means whereby the therapist presents his self-consistent and unshakable value system to the patient and demonstrates his mastery of a body of theory and technique. In these ways they further contribute to the therapist's influence.

The possibility that interpretations might directly influence the patient's productions has long been recognized. Psychoanalysts in particular have sought to deny that interpretations can operate as suggestion in this sense.[38] The material just cited as well as evidence from psychoanalysis itself casts considerable doubt on this contention. Freud's well-known statement that ". . . we are not in a position to force anything on the patient about the things of which he is ostensibly ignorant or to influence the products of the analysis by arousing an expectation," was made before his discovery that patients fabricated infantile memories in accord with his theories.[39] Glover went to some lengths to draw a distinction between correct and incorrect interpretations, agreeing that the latter might operate by suggestion but offering elaborate reasons why the former did not. That he did not entirely convince himself is suggested by the following quotation, from an article written some twenty years later: ". . . despite all dogmatic and puristic assertions to the contrary we cannot exclude or have not yet excluded the transference effect of 'suggestion through interpretation.' "[40] Recently Carl Rogers has agreed that even his "client-centered" techniques "institute certain attitudinal conditions, and the client has relatively little voice in the establishment of these conditions. We predict that if these conditions are instituted, certain behavioral consequences will ensue in the client. Up to this point this is largely external control."[41]

Operant conditioning offers a mechanism for explaining the repeated observation that patients tend to express their problems and attitudes in the therapist's language. Stekel said long ago, "Dreams are 'made to order,' are produced in the form that will best please the analyst."[42] Patients treated by Carl Rogers' group show a shift of their perceived self toward their ideal self.[43] Those treated by Murray, who operates in a framework of learning theory, show a decrease in defensive verbalizations and an increase in direct expression of feeling.[44] Patients in psychoanalysis express increasing amounts of hitherto unconscious material as treatment progresses. Heine found that veterans who had undergone psychotherapy expressed the reasons for their improvement in terms of the theoretical systems of their therapists.[45] Rosenthal found that improved patients showed a shift in their value system to those held by the therapist.[46]

It may be tentatively concluded that the elimination of suggestion in the crude sense of directly implanting ideas in the patient does not exclude reinforcement which may influence his productions in the directions expected or desired by the therapist. It would be a mistake, however, to generalize too hastily from these scanty findings. They apply only to what the patient says, not to how he actually feels. In psychotherapy as in thought reform, the extent to which changes in verbalizations represent mere compliance or internalization of the attitudes expressed is unknown.[47] There is a distinct possibility, however, that a person's attitudes may be significantly influenced by his own words. Most persons cannot indefinitely tolerate a discrepancy between communicative behavior and underlying attitudes because such deceit is incompatible with self-respect, and under some conditions it is the attitudes which yield. [48]

The chief interest of operant conditioning for psychotherapy at this point is that it can work through cues of which the therapist is unaware, as in the case of Herbert Bryan. This may lead the therapist erroneously to assume that the patient's productions reflect actual attitudes or experiences, thereby independently verifying his theories, whereas in fact they are responses to his expectancies.

In operant conditioning no learning occurs unless the reinforcement satisfies a need of the animal's. A hungry pigeon will quickly learn to peck at a target if his pecks release pellets of food, but a satiated one will not. By analogy it seems likely that certain behaviors of a person will be conditioned only if they are followed by a reinforcement which meets some motivation in him. Greenspoon's graduate students probably were trying to please him by being good experimental subjects. In this connection Verplanck found that students had only "indifferent" success in trying to condition each other. The successful students seemed to have prestige, suggesting that the procedure succeeded if the subject "cared" about the experimenter's behavior. [49] Apparently very slight motivation may suffice if the subject has no objection to learning the new behavior.

When a person does object to the behavior to which others desire to condition him, presumably the strength of his motive to learn the new behavior would have to be sufficient to outweigh the strength of his resistance. Prisoners undergoing thought reform usually had to be made to feel that pleasing the interrogator offered the only hope of escape from an intolerable situation before they responded to his pressures. Psychiatric patients, like political prisoners, are usually committed to a certain view of the world. Sometimes this view may accord with the therapist's, but this could not account for the fact that therapists of all schools obtain confirmatory material from their patients. In some cases, at any rate, the therapist's viewpoint must conflict with the patient's initial one. The apparent ease with which such patients learn to make statements in line with the therapist's expectancies suggests that they are strongly motivated to win his approval. The most likely source of this motivation would appear to be their expectation that he will relieve their distress.

Direct Effects of Favorable Expectation on the Duration and Outcome of Psychotherapy

Any discussion of the effects of psychotherapy involves the thorny issue of how to define and evaluate improvement. Until general agreement is reached on the criteria of improvement and adequate follow-up data are available, many crucial questions cannot be answered. These include, for example, whether the changes brought about by different forms of psychotherapy are the same or different and whether some types of change are more permanent or basic than others. Under the circumstances I believe that progress can best be made by confining the term *improvement* only to explicitly reported or demonstrable favorable changes in a patient's objective or subjective state. This view regards other commonly used criteria of improvement—for example, greater maturity or personality reorganization—as inferences about the causes of the observed behavioral and subjective changes, or ways of summarizing a group of these changes.[50] In this section, various criteria of improvement are used, depending on the material being reviewed. These are disappearance of a bodily lesion such as a wart or a peptic ulcer, beneficial change in a person's attitudes and life pattern as in religious conversions, and changes in certain experimental measures such as a symptom check list or a self-ideal Q sort.[51] The meager evidence available on the duration of such changes will be presented. No attempt is made to evaluate them in terms of 'depth' or 'extent,' and the reader is left free to draw these inferences for himself.

The Temporal Course of Treatment

That the therapist's expectancies, transmitted to the patient, affect the amount of treatment in relation to improvement is suggested by Clara Thompson's observation that frequency of sessions, over a fairly wide range, seems not to affect either the duration or outcome of therapy. She points out that American psychoanalysts, possibly because they liked long weekends, soon dropped the frequency of sessions from six to five per week. Later, under increasing pressure from the hordes of patients seeking treatment, they reduced the frequency to three times, or even once a week. She states that effective psychoanalysis can be done, in rare cases, even at the latter rate. Moreover, "in actual duration of treatment, in terms of months and years, the patient going five times a week takes about as long to be cured as the patient going three times."[52] She concludes that the passage of time required for the patient to consolidate new insights and incorporate them into his daily living is the crucial variable, rather than amount of therapeutic contact. In view of the previous discussion, an alternative conclusion might be that some therapists have changed their expectancies as to the frequency of visits necessary to relieve their patients but not as to the total duration of treatment required. The patients have obliged by taking as long to get well but not needing to be seen as often.

This leads to consideration of some evidence that the speed of the patient's improvement may be influenced by his understanding of how long treatment will last. There has been a tendency for psychotherapy to become increasingly prolonged when there are no external obstacles to its continuance. Psychoanalyses now often last five or six years. At the Counselling Center of the University of Chicago the average number of sessions increased from 6 in 1949 to 31 in 1954.[53]

This development may be a manifestation of the therapist's need to maintain confidence in his form of treatment and thereby the patient's confidence in him. Rather than admit defeat he keeps on trying until he, the patient, or both are exhausted, or until treatment is interrupted by external circumstances, leaving open the possibility that it might have been successful if the patient could have continued longer. In any case, length of treatment probably reflects in part the therapist's and patient's expectancies. Those who practice long-term psychotherapy find that their patients take a long time to respond; those who believe that good results can be produced in a few weeks claim to obtain them in this period of time.[54] There is no evidence that a larger proportion of patients in long-term treatment improve, or that the improvements are more permanent than in patients treated more briefly. On the other hand, there is some experimental evidence that patients respond more promptly when they know in advance that therapy is time-limited.

Particularly interesting in this regard are two papers on the group treatment of peptic ulcer patients. Fortin and Abse treated nine college students with peptic ulcer, demonstrated by X-ray, with an analytic type of group therapy for one and one-half hours twice a week for about a year. The patients simultaneously received medical treatment for relief of discomfort. In these groups "discussion of ulcer symptomatology was ignored and attention became focussed on basic personality problems."[55] Most of the patients had a flare-up of symptoms during the first month, and three required bed rest in the infirmary. However, during the later part of group psychotherapy—presumably after several months—in addition to favorable personality changes the ulcer symptoms lessened in intensity and frequency. Fortin and Abse state that at the end of the year, "Among the four members who were diagnosed initially prior to group therapy, no recurrence was reported; among the remaining six members with chronic peptic ulcers, where the expected rate of recurrence is over 75 percent for a period of three years' observation, only one student reported a hemorrhage."[56]

Chappell, Stefano, Rogerson, and Pike treated 32 patients with demonstrated peptic ulcers, which had been refractory to medical treatment, by a six-week course of daily didactic group therapy sessions in addition to medical treatment, and compared the results with a matched control group receiving medical treatment only.[57] The therapy group stressed ways of promoting "visceral rest." They report that all but one of the experimental subjects became symptom-free within three weeks, the period during which Fortin's patients were suffering exacerbations. At the end of three months all but two were symptom-free.[58] In contrast, 18 of the control group of 20, after an initial good response to the medical regimen, had had full recurrences of symptoms within this period. At the end of three years, 28 of the experimental group were re-examined, and 24 "considered themselves to be healthy." Of these 15 were symptom-free or nearly so. Only two were as sick as at the start. Thus Chappell's patients began to get better while Fortin's were getting sicker, and the end results seem equally good and at least equally durable.[59]

That patients' expectations concerning the duration of treatment affect the speed of their response is suggested by a finding of a research study on psychotherapy of psychiatric outpatients.[60] Patients were assigned at random to three psychiatric residents for individual therapy at least one hour a week, group therapy one and one-half hours a week, or "minimal individual therapy," not more than one-half hour every two weeks. Each resident conducted all three types of treatment. The residents' obligation extended only to six months of treatment, at which time they were free to drop the patients. The patients were told that at the end of six months a decision as to further treatment would be made by patient and therapist. Two scales were used to measure patients' progress. One was a symptom check list filled out by the patient as a measure of his subjective state. The other was a social ineffectiveness scale, a measure of the adequacy of social functioning, filled out by the research staff on the basis of interviews with both the patient and an informant. At the first re-evaluation, at the end of six months, there was a sharp average decline in both symptoms and social ineffectiveness. The decline in symptoms was unrelated to type of therapy or therapist; improvement in social effectivness was greater, the greater the amount of treatment contact over the six-month period. Although individual variations were marked, discomfort scores and ineffectiveness scores at the end of two years were on the average no higher than they were at the end of six months, regardless of whether or not patients continued in psychotherapy. This raises the possibility that many of these patients achieved their improvement in six months because they understood this to be the designated period of treatment.

Support for this is offered by Schlien. In a preliminary study which is being checked at this writing, he compared the improvement on certain measures of a group of clients who were told at the start that they would receive only 20 therapeutic sessions over a ten-week period with a group who continued in treatment until voluntary termination. Both groups received client-centered therapy, and the same improvement measures were used for both. The groups were closely matched at the start of therapy by the criteria used. The group receiving time-limited therapy reached the same average level of improvement on these measures at 20 interviews as the others did in 55. Moreover, at the end of the latter period, the group receiving time-limited therapy had maintained their improvement, even though they had been out of treatment several months. [61]

These studies all suggest that speed of improvement may often be largely determined by the patient's expectancies, as conveyed to him by the therapist, as to the duration of treatment, and that a favorable response to brief therapy may be enduring.

Faith as a Healing Agent

For a patient to rely on his therapist for help, he must at least have hope that something useful will transpire. The therapist usually tries to inspire more than this; he seeks to win the patient's trust, confidence, or faith. Many therapists feel that in the absence of such an attitude little can be accomplished; and there is some evidence that this state of mind in itself can have important therapeutic effects.

It is generally agreed that a patient's hope for a successful outcome of treatment can make him feel better, but it is usually assumed that improvement based solely on this is transient and superficial. An example of this type of response is afforded by an obsessional patient who tried several forms of psychotherapy, each lasting many months. He stated that as long as he hoped that the treatment would help him, his symptoms greatly improved. When his hope eventually waned, his symptoms would recur and he would seek another therapist.

Changes following brief therapeutic contact, however, in which little seems to have occurred beyond the arousal of the patient's faith in the therapist, are sometimes deep-seated and persistent. The most plausible explanation for the permanence of these "transference cures" is that the relief the patient experiences from this relationship frees him to function more effectively. [62] He becomes better able to utilize his latent assets and find the courage to re-examine himself and perhaps to modify his habitual maladaptive ways of responding, leading to genuine personality growth.

There is a good possibility, however, that the emotional state of trust or faith in itself can sometimes produce far-reaching and permanent changes in attitude or bodily states, although the occurrence of this phenomenon cannot be predicted or controlled. The major evidence for this lies in the realm of religious conversions and miracle cures.

It is common knowledge that faith in its religious form can have profound and lasting effects on personality, attitudes, and values. After a conversion experience the convert may have changed so much as to be scarcely recognizable as the person he was before this experience. This is seen not only in persons like St. Augustine and St. Francis but even in an occasional denizen of skid row who becomes "saved" at a Salvation Army meeting. [63] Most such conversions are transient, of course, and backsliding is the rule. In this they resemble the transference cures already discussed. As with such cures, perhaps a conversion sticks when it leads to new forms of behavior which yield more rewards than the old patterns. For purposes of this discussion, the only important points are that religious conversions can lead to profound and permanent changes of attitude in persons who have undergone prolonged hardship or spiritual torment and that they usually involve intimate, emotionally charged contact with a person or group representing the viewpoint to which the convert becomes converted. Conversions which occur in isolation are often, perhaps always, preceded by such contacts. [64] According to William James, "General Booth, the founder of the Salavation Army, considers that the first vital step in saving outcasts consists in making them feel that some decent human cares enough for them to take an interest in the question whether they are to rise or sink." [65] The role of divine intervention in producing conversion experiences may be left open. The significant point for this discussion is that they are usually accompanied or preceded by a certain type of relationship with other human beings, which in some ways resembles the psychotherapeutic one. The psychotherapist, too, cares deeply whether his patient rises or sinks.

That faith can also produce extensive and enduring organic changes is amply attested to by so-called miracle cures. There can be little doubt that these cures can activate reparative forces which, in rare instances, are powerful enough to heal grossly damaged tissue. The best documented cases are those healed at Lourdes, and evidence for these is as good as for any phenomena that are accepted as facts. [66]

Patients claiming to have been miraculously cured at Lourdes are examined by a bureau of non-Catholic physicians, who certify that a cure has occurred only when there is unquestioned evidence of organic pathology previous to the cure. The cures include healings of chronic draining fecal fistulas, union of compound fractures which had remained unhealed for years, and similar quite convincing manifestations. Although the consciousness of being cured comes instantly and healing is rapid, it occurs by normal reparative processes. A cachectic patient takes months to regain his weight. An extensive gap in tissues is filled by scar tissue as in normal healing, and this repair may take hours or days.

For various reasons the actual number of cures of this type at Lourdes cannot be accurately calculated. The most conservative figures is the number of cures certified by the Church as miraculous, which by 1955 was only 51. This is an infinitesimal percentage of the millions of pilgrims who visited Lourdes up to that time. By the most liberal criteria, only a small fraction of one percent of the pilgrims have been healed. This raises the possibility that similar cures occur with at least equal frequency in ordinary medical practice but are overlooked because no one physician has a large enough sample of patients. Questioning of colleagues, many of whom report having actually treated or at least having heard of one such case, tends to bear out this supposition. In any case, it is clear that faith cures occur, regardless of the object of the patient's faith. All religions report them, and they are also produced by persons who, by the accepted standards of society, are charlatans. That is, the healing force appears to reside in the patient's state of faith or hope, not in its object. This point has been neatly illustrated by an experiment performed by Rehder with three chronically and severely ill bedridden elderly women patients.[67] One had chronic inflammation of the gall bladder with stones, another had failed to recuperate from an operation for pancreatitis and was a mere skeleton, and the third was in the last stages of metastatic uterine carcinoma. He permitted a local faith healer to try to cure them by absent treatment, without the patients' knowledge. Nothing happened. He next told the patients about the faith healer, built up their expectancies over several days, and then assured them that the faith healer would be treating them from a distance at a certain time the next day. This was a time during which the faith healer did *not* operate. All three women showed dramatic and remarkable improvement at the suggested time. The second was permanently cured; the other two were not, but showed striking temporary responses. The cancer patient, for example, lost massive edema and ascites, her anemia markedly improved, she became strong enough to go home and be up and about, and she continued virtually symptom-free until her death. These three patients were greatly helped by a belief which was false—that the faith healer was treating them from a distance.

Certain features are common to most miracle cures. The patients are usually chronically ill, debilitated, and despondent. Their critical faculty has been weakened, and they are ready to grasp at straws. The journey to the shrine is long and arduous—persons who live in the vicinity of the shrine having proved poor candidates for cures. After arrival there are many preliminaries before the patient can enter the shrine, and during the preparatory period the patient hears about other miraculous cures and views the votive offerings of those healed. As Janet says, "all these things happen today at Lourdes just as they used to happen of old at the temple of Aesculapius."[68] In his despair the patient's state of mind is similar to that of the victim of thought reform, and the symbols of cure are present, as in the psychiatrist's office, although in much more potent form. Finally, all three types of experience are similar in that another person or group of persons is involved who represents the promise of relief.

Since it is the state of hope, belief, or faith which produces the beneficial effects rather than its object, one would expect to find the same phenomena in a nonreligious framework, and this is indeed the case. For example, according to Harold Wolff, hope had definite survival value for prisoners in concentration camps: ". . . prolonged circumstances which are perceived as dangerous, as lonely, as hopeless may drain a man of hope and of his health; but he is capable of enduring incredible burdens and taking cruel punishment when he has self-esteem, hope, purpose, and belief in his fellows."[69]

In the realm of medicine evidence abounds that faith can facilitate bodily healing. In these cases the patient's faith is activated by the doctor's administration of an inert pharmacological substance, which symbolizes his healing function. Such remedies are called placebos, implying that they are means of placating the patient and therefore not genuine treatment. But placebos can have deep and enduring effects.[70] An instructive example of the power of the placebo is the lowly wart. Warts have been shown by several dermatologists to respond to suggestion as well as to any other form of treatment. One of the most careful studies is that of Bloch.[71] He was able to follow 136 cases of common warts and 43 cases of flat warts over a period of two and one-half years. Of the former group 44 percent, of the latter 88 percent were healed by painting them with an inert dye. About half of the cures occurred after one treatment, while less than 3 percent required more than three sessions. Bloch found that cases which had previously been treated unsuccessfully by the usual means responded just as well as untreated cases, and he adequately ruled out the possibility that his cure rates might represent the percentage that would have healed without any treatment. Since warts are a definite tissue change caused by an identifiable virus, this cure by placebo may serve as a prototype of an organic disease cured by faith. In this case the faith seems to operate to change the physiology of the skin so that the virus can no longer thrive on it.

Placebos can also heal more serious tissue damage, if it is directly related to the patient's emotional state. In a recently reported study two groups of patients with bleeding peptic ulcer in a municipal hospital in Budapest were compared.[72] The placebo group received an injection of sterile water from the doctor, who told them it was a new medicine which would produce relief. The control group received the same injection from nurses who told them it was an experimental medicine of undetermined effectiveness. The placebo group had remissions which were "excellent in 70 percent of the cases lasting over a period of one year." The control group showed only a 25 percent remission rate. The cure of warts and peptic ulcers by suggestion is not as spectacular as religious miracle cures, but qualitatively the processes involved seem very similar.

Just as placebos can benefit organic conditions, they can help subjective complaints, and the beneficial effects are not necessarily transient. Evidence to support this contention is still scanty. One scrap is that in a controlled study of the effects of mephenesin and placebo on psychiatric outpatients, it was found that the relief of symptoms by placebo persisted undiminished for at least eight weeks, at which time the experiment was terminated.[73]

Miracle cures and placebo responses suggest the probability that a patient's expectancy of benefit from treatment in itself may have enduring and profound effects on his physical and mental state. It seems plausible, furthermore, that the successful effects of all forms of psychotherapy depend in part on their ability to foster such attitudes in the patient. Since it is the patient's state which counts, rather than what he believes in, it is not surprising that all types of psychotherapy obtain roughly equal improvement rates.[74] This finding also suggests that the generic type of relationship offered by the therapist plays a larger part in his success than the specific technique he uses. The aspects of the therapist's personality that affect his healing power have not yet been adequately defined, but it seems reasonable to assume that they lie in the realm of his ability to inspire confidence in his patients. In this connection the findings of Whitehorn and Betz[75] may be pertinent—that therapists whose relationship with their schizophrenic patients was characterized by active personal participation obtained very much better results than those who failed to show this attitude. The therapeutic forces in such a relationship are complex, but one may well be that the therapist's attitude conveys his belief in the patient's capacity to improve, which in turn would strengthen the patient's faith in the treatment procedure, as mentioned earlier. That psychotherapy produces its effects partly through faith is also suggested by the fact that sometimes these effects occur rapidly, as already discussed, and that the speed of cure need bear no relation to its depth or permanence.

The hypothesis that some of the favorable results of psychotherapy may be primarily produced by the patients' favorable expectancies has led some colleagues and myself to study similarities between the effects of psychotherapy and placebo, with the eventual aim of being able to sort out those effects of psychotherapy which cannot be explained on this basis.[76] Two preliminary findings are of interest in this connection. A subgroup of the psychiatric outpatients who were symptomatically improved after six months of psychotherapy, but whose scores on the symptom check list had gradually climbed back to close to the pretreatment level over a two-year follow-up, were then given placebos. After two weeks, their average score on the symptom check list had again dropped back to the level of the period immediately after psychotherapy.[77] The finding that psychotherapy and placebos have similar effects on this measure has led to questions about the meanings of a patient's report of symptoms, which are now being explored. The other tentative finding which has suggested further lines of research is that a group of patients who improved the most on discomfort and ineffectiveness after six months of psychotherapy had personal characteristics surprisingly similar to those found by other investigators in surgical patients whose pain was alleviated by placebos.[78]

In pulling together the evidence that the patient's attitude of trust or faith may play a significant part in his response to all forms of psychotherapy, I do not contend that all or even most of the processes or effects of psychotherapy can be explained on this basis alone. There are obviously many important determinants of the processes and outcomes of treatment besides the direct influence of the therapist based on patients' trust in him. In this presentation, however, I have attempted to focus on two interrelated themes. One is that because of certain properties of all therapeutic relationships, the therapist inevitably exerts a strong influence on the patient. This influence arises primarily from the patient's hope or faith that treatment will relieve his distress. This favorable expectation is strengthened by cultural factors, aspects of the referral or intake process, cues in the therapy situation which indicate that help will be forthcoming, and the therapist's own confidence in his ability to help, springing from his training and his methods. Analogies between psychotherapy and thought reform have been used to clarify some of the sources and modes of operation of the influencing process in the former. Some examples of the influence of the therapist's expectations on the patient's productions and on the duration of therapy have been given.

The other theme is that the patient's favorable expectation, which is a major determinant of the therapist's influence over him, may have direct therapeutic effects which are not necessarily transient or superficial. Certain implications of these propositions for practice and research may be briefly mentioned.

Since this review points out areas of relative ignorance which need further exploration rather than areas of knowledge, its implication for psychotherapeutic practice must be regarded as extremely tentative. It should be noted first that the likelihood of a common factor in the effectiveness of all forms of psychotherapy does not imply that all methods or theories are interchangeable. It may well turn out that the specific effects of different approaches differ significantly and that different types of patients respond differentially to different therapeutic techniques. Until these questions are clarified, it is important that every therapist be well versed in his theoretical orientation and skilled in the methods most congenial to him, in order to maintain his self-confidence and thereby the patient's faith in him. Since the leading conceptual systems of psychotherapy are not logically incompatible, but represent primarily differences in emphasis or alternative formulations of the same ideas,[79] adherents of each school need feel no compunction about holding to their own positions, while tolerant of alternative views, pending the accumulation of facts which may make possible decisions as to the specific merits and drawbacks of different approaches.

If the common effective factor in all forms of psychotherapy is the patient's favorable expectancy, this suggests that psychotherapists should deliberately mobilize and utilize patients' faith in the treatment they offer. The problem here is where to draw the line. The psychotherapist obviously cannot use methods in which he himself does not believe. Moreover, reliance on the healing potentialities of faith to the neglect of proper diagnostic procedures would obviously be irresponsible. Treating tuberculosis or cancer by faith healing alone is none the less reprehensible because it may work occasionally. But a large component of the illnesses which bring patients to psychiatrists—how large is still unclear—consists of harmful emotional states such as anxiety, apprehensiveness, and depression, and for these faith or trust may be a specific antidote. In such conditions, the strengthening of the patient's trust in his therapist, by whatever means, may be as much an etiological remedy as penicillin for pneumonia.

The psychotherapist should be prepared, therefore, to modify his approach, within limits possible for him, to meet the expectancies of different types of patients. Interview types of therapy, for example, tend to fit the expectations of most middle-class patients, but many lower-class patients cannot conceive of a doctor who does not dispense pills or jab them with needles. These patients are very apt to drop out of interview psychotherapy because they cannot perceive it as treatment for their ills.[80] For them the tactics of therapy may involve accommodating to their initial expectations so that they will return for more treatment. The developing therapeutic relationship may then lead to modification of the patients' expectancies in a more psychotherapeutically useful direction. Thus it may be hoped that adequate diagnosis will eventually include an estimate as to the type of therapeutic approach most likely to mobilize the patient's faith.

This review also suggests the desirability that psychotherapists be more aware of the extent of their influence on patients. The physician cannot avoid influencing his patients—the only question is whether he should use this influence consciously or unconsciously.[81] As Modell says, "It would be well to remember that in all therapy trouble is apt to follow the ignorant application of important forces,"[82] and this applies particularly when the important force is the therapist himself.

It might be objected that the therapist's direct use of influence tends to intensify the patient's dependency and thereby impede genuine progress. There is no question as to the desirability of helping patients to independence, but the real problem is to determine when this goal is better achieved by freely accepting their initial dependency and using it, and when by resisting this attitude from the start.[83] It is easy for patient and physician to become absorbed in a struggle over this issue, to the detriment of therapeutic movement. For example, sometimes giving a patient a symptomatic remedy he requests may improve the therapeutic relationship and permit discussion to move to more fruitful topics, whereas withholding it impedes all progress.[84] In order to become genuinely self-reliant, a child needs to feel securely dependent on his parents. From this he develops the confidence in the dependability of others which enables him to forge ahead. The same consideration may often apply to patients.

Validation of these tentative implications for practice awaits the accumulation of more knowledge. This review suggests two hopeful directions in which to seek this knowledge. One is the study of conditions contributing to the patient's faith in his therapist, and the effects of this on the processes and effects of treatment. Psychiatry, in its preoccupation with illness, has concerned itself almost exclusively with pathogenic feelings such as fear, anxiety, and anger. It is high time that the 'healing' emotions such as faith, hope, eagerness, and joy received more attention.[85] Of these, the physician-patient relationship affords a special opportunity to study the group of emotions related to expectancy of help which may be grouped under the generic term *faith*. A promising experimental approach to elucidating the determinants, psychological and physiological concomitants, and effects of these emotions lies in study of the placebo effect, since the placebo, under proper circumstances, symbolizes the physician's healing powers. Study of the relationships between the placebo response and response to psychotherapy in psychiatric patients may help to isolate and define the role of the faith component in therapy.

The second promising line of research lies in experimental studies of the ways in which the therapist transmits his expectancies, goals, and values to the patient, and the effects of these on the patient's responses in therapy. Until this matter is elucidated, great caution is advisable in drawing conclusions as to the etiology of mental illness from patients' productions in therapy.

It is now clear that psychotherapists of different schools may elicit from their patients verbal productions confirming the theoretical conceptions of that school and that patients sometimes accommodate their memories and dreams to the expectations of the therapist to the point of outright confabulation. The possibility that the patient may be responding to the therapist's cues and telling him what he wants to hear must always be kept in mind, especially since it can occur without either being aware of it. Hypotheses about interpersonal factors in mental illness require validation by observations outside the therapeutic situation.[86]

By the same token, one must be cautious about attributing improvement to other causes until more is known about the limits of the direct effects of the patient's positive expectancies on his state of health, and the expectancies of the psychiatrist as related to them. Until more is known about the factors in the patient, therapist, and treatment situation which determine the degree and form of influence exerted by the therapist, and about the effects of this influence on the patient's behavior and the nature and duration of his improvement, it is impossible adequately to isolate either the factors specific to each form of psychotherapy or those involved in all forms of psychotherapy. In the meantime there is a danger of falling into the trap of attributing the patient's improvement to the particular kinds of productions he gives in a given kind of treatment, overlooking the possibility that both the productions and the improvement may be determined, at least in part, by his faith in the therapist.

Acknowledgments

This paper has grown in part out of research studies supported by the United States Public Health Service (M–532, C–2) and the Ford Foundation. Many of the ideas have been developed and clarified through discussion with Lester H. Gliedman, M.D., Stanley D. Imber, Ph.D., Earl H. Nash, Jr., M.S., and Anthony R. Stone, M.S.S.W., members of the Henry Phipps Psychiatric Clinic of the Johns Hopkins Hospital psychotherapy research staff, to whom the writer expresses his appreciation.

References and Notes

1. See, for instance, Talcott Parsons, "Illness and the Role of the Physician: A Sociological Perspective," *Amer. J. Orthopsychiatry* (1951) 21:452–460. Sebastian DeGrazia gives a brilliant if biased analysis of cultural and other factors contributing to the psychotherapist's influence over his patients. See DeGrazia, *Errors of Psychotherapy;* New York, Doubleday, 1952.

2. Norman Reider, "A Type of Transference to Institutions," *J. Hillside Hosp.* (1953) 2:23–29. For an interesting account of experimental studies on the context of a situation as an important determinant of influence see Robert R. Blake and Jane S. Mouton, "The Dynamics of Influence and Coercion," *Internat. J. Social Psychiatry* (1957) 2:263–274.

3. Sigmund Freud, *A General Introduction to Psychoanalysis;* New York, Liveright, 1920; p. 212.

4. Josef Breuer and Sigmund Freud, "Studies on Hysteria," in *The Complete Psychological Works* 2:3–305; London, Hogarth, 1955; p. 265.

5. Leslie Schaffer and Jerome K. Myers, "Psychotherapy and Social Stratification," *Psychiatry* (1954) 17:83–93.

6. John C. Whitehorn and Barbara J. Betz, "A Study of Psychotherapeutic Relationships between Physicians and Schizophrenic Patients," *Amer. J. Psychiatry* (1954) 111:321–331.

7. See, for instance, George Winokur, "'Brainwashing'—A Social Phenomenon of Our Time," *Hum. Organization* (1955) 13:16–18 and Frederick Wyatt, "Climate of Opinion and Methods of Readjustment," *Amer. Psychologist* (1956) 11:537–542.

8. Edward Glover, "Research Methods in Psycho-Analysis," *Internat. J. Psycho-Anal.* (1952) 33:403–409.

9. Werner Wolff, "Fact and Value in Psychotherapy," *Amer. J. Psychotherapy* (1954) 8:466–486.

10. Kenneth E. Appel, William T. Lhamon, J. Martin Myers, and William A. Harvey, "Long Term Psychotherapy," *Research Publ. Assn. N. and M. Disease* (1951) 31:21–34.

11. See note 9; p. 470.

12. Henri Ellenberger, "The Ancestry of Dynamic Psychotherapy," *Bull. Menninger Clin.* (1956) 20:288–299; p. 290.

13. Jerome D. Frank, Lester H. Gliedman, Stanley D. Imber, Earl H. Nash, Jr., and Anthony R. Stone, "Why Patients Leave Psychotherapy," *AMA Arch. Neurol. and Psychiat.* (1957) 77:283–299. The results mentioned are reported in more detail in Imber, Frank, Gliedman, Nash, and Stone, "Suggestibility, Social Class and the Acceptance of Psychotherapy," *J. Clinical Psychol.* (1956) 12:341–344, and Imber, Nash and Stone, "Social Class and Duration of Psychotherapy," *J. Clinical Psychol.* (1955) 11:281–284.

14. See note 5.

15. Frank and others, note 13; p. 294.

16. With psychotics the suggested relation between degree of distress and willingness to trust the therapist often does not hold, because their distrust of others, especially those who seem to be offering help, is so profound. With such patients, the common core of successful psychotherapy may be the ability to break through this attitude and establish a trusting, confidential relationship. See, for example, John C. Whitehorn and Barbara J. Betz, "A Comparison of Psychotherapeutic Relationships between Physicians and Schizophrenic Patients When Insulin Is Combined with Psychotherapy and When Psychotherapy Is Used Alone," *Amer. J. Psychiatry* (1957) 113:901–910. This common feature may explain the equally good results claimed by advocates of apparently incompatible therapeutic approaches. See, for example, *Psychotherapy with Schizophrenics,* edited by Eugene B. Brody and Frederick C. Redlich; New York, Internat. Universities Press, 1952.

17. See note 9.

18. This point is interestingly discussed by B. F. Skinner in Carl R. Rogers and B. F. Skinner, "Some Issues Concerning the Control of Human Behavior: A Symposium," *Science* (1956) 124:1057–1066.

19. The description of brainwashing in this paper is based on: L. E. Hinkle, Jr., and H. G. Wolff, "Communist Interrogation and Indoctrination of 'Enemies of the State,'" *A.M.A. Arch. Neurol. and Psychiat.* (1956) 76:115–174; Robert J. Lifton, "'Thought Reform' of Western Civilians in Chinese Communist Prisons," *Psychiatry* (1956) 19:173–195; Lifton, "Chinese Communist Thought Reform," pp. 219–312; in *Group Processes: Transactions of the Third Conference;* New York, Josiah Macy, Jr. Foundation, 1957; Edgar H. Schein, "The Chinese Indoctrination Program for Prisoners of War," *Psychiatry* (1956) 19:149–172. See also W. Sargant, *Battle for the Mind;* New York, Doubleday, 1957. He suggests that thought reform, religious revivals, and certain psychiatric treatments facilitate attitude change by producing excessive excitation, leading to emotional exhaustion and hypersuggestibility.

20. This reinforcement of certain of the prisoner's responses is analogous to operant conditioning, as will be discussed more fully below, in connection with psychotherapy.

21. Schein, note 19; p. 163, and footnote.

22. Schein, note 19; pp. 162–163.

23. Lifton, *Group Processes*, note 19; p. 269.

24. See note 19; p. 171.

25. Erving Goffman, "Interpersonal Persuasion," pp. 117–193; in *Group Processes: Transactions of the Third Conference;* New York, Josiah Macy, Jr. Foundation, 1957.

26. Lawrence S. Kubie, *Practical Aspects of Psychoanalysis;* New York, Norton, 1936; p. 140.
27. See note 26; p. 145.
28. Freud, note 3; pp. 319, 321 (Freud's italics).
29. Albert Stunkard, "Some Interpersonal Aspects of an Oriental Religion," *Psychiatry* (1951) 14:419–431.
30. Hadley Cantril, *The Psychology of Social Movements;* New York, Wiley, 1941.
31. Edward S. Bordin, "Ambiguity as a Therapeutic Variable," *J. Consulting Psychology* (1955) 19:9–15.
32. For a brilliant analysis of compliance, identification and internalization in the influencing process see Herbert C. Kelman, "Compliance, Identification and Internalization: Three Processes of Attitude Change," *J. Conflict Resolution* (1958) 2:51–60.
33. Ernest R. Hilgard, *Theories of Learning;* New York, Appleton-Century-Crofts, 1948; Ch. 4, pp. 82–120.
34. Jurgen Ruesch, "Psychotherapy and Communication," pp. 180–187; in *Progress in Psychotherapy, 1956,* edited by Frieda Fromm-Reichmann and J. L. Moreno; New York, Grune and Stratton, 1956; p. 183.
35. Joel Greenspoon, "The Reinforcing Effect of Two Spoken Sounds on the Frequency of Two Responses," *Amer. J. Psychology* (1955) 68: 409–416.
36. Kurt Salzinger and Stephanie Pisoni, "Reinforcement of Affect Responses of Schizophrenics During the Clinical Interview," *J. Abnormal and Social Psychol.* (1958) 57:84–90.
37. Edward J. Murray, "A Content-Analysis Method for Studying Psychotherapy," *Psychological Monographs* (1956) 70, Whole No. 420. The "Herbert Bryan" protocol is in Carl R. Rogers, *Counseling and Psychotherapy;* New York, Houghton Mifflin, 1942; pp. 259–437.
38. See, for instance, Kubie, note 26; Ch. 7.
39. Breuer and Freud, note 4; p. 295.
40. See Glover, note 8; p. 405, and "The Therapeutic Effect of Inexact Interpretation: A Contribution to the Theory of Suggestion," *Internat. J. Psycho-Anal.* (1931) 12:397–411. Other psychoanalytic writers have stressed the "hypersuggestibility" of the patient in analysis, seeing in the transference an analogy to hypnotic rapport. See, for example, Ida Macalpine, "The Development of the Transference," *Psychoanalytic Quart.* (1950) 19:501–539; Herman Nunberg, "Transference and Reality," *Internat. J. Psycho-Anal.* (1951) 32:1–9; C. Fisher, "Studies on the Nature of Suggestion: Pt. 1, Experimental Induction of Dreams by Direct Suggestion," *J. Amer. Psychoanal. Assn.* (1953) 1:222–255.
41. Rogers, note 18; p. 1063.
42. Wilhelm Stekel, *Interpretation of Dreams;* New York, Liveright, 1943, quoted by Werner Wolff in "Fact and Value in Psychotherapy," *Amer. J. Psychotherapy* (1954) 8:466–486; p. 466.
43. Carl R. Rogers, "A Research Program in Client-Centered Therapy," *Research Publ. Assn. N. and M. Disease* (1951) 31:106–113.
44. Murray, note 37.
45. Ralph W. Heine, "A Comparison of Patients' Reports on Psychotherapeutic Experience with Psychoanalytic, Nondirective and Adlerian Therapists," *Amer. J. Psychotherapy* (1953) 7:16–23.
46. David Rosenthal, "Changes in Some Moral Values Following Psychotherapy," *J. Consulting Psychol.* (1955) 19:431–436. For historical examples of "doctrinal compliance"

see Jan Ehrenwald, "The Telepathy Hypothesis and Doctrinal Compliance in Psychotherapy," *Amer. J. Psychotherapy* (1957) 11:359–379.

47. For example, in an experimental study of psychotherapy with a schizophrenic, M. B. Parloff found that ". . . although topic choice appeared to follow the therapist's values remarkably closely, the patient's own evaulation of these topics in some instances, moved quite independently. . . . This finding suggests that the patient may be superficially compliant to the unconsciously expressed expectations of the therapist, without, however, internalizing such values." M. B. Parloff, "Communication of Values and Therapeutic Change," paper read at the American Psychological Association meeting, New York, 1957.

48. Bruno Bettelheim, "Remarks on the Psychological Appeal of Totalitarianism," *Amer. J. Economics and Sociology* (1952) 12:89–96. Recent experimental studies have found that inducing a person to speak overtly in favor of some position changes his private opinion in the direction of the one he had publicly stated. See Irving L. Janis and Bert T. King, "The Influence of Role-Playing on Opinion Change," *J. Abnormal and Social Psychol.* (1954) 49:211–218; Bert T. King and Irving L. Janis, "Comparison of the Effectiveness of Improvised Versus Non-Improvised Role-Playing in Producing Opinion Changes," *Hum. Relations* (1956) 9:177–186.

49. W. S. Verplanck, "The Operant Conditioning of Human Motor Behavior," *Psychological Bull.* (1956) 53:70–83.

50. Morris B. Parloff, Herbert C. Kelman, and Jerome D. Frank, "Comfort, Effectiveness, and Self-Awareness as Criteria of Improvement in Psychotherapy," *Amer. J. Psychiatry* (1954) 111:343–351.

51. See note 13. See also Rogers, note 43.

52. Clara Thompson, *Psychoanalysis: Evolution and Development*; New York, Hermitage House, 1950; p. 235.

53. J. Seeman, quoted in J. M. Schlien, "Time-Limited Psychotherapy: An Experimental Investigation of Practical Values and Theoretical Implications," *J. Counseling Psychol.* (1957) 4:318–322.

54. See, for instance, Jacob H. Conn, "Brief Psychotherapy of the Sex Offender: A Report of a Liaison Service Between a Court and a Private Psychiatrist," *J. Clinical Psychopathol.* (1949) 10:1–26; Jacob H. Conn, "Hypnosynthesis III: Hypnotherapy of Chronic War Neuroses with a Discussion of the Value of Abreaction, Regression, and Revivication," *J. Clinical and Experimental Hypnosis* (1953) 1:29–43.

55. John N. Fortin and D. W. Abse, "Group Psychotherapy with Peptic Ulcer," *Internat. J. Group Psychotherapy* (1956) 6:383–391; p. 385.

56. Fortin and Abse, note 55; p. 390 and following.

57. M. N. Chappell, J. J. Stefano, J. S. Rogerson, and F. H. Pike, "The Value of Group Psychological Procedures in the Treatment of Peptic Ulcer," *Amer. J. Digestive Diseases and Nutrition* (1937) 3:813–817.

58. One patient could not be located.

59. Unfortunately Fortin and Abse do not state how many of the patients had mild recurrences, and Chappell and his colleagues do not give the improvement rate at the end of a year, so the results of the two treatment programs cannot be strictly compared. Assuming that the student who hemorrhaged in the first study is equivalent to the "relapsed" patients in the second, Chappell had the same recurrence rate at the end of three years that Fortin and Abse had at the end of a year—about 10 percent in each series. On the unlikely assumption that the 4 patients lost to the Chappell study had relapsed, their three-year recurrence rate is about 20 percent. Including the mild recurrences this brings

the Chappell three-year relapse rate to about 50 percent. Even this figure is well below the expected recurrence rate of over 75 percent mentioned by Fortin and Abse.

60. Jerome D. Frank, Lester H. Gliedman, Stanley D. Imber, Anthony R. Stone, and Earl H. Nash, Jr., "Patients' Expectancies and Relearning as Factors Determining Improvement in Psychotherapy," *Amer. J. Psychiatry*, in press.

61. J. M. Schlien, "An Experimental Investigation of Time Limited, Client Centered Therapy," University of Chicago Counselling Center Discussion, Papers, Vol. 2, 1956. According to Schlien (see footnote 53), patients on time limited therapy showed changes on TAT scores in the follow-up period which were interpreted as undesirable, despite their maintained improvement on the other indices. The sources of this discrepancy are now under study.

62. Franz Alexander, "Discussion of 'Aims and Limitations of Psychotherapy' by Paul H. Hoch," pp. 82–86; in Fromm-Reichmann and Moreno, note 34; p. 82.

63. For interesting biographical vignettes of nine such converts, see H. Begbie, *Twice-Born Men*; London, Revell, 1909.

64. Benjamin Weininger, "The Interpersonal Factor in the Religious Experience," *Psychoanalysis* (1955) 3:27–44.

65. William James, *The Varieties of Religious Experience*; New York, The Modern Library, 1936; p. 200.

66. Pierre Janet's discussion of "Miraculous Healing," Ch. 1 in *Psychological Healing*, Vol. 1 (New York, Macmillan, 1925) is the best account of miracle cures which has come to my attention. A very good recent account is found in Ruth Cranston, *The Miracle of Lourdes*; New York, McGraw-Hill, 1955.

67. H. Rehder, "Wunderheilungen, Ein Experiment," *Hippokrates* (1955) 26:577–580.

68. Janet, note 66; p. 48.

69. H. Wolff, "What Hopes Does for Man," *Saturday Review of Literature*, January 8, 1957, p. 45.

70. A. A. Kurland, "The Drug Placebo—Its Psychodynamic and Conditional Reflex Action," *Behavioral Science* (1957) 2:101–110, offers a recent survey of knowledge as to the effects of placebos.

71. B. Bloch, "Ueber die Heilung der Warzen durch Suggestion," *Klin. Wochenschr.* (1927) 6:2271–2325.

72. F. A. Volgyesi, "'School for Patients,' Hypnosis-Therapy and Psycho-Prophylaxis," *British J. Medical Hypnotism* (1954) 5:8–17.

73. J. L. Hampson, David Rosenthal, and Jerome D. Frank, "A Comparative Study of the Effect of Mephenesin and Placebo on the Symptomatology of a Mixed Group of Psychiatric Outpatients," *Bull. Johns Hopkins Hosp.* (1954) 95:170–177.

74. Appel and others; see note 10.

75. See note 6.

76. David Rosenthal and Jerome D. Frank, "Psychotherapy and the Placebo Effect," *Psychological Bull.* (1956) 53:294–302. See also the editorial by J. C. Whitehorn, "Psychiatric Implications of the 'Placebo Effect,'" *Amer. J. Psychiatry* (1958) 114: 662–664.

77. Lester H. Gliedman, Earl H. Nash, Anthony R. Stone, and Jerome D. Frank, "Reduction of Symptoms by Pharmacologically Inert Substances and by Short Term Psychotherapy," *AMA Arch. Neurol. and Psychiat.* (1958) 79:345–351.

78. L. Lasagna, F. Mosteller, J. M. von Felsinger, and H. K. Beecher, "A Study of the Placebo Response," *Amer. J. Medicine* (1954) 16:770–779.

79. See, for example, the contributions to *Progress in Psychotherapy*, 1956, note 34.

80. Frank, and others, note 13.

81. M. Balint, "The Doctor, His Patient, and the Illness," *Lancet* (1955) 268:683–688.

82. Walter Modell, *The Relief of Symptoms*; Philadelphia, Saunders, 1955; p. 56.

83. Sydney G. Margolin advocates deliberately fostering regression of certain patients in "On Some Principles of Therapy," *Amer. J. Psychiatry* (1958) 114:1087–1096.

84. Jerome D. Frank, "Psychotherapeutic Aspects of Symptomatic Treatment," *Amer. J. Psychiatry* (1946) 103:21–25.

85. Sandor Rado sees as one of the critical tasks in the treatment of behavior disorders, "to generate in [the patient] an emotional matrix dominated by the welfare emotions [pleasurable desire, joy, affection, love, self-respect and pride]"; see *Psychoanalysis of Behavior*; New York, Grune and Stratton, 1956; p. 253. Perhaps faith should be included in the list.

86. For a penetrating discussion of this issue, see Ernst Kris, "Psychoanalytic Propositions," Ch. 22, pp. 332–351; in *Psychological Theory*, edited by M. H. Marx; New York, Macmillan, 1951.

24

Prepaid Group Practice and the New "Demanding Patient"

Eliot Freidson

The future dimensions of medical practice in the United States are beginning to emerge now, both through the steady increase in prepaid insurance coverage for ambulatory care, and through the pressure on physicians to work together in organizations. But what will be the impact of those changes on the people involved, and on their relationships with each other? What will be doctor-patient relationship be like? There can be little doubt that prepaid medical care insurance plans will, by changing the economic relationship between doctor and patient, also change many ways in which they interact with each other. And there can also be little doubt that when physicians routinely work in organizations where they are cooperating rather than competing with colleagues, other elements of their relationships with patients and colleagues will change.

Obvious as it is that change will occur, we have rather little information relevant to anticipating its human consequences. We have fairly good estimates of the economic consequences of those changes in the organization of medical care, and we have hopeful evidence on how the medical quality of care might be affected, but between the input and output measures there is only a black box: we have little information on how the human beings in medical practice produce the results which are measured, on the quality of their experience in practice, and on the characteristic ways they try to manage their problems at work. Without knowing something about that, it is rather difficult to anticipate how doctor-patient relationships will change and what problems will be embedded in them.

This paper is an attempt to provide some information about how the participants in a medical care program which anticipated present-day trends responded to each other and to the economic and social structure of practice. The data upon which I

SOURCE: *Milbank Memorial Fund Quarterly / Health and Society* 51, no. 4 (Fall 1973): 473–88.

shall draw come from an eighteen-month-long field study of the physicians who worked in a large, prepaid group practice. Most of the primary practitioners (internists and pediatricians) worked on a full-time basis in the medical group, and most of the consultants worked part-time, but all fifty-five of them were on salary, officially employees of the institution. Their medical group contracted with an insurance organization to provide virtually complete care to insured patients without imposing on them any out-of-pocket charges. In studying the physicians of the medical group, a very large amount of observational, documentary, and direct evidence was collected in the course of examining files, attending all staff meetings, listening to luncheon-table conversations, and carrying out a series of intensive interviews with all the physicians in the group. The research obtained a systematic and comprehensive view of how the group physicians worked and what their problems were. Because of a lack of space here, however, only a summary of findings bearing on a single issue is possible.

The Administrative Structure of the Group

To understand practice in the medical group, it is necessary to understand the framework in which it was carried out. The group did not have an elaborate administrative structure, since it lacked clear gradations of rank and authority and had rather few written, formal rules. It was not organized like a traditional bureaucratic organization. The few rules which were bureaucratically enforced all dealt in one way or another with the *terms* of work—with how and what the physician was to be paid, and the amount of time he was to work in return for that pay. Ultimately, the terms of work were less a function of the medical group administration than of the health insurance organization with which the medical group entered into a contract. The absolute income available for paying the doctors derived primarily from the insurance contract, which specified a given sum per year per insured person or family, plus additional sums by a complicated formula not important for present purposes. The administration of the medical group could decide how to divide up the contract income among the physicians but had to work within the absolute limits of that income.

By the same token, critical aspects of the *conditions* of work stemmed more from the terms of the service contract than from the choice and action of the group administration. The most important complaint of the physicians about the conditions of work in the medical group was of "overload"—having to provide more services in a given period of time than was considered appropriate. Such "overload" was a direct function of the prepaid service contract, which freed the subscriber from having to pay a separate fee for each service he wished, and encouraged many physicians to manage patient demands by increasing referrals and reappointments.

It was around these externally formulated contractual arrangements that we found the administration of the medical group establishing and enforcing the firmest bureaucratic rules, perhaps because it had no other choice than to do so in order to satisfy its contract to provide services. The prepaid service-contract arrangement could be conceived of as purely economic in character—simply a rational way of *paying* for health care, which did not influence health care itself. But it was much more than that, since it organized demand and supply, the processes by which health care takes place. In fact, it was closely connected with many of the problems of practice in the group. This is not to say that it created those problems in and of itself. Rather, it gave rise to new possibilities for problematic behavior on the part of both patient and physician and prevented the use by both of traditional solutions. To understand its relationship to the problems of practice in the medical group, to the way the physicians made sense of their experience, and to the ways they attempted to cope with it, let us first examine the way the physicians responded to the differences they perceived between prepaid service-contract group practice and private, fee-for-service solo practice.

The Meanings of Entrepreneurial and Contract Group Practice

All of the physicians interviewed, including those who had left the group and were solo practitioners at the time of being interviewed, had at one time or another worked on a salary in the medical group. Thus, they reported on circumstances in which they could not themselves charge the patient a fee for the services they rendered. Their income was independent of the services they gave, just as the cost to the patient was independent of the services he received. The patient demanded and the physician supplied services on the basis of a prepayment contract which established a right for the patient and an obligation for the physician. Furthermore, the group was organized on a closed-panel basis, so that in order to obtain services by the terms of his contract, without out-of-pocket cost, the patient had to seek service only from the physicians working at the medical group, and no others.

Virtually all of the physicians interviewed had also had occasion to work on the traditional basis of solo, fee-for-service "private" practice. In that mode of organizing work and the marketplace, the physician makes a living by attracting patients and providing them with services paid for by a fee for each service. The physician's income is directly related to the fee charged and the number of services provided. He has no contractual relationship with patients. He must attract them by a variety of devices—accessibility, reputation, specialty, referral relations with colleagues— and maintain a sufficiently steady stream of new or returning patients to assure a stable if not lucrative practice. In theory, the patient is free to leave him for another physician, and relations with colleagues offering the same services are at least nominally competitive.

How did the physicians interpret these different arrangements and what did they emphasize in their experience with each? In the interviews, the prepaid group physician was often represented as helpless and exploited, with words like "trapped," "slave," and "servitor" used to describe his position. Since the contract was for all "necessary" services, however, it was hardly accurate to say that the physicians had to provide every service the patient demanded. They could have refused. But at bottom it was not really the formal contract which was the issue. Rather, the physicians were responding to the absence of a mechanism to which they were accustomed, a mechanism which, by attesting to the value of the physician's services in the eyes of the patient, and by testing the strength of the patient's sense of need, precluded the necessity of actually refusing. The physicians were responding to the absence of the out-of-pocket fee which is a prerequisite for service in "private practice."

The fee was seen as a useful barrier between patient and doctor which forced the *patient* to discriminate between the trivial and the important before he sought care. The assumption was that if the patient had to pay a fee for each service, he would ask only for "necessary" services, or, if he were too irrational or ignorant to discriminate accurately, he would at the very least restrict his demands to those occasions when he was really greatly worried. The fee served as a mechanical barrier which freed the physician of the necessity of having to refuse service and of having to persuade the patient that his grounds for doing so were reasonable. Since a fee operates as a barrier in advance of any request for service, it reduces interaction between physician and patient. In the prepaid plan, the physicians were not prepared for the greater interaction which the absence of a fee encouraged.

In addition to the service contract, there was also the closed-panel organization of the medical group. The physicians themselves were aware that some patients often felt trapped, since, in order to receive the benefits of their contract, they had to use the services only of a physician employed by the medical group. If he wanted to be treated by a particular individual in the group, he might nonetheless have had to accept another because of the former's full panel or appointment schedule. And when patients were referred to consultants, they were supposed to be referred to a specialty, not to an individual specialist. Some of the physicians themselves found this situation unsatisfactory because they were not personally chosen by patients, but were seen by patients because they happened to have appointment time free or openings on their panel, not because of their individual reputation or attractiveness.

Finally, there was the issue of group practice itself, of the constitution of a cooperative collegium rather than, as in entrepreneurial practice, an aggregate of nominally competing practitioners. In the latter case, the physician may be "scared that somebody would . . . take his patient away," or that the patient may "walk out the door and you may never see him again." Nevertheless, if he can afford it, the physician in fee-for-service solo practice can choose to refuse to give the patient what he asks for, and can even discourage him from returning. But in the group practice, the physicians did not generally have the option of dropping a patient with whom they had difficulty. The reason was not to be found in any potential economic loss, as in entrepreneurial practice, but rather in the closed-panel practice within which colleagues were cooperating rather than competing. When physicians form a closed-panel group, they cannot simply act as individuals, "drop" a patient who is troublesome, and allow him to go to a colleague, for if each of the group dropped his own problem patients, while he would indeed get rid of the ones he had, he would get in return those his colleagues had dropped, as his colleagues would get his. And so the pressure was to "live" with such patients and try to manage them as best one could—something for which the physician with ideological roots in private practice was poorly prepared.

From the view which the physicians presented, it seemed that the medical group involved them in a situation in which traditional safety valves had been tied down and the pressure increased. The service contract was thought to increase patient demand for services, while at the same time it prevented the physician from coping with that demand by the traditional method of raising prices. The closed-panel arrangement restricted the patients' demands to those physicians working cooperatively in the medical group, so the physicians could not cope with the pressure by the traditional method of encouraging the troublesome patient to go elsewhere for service. Confrontation between patient and physician was increased, and both participants explored new methods for resolving them. Indeed, the insurance scheme itself provided the resources for some of those new methods of reducing the pressure on demand and supply.

Paradigmatic Problems and Solutions

The basic interpersonal paradigm of a problematic doctor-patient relationship may be seen as a conflict between perspectives and a struggle for control or a negotiation over the provision of services. From his perspective the patient believes he needs a particular service; from his, the physician does not believe every service the patient wishes is necessary or appropriate. The content of this conflict between perspectives is composed of conceptions of knowledge, or expertise, the physician asserting that he knows best and the patient insisting that he is his own arbiter of need.

The conflict, however, takes place in a social and economic marketplace which provides resources that may be used to reinforce the one or the other position. In the case of medicine in the United States, that marketplace has in the past been organized on a fee-for-service basis, practitioners being entrepreneurs competing with each other for the fees of prospective patients. The fee the patient is willing and able to pay, in conjunction with the physician's economic security, constitute elements which are of strategic importance to private practice. If the physician's practice is well enough established, he can refuse service he does not want to give or does not believe necessary to give, even though he loses a fee and possibly a patient. On the other hand, if he desires to gain the fee and reduce the chance of "losing" the patient, he may give the patient the service he requests even if he believes it to be unnecessary. Like a merchant, he is concerned with pleasing his patients by giving them what they want, suspending his own notions of what is necessary and good for them in favor of his gain in income should he desire such gain.

The patient, on the other hand, has his fee as a resource (if he is lucky), and the freedom to turn away from the practitioner who does not provide him with the service he wants and pay it instead to the physician who does. He may take his trade elsewhere, but before he does he may introduce pressure by implying that if he does not get what he wants he will find someone else. In essence, the patient can play "customer" to the physician's merchant.

In contrast to these marketplace roles, there are those more often ascribed to doctor and patient by sociologists—that of expert consultant and layman. The layman is defined as someone who has a problem or difficulty he wishes resolved, but who does not have the special knowledge and skill needed to do so. He seeks out someone who has the necessary knowledge and skill and cooperates with him so that his diffculty can be managed if not resolved. In dealing with the expert, the layman is supposed to suspend his own judgment and instead follow the advice of the expert, who is considered to have superior knowledge and better judgment.

When there are differences of opinion of such character that the patient cannot bring himself to cooperate, the *generic* response of the expert is to attempt to gain the patient's cooperation by persuading him, on the basis of evidence which the expert produces, that it would be in his interest to cooperate and follow the recommended course. To *order* him to comply, or to gain compliance by some other form of coercion or pressure, is a contradiction of the essence of expertise and its "authority." Analytically, expertise gains its "authority" by its persuasive demonstration of special knowledge and skill relevant to particular problems requiring solution. It is the antithesis of the authority of office.

As a profession, however, medicine represents not only a full-time occupation possessed of expertise which participates in a marketplace where it sells its labor for a profit, but more particularly an occupation which has gained a specially protected position in the marketplace and a set of formal prerogatives which grant it some degree of official authority. For example, the mere possession of a legal license to practice allows the physician to officially certify death or disability, and to authorize pharmacists to dispense a variety of powerful and dangerous drugs. Here, albeit in rudimentary form, we find yet a third facet by which to characterize a third kind of doctor-patient relationship—that of the bureaucratic official and client. The latter seeks a given service from the former, who has exclusive control over access to services. The client seeks to establish his need and his right, while the official seeks to establish his eligibility before providing service or access to goods or services. In theory, both are bound by a set of rules which defines the rights and duties of the participants, and each makes reference to the rules in making and evaluating claims. In a rational-legal form of administration, both have a right of appeal to some higher authority who is empowered to mediate and resolve their differences.

In the predominant form of practice in present-day United States, the physician is more likely to be playing the role of merchant and expert than the role of official, though the latter is real enough and too important to be as ignored as it has been by sociologists and physicians alike. It is, after all, his status as an official which gives the physician a protected marketplace in which to be a merchant. Nonetheless, to be a true official virtually precludes being a merchant, so that only in special instances in the United States can we find medical practice which offers the possibility of taking the role of official on an everyday rather than an occasional basis.

The medical group we studied was just such a special instance, for it eliminated the fee and discouraged the profit motive, while setting up its physicians as official gatekeepers to services specified in a contract with patients, through an insurance agency with supervisory powers of its own. The contractual network specified the basic set of systematic rules, and established the official position of the physician. Under the rules, the physician served as an official gatekeeper to and authorizer of a whole array of services—not only his own, but also those of consultants who, even though "covered" in the contract, would not see a patient without an official referral, and those of laboratories, which do not provide "covered" tests without an official group physician's signature. In other reports of this study I show how the physicians were led to use their official powers to cope with problems of work, and how they exercised their role of expert. I also show how some railed against a situation which prevented them from using the more familiar techniques of the merchant to resolve their problems.

Here, however, I wish to point out that in the medical group the physician was not the only participant to whom a new role was made available. The situation, which left open the option of official and closed the option of merchant for physicians, also left open the option of bureaucratic client and closed the option of shopper or customer for patients. And when the patients acted as bureaucratic clients they posed different problems to the physician than they did when they acted as a customer, or as a patient: they asserted their rights in light of the rules of the contract. This untraditional possibility for patient behavior was one which upset the physicians a great deal and served as the focus for much of their dissatisfaction. Most of their problems of work stemmed ultimately from their relationships with patients and tended to be characterized in terms of the patient, so that it is important to understand the way the physicians saw their patients. Typically, work problems stemmed from patients who "make demands"; "the demanding patient" was seen to lie at the root of those difficulties.

Three Types of "Demanding Patients"

It is very easy to get the impression from this analysis that the work-lives of the group physicians were constantly fraught with pressure and conflict. Such an impression stems partially from the strategy of analysis I have chosen, a strategy which focuses on work problems rather than on the settled, everyday routines which stretch out on either side of occasional crises. Without remembering that most medical work is routine rather than crisis, one could not understand how physicians manage to get through their days. Indeed, the kinds of medical complaints and symptoms which are most often brought into the office were such that the daily routine posed a serious problem of boredom to the practitioners. Furthermore, most patients were not troublesome. As members of the stable blue- and white-collar classes, most knew the rules of the game, respected the physicians, and were more inclined than not to come in with medically acceptable (even if "trivial") complaints.

Nonetheless, the fact of routine, even boredom, would be difficult to discern in the physicians' own conversations. They did not talk to each other, or to the interviewers, about their routines; they talked about their crises. They did not talk about slow days, but about those when the work pressure was overwhelming. They rarely talked about "good" patients unless they received some unusual letter of thanks, card, or gift of which they were proud; they talked incessantly about troublesome or demanding patients. They almost never talked about routine diagnoses and their management, but talked often about the anomaly, the interesting case, or one of their "goofs." So the analytical strategy for reporting this study is not arbitrary, since it reflects the physicians' own preoccupations. It was by the problematic that they symbolized their work and it was in terms of the problematic that they evaluated their practice. Even though all agreed that "demanding patients" were statistically few in number, many who left the medical group ascribed their departure to their inability to bear even those few patients.

Most important for present purposes was the fact that, upon analysis of the physicians' discussion of "demanding patients," it was discovered that the most important type was a new one for them. They posed demands which the physicians were unaccustomed to dealing with, for the demands stemmed from the contractual framework of practice in the medical group and were generic to the role of the bureaucratic client rather than the customer or layman. Perhaps this was why they seemed so outrageous and insulting, for such demands treated the physicians as if they were officials rather than "free professionals." The distinction between that kind of demandingness and others was more often implicit than explicit in the physicians' talk when they were asked to characterize demanding patients. The tendency, however, was to distinguish one kind of demanding patient as dictatorial and another as essentially the opposite—eternally supplicant.

Of the two kinds of demanding patients, one would be familiar to the informed reader as the ambulatory practice version of the "crock" met in complaints by medical students and the house staff in the clinics of teaching hospitals. The crock was the person who played the respectful patient role, but presented complaints for which the physician had no antibiotic, vaccine, chemical agent, or technique for surgical repair. All the physician could provide for such complaints was what he considered "palliative" treatment rather than "cure." He neither learned anything interesting by seeing some biologically unusual condition nor felt he accomplished successful therapy. And he worried that he might overlook something "real."

Clearly, this kind of demanding patient was irritating because he had to be babied rather than treated instrumentally and because the doctor had to devote himself to "treating people [whom he considers to be] well, or have the same kind of anxieties we all have." Furthermore, he confronted the doctor with failure: he "can never be reassured. You know you are not getting anywhere with him and you just have to listen to him, the same chronic minor complaints and the same business." "I'm just not satisfied with my results, and the patient just keeps coming back, worse than ever."

In light of the distinctions I made earlier, it should be clear that this kind of demanding person was not playing either the role of bureaucratic client or that of customer. The role of the helpless layman was adopted, which did not contradict the role the physician wished to play. The problem was that the nature of the complaints was such that the medical worker could not play his role in a satisfying way—he could not really help, and his advice that there was no serious medical problem was refused.

The other kind of demanding patient was quite different, however, for he did not ceaselessly *beg* for help so much as *demand* services on the basis of his economic and contractual rights. Such rights do not, of course, exist in fee-for-service solo practice, but the analogue in such practice would be the demanding customer. Such a person is more likely to shop around from one physician to another rather than stick to one and demand his service. Given the structure of fee-for-service solo practice, we should expect in it rather less confrontation with demanding customers, though the physicians did tell stories about some who openly threatened to take their business elsewhere if they did not get what they wanted. Rare as such confrontation was, when it did occur, it was described with the same shock and outrage as was observed in the physicians' stories about demanding contract patients.

The "power of the contract" which one physician spoke of implied correctly that some patients, playing the role of bureaucratic client, threatened to and on occasion actually employed the device of an official complaint. They could complain either to the administration of the medical group or to an office established by the insuring organization to receive and investigate complaints. After all, if one has a contract, one also has the right to appeal decisions about its benefits. And naturally, the more familiar and effective with bureaucratic procedures the patients were, the more were they able to make trouble. The seventeen physicians who generalized about the social characteristic of demanding patients yielded in sum a caricature of the demanding patient as a female schoolteacher, well educated enough to be capable of articulate and critical questioning and letter writing, of high enough social status to be sensitive to slight and to expect satisfaction, and experienced with bureaucratic procedures. In the physicians' eyes, they were also neurotically motivated to be "demanding."

Also specially nurtured in the framework of the prepaid group practice—contrary to the ideal of bureaucracy but faithful to its reality—was the use by the bureaucratic client of "pull" or political influence to reinforce his demands and gain more than nominal contract benefits. Analogous to political influence in the free medical marketplace is the possession of wealth or prestige, making one a desirable customer who may refer his friends to the physician. Another form of "pull" lies in having connections with an especially influential and prestigious medical colleague. Both types of patients gain special handling in solo practice. In the medical group, however, "pull" was more related to influence in those segments of the community engaged in negotiating insurance contracts. There were occasional instances when a demanding patient was also an important member of a trade union, or had friends in high political places. Managing such patients was particularly difficult for the administration, since it was unable to protect its own staff in the face of such political influence.

Managing Demanding Patients in the Future

In this paper I have assumed that a prepaid service-contract medical group has important characteristics which will become more common in the future and which, therefore, allow us to make plausible and informed anticipations of the problems of medical practice in the future. On the basis of extensive interviews with physicians who worked in such a medical group, I suggested that a new kind of problem of management was posed to them by the social and economic structure of their practice. Ostensibly, the problem was the familiar and traditional one of the "demanding patient." Looking more closely at the usage of that phrase, however, led to the conclusion that there was more than one kind of "demanding patient." Indeed, on the basis of the physicians' discussions of their problems, I suggested that there were three types of demanding patients, each posing a different problem of management and a different challenge to medical self-esteem.

Virtually unmet in the medical group (but mentioned by the physicians) were those who acted like demanding customers by insisting on either obtaining the services they wished or of taking their business (and fees) elsewhere. Such a strategy is of course generic to entrepreneurial practice, and most effective with weakly established practitioners in a highly competitive medical market. The second type of demanding patient was the traditional "crock," what a spokesman for Kaiser-Permanente once called "the worried well." Such a patient persisted in seeking consultation for complaints which the physicians felt were trivial and essentially incurable. They were a more serious problem in the medical group than they were reported to be in fee-for-service solo practice because their demands could not be reduced by the imposition of a fee barrier or by suggesting that they go elsewhere for service. The third type of demanding patient was new and particularly disturbing to the physicians—the patient who demanded services which he felt he had a right to under the terms of his prepaid service contract and who had recourse to complaining about the deprivation of his rights to the bureaucratic system of appeal and review.

In the future, with prepaid group practice far more common, we should expect new problems in the doctor-patient relationship as that new kind of demanding patient is met with by more physicians. Insurance coverage in the future may be such as to maintain some kind of fee barrier (as in prepaid plans which now impose small charges for house calls), but the barrier will be less than that to which physicians were accustomed in fee-for-service practice and will be less effective in discouraging demandingness. In addition, since he will be working cooperatively with colleagues in group practice, the physician will be less able to simply "drop" his demanding patients. Unable to use money or evasion to cope with his relationship to problem patients, the physician will have to use other methods. What options are open to him?

Just as the structure of fee-for-service solo practice produces the possibility of using mechanical financial solutions, so does the structure of prepaid service-contract practice also produce the possibility of using mechanical solutions. The mechanical solutions observed in the medical group studied lay in providing all services covered by the contract which were not inconvenient to the practitioner—office visits, referrals, and laboratory tests. (The house call was not convenient, and was resisted strongly.) But whereas the former solutions were traditional and so regarded as "natural" and "reasonable," the use of the latter was regarded as "giving in," and treated with resentment and concern. Both are, analytically, equally mechanical, an equally passive reflex to the organization of the system of care.

The consequences of passive response to the new conditions by which patient demand will be structured are already clear. In the face of rising services and costs, strong administrative, financial, and peer-review pressures will force the physician to limit his "giving in" and restrict the supply of demanded services. But how exactly can the physician limit services, and what kind of interaction will go on between him and his patient under such circumstances? I cannot provide empirical evidence from my study because in the medical group there was rather little organized pressure to limit services. The physicians could "give in" when they chose to. But the logic of my analysis would lead me to expect that when there is pressure to limit service to demanding patients in a structure like that of the medical group, the structure taken by itself provides the opportunity for doing so on the bureaucratic grounds to the official authority of the physician as a gatekeeper to benefits. He can simply refuse the patient, standing on the official position which the structure provides him.

But it need not be that way. While the prepaid service-contract group practice virtually precluded the adoption by physician and patient of a merchant-customer relationship, and allowed the adoption of an official-client relationship which was precluded in private solo practice, it did not *force* the practitioners to manage their problems that way. Some chose to adopt the interactional strategy which is an inherent possibility in medical practice no matter what the historical framework in which it takes place—the strategy of the expert consultant who relies neither on his position in the marketplace nor on his official position in a bureaucratic system but on his knowledge and skill. Some physicians were persuaded that if they invested extra attention and energy in "educating" their patients and developing a relationship of trust they would ultimately have fewer "management" problems. To cope with suspicion on the part of the patient they initially provided services on demand in order to show that they recognized the legitimacy of the patient's contractual rights, and that they were not motivated to withhold services from them. At the same time, however, they tried to explain to the demanding patient the grounds for their judgment that the services were medically unnecessary. They undertook, in other words, to persuade and demonstrate, and avoided mechanical solutions to the problem of demandingness. The social, moral, and technical quality of the medical care of the future will depend on whether medical practice will be organized in such a way as to encourage such a positive mode of responding to patient demands, or whether it will, like traditional practice, be merely a fiscally and technically functional structure which does not take cognizance of the human qualities of those it traps.

Acknowledgment

The study reported here was partially supported by USPH grants RG–7882, GM–07882, CH00025, CH–00414, and HS–00104.

Note

This article is an abridged version of a chapter of a work in progress at the time of publication. Detailed data and more elaborate analysis are to be found in Eliot Freidson, *Doctoring Together: A Study of Professional Social Control* (New York: Elsevier Scientific Publishing Co., 1975).

25

Children, Stress, and Hospitalization

A Field Experiment

James K. Skipper, Jr., and Robert C. Leonard

This paper reports an experimental study concerned with the reduction of some of the effects of hospitalization and surgery—physiological as well as social and psychological—in young children. Usually much of children's behavior while hospitalized for surgery is presumed to be a response to psychological and physiological stress. This research offers evidence demonstrating the effects of *social interaction* on children's response to hospitalization for a tonsillectomy operation.

When illness is serious enough to warrant an individual's confinement to a hospital, the process of hospitalization may produce stress (for all concerned) independent of that precipitated by the illness itself. Illness may be a stress-provoking situation not only for the stricken individual, but also for the members of his immediate family. Of special interest here is the stress in the patient role resulting from discontinuities, ambiguities and conflicts in the network of role relationships in which the patient becomes involved when he enters the hospital care and cure system. Stress seems to be especially high for both the staff and the patient and his family in cases involving surgery on young children.

One of the most common causes of hospitalization and surgery in preteenage children is tonsillectomy. It has been estimated that over two million of these operations are carried out each year. They constitute about one-third of all operations in the United States. Often it represents the child's first admission to a hospital, his first separation from the security of his parents and home, and his first real experience involving loss of consciousness and bodily parts. The stress produced by this type of hospitalization and surgery results from loneliness, grief, abandonment, imprisonment, and the threat of physical injury, as well as intense needs for

SOURCE: *Journal of Health and Social Behavior* 9 (December 1968): 275–87. Copyright © 1968 by the American Sociological Association. Reprinted by permission of the publisher and the authors.

love, affection, and maternal protection. The experience may even lead to grave psychological problems years after the child has been discharged.[1]

The data in this report are based on a field experiment designed to test the effects on the behavior of hospitalized children of nurses' interaction with the children's mothers. It was hoped that the experiment would develop a method of reducing the children's stress indirectly by reducing the stress of their mothers. The study is a logical extension of a series of small sample experiments used to measure the effects of nurse-patient interaction on the behavior of patients. Evidence from these studies indicates that interaction with a patient-centered nurse trained in effective communication often results in large reductions in the stress experienced by the patient and a large decrease in somatic complications. (Leonard et al., 1967)

We postulate that hospitalization for a tonsillectomy operation is likely to produce a great deal of stress for child patients and their mothers. For the children this stress is likely to result in: elevated temperature, pulse rate and blood pressure; disturbed sleep; postoperative vomiting; a delayed recovery period; and other forms of behavior which deviate from the medical culture's norms of "health" and normal progress of hospitalization and treatment.

We conceptualize these patient behaviors to be simply instances of individual human behavior, which therefore can be affected by the patient's attitudes, feelings, and beliefs about his medical treatment, hospital care, and those who provide it. This is not to disregard physical and physiological variables as stimuli for the patient's response, or to deny that the response may be "physiological." Rather, we reason that in addition the meaning the patient attaches to the stimuli, will also affect his response. For instance, some (stressful) definitions of the patient role and the hospital situation may result in deviant patient behavior in spite of all atempts at control by medication, anesthesia, or variations in medical technology.

Past attempts at reducing children's stress in the hospital have not fully considered the effect that parents and especially the mother may have on the child's level of emotional tension. (Prugh et al., 1953) The mother is a prime factor in determining whether changes in the child's emotions and behavior will be detrimental or beneficial to his treatment and recovery. If she is affected by severe stress herself, her ability to aid her child may be reduced. Moreover, in her interaction with the child her feeling state may be communicated and actually increase the child's stress.[2]

If the mother were able to manage her own stress and be calm, confident and relaxed, this might be communicated to the child and ease his distress. Moreover, the mother might be more capable of making rational decisions concerning her child's needs and thus facilitate his adaptation to the hospital situation. An important means of reducing stress from potentially threatening events is through the communication of information about the event. (Janis, 1958) This allows the individual to organize his thoughts, actions, and feelings about the event. It provides a framework to appraise the potentially frightening and disturbing perceptions which one might actually experience. An individual is able to engage in an imaginative mental rehearsal in which the "work of worrying" can take place. According to Janis (1958) the information is likely to be most effective if communicated in the context of interest, support, and reassurance on the part of authoritative individuals.

Regular and Experimental Conditions

As has been noted in the literature in a variety of different contexts, the modern hospital is a notoriously poor organization for eliciting information, providing support, or generating a reassuring atmosphere. From the patient's point of view, the lack of information and lack of emotional warmth from physicians and nurses are among the most criticized aspects of patient care. (Skipper, 1965; Mumford and Skipper, 1967) For whatever reasons, to the extent medical and nursing personnel do not engage in expressive interaction with patients and provide them with information, they contribute to, or actually become sources of stress.

We can describe the usual routine staff approach to tonsillectomy patients and their mothers from the experience of members of our research team who worked for several months in advance of the study on the ward where our experiments were conducted. Typically, the staff approached the patient as a work object on which to perform a set of tasks, rather than as a participant in the work process or an individual who needs help in adjusting to a new environment. The attending surgeon's interaction with the child was limited primarily to the performance of the operation and release from the hospital. The nursing staff tended to initiate interaction only when they needed some data for their charts or had to perform an instrumental act such as taking blood pressure, checking fluid intake, or giving a medication. The typical role was the bureaucratic one of information gatherer, chart assembler, and order deliverer. They offered very little information and were usually evasive if questioned directly. If the mother displayed stress, the staff tried to ignore it or to get her to leave the ward.

For our research purposes, actual practice made a good comparison condition against which to test the hypothesis that:

the childrens' stress can be reduced indirectly by reducing the stress of the mothers.

The experimental approach began with the admission of the mother and child to the hospital. Although the child was present, the focus of interaction was the mother. No more attention was paid to the child than under routine (control) admission conditions. The special nurse attempted to create an atmosphere which would facilitate the communication of information to the mother, maximize freedom to verbalize her fear, anxiety and special problems, and to ask any and all questions which were on her mind. The information given to the mother tried to paint an accurate picture of the reality of the situation. Mothers were told what routine events to expect and when they were likely to occur—including the actual time schedule for the operation.

The experimental interaction may be characterized as expressive, yet affectively neutral, person-oriented rather than task-oriented, nonauthoritarian, specific (not diffuse) and intimate. The special nurse probed the mother's feelings and the background of those feelings as possible causes of stress regardless of what the topic might be, or where it might lead. In each individual case the special nurse tried to help the mother meet her own individual problems.

With the experimental group, the process of admission took an average of about 5 minutes longer than regular admission procedures. In addition to the interaction which took place at admission, the special nurse met with the mothers of the first 24 experimental group patients for about 5 minutes at several other times when potentially stressful events were taking place. These times were: 6:00 and 8:00 p.m. the evening of admission; shortly after the child was returned from the recovery room the next morning; 6:00 and 8:00 p.m. the evening of the operation; and at discharge the following day. The remaining 16 experimental group mothers were seen only at admission. For purposes of analysis the first 24 patients and their controls constitute Experiment I, and the remaining 16 patients and their controls Experiment II.

Our theory predicts that: providing the experimental communication for the mothers of children hospitalized for tonsillectomy would result in less stress, a change in the mothers' definition of the situation, and different behavioral responses. This in turn would result in less stress for the child and, hopefully, a "better" adaptation to the hosptialization and surgery. If this could be demonstrated, not only might it be a practical means of reducing the stress of young children hospitalized for tonsillectomy, but it would also provide direct evidence on the effect of social interaction on behaviors often assumed to be responses to psychological stress.

Research Methodology

To test these hypotheses an experiment was conducted at one large teaching hospital, in a four-month period during the late fall and winter. The sample included all patients between the ages of 3 and 9 years admitted to the hospital for tonsillectomy and having no previous hospital experience. Patients were excluded from the sample if there were known complicating medical conditions, their parents did not speak English, or their mothers did not accompany them through admission procedures. A total of 80 patients qualified for the sample. Forty-eight of the children were male, and 32 were female. Thirty-six were between the ages of 3 and 5, and 44 between the ages of 6 and 9. Thirty-three of the mothers had more than 12 years of formal education, 45 between 10 and 12 years and 2 less than 10 years. All the families were able to pay for the cost of the operation and the hospitalization.

Children were admitted to the hospital late in the afternoon the day before surgery was performed. At admission each child received a physical examination which included securing samples of blood and urine and a check on weight, blood pressure, temperature and pulse rate. When the admission procedures were completed the child was dressed in his night clothes and taken to one of two four-bed rooms limited to children who were to undergo a tonsillectomy. Control and experimental patients were not separated, but placed in rooms with each other to eliminate any systematic peer influence. From midnight until their return to the room after surgery, the children were not allowed to take fluids. The next morning, starting at 8 o'clock, the children were taken to the operating room, one every half-hour. Each child voided before the surgery. Following the operation they were taken to the recovery room where they remained until awake. Then they were returned to their room where they stayed until their discharge late the following morning. Only six of the mothers gained permission to "room in" with their child overnight. Three of these were in the control group and three were in the experimental group. All but one of the remaining mothers was able to spend most of the operation day at the hospital. However, a record was not kept of the actual amount of time spent with her child. In fact it was beyond the resources of this investigation to obtain systematic data on the mother-child interaction; that is, the actual differences in frequency, timing and quality of interaction between control and experimental group mothers with their children.

The study was experimental in the sense that R. A. Fisher's (1947) classic design was used. The children were randomly assigned to control and experimental groups. No significant differences were found in the composition of the groups on the bases of: sex, age or health of the children, age of the mothers, class background, religious affiliation, and types of anesthesia used during the operation. Since the children were randomly assigned, antecedent variations and their consequences are taken into account by the probability test.

Correlated measurement bias may be a much more important source of mistaken conclusion than bias in the composition of the groups. One way of gaining some control of this type of bias is a "blind" procedure in which the individual measuring the dependent variables does not know which treatment the subjects have been assigned. With one exception, blind procedures were employed in this research.

The independent variable in the experiment was interaction. The experimental manipulations were all communicative—affective as well as cognitive. They emphasized the communication of information and emotional support to the mothers. The dependent variable was the behavior of the children. Thus the experimental variation was the interaction under usual hospital conditions compared with what was added experimentally.

All patients and their mothers whether in control or experimental group were subjected to regular hospital treatment and procedures. In addition, experimental group patients and mothers were admitted to the hospital by a specially trained nurse. Admission is a crucial time to introduce the experimental communication. Entry into any new social situation can be a tense experience. Lack of attention to the patient's definition of the situation in the admission process not only does not relieve stress but may actually increase it. Previous experimentation (Leonard et al., 1967) has indicated the potential effect of providing such attention on immediate stress and also the patient's adjustment to the hospital experience.

The regular nursing staff was informed that a study was in progress and asked to complete a short questionnaire regarding the behavior of the child and mother, as well as making charts and records available. They did not know which patients were in the control and experimental groups. The study was conducted at a teaching hospital, and the staff was used to having all sorts of projects taking place on the ward. They had become immune to them and ignored them unless they seriously interfered with their work. The staff was also familiar with the research personnel, who had been working on various projects on the ward on and off for over a year.

At admission, regardless of group, each mother was asked if she would be willing to complete a short questionnaire which would be mailed to her 8 days after her child was discharged, and would concern the hospital experience and its aftermath. None of the mothers refused. The mothers were not aware of whether they were in the control or experimental group. The questionnaire asked for the mothers' perception of: her own level of stress before, during and after the operation, as well as her possible distress about a future similar operation; her desire for information during the hospitalization and her feeling of helpfulness; her trust and confidence in the medical and nursing staff; and her general satisfaction with the hospital experience. By means of a second questionnaire administered to the regular nursing staff, an independent measure of each mother's level of stress and general adaptation to the hospital experience was secured. To discover the effects of hospitalization on the child after discharge, a section of the mailback questionnaire to the mother also concerned aspects of the child's behavior during his first 7 days at home. Items were related to such matters as whether the child ran a fever, whether it was necessary to call a physician, and whether the child recovered during the first week at home. In addition, mothers were asked if their child manifested any unusual behavior which might be regarded as an emotional reaction to the operation and hospitalization such as disturbed sleep, vomiting, finicky eating, crying, afraid of doctors and nurses, etc.

Based on previous research several somatic measures of children's stress in the hospital were selected. Each child's temperature, systolic blood pressure and pulse rate were recorded at four periods during the hospitalization: admission, preoperatively, postoperatively, and at discharge. The normal variability of these vital signs is not great in children between the ages of 3 and 9. Children at this age have not developed effective inhibiting mechanisms, so that an increase in excitement, apprehension, anxiety and fear, etc. will be reflected in the level of these indicators. Inability to void postoperatively and postoperative emesis also may be responses to stress over which a child has little conscious control. The time of first voiding after the operation was recorded as well as the incidence of emesis from the time the child entered the recovery room until discharge. Finally, the amount of fluids a child is able to consume after the operation may be related to the mother's understanding of its importance and her ability to get the child to cooperate. Fluid intake was recorded for the first 7 hours upon the child's return from the recovery room. This period represented the shortest time that any mother in the study stayed with her child after the operation.

Systolic blood pressure was measured and recorded by the special nurse. Checks on the objectivity and reliability of the special nurse were made periodically. Data on pulse rate, temperature, postoperative vomiting, ability to void postoperatively, and oral intake of fluids were collected and recorded by staff nurses who had no knowledge of which children had been assigned to the control and experimental groups.

Data were complete on all patients and mothers with two exceptions. First, since reliability checks were not made on the special nurses' measurement of systolic blood pressure for several patients in Experiment II, these were not used. Second, the regular nursing staff's estimate of the mothers' stress and adaptation was not available for two mothers in Experiment II. The response rate to the mailback questionnaire was over 92 per cent, 74 of the 80 mothers returning the questionnaire. Four of the nonreturns were control group mothers (2 in Experiment I and 2 in Experiment II) and 2 experimental group mothers (Experiment I).[3] All hypotheses predicted the direction of differences between control group mothers and experimental group mothers and children.

Findings

In a previous paper (Skipper et al., 1968) the effect of the special nurse's interaction with the mothers was presented in detail. In summary, according to the mothers' reports on the mail-back questionnaire, experimental group mothers suffered less stress than control group mothers during and after the operation. This finding was substantiated by the independent evaulation of the regular nursing staff. The regular nursing staff also estimated each mother's difficulty in adapting to the hospitalization. Experimental group mothers were rated as having less over-all difficulty in adaptation. This agreed with the mother's own self-evaulation. Experimental group mothers, as compared to control group mothers, reported: less lack of information during the hospitalization; less difficulty in feeling helpful to their child; and a greater degree of satisfaction with the total hospital experience. Taken together these measures provide evidence in support of the hypothesis that social interaction with the special nurse was an effective means of changing the mothers' definition of the situation to lower stress levels, thus allowing them to make a more successful adaptation to the hospitalization and operation.

In this paper we are concerned with the effect of the nurse-mother interaction on the children. Tables 1–3 compare the mean systolic blood pressure, pulse rate, and temperature of control and experimental sets of children at four periods during hospitalization—admission preoperatively, postoperatively, and discharge.

At admission, the differences in systolic blood pressure were, of course, random, with the experimental mean actually slightly higher than the control (Table 1). This difference was reversed after the experimental treatment, and the control children continued to have higher average blood pressure throughout their hospital stay. In Experiment I the mean for experimental group children at admission, 111.5, dropped preoperatively to 109.1, remained relatively the same postoperatively, 109.7, and then dropped sharply at discharge to 104.7. The discharge mean was lower than the admission mean. The mean for control group children at admission, 110.4, rose to 120.3 preoperatively, and continued to rise to 127.8 postoperatively, before falling to 120.9 at discharge. The discharge mean was much higher than the

TABLE 1. Mean Systolic Blood Pressure of Control and Experimental Group Children at Four Periods during Hospitalization

	Admission	Preoperative (8:00 P.M.)		Postoperative (8:00 P.M.)		Discharge		Total N
	$\bar{x}$	$\bar{x}$	t^*	$\bar{x}$	t^*	$\bar{x}$	t^*	
Experiment I								
Experimental	111.5	109.1	4.81	109.7	7.73	104.7	6.81	24
			$P<.0005$		$P<.0005$		$P<.0005$	
Control	110.4	120.3	....	127.8	....	120.9	....	24

*One-tailed test.

TABLE 2. Mean Pulse Rate of Control and Experimental Group Children at Four Periods during Hospitalization

	Admission	Preoperative (8:00 P.M.)		Postoperative (8:00 P.M.)		Discharge		Total N
	$\bar{x}$	$\bar{x}$	t^*	$\bar{x}$	t^*	$\bar{x}$	t^*	
Experiment I								
Experimental	103.6	95.8	5.10	101.6	6.31	95.2	5.08	24
			$P<.0005$		$P<.0005$		$P<.0005$	
Control	104.6	110.8	....	122.2	....	110.8	....	24
Experiment II								
Experimental	105.6	100.2	1.38	117.1	.83	105.4	2.13	16
			$P<.10$		$P>.10$		$P<.025$	
Control	104.9	107.5	....	123.1	....	116.8	....	16

*One-tailed test.

admission mean. The mean differences between the control and experimental group children reached a level of statistical significance of beyond .005, preoperatively, postoperatively, and at discharge.[4] As mentioned previously, the data for Experiment II are not presented since reliability checks on the special nurses' measurement of systolic blood pressure were not available for several patients. However, the data that were available followed the same patterns as described in Experiment I.

We see in Table 2 that in both Experiments there was little difference at admission between the mean pulse rate of control and experimental group children. In Experiment I the mean for experimental group children at admission, 103.6, dropped to 95.8 preoperatively, rose to 101.6 postoperatively, and then fell to 95.2 at discharge. The discharge mean was lower than the admission mean. The control group mean at admission, 104.6, rose preoperatively to 110.8 and continued to rise to 122.2 postoperatively, before falling only to 110.8 at discharge. The discharge mean in the control set was much greater than the admission mean. The mean difference between the two groups reached a statistical level of significance

TABLE 3. Mean Temperature of Control and Experimental Group Children at Four Periods during Hospitalization

	Admission	Preoperative (8:00 P.M.)		Postoperative (8:00 P.M.)		Discharge		Total N
	$\bar{x}$	$\bar{x}$	t^*	$\bar{x}$	t^*	$\bar{x}$	t^*	
Experiment I								
Experimental	99.4	99.1	1.13	100.1	2.48	99.2	1.68	24
			$P>.10$		$P>.01$		$P<.05$	
Control	99.5	99.8	....	100.7	....	99.8	....	24
Experiment II								
Experimental	99.3	98.9	2.65	99.3	1.93	99.3	.85	16
			$P>.01$		$P<.05$		$P>.10$	
Control	99.3	99.4	....	99.9	....	99.7	....	16

*One-tailed test.

beyond .005 at each of the periods. Exactly the same pattern appeared in Experiment II, but the differences between the group means were considerably less and did not reach as high a level of statistical significance.

Table 3 shows that in both Experiments I and II at admission there was little difference between the mean temperature of control and experimental children. In Experiment I the experimental group mean at admission, 99.4, fell to 99.1 preoperatively, rose to 100.1 postoperatively and dropped to 99.2 at discharge. Again, as in the case of systolic blood pressure and pulse rate, the discharge mean was lower than the admission mean. The control group mean at admission, 99.5, rose to 99.8 preoperatively and continued to rise to 100.7 postoperatively before falling to 99.8 at discharge. Again the mean discharge figure for the control group children was higher than the admission mean. The same pattern appeared in Experiment II.

In addition to systolic blood pressure, pulse rate, and temperature the childrens' postoperative emesis, hour of first voiding, and oral intake of fluids were checked. Tables 4 and 5 present these data. Table 4 shows that in Experiment I, 10 of the children vomited after the operation, 7 of them more than once, while only 3 experimental group children vomited, none of them more than once. Although the incidence of postoperative emesis was not as great in Experiment II as Experiment I, the same pattern appeared. Control group children experienced more emesis than experimental group children. As can be seen from Table 5, control group children did not void as rapidly after the operation as experimental group children. In Experiment I the mean hour of first voiding for control group children was well over 7½ hours compared to 4½ for experimental group children. In Experiment II the corresponding figures were: control group children approximately 6¾ hours and experimental group children 5¾ hours. Moreover, in both Experiments control children consumed much less fluid during the first 7 hours after the operation than experimental group children (Table 5).

Taken together these physiological measures indicate that the level of stress among experimental children was much lower. This was true for both Experiments. Experimental children had lower mean levels of systolic blood pressure, pulse rate and temperature preoperatively, postoperatively, and at discharge than control group children. Experimental group children had less postoperative emesis, voided earlier, and drank more fluids than control group children. These data lend support to the hypothesis that the experimental nurse-mother interaction would reduce

TABLE 4. Incidence of Postoperative Emesis for Control and Experimental Group Children

	None		Once		More Than Once		Total N	χ^2
	N	%	N	%	N	%		
Experiment I								
Control	14	58	3	12	7	29	24	8.40
Experimental	21	88	3	12	0	0	24	P<.01
Total	35	73	6	12	7	15	48	
Experimental II								
Control	12	75	1	6	3	19	16	1.15
Experimental	14	88	1	6	1	6	16	P<.10
Total	26	81	2	6	4	12	32	

TABLE 5. Mean Number of Hours from the End of the Operation to the Hour of First Voiding and Mean Intake of Fluids Postoperatively for Control and Experimental Group Children

	Mean Hours before First Voiding		Mean Fluid Intake (no. of c.c. after 7 hours)		Total N
	$\bar{x}$	t^*	$\bar{x}$	t^*	
Experiment I					
Experimental	4.54	5.94	629.17	4.81	24
Control	7.63	$P<.0005$	413.13	$P<.0005$	24
Experiment II					
Experimental	5.75	.58	520.00	3.62	16
Control	6.81	$P>.10$	351.56	$P<.005$	16

*One-tailed test.

mothers' stress and increase their ability to adapt rationally to the hospitalization, which, in turn, would have profound effects on their children. The hypothesis is further supported by the regular nursing staffs' evaluation of the children's general over-all adaptation to the hospitalization. By means of a short questionnaire each staff nurse who had the most contact with a child was asked to judge whether she considered the child's adaptation to be high, average or low. The staff nurses had no knowledge of whether a child was in the control or experimental group. Table 6 presents these data. In Experiment I, 50 per cent of the experimental group children were judged as making a high adaptation to the hospitalization compared to only 17 percent of control group children. The corresponding figures for Experiment II were: experimental group children 56 per cent high adaptation and control group children 31 per cent high adaptation.

The mail-back questionnaire to the mothers provides data on the children's condition and behavior at home during the first week after discharge (Table 7). In both experiments over 50 per cent of control group mothers reported that their child ran a fever during the first week at home while less than one third of the experimental group mothers reported this. None of the experimental group mothers reported their child vomiting, but this was reported by four control group mothers, two in

TABLE 6. Regular Nursing Staffs' Evaluation of Control and Experimental Group Children's Adaptation to the Hospitalization

	High Adaptation		Average Adaptation		Low Adaptation		Total N	χ^2
	N	%	N	%	N	%		
Experiment I								
Control	4	17	15	62	5	21	24	6.00
Experimental	12	50	9	38	3	12	24	$P<.02$
Total	16	33	24	50	8	17	48	
Experiment II								
Control	5	31	5	31	6	38	16	3.14
Experimental	9	56	5	31	2	12	16	$P>.10$
Total	14	44	10	31	8	25	32	

TABLE 7. Fever, Emesis, Condition Requiring Mother to Call Physician, and Recovery Time during First Week at Home, for Control and Experimental Group Children

	Fever Reported			Emesis Reported			Called Physician			Recovery Time within One Week		
	N	%	*χ^2	N	%	*χ^2	N	%	*χ^2	N	%	*χ^2
Experiment I												
Control	11	50		2	9		9	41		11	50	
Experimental	6	27	2.39 P<.07	0	0	.51 P>.10	3	14	2.86 P<.05	22	100	12.12 P<.0005
Total	17	39		2	4		12	27		33	75	
Experiment II												
Control	8	57		2	14		6	43		5	36	
Experimental	5	31	1.07 P>.10	0	0	.22 P>.10	3	19	1.08 P>.10	15	94	8.83 P<.002
Total	13	43		2	7		9	30		20	67	

*Corrected for Continuity, one-tailed test.

TABLE 8. Unusual Fear of Hospitals, Physicians and Nurses, Crying More Than Usual, and More Disturbed Sleep Than Usual during the First Week after Discharge, for Control and Experimental Group Children

	Unusual Fear			Crying More Than Usual			Disturbed Sleep More Than Usual			Total N
	N	%	$^*\chi^2$	N	%	$^*\chi^2$	N	%	$^*\chi^2$	
Experiment I										
Control	8	36	5.02	10	46	2.63	15	68	11.38	22
Experimental	1	4	$P<.05$	4	18	$P<.06$	3	14	$P<.0005$	22
Total	9	20		14	32		18	41		44
Experiment II										
Control	7	50	7.81	8	57	2.00	11	79	6.56	14
Experimental	0	0	$P<.0003$	4	25	$P<.08$	4	25	$P<.005$	16
Total	7	23		12	40		15	50		30

*Corrected for Continuity, one-tailed test.

Experiment I and two in Experiment II. Almost 41 per cent of control group mothers in Experiment I and almost 29 per cent in Experiment II indicated that they were worried enough about their child's condition to call a physician. Less than 14 per cent of experimental group mothers in Experiment I and less than 19 per cent in Experiment II indicated it was necessary to call a physician. Finally, and perhaps most significantly, 100 per cent of experimental group mothers in Experiment I and 94 per cent in Experiment II reported that their child had recovered from the operation before the end of the first week after discharge. Only 50 per cent of control group mothers in Experiment I and 36 per cent in Experiment II claimed their child recovered during the first week. In other words, based on mother's reports all but one of the experimental group children recovered from the operation during the first week after discharge, in contrast to less than half of the control group children.

These data indicate the experimental group children seemed to experience, physiologically, less ill effects from the operation and hospitalization and made a more rapid recovery than control group children. In addition, there were differences in the social and psychological behavior of the two groups. Major differences were found in three areas: excessive crying, disturbed sleep, and an unusual fear of doctors, nurses, and hospitals (Table 8). In both experiments, twice as many control as experimental mothers reported their child cried more than usual during the week after his discharge. Over 68 per cent of control group mothers in Experiment I, and over 78 per cent in Experiment II indicated their child suffered unusual sleep disturbances at night. This was compared with just 14 per cent of experimental mothers in Experiment I and 25.0 per cent in Experiment II. Of all the effects of the operation and hospitalization at home, disturbed sleep appeared to be the most common and the most severe.

Although only one experimental mother (Experiment I) reported her child seemed to have an unusual fear of the hospital and its personnel, 36 per cent of control mothers in Experiment I and 50 per cent in Experiment II reported that their child did. Often fear of the hospital, disturbed sleep, and excessive crying occurred in combination with one another. A written comment by one of the control group mothers aptly illustrates this:

> My child has had nightmares ever since he left the hospital. This is very unusual for him. He wakes up in the middle of the night yelling and screaming and crying his heart out. He is afraid someone will put him back in the hospital and leave him forever.

In addition to excessive crying, disturbed sleep, and fear of the hospital, slight differences were discovered in a number of other behavioral areas. According to mothers' reports, control group children had greater difficulty than usual in eating, drinking, and relating to others, as well in manifesting more regressive behavior (thumb sucking, bed wetting, etc.) than experimental group children.[5]

Conclusion and Implications

The control group data confirms our hypothesis that under prevailing conditions the social environment of the hospital is likely to produce a great deal of stress for child patients and their mothers. For the children this stress is likely to result in elevated temperature, pulse rate and blood pressure, disturbed sleep, fear of doctors and nurses, a delayed recovery period, and other forms of behavior which deviate from the medical culture's norms of "health" and normal progress of hospitalization. The experimental group data indicate that a change in the quality of interaction between an authoritative person such as the experimental nurse and the hospitalized child's mother can lower the mother's level of stress and produce changes in the mother's definition of the situation. Due to the mother's intimate relationship and interaction with the child, a reduction in her level of stress and changed definition of the situation alters a salient component of the child's social environment. The data support the hypothesis that this may result in less stress for the child and consequently a change in his social, psychological, and even physiological behavior.

In Experiment I the special nurse interacted with the experimental group mothers at admission and at several other times during the hospitalization. In Experiment II the interaction was limited to the admission process. The observed effects of the experimental interaction on the childrens' behavior were in the predicted direction for both experiments, although the magnitude of the relationship was generally slightly higher in Experiment I. Although this finding highlights the effectiveness of the initial interaction and/or suggests that admission may be the crucial time and place to begin stress reducing interaction, it also suggests that further interaction throughout the hospitalization has important effects.

According to general sociological theory much of the important variation in individual human behavior is explained by variation in the culture and structure of the group to which the individual belongs. Additional variation is explained by the individual's status and position within the group. On occasion sociologists implicitly or explicitly specify intervening psychological states and processes that mediate group effects on individual behavior. When psychological variables are included their source is usually hypothesized in the socialization process or simply in social interaction. Indeed, sociology is often defined as the study of human interaction. However, many times sociologists do not find it convenient in their research to observe interaction, or the actual behavior that is supposedly affected by interaction. Self-reported values, statuses, role definitions, individual psychological states and behavior have been more accessible for study. Thus sociologists have accumulated data suggesting that status inconsistency or low status crystallization is likely to result in strong liberal political attitudes, voting for the democratic party, or, depending on the type of inconsistency under discussion, higher frequency of self-reported psychosomatic symptoms. Although this line of research does not appear to have been explicitly linked to the "social structure and anomie" theories of deviant behavior stemming from Durkheim, it has been linked to the "status integration" suicide research which also derives from Durkheim and with the psychological theories of cognitive dissonance.[6] Most previous research has relied on static macro-level correlations using census-type statistics for infrequent events such as suicide, or on survey analyses of self-reported physiological stress symptoms correlated with various indexes of individual status consistency. The intervening social process activating the psychological inconsistencies has not explicitly figured in the research, nor has the research been experimental. Obviously, it is extremely difficult in most cases to manipulate these structural variables. The research reported above, by focusing on the effects of the immediate social environment rather than on more permanent social structural determinants or long-term personalities changes points the way to nonlaboratory experimental tests of social environmental stress theory.

In addition to its potential contribution to social psychological theory, this type of research can form an interesting chapter in applied sociology. It has immediate implications for the control of stress, since control lies in the dyadic interaction which can be manipulated by individual practitioners. The results of this research suggest that even just one such practitioner out of the dozens with whom a patient may come in contact may be able to have a major effect. In contrast, manipulation of either relatively permanent statuses, major structural features of the organization, or deep-seated personality traits must be more difficult.

Specifically, if supported by further, more extensive research, the data suggest that some of the after-effects of hospitalization and surgery in young children, physiological as well as social and psychological, may be alleviated through a relatively simple and inexpensive social process. An authoritative figure, by establishing an expressive relationship with the mother of a child, and providing her with information, may reduce the mother's stress and allow her to make a more rational adaptation to the child's problems and take a more active role in aiding him. The change in the mother's behavior may then have a profound effect on the child's behavior. We suggest that this process might be an effective and efficient procedure which could easily be added to the arsenal of ways and means which health professionals may have at their disposal for combating the stress of hospitalization and surgery on both mother and child.

Acknowledgments

This research took place at the Child Study Center, Yale University, in cooperation with the Yale School of Nursing and the Yale New Haven Community Hospital. It was supported in part by a grant to the senior author from the Yale Medical School. The authors would like to express their appreciation to Julina Rhymes, Perry Mahaffy, Jr., Margaret Ellison and Powhatan Wooldridge for their helpful assistance during the data collection stage of the research.

Notes

1. Lipton (1962) summarizes much of the literature concerning the nature, extent, and psychological effects of tonsillectomy operations. However, recent evidence is leading many physicians to question the need for tonsillectomy at all, especially in routine cases. (McKee, 1963).
2. Escalona (1953) points out that the communication of feeling states between a mother and her child may take place on a non-verbal as well as verbal level, may occur at even a very early age in the life of the child, and may not be fully subject to the voluntary control of the mother.
3. The actual design of the questionnaire and the return rate is described and discussed in (Skipper and Ellison, 1966).
4. The reader should keep in mind that statistical significance does not necessarily indicate practical significance. For the most part variations in the somatic indicators are within what might be considered the normal range. Their importance lies in the fact that they are symptomatic of the degree of stress suffered.
5. When all the results from the mail-back questionnaire were controlled for the age and sex of the child, and the education of the mother, one important association was discovered. Regardless of treatment (control or experimental) children age 6 and under suffered more from disturbed sleep during the first week after the operation than those age 7 and over.
6. Much of the literature on this topic is summarized in Martin's (1965) cogent review of theories of stress.

References

Escalona, S.
    1953 Emotional Development in First Year of Life. pp. 11–92 in Milton J. E. Senn (ed.), Problems of Infancy and Childhood. Packanack Lake, N.J.: Foundation Press.
Fisher, Ronald.
    1947 The Design of Experiments. Edinburgh: Oliver & Boyd.
Janis, Irving.
    1958 Psychological Stress. New York: Wiley.
Leonard, R., J. Skipper, and P. Woolridge.
    1967 "Small sample field experiments for evaluating patient care." Health Services Research 2 (Spring): 46–60.
Lipton, S.
    1962 On the Psychology of Childhood Tonsillectomy. pp. 363–417 in Ruth Eissler et al., (eds.), The Psychoanalytic Study of the Child. New York: International Universities Press.
Martin, W.
    1965 "Socially induced stress: some converging theories." Pacific Sociological Review 8 (Fall): 63–69.
McKee, W.
    1963 "A controlled study of the effects of tonsillectomy and adenoidectomy in children." British Journal of Preventive and Social Medicine 17, 2:46–69.

Mumford, Emily and James K. Skipper, Jr.
  1967 Sociology in Hospital Care, New York: Harper and Row 117–139.
Prugh, D., E. Staub, H. Sands, R. Kirschbaum and E. Lenihan.
  1953 "A study of the emotional reactions of children and families to hospitalization and illness." American Journal of Orthopsychiatry, 23:70–106.
Skipper, J.
  1965 Communication and the Hospitalized Patient. pp. 61–82 in James K. Skipper, Jr., and Robert C. Leonard (eds.), Social Interaction and Patient Care. Philadelphia: Lippincott.
Skipper, J. and M. Ellison.
  1966 "Personal contact as a technique for increasing questionnaire returns from hospitalized patients after discharge." Journal of Health and Human Behavior 7 (Fall): 211–214.
Skipper, J., R. Leonard and J. Rhymes.
  1968 "Child hospitalization and social interaction: An experimental study of mothers' stress, adaptation and satisfaction." Medical Care (in press).

26

An Experimental Study in Nurse–Physician Relationships

Charles K. Hofling, Eveline Brotzman,
Sarah Dalrymple, Nancy Graves,
and Chester M. Pierce

As physicians move increasingly out of their traditional channels of functioning and into broader areas of the community, their relationships with members of the other health disciplines assume increasing significance. Similarly the intradisciplinary conflicts which beset these other professionals become of greater concern to the physician, since his own effectiveness comes to depend more and more upon others. This paper is an account of the way in which a group of psychiatrists and nurses have attempted to obtain a picture in depth of the effect of certain aspects of the nurse-physician relationship.

There is no doubt that the professional status and standards of nurses are at times challenged by the behavior of doctors (1, 3, 8). From a consideration of naturally occurring situations in which such challenges occur, two particularly significant categories appear to be: 1) the situation in which the doctor violates an accepted procedure of which the nurse is customarily in charge (*e.g.*, entering an isolation unit without taking the proper precautions); and 2) the situation in which the doctor directs the nurse to carry out a procedure which is in some fashion against her professional standards (*e.g.*, ordering the nurse to administer intravenous medication in a hospital where nurse-administrative policy opposes such action). Since the former situation can take place without the nurse's attention necessarily being directed to the problem, we selected the latter as the type of incident to create experimentally and to study.

Method

It was decided to construct the incident around an irregular order from a doctor to a nurse for her to administer a dose of medication.

SOURCE: *Journal of Nervous and Mental Disease* 143 (August 1960): 171–80. Copyright © 1960, The Williams & Wilkins Co. Reprinted by permission.

Ingredients of the experimental conflict. 1) The nurse would be asked to give an obviously excessive dose of medicine. For reasons of safety it was decided to use a placebo. 2) The medication order was to be transmitted by telephone, a procedure in violation of hospital policy. 3) The medication would be "unauthorized," *i.e.*, a drug which had not been placed on the ward stock-list and cleared for use. 4) The order would be given to the nurse by an unfamiliar voice.

Overall approach. The conflict situation was contrived at a public and a private hospital on 12 and ten wards, respectively. A questionnaire was administered to a group of nurses at a third hospital as a matched control. The control subjects were asked what they would do if confronted with the circumstances of the experimental conflict. A group of student nurses was also given the questionnaire, in order to see how less experienced nurses thought they would react.

Experimental Design

Ward Incident

Pill boxes bearing hospital labels were marked as follows:

ASTROTEN

5 mg. capsules
Usual dose: 5 mg.
Maximum daily dose: 10 mg.

These were placed on the wards. Each box contained pink placebo capsules filled with glucose. To standardize the telephone order, a written script was prepared for the caller. In order to standardize the stimulus call as much as possible, a set of standardized replies to the likeliest responses of the nurse was composed and closely adhered to.

It was decided that the emotional tone conveyed by the caller would be one of courteous, but self-confident firmness. As a precaution against unintentional departures from this tone, it was arranged to have the calls monitored by another member of the research team, whose function it would be to signal to the caller if he started to vary from the prescribed tone.

All telephone calls were tape-recorded. It was arranged to have a colleague, an expert in verbal behavior, listen to the tape after the experiment and mark as invalid any calls in which he perceived an appreciable variation from the prescribed tone or any cues suggesting that the call was not genuine.

Termination points for the telephone conversation were as follows: 1) compliance upon the part of the subject; 2) a clear-cut, sustained refusal; 3) insistence upon calling or talking to any third party of equal or superior rank in the hospital hierarchy: 4) the subject's becoming emotionally upset; 5) inability to find the medication in two attempts; and 6) prolongation of the telephone call—by any means—to ten minutes.

To study the subjects' environment and their nonverbal behavior as well as to halt the experiment before the involvement of any patient, an observer—a staff psychiatrist—was placed on each unit selected. It was his function to terminate the

situation by disclosing its true nature when: 1) the nurse had "poured" the medication and started for the patient's bed; 2) she had ended the telephone conversation
with a refusal to accept the order; 3) she began to telephone or otherwise contact
another professional person; or 4) at the expiration of ten minutes following the end
of the call if none of the foregoing alternatives had been adopted.

It was anticipated that a post-incident conversation between observer and subject
would allow the observer to assume two additional functions. He could obtain some
further material from the subject (as to her inner responses to the experience), and
he could offer psychiatric "first-aid" if indicated, to allay any disquieting feelings
which might be mobilized by the experiment.

The experiment was conducted during the period from shortly before to shortly
after evening visiting hours (7:00–9:00 P.M.) and was performed on medical, surgical, pediatric and psychiatric wards. This period was selected because it is a time
when the administration of therapeutic measures is at a minimum. It is also (re-
grettably) a time when interns and residents tend to absent themselves from the
wards; thus the nurse would have to make her own immediate decision regarding
the telephone calls.

It was arranged that, as soon as the doctor-observer decided that the ward conditions safely permitted the experiment, he would give a signal by calling in from the
ward telephone to the office being used by the investigators, using a code sentence.

One of the nurse investigators visited all of the experimental sites in succession
within a half-hour of the incident. She explained the value of further information
and requested an appointment for follow-up interview (for which the subject would
be offered payment at extra-duty rates). To avoid undue retrospective distortion, the
appointments were all made for interviews within 48 hours of the critical incident.

These follow-up interviews, of about 45 minutes each, were relatively unstructured. However, the nurse-investigator had, in the meantime, reviewed the telephone recordings and the reports of the psychiatrist-observers, and she endeavored
to cover the following points in her interviews, as opportunity was afforded.

1. Unguided narrative: ("Please tell me what happened last night, starting with
   whatever you were doing just before the phone call about Astroten.")
2. Emotions: ("What were your feelings at the point where. . . .")
3. Discrepancies, if any: ("Are you sure it happened just that way?")
4. Comparable naturally occurring experiences: ("Try to leave out, for the moment, your present knowledge that the incident was experimental. Suppose it
   to have been 'real.' Can you think of similar situations which you have
   experienced? Tell me about them.")
5. Retrospective view: ("What are your feelings about the incident now? What
   are they about the experience as such?")
6. Eliciting biographical data not otherwise mentioned: age, religion, marital
   status, children, place(s) of birth and of growing up, nursing experience, other
   work experience, professional ambitions.
7. Offering support and reassurance if indicated: renewing assurance of subject's
   anonymity if indicated.

Graduate Nurse Questionnaire

The hospital chosen for the questionnaire phase was a general hospital, as were the first two. Like the others, it had over 500 beds and was located in the Midwest. The subjects given the hypothetical situation were closely matched with the experimental subjects at the public hospital as to: age, sex, race, marital status, length of work week (part-time or full-time), amount of professional experience, type of nursing education (three-year or four-year program), and geographical area of origin. There were 12 graduate nurses in the control group.

The questionnaire was administered in a large conference room with the subjects being provided with writing materials and seated at widely spaced intervals from one another.

The investigator, a physician, spoke to the subjects as follows:

I should like you to imagine yourself, as vividly as possible, in this situation. You are a staff nurse, working 3:00 P.M. to 11:00 P.M. on a ward of a general hospital, and in charge of the ward during that period.

It is the official policy of this hospital that medication orders are to be written by the physician before being carried out by the nurse. This policy fairly often is not adhered to.

You are the only nurse on the ward, the head nurse and the departmental supervisor having left the hospital. None of the house doctors are on ward, which is moderately busy.

Dr. Smith is known to be on the staff of the hospital, but you have not met him. Mr. Jones is one of the patients on your ward.

At about 8:00 P.M. you receive the following telephone message:

"This is Dr. Smith, from Psychiatry, calling. I was asked to see Mr. Jones this morning, and I'm going to have to see him again tonight—I don't have a lot of time, and I'd like him to have had some medication by the time I get to the ward. Will you please check your medicine cabinet and see if you have some Astroten? That's ASTROTEN."

Your medicine cupboard contains a pillbox, bearing the label of the hospital pharmacy, and reading as follows:

ASTROTEN

5 mg. capsules
Usual dose: 5 mg.
Maximum daily dose: 10 mg.

You return to the telephone, and the message continues as follows:

"You have it? Fine. Now will you please give Mr. Jones a stat dose of 20 milligrams— that's four capsules—of Astroten. I'll be up within ten minutes, and I'll sign the order then, but I'd like the drug to have started taking effect."

The nurses were then handed sheets of paper upon which was printed everything which had just been read to them. They were invited to read these sheets, being told that this was merely to help them keep the details in mind.

The investigator then said to the subjects: "Please write down exactly what you would say and do."

After this answer was completed, the investigator said to the subjects, "Please write down the rationale for what you said and did in this episode, that is to say, the considerations influencing your decision."

The next question presented to the subjects was, "What do you think a majority of nurses would have done in this situation?"

The last question offered the subjects was, "What do you think a majority of this group will have written?"

Nursing Student Questionnaire

To compare and contrast with what graduate nurses did in the stress situation and with what they thought they would do in it, the hypothetical case was presented to a group of 21 degree-program nursing students. The method of presentation of the hypothetical situation and of presenting the questionnaire was the same as has been described for the graduate nurse.

Results

Ward Incident

In all, a total of 22 subjects can be reported: 12 from the municipal hospital and ten from the private hospital.

(1) Twenty-one subjects would have given the medication as ordered.

(2) Telephone calls were invariably brief. Exclusive of time spent in looking for the medication the calls averaged only two minutes in duration. Essentially no resistance to the order was expressed to the caller.

The transcript of a typical telephone call runs as follows:[1]

Nurse: Ward 18; Miss Rolfe.
Caller: Is this the nurse in charge?
Nurse: Yes, it is.
Caller: This is Dr. Hanford, from Psychiatry, calling. I was asked to see Mr. Carson today, and I'm going to have to see him again this evening.
Nurse: Yes.
Caller: I haven't much time and I'd like him to have received some medication by the time I get to the ward. Will you please check the medicine cabinet and see if you have some Astroten.
Nurse: Some what?
Caller: Astroten. That's ASTROTEN.
Nurse: I'm pretty sure we don't.
Caller: Would you take a look, please?
Nurse: Yes, I'll take a look, but I'm pretty sure we don't.

(45 seconds' pause)

Nurse: Hello.
Caller: Well?
Nurse: Yes.
Caller: You have Astroten?
Nurse: Yes.
Caller: O.K. Now, will you give Mr. Carson a stat dose of twenty milligrams—that's four capsules—of Astroten. I'll be up in about ten minutes, and I'll sign the order then, but I'd like the medicine to have started taking effect.
Nurse: Twenty cap . . . Oh, I mean, twenty millgrams.

Caller: Yes, that's right.
Nurse: Four capsules. O.K.
Caller: Thank you.
Nurse: Surely.

(3) There was little or no conscious attempt at delay. Twenty-one of the subjects offered no delay after conclusion of the call.

(4) On interview, 11 of the subjects expressed their having had an awareness of the dosage discrepancy. The remainder professed lack of awareness of it.

(5) During the telephone conversation none of the subjects insisted that the order be given in written form before implementation, although several sought reassurance that the "doctor" would appear promptly. On interview, 18 of the subjects indicated a general awareness of the impropriety of nonemergency telephone orders. Most of the subjects agreed, however, that it was not an uncommon impropreity.

(6) In 17 cases phenomena falling into the category of "psychopatholgy of everyday life" were noted in the course of the observations. That is to say, the subjects exhibited such behavior as mishearing, misplacing of familiar objects, temporary forgetting, and the like, during the time beginning with the stress telephone call and ending when the on-the-spot observer terminated his conversation with the subject and left the ward.

An example of "psychopathology" of this type is afforded by the transcript of a telephone call given above. When the nurse, in response to the caller's last long statement, begins to say, "twenty capsules," this is undoubtedly an unconsciously determined slip and not a simple misunderstanding.

A very frequent example is the one referred to in paragraph 4, namely the repression of awareness of the dosage discrepancy.

A third example—also frequent—has to do with the subjects' not being able to see the Astroten boxes when they first looked for them. In all cases, the boxes had been placed in prominent locations in the medicine cabinets shortly before the experiment. Yet several times the nurses were unable to locate the boxes at the first trial. When a second trial was insisted upon, the boxes were found rather rapidly.

(7) None of the subjects became overtly hostile to the telephone caller or to the observer. Only one of the subjects, the one who refused to accept the order, indicated to the observer that she felt some hostility to the caller during the call.

(8) The overt emotional tones of the subjects' responses upon disclosure of the experiment as such varied considerably. The range was from mild scientific interest, through chagrin and mild confusion, to anxiety and some sense of guilt, and, in a few instances, irritation or veiled anger. The modal response could be said to involve chagrin, mild anxiety, and a hint of guilt.

(9) Opinions differed as to the details of a "correct" response, but 16 of the subjects felt that the response should have involved greater resistance to the telephone order.

(10) Sixteen subjects felt quite unsure that their responses had been typical.

(11) On interview, 15 of the subjects spontaneously recalled similar naturally occurring experiences. The remainder could recall such experiences when asked if

they had occurred. A majority of the subjects referred to the displeasure of doctors on occasions when nursing resistance had been offered to instructions which had been considered improper.

(12) Only one of the subjects seriously questioned the identity of the observer or the propriety of his presence on the ward (before his having identified himself).

Graduate Nurse Questionnaire

The results obtained from the subjects in the hypothetical situation may be summarized as follows:

(1) Ten of the 12 subjects reported that they would not have given the medication; two of the subjects said that they would have given the medication.

(2) In discussing the rationale for what they would have done, seven subjects referred to the dosage discrepancy in one way or another. Four of the ten subjects who said that they would have refused to give the drug mentioned the dosage discrepancy as the principal reason; the others gave greater emphasis to "hospital policy" or the "necessity for a written order."

(3) Seven subjects said they thought that a majority of nurses would handle the situation in the way that they would do. Two subjects said that they thought a majority of nurses would not have handled the situation in their way. Three responses were equivocal.

(4) Ten nurses said that they thought a majority of the nurses present would have responded in the same way that they did.

Examples of the subjects' reports as to what they would say and do in the situation presented are as follows:

> I'm sorry, but I cannot give the medication until the order is written. If you can't come down, perhaps you could have another doctor come and write the order. I would then be very happy to carry it out. I'm wondering, too, if your order refers to the same Mr. Jones here on my ward, as the label on this box of Astroten states that ten milligrams is the maximum daily dose, and you have stated that you would like for the patient to receive twenty milligrams.

> I'm sorry, Dr. Smith, but I cannot give this medication without a written order. This is the policy of the hospital.

Student Nurse Questionnaire

(1) Of the 21 nursing students, all believed that they would not have given the medication as ordered.

(2) Eight students gave as the principal reason for refusing to accept the order their concern lest the patient suffer ill effects from the apparently excessive dosage.

(3) Nineteen of the subjects—either in the fantasied telephone conversations or in giving the rationale for their behavior—specifically referred to the apparently excessive dosage, although in 11 of these instances this concern was not given as the chief objection.

(4) In most instances, the conversation which the nursing student fantasied herself holding with the caller was more extended and more illuminating than were any of the actual conversations recorded in the experiment. Even the brief refusals

typically included a statement recognizing some of the principal features of the situation.

(5) Nearly all replies were distinctly courteous; none were discourteous.

Examples follow of the students' reports as to what they imagined themselves saying and doing in the situation.

> Upon finding the medication in the cupboard, I would question the dosage of the medication being twenty milligrams when the maximum dose was ten milligrams. I would not administer the medication unless the supervisor was present to o.k. the order, because I did not know the doctor who phoned in the order and am not accustomed to give any medication unless it is a written order; also, because the medication is one that I am not familiar with, I would be also unfamiliar with the toxic effects.
>
> I'm sorry, sir, but I am not authorized to give any medication without a written order, especially one so large over the usual dose and one that I'm unfamiliar with. If it were possible, I would be glad to do it, but this is against hospital policy and my own ethical standards. If you would come to the ward and write the order, I would be glad to administer the drug. In addition to the above, I would include something about the actual dosage.

Discussion

Perhaps the first point to be stressed is that the primary, overt response of the subjects was unexpected and, in particular, unexpectedly uniform. None of the investigators and but one of the highly experienced nurse consultants with whom the project had been discussed in advance predicted the outcome correctly.

It has long been recognized that when there is friction between doctors and nurses, it is the patients who chiefly suffer (7). However, the present study underscores the danger to patients in unresolved difficulties of the nurse-doctor relationship even when there is little or no friction in the usual sense of the word. In a real-life situation corresponding to the experimental one, there would, in theory, be two professional intelligences, the doctor's and the nurse's, working to ensure that a given procedure be undertaken in a manner beneficial to the patient or, at the very least, not detrimental to him. The experiment strongly suggests, however, that in the real-life situation one of these intelligences is, for all practical purposes, nonfunctioning.

The experiment indicates quite clearly that, insofar as the nurse is concerned, the psychological problems involved in a situation such as the one under discussion are operating to a considerable extent below the threshold of consciousness. Perhaps the most striking evidence of this is the fact that, whereas nearly all of the subjects quite correctly either repeated the dosage ordered or asked that it be repeated, none of them gave any evidence of conscious concern at the discrepancy between the dose ordered and the alleged maximum safe dose.

Since there is so little evidence of *conscious* conflict in the situation, one may perhaps be inclined to question the existence of appreciable conflict at any level. For a small minority of the subjects, it may indeed be true that their adaptation to situations like the experimental one had reached the point that they experienced no significant conflict, at any level, but, for a majority, the evidence of preconscious or unconscious conflict is persuasive.

It is clear that the subjects, when interviewed, were reacting to at least a double stimulus: to the realization that 1) their behavior, irrespective of what it had been, had been professionally observed without their prior knowledge; and 2) their *specific* behavior had been noted. It was believed, on careful questioning, that the embarrassment, irritation, and such anger as was present were in response to the first portion of the stimulus, namely, the disclosure of observation *per se*. On the other hand, in the face of an attitude on the part of the interviewers which was sympathetic rather than purely neutral, *a majority of the subjects were clearly defensive of their specific handling of the situation.* Moreover, all of those slips of behavior which we have called "psychopathology of everyday life" and of which one or more examples were offered by 17 of the 21 subjects, are indicative of preconscious or unconscious conflict. With the disclosure of the experiment as having been such, elements of the conflict moved into consciousness, as was attested by those reactions which included anxiety, chagrin, and a sense of guilt.

Even in the hypothetical presentation of the critical incident, a considerable amount of subsurface tension was induced. One example of the effects of this tension was the *non sequitur* uttered by the nurse who said, "I'm wondering, too, if your order refers to the same Mr. Jones here on my ward, as the label on this box of Astroten states that ten milligrams is the maximum daily dose, and you have stated that you would like for the patient to receive twenty milligrams." This statement is not far removed from the phenomena referred to in the actual test situation as "psychopathology of everyday life."

There is evidence that a considerable amount of self-deception goes on in the average staff nurse. In nonstressful moments, when thinking about her performance, the average nurse tends to believe that considerations of her patient's welfare and of her own professional honor will outweigh considerations leading to an automatic obedience to the doctor's orders at times when these two sets of factors come into conflict.

Insofar as these matters are concerned, there is in some respects a close correspondence between the way in which nursing students have been taught to think of themselves and their professional functions (*i.e.*, the "official" faculty position),[2] the way in which they actually do think of these things as upperclassmen, and the way in which they will think of them—in moments free of stress—several years later as staff nurses. Concern has been expressed as to the degree to which this view corresponds to reality (4). This investigation tends to show that the view involves an illusion, which, although perhaps shallow, is widespread and enduring. This illusion is, of course, that the nurse will habitually defend the well-being of her patients as she sees it and strive to maintain the standards of her profession.

The present investigation surely has among its implications the idea that all is not well in the professional relationships of nurses and physicians and that these difficulties, whatever they may be, exert a limiting effect upon the nurse's resourcefulness and, in some situations, increase the hazard to which the patients undergoing treatment are exposed. Just because these implications are very strong, it is correct to point out that there is another side to the professional relationship of nurses and physicians, as disclosed in this investigation, and another set of comments to be made about the nurses' effectiveness in crisis situations.

There is no question but that the physician, whether he deserves it or not, is still the recipient of certain quite positive attitudes on the part of the nurse (2, 8). During the data-gathering phase of the present investigation, transcripts were made of 27 nurse-physician telephone conversations, and written records were obtained of 35 fantasied nurse-physician (or nursing student-physician) conversations. In a very great majority of these conversations, a note of courtesy and respect on the part of the nurse toward the physician was unmistakable.

Then there is the matter of trust. The inference is very strong that the nurses' almost invariable acceptance, in the actual stress situation, of the caller as being what he said he was and of doing what he said he was going to do involved a definite (generalized) element of trust.

There is also the matter of efficiency. It has been mentioned that, in the actual test situation, there was a strong, almost uniform tendency for the nurses to implement what they took to be the doctor's wishes promptly and with minimum wasted effort.

It is necessary to recognize that all of these characteristics can, in their place, be of inestimable value to physicians and to their patients. It is easy to recall crisis situations in which the nurse's loyalty to the physician, her appreciation of the value of his judgment, and her willingness and ability to act promptly and efficiently without wasting precious time in discussion have made the difference between life and death for the patient.

The present investigation does not imply that these values should be sacrificed. Rather, it implies that it would be worth an extensive effort on the part of the nursing and medical professions to find ways in which these traditional values can be reconciled with the nurse's fuller exercise of her intellectual and ethical potentialities.

We believe that the typical nurse of today has certain conscious motivations—aspirations and ideals—with respect to her position and functions which may be summarized as the wish both to be and to be considered a professional person in her own right (5). This wish involves several component desires and strivings: mastery of a body of scientific knowledge, application of intelligence, exercise of judgment, assumption of responsibility for patients while offering services to them, gaining the respect of colleagues in related disciplines. All these motivations were expressed by our nurse-subjects collectively, and many of them were expressed by each subject individually.

On the other hand, the nurse retains another group of (largely conscious) motivations with respect to her relationship with the doctor. These include the wish to be liked by him, to receive his gratitude, praise and approval, and to avoid blame and recriminations. These strivings are indicated in various portions of the experimental material: in the courtesy of the telephone conversations (usually ending with a "thank you"), in the unquestioning attitudes; in the promptness of execution of the order; and in the fear of disapproval upon disclosure.

It is to be noted that the first set of motivations is currently being strongly reinforced by nursing education, particularly in its more formal aspects (5, 6). The second set receives reinforcement in the expectations and responses of a majority of physicians. The first set is best served by an intellectual and emotional orientation which is, in many ways, quite active. The second set requires an orientation which is, in some ways, distinctly passive.

The duties and responsibilities of a nurse are, of course, sufficiently extensive and varied to afford opportunity for the gratification of each set of motivations at one time or another. The present study indicates, however, that the two sets can be—or can appear to the nurse to be—mutually incompatible and thus that a state of conflict can be produced on certain occasions when they are stimulated simultaneously. The study indicates further that, in such situations, the second set of motivations will win out in a very great majority of instances. Crucial to this conflict is the fact that in hospital psychodynamics most doctors are male and most nurses are female. Thus the nurse has biocultural as well as politico-legal reasons to be passive to the doctor's wishes.

Since this investigation does not shed light upon the motivational states of physicians in their relationships to nurses, it would be premature to offer much comment on the degree to which the conflict in the nurse is reality-based, rather than based upon inferences of questionable accuracy. However, one can assert with confidence the general truth that inner conflict is productive of anxiety and that, beyond a certain low intensity, anxiety tends to reduce the versatility and inventiveness of a personality. Thus, one can feel reasonably certain that, in situations such as the experimental one, solutions affording gratifications to both sets of the nurses' strivings are found far less often than is theoretically possible.

Perhaps the last statement can be clarified by returning to specifics. Any attempt to submit an "ideal solution," a formula of conduct, for the handling of situations like the experimental one would, of course, be unduly rigid and arbitrary. Yet one has the distinct impression that the observance of professional courtesy and loyalty need not have precluded the making of relevant inquiries. It need not have precluded the nurses' making some sort of *appraisal* of the situation and then arriving at a *conscious decision* instead of an automatic response. Whether such a decision would lead to eventual compliance, to refusal, or to some temporizing measure is not pertinent to the present question. The point is that there appears to be room for greater intellectual activity—the pursuit of which need not be aggressive, destructive, or (to speak of the majority of nurses) unfeminine. One can feel quite sure that, whatever its precise, overt nature, a response based upon a sense of appraisal and decision would be far less likely to produce inner tension than one reached quasi-automatically on the basis of barely perceived inner forces.

This last statement reverts once again to the recognition that the conflict state, in both its interpersonal (nurse versus doctor) and intrapersonal (nurse versus herself) aspects, appears to involve components which do not reach the level of full awareness.

At this point the current presentation reaches something of a dilemma: to conclude without further reference to the nature of these unconscious components may give the false impression that they seem of little significance; to attempt a further discussion of these elements—a discussion based very largely upon inference—may give a false sense of assurance that they have been fully and correctly identified.

What follows, therefore, is offered tentatively and merely as the line of speculation which appears best to fit the limited data.

If one accepts the view that the subjects' emotions of shame, embarrassment, and guilt following the experimental incident were derived, at least in part, from the nature of their activities and fantasies during the incident, one has a clue to these less obvious forces. It must be remembered that: 1) the subjects had not behaved in an unusual manner during the incident, but, rather, in their customary fashion; 2) very few of the subjects had any reason to suppose they had behaved differently from the great majority of subjects; 3) neither the psychiatrist-observer nor the nurse-interviewer expressed thoughts or feelings other than those of friendly curiosity, and, of course; 4) in no instance was there the faintest possibility that patient-care had suffered.

Yet the emotions were unmistakable. The question thus becomes, "What subsurface motivations led the nurse to feel ashamed, embarrassed and and guilty?" One can dismiss out of hand the speculation that hostile feelings toward the patient (leading to a sense of guilt and thus to a need for punishment or abuse) were of great significance: the life-patterns, the personal and professional adjustments of the subjects make this clear. If a further argument were needed, one is readily at hand: the individual patients in the experimental situation varied from nurse to nurse and varied widely, yet some elements of the emotional response remained qualitatively almost constant.

Although it rests upon inference and only indirectly upon the data, the likeliest answer to the above question appears to be that the nurse is responding, in situations like the experimental one, on the basis of transference to the doctor. The transference seems typically to involve both an erotic and an aggressive component. On this view, the preconscious or unconscious wish to win the doctor's love and the utilization of reaction-formation against aggressive impulses toward him, born of frustration, lead the nurse at times to compromise her conscious professional standards.

Notes

1. All proper names and the designation of the ward have been changed.
2. A point not demonstrated experimentally, but brought out in individual discussions with faculty members.

References

1. Bullock, R. P. Position, function and job satisfaction of nurses in the social system of a modern hospital. Nurs. Res., *11*: 4–14, 1953.
2. Johnson, M. and Martin, H. A sociological analysis of the nurse role. Amer. J. Nurs., *58*: 373–377, 1958.
3. Loeb, M. B. Role definition in the social world of a psychiatric hospital. In Greenblatt, M. *et al.*, eds. *The Patient and the Mental Hospital*, pp. 14–19. Free Press, Glencoe, Illinois, 1957.
4. Mauksch, H. Becoming a nurse: A selective view. Ann. Amer. Acad. Polit. Soc. Sci., *346*: 88–98, 1963.
5. Newton, M. E. Nurses' caps and bachelors' gowns. Amer. J. Nurs., *64*: 73–77, 1964.

6. Peterson, F. K. The new diploma schools. Amer. J. Nurs., *64*: 68–72, 1964.
7. Ruesch, J., Brodsky, C. and Fischer, A. *Psychiatric Care*, pp. 135–136. Grune & Stratton, New York, 1964.
8. Rushing, W. A. Social influence and the social-psychological function of deference: A study of psychiatric nursing. Soc. Forces, 41: 142–148, 1963.

VI

Health Care
and Social Policy

Finally, three readings provide glimpses of the issues and debates characteristic of social-policy concerns. Social policy and health is a very large area and involves almost every aspect of medical and public health activity as well as issues not directly related to medical care, such as environmental control, unemployment, and income maintenance. The area, of course, is highly political and thus is inevitably involved with political ideologies and coalition formation.

In reading 27, Robert Alford presents a general discussion of the political dynamics in the health field, which has been expanded into a successful book entitled *Health Care Politics* (University of Chicago Press, 1975). Alford provides some sense of the powerful political interests in the health arena, although in my view he exaggerates their monolithic power and control and underestimates the extent of real achievements and improvements in health-care provision. Moreover, in addressing the issue abstractly, he never defines criteria by which he measures lack of progress, nor does he suggest clear options that would produce better results. Yet the discussion is valuable because Alford illustrates how pluralistic politics and the emergence of powerful interest groups make it exceedingly difficult to bring about fundamental changes in the organization of health care.

If Alford writes from a radical perspective, Aaron Wildavsky has a more conservative viewpoint. In reading 28, he describes some of the dilemmas of the health-care arena and then examines in a humorous but serious analysis what planning can achieve. Directing his attention to recent legislation that establishes health-systems agencies throughout the country, Wildavsky contrasts the ideals of planning with what he believes is likely to occur. Planning, Wildavsky argues, will have perverse consequences, making even worse some of the problems that the plans have been developed to solve. Wildavsky's is, of course, not the last word on the subject, and his treatment of the issues is polemical. But he provides a great deal of food for thought and gives the student an opportunity to match his wits against Wildavsky's in thinking about counterarguments. For the student wishing to follow up this type of policy matter, I recommend two of my recent books: *Future Issues in Health Care* (New York: Free Press, 1979) and *The Growth of Bureaucratic Medicine* (New York: Wiley-Interscience, 1976).

The last reading in this book is by Victor Fuchs and is particularly appropriate because it attempts to define the problems and choices we must face as we think about health care in the future. Fuchs makes clear that although economics is important to all of these problems, the decisions that must be made are social and a matter of values. Thus there are no technical answers to our dilemmas. The technical knowledge provided by the social scientist may help us clarify our choices, but in the end we must make them on the basis of what we care about and in terms of the human values we wish to promote. This is not the end of your study; it simply takes you back to the beginning.

27

The Political Economy of Health Care

Dynamics without Change

Robert R. Alford

Health care in the United States is allegedly in a state of crisis. High and rising costs, inadequate numbers of medical and paramedical personnel, a higher infant mortality rate in 1969 than thirteen other countries, a lower life expectancy in 1965 for males than seventeen other countries, and poor emergency room and ambulatory care are among the diverse facts or allegations which have justified a wide variety of proposed reforms. And yet the numbers of health personnel, the proportion of the gross national product spent on health care, and the sheer quantity of services rendered have grown considerably faster than the economy as a whole.[1]

If health care is in "crisis" now, then it was in crisis ten, twenty, and forty years ago as well. Several qualified observers have commented on the similarity between the 1932 analysis by the Committee on the Costs of Medical Care[2] and reports issued thirty-five or more years later. Dr. Sumner N. Rosen, an economist on the staff of the Institute of Public Administration in New York City, has said that the "catalogue of problems drawn up almost forty years ago strongly resembles the latest list—inadequate services, insufficient funds, understaffed hospitals. Virtually nothing has changed."[3] Economist Eli Ginzberg, summarizing the results of his study of New York City, concludes that "While changes have occurred in response to emergencies, opportunities, and alternatives in the market place, the outstanding finding is the inertia of the system as a whole."[4]

The overwhelming fact about the various reforms of the health system that have been implemented or proposed—more money, more subsidy of insurance, more manpower, more demonstration projects, more clinics—is that they are absorbed into a system which is enormously resistant to change. The reforms which are suggested are sponsored by different elements in the health system and advantage

SOURCE: *Politics and Society* 2 (Winter 1972): 127–64. Reprinted by permission of Geron-X, Inc., Publishers.

one or another element, but they do not seriously damage any interests. This pluralistic balancing of costs and benefits successfully shields the funding, powers, and resources of the producing institutions from any basic structural change.

This situation might well be described as one of "dynamics without change." This paper argues that both the expansion of the health care industry and the apparent absence of change are due to a struggle between different major interest groups operating within the context of a market society—professional monopolists controlling the major health resources, corporate rationalizers challenging their power, and the community population seeking better health care.

Although the paper generalizes from the scholarly literature as well as from documents and from interviews which took place in New York City, it should be regarded as a set of "outrageous hypotheses," in the spirit of Robert S. Lynd's classic *Knowledge for What?*,[5] rather than as a theory inferred from reliable empirical findings.

Market versus Bureaucratic Reform

Pressures for change come largely from three types of reformers, of which the first two are most important. The first, whom I shall call the "market reformers," would expand the diversity of facilities available, the number of physicians, the competition between health facilities, and the quantity and quality of private insurance. Their assumptions are that the public sector should underwrite medical bills for the poor and that patients should be free to choose among various health care providers. The community population is regarded as consumers of health care like other commodities and is assumed to be able to evaluate the quality of service received. Market pressures will thus drive out the incompetent, excessively high priced or duplicated service, and the inaccessible physician, clinic, or hospital. The market reformers wish to preserve the control of the individual physician over his practice, over the hospital, and over his fees, and they simply wish to open up the medical schools to meet the demand for doctors, to give patients more choice among doctors, clinics, and hospitals, and to make that choice a real one by providing public subsidies for medical bills.

These assumptions are questioned by the "bureaucratic reformers." They stress the importance of the hospital as the key location and organizer of health services and wish to put individual doctors under the control of hospital medical boards and administrators. The bureaucratic reformers are principally concerned with coordinating fragmented services, instituting planning, and extending public funding. Their assumption is that the technology of modern health care requires a complex and coordinated division of labor between ambulatory and in-hospital care, primary practitioners and specialists, and personalized care and advanced chemical and electronic treatment. The community population is regarded as an external constituency of the health providers to be organized to represent its interests if necessary to maintain the equilibrium of the system.

These contrasting modes of reform are partly illustrated by recent articles by Harry Schwartz of the *New York Times* and Dr. Milton I. Roemer of UCLA, who represent the market and bureaucratic reform views, respectively.[6] Both recognize the rocketing costs, criticize duplicated facilities, and call for such reforms as health insurance. But they differ sharply both in their image of the health system and in their proposals for reform.

According to Schwartz, "these needed and useful improvements can be made within the context of a continued pluralistic system. Different people have different tastes and different needs. Those who want to use prepaid groups should be permitted to do so; those who want to go to a physician and pay him each time should be free to do so, too. The result may not seem to be as neat on an organization chart as a uniform national system, and it may have seeming inefficiencies and duplications. But the right of choice for doctors and patients alike is worth such costs—at least in a really humane society."[7]

Schwartz argues that the pluralistic market society in the United States not only "provides choices for both physician and patients," but also "gives [the physician] an economic interest in satisfying the patient" and provides "reassurance and psychological support" to the patient because of the "intimate and humane" contact between physician and patient. He argues that a "nationalized and bureaucratic" system like that in Britain will reduce the amount of choice, reduce the incentives to please the patient, and thus depersonalize treatment.

This position is essentially a defense of the present system or an advocacy of further extension of the market principle. Critics of this position argue that the choices allegedly provided by the plurality of health care providers are not real for most people, that the economic incentives to physicians result in much over-doctoring, over-hospitalization, and over-operating, and that the alleged "intimate and humane" quality of most doctor-patient relationships is a myth.

Thus, Dr. Roemer, in sharp contrast to Schwartz, asserts that indeed "[o]ur spectrum of health services in America has conventionally been described as 'pluralistic.' More accurate would be to describe it as an irrational jungle in which countless vested interests compete for both the private and the public dollar, causing not only distorted allocations of health resources in relation to human needs but all sorts of waste and inefficiency along the way."[8]

The image of the ideal health system presented by Dr. Roemer is worth summarizing, because it appears in many reports and studies aimed at "coordinating" health facilities and services. Integrating the system is advocated simultaneously with differentiating its components into a rational division of labor. The ideal system provides "primary health centers" for every neighborhood, close to people's homes, staffed by general practitioners and "medical assistants," to provide basic diagnoses and preventive services. "Each person served by this health center would be attached to a particular doctor and his team of colleagues."[9] "For each four or five such health centers . . . there should be a district hospital" with 120 to 150 beds to handle relatively common conditions: maternity cases, trauma, less complex surgery. For the service areas of about 10 district hospitals, there would be a regional hospital with about 500 beds serving even "more complex medical or surgical problems" and engaged actively in medical research. "At the highest echelon, serving the population coming under three to five regional hospitals (that is, from

1½ million to 2½ million people), should be a university medical center" providing basic medical training and treating all types of cases as part of their research and teaching objectives.

According to Dr. Roemer, "Ideally health care should be a public service like schools or roads, paid for from general tax revenues." All professional personnel would be salaried, with salaries varying "according to qualifications, skills and responsibilities." The quality of medical care would be assured by a "framework of authority and responsibility, backed up by continuous education. Surveillance and reasonable professional controls would also be provided, with rewards and penalties as necessary." In charge of the system would be a hierarchy of officials, beginning with the district hospital director who would serve as a "public health director" in the "broadest social sense," being responsible for seeing to it that "the whole health service operates effectively.... He would be responsible for coordination of the several parts of the system, through proper use of records, statistics and information exchange.... He would be responsible to a health official above him."[10]

Another plan for bureaucratic reform envisions automated multiphasic screening of patients upon first contact in order to use scarce medical manpower efficiently, and an integrated system of health maintenance organizations, clinics, and specialized hospitals. The greater supervision and checking of medical decisions in the hospital context is seen as far outweighing the possible loss of personal contact.[11]

Contrasting images both of present institutions and of the viability of reform are seen in Schwartz's and Roemer's analogy of health to education. Dr. Roemer cites the public school system as an "achievement" of the American political system which did not require a revolution, along with a sharply graduated income tax and an extensive social security program. These achievements constitute grounds for his optimism that a reorganized health system can be achieved without a fundamental modification of American political and economic institutions. Harry Schwartz, on the other hand, cites the public school system as a "debacle" and says that "[i]n every community, public school education is free to the recipients; yet, everywhere—or almost everywhere—there is bitter complaint of the failure of this system to teach effectively or to satisfy the psychological needs of our young people."[12]

These two contrasting diagnoses, images of the future, and proposals for reform of health care are not opposing political ideologies which can be accepted or rejected only in terms of one's moral and political values. They are also analyses of the structure of health care resting upon different empirical assumptions about the nature of and power of the medical profession, the nature of medical technology, the role of the hospital, and the role of the patient (or the "community") as passively receiving or actively demanding a greater quality and quantity of health care.

Major Interest Groups

Strategies of reform based on either "bureaucratic" or "market" models are unlikely to work. Each type of reform stresses certain core functions in the health system and regard others as secondary. But both neglect the way in which the groups representing these functions come to develop vital interests which sustain the present system and vitiate attempts at reform.

For the market reformers, supplying trained physicians, innovating through biomedical and technological research, and maintaining competition between diverse health care producers are the main functions to be maintained. They view the hospitals, medical schools, and public health agencies as only the organizational framework which sustains the primary functions of professional health care and biomedical research. However, these types of work become buttressed through institutional mechanisms which guarantee professional control, and come to constitute powerful interest groups which I shall call the "professional monopolists." Because these interest groups are at present the dominant ones, with their powers and resources safely embedded in law, custom, professional legitimacy, and the practices of many public and private organizations, they do not need to be as visibly active nor as cohesively organized as those groups seeking change.

For the bureaucratic reformers, the hospitals, medical schools, and public health agencies at all governmental levels perform the core functions of organizing, financing, and distributing health care. Hospitals are seen ideally as the center of networks of associated clinics and neighborhood health centers, providing comprehensive care to an entire local population. The bureaucratic reformers view physicians and medical researchers as performing crucial work, but properly as subordinated and differentiated parts of a complex delivery system, coordinated by bureaucrats, notably hospital administrators. However, these large-scale organizations also become powerful interest groups, which I shall call the "corporate rationalizers." These interest groups are at present the major challengers of the power of the professional monopolists, and they constitute the bulk of the membership of the various commissions of investigation and inquiry into the health care "crisis."

A third type of reformer is relatively unimportant in the American context as yet: the "equal-health advocates," who seek free, accessible, high-quality health care which equalizes the treatment available to the well-to-do and to the poor. They stress the importance of community control over the supply and deployment of health facilities, because they base their strategies upon a third set of interest groups: the local population or community affected by the availability and character of health personnel and facilities. The community population is not as powerful or as organized as the other two sets of interest groups, but has equally as great a stake in the outcomes of the operations of health institutions.

Each of these three major interest groups is internally heterogeneous. The professional monopolists include biomedical researchers, physicians in private or group practice, salaried physicians, and other health occupations seeking professional privileges and status, who differ among themselves in their realtionships to each other, as well as to hospitals, medical schools, insurance plans, and government agencies, and thus their interests are affected differently by various programs of reform. But they share an interest in maintaining professional autonomy and control over the conditions of their work, and thus will—when the autonomy is challenged—act together in defense of that interest.

The corporate rationalizers include medical school officials, public health officials, insurance companies, and hospital administrators, whose organizational interests often require that they compete with each other for powers and resources. Therefore, they differ in the priority they attach to various reform proposals. But they share an interest in maintaining and extending the control of their organizations over the conditions of work of the professionals (and other employees) whose activities are key to the achievement of organizational goals.

The community population constitutes a set of interest groups which are internally heterogeneous with respect to their health needs, ability to pay, and ability to organize their needs into effective demands, but they share an interest in maximizing the the responsiveness of health professionals and organizations to their concerns for accessible, high-quality health care for which they have the ability to pay.

My assumption in making these key distinctions is that the similarities of structural location and interests vis-à-vis each other of each of these interest groups warrant an emphasis on the common interests within each group rather than on their differences. If my concern were to explain the actions of various individuals and groups with respect to a particular piece of legislation or administrative decision, lumping these diverse groups and individuals together into three such internally diverse groups would be entirely too crude. But for explaining the main contours of the present system and its resistance to change, finer distinctions would entail a short-term time perspective. Differences which are extremely important for tactics may be relatively unimportant in the long run.[13]

The danger of this mode of analysis, however, is that the internal contradictions within each interest group may be the source of potential strategic alliances which may have great long-term implications. For example, the vision of an ideal health system which erases the distinction between those who pay and those who don't is held up by the bureaucrtic reformers as well as by the equal-health advocates. And, in the abstract, both the value of personalized care (defended by one group as viable only through fee-for-service medicine) and the value of coordinated, comprehensive care (defended by another group as possible only through hospital-organized health care) are hard to question.

But whether or not these values of personalized service and comprehensive care are sheer ideological rationalizations by one or another interest group of its power and privileges may be irrelevant if they can be used as a weapon for critical attack upon the inadequacies of health care. The corporate rationalizers properly accuse the professional monopolists of not providing the personalized care which justifies their claim to fee-for-service practice. The professional monopolists properly accuse the corporate rationalizers of not being concerned with personalized care in their drive for efficient, high-technology health care. The contradictions in both cases between rhetoric and performance provide an opportunity to the equal-health advocates to show the deficiencies in analysis and program of the dominant interest groups.

Differences between these interest groups should not be overemphasized, because both the professional monopolists and the corporate rationalizers are operating within the context of a market society. Both have a concern to avoid encroachments upon their respective positions of power and privilege, which depend upon the continuation of market institutions: the ownership and control of individual labor, facilities, and organizations (even "nonprofit" ones) by autonomous groups and individuals, with no meaningful mechanisms of public control. (The instruments of alleged political control available to the community population are discussed later.)

The corporate rationalizers may thus favor certain market reforms, if that will provide them with more doctors for their hospitals, more researchers for their medical schools, and more potential workers for medical corporations, and will subject these workers to market pressures which in turn will make them tractable employees. The professional monopolists may thus favor certain bureaucratic reforms, particularly those aspects of planning and coordination which safeguard their interests, or administrative rules in hospitals which guarantee their continued dominance of medical practice.

Nor should the seeming rationality implied by the term "interest group" be overemphasized, because one basic consequence of the plurality of interest groups is that health institutions in a real sense are out of control of *both* the professionals and the bureaucrats. A hospitalization that could be terminated in one week lasts two, because there is a week's waiting time for a barium enema. Or one-third of a high-cost ward may be occupied because convalescent or chronic care facilities are unavailable. These failures of "coordination" or "planning" are not due to a conspiracy, vested interests (except in a very narrow sense), or failures of information (the horror stories are endless).[14]

Investigations of the Health System

It is significant that most definitions and diagnoses of the "crisis" do not come from the health professionals. The AMA and other professional associations have largely reacted defensively, proposing alternatives and compromises only when other interest groups have raised challenges to existing practices. When institutions and laws continuously serve the interests of dominant interest groups, challenge must come from elsewhere.

From where has the challenge come? A clue lies in the composition of the numerous commissions of inquiry which have investigated the health delivery system is the last twenty years and made many recommendations for public policy. I can cite only a few examples here, but they are typical.[15] The thirty-six-member "Heyman Commission" which issued its report on New York City health services in 1960 included five city officials, twelve hospital administrators and executives of health associations or medical research institutes, fifteen corporate or bank executives or directors, one university president, one labor representative, and two persons representing private medical practice (both presidents of county medical societies). Of the corporate group, at least five were directors of voluntary hospitals or pre-paid health plans.[16]

Seven years later, the so-called "Piel Commission" reported its findings to Mayor Lindsay, and recommended the establishing of the Health Services Administration (1967) and the Health and Hospitals Corporation (1970). Its seven members included one publisher, one university professor, and five corporate and banking representatives, all of whom happened to hold directorships of voluntary hospitals or other health associations.[17] Of the fourteen M.D.'s comprising the "medical advisory committee" to the commission, four represented hospitals, six university medical centers, two the New York Academy of Medicine, one a health institute, and only one a county medical society.

At the federal level, such commissions are similar in composition. To take only one example, the Task Force on Medicare and Related Programs was composed of twenty-seven persons, five of whom held M.D.'s. Only one of these (according to the list of the affiliations in the report) was an unattached physician. Four others were associated with city or state health agencies or were directors of hospitals or medical schools. Of the remaining twenty-two members, seven were corporation executives (one a proprietary hospital chain), six were connected with universities (including medical schools), three with community or state health agencies, and three with hospitals.[18] The chairman of the task force was the president of Blue Cross, a private hospital insurance association.

While I may not have accurately classified the members' multiple affiliations, the relative absence of physicians, and especially physicians in private practice, is striking. Predominant in all of these commissions are hospital administrators, hospital insurance executives, corporate executives and bankers, medical school directors, and city and state public health administrators. These organizations represent a coalition of interest groups which I have called the "corporate rationalizers." They favor what the AMA attacked as the "corporate practice of medicine,"[19] favoring the coordination of health services by a combination of private and public health agencies, principally the hospital.

The analyses of the health "crisis" in these reports follow a number of common themes. A brief summary of one of them will illustrate both the character of the diagnosis of the crisis and the nature of the recommendations. The most recent example available from New York State is Governor Rockefeller's Steering Committee on Social Problems,[20] composed of seventeen members, only one of whom had an M.D. Of the sixteen men who took part in the study, fourteen were high executives of some of the country's largest corporations, banks, or brokerage firms, including U.S. Steel, Pan American World Airways, duPont, Equitable Life, AT&T, as well as Xerox and General Foods. The one M.D. was on the Yale medical school faculty; the other noncorporate executive was the president of the Committee for Economic Development.

Their report emphasizes that the health "crisis" is *not* a result of a shortage of anything, whether beds, physicians, dollars, or physician assistants (allied health manpower). Although the report does not generalize in this way, this overabundance might be termed an "anarchy of production," almost in the classic image of a capitalist economy.

With respect to manpower, "Boston, for example . . . has one of the nation's greatest complexes of medical institutions [but] a severe shortage of general care practitioners."[21] Two percent of medical school graduates in 1970 became general practitioners.[22] There are also "too many ancillary personnel—but . . . they are not adequately trained and not effectively deployed." . . .[23]

With respect to beds, "[w]e estimate that we need 450,000 short-term hospital beds—we now have 800,000 such beds."[24]

With respect to duplication of facilities, "[n]eedless competition [by hospitals for costly but under-used equipment] results in tremendous waste of scarce resources and funds."[25] And mortality rates were sharply higher in hospitals where surgeons performed few operations such as open-heart surgery.

With respect to funds, increasing costs and subsidies act as an incentive to expand facilities and add to inflation. Total expenditures on health rose from twenty-six billion dollars in 1960 to sixty-seven billion in 1970, from 5.3 percent of the gross national product to 7 percent. Two-thirds of the 1970 total was personal health expenditures, with half of this due to price increases, not more use of services or more advanced technology.

This "overproduction" of health manpower and facilities is distributed in such a way as to maintain a "two-class health system—one for the poor and a better one for those able to pay their own way. . . . The nation's poor people have been receiving inadequate and, at times, inexcusable care and treatment."[26]

Using the words of the 1967 National Advisory Commission on Health Manpower, the report summarizes the state of affairs: "Medical care in the United States is more a collection of bits and pieces (with overlapping, duplication, great gaps, high costs and wasted effort) than an integrated system in which needs and efforts are closely related." But, according to the Rockefeller committee, "The situation is more acute than four years ago, and deteriorating rapidly."[27]

This picture is restated in every diagnosis of the "crisis" of the health system. The figures portray dynamics without change: a rapid increase in almost every index of growth—dollars, manpower, programs—except those pertaining to quality, distribution, accessibility, and reasonable cost to the consumer.

It should be noted that the empirical criteria and basis for the judgments of quality and the adequacy of quantity and distribution are not given in this report, nor are the basic data available which would be necessary to evaluate either a specific health service or the character of coordination of diverse health institutions. The reasons for this absence of information will be discussed later in a more theoretical context, but the point is that the many critiques of the health "system" are not cumulative nor based on solid research, and thus have an ideological character, rooted in images and theories about the proper way to reorganize and coordinate the "system."

The Rockefeller committee, without quite saying so, attributes many of the defects of health care to the interests of the physicians, the "dominant profession."[28] The physicians have defined "health and medical care in very restricted terms," leaving out preventive medicine.[29] "Most clinics serving poor people are structured for the convenience of the doctor, not the patient."[30] "Much care now given by a physician does not require a physician's level of training and education."[31] The physicians, and especially those allied occupations which have not yet achieved similar professional controls over their incomes and work, exhibit a "great deal of sensitivity about professionalism and status."[32] As a result, "[w]e are impressed with the number of meritorious proposals for change which have been ignored, and with the tendency of the health care establishment to resist such change."[33]

In a barely concealed attack on the interests of the professional monopolists in maintaining their power and privileges, the Rockefeller committee recommended coordinating all health services around hospitals, or "Health Center Complexes," employing "modern management approaches"[34], utilizing machinery for "internal planning and systems development," and, perhaps most important, establishing "utilization controls." The system recommended would, ideally, cover the entire population for seventy-five percent of their medical bills (one hundred percent for the poor).[35]

While not expressly advocating salaries for physicians, the utilization controls would exclude any public funds being used for health care services "found to be unnecessary in accordance with generally accepted practice"; nor would any charge be honored which "extends the prevailing level of charges in the community."[36]

It is quite clear that the committee accepts the hospital as the central health provider in our society. They see the hospital, with some qualifications, as the "core of a broader health care corporation responsible for assuring comprehensive health care to a defined service area."[37] It should be franchised or licensed by a state and participate meaningfully in "area, state and regional health care planning and regulation."[38] The result will be a network of community preventive services, ambulatory and home care, integrated with in-hospital care, and linked to nursing homes and extended care facilities.

There is little to object to in this abstract image of an ideal health system, which is quite similar to Dr. Roemer's. The point here is not to criticize its assumptions, but to suggest that it is in fact a challenge by the corporate rationalizers of the professional monopolists. The proposals by the committee to end restrictive licensing of health professionals would challenge their attempts to control their markets and their own supply. The proposals to open up medical schools and reduce the length of time for training an M.D. also challenges professional control over their own supply.[39]

The proposals to establish physician assistants (or "surrogates"—a significant substitute term) would challenge the monopoly of M.D.'s over important areas of primary health care. As the report says, a Washington pilot program indicates that "such men can perform a series of jobs with even greater skill than most physicians."[40]

The proposals to expand prepaid group practice and review utilization and fees challenge the sole control by M.D.'s over their conditions of work and incomes, and thus directly undercut their professional monopoly.[41]

The proposal to allocate health professionals after their first training to areas short of health manpower, in return for waiving of loans, constitutes an invasion by government of the right of the new physician to choose his own area of practice.[42]

Thus, major proposals to reorganize and coordinate the health delivery system constitute several important challenges to the professional monopoly of the physicians.

What is the likely course of change? Given the central interests of each set of groups and the ease with which the equal-health advocates can be co-opted, change is extremely difficult. The interrelated activities of these groups account for the expansion of health care in providing units at the "bottom" of the system and the elaboration of bureaucratic machinery at the "top." Explanation of the "dynamics without change" of these processes are now my major concern, not the character of private medical practice.

The Professional Monopolists

The professional monopolists are mainly physicians, specialists, and health research workers in medical schools and universities (but not hospital administrators, even if they have M.D.'s), who usually have an advanced degree and also a position—either an entrepreneurial one guaranteed by law and custom or an official one defined by the hierarchy of statuses within an organization—which entitles them to monopoly over certain kinds of work. Their incomes are derived from private practice or from foundations, governments, and universities, but they are able to exploit organizational resources for their personal and professional interests. They can be called "monopolistic" because they have nearly complete control over the conditions of their work, buttressed by the traditions of their professions and/or institutions, and because usually there is no other way to show effectiveness except through a demonstration grant, research project, or contract to them, or by contracting with them to perform their professional services. Frequently a clinic or health center will be set up which, although providing services, is established mainly for other purposes of the persons who hold power (not always or even usually the operating staff): research, training, professional aggrandizement, power within their home" institutions, the prestige of extending their professional empire, and so forth.

The major consequence of the activity of the professional monopolists is a continuous proliferation of programs and projects which are established in a wide variety of ways, under many auspices, and with many sources of funding, and which undoubtedly in most cases provide real services of some kind. The reason it is so difficult to describe or explain how these work is that the professional monopolists who set them up attempt to provide a symbolic screen of legitimacy while maintaining power in their own hand through various organizational devices. A continuous flow of symbols will reassure the funding of allegedly controlling publics or constituencies about the functions being performed, while the individuals or groups which have a special interest in the income, prestige, or power generated by the agency are benefiting from its allocations of resources.

Thus, the symbolic screen will put off attempts at control or supervision by making them difficult as well as less likely (because the nominally superior agency will be reassured). It is almost impossible to plan or coordinate or integrate the activities of the myriad projects and programs because important interests of the individuals and groups which establish and maintain them contradict the goals of those who wish to coordinate, plan, and integrate all of the functions implied or defined by the master symbols of the project: its title, the funding agency's contract with it, its annual report, and so on.

The professional monopolists, by and large, are satisfied with the status quo and do not form part of the "market reformers" who regard them as performing the core health functions. The physicians and biomedical researchers are not in the vanguard proposing reforms, except when their powers and prerogatives are threatened by others. That physicians are not heavily represented on the various reformist committees and that the AMA is losing membership and is continuously criticized for its political stance do not mean that physicians are losing power. The physicians in private practice and the voluntary hospitals still constitute the core of the health system. All of the federal, state, and local programs and projects which occupy so much time and energy of both types of reformers are still on the periphery of the health system. Almost none of the reports, commissions of investigation, presidential task forces, and so forth, which attempt to define the crisis and recommend solutions, ever mention invading the powers and territory of the private physicians and the voluntary hospitals.

The continuous control of the medical profession over the provision of medical services is a basic element of the American health system. As one author put it in 1932, "The legal ownership and ultimate control of the great bulk of capital invested in the practice of medicine in hospitals lies with the lay public, but the medical profession exercises a pervasive and in most instances a determining influence over the utilization of this capital and over the kinds of service which, through the use of this capital investment, are furnished to the community."[43] Twenty-three years later, the same author asserted that "the predominance of social capital has continued. Proprietary hospitals have diminished in absolute and relative importance. . . . More capital per physician is required than formerly."[44]

But in 1955 a third of American doctors worked entirely with organizations full time, and "a much larger number—about five-sixths, including the preceding group—work part time or full time with organizations—especially hospitals and clinics."[45] This trend has undoubtedly continued.

Thus, medicine seems to be a classic case of the socialization of production but the private appropriation of the "surplus" by a vested interest group—the doctors—who maintain control through their professional associations of the supply of physicians, the distribution of services, the cost of services, and the rules governing hospitals. The gradual decline of solo practice has created the social conditions for the challenge of this professional monopoly by the corporate rationalizers.

This generalization probably applies mainly to larger cities and perhaps most to New York City. In smaller cities the physicians still control the hospitals through the county medical societies. Administrators of the small-town hospitals are less professionalized than those in big-city hospitals and thus have a less independent view of the way their hospital should be run. A small town is also not likely to have a medical school, so that a potential coalition of corporate rationalizers from a medical school, hospital administrators, insurance companies, and public health agencies does not have the organizational or political base to challenge the control by the solo physicians of medical practice in the hospital.

Potential mavericks among the doctors are controlled by the power of the county medical board to refuse an appointment in the hospital. Small cities are less likely to have more than one hospital, so that a dissident physician has no place to go, except to change his place of practice.

Thus, small cities are less likely to exhibit open conflict over the organization, quantity, and quality of health care than large cities. (In the pluralist sense, no "power" is being exercised.) But there may actually be more unequal allocation of health care to various segments of the community and more chance that doctors and professional associations are unchallenged than in larger cities, where opposing interest groups have reached some threshold of effective organization.

The Corporate Rationalizers

The corporate rationalizers are typically persons in top positions in "health" organizations: hospital administrators, medical school directors, public health officials, directors of city health agencies, heads of quasi-public insurance (Blue Cross), state and federal health officials. Their ideology stresses a rational, efficient, cost-conscious, coordinated health care delivery system. They see the medical division of labor as arbitrary and anachronistic in view of modern hospital-based technology. The more successful they are in unifying functions, powers, and resources under a single glorifying symbol ("medical center," "comprehensive health planning"), the greater their incomes are likely to be and the higher their community and professional prestige. Thus, there are ample incentives for these individuals to attempt to expand the powers fo their home institutions or organizations.

Sometimes the corporate rationalizers ally themselves with the professional monopolists within their own institutions as a way of gathering more financial resources and legitimacy, and also as a way of bringing more and more health care units into their domain, even if not under their control. But usually it is in the interests of the corporate rationalizers to attempt to control the conditions of work, the division of labor, and the salaries of their employees, in view of the exigencies of funding and the need to adopt technical and organizational innovations without the built-in resistances of professional (or union, for that matter) jurisdictions over tools and tasks. They, therefore, attempt to convert professionals, mainly physicians, into employees and in a variety of ways to circumscribe their power in the hospital.

Although great size and resources are equated with capability and performance in order to legitimate extending the domain of control of the corporate rationalizers, there is little evidence that even the internal structure of the giant hospital complexes is planned, integrated, and coordinated for the effective delivery of health services to a given target population, let alone the public as a whole.

"Outreach" neighborhood health centers established by a medical center may be advertised as a rational step toward coordination and integration, but instead are really needed as a source of patients and surgical material. Because of Medicare, physicians assume they will be reimbursed, and thus need not send poor patients with interesting diseases on to a university hospital. The goal in establishing a neighborhood health center is thus not coordination, but patients. Other cases of supposed coordinating mechanisms—ambulance services, referrals, communication of records and patient information—are notoriously poor in operation, and there is little evidence that the extension of control by one organization, whether via formal merger or not, results in more comprehensive care.

Even if the target of the corporate rationalizers' activity is to coordinate and integrate a number of organizations into a cohesive whole, the successful instituting of such bureaucratic controls means that democratic planning and coordination of the larger health system becomes *more* difficult. Generating enough power to integrate a portion of it successfully means, almost by definition, that this part is now insulated from outside influence and can successfully resist being integrated into a still larger system.

The rhetoric of the corporate rationalizers conceals this consequence by suggesting that social or political mechanisms can be created to unify and integrate the entire system. But such mechanisms do not exist—in government or anywhere else. The mere passage of legislation establishing "comprehensive health planning," for example, does not provide them with the necessary power and resources. If this is the case, then the act of creating another agency further complicates the system. As will be discussed later in more detail, historically legislators have responded to pressures for reform by establishing a series of agencies—none of which has sufficient power to do its job. Few of these are abolished, and subsequent legislation incorporates the previous agencies into the list of those to be "coordinated," thereby further complicating the system. The resources made available to these agencies, charged with planning and coordinating other agencies, frequently become part of the budgets controlled by the corporate rationalizers.

A major consequence of the activity of the corporate rationalizers is a constant expansion of the functions, powers, and resources of their organizations. One organizational device for doing that is the institution of a bureaucratic stratum designed to coordinate and integrate the component units. Unfortunately, this new stratum cannot carry out this function because it is a staff operation with little power and is usually the instrument of one particular leadership faction within the organization. Thus, their recommendations frequently fail to carry enough weight to be implemented. Also the planning or research staff tends to be drawn, because of lack of any other source of personnel, from the ranks of the professional monopolists, who have little stake in truly rationalizing the operation and see the planning or research functions partly as instruments for their own personal and professional ends. Where the goals of the professional monopolists within the organization and the sponsoring faction of the corporate rationalizers coincide, an effective staff function will be performed. In that case, the committed and motivated staff will usually come into conflict with a powerful element in the top officialdom of the organization—either another group of professional monopolists whose toes they are stepping on, or a faction among the corporate rationalizers.

Thus, the net effect of the activities of the corporate rationalizers is to complicate and elaborate the bureaucratic structure. The relationship between them and the professional monopolists is symbiotic in that the ever-increasing elaboration of the bureaucratic structure is justified by the need to coordinate the expansion of health care providing units at the bottom. No group involved has a stake in the coordination and integration of the entire system toward the major goal of easily accessible, inexpensive, and equal health care.

The Community Population

The third major set of interest groups comprises the community population affected by or needing health care. Their spokesmen are the "equal-health advocates," comprising various "community control" groups in both black and white communities, full- or part-time organizers, and some intellectuals. Because they are not part of the network of health institutions and agencies, they are free to demand more and better health services and also some voice in the decisions and policies which might affect health care. City bureaucracies, public health agencies, and the medical schools usually contain some supporters.

The efforts of these diverse individuals and groups, whether aimed at specific or general reforms, are likely to fail. If their demands are focused upon a particular program or need, the response is likely to be the establishment of a particular kind of program or clinic—drug, alcoholism, mental health. The professional monopolists will seize upon the demand as an opportunity to legitimate their efforts to establish another project or program. While some tangible services to some people may be the outcome, the overall result is the expansion and proliferation of still more highly specialized clinics, demonstration projects, or health centers which confuse people trying to find care and are highly expensive in both staff and administrative costs and, thus, lead to a further elaboration of the overriding bureaucratic structure.

If the demands of the equal-health advocates are directed toward reorganizing the health system, the activities of the corporate rationalizers are legitimated. New planning committees and new coordinating councils will be set up with representation from the community groups and with the avowed goal of rationalizing the system. But the community representatives do not have the information necessary to play an important political role; they do not know the levers of power, the interests at stake, and the actual nature of the operating institutions, and they do not have the political resources necessary to acquire that information since they are only minority members of advisory committees. The presence of equal-health advocates on one or another committee or council is a sign of legitimacy being claimed by either a set of professional monopolists or corporate rationalizers, or sometimes both, in their battle for resources and power.

Because the community is not self-conscious and knowledgeable about health facilities, and because the members of the community are likely to give food, jobs, housing, and schools priority over doctors and hospitals—since only a small proportion of the community needs health care at any given time—the equal-health advocates are likely to have a great deal of autonomy in representing community needs to official agencies. Advocates are not under much surveillance, there is little reaction to their decisions, and their victories have little collective impact. Thus, the isolation of equal-health advocates from the community increases the chances of their being co-opted into advisory boards, planning agencies, and other devices for advertising the representative character of "community participation" without much chance, let alone guarantee, that the community will be able to evaluate and control the actions of their advocates, let alone the health providers.

Thus, the major consequence of the activity of the equal-health advocates is to provide further legitimacy for both the expansion of specific research or service units controlled by professional monopolists and the expansion of the layers of bureaucratic staff under the control of the corporate rationalizers. Given the enormous discrepancy between the output of actual health services and their claims, there will be a continuous supply of persons from community groups ready to serve as equal-health advocates. However, persons who have played that role for some time are likely to become discouraged and leave, or will be co-opted into one of the established health organizations. Other persons will arise from community organizations to replace them for a wide variety of motives: prestige as a community representative, a chance to mingle with high city and other officials and community leaders, and possibly a chance for a better job or a political career. This chance for mobility may be good for the individuals involved, but may be disastrous for the accumulation of political and organizational experience by community groups, if their leaders are constantly either being absorbed into the existing health system or dropping out of activity.

Given the original diversity of health providers and the personal and organizational stakes of the interdependent, although conflicting, network of professional monopolists and corporate rationalizers, the demands of the equal-health advocates are almost inevitably frustrated. In fact, the system as a whole, as a result of their activities, moves in a direction exactly opposite to that which they envision. Costs go up as a result of the establishment of new, expensive programs. The accessibility of care goes down as a result of the proliferation of specialized, high-technology, research- or teaching-oriented health care units.

This description of a system in equilibrium is of course only partial. The legitimacy gained for the dominant interest groups by the activity of the equal-health advocates is precarious because it rests upon a continuous contradiction between rhetoric and performance. Legitimacy is purchased at the escalating cost of constantly expanding provider units which duplicate each other and of continuously establishing new agencies which purport to coordinate and integrate. To the extent to which equal-health advocates can create consciousness among the community population of the causes of the situation, the groundwork is laid for a more fundamental challenge to the powers and privileges of the dominant interest groups.

The Consequences of a Community "Victory"

The preceding discussion of the activities of the equal-health advocates has argued that their attempts to increase the quality and quantity of health services available to them are likely to fail. Either they will become absorbed with no real power in an "advisory committee" to existing agencies, or they will play a minority role in planning committees for new health facilities which take years to come to fruition. While some community participation may lead to greater political consciousness, under present conditions co-optation and stalemate are most likely.

Even if community groups become involved in planning committees for new facilities, one highly likely consequence is that their activities by themselves will block new programs and projects. Once community groups are mobilized, they tend to conflict with each other and with the professionals in health organizations over funding, priorities, timing, sites, and control. Community participation is a classic instance of the "veto group" process leading to stalemate.

Such a typical pattern is no accident. The structure of participation maximizes the chances of stalemate by setting up the rules of decision making in such a way as to prevent any major interest group from being seriously damaged (the requirement of "consensus"), and by failing to allocate enough power to the decision-making bodies on which community groups are represented. Because these bodies are not given enough power, there is little incentive to set up procedures and create a composition which will lead to effective decision-making processes. Just the opposite incentives exist: to make them large and unwieldy—as "representative" as possible—so that all points of view will be heard but none implemented, save those interest groups who already hold power. The net result is many meetings, speeches, and reports. Committees are set up which plan, coordinate, and communicate— and ultimately evaporate when the planning grant runs out.

One consequence of this particualr scenario is that even the professionals who started the project with a sincere desire to "get the community involved" will become cynical about the competence and skills of community groups and leaders. The next time around they will join the ranks of those who try to make the mechanisms of community representation as fictitious as possible in order to preserve at least some chance of getting a health facility organized, funded, and built.

But let us assume that, as a result of sustained community organization and pressure, a "neighborhood health center" is, at long last, established to provide accessible, inexpensive, and high-quality care. What are the consequences? Will it continue to do so? No, for several reasons: the consequences of excessive *demand*, its establishment as part of a two-*class* health system, and the likelihood of short-term *funding*. Each of these reasons why a community "victory" is likely to be short-lived is worth a brief discussion.

Neighborhood health centers are selected as the example of a community victory because of their recent emergence as the focus of demand in New York City and their actual funding under specific federal legislation; but there have been parallel programs in the past, and there will be others in the future under such names as comprehensive health center, district health center, health maintenance organization, neighborhood family care center, ambulatory care service, child health station, and mental helath clinic. Such a "center" is likely to be set up only in an area where few M.D.'s are in private practice, where there are few hospitals, and where there is a heavy concentration of poor people. The market reformers can applaud such an innovation because it meets demand in a flexible way, establishes diversity in the system, and uses government resources where the private market has no incentive to compete. The bureaucratic reformers hail such a development because it usually will be established as an "outreach" clinic by an existing hospital, under public funding, and therefore add to the resources of the seeming movement toward integration and coordination.

Demand. Because of the inadequacy of other health facilities in poor areas, the very success of a neighborhood health center is likely to be its downfall. If it attempts to "deal comprehensively with patients' problems," the center becomes the "repository for all the unmet needs of our patients. . . ." The consequence of the "lack of adequate social services in our community will inevitably deaden staff's responsiveness to their problems."[46] Thus, even though the staff may have begun work there in the full flush of idealism, ready to serve the community's needs with great energy and devotion, their very commitment will cause patients to flood in demanding care. The resulting overload of work will reduce the quality of care, the enthusiasm of the staff, and the sense of gratitude of the patients.

Establishing a facility in a poor area which provides—at its beginning—easily accessible, inexpensive, and high-quality care will thus generate enormous demand, reflecting great unmet needs, which soon reduces both accessibility and quality. Thus, the activities of the equal-health advocates, if successfully focused upon the "realistic" end of getting an OEO grant for a neighborhood health center, let us say, are likely to be fruitless from the point of view of the system as a whole. If the total quantity of health services available to the population is increased, it can then be argued plausibly that the community is better off than it was before. But if the same characteristics—long waits, hurried physicians, and so forth—are reproduced after a while, the net effect may be cynicism on the part of the previously idealistic staff and a new sense of hopelessness in the population, which has been led to expect real improvement.

Where the poor community has become apathetic because of the successive failure of previous attempts to install new facilities, it may be difficult for the latest one, no matter how well-intentioned and well-staffed at the outset, to generate usage. If so, this becomes an obvious argument for dismantling the health center, particularly since it is likely to be set up as a demonstration project. *Lack* of demand thus will kill the facility.

Class. The same characteristics of the "old" system are reproduced not only by the demand on the facilities but also by the maintenance of a two-class system. In the case of the OEO neighborhood health centers, the requirement that service be only to the poor has meant "heavy-handed insistence"[47] by OEO on a means test, with all of the resulting downgrading of respect for the patients, lower status for the staff, and other characteristics of institutions designed for the poor.

Attempting to build health care institutions for *all*, providing free, accessible, and high-quality care, runs into an objection. Why serve the middle class? They can pay for it. Why not reserve these scarce resources for the poor who need it most? If you open up health care to all on the same basis, the argument runs, the middle class will monopolize services since they have the information and the resources to take advantage of the available facilities. This is a plausible argument, especially if one takes the position that political realism argues for a piecemeal approach to reform.

But, as already suggested, the consequences of a two-class institution are likely to be the extension of more of the same kind of services as before. To the extent that the sheer production of more health care facilities is better, such additions of facilities may be worthwhile, but they do not constitute reforms of the health system.

Funding. The argument that more is better assumes, for its plausibility, that these neighborhood health centers become part of the established array of health facilities available to the public, even on terms of existing costs, accessibility, and quality. This is not the case, however. The magic wand of financing moves from health area to health area and from crisis to crisis, causing one kind of facility to grow and flourish for a time, then another, leaving the first to dwindle or wither away. Community mental health centers, neighborhood health centers, and methadone clinics have each felt the impact of public concern.

Precisely because of community pressures, funding tends to flow to the kinds of facility which can be advertised as a legitimate response to community needs. When the "old" agency or facility fails to meet those needs, community pressure builds up again after a time, and a new agency surges forward, leaving the hollow shell of an under-financed, struggling agency in its wake. The old agencies are struggling partly because their failure to meet the needs has become obvious; they lose political clout, and their budgets are cut to make resources available to the new agencies, or at least they are not increased enough to enable them to do their jobs. Thus, they are further paralyzed.

The lack of permanent governmental commitment to such programs as the OEO neighborhood health centers—their definition as peripheral and supplemental programs to the main body of the private health sector—means that they are eternally precarious and starved for funds. The consequences for their internal operations are serious. They must seek the short-term payoff, the program which will bring in the maximum number of patient visits as tangible evidence that they are playing the political role which originally generated them: cooling out the community. If they seek maximum short-term "productivity" in terms of patient visits, they run the danger of overloading their facilities which were probably under-financed and under-staffed in the first place. Overloading, as we have seen, in turn reduces the impact on the community and the likelihood of community pressure demanding the project's continuation. In effect, the health center becomes after a few years just another component of the two-class health system, and its theoretical goal of providing comprehensive health care is contradicted by practice.

Another consequence of dependence on short-term financing—itself also a result of the strategy of getting something rather than nothing for the poor—is that costs are likely to be high. In the first few years of any program, the setting-up costs— hiring, training, capital investment in buildings and facilities—are high. But in the context of "demonstration projects," where an evaluation of the costs will, at least seemingly, be one of the bases for judging whether or not the project will continue, these high initial costs become one of the negative features in the evaluation. A common point made about demonstration projects is that they are expensive and therefore cannot be continued.

Another reason that such projects are expensive is that the poor community has many sick, untreated people. If they ask for care once it is made available, the new, ambitious, and committed (let us assume) staff is put in a double bind. If they seek to meet all of these needs, they will quickly subject themselves to difficult work conditions, with all of the consequences listed above. If they attempt to insulate themselves against only the most pressing medical needs, and try to meet those needs in a humane, careful, and thoroughly professional manner, they inevitably set up barriers to treatment for the rest. Poor patients asking for help (and also testing the new facility for its humanity) will again be subjected to "official" treatment: the appointment hassle, the inquiries (Are you really sick?), and the not-so-subtle attitudes (What do you expect for nothing?). While the health care for those persons who ultimately reach a physician in the health center may be careful and competent, the cost of making it possible for their care to be of high quality may reduce the accessibility of care to many others. This consequence is a direct result of inadequate manpower and resources.

The auspices under which the neighborhood health center is organized might seem to make a difference. It is sometimes argued that linking such centers to medical schools will increase the chances of better care for the poor. This is not necessarily the case because of the exploitation of the poor for teaching purposes. The poor patients with rare diseases may, indeed, be selected for special and even superb treatment, but may be subjected to untested medicines or operations (for legitimate research and teaching purposes, of course) by inexperienced persons (medical students), who would never be allowed to practice their skills in that way on wealthy patients. The remainder of the patients, the poor with ordinary, uninteresting diseases which are useful for neither research nor training, are subjected to the normal indignities found in charity institutions of all types.

But the poor are not better off if the neighborhood health center is not connected to a medical school. In this case the medical staff, working in a lower-status facility precisely because it serves the poor and is not connected to a medical school, tends to be composed of foreign doctors, many of whom are not well-trained, below-average medical school graduates who cannot get better jobs or practices, young idealists who get discouraged after a few years and leave, or a few good physicians who have taken the job as part of their career but intend to move on as soon as possible. The staff tends to have a high turnover, and thus is relatively unable to build up continuous relationships with families in the area.[48]

To conclude, even if the equal-health advocates are victorious in their long struggle to get more health facilities in a poor area, the principles by which the rest of the health system already operates become reproduced in the new facility. The disillusionment which follows leads either to apathy or greater militance, depending on the concrete character of the experiences of the community population, the political skills of the equal-health advocates, and the broader social and political situation at the time.

The Role of the Political System

Up to this point we have dealt only with the interest groups active at the local level, and the resources for which they compete have been regarded as exogenous factors. The points might be made that all of the processes summarized above are due to vacillating financial support and that regular funding for health services would solve many problems, even if they were organized as at present. This may indeed be true, but then it is necessary to see if the sudden spurts of funds for new programs and then their drying up, and the continuous creation of new but under-funded and under-powered agencies, are characteristics of the political system which can be easily rectified.

Most new urban health programs depend on vacillating commitments under federal and state legislation. But most of the analyses of New York City's (or any other community's) programs regard these characteristics of the political system as exogenous factors to be taken account of, but almost like fate or the weather. The Ginzberg study, discussing ambulatory services and the city's plans for "neighborhood family care centers," says, "In the presence of persisting financial strictures that are not likely to be loosened by the current federal administration . . . the city has nonetheless committed itself to a priority program. . . ." And the city's "ambitious program to establish neighborhood family care centers throughout the city was scarcely off the drawing board when it was undermined by Medicaid cutbacks at the state and federal levels as early as 1968."[49]

The federal government has been seen as a major force in reforming health care. Yet federal activity has intensified the problems. Government agencies are not independent forces for the public interest, regulating, coordinating, mediating, and planning. Instead, government agencies are likely to become instruments for one or another part of the private sector. The Small Business Administration, for example, has been used on a number of occasions by one group of hospital interests to finance expansion, even while the Hill-Burton Agency has been financing the expansion of another nearby hospital.[50]

And at the federal level, according to Dr. James A. Shannon, former director of the National Institutes of Health, health programs are a "broadly decentralized" and "highly fragmented" set of "patchwork" activities that make it "difficult to consider broad issues in a coherent manner." These activities touch on every problem of health care and delivery "without dealing decisively with any one," he said.

Federal programs have "come into being sequentially as unbearable defects are uncovered" in private health care systems, rather than as "elements in a complete and unified system." During the Johnson administration alone, the Congress enacted fifty-one pieces of health legislation that provided for some 400 "discrete" authorities. The establishment of Regional Medical Programs in 1965 and Comprehensive Health Planning Programs in 1966 are additional cases in point. According to Dr. Shannon, elements of these two programs are in "direct conflict" with each other.[51]

As the Task Force on Medicaid put it, "The existing programs that directly influence new development or change (Partnership for Health, Regional Medical Programs, National Center for Health Services Research and Development, Maternal and Child Health, Neighborhood Health Center, Community Mental Health Centers, and Hill-Burton) have each been established by specific legislation that limits and defines eligible populations, services and the roles that demonstration, experimentation, and research can play. Consequently, each program has its own grant policies, funding cycles, and requirements for review, reporting and accounting; and any group trying to develop comprehensive health care at the local level must thread its way through a maze of multiple grant applications, multiple sets of books, and inflated administrative cost—all too often to be rewarded with fragmented assistance."[52]

According to the Rockefeller committee, at the federal, state, and local levels, there are "68 different controlling agencies in the field. . . ."[53] The U.S. Department of Health, Education and Welfare is "replete with overlapping and duplicating funding programs which not infrequently work in contradiction to each other. . . . 25 major programs within HEW, funded at a current cost of $12.7-billion . . . bear upon various aspects of the health care problem and . . . operate largely independently of each other. More importantly, many of the programs have outlived their usefulness. . . ."[54]

Also, HEW has been "too politically defensive and not sufficiently assertive. Too frequently, it reacts to individual Congressional initiative, and, in the absence of an overall health strategy of its own, fails to provide... leadership.... Many of its programs address old issues, which have been inherited from earlier days and not been re-tooled to keep abreast of contemporary needs. Overlays are put on overlays, and instead of reform and new structures, old programs are continued in their old style while new ones are added as needed—and as legislative expediency permits."[55]

Congress cannot be looked to for help. "Congress... many years ago succumbed to categorical 'disease' programs and patterns [and] has, by its actions and control over appropriations through a variety of subcommittees, contributed to many of the problems of fragmentation which now plague the present system."[56]

The main consequences of Medicare and Medicaid have been the same. As a prominent medical sociologist says, "Whatever the merits of Medicare and Medicaid, they impressively illustrate that to increase substantially investments in health care without altering the framework in which services are delivered will only exacerbate the inefficiencies and absurdities of the current organization of medical care in America."[57]

Given the functions performed by the basic structure of the health care system for the dominant interest groups, legislation which allegedly establishes new principles of operation and explicitly is designed to change the "system" is almost inevitably distorted in ways which reinforce the present system. For example, in commenting on the community mental health centers established by federal legislation in 1963, Connery et al. say, "Something appears to have been lost since the community centers program was initiated. The 'bold new approach' of 1963 shows great promise of becoming merely an expensive expansion of decentralized facilities closely resembling the outpatient clinics predating its adoption."[58]

But the corporate rationalizers have faith in the power of the federal government, despite their own account of its complex and fragmented structure. I intentionally omitted some of the optimistic rhetoric surrounding some of the above critique. The Rockefeller committee softens its criticism of HEW above by asserting that HEW "fails to provide the leadership it can and should be expected to give." Elsewhere it speaks of the "vital, major role" to be played by HEW in "helping to shape and rationalize the health care system."[59] And the Task Force on Medicaid asserts, "We must focus these programs around a common Federal health-service policy, coordinate financial and administrative requirements, integrate technical services and spend what we save on new and improved services."[60] This brave rhetoric is nearly meaningless. Why?

The answer is that politicians have to respond to crises. The "solution": a continuing series of new programs which promise to respond to the crisis. When one program fails, another will be offered, sometimes by the same incumbent party and politician, sometimes by the next incumbent who may have been propelled into office by his promises to provide leadership which will solve the problems his predecessor promised to solve and didn't.

Thus, each impending election produces a spate of new programs which show either or both how much the incumbent has achieved or how much his challenger will achieve. Given the frequency of elections and the need to provide patronage which will solidify the support of local constituencies, each set of officials will attempt to institutionalize his programs in a new set of agencies. The liberals go along, and even become the main proponents of these "solutions" because of a politically realistic, pragmatic assessment of the situation.

Thus, new programs are sold; they become political commodities on the electoral market. But like other commodities their exchange value for electoral support is more important than their use value—how much actual health care is provided. Once their price has been realized in the political market, new programs lose much of their value, except insofar as something tangible must be demonstrated at the time of the next election. But what is "tangible"? An agency, a building, a staff, a budget, funds being spent, but not, unfortunately, actual improvements in health services. In fact, attempts to demonstrate actual improvements are likely to show only the discrepancy between intentions (or claims) and performance and are, therefore, politically dysfunctional.

But this description seems to contradict the oft-made point that legislatures are losing control as more and more programs become firmly embedded in bureaucratic agencies. This is true, but does not contradict my thesis. Legislatures which fund new programs are, indeed, interested in maintaining their fiscal and statutory control over as much government activity as possible. This control is steadily weakening as more and more agencies become securely established and remove bigger and bigger chunks of the budget (whether city, state, or federal) from legislative power. What accounts for this contradiction?

The interest of the legislature as a whole in maintaining control over budgets and agencies is contradicted in specific cases by the interests of a given faction within it, which wishes to turn over programs to a permanent agency, stably representing in its policies and decisions the interest of a specific constituency. As a result of logrolling between various factions within the legislature, such bills are ultimately passed in many cases. Every faction, whether liberal or conservative, wants to institutionalize its own programs—embed them in permanently funded agencies beyond the reach of "political" decisions—and prevent other factions from doing the same for their interest groups. But the consequence of continuous expansion of such bureaucratic agencies—by definition, those which are renewed or refunded with little or no debate—is to reduce the power of the legislature as a whole.

The compromise which frequently resolves this contradiction, decision by decision, is to vote to establish a new program, thus responding to constituent demands, but on a "demonstration project" or year-by-year basis. This "solution" creates additional problems for legislative operations because it means that many programs must be brought up frequently for "review," cluttering up the legislative schedule. But at the cost of much seemingly ritualistic behavior (passing renewal legislation or another biennial budget by a unanimous vote), the legislature maintains control over as much of the budget and agencies as possible. If at any time a given program loses political support, becomes a liability, or becomes too "expensive" or "obsolete," it can be cut back or eliminated.

There is one sense in which it is in the interests of legislators to create public bureaucracies. Creation of an agency is a way of getting political pressure from interest groups off their backs. Depending on the cohesion, political resources, and consistency of the demands of the interest group with the dominant institutions of the society, the new agency will be substantive rather than symbolic response to the demands.[61]

New agencies thus simultaneously reduce the power of the legislature vis-à-vis the proliferating array of public bureaucracies, but also are a sign of the power of those majority coalitions within the legislature which succeed in establishing the agency and in providing it with the power to respond substantively to outside constituencies. The point here is that the long-range effect of the actions of legislatures is to decentralize power into a wide variety of public bureaucracies. This is a necessary form of administrative fragmentation in a pluralist system, because it reduces "demand overload" on the legislature. The various recommendations to create instrumentalities to "coordinate" and "integrate" services ignore these political functions.

The consequence at the *operating* levels of health agencies of these processes at the *legislative* level is to create continuous uncertainty among the staff. Considerable time must be diverted from program into preparation of the annual budget report, grant application, or whatever other document must demonstrate the need for continuation of the project or program. To some extent, it might seem that this need continually to justify the program would maintain the priority of the original goals which established the program. This may in some cases be true. But also likely is a concern with tangible and manifest aspects of the program, those most easily measured in quantitative terms, such as adding new staff members, spending more money, adding divisions or departments which have new names, or building offices and new facilities. None of these has any necessary relationship to the presumed goals of the organization, but forms a visible part of the description of its recent achievements. Growth, expansion, and increased complexity can all be defined as progress toward the goals.

In addition to the pressure to develop these indicators of performance, there must be a continuing escalation of the rhetoric of claims of past performance and the promises for the next period of funding. In many situations, funds will be scarce, and different agencies will be competing against each other for them. Pressure is thereby created to exaggerate both reports and plans in order to create a favorable comparison. Because the granting agency does not want to lose its own control over decisions, it is not likely to release information about how generous the available funds are in any given year, and therefore how "honest" the applying agency need be in order to compete effectively with other applying agencies. In any case, the applying agency (whether for funds, legislation, a new program, or any other authority being requested) has nothing to gain from being honest, because it never knows at what moment a revelation of the shortcomings of a program—even if clearly provable to be out of control of the staff—will be used against it by one or another faction higher in the organization which holds a different conception of the relative importance of one or another component department or agency.

This pluralistic competition exists because there can be no central control mechanism for making national health policy which is in the general or "public" interest. While legislatures have the symbolic role, they are a congeries of representatives of specific interest groups. Sometimes bureaucratic agencies are regarded as "above politics," even if legislatures cannot be, and thus are potentially able to formulate general public policy. Many reforms aim at removing decisions from the legislature or the executive and placing them in a bureaucratic agency, for the reasons and with the consequences outlined above. These efforts assume that such agencies can become neutral instruments of general interests, but ignore the continuous distortion of their substantive decisions in directions which fit the pervasive presence of private economic and social power. In fact, the more apparently separate the agency is from legislative representative institutions, the more vulnerable it is to influence from private organizations and groups, such as the doctors and the voluntary hospitals, in the case of the health system.

Given this sketchy outline of the structure and the processes by which it changes, one might imagine that it would quickly become both bottom- and top-heavy and collapse. That is, the multiplicity of organizational units and the differentiation of existing ones in response to the pressures summarized above would cause such a high level of overlapping, costs, complexity, and inaccessibility that a fantastically expensive chaos of organizations failing to accomplish their stated goals would result. At what point such a system would become politically and socially unbearable is difficult to say. We may be close to that point.

But there is at least one political mechanism which militates against this process and serves to maintain some equilibrium. Although this is not their intention, one consequence of the legislatures' maintaining veto power over agencies by not making them permanent is to allow the dying off (or the killing off) of a certain proportion of agencies, programs, and projects.[62] Some agencies are eliminated, and some projects disappear, remarkable as it seems. There may be little or no correlation between the tangible services which an agency performs and the likelihood of its not being refunded. Certainly one should not assume from the cries of agony which are raised by the staff, its clientele, or its political sponsors when an agency is in imminent danger of being killed that, in fact, its continuation would be the best possible use of the human and material resources involved.

But from the point of view of the continuation of the existing system, the periodic elimination of some organizations may compensate for the continuous creation of new ones. Like political regimes, bureaucratic organizations may either accumulate so many liabilities that they lose political support, or they become so rigid—so "bureaucratic" in the pejorative sense—that they are no longer able to adjust to a situation to which their political sponsors want them to respond. In that case, even if the need which generated the organization remains unfulfilled, an existing organization may be allowed to die, and a new one may be created in its place. The new one may also be, as the old one may have been, merely a symbolic response to the need. But it is a response; the organization has a fresh new name and a fresh new staff—even though their jobs may be part of political patronage—and can thus be advertised as the actions of a responsible and innovative leadership.

The life history of any organization and the interests it serves thus cannot be seen in a vacuum. The organization, no matter how seemingly securely established by law, custom, or funding, will continue to exist only so long as the coalition of interest groups who benefit from its existence continue to support it. The more stable an organization seems, say one of the great voluntary hospitals in New York City, the more likely it is that its activities are continuously serving the interests of certain groups. Emerging conflict over the existence, purpose, funding, size, location, or any other characteristic indicates that the interests the organization has been serving are withdrawing their support, becoming weaker, or being challenged. Only when there is some chance of altering the balance of power and control over the organization are other groups likely to challenge its existence or character.[63]

Consequences for Health Research

The seemingly confident factual assertions above do not rest upon well-confirmed and repeated studies of health institutions, but are only hypotheses seeking to link scattered observations. In fact, little knowledge exists about how the present system works or what alternatives might be feasible. The 1967 "Report of the National Advisory Commission on Health Manpower" concluded that "there is a serious lack of the consistent and comprehensive statistical information that is required for rational analysis and planning, despite a surfeit of numbers about health."[64] The research director of the Kaiser Foundation Hospitals in Portland, Oregon, commenting like others on the lack of significant change between 1933 and 1967, added that, although many "conferences and papers" in thirty-five years have pointed out the "need for adequate medical care research," we still do not have "comprehensive, coordinated, and reliable research, systematically carried on to help solve the many complex problems in the organization of health care services."[65]

Although the community population has a real stake in accurate information on the quality and quantity of services and their costs, and also information on a structure of controls which would be responsive to community health needs, they have no resources with which to command that information. The main information which the system generates is internal management information for billing and tax purposes, individual patient data, and research data useful for certain professional and scientific problems, but not for assessment of outputs and the performance of the organization. But outside groups cannot easily obtain even these data to analyze for their own purposes, since the data might be used to show the ways in which the various parts of the organizations fail to achieve their ostensible goals, advertised far and wide in the efforts to achieve more funds. Even if available, information could not easily be aggregated with information from other sources to estimate the causal relationships between the inputs of money and manpower from one organization to another and the outputs of tangible health services. The professional monopolists, who tend to be strategically located in data-gathering and -processing positions, also have no incentive to release information to outside groups who might challenge their power to define their own work.

Because there is *no* "system" in the sense operations researchers define it, the oft-repeated solution of better information and better communication is no solution at all. Thus, while obeisance may be made to information gathering and data processing, these symbolic claims again serve to screen the absence of the basic data which could be used to measure the character of services and the performance of organizations. For the same reasons, the data do not exist which could allow the study of the health system as a whole. Almost no studies have been done which take as problematic the structure of health-care-providing institutions—their funding, control, relationships to each other, and impact on the quality and quantity of services. Most studies of the "delivery system" focus on the utilization of health services by different income, occupational, and ethnic groups, on the socialization of physicians and nurses, or on the impact of the internal organization of a hospital upon patient care. While all of these studies can be justified in their own terms, they do not touch the core problem of the structure of the *producing* institutions, but focus instead either upon the *consumers* of health care or upon a specific institutional, organizational, or professional context in which a particular kind of care is provided. Such a paucity of studies is no accident; such studies would challenge the primary interests of both the professional monopolists and the corporate rationalizers in maintaining the structure of health institutions as they now exist and in directing its "orderly" expansion.

Crisis and the Political Economy of Health

Periodic crises, notably those in the last ten years in New York City, have been precipitated by the corporate rationalizers in an attempt to arouse support for their goals, although media exposure which defines a crisis usually has nothing to do with any change in the basic performance of the health system. The series of investigations in New York City by private, city, and state agencies from 1950 to 1971 stress the fragmentation and lack of coordination of the system, a sure sign of the ideology of corporate rationalization—as are the various reorganizations of the hospitals carried out in the last decade. But none of the reforms has touched the basic power of the private sector and its institutions.

A few crises have been precipitated by equal-health advocates moving outside the established framework of representation and influence to take disruptive, militant action. These have produced specific responses, usually in the form of new programs or still more "representation," taking the forms already described.[66]

Both market and bureaucratic reformers are likely to be upper middle class in their social origins, incomes, and occupational prestige, and thus they share an interest in moderating conflict and blunting "community" demands even if they are bitterly divided among themselves over the timing and scope of reforms. Noisy debate conceals an underlying unity of commitment to working through existing political channels, which may account for the unwillingness of the bureaucratic reformers—visibly more dissatisfied with the present organization of health care—to mobilize potential allies with the rhetoric and political tactics which could generate an effective movement for change. The ambiguous analyses of the various investigations recommending "coordination" and "planning"—and the fatal compromises which result (as in the case of the Health and Hospitals Corporation in New York City)—are the ideological corollary of a political commitment not to challenge the essential power of the professional monopolists.[67]

As Eli Ginzberg put it, "Each of the major parties insists that its essential power remain undiminished as a result of any contemplated large-scale change. . . . Inherent in pluralism is an overwhelming presumption in favor of incremental rather than large-scale reforms."[68]

An explanation of the deep-rooted character of the dynamics without change must thus ultimately go back to the dominance of the private sector and the upper middle class. As Ginzberg also says, "The industry remains dominated by the private sector—consumers, private practitioners, voluntary hospitals."[69] Thus, a major characteristic of the public sector is that it does not have the power to challenge the domination of the private sector. Given this domination, it seems a reasonable assumption that major characteristics of the health system are due to private control. Government policy is not fundamentally important, except insofar as the policy is *not* to interfere with the private sector, or only to come forth with financial subsidies for the private sector.

To say this does not mean that *any* program which increases the government's role will be an advance since any specific government policy may affirm the dominance of the private sector, provide additional subsidies for it, or further institutionalize the dichotomy between the public and private sectors. It would be possible, for example, to separate the public sphere of subsidies for the poor, or even government-owned clinics and hospitals, even further from the private sector; and this could be advertised as a step forward in public support for health services for the poor. But if the results were further to insulate the private sector from public mechanisms of funding and control, to set up new public institutions subject to the vacillating funding already discussed, and, further, to perpetuate a two-class system of care, these alleged reforms might be better regarded as a setback.

It is important to emphasize that Ginzberg in the quotation above includes the "consumers" as part of the private sector. If the upper middle-class consumers of the health care provided by fee-for-service practitioners and hospitals are, in fact, securing most of the medical services they need, then these particular consumers have no incentive to change the system, and, in fact, have compelling incentives to keep it the way it is. From their point of view, the only result of a merger of the private with the public sectors would be to *reduce* their capacity to buy care, because their access to the medical and hospital market would be restricted. And this would be most true for the richest consumers. If there were a move to open up the best hospitals and the best surgeons to the public on the basis of need rather than on the basis of the ability to purchase care, the only possible result would be to reduce their access to the market, unless the supply of manpower, beds, and machines were expanded to the point where all, regardless of income, had access to equivalent care. That, of course, would be enormously expensive.

For this reason, intrinsically related to the class structure of American society, the vision of merging the two systems—having only one set of offices, clinics, hospitals, beds, wards—is undoubtedly utopian. The symbiosis of upper middle-class consumers of health care, their private physicians, and their voluntary hospitals, constitutes a coalition of interest groups too strong to be defeated by hospital reorganization, comprehensive health planning legislation, or new neighborhood health centers—if the goal is equality of health care.

Given a system which cannot provide decent care for all because of the domination by the private sector, and thus a continuing "crisis," there is increasing pressure upon government to step in. But, again, because of the dominance of the private sector, government cannot act in a way which could change the system without altering the basic principle of private control over the major resources of the society.

Thus, the health system exhibits a continuous contradiction between the expectations of the people for decent health care, the impossibility of the private sector to provide decent and *equal* health care for all, and the impossibility of the public sector to compensate for the inadequacies of the private sector.

Conclusions

To summarize and conclude the argument, the "crisis" of health care is *not* a result of the necessary competition of diverse interests, groups, and providers in a pluralistic and competitive health economy, nor a result of bureaucratic inefficiencies to be corrected by yet more layers of administration established by government policy. Rather, the conflicts between the professional monopolists—seeking to erect barriers to protect their control over research, teaching, and care—and the corporate rationalizers—seeking to extend their control over the organization of services—account for many of the aspects of health care summarized above.

These conflicts stem, in turn, from a fundamental contradiction in modern health care between the character of the technology of health care and the private appropriation of the power and resources involved. Health care, from the point of view of the most advanced technology, is a complex division of labor, requiring highly specialized knowledge at some points, routine screening at others, highly personalized individual care at still others. The integration of all aspects of the health care system—preventive care, outpatient checkups, routine treatment for specific minor illnesses, specialized treatment for rare diseases requiring expensive machines, long-term care for chronic conditions—would require the defeat or consolidation of the social power that has been appropriated by various discrete interest groups and that preserves existing allocations of social values and resources. Government is not an independent power standing above and beyond the competing interest groups.

An institutional and class structure creates and sustains the power of the professional monopolists and the corporate rationalizers. Dynamics are likely to continue in the direction proposed by the latter coalition. Change is not likely without the presence of a social and political movement which rejects the legitimacy of the economic and social base of pluralist politics.

Acknowledgments

This paper was prepared under a grant to the Center for Policy Research, New York, from the National Center for Health Research and Development, National Institute of Mental Health. I am indebted to the Center for Policy Research for providing research facilities, and particularly for making it possible for Ann Wallace to serve as my research associate during 1970–71.

I wish to thank the National Conference of Social Welfare for permission to use part of an earlier version which appeared in *The Social Welfare Forum* (New York: Columbia University Press, 1971).

Too many friends and colleagues have commented on the paper by this time to allow their names to be mentioned here, but I hope they will recognize their impact on the final version and realize that their sometimes severe criticisms have been appreciated if not always heeded.

References and Notes

1. For a collation of a wide variety of health statistics, see the Committee on Ways and Means, U.S. House of Representatives, *Basic Facts on the Health Industry* (Washington, D.C.: U.S. Government Printing Office, June 28, 1971).

2. *Medical Care for the American People*, the final report of the Committee on the Costs of Medical Care, adopted October 31, 1932. (Reprinted, 1970, by the U.S. Department of Health, Education and Welfare.)

3. Sumner N. Rosen, "Change and Resistance to Change," *Social Policy* 1 (January/ February 1971):4.

4. Eli Ginzberg et al., *Urban Health Services* (New York: Columbia University Press, 1971), p. 224.

5. Robert S. Lynd, *Knowledge for What?* (Princeton: Princeton University Press, 1939).

6. Harry Schwartz, "Health Care in America: A Heretical Diagnosis," *Saturday Review*, 14 August 1971, pp. 14–17, 55; and Milton I. Roemer, "Nationalized Medicine for America," *Trans-Action*, September 1971, pp. 31–36. These articles merely provide concrete illustrations of certain points, and it cannot be assumed that either man holds any views which I summarize under the general categories except those specifically quoted.

7. Schwartz, op. cit., p. 55.

8. Roemer, op. cit., p. 36.

9. Ibid., p. 34.

10. Ibid., p. 36.

11. See Sidney Garfield, "The Delivery of Medical Care," *Scientific American* 222 (April 1970): 15–23, for another model along these lines, which is criticized by Schwartz, op. cit.

12. Schwartz, op. cit., p. 55.

13. I assume also that there is a reasonably high correlation between ideologies and personal incentives of doctors, researchers, administrators, and the organizational interests of the medical profession, hospitals, or public health associations. That is, there is a high probability that elites will take a public position consistent with the interests of their organization. Career incentives probably require that collective myths be publicly sustained, even if there is considerable private cynicism or disbelief. More detailed analyses of particular events and conflicts would require taking into account contradictions and discrepancies between ideology, personal incentives, and organizational interests.

    A further distinction can also be drawn between the objective interests of an individual or group (the consequences of certain policies) and its subjective interests (beliefs about those consequences). A group may be affected in important ways by the operations of an institution, but its members may not be conscious of those consequences and thus may not act either to defend themselves or to change the structure which produces the consequences. Or even if conscious of the consequences, the members may be unwilling or unable to act for a variety of reasons. See Isaac D. Balbus, "The Concept of Interest in Pluralist and Marxian Analysis," *Politics and Society* 1 (February 1971): 151–177, for a recent discussion of this point, and for an earlier but similar statement, Harry Eckstein, *Pressure Group Politics: The Case of the British Medical Association* (Stanford: Stanford University Press, 1960), pp. 9–12.

14. I am indebted to Dr. Joel Hoffman for some of these points.

15. For a content analysis and evaluation of seven of the some fifteen such reports dealing with health care in New York City between 1950 and 1971, see Robert R. Alford, *Interorganizational Outputs: Case Studies of Health Care in New York City* (New York: Center for Policy Research, 1972).

16. See the "Report of the Commission on Health Services of the City of New York," July 20, 1960.

17. See the report and staff studies of the Commission on the Delivery of Personal Health Services, *Community Health Services for New York City* (New York: Frederick A. Praeger, 1969). The report was officially released on December 19, 1967.

18. "Report of the Task Force on Medicaid and Related Programs," U.S. Department of Health, Education and Welfare (Washington, D.C.: U.S. Government Printing Office, June 29, 1970), cited henceforth as "Task Force."

19. Quoted in Herman M. Somers and Anne R. Somers, *Medicare and the Hospitals: Issues and Prospects* (Washington, D.C.: The Brookings Institution, 1967), p. 136.

20. See the "Preliminary Report of the Governor's Steering Committee on Social Problems on Health and Hospital Services and Costs," April 15, 1971, henceforth referred to as "Preliminary Report."

21. Ibid., p. 12.

22. Ibid., p. 14.

23. Ibid., p. 22.

24. Ibid., p. 21.

25. Ibid., p. 13.

26. Ibid., pp. 8, 15.

27. Ibid., p. 41.

28. See Eliot Freidson, *Professional Dominance* (New York: Aldine, 1971), for a critique of the professional division of labor in health care.

29. "Preliminary Report," op. cit., pp. 18, 64.

30. Ibid., p. 38.

31. Ibid., p. 64.

32. Ibid., p. 65.

33. Ibid., p. 23.

34. Ibid., p. 57.

35. Ibid., p. 76.

36. Ibid., pp. 57–58.

37. Ibid., p. 52.

38. Ibid., p. 54.

39. Ibid., p. 68.

40. Ibid., p. 70.

41. Ibid., p. 82.

42. Ibid., p. 72.

43. Michael M. Davis and C. Rufus Rorem, *Crisis in Hospital Finance* (Chicago: University of Chicago Press, 1932), p. 76.

44. Michael M. Davis, *Medical Care for Tomorrow* (New York: Harper and Brothers, 1955), p. 34.

45. Ibid., p. 35.

46. Martin Luther King Neighborhood Health Center, New York City, *Annual Report*, 31 December 1969, p. 15.

47. Ibid., p. 14.

48. The same problems plague the "free-clinic" movement as well. Sponsorship of a neighborhood health center in a poor area with few health facilities thus has little to do with the structural causes of its failure to become a long-range solution. See, for example, Health-PAC *Bulletin*, no. 34, October 1971.

49. Charles M. Brecher and Miriam Ostow, "Ambulatory Services," in Ginzberg et al., op. cit., pp. 155–157.

50. *Federal Role in Health,* report of the Subcommittee on Executive Reorganization and Government Research, Committee on Government Operations, U.S. Senate, 91st Cong., 2d sess., Rept. 92–809 (Washington, D.C.: U.S. Government Printing Office, 1970), pp. 25–26.

51. Ibid., pp. 18–19.

52. "Task Force," op. cit., p. 29.

53. "Preliminary Report," op. cit., p. 16.

54. Ibid., p. 17.

55. Ibid., p. 33.

56. Ibid., p. 17.

57. David Mechanic, reivew of Barbara Ehrenreich and John Ehrenreich, *The American Health Empire: Power, Profits, and Politics,* and Selig Greenberg, *The Quality of Mercy,* in *Science* 172 (14 May 1971): 701–703.

58. Robert H. Connery et al., *The Politics of Mental Health: Organizing Community Mental Health in Metropolitan Areas* (New York: Columbia University Press, 1968), p. 501

59. "Preliminary Report," op. cit., p. 33.

60. "Task Force," op. cit., p. 29.

61. See Murray Edelman, *The Symbolic Uses of Politics* (Urbana: University of Illinois Press, 1964), and by the same author, *Politics as Symbolic Action: Mass Arousal and Quiescence* (Chicago: Markham Publishing Co., 1971), for an elaboration of this point.

62. I am indebted to Jonathan Cole for suggesting this possibility to me.

63. See Richard D. Alba, "Who Governs—The Power Elite? It's All in How You Define It," in *The Human Factor* (Journal of the Graduate Sociology Student Union, Columbia University) 10 (Spring 1971): 27–39, for an elaboration of this point. Although it may be obvious, it should perhaps be made more explicit that my position here directly contradicts those who assert that power is seen or manifest only in instances of conflict, and that assessment of who wins in such conflicts is an adequate measure of power.

64. "Report of the National Advisory Commission on Health Manpower," 2 vols. (Washington, D.C.: U.S. Government Printing Office, 1967), 1:4.

65. Merwyn R. Greenlick, "Imperatives of Health Services Research," *Health Services Research,* 4 (Winter 1969): 259.

66. See Barbara Ehrenreich and John Ehrenreich, *The American Health Empire: Power, Profits and Politics* (New York: Vintage Books, 1971), a publication of the activist New York group Health-PAC, for a similar perspective, although the authors are more optimistic about the prospects for and consequences of militant community action isolated from broader movements than my argument would lead me to be. Michael Halberstam, "Liberal Thought, Radical Theory, and Medical Practice," *The New England Journal of Medicine* 284 (27 May 1971): 1180–1185, criticizes the "radical" position on health care for essentially accepting the position I have called "bureaucratic reform." Interestingly, this criticism would apply also to the proposals advanced by Robb Burlage, one of the founders of Health-PAC. (See his *New York City's Municipal Hospitals: A Policy Review* [Washington, D.C.: Institute for Policy Studies, 1967].) Halberstam, an M.D. himself, stresses the importance of reducing alienation and depersonalization and believes that only committed individual responsibility to a patient by a health professional can provide such personalized care. In this respect the "radical" position exhibits a curious schizophrenia between a faith in the potential rationality of large-scale organization and a faith in the redeeming power of community control. Perhaps the two can be reconciled, but there have been few serious efforts to think through the problem.

67. See Edmund O. Rothschild, "The Level of Health Care in Municipal Hospitals Is Shocking," *New York Times*, 27 November 1971, p. 131, for the most recent surfacing of the same old situation in the New York City hospitals, allegedly to be cured by the bureaucratic reforms recommended by the Piel Commission (op. cit.), including the Corporation. Rothschild was at the time he wrote the article an attending physician at Memorial Hospital for Cancer and a member of the board of directors of the Corporation.
68. Ginzberg et al., op. cit., p. 226.
69. Ibid.

28

Can Health Be Planned?

Aaron Wildavsky

Mother was right! You should eat a good breakfast every day; you shouldn't smoke and you shouldn't drink; you should sleep seven or eight hours a day and not four or fourteen; and you shouldn't worry because it's bad for you. The rich person who does all these things is likely to be slightly healthier than the poor person who does them all, but the poor one who does not do all or most will be much healthier than the rich one who does half or less. The moral of this story is not surprising: health is a product of who we are—our genetic inheritance—and how we live—the air we breathe, the food we eat, the exercise we don't get—not how often we see a doctor.

Evidently what is euphemistically called the delivery of health services (as if the welcome wagon lady were to drive up and present people with packages of health) must be radically reevaluated. We are not talking about peripheral or infrequent aspects of human behavior. We are talking about some of the most deeply rooted and often experienced aspects of human life—what one eats, how often and how much; how long, how regularly and how peacefully one sleeps; whether one smokes or drinks and how much; even the whole question of personality. Delivering health, then, in the absence of a technological breakthrough (the famous pill that's good for all that ails you and only has to be taken once) is a product of innumerable decisions made on a daily basis. To oversee these decisions would require a larger bureaucracy than anyone has yet conceived and methods of surveillance bigger than big brother. The seat belt buzzer that screeches at us if we do not modify our behavior would be but a mild harbinger of the forces that would have to be brought to bear to improve health habits. When the magnitude of the task is understood—that delivering health involves revolutions in human conduct—it is no wonder that we fail.

Speaking of the delivery of health services is a fundamental misnomer, as if

SOURCE: Michael M. Davis Lecture, Center for Health Administration Studies, Graduate School of Business, University of Chicago, 1976. Reprinted by permission.

defining a (medical) process by its (health) purpose could, by some verbal sleight of hand, guarantee achievement. Health can be delivered only in small part; it must largely be lived.

What can be delivered? Medical services and medicines, although, of course, that is no guarantee they will be used. If medicine can be delivered, however, what is it worth when it gets where it's supposed to go? What, in a word, is the realtionship between medicine and health?

According to *The Great Equation*: Medical Care = Health.[1] But the great equation is wrong. More medical care does not equal better health. The best estimates are that the medical system (doctors, drugs, hospitals) affects only a small proportion of the usual indices for measuring health—whether you live at all (infant mortality); how well you live (days lost due to sickness); how long you live (adult mortality). Health rates are determined by factors over which doctors have little or no control, from individual life style (smoking, exercise, worry) to social conditions (income, eating habits) to the physical environment (air and water quality). Most of the bad things that happen to people are presently beyond the reach of the medical system. In the absence of medical knowledge gained through new research, or of new administrative knowledge to convert common practice into best practice, therefore, current medicine has gone as far as it can. Hence the marginal value of spending one or ten billion additional dollars on medical care in order to improve health would be close to zero.

The fallacy of *The Great Equation* is based on the *Paradox of Time:* past successes lead to future failures. As life expectancy increases and as formerly disabling diseases are conquered, medicine is faced with an older population whose disabilities are more difficult to defeat. Former victims of tuberculosis are today's geriatric problems. Thus time converts one decade's achievements into the next decade's dilemmas.

The Great Equation is rescued by the *Principle of Goal Displacement*, which states that any objectives that cannot be attained will be replaced by ones that can be approximated. Every program needs an opportunity to be successful; if it cannot succeed in terms of its ostensible objectives, its sponsors may shift to goals they can achieve. The process subtly becomes the purpose. The input becomes a surrogate for the output. And that is exactly what has happened as "health" has become equivalent to "equal access" to medicine.

When government goes into public housing, it actually produces apartments; when government goes into health, all it can make available is medicine, which is far from health. But the government can try to equalize access to medicine, whether or not that access is related to improved health. If the question is: "Does health increase with government expenditure on medicine?" the answer is likely to be negative. Just alter the question to: "Has access to medicine been improved by governmental programs?" and the answer is most certainly, though not yet entirely, positive.

Wait a minute, says the medical sociologist, pain is just as real when it's mental as when it's physical. If people want to know somebody loves them, if today they prefer Doctors of Medicine to Doctors of Theology, they are entitled to get what they want. One can always argue that even if the results of medical treatment are illusions, the poor are entitled to their share. This is a powerful argument but it neglects the inevitability of rationing.

"No system of care in the world is willing to provide as much care as people will use, and all such systems develop mechanisms that ration . . . services," says David Mechanic, summing up the *Axiom of Allocation*. But why do people want more medical service than any system is willing to provide?

If Medicine is only partially and imperfectly related to health, it follows that doctor and patient often must be uncertain as to what is wrong or what to do about it. Otherwise medicine would be perfectly related to health and there would be no health problem, or it would be quite different: health rates would be on one side and health resources on the other. Costs and benefits could be neatly compared. But they can't because knowledge is often lacking on how to produce the desired benefits. Uncertainty exists because medicine is a quasi-science—more science than, say, political science, less so than physics. How participants in the medical system resolve their uncertainties matters a great deal.

The *Medical Uncertainty Principle* states there is always one more thing that might be done—another consultation, a new drug, a different treatment. Uncertainty is resolved by doing more, the patient by requesting and the doctor by ordering, more service. A simple rule for resolving patient uncertainty is for the patient to seek care up to the level of his insurance or subsidy. If everyone uses all the care he can, total costs will rise; but the individual has so little control over the total that he does not appreciate the connection between his individual choice and the collective result. A corresponding phenomenon occurs among doctors. They can resolve uncertainty by prescribing up to the level of the patient's insurance or subsidy, a rule reinforced by the high cost of malpractice. The patient is anxious, the doctor insecure; this combination is unbeatable unless the irresistible force meets the immovable object—the *Medical Identity*.

This law states that use is limited by availability. Only so much can be gotten out of so much. If *Medical Uncertainty* suggests that existing services will be used, the Identity reminds us to add the words "up to the available supply." That supply is primarily doctors, who advise on the kind of care to be sought, the number of hospital beds (only one person in a bed at a time in our culture), and the number of patients making demands. Considering only his own desire to call upon medical services in time of need, each individual wants to maximize supply. For this reason expenditures on medical care are always larger than any estimate of the social benefit received. Now we can understand, by combining into one law the previous principles and identity, why costs rise so far and so fast.

The Law of Medical Money is that expenditures rise to the level of insurance and subsidy. The medical system absorbs all inputs. Broadly speaking, payments will equal the total of all private insurance and government subsidy. Since these resources expand faster than the factors of production, prices rise.

What process ultimately limits medical costs? If the *Law of Medical Money* predicts that expenditures will increase to the level of available funds, then that level must be limited to keep costs down. Insurance may stop increasing when out-of-pocket payments exceed the growth in the standard of living, so that individuals are not willing to buy more. Subsidy may hold steady when government wants to spend more on other things or to keep its total tax take down. Expenditures will be limited when either individuals or governments reduce their inputs into medicine. The fact that both lack incentive to reduce inputs is responsible for creating the sense of crisis over health policy.

Surveys show that more than three-quarters of the population are satisfied with their medical care. Every subgroup in the population is healthier than it was in past decades: rich and poor, black and white, now see doctors about the same number of times a year. The vast majority are generally satisfied but they specifically wish medical care didn't cost so much and they would like to be more certain of contact with their own doctor. So far as the people are concerned, then, the basic problems are cost and access.

But how can larger proportions of people in need of medicine be getting it at the same time as there is universally agreed to be a crisis in health care? The "bads" we face are a direct consequence of the "goods" we have tried to accomplish. Medicaid for the poor and Medicare for the elderly have increased use of the medical system, as they were intended to do, thus making it more crowded and, according to the *Law of Medical Money*, more expensive. Governments are faced with phenomenal expediture increases. Administrators alternately fear charges of incompetence in restraining real financial abuse and niggardliness toward the needy. Doctors fear federal control because efforts to lower costs lead to more stringent regulations. The proliferation of forms makes them feel like bureaucrats; the profusion of review committees threatens to keep them permanently on trial. New complaints increase faster than old ones can be remedied. If money is a barrier to medicine, the system is discriminatory. If money is no barrier, the system gets overcrowded. If everyone is insured, costs rise to the level of the insurance. If many remain underinsured, their income falls to the level of the disaster that awaits them. The better government tries to be, it seems, the worse it is criticized. The more we-the-people do collectively, the less we like it individually. Why can't we break out of this bind?

Basically there are two sites for relating cost to quality, that is, for measuring needs, which may be infinite, against resources, which are limited. One is at the level of the individual and the other at the level of the collectivity. By comparing individual desires with personal resources, through the private market, the individual internalizes an informal cost-effective analysis. Other valued objects—say, a vacation—might compete with medicine, thus reducing the inputs into (and the total expenditures of) the medical system. Even if apparently knowledgeable doctors make consumption decisions for evidently ignorant patients, they would both have to consider their joint limits of time to spend on medicine versus limits of income to support it. This creative tension may also be had at the collective level—a tension between some public services like medicine, and others like welfare, a tension between the resources left in private hands and those devoted to the public sector. If all health expenditures were shifted to the central government, it would be so large—well over a hundred billion dollars—that government would be motivated to reduce its inputs. And once government set its contribution, there would have to be real resource allocation because it would no longer be possible to shift costs to other parties; the "buck" would stop with the federal government because its appropriation would be all the medical system could spend. The fatal defect of the mixed (public and private) system, a defect that undermines the worth of its otherwise valuable pluralism, is that it does not impose sufficient discipline either at the individual or at the collective level. The individual need not face his full costs and the government does not carry the entire burden of expenditure.

But we-the-people are not willing to have either a purely private or a gigantic governmental medical system. To our credit, we will no longer allow money to be the main mechanism of access to medicine. Because of our desirable devotion to freedom of choice, we will not forbid the private practice of medicine. Thus a mixed system is inevitable. Truly it reflects our willingness to embrace contradictions: more medicine at lower costs and higher quality. We-the-people call the tune, but we are not willing to pay the piper. That is why we insist government do more, but when it does, we like it less.

What else can government do that it has not yet done? Send our medical problem children on a visit to distant relatives by turning the problem (though not, of course, the money) over to regional or local authorities. As the old joke has it, "Let his mother worry." Does this approach appear flippant? Don't worry. We have a plan.

Planning is the ability to control the future through present acts; the more future consequences one controls, the more one can be said to have planned effectively.[2] control of the future requires knowledge (so one knows what one is doing) and power (so one can compel others to do what one wishes). But there does not have to be a plan to have planning. Any process of decision that effects behavior whether it be a market or an administrative mechanism, may be thought of as a plan, insofar as it provides incentives for generating one sort of future behavior rather than another. Normally, the planners problem is that they lack both power and knowledge; they cannot control the behavior of others and, if they could, the desired consequences would not ensue. When knowledge is missing and power is absent, planning becomes a word for the things we would like to do but do not know how to do or are unable to get others to do. Planning need not be a simple solution; it can be, and often is, a convoluted way of restating the problem: Can we increase quantity and quality of medical services while decreasing costs? The answer is "we can't," as the National Health Planning and Resources Development Act of 1974, establishing health system agencies (HSAs), will prove once again.

The main power of some two hundred HSAs now being established is negative: by refusing to approve certificates of need (or otherwise objecting), HSAs can delay or prevent the construction of regional medical facilities and therefore the provision of medical services. Toward this end, HSAs are given administrative funds of their own and a local power base, in that their membership must comprise at least one-third of medical providers and perhaps a half of consumer representatives.

The Act of 1974 is a plan in that it creates incentives encouraging certain types of behavior. But the plan is perverse. HSAs are mandated to reduce costs and improve the delivery of health services. They will actually increase costs and transfer ineffective service delivery from the have-littles to have-nots. Why? Because they do nothing to affect the law of medical money—that expenditures and costs rise to the level of insurance and subsidy; on the contrary, they enhance the force of that law by creating incentives to increase rather than to decrease use of medical resources. Every decision they make will be paid for elsewhere by someones else—patients, insurance companies, taxpayers. No actors will limit inputs into the medical system because they are not in charge of any fixed sum of money that would have to be allocated. All will continue to make internal decisions, secure in the knowledge that the costs they generate will ultimately be passed on to others and that these others, because costs are so widely diffused over so many people, will lack sufficient under- standing and interest in these decisions to exert a restraining influence.

HSAs will immediately espouse the doctrine of the three increases—more professionals, more lawyers, more data. It is self-evident that establishment of HSAs will lead to an enormous increase in demand for health professionals, thereby bidding up their price. As they have in all other major policy initia- tives in recent decades, lawyers will be involved in greater numbers and with enhanced authority in order to straighten out conflicts among previous acts and among new regulations, particularly criteria and procedural safeguards made more complex by interaction with various private and public agencies at different levels of government. HSA lawyers will generate countervailing action on the part of pro- viders and consumers, thus making more work for all. What will they produce? More data. There will be vast proliferation of data on efforts, because that is what will be produced, but not, of course, on effects, because there won't be any, at least not relating to changes in health rates. Like the Humpty Dumptys they resemble, HSAs cannot put the great equation—medical care equals health—back together again. To do that they would have to do less, but they are designed to do more.

In the beginning, one can imagine, various providers will be directed to join with their neighbors in combining facilities that are regarded to be in oversupply. The HSAs will issue orders but these orders will not be obeyed. HSAs can say "no" but they cannot mandate "yes." They cannot command, so they will have to bargain. What will they give up to get what they want? The answer is the same as that given to investors who want to reduce their risks—other peoples' money. HSAs will, in effect, levy a toll on taxpayers and holders of medical insurance policies who will, "in real life," pay for the increased availability and/or use of medical goods and services by other people.

The self-evident fact that administrative expenses will increase is not the main reason for expecting a substantial rise in individual costs and total system expendi- tures. For this conclusion my case rests on the incentives HSAs have for resolving internal differences by the time-honored political method of log-rolling (or, you scratch my back and I'll scratch yours). If there were a fixed sum to distribute among applicants, of course, more for one would mean less for another. But since there is not, the interests of the main parties will lead them to resolve their differences by providing more rather than less largesse.

First the providers. It will be difficult for providers of medical services to maintain a united front if resources like beds are taken away from some and given to (or left with) others. They will find a better way of solving this problem by trading beds for machines and other facilities. I don't know how many CATs (Computerized Axial Tomography) equal how many beds or kidney machines or heart units, but talented professionals will find a common currency as well as a common language. The costs will be spread around by increasing bed rates, by the usual practice of cross-subsidization in which simpler forms of surgery pay for the more complex kinds, and by finding more treatments for which these devices are relevant. Despite innumerable administrative controls, cost overruns will not be curtailed because somebody else has to pick up the tab.

Next the consumers. They believe the people they represent need health services and that health delivery could certainly be improved. With this providers will agree. But consumers are not likely to have accurate cost information or know how to interpret it or, worst of all, feel its impact directly on themselves. Faced with a choice between fighting for lower costs for all, with its implication of lesser services for their clients, and agreeing to support superior services for themselves without worrying about others, they will invariably choose the path of least resistance. They will negotiate with providers for larger packages in which their constituents can get more services, and perhaps jobs as well, in return for going along with the latest provider interests. Why should producer and consumer conflict when they can coalesce by giving every someone something: you co-opt me and I'll co-opt you and we will all co-opt each other.

Alain Enthoven tells an instructive story:

> . . . about a man who left the presidency of a medical products company to become a professor of management. One day he decided it would be fun to see some of his old associates from business days, so he organized a lunch at a nice restaurant. At the end of the meal, from habit, he reached for the check, but his successor as company president took it and said, "Let me have it; for us it's a deductible expense and the government will pay half of it through reduced corporate profits tax." But the local hospital administrator took it out of his hand saying, "No, let me take it; this will be an allowable conference expense, and we can put the whole thing in our overhead and get it back from Blue Cross and Medicare." But his neighbor took the check from him and said, "Let me have it; after all, I'm a cost-plus contractor to the government and not only will we get the cost reimbursed, but we'll get a fee on top of it." But the fifth man at the table got the check: "Look friends, I'm from a regulated industry, and we're about to go in for a rate increase. If I can put this lunch in our cost base, it will help justify a higher rate not only this year, but projected on out into the future."[3]

The moral of the story is that regulation is taxation, taxation with representation to be sure, but still a hidden form of taxation.

Consider the HSAs combination of log-rolling with barriers to entry. Naturally, HSAs will be composed of providers and consumers who are already there. They can be expected to give future providers and consumers a hard time. The most likely loser will be new proponents of health maintenance organizations. Either they will be denied certificates of need, because everything that needs to be done is ostensibly being done by those who are already there, or, if HMOs cannot be resisted, they will be added on to what already exists. Every innovation that challenges existing interests will either be attacked as unnecessary or added on, to maintain harmony. One cannot say exactly what will happen except that we know in advance the one important thing that will not happen: old services will not give way to new ones.

The trouble with failure is that it can happen to anyone. If failure by medical providers were possible before, with old facilities dying when they had outlived their usefulness, it will no longer be permitted. Providers will understand their mutual interest in insuring against failure by agreeing to bail out each other at public expense. Medical providers and their consumer customers may not be able to improve mortality rates of the population but they will certainly be able to keep each other alive.

Who wins is obvious, at least in the short run. But who loses? The answer depends on who is least able (a) to pass on costs or (b) to lobby effectively for subsidy. To no one's great surprise, the near-poor will get it in the neck again. The upper class will find ways to reduce taxes and the middle class will improve their insurance; the poor will get a superior subsidy. Both the top and the bottom exert influence in different ways, but they are influential. Only the near-poor lack either a governmentally protected program or market leverage. Hence HSAs will transfer income from the near-poor to the officially designated poor.[4]

Presumably HSAs are designed to take the heat off the central government—don't harass your Congressman, picket your local HSA instead!—by adopting the time-honored method of diffusing conflict over large numbers of areas. Presumably, this intended effect will occur for a while if only because the confusion will be so great, the actors so numerous, the consequences so elusive, that most energies will be absorbed in figuring out whether HSAs work. When it becomes clear that they don't and won't, the conclusion is unlikely to be that collective regulation is bad but that private or pluralistic medicine has failed. By loading the medical market with the burden of regulation—capture by the interests most immediately affected, delay in adaptation to emerging conditions, passing the price of monopoly on to others—it will be condemned for its high cost and lack of responsiveness. The lesson will be that the private market has failed and that only public administration can save us. The lesson should be that doctors should do less and that we-the-people should do more about our own health.

Notes

1. The general theory about health policy presented here (though not the later application to Health System Agencies) is a summary of ideas presented in "Doing Better and Feeling Worse: The Political Pathology of Health Policy" to be published in *Daedalus* and in a volume sponsored by the Rockefeller Foundation, which sponsored my research.
2. This paragraph is adapted from my "If Planning Is Everything, Maybe It's Nothing," *Policy Sciences* 4 (1973): 127–53.
3. Alain C. Enthoven, draft of "National Health Insurance and the Cost of Medical Care," an address to the Detroit Academy of Medicine, May 13, 1975, pp. 10–11.
4. For further findings on how and why the near-poor lose out, see Frank Levy, Arnold Meltsner, and Aaron Wildavsky, *Urban Outcomes* (University of California Press, 1974).

29

Problems and Choices

Victor R. Fuchs

The Problems We Face

In recent years, almost every American family has become acutely aware of the soaring costs of medical care, the difficulties of access to physicians, and the mounting health problems of our society. According to many observers, the U.S. health care system is in "crisis." But a crisis is a turning point, a decisive or crucial point in time. In medicine the crisis is that point in the course of the disease at which the patient is on the verge of either recovering or dying. No such decisive resolution is evident with respect to the problems of health and medical care. Our "sick medical system," to use the headline of numerous magazine and newspaper editorials, is neither about to recover nor to pass away. Instead, the basic problems persist and are likely to persist for some time to come.

What are these problems? Many of them are related to the *cost* of care. Indeed, one close observer of the Washington scene has argued that "the medical 'crisis' . . . is purely and simply a crisis of cost. The inflationary rise in medical costs is the key concern of congressmen and consumers, a fundamental political and economic fact of life for both."[1] Another category of problems concerns *access* to care; while a third major set involves the determinants of *health levels*. Let us look briefly at each of the problems in turn.

Cost

In 1973 Americans spent an average of $450 per person for health care and related activities such as medical education and research. This was almost 8 percent of the GNP (the gross national product is the total value of all goods and services produced in the nation). Twenty years before, health care represented only 4.5 percent of the nation's output, and even as recently as 1962 the proportion was only 5.6 percent. Thus from 1963 to 1973 health expenditures rose at the rate of 10 percent annually while the rest of the economy (as reflected in the GNP) was growing at only 6 to 7 percent.

One often reads or hears that costs have become so high that the average family can no longer pay for health care and that some other way must be found to finance it. This is pure nonsense. The average family will always have to pay its share of the cost one way or the other. Payment may take many forms: fee-for-service, insurance premiums, or taxes. If the system is financed by taxes on business, then people pay indirectly, either through higher prices for the goods and services business produces or through lower wages. True, a highly progressive tax could result in some redistribution of the burden. But given the likely pattern of tax incidence, the only meaningful way to ease the cost burden on the average family is to moderate the increase in total expenditures.

Not only is *average* cost of health care high and growing at a rapid rate, but there is also the problem of *unusual* cost. It is clear that in any particular year a relatively small number of families make extensive use of health services, and if payment is on a fee-for-service basis, the cost to them is exceedingly high. Renal dialysis for one individual, for instance, may cost ten thousand dollars a year; some surgical procedures cost even more. But the remedy for this problem has been known for a long time—some form of insurance or prepayment. This will not help the *average*-cost problem—indeed, it would aggravate it if insurance were to induce additional utilization—but it does take care of those individuals who require unusually large amounts of care.

Note that these two cost problems have little to do with one another. If average costs were half their present levels or rising at half their present rate, some families would still experience mammoth medical care bills in any given year. Similarly, even if every family had complete protection against unusual costs through major-risk insurance, the problem of slowing the escalation of rising average costs would remain. They are separate problems and require separate solutions.

Why has average cost grown so rapidly, and what can be done about it? One useful approach is to realize that cost, measured by total expenditures, is equal to the *quantity* of care utilized multiplied by the *price* per "unit" of care. Utilization, measured by number of visits, prescriptions, tests, days in hospital, and the like, depends upon the *health condition* of the population as well as its *propensity to use health services* for any particular health condition. This propensity depends in part on the patient, who, in most instances, must initiate the care process and consent to its continuance. But it also depends on the physician who, because of his presumed superior knowledge, is empowered by law and custom with the authority to make decisions concerning utilization. It is the physician who sends the patient to the hospital and sends him home, who recommends surgery, who orders tests and X rays, and who prescribes drugs.

So much for utilization. What about price? The price of a given "unit" of medical care depends on the relative *productivity* (i.e., output per unit of input) of the labor and capital used to produce it and on the *prices paid* for this labor and capital. Productivity depends on such factors as the appropriateness of the scale and type of organization in question, on the amount of excess capacity, on technological advance, and on the effectiveness of incentives and training. Thus productivity is directly affected if a hospital is either too large or too small to be efficient, or if the community has more hospital beds than it needs, or if there are less expensive ways of performing laboratory tests.

The physician can have considerable influence on productivity because of his broad powers of decision making. For instance, the physician decides how many and what kinds of auxiliary personnel work with him in his practice. And committees of physicians make many of the critical decisions that affect productivity in the hospitals they are affiliated with. The patient can also affect productivity through his cooperation and general behavior. For instance, a patient who gives a physician a full and reliable medical history and who complies with the latter's instructions regarding drugs and diet can contribute substantially to the efficiency of the care he receives. Furthermore, although the prices paid for labor and capital used in health care are largely governed by forces at work in the economy at large, special circumstances within the health field, such as the unionization of hospital employees, can affect wages and thus costs.

Any explanation for the rise in the average cost of health care and any proposal for containing or lowering this cost can be analyzed within the accounting framework just described, for nothing affects cost that does not first affect the health of the population, the propensity of people to use health services, the productivity of the factors of production (labor and capital) used in medical care, or the prices paid for those factors. It should be stressed, however, that this is an *accounting* framework; it cannot provide a behavioral explanation of cost change. That can only come through an analysis of the actual behavior of patients, physicians, hospital administrators, government officals, and other decision makers.

It is not easy to say how much of the increase in cost in the past decade is due to the increased quantity of health care and how much to higher prices. Price should refer to some well-defined unit of service, but in fact the "content" of a physician's visit, or of a day in the hospital, keeps changing over time. The official price index for medical care, which is an average of changes in the price of a hospital day, a physician visit, and other elements of care and is published by the U.S. Bureau of Labor Statistics, shows an annual increase of 5 percent since 1962. This implies that there was also a 5 percent annual increase in *quantity* of these goods and services over the same period (for the sum of the two must equal the 10 percent annual increase in total medical expenditures cited at the beginnning of this section). But because the official price index makes little allowance for changes in health care *quality* (i.e., the effects on health or the amenities associated with care) it may give a misleading picture of the true changes in *quantity*. To the extent that the quality of care has increased, the price index is overstated; if quality has decreased, it is understated.

Part of what we know to be an increase in quantity is due to the growth of population which has been about 1 percent annually since 1962. The balance must reflect either an increased propensity to use health services or adverse changes in the health condition of the population because of pollution, smoking, increased numbers of accidents, and the like.

The price of medical care has been growing more rapidly than the overall price index and at about the same rate as the price index for all services. This reflects higher prices for the inputs used in medical care, particularly the labor of physicians, nurses, and other personnel. It also reflects our inability to increase productivity in health care as rapidly as in the economy as a whole.

Most proposals for medical care reform seek to contain costs, but there are important differences in the strategies proposed for accomplishing this. These strategies, which will be discussed in more detail in subsequent chapters, are introduced briefly here.

The first strategy looks to *changes in supply* to drive down price and ultimately cost. According to this view, a substantial increase in the number of hospitals and physicians would force significant reductions in charges and fees, presumably either by stimulating increases in productivity or decreases in prices and wages.

A second strategy would reduce utilization by *improving the health* of the population. Advocates of this approach argue that more preventive medicine, health education, and environmental improvements could reduce the need for hospitals, physicians, and drugs.

A third approach would depend upon administrative *controls and planning* to contain costs. Such devices as hospital planning councils, utilization review committees, and drug formularies fall into this category, as do more direct interventions such as wage and price ceilings. Some controls are intended to reduce utilization, others to improve productivity, and still others to limit prices paid to the factors of production.

A fourth strategy attempts to induce *greater cost-consciousness* in consumers by modifying health insurance to include substantial deductibles (amounts the patient must pay before the insurance becomes effective) and coinsurance (partial payment by the patient after the insurance becomes effective). The goal here is to reduce the propensity to use health services for any given health condition, and also to increase the consumer's incentive to maintain his health.

Finally, there are those who look to the *physician to control costs*; changing the method of compensation, according to this strategy, would give him a strong incentive to do so. For instance, it is argued that payment on a capitation[2] basis, rather than fee-for-service, would reduce the number of unnecessary operations.

In order to evaluate these diverse strategies, one needs a good understanding of the determinants of health and of the workings of the health care market. My own view is that decentralized administrative controls and modification of patient behavior both have something to contribute, but I would put greatest emphasis on the physician. My reasons for emphasizing the physician as the key to controlling costs are developed in subsequent chapters.

Access

The problems of access to health care fall into two main categories, which may be labeled "special" and "general." The special problems of access are those faced by particular groups in society—the poor, the ghetto dwellers, and the rural population. The general problem of access is one that is felt even by individuals and families who have enough income or insurance to pay for care and are not disadvantaged by reason of location or race. For them the problem is simply to get the kind of care they need when they need it.

The problems the poor face in getting access to medical care are similar to those they face in obtaining other goods and services. To be poor is, by definition, to have less of the good things produced by society; if they did not have less they would not be poor. There are many people, however, who argue that medical care is special, that access to care is a "right" and should not be dependent upon income. Opposed to this is the view that if one wishes to help the poor, the best way to do so is to give them more purchasing power and let *them* decide how they want to spend it. According to this view, it makes little sense to use hard-to-raise tax money to lift the poor up to some arbitrarily high standard of medical care while they have grievous deficiencies in housing, schooling, and other aspects of a good life. A more systematic look at this question is presented later in this chapter.

Poverty explains part of the access problem for the rural population, but not all of it. Even in rural areas with substantial purchasing power, the physician-population ratio is typically much lower than in the cities. This is true not only in the United States but in almost every country in the world. It is true in Israel, which has a very large supply of physicians because of immigration; it is true in Sweden, which is frequently said to have a model health care system; it is even true in the Soviet Union, where physicians are government employees and supposedly must practice wherever they are sent.

The reason for the access problem in rural areas is very clear: physicians prefer to practice in highly urbanized areas. They do so partly for professional reasons such as the desire to practice with colleagues, use up-to-date facilities, and concentrate on a specialty. They also generally prefer the educational, cultural, and recreational facilities available for themselves and their families in metropolitan areas.

What, if anything, to do about the rural access problem is less clear. Should physicians be forced to go to rural areas? Should they be bribed to go there with very high incomes financed by taxes on citydwellers? One popular proposal is to subsidize medical education on condition that the student promise to practice in a rural area. In the absence of any demonstration that health is worse in rural areas, however, I do not see any strong case for adopting special measures aimed solely at changing physicians' location decisions. If, however, such decisions were to be influenced by broader programs aimed at rural poverty, or at a wider dispersion of the population, that would be a different matter.

The access problem for blacks and some other minority groups is largely a question of poverty. Many members of minority groups with adequate incomes and insurance do not experience any unique problems with respect to health care. Where discrimination in housing is severe, however, and middle- and upper-income blacks are locked into low-income ghettos, they probably will experience access problems because the supply of services is geared to the low average level of income in the area. The best solution for this problem is to eliminate discrimination in housing. Another distinct problem arises when blacks (or Chicanos or Indians) prefer to be treated by other blacks (or Chicanos or Indians); this can only be solved by increasing the number of health professionals from these minority groups.

The *general* problem of access . . . is a complex phenomenon that in the broadest sense represents a failure of the medical care market to match supply and demand. While the term *general problem* implies that it is experienced by the population generally and not only by particular groups, it must not be thought that the problem is general in the sense of applying to all kinds of physicians. . . . There are actually substantial surpluses of some types of physician specialists, such as surgeons. The general problem of access exists mainly with respect to primary care, emergency care, home care, and care outside customary working hours. And so the solution . . . does not lie in simply increasing the number of physicians.

Health Levels

Concern about health levels in the United States primarily takes two forms. First, there is concern that health levels in this country are not as high as in many other developed nations. The principal evidence for this is found in comparisons of age-specific death rates and of life expectancies (life expectancy is a summary measure of these death rates). The excess of death rates in the United States over those elsewhere is, in some cases, striking. For instance, the death rate for males ages 45 to 54 is almost double the Swedish rate. Of every hundred males in the United States who turn 45, only ninety will see their fifty-fifth birthday. In Sweden, ninety-five will survive the decade. Granted, there are many dimensions of health besides mortality, but the lack of adequate measures precludes their use for comparisons among populations. In any case, there seems little reason to believe that examination of these other dimensions would reverse conclusions based on mortality. Most deaths, after all, are preceded by illness, either physical or mental.

Infant mortality is another frequently used index of health. This indicator usually falls as income rises, but the United States, which has the highest per capita income in the world, does not have the lowest infant death rate. Indeed, the rate in this country is one-third higher than in the Scandinavian countries and the Netherlands.

The other principal cause for concern regarding health levels is that they vary greatly among different groups in the United States. For instance, the disparity between whites and blacks is very great. Black infant mortality in this country is almost double the white rate, and black females ages 40–44 have two-and-one-half times the death rate of their white counterparts. Other minority groups (e.g., the Indians) also have very poor health levels, while still others, such as the Japanese and the Mormons, enjoy levels that are considerably above the national average.

The most important thing to realize about such differences in health levels is that they are usually *not* related in any important degree to differences in medical care. Over time the introduction of new medical technology has had a significant impact on health, but when we examine differences among populations at a given moment in time, other socioeconomic and cultural variables are now much more important than differences in the quantity or quality of medical care.

Medical advances beginning in the 1930s and extending through the late 1950s brought about significant improvements in health, especially through the control of infectious diseases. These advances have been widely diffused among and within all developed countries and even some of the less developed ones. For more than a decade, however, the impact of new medical discoveries on overall mortality has been slight; indeed, the death rate for U.S. males at most ages, except the very young and the very old, has actually been rising. The chief killers today are heart disease, cancer, and violent deaths from accidents, suicide, and homicide. The behavioral component in all these causes is very large, and until now medical care has not been very successful in altering behavior.

The preceding discussion of the problems of cost, access to medical care, and health levels indicates why there is so much concern about health care and so many proposals for changes in its organization and financing. In appraising such proposals it is useful to keep in mind the central economic problem of allocating scarce resources among competing needs. The promises of the planners and the panaceas of the politicians, then, must be seen against the reality of difficult choices.

The Choices We Must Make

An appreciation of the inevitability of choice is necessary before one can begin to make intelligent plans for health-care policy, but more than that is required. Some grasp of the variety of levels and kinds of choices we make is also essential. All of us, as individuals, are constantly confronted with choices that affect our health. In addition, some choices must be exercised collectively, through government.

Health or Other Goals?

The most basic level of choice is between health and other goals. While social reformers tell us that "health is a right," the realization of that "right" is always less than complete because some of the resources that could be used for health are allocated to other purposes. This is true in all countries regardless of economic system, regardless of the way medical care is organized, and regardless of the level of affluence. It is true in the communist Soviet Union and in welfare-state Sweden, as well as in our own capitalist society. No country is as healthy as it could be; no country does as much for the sick as it is technically capable of doing.

The constraints imposed by resource limitations are manifest not only in the absence of amenities, delays in receipt of care, and minor inconveniences; they also result in loss of life. The grim fact is that no nation is wealthy enough to avoid all avoidable deaths. The truth of this proposition is seen most clearly in the case of accidental deaths. For instance, a few years ago an airplane crashed in West Virginia with great loss of life. Upon investigation it was found that the crash could have been avoided if the airport had been properly equipped with an electronic instrument landing device. It was further found that the airport was fully aware of this deficiency and that a recommendation for installation of such equipment had been made several months before the crash—and turned down because it was decided that the cost was too high.

Traffic accidents take more than fifty thousand lives each year in the United States, and because so many of the victims are young or middle-aged adults,[3] the attendant economic loss is very high. As a first approximation, the relative economic cost of death can be estimated from the discounted future earnings of the deceased if he had lived. According to such calculations, the death of a man at twenty or thirty is far more costly than death at seventy. Many of these traffic deaths could be prevented, but some of the most effective techniques, such as the elimination of left turns, are extremely expensive to implement. The same is true of deaths from other causes—many of them are preventable if we want to devote resources to that end. The yield may be small, as in the case of a hyperbaric chamber[4] that costs several million dollars and probably saves a few lives each year, but the possibilities for such costly interventions are growing. Current examples include renal dialysis, organ transplants, and open-heart surgery. Within limits set by genetic factors, climate, and other natural forces, every nation chooses its own death rate by its evaluation of health compared with other goals.

But surely health is more important than anything else! Is it? Those who take this position are fond of contrasting our unmet health needs with the money that is "wasted" on cosmetics, cigarettes, pet foods, and the like. "Surely," it is argued, "we can afford better health if we can afford colored telephones." But putting the question in this form is misleading. For one thing, there are other goals, such as justice, beauty, and knowledge, which also clearly remain unfulfilled because of resource limitations. In theory, our society is committed to providing a speedy and fair trial to all persons accused of crimes. "Justice delayed is justice denied." In practice, we know that our judicial system is rife with delays and with pretrial settlements that produce convictions of innocent people and let guilty ones escape with minor punishment. We also know that part of the answer to getting a fairer and more effective judicial system is to devote more resources to it.

What about beauty, natural or manmade? How often do we read that a beautiful stand of trees could be saved if a proposed road were rerouted or some other (expensive) change made? How frequently do we learn that a beautiful new building design has been rejected in favor of a conventional one because of the cost factor? Knowledge also suffers. Anyone who has ever had to meet a budget for an educational or research enterprise knows how resource limitations constrain the pursuit of knowledge.

What about more mundane creature comforts? We may give lip service to the idea that health comes first, but a casual inspection of our everyday behavior with respect to diet, drink, and exercise belies this claim. Most of us could be healthier than we are, but at some cost, either psychic or monetary. Not only is there competition for resources as conventionally measured (i.e., in terms of money), but we are also constantly confronted with choices involving the allocation of our time, energy, and attention. If we are honest with ourselves there can be little doubt that other goals often take precedence over health. If better health is our goal, we can achieve it, but only at some cost.

Stating the problem in this fashion helps to point up the difference between the economist's and the health professional's view of the "optimum" level of health. For the health professional, the "optimum" level is the highest level technically attainable, regardless of the cost of reaching it. The economist is preoccupied with the *social optimum*, however, which he defines as the point at which the value of an additional increment of health exactly equals the cost of the resources required to obtain that increment. For instance, the first few days of hospital stay after major surgery might be extremely valuable for preventing complications and assisting recovery, but at some point the value of each additional day decreases. As soon as the value of an additional day's stay falls below the cost of that day's care, according to the concept of social optimum, the patient should be discharged, even though a longer stay would be desirable if cost were of no concern. The cost reminds us, however, that those resources could be used to satisfy other goals.

The same method of balancing *marginal benefit* and *marginal cost*[5] is equally applicable in choosing the optimum number of tests and X rays, or in planning the size of a public health program, or in making decisions about auto-safety equipment. Indeed, the concept of margin is one of the most fundamental tools in economics. It applies to the behavior of consumers, investors, business firms, or any other participant in economic life. Most decisions involve choosing between a little more or a little less—in other words, comparing the marginal benefit with the marginal cost. The optimum level is where these are equal and the marginal cost is increasing faster (or decreasing slower) than the marginal benefit.

Medical Care or Other Health Programs?

But weighing individual and collective preferences for health against each and every other goal is only the first choice. There is also a range of choices within the health field itself. Assume that we are prepared to devote x amount of resources to health. How much, then, should go for medical care and how much for other programs affecting health, such as pollution control, fluoridation of water, accident prevention, and the like? There is no simple answer, partly because the question has rarely been explicitly asked. In principle, the solution is to be found by applying the economist's rule of "equality at the margin." This means relating the incremental yield of any particular program to the incremental cost of the program and then allocating resources so that the yield per dollar of additional input is the same in all programs.

Expenditures for any type of health-related activity, be it a hyperbaric chamber for a hospital or a rat-control program in the ghetto, presumably have some favorable consequences for health which can be evaluated. It is not easy to measure these consequences, but we could do a lot better than we are doing and thus contribute to more rational decision making.

Note that decisions about expanding or contracting particular programs should be based on their respective *marginal* benefits, not their *average* benefits. Thus, while a particular health program—say, screening women once a year for cervical cancer—may be particularly productive (that is, yield a high average benefit per dollar of cost), it does not necessarily follow that expanding that program twofold—for example, screening women twice a year—will be twice as productive. Some other program—say, an antismoking advertising campaign—might not show as high an average return as the screening program, yet the marginal return to *additional* expenditures might exceed that obtainable from additional cancer screening. In the following hypothetical numerical example, cancer screening has a higher average benefit than the antismoking campaign at every expenditure level,

TABLE 1. Hypothetical Illustration of Distinction between Average and Marginal Benefit

	Expenditures	Value of Benefits	Average Benefit per Dollar of Expenditures	Marginal Benefit per Dollar of Expenditures
	$10,000	$ 50,000	$5.00	
	20,000	80,000	4.00	$3.00
Cancer	30,000	100,000	3.33	2.00
Screening	40,000	120,000	3.00	2.00
Program	50,000	130,000	2.60	1.00
	60,000	135,000	2.25	.50
	$10,000	$ 30,000	$3.00	
	20,000	50,000	2.50	$2.00
Antismoking	30,000	70,000	2.33	2.00
Program	40,000	90,000	2.25	2.00
	50,000	105,000	2.10	1.50
	60,000	115,000	1.92	1.00

but the *incremental* yield from additional expenditures at any level above $40,000 is higher for the antismoking program. Thus if both programs were at the $40,000 level, it would be preferable to expand the second one rather than the first.

An objection frequently raised to such an approach is that "we can't put a price on a human life." One answer to this is that we implicitly put a price on lives whenever we (or our representatives) make decisions about the coverage of a health insurance policy, the installation of a traffic light, the extension of a food stamp program, or innumerable other items. A second answer is that it may be possible to choose from among health programs *without* placing a dollar value on human life; it may be sufficient to compare the marginal yield of different programs in terms of lives saved in order to determine the allocation of resources that yields the more significant social benefits.

Physicians or Other Medical Care Providers?

But that is not the whole story. Even if we could make intelligent choices between medical care and other health-related programs, we would still be faced with a significant range of decisions concerning the best way to provide medical care—that is, the best way to spend the medical care dollar. One of the most important of these decisions . . . concerns the respective roles of physicians and such other medical care providers as physician assistants, nurses, clinicians, midwives, and family-health workers. A related set of decisions concerns the optimal mix between human inputs (whether physicians or others) and physical capital inputs, such as hospitals, X-ray equipment, and computers.

In short, if we are concerned with the best way to produce medical care, we must be aware that the solution to the problem requires more than medical expertise. It requires consideration of the relative prices, of various medical care inputs, and of their contribution (again at the margin) to health. The argument that these inputs must be used in some technologically defined proportions is soundly refuted by the evidence from other countries, where many health systems successfully utilize doctors, nurses, hospital facilities, and other health inputs in proportions that differ strikingly from those used in the United States.

How Much Equality? And How to Achieve It?

One of the major choices any society must make is how far to go in equalizing the access of individuals to goods and services. Insofar as this is a question of social choice, one cannot look to economics for an answer. What economic analysis can do is provide some insights concerning why the distribution of income at any given time is what it is, what policies would alter it and at what cost, and what are the economic consequences of different distributions.

Assuming that some income equalization is desired, how is this to be accomplished? Shall only certain goods and services (say, medical care) be distributed equally, or should incomes be made more equal, leaving individuals to decide how they wish to adjust their spending to take account of their higher (or lower) income?

For any given amount of redistribution the welfare of all households is presumably greatest if there is a general tax on the income of some households and grants of income to others, rather than a tax on particular forms of spending or a subsidy for particular types of consumption. Common sense tells us that if a household is offered a choice of either a hundred dollars in cash or a hundred dollars' worth of health care, it ought to prefer the cash, because it can use the entire sum to buy more health care or health insurance (if that is what it wants) or, as is usually the case, increase consumption of many other commodities as well. By the same reasoning, if a household is offered a choice between paying an additional hundred dollars in income tax or doing without a hundred dollars' worth of health care, it will opt for the general tax on income, and then cut back spending on the goods and services that are, in its opinion, most dispensable.

Despite the obvious logic of the foregoing, many nonpoor seem more willing to support a reduction in inequality in the consumption of particular commodities (medical care is a conspicuous example) than toward a general redistribution of income. In England, for instance, everyone is eligible to use the National Health Service, and the great majority of the population gets all of its care from this tax-financed source. At the same time, there is considerable inequality in other aspects of British life, including education and income distribution in general.

Support for the notion that medical care ought to be available to all, regardless of ability to pay, is growing in the United States. There is, however, also growing recognition of marked disparities in housing, legal services, and other important goods and services. Whether these disparities should be attacked piecemeal or through a general redistribution of income is one of the most difficult questions facing the body politic. . . .

Today or Tomorrow

One of the most important choices every individual and every society has to make is between using existing resources to satisfy current desires or applying them to capital-creating activities in anticipation of future needs. Economists call the former *consumption* and the latter *investment*.

This broad concept of investment should not be confused with the narrow use of the term in financial transactions—e.g., the purchase of stock. Broadly speaking, investment takes place when a tree is planted, when a student goes to school, when you brush your teeth, as well as when you build a house, a factory, or a hospital. Any activity that can be expected to confer future benefits is a form of investment. (To be sure, sometimes a single activity—such as education—will have elements of consumption—that is, provide current satisfaction—along with those of investment.)

Such investment can be in both physical or human capital.[6] Thus health is a form of capital: health is wealth. Investment in health takes many forms. Immunization, annual checkups, exercise, and many other activities have current costs but may yield health benefits in the future. Medical education and medical research, both involving expenditures of billions of dollars annually, are prime examples of investment in the health field that results in the diversion of resources (physicians and other personnel) from meeting current needs in order to reap future rewards.

How far should we go in providing for tomorrow at the expense of today? As with all economic decisions, price plays a role here, too. Specifically, in making decisions concerning health investments, we must somehow take into account the fact that people discount the future compared with the present. Using the concept of the special kind of price called *rate of interest* or *rate of return* answers that need.

No investment in health is undertaken unless the investor believes it will yield a satisfactory rate of return. Health professionals frequently despair over the failure of some people to invest in their own health; such behavior, they assert, is irrational. But this need not be the case. If a person discounts the future at a high rate, as evidenced by a willingness to pay 20 or 30 percent annual interest for consumer loans or installment credit, it would not be rational for him to make an investment in health that had an implicit return of only 15 percent.

It is abundantly clear that poeple differ in their attitudes toward the future; that is, they have different *rates of time discount*.[7] The reasons for these differences are not known. They may be related to perceptions about how certain the future is, and they may depend upon how strongly rooted is one's sense of the past. Young children, for instance, characteristically live primarily in the present; they lack both a historical perspective and a vision of the future. Thus it is often difficult to get children to undertake some unpleasant task or to refrain from some pleasureable activity for the sake of a beneficial consequence five or ten years away. Some adults, too, set very little store in the future compared with the present; they have a very high rate of time discount.

Most health-related activities—smoking, exercise, diet, periodic checkups and so forth—have consequences which are realized only after long periods of time. One possible reason for the high correlation between an individual's health and the length of his schooling . . . is that attending to one's health and attending school are both aspects of investment in human capital. Thus the same person who has accumulated a great deal of human capital in the form of schooling may, for the same reasons, have made (or had made for him) substantial investments in health.

Your Life or Mine?

Suppose a small private plane crashes in an isolated forest area and no one knows whether the pilot is dead or alive. How much of society's resources will be devoted to searching for him? How much "should" be devoted to the search? If the pilot is a wealthy or prominent man, the search is likely to be longer and more thorough than if he is not. If he is wealthy, his family's command over private resources will make the difference; if he is a prominent government official, it is likely that publicly owned resources will be utilized far more readily than if the pilot were unknown and poor.

We see in this simple example one of the basic dilemmas of modern society. On the one hand, we believe that all people should be treated as equals, especially in matters of life or death. Against this we have what Raymond Aron calls the imperative "to produce as much as possible through mastery of the forces of nature,"[8] a venture requiring differentiation, hierarchy, and inevitably unequal treatment. The problem arises in all types of economic systems, and in all systems the response is likely to be similar.

If the family of a wealthy man wants to devote his (or their) wealth to searching for him, thereby increasing his probability of survival, is there any reason why the rest of society should object? (If the family used their command over resources for some frivolous comsumption, would anyone else be better off?) Suppose, however, that instead of a plan crash the threat of death came from an ordinarily fatal disease? Would the same answers apply? The capacity of medical science to intervene near the point of death is growing rapidly. Such interventions are often extremely costly and have a low probability of long-term success—but sometimes they work. Whose life should be saved? The wealthy man's? The senator's? Society cannot escape this problem any more than it can avoid facing the other choices we have discussed.

A related dilemma concerns the allocation of resources, either for research or care, among different diseases and conditions. The potential for social conflict here is high because the relative importance of different diseases is perceived differentially by groups according to their income level, race, age, location, and other characteristics.

A particularly striking example of this problem is sickle-cell anemia, a disease which in the United States affects primarily blacks. Recently there has been a substantial increase in the amount of funds available for research on this as-yet-incurable disease, primarily as a result of the growing political strength of the black community.

Many other diseases have a particularly high incidence among specific groups. Thus cigarette smokers have a much greater stake in research or services for lung cancer than do nonsmokers. And in the case of occupation-related diseases, the interests of workers and employers directly affected are much greater than those of the general public.

Economics cannot provide final answers to these difficult problems of social priorities, but it can help decision makers think more rationally about them. In allocating funds for medical research, for instance, economic reasoning can tell the decision maker what kind of information he ought to have and how to arrange that information so as to find the probable relative value of various courses of action.

Contrary to the opinion of many medical researchers, the criterion of "scientific merit" is not sufficient to form the basis for a rational allocation of medical research funds. Certainly decision makers should consider the relative importance the scientific community attaches to particular problems. But other kinds of information—such as the number of persons affected by a particular disease, the economic cost of the attendant morbidity[9] and mortality, and the cost of delivering preventive or therapeutic services if research is successful—should also be considered. The last item is particularly important when funding applied as opposed to basic research, because the development of a "cure" that is enormously expensive to implement probably has a low return and creates many serious social problems as well. For example, if a cure for cancer were discovered tomorrow but cost $150,000 per case to implement, the resulting controversies over the method of financing and the selection of cases to be cured might be so great as to make one view the cure as a mixed blessing.

The Jungle or the Zoo?

One of the central choices of our time, in health as in other areas, is finding the proper balance between individual (personal) and collective (social) responsibility. If too much weight is given to the former, we come close to recreating the "jungle"—with all the freedom and all the insecurity that the jungle implies. On the other hand, emphasizing social responsibility can increase security, but it may be the security of the "zoo"—purchased at the expense of freedom. Over the centuries man has wrestled with this choice, and in different times and different places the emphasis has shifted markedly.

Nineteenth-century Western society idealized individual responsibility. This was particularly true in England and the United States, where a system of political economy was developed based on the teachings of Locke, Smith, Mill, and other advocates of personal freedom. As this system was superimposed on a religious foundation which exalted hard work and thrift, the result was an unprecedented acceleration in the rate of growth of material output. Each man's energies were bent to enhancing his own welfare, secure in the knowledge that he and his family would enjoy the fruits of his efforts and in the conviction that he was obeying God's will.

That the system worked imperfectly goes without saying. That the outcome for some individuals was harsh and brutal has been recounted in innumerable novels, plays, histories, and sociological treatises. But when set against man's previous history, the material benefits and the accompanying relaxation of social, religious, and political rigidities were extraordinary.

By the beginning of this century, however, reactions to such uninhibited "progress" has arisen in most Western countries. Since then a variety of laws have been passed seeking to protect individuals from the most severe consequences of unbridled individualism. Laissez-faire is dead, and only a few mourn its passing. In fact, the attitude of many intellectuals and popular writers on political economy seems to have swung to the other extreme. In the 1920s R. H. Tawney, surveying the eighteenth- and nineteenth-century attitudes toward poverty, wrote that "the most curious feature in the whole discussion . . . was the resolute refusal to admit that society had any responsibility for the causes of distress."[10] Some future historian, in reviewing mid-twentieth-century social reform literature, may note an equally curious feature—a "resolute refusal" to admit that individuals have any responsibility for their own distress.

From the idealization of individual responsibility and the neglect of social responsibility we have gone, in some quarters, to the denial of individual responsibility and the idealization of social responsibility. The rejection of any sense of responsibility for one's fellow men is inhuman, but the denial of any individual responsibility is also dehumanizing.

Moreover, with respect to health such a view runs contrary to common sense. As Henry Sigerist, an ardent advocate of socialized medicine and other expressions of social responsibility, has observed: "The state can protect society very effectively against a great many dangers, but the cultivation of health, which requires a definite mode of living, remains, to a large extent, an individual matter."[11] Most of us know this is true from personal experience. As long as we believe that we have some control over our own choices, we will reject theories that assume that "society" is always the villain.

A great deal of what has been written recently about "the right to health" is very misleading. It suggests that society has a supply of "health" stored away which it can give to individuals and that it is only the niggardliness of the Administration or the ineptness of Congress or the selfishness of physicians that prevents this from happening. Such a view ignores the truth of Douglas Colman's observation that "positive health is not something that one human can hand to or require of another. Positive health can be achieved only through intelligent effort on the part of each individual. Absent that effort, health professionals can only insulate the individual from the more catastrophic results of his ignorance, self-indulgence, or lack of motivation."[12] The notion that we can spend our way to better health is a vast oversimplification. At present there is very little that medical care can do for a lung that has been overinflated by smoking, or for a liver that has been scarred by too much alcohol, or for a skull that has been crushed in a motor accident.

The assertion that *medical care* is (or should be) a "right" is more plausible. In a sense medical care is to health what schooling is to wisdom. No society can truthfully promise to make everyone wise, but society can make schooling freely available; it can even make it compulsory. Many countries have taken a similar position with respect to medical care, although the compulsory aspects are sharply limited. Our government could, if it wished to, come close to assuring access to medical care for all persons. But no government now or in the foreseeable future can assure health to every individual.

Because utilization of medical care is voluntary, the mere availability of a service does not guarantee its use. The discovery of polio vaccine was rightly hailed as a significant medical advance, but in recent years there has been a sharp drop in the proportion of children receiving such vaccinations. At present, probably one-third of the children between 1 and 4 years of age are not adequately protected. The problem is particularly acute in poverty areas of major cities, where as many as half the children probably are without full protection against polio. There are undoubtedly many difficulties facing poor families that make it more difficult for them to bring their children to be vaccinated, but the service itself is available in most cities.

Another example of a gap between availability and utilization comes from a study of dental services covered by group healh insurance. The study reported that white-collar workers and their families used significantly more preventive services than their blue-collar counterparts even though the insurance policy provided full coverage for all participants. The only dental service used more frequently by blue-collar families was tooth extraction—a procedure which is usually a consequence of failure to use preventive services, such as repair of caries.

If people have a *right* to care, do they also have an *obligation* to use it? This complex question will assume greater significance as the collective provision of care increases. In our zeal to raise health levels, however, we must be wary of impinging on other valuable "rights," including the right to be left alone. Strict control over a man's behavior might well result in increased life expectancy, but a well-run zoo is still a zoo and not a worthy model for mankind.

As we attempt to formulate responsible policy for health and medical care, we should strive for the balance advocated by Rabbi Hillel more than two thousand years ago when he said, "If I am not for myself, who will be for me, but if I am for myself alone, what am I?"

The preceding discussion of the choices that face our society helps to put the major problems of health and medical care in proper perspective. These problems, as perceived by the public, are high cost, poor access, and inadequate health levels. In order to attack them intelligently, we must recognize the scarcity of resources and the need to allocate them as efficiently as possible. We must recognize that we can't have everything. In short, we need to adopt an economic point of view.

The discussion of choices also reveals some of the limits of economics in dealing with the most fundamental questions of health and medical care. These questions are ultimately ones of value: What value do we put on saving a life? on reducing pain? on relieving anxiety? How do these values change when the life at stake is a relative's? a neighbor's? a stranger's?

Nearly all human behavior is guided by values. Given the values, together with information about the relationship between technological means and ends, about inputs and constraints (resources, time, money), economics shows how these values can be maximmized. To the extent that individual behavior attempts to maximize values, economic theory also possesses significant power to predict behavior. If and when values change and these changes are not taken into account, however, economics loses a good deal of its predictive power. The most difficult part of the problem is that values may change partly as a result of the economic process itself.

According to one well-known definition, "economics is the science of means, not of ends": it can explain how market prices are determined, but not how basic values are formed; it can tell us the consequences of various alternatives, but it cannot make the choice for us. These limitations will be with us always, for economics can never replace morals or ethics.

Notes

Documentary and explanatory notes, originally presented by means of a dual system, are here combined in a single enumeration. Thus note numbers given here vary from those in the source.

1. Jonathan Spivak, "Where Do We Go from Here," in Robert D. Eilers and Sue S. Moyerman, eds., *National Health Insurance* (Homewood, Ill.: Richard D. Irwin, 1971), p. 272.
2. A system in which the physician receives a fixed amount per year regardless of the amount of care actually delivered.
3. The motor accident death rate reaches its peak in the late teens and early twenties.
4. A specially constructed facility for raising the oxygen content of air in order to treat more effectively certain rare diseases.
5. Marginal (or incremental) benefits and costs are those resulting from small changes in inputs.
6. The development of the theory of human capital by Gary Becker, Jacob Mincer, T. W. Schultz, and others and its application in fields such as education and health is one of the great advances in economics in the past quarter-century.
7. Rate of time discount is a measure of how willing people are to incur present costs or defer present benefits in order to obtain some benefit in the future.
8. Raymond Aron, *Progress and Disillusion* (New York: Praeger, 1968), p. 3.
9. Morbidity is the extent of an illness in the population.
10. R. H. Tawney, *Religion and the Rise of Capitalism* (New York: Harcourt Brace, 1920), p. 270.
11. Henry Sigerist, *Medicine and Human Welfare* (New Haven: Yale University Press, 1941), p. 103.
12. J. Douglas Colman, "National Health Goals and Objectives" (speech delivered to the National Health Forum, Chicago, Illinois, March 20, 1967).

Index